Hospitality Management and Organisational Behaviour

Fifth edition

Laurie J. Mullins

Penny Dossor

PEARSON

Harlow, England • London • New York • Boston • San Francisco • Toronto • Sydney
Auckland • Singapore • Hong Kong • Tokyo • Seoul • Taipei • New Delhi
Cape Town • São Paulo • Mexico City • Madrid • Amsterdam • Munich • Paris • Milan

Pearson Education Limited
Edinburgh Gate
Harlow CM20 2JE
United Kingdom
Tel: +44 (0)1279 623623
Web: www.pearson.com/uk

First published (as *Hospitality Management: A human resources approach*) 1992 (print)
Second edition 1995 (print)
Third edition (published as *Managing People in the Hospitality Industry*) 1998 (print)
Fourth edition (published as *Hospitality Management and Organisational Behaviour*)
2001 (print)

This edition published 2013 (print and electronic)

ISBN: 978-0-273-75837-2 (print)
         978-0-273-78112-7 (eText)
         978-0-273-75841-9 (eBook)

British Library Cataloguing-in-Publication Data
A catalogue record for the print edition is available from the British Library

Library of Congress Cataloging-in-Publication Data
A catalog record for the print edition is available from the Library of Congress

Typeset in 9.5/12.5 pt Charter ITC Std by 32

NOTE THAT ANY PAGE CROSS REFERENCES REFER TO THE PRINT EDITION

ARP Impression 98
Printed in Great Britain by Clays Ltd, St Ives plc

Contents

About the authors

Laurie Mullins is a consultant and author specialising in management and organisational behaviour, and managing people at work. Before taking early retirement, Laurie was a principal lecturer at the University of Portsmouth Business School where he led the behavioural and human resource management group.

Laurie has experience of business, local government and university administration and human resource management. For a number of years he was also a member of, and an instructor in, the Territorial Army.

He has undertaken a range of consultancy work including as an adviser with the United Nations Association International Service (UNAIS); served as a visiting selector for Voluntary Service Overseas (VSO); acted as adviser and tutor for a number of professional and educational bodies including UNISON Education; and served as an external examiner for university degree and postgraduate courses, and for professional organisations.

Laurie has undertaken a year's academic exchange in the Management Department, University of Wisconsin, USA and a visiting fellowship at the School of Management, Royal Melbourne Institute of Technology University, Australia, and he is a visiting lecturer in the Netherlands.

Laurie is also author of *Management and Organisational Behaviour* and *Essentials of Organisational Behaviour*, both published by Pearson Education. Laurie's books have featured regularly in the best-selling business books.

Penny Dossor is a principal lecturer at the University of Portsmouth Business School where she is course leader for the hospitality programmes alongside teaching hospitality management, organisational behaviour and cross-cultural awareness. She has a particular interest in the integration of international students and is currently course leader for some international courses and faculty coordinator for foreign student exchanges.

Before starting her teaching career on a range of hospitality courses in 1982, Penny undertook a Hotel and Catering Management degree, which she followed with a number of hotel and hospitality management and personnel management appointments in both public and private sectors. Her hospitality experience includes time working in Switzerland.

Dedications

From Laurie

To Pamela, and for Kelvin and Jake

From Penny

To John

In acknowledgement and appreciation

From Laurie Mullins

Special tribute to my wife Pamela, children and family for their continuing support.

From Penny Dossor

A special thank you to my husband, John Baldry, for his help, support and substantial contribution in the final stages of the compilation of this new edition.

Acknowledgements

Thanks and gratitude to:

- Nina Becket, Oxford Brookes University Business School
- Colleagues at the Business School, University of Portsmouth – Gerry Banks, Gill Christy, Robin Shepherd
- Martin Brunner, Independent Consultant
- Those hospitality managers who kindly gave permission to use information from their own organisation, including: Kathy Budd, Vic Laws, Chris Moore, Andrew Morgan, Tony Mullan, Gerard Ryan, Claire Timmins, Vicky Williams, Angela Wyer
- Fred. Olsen Cruise Lines
- The team at Pearson Education including Rufus Curnow, Rachel Gear and Priyadharshini Dhanagopal

Publisher's acknowledgements

We are grateful to the following for permission to reproduce copyright material:

Figures

Figure 4.13 from Informal organisations, *The British Journal of Administrative Management* (Kenneth L. 1997); Figure 6.8 from A good fit is essential, *Professional Manager*, 15, p. 38 (Cutler A. 2005), Chartered Management institute; Figure 8.4 from *Interactive Behavior at Work*, Financial Times Prentice Hall (Guirdham M. 2002) p. 119, Reproduced with the permission of Pearson Education Ltd.

Photographs

(Key: b-bottom; c-centre; l-left; r-right; t-top)
Clink Charity: 427b, 428t; **FLPA Images of Nature**: John Eveson 105b; **Getty Images**: Greg Zabilski/ABC 228b; **Walt Disney World Swan and Dolphin**: 466b
All other images © Pearson Education

In some instances we have been unable to trace the owners of copyright material, and we would appreciate any information that would enable us to do so.

Preface

However the nature of the hospitality industry is viewed, it is an inescapable fact that an overriding determinant of successful organisational performance is the actions and behaviour of its members of staff. The concepts and ideas presented in this book provide you with a basis for the critical analysis of the structure and management of hospitality organisations, and interactions among people who work in them.

The central theme is improved organisational performance through the effective management of the people resource. This involves an understanding of individual and group behaviour, and factors influencing the effective management of people. There are many aspects to management but the one essential ingredient of any successful manager is the ability to handle people effectively.[1]

This book provides a foundation for the critical appraisal of organisational and managerial processes. Managers within the hospitality industry today are faced with managing an increasingly diverse and multicultural workforce and the nature of the economic realities facing the industry. These and other contemporary issues in modern hospitality management are addressed by this text.

We hope you will be encouraged to think about what you have read and to explore specific applications that will enhance your awareness and understanding of hospitality management and organisational behaviour.

Aims of the book

The aims of this book are to:

- examine the relevance and applications of general concepts of management and organisational behaviour to hospitality organisations;
- present an integrated approach to the subject area embracing both theory and practice;
- balance academic rigour with a pragmatic approach to the subject area;
- indicate ways in which performance may be improved through a better understanding of the effective management of people.

It is intended that this book will appeal to students at undergraduate, professional or post-experience level who are aspiring to a managerial position. It is also hoped that the book will appeal to practising managers and supervisors who wish to extend their knowledge of the subject area.

---

[1]For a fuller discussion, see Mullins L. J., *Management and Organisational Behaviour*, 10th edn, Financial Times Pitman Publishing (2013).

Plan of the book

The book is divided into ten interrelated chapters.

Chapter 1 – Nature and scope of the hospitality industry

Chapter 2 – Understanding the nature of the workforce

Chapter 3 – Diversity management

Chapter 4 – Organisational goals and structure

Chapter 5 – Defining management

Chapter 6 – Nature of leadership

Chapter 7 – Workforce motivation and involvement

Chapter 8 – Managing through groups and teams

Chapter 9 – Managing challenging situations

Chapter 10 – Managing the changing environment

No one book of manageable size could hope to cover adequately all sectors of the industry or all aspects of such a wide and diverse area of study. In order to attain a reasonable depth, the book concentrates on selected topics of particular relevance to the effective organisation of work and an understanding of the behaviour and management of people. This is supported with specific hospitality contexts, situations and examples.

Your study of this book

The format of the book is clearly structured and written with a minimum of technical terminology. Each chapter is fully supported with diagrams and contains:

- a brief introduction and set of learning outcomes;
- a series of critical review and reflections;
- practical examples and scenarios throughout the text;
- assignments and case studies at the end of each chapter;
- a summary of key points;
- review and discussion questions; and
- comprehensive notes and references.

There is a logical flow to the sequence of topic areas with appropriate cross-referencing between chapters. However, each chapter is self-contained, and the selection and order of chapters can be varied to suit personal preferences or the demands of your particular course of study. Main sections are identified clearly with detailed headings and sub-headings.

The **Critical review and reflections** through each chapter are intended to provoke critical thinking, inspire personal reflection about areas you have studied and to question what happens in your own organisation.

The **Review and discussion questions** provide a basis for revision, and a test of your understanding and knowledge of the chapter contents.

The **Assignments and Case studies** provide an opportunity to relate ideas and principles to specific work situations; to think about the major issues of each chapter, and to discuss and compare views with colleagues.

The **Notes and references** at the end of each chapter should help you to pursue further any issues of particular interest. In order to provide more detailed and specific referencing, and to keep the main text uncluttered, a simple numbering system has been chosen. This system appears to be favoured by most readers. The thoughts and ideas of other people are not always clearly distinguishable from one's own. While every effort has been made to give references to the work of other writers, we apologise to any concerned if acknowledgement has inadvertently not been recorded.

You are encouraged to complement your reading of the book by drawing upon your own practical experience. Search for good and bad examples of the management of people within the hospitality industry, and consider reasons for their apparent success or failure.

We hope you will find satisfaction and also some measure of enjoyment from this book.

Laurie Mullins and Penny Dossor

Chapter 1

Nature and scope of the hospitality industry

Learning outcomes

After completing this chapter you should be able to:

- define the broad nature, scope and environmental context of the hospitality industry;
- explain the term *hospitality*;
- apply relevant general management theory to managing people in the hospitality industry;
- detail aspects that make the hospitality industry unique;
- identify the nature of research in hospitality and the contribution it makes;
- explain the terms *service culture* and *service industries*;
- relate the open systems model of organisations to hospitality.

Introduction

This chapter explores the context in which management of people within the hospitality industry takes place. The hospitality industry has a number of characteristic features, but it also shares important common features with other business industries and faces the same general problems of organisation and management. Attention should be given to ways in which ideas drawn from general management theory and practice can be applied with advantage to the hospitality industry.[1]

Critical review and reflection

'It is impossible to define "the hospitality industry". It is a combination of many industries.'

How would you describe the hospitality industry?

The scope and size of the hospitality industry

The scope of the hospitality industry

In recent years the term 'hospitality' has become increasingly popular as an all-embracing nomenclature for a larger grouping of organisations including hotels. As a collective term, the hospitality industry may be interpreted in a number of ways. For example, according to a British Hospitality Association report the hospitality sector of the economy includes:

- hotels and related services, which includes camping grounds and other accommodation.
- restaurants and related services, which includes pubs, takeaway food shops, licensed clubs; (this is seen to include motorway service areas, where hospitality services are the main activity).
- catering (including contract catering to both private and public sector clients, and in-house catering across non-hospitality direct sectors such as health and education).
- event management (including conference and exhibition organisers).
- temporary agency employment in these areas is also seen as part of the hospitality economy.[2]

The catering sector of the industry is particularly diverse. Davis and Stone[3] comment that food and beverage management is characterised by its diversity, including public and private provision, and cooling everything from a range of small independently owned private hotels and operated units to large multinational corporations managing global brands, such as Hilton and Starbucks, and from prison catering to the most luxurious hotels and providing refreshments in estashblishment ranging from cathedrals to casinos.

People 1st is the sector skills council for hospitality, passenger transport, travel and tourism in the UK.[4] It defines its role as being to:

transform skills in the sector, particularly in the areas of management and leadership, customer services and craft/technical skills. We are committed to ensuring that public funds support the industry to develop only those qualifications and programmes that meet the needs of employers.[5]

People 1st indicates 14 relevant industries that make up the hospitality, leisure, travel and tourism sector:

- contract food service providers
- events
- gambling
- holiday parks
- hospitality services
- hostels
- hotels
- membership clubs
- pubs, bars and nightclubs
- restaurants
- self catering accommodation
- tourist services
- travel services
- visitor attractions

People 1st suggests that each industry is unique in many respects, which is clearly the case, although there is often a close overlapping of hospitality and tourism activities, thus making it difficult to establish where one sector commences and the other ends. However the various activities are owned and operated, the sector is closely bound to ensure a high standard of customer service and a quality 'visitor' experience.

> The visitor is at the heart of the sector and further synergy is found in common 'vertical and horizontal ownership', which means that many operators can be found in more than one industry.

(People 1st 2011)

Critical review and reflection

Which of the 14 relevant industries that People 1st identify do you think 'belong in the hospitality sector'?

How can you justify your analysis?

Attempting to separate the businesses into the various sectors is clearly problematic. One might consider theme parks such as Legoland and Chessington, which, while being tourist attractions, also provide hotel accommodation and catering as part of their overall offerings.

Even within a narrower definition of hospitality, without a tourism element, it should be noted that there are significant differences as well as similarities. Although there are some common factors among the different divisions, and some movement of staff from one division to another, the hospitality industry comprises separate and distinct sectors. The hotel sector and the catering sector, for example, are in many respects entirely different businesses and have their own characteristics.

The context of the hospitality industry

The UK hospitality industry, with its ever-developing range of products and services, has seen vast growth in recent years.[6] In the 2010–11 British Hospitality Association annual report it is stated:

> Hospitality is one of the main pillars of the UK economy and the economic driver of almost every region in the country. It is the fifth largest industry in the UK, directly employing over 2.4 million people and, indirectly, a further 1.2 million.[7]

The hospitality, leisure, travel and tourism sector employs more than two million people: one in 14 of UK jobs.[8] Of these, 58 per cent are female and 42 per cent male.

Reasons for the growth in hospitality include the improved standard of living and increased discretionary income that most people enjoy. This has enabled many to enjoy the hospitality offerings that, formerly, were restricted to the wealthy minority[9] (see the Case Study at the end of this chapter, Fred.Olsen cruise lines').

It is likely that increased awareness of the pleasures of fine dining, through a raised media profile, has something to do with the popularity of eating out. The hotel sector has also reacted to the increased spending power of many people, by refining its offerings to include weekend and mini breaks, some of which are specifically tailored to interest groups. Whilst there are fluctuations in demand, depending on the general economic situation, overall longer-term trends have been positive. However, it should be noted that along with the growth in the industry has come increased competition, which often expresses itself in keen pricing.

The industry as a whole remains labour-intensive. Despite some technological advances, customers in all aspects of the hospitality industry are buying service which hospitality employees are required to provide.

Whilst increased demand should, perhaps, lead to increased profitability, many hospitality products are price-sensitive, and there is often heavy capital investment, leading to a requirement to maintain market share. This can often only be achieved in the highly competitive market by competitive pricing. Because the industry is so labour-intensive, it is necessary that labour costs are controlled in order to maintain profit margins.

Boella and Goss-Turner point out the implications of the above analysis for wages in the industry.

> Admittedly at the top of the scale, some highly skilled workers such as chefs, who are in short supply, can command very high wages, but at the other end of the scale, kitchen porters and cleaners, for example, would earn considerably higher wages for broadly similar work in other employment sectors.[10]

The relatively low wages paid in the industry, particularly to employees such as cleaners and kitchen porters, have contributed to the nature of the workforce, which is highly transient, with much migrant labour (21 per cent born overseas, of whom 64 per cent come from outside the European Economic Area).[11] The sector has one of the highest figures for labour turnover of any industry in the UK, currently 23 per cent.[12]

What is hospitality?

From a survey of the literature for the historical and sociological bases of hospitality, King describes hospitality in general as having four attributes:

- a relationship between individuals who take the roles of host and guest;
- this relationship may be commercial or private (social);
- the keys to successful hospitality in both the commercial and private spheres include knowledge of what would evoke pleasure in the guest; and
- hospitality as a process that includes arrival, providing comfort and fulfilment of the guest's wishes, and departure.

King suggests that commercial hospitality has several key elements that must be included in a model of hospitality including host-employee and guest-customer who are involved in face-to-face interactions[13] (see Figure 1.1).

From insights into the natural processes of hospitality relating to modern commercial hospitality organisations, Guerrier explains the provision of hospitality as:

- providing basic human needs for food, drink and somewhere to sleep for people who are not regular members of the family;
- rewarding hosts by enhanced prestige in the community if they provide lavish hospitality to guests; and
- an exchange for the mutual benefit of the host and the guest.[14]

Walker suggests there are many definitions of hospitality, but the industry includes 'a wide range of businesses each of which is dedicated to the service of people away from home', with the purpose of each being 'the cordial and generous reception of guests'.[15]

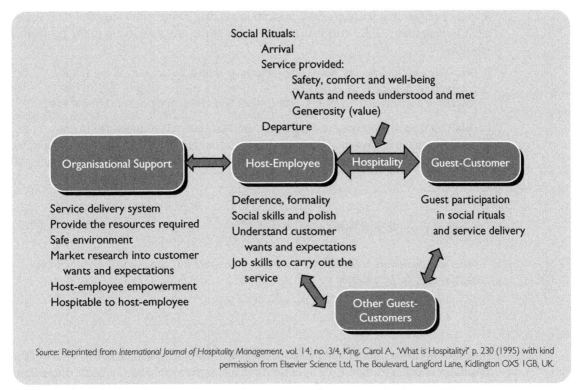

Source: Reprinted from International Journal of Hospitality Management, vol. 14, no. 3/4, King, Carol A., 'What is Hospitality?' p. 230 (1995) with kind permission from Elsevier Science Ltd, The Boulevard, Langford Lane, Kidlington OX5 1GB, UK.

Figure 1.1 Hospitality model

Lashley and Morrison suggested that hospitality can be better understood, if the 'three domains' that comprise it are first identified and then considered separately. They proposed that hospitality needs to be analysed by:

> reflecting insights into the study of hospitality that encompass the commercial provision of hospitality and the hospitality industry, . . . (recognizing that) . . . hospitality needs to be explored in a private domestic setting and . . . (studie) . . . hospitality as a social phenomenon involving relationships between people.[16]

(In this model the 'three domains' are the commercial provision of hospitality, private domestic hospitality, and hospitality as a social relationship between people.)

In essence, Lashley and Morrison are suggesting that what takes place in the hospitality industry needs to be seen in the context of what happens domestically. People who entertain their friends at home are, essentially, being hospitable. The social relationship is that they are the hosts and their visitors are guests, and as hosts they put their guests' comfort and needs first, by concentrating on providing an enjoyable experience. The commercial hospitality organisation, despite selling its products and service, needs, according to the authors, to be hospitable to its guests.

There has been considerable academic debate over this analysis. Slattery is critical of the 'three-domains' approach. He cites Lashley and Morrison's definition of hospitality as:

> a contemporaneous human exchange which is voluntarily entered into and designed to enhance the mutual well being of the parties concerned through the provision of accommodation, and/ or food, and/or drink... (which) captures the generic essence of hospitality, placing the issue of human exchange at the very heart of the hospitality concept.

Slattery believes that Lashley's false assumption is that if customers pay then their enjoyment is compromised. He criticises the relevance of the private domain to the hospitality business.[17]

> First, the very idea of the hospitality industry is that it occurs out of the home . . . The provision of hospitality to outsiders in the home is a marginal family activity, while in the hospitality business renting rooms, selling meals and selling drinks is the *raison d'être*.

For Slattery then, the purpose of the hospitality organisation is commercial, to make a profit, not primarily to be hospitable (although it is reasonable to suggest that being hospitable and providing an enjoyable experience may encourage repeat business and commercial success).

Critical review and reflection

What do you believe should be the purpose of a hospitality organisation? Is it to be commercial or to be hospitable?

Justify your view by reference to the above debate.

The following article, submitted by Robin Shepherd, develops the ideas of the nature of the hospitality industry further. He is interested to explore the social and emotional dimensions of the consumer experience and the notion of host and guest collaborating as co-creators of the hospitality experience.

Exhibit 1.1 The respect economy – the personalisation of the modern hospitality service encounter

Hospitality would appear to be a simple thing. When asked, most people would think of their favourite restaurant, pub, hotel and smile as they remembered the companionship and laughter that accompanied their visit to drink, to eat, to stay. Most often, the details of the meal or the quality of the beer or the cleanliness of the room will remain pleasantly hazy, while the sense of security, warmth and belonging – the emotional experience – stays sharply focused. It is this that the successful exponents of the hospitality 'product' know and have always known.

So why, if this is so well known, has it become so difficult to achieve for many of the hospitality industry's modern multiple operators? To understand this it is necessary to have a grasp of the shifts in economic offering driven by consumers whose needs and wants have changed over time, thus defining the demands businesses must meet to gain a competitive advantage in increasingly competitive markets.

The 1960s ushered in the period of modern mass consumption driven by a plethora of both social and technological innovation that revolutionised the perception of value. An explosion of new products delighted and surprised the increasing numbers of new male and female consumers who had greater discretionary income than any previous generation. The way to achieve market share in this new 'product economy' was by the invention and innovation of 'things' to buy.

Of course, as the number of companies producing 'things' grew and the number of new 'things' grew less numerous, the products became less distinct so that increased market share became more difficult to achieve. Thus, while new products continued to be developed, albeit less frequently, a new way to differentiate them became imperative.

Service provided this step up in economic value and so the 'service economy' dawned. Service in itself was not a new concept: the intangible element of the Hospitality product was and is anticipated and expected by consumers. The problem was how to achieve a consistent level of service across increasingly large, multi-unit corporations, and so to define an entire brand with this new differentiator.

The answer, in spite of much-published aspiration to levels of service excellence, was to introduce process and system to standardise service to achievable levels and so reduce its perceived inherent instability. SERVQUAL was the most commonly adopted system of service quality assurance but in spite of its original good intention and one of its fundamental dimensions being empathy, which is concerned with understanding the customer's needs and the ability to provide an individualised service,[18] it was sadly reduced in many instances to a series of quality audits designed to tightly control employee initiative as they delivered to the achievable median quality standard. As Riley et al.[19] described it, 'getting the balance of trust and control is what managing people is about'.

However, as all organisations adopt the same approach and as consumers' expectations and demands rise, the delivery of service quality becomes the 'norm'. It becomes a 'hygiene' factor that merely satisfies the customers' basic needs and expectations but does not drive loyalty, as satisfied customers can easily defect to competing providers of similar, homogenised services.[20]. This view is confirmed by Morgan[21] who suggests that as service quality is taken for granted it becomes commoditised and no longer offers a competitive advantage for organisations.

Unsurprisingly, it was not long before the search for new economic value began again. Pine and Gilmore[22] identified this as the move to an 'experience economy'. They believe that in the experience economy the only way to sustain a competitive advantage and avoid becoming commoditised is by turning services into memorable experiences that involve the customer as a participant.

These memorable experiences can be achieved by staging the services as in a theatrical play where the drama is the business strategy, actors are the employees, the scripts are the processes and the performance is the service delivery[23]. These theatrical elements are used to engage the individual customer in a personal way that creates a memorable event.[24] Hemmington[25] points out that hospitality services have the opportunity to be more experiential than theatre by stimulating all five senses – sight, sound, taste, touch and smell – to heighten the experience and make it even more memorable. You can 'visit with' Mickey Mouse (www.disneyland.disney.go.com/disneyland/mickeys-house), have dinner in the sky, hanging from a huge crane 150 metres up[26] and drink vodka from a glass made of ice on a seat of ice in a bar in a hotel made entirely from ice![27]

Toffler[28] (1970, cited by Morgan et al., 2008) predicted that, as technological development accelerated, people would become more concerned with collecting experiences than owning products. Owning 'things' used to provide the individuals with a certain status, but in the experience economy people want to share their memorable experiences, tell stories to 'achieve a status dividend from their purchases'.[29] As a result, physical experiences have often become commoditised through digitisation; experiences are made solid by their digital capture, often to be published and shared through social media. As a consequence these experiences are no longer truly unique and personal to the individual and have become commoditised.

Thus, instead of companies developing or staging experiences for customers, which is to a large extent the view of Pine and Gilmore, Prahalad and Ramaswamy[30] suggest that companies should be co-creating experiences with customers. This requires a personalised co-creation of experiences that result in value that is unique to each individual consumer. This value is reinforced with a deliberate coinciding of corporate culture with individual consumer mores, by the development of an authentic emotional connection between the company and the consumer. Kevin Roberts, CEO of Saatchi & Saatchi,[31] describes this as delivering the consumer 'loyalty beyond reason'. It is the emotional memories that the customer will remember and it is the emotional connection that strengthens the long-term relationship development removing any notion of commoditisation.[32]

In Ramaswamy's later work[33] he focuses on co-creation with 'internal' customers, the employees, and how organisations must transform the nature of engagement and value creation within the organisation, from top to bottom, in order to become a true co-creative, individual customer-centric organisation.

Successful personalisation and co-creation experiences are highly dependent on individual staff members and their ability to deal with customers in various different service encounters. In order to maximise staff's contribution in service encounters, organisations must create a work environment that promotes dignity, pride and satisfaction.[34] It is essential for organisations to be run in a way that makes it attractive to the right type of people the business wants to hire,[35] and a mutual trust and respect between internal customer (the employee) and management must be ensured, before a genuine customer care can be communicated externally.[36]

Employees should be encouraged and given the flexibility to come up with new creative ideas as they have to fulfil the needs of guests in more unusual and exciting ways to create memorable experiences and emotional connections.[37] For successful empowerment to be achieved, management has to be able to 'let go', avoid setting too strict policies and procedures so as to allow creativity. Companies must demonstrate trust in and respect for their employees so that they will feel supported by the management to act in the right way.[38]

Staff's ability and willingness to recognise, understand and respond to customers' individual needs at various 'touch points' will determine the success of the personalisation experience.[39] If staff possess high emotional intelligence they are able to perceive and generate emotions, communicate effectively, build relationship bonds[40] and are therefore likely to ensure successful and memorable personalised service experience.

It is by adoption of the tenets of what is now tentatively described as the respect economy that hospitality businesses seek to deliver to each one of their customers the emotional warmth and security that will so differentiate them from their competitors and deliver a 'loyalty beyond reason' to their products, service and experiences.

Source: The authors are grateful to Robin Shepherd for this contribution.

Critical review and reflection

'Hospitality businesses seek to deliver to each one of their customers the emotional warmth and security that will so differentiate them from their competitors and deliver a "loyalty beyond reason" to their products, service and experiences.'

Do you agree? Can this approach be instilled in all hospitality organisations?

The emotional warmth and security, referred to above, can only be provided by the people who work in an organisation. Therefore alongside the commercial, contractual, relationship that exists between the organisation and the customer there is the human relationship between the person who, for example, orders the food and the person who serves it.

Hornsey and Dann[41] point out that an individual employee's relationship with a customer may be seen as separate to that of the relationship of the customer with the core organisation. The point is that the customer may seek, and/or reward, exceptional service through the practice of tipping the employee who provides the service. The practice has been unofficially institutionalised in organisations where employees in some customer-facing roles find their tips far more lucrative than their official wage.

Exhibit 1.2 Tipping

Porters at a famous London hotel are known to have uniform trousers made with very deep pockets, so that they have somewhere to keep the tips that they are given. At one evening function for 400, the porter was taking coats from arriving guests who typically tipped £1. The deep pockets meant that the porter could continue at his station without having to return to his locker to deposit the tips.

But it is not only the big London hotels where some people get tipped handsomely. A former manager of a regional hotel relates that when responsible for the payroll, often she had to remind the portering staff to collect their wages, since the tips they received made the wages somewhat irrelevant.

Tipping is a relatively common practice in the USA but is even more prevalent in the USA, leading to a more service-orientated approach.

General management theory

Managers in hotels and catering tend often to view the industry as unique, to regard it as somehow special and unlike any other industry. To what extent is such a view justified? According to Fearn, writing in 1971, management in the hotel and catering industry had not developed at the same pace as in other industries:

> little progress has been made in terms of management attitudes, knowledge and thinking. When one considers the astounding management progress in industries which have been created during this century it is difficult to account for the lack of progress and change in the hotel and catering industry.[42]

Developments have clearly been made since that time and increasing emphasis is being placed on ways in which ideas drawn from general management theory may be applied to the industry.[43] In 1994 Medlik made the point that 'only limited progress has been made in the translation of business and management theory from manufacturing to service industries generally and to hotels in particular'.[44]

However, the hospitality industry differs from other industries in the extent to which it is service related and labour-intensive. While new systems may be introduced, along with some new technology, particularly related to bookings and record systems, the essential nature of the industry remains unchanged. This might go some way to answering the points that Fearn and Medlik have made; however, though some progress has certainly been made, it is clear that there is still scope for further development.

Hospitality education and research

From a review of the development of hospitality education and research in 1996, Jones posed the question: 'Is there such a thing as hospitality research?' to which he suggested the answer was an unequivocal 'Yes'. However, Jones did go on to argue that hospitality research was not truly discrete and distinctive, and there was little work that does not derive from other disciplines.[45]

The Council for Hospitality Management Education (CHME), which was founded in 1979, aims 'to contribute to the professional development and status of UK hospitality management education, through the sharing of best practice in scholarship and pedagogy' and has encouraged developments in research in the hospitality industry. CHME is a non-profit organisation representing UK universities and colleges offering higher education programmes in the fields of hospitality studies, hospitality management and related fields. In addition to its interest in management education it has produced a number of research reports of interest to the industry. However, the question remains: to what extent is the industry open to new ideas and developments? Academic research is only of value to an industry if the organisations comprising the industry are prepared to consider recommendations made.

Tom Baum, speaking at HTMi Hospitality Research, Switzerland in December 2010, said that the industry 'is incredibly information-rich and the managers don't necessarily have the time or the skills to interpret that information'.[46]

Focusing on the nature of academic research within UK hospitality management, Taylor and Edgar take the view that there is some evidence that hospitality research is still somewhat embryonic and although considerable progress may have been made in recent years in terms of both the quantity and quality of research, the field has yet to reach a state of maturity.[47]

From a survey of 156 books and articles on organisational behaviour and human resource management in the hospitality industry, Guerrier and Deery concluded that researchers were primarily engaged in applying mainstream ideas to the hospitality industry rather than influencing mainstream research. The industry provides a wonderful environment in which to explore current issues in organisational studies and human resource management. However, although there is a considerable body of knowledge about hospitality management, even here there are gaps and compared with the rhetoric, little is known about the real nature of management work.[48]

So is the hospitality industry unique?

A number of writers suggest a strong case for viewing the hospitality industry as 'unique'.[49] However, it can also be argued strongly that every industry is of course unique in the strict sense of the word. The important point is that all industries share common features but they also differ in many important respects.

Accordingly, the questions to be examined are:

1 What are the common features that the hospitality industry shares with other industries?

2 To what extent is the industry different in significant respects from other industries?

3 Are these differences sufficient to mark the hospitality industry as unique, and to restrict the application of general management theory and practice?

In order to examine these questions some perspective is needed in which to attempt a meaningful comparison of hospitality operations with those in other industries. We need to consider the nature of the organisational setting.

The organisational setting

The process of management does not take place in a vacuum but within the context of an organisational setting. Organisations are diverse and come in all forms, shapes and sizes. The structure, management and functioning of organisations will vary because of differences in their nature and type, goals and objectives, external environment, goods and/or services supplied, customers, and the behaviour of people who work in them.

By way of an extreme example let us consider just two types of organisation towards the opposite ends of a possible continuum – say a maximum security prison and a university largely concerned with research – as a framework within which to focus our attention. We can appreciate readily that, although both types of organisation will be concerned with the basic activities of management, their actual procedures and methods of operation, structure, systems and styles of management, and orientation and behaviour of members will differ considerably.

We can therefore bear such a comparison in mind when exploring both the general and distinctive features within the organisational setting of the hospitality industry.

Common factors in organisations

Despite the differences among various organisations there are at least four common factors in any work organisation:

- people;
- objectives;
- structure;
- management.

It is the interaction of **people** in order to achieve **objectives** which forms the basis of an organisation. Some form of **structure** is needed by which people's interactions and efforts are channelled and coordinated. It is through the process of **management** that the activities of the organisation and the efforts of its members are directed towards the pursuit of objectives.

The effectiveness of the organisation will depend upon the quality of its people, its objectives and structure, and the resources available to it. There are two broad categories of resources:

- **non-human** – physical assets, materials, equipment and facilities; and
- **human** – members' abilities and influence, and their management.

The interrelationship of people, objectives, structure and management, together with the efficient use of resources, will determine the success or failure of the organisation and the extent of its effectiveness (Figure 1.2).

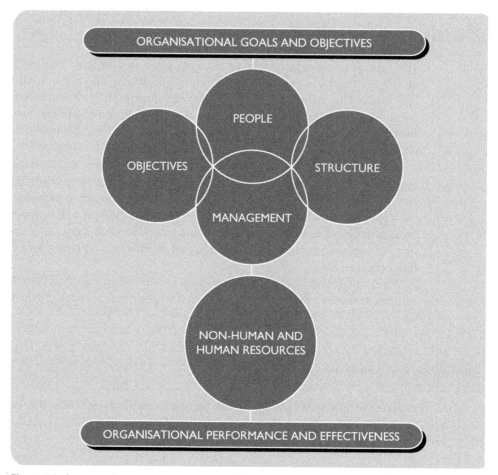

Figure 1.2 Common factors in work organisations

Hotel operations and the hospitality industry

The broad and variable nature of hotel operations means that they can be seen to embrace, to a greater or lesser extent, elements of associated sectors of the hospitality industry such as the licensed trade, catering and leisure activities and to an increasing degree, event management. In general terms, then, the hotel sector is also likely to exhibit a wider and more diverse range of organisational and staffing characteristics than might necessarily be found in other sectors of the hospitality industry.

Types of hotels

There are, however, many different types of hotels, and many different ways of attempting to distinguish between them and to categorise them. Medlik, for example, adopts the following criteria for classifying the main types of hotels.[50]

- The **location**, for example cities, towns, coastal resorts or country; and **position** within its location, for example city or town centre, along the beach or a motorway.

- The relationship with a particular **means of transport**, for example motels, railway hotels or airport hotels.

- The **purpose of visit** and main reason for the guests' stay, for example business hotels, convention hotels, holiday hotels, activity and sport hotels.

- A pronounced tendency to a **short or long duration** of guests' stay, for example a transit or a residential hotel.

- The **range of facilities and services,** for example open to residents and non-residents, provision of overnight accommodation and breakfast only, or an apartment hotel.

- The distinction between **licensed** and **unlicensed hotels.**

- The **size** of hotel, for example by number of rooms or beds – a large hotel would have several hundred beds or bedrooms.

- The **class** or **grade** of hotel as in hotel guides and classification and grading systems, for example a five-star luxury or quality hotel, or a one-star basic standard hotel.

- The **ownership** and **management** of the hotel, for example chain or group hotels, or individually owned independent hotels.

Exhibit 1.3 The Savoy Hotel, London – a personal perspective

The Savoy Hotel in London is the foremost quality and customer-focus-driven hotel in the world. 'For excellence we strive' is the motto and every staff member knows it and lives it throughout every day of employment.

What I remember so vividly is the feeling that I got when I started my very first shift as a commis waiter in the 'River Room' restaurant. When I served my first guest there was nothing that was going to stop me giving the best service this customer had ever had. I didn't know why, it was something in the atmosphere that spurred me on to do it. I noticed this throughout my whole time there. If it is possible to say, it was almost like the staff fed off the teamwork and generated motivation, no matter how busy we were or how tired. The result of this was finishing a shift feeling completely drained but overwhelmingly satisfied with what we had achieved.

The Savoy is a frightening place to work in, partly due to the superstition and history that surround it and given the fact that few people ever get the chance to go there in their lifetime. For the staff, however, it is a rare opportunity to be taught the basics by the best in the world. This was the reason, I feel, that the staff gave their all. It is seen as a platform where careers are either launched or destroyed, such is its power. Those who succeed in completing their training there have really accomplished a great deal and something to be rightly proud of.

From my own perspective there were countless times when after a shift starting at 6 am and ending at 11 pm all I wanted to do was hand in my resignation and say that it was all over. However, this was compensated for when, after a 13-hour day of continuous walking, carrying, cleaning and serving, you had the opportunity to stay in a staff room on the top floor of the hotel if you were on an early shift the next day. All for free.

What more can I say? Sought-after days off were cancelled at short notice, double shifts back to back were not uncommon, but you rarely heard anyone complain or argue. It never occurred to me why.

Training was on the job. You looked and listened to everyone and the speed at which you learnt was your own personal task. Most certainly you learnt fast. There was no opportunity to slacken off as it was reiterated time and time again that there was always something to do. Someone once told me he had worked out that in a day he would walk nearly five miles. So comfortable shoes were an essential.

A typical day at the Savoy started for me at 4.30 am. Arriving at work at 5.50 am, I would then change into black trousers, a clean white waiter's jacket, ensuring that all buttons were polished, and black shoes, also polished. Dirty jackets and/

or shoes were not acceptable and failure to have a clean jacket would either mean that you would be sent back to the changing room or kept well out of the way of the guests. I would arrive in the restaurant at around 6 am and begin to prepare the station. Once all the silver cutlery had been cleaned and the bread baskets filled with fresh rolls and Danish pastries we would all go for breakfast in the table room at 7 am. Half an hour later we would begin service. As a commis waiter there was nothing else to do except follow orders from the *chef de rang* (head of the station). The commis would run back and forth from the kitchen collecting orders, clearing tables, re-laying tables with fresh linen and getting countless pots of tea and coffee. Taking an order from a guest was a real honour and from a commis point of view it was an experience not to be forgotten.

I remember one instance when I realised how extraordinarily high the standards were at the Savoy when, upon a guest spilling a glass of orange juice over their table, I was asked by the *chef de rang* to re-lay the table while the guest was reseated at another one. There was a knack to changing a tablecloth whereby the guests never saw the green baize of the table. On this occasion, however, I saw fit to place an old menu underneath the table cloth to stop the dampness on the baize seeping through to the new table cloth. It seemed that one of the guests saw the green baize of the table, for what could have only been seconds. Twenty minutes later I was up in front of the Food and Beverage Manager and had to explain my actions and reassure him that it would not happen again. You could say that this was absurd but it seemed that this was common procedure.

I look back at my training at the Savoy with great pride and honour. There is no place else where such an exceptional level of training could be given. It seemed almost as though no guest had a bad experience there. The Savoy is a time capsule where everyone works to their limits to achieve the ultimate, if that is possible. I have served princes and kings, pop stars and politicians and I thank the Savoy, hard though it was, for the opportunity to do so.

Source: the author is grateful to Christian Ternofsky for providing this contribution.

Exhibit 1.4 Stress and the airport hotel

High stress abounds in airport hotels due to a number of factors, which are in some ways unique to these properties.

A high proportion of hotels around an airport means that the labour pool is usually smaller than the area requires, bearing in mind that more money could be earned doing unskilled jobs within the airport than working for a hotel as a chambermaid, for instance. Staff tend to move around the hotels. Staff shortages are common, especially with hourly paid jobs – workers will follow the highest bidder.

Airport hotels are busy on a 24-hour basis. Food outlets must be operational for up to 18 hours a day. Room service has to be 24-hour. Guests can be ill-tempered due to delays or jet lag. Food requirements can be obscure because international travellers are in the wrong time zone, i.e. an American traveller may demand breakfast during lunch service. Air crews are commonplace and they require early and accurate wake-up calls, quiet rooms and low room rates.

Delayed flights cause untold upheaval to catering outlets because of the large number of people descending on coffee shops and bars with very short notice. They are usually issued with a meal voucher; they are often cross with the delay. Children can cause havoc to other guests.

Car parks must be manned to prevent free parking for weeks on end. Security needs to be of a high standard as the high turnover of guests and the international factor add to the risks.

Organisational and staffing characteristics

Hotels, then, are not a homogeneous grouping. It is, however, possible to summarise a number of important organisational and staffing features which are characteristic of hotels in general, and which, in part at least, may be a feature of other sectors of the hospitality industry. For example:

- large numbers of individual units of varying size and many different types are located throughout the whole of the country and internationally;
- many units operate for 24 hours a day, seven days a week;
- there are high fixed costs, a fixed rate of supply but a fluctuating, seasonal and often unpredictable demand;
- it is both a production and service industry;
- production and sales are combined on the same premises;
- there is a diverse range of customers seeking to satisfy a variety of needs and expectations;
- services are supplied direct to the customer on the premises and the customer leaves with no tangible product;
- a wide range of operations are combined, many of which are provided simultaneously;
- a high degree of coordination is required, often measured over very short time scales;
- managers are expected to demonstrate proficiency in technical and craft skills as well as in management areas;
- staff may live on the premises;
- many different skills are required but there are also high numbers of unskilled staff;
- the majority of staff receive low pay;
- staff are often expected to work long and 'unsocial' hours;
- there is a large proportion of young, female, part-time, agency and casual staff;
- there is also a high proportion of staff from other countries;
- there are many trade unions but generally trade union membership is low;
- there is high mobility of labour within the industry, and a high turnover of staff joining and leaving the industry.

Distinctive nature of the hotel industry

It is these characteristics which collectively determine the distinctive nature of the hotel industry, which shape organisational design and structure, and largely determine managerial policies, procedures and behaviour.[51] It is the combination of these organisational and staffing characteristics which determines the process of management and which has a distinctive effect on the behaviour of staff and on employee relations.[52] As an example of the nature of work in the hospitality industry, Figure 1.3 gives an insight into the job of a room attendant at the Four Seasons Hotel, London as seen through the eyes of her daughter's diary as part of 'Take Your Daughter to Work Day'.

Marjorie Williams, 41, is a chambermaid at the Four Seasons Hotel, Park Lane, London. She works a 40-hour week and is responsible for cleaning and overseeing the standards of rooms.

ALISON'S DIARY

9am Went to collect my uniform. I enjoyed wearing it – it helped me think my way into the job.

9.30am Went to the morning meeting to go through the night manager's log and find out what has happened in the hotel the night before. It says if a guest has complained or if anything unusual happened that needs to be looked at. Then department heads went through a list of things happening today which will affect the running of the hotel – things you might not even think of, like a march outside, or famous guests booked in. I hope someone famous comes in today.

11am I went with Mum to help clean and check the rooms. She has to get everything just right and exactly the same in every room – even the space between the phone and the note pad. Everything has to be done to the hotel's set standard, and you can't overlook anything. I didn't think Mum would have to work so hard or have to remember so many things – it's no wonder she thinks I'm so untidy at home. I cleaned the coffee table – about eight times – and helped make up the bed. Replaced all those little shampoo and bath supplies that guests use – or take home with them!

12noon Got changed into a different uniform and went to work as a doorman – or door girl. I couldn't carry the cases, but showed people where to check in. Some guests are so nice and smile or chat, and some ignore you completely – you are just someone to wait on them. The trouble is, you can't tell from just looking at them which sort they are. Someone said I looked cute in my hat.

It gets so busy at lunch time. Ernie Wise and Alan Whicker turned up, but I was too shy to speak to them. They seemed so normal, even though they were famous. Perhaps I should have told them I'd like to be an actress – they might have given me my big break.

1pm Grabbed some lunch – fish and chips – in the canteen with some of the other girls. We swapped stories about the guests we had seen but we were all feeling quite tired already. I think half a day at work might be enough for me.

2pm It was much quieter in the afternoon, but I still had to look attentive and be on my best behaviour. When you are on show, you can't afford to relax. Thank goodness it wasn't January – I would have frozen to death.

3pm Did a shift on room service and in the kitchens. It's amazing what guests need brought up to their rooms. The activity never seems to stop; the service runs 24 hours a day. At least at school you get breaks and the chance to gossip with your friends; here, you barely have time to nip to the loo.

3.30pm Review meeting. I can't decide whether it's better to be at work or at school. When it was really busy I kept wanting to be back at school for a rest but then, when it was quieter, I really enjoyed watching how everyone works in a team. What Mum does is just as important as anyone in the management. The first thing guests judge in a hotel is their room and my mum is responsible for making sure their first impressions are good ones. That makes me really proud of her, and I wish more people would realise that. Some guests really appreciate what she does and leave tips, others ignore her.

Went back after the meeting to 'help' Mum but I wasn't in a fit state to do anything so I just put my feet up until it was time to go home.

> 'I didn't think Mum would have to work so hard or remember so much. No wonder she thinks I'm untidy'

Source: Reprinted with permission of Solo Syndication from *YOU Magazine*, 20 April 1997, p. 32.

Figure 1.3 So this is what Mum does all day

Clearly, however, not all of these characteristics will apply, necessarily, to every hotel. It is important to remind ourselves of the importance of the organisational setting, of the diverse nature of the industry, and, to repeat, that **hotels are not a homogeneous grouping**. For example, large city-centre hotels are likely to have a wider range of operations, more bureaucratic procedures, narrower and more specialised areas of responsibilities, and a proportionally higher level of mobility and staff turnover than smaller country hotels. Particular types of hotel will exhibit more specific characteristics; for example, retirement hotels will have a narrower range of customer, and provide a range of facilities and services directed specifically to their particular needs and expectations.

The hospitality industry is also very cosmopolitan and hospitality organisations exist in all parts of the world. It is therefore important to recognise the significance of national, cultural and ethnic values, and socio-political influences.[53]

Small-size establishments

Major hotel groups provide a significant number of rooms and much of the 'theory' of hospitality management is grounded in the study of large-scale organisations. However, it is important to remember that a characteristic feature of the industry is the predominant number of small, independent businesses which often may be operated and managed by the proprietors. Such organisations provide an equally important area of study into organisational behaviour and the effective management of people.[54]

Exhibit 1.5 Running a small hotel

The following original commentary has been provided by the owners/managers of a six-bedroom country house hotel.

In the running of a small establishment as opposed to a larger organisation one of the first points to consider is what type of guest you wish to attract. This is not so narrow-minded as it might appear. There are many people with like tastes and interests across the population no matter what class or creed and in a small establishment you need an easy mix of characters to create a comfortable atmosphere. This means, therefore, giving careful thought as to where and how you will advertise. For instance, we accentuate the aspect of wildlife, and peace and quiet with adults only. Once you have decided to stipulate any limitation, such as, for example, no children or pets, it is essential not to waver for many guests will often choose your establishment because of that stipulation.

Most small hotels are run by the owners who probably do most of the work involved, if not all of it. This means you have to be well organised, able to turn your hands to all tasks and trades, and most importantly of all not panic if things go wrong as they are bound to from time to time. When people choose a small family-run hotel they expect to receive personal attention which means you have to be around and in view for most of the day and evening with a pleasant expression, and prepared to spend time with your guests, not just the passing hello or pleasantry.

The job, which it is really, requires an abnormally high degree of dedication and input but can be most rewarding. If you are successful at putting yourself and your establishment across, your return rate of guests takes a lot of hard work from you because they will usually chat among themselves, therefore setting the stage for a relaxed and happy atmosphere. Small additions to the furnishings and surroundings can add greatly to the well-being of your guests without being costly, for instance small ornaments, pictures or even photographs or personal portraits.

Finance and profitability are of course very important and require a lot of thought. Small establishments are not normally vastly profitable and most owners are happy if they can make a reasonable living from the business. Do not neglect the bookkeeping side of the business. If your accounts are in a mess then very likely your finances will be also. Try to keep on top of your bills and remember to put aside any VAT that will be due. We find it helpful to put this into a separate account and try to forget it is there until payment is due. Always look after and pay the small local traders you deal with. They are probably struggling too and you are more likely to get excellent service if you remember this.

Food is obviously very important and probably a high proportion of your outgoing commitments. We found that we could give a good, varied choice by displaying our menu each morning and asking guests, if they were dining with us, if they could possibly let us know and choose their meal at least an hour before dinner time. It is amazing how obliging people can be and often we know in the morning what to prepare as guests have already made their choice. This method not only cuts down on waste enormously but also ensures the dishes are freshly cooked and appetising.

Another important point is flexibility. If guests would like a slight variation from the menu this should be available and can easily be achieved in a small establishment. While it is understandable that there is the need to be cost effective, do not be meagre in portioning the meals. For example, a good cheeseboard always receives favourable comment. You will have far happier customers if they leave the table fully satisfied rather than still feeling peckish.

If you are fortunate enough to be able to employ staff, make it clear what you require of them and then trust them to get on with the job. Nobody likes to be continually monitored and it can cause bad feeling if you are always looking over their shoulders. This does not mean that you do not check their work. This can be done quite surreptitiously and if found to be lacking then a quiet word is often sufficient to rectify any shortcomings.

Should your staff at any time seem to be struggling with a task (perhaps, for example, they may not feel well) then you should be able to muck in and help. This will gain you respect apart from showing that you can do the job as well as give orders. Often this can work as a bonus as when you are pushed for time the help will be reciprocated. Build up a trust with your staff and be prepared to back them unless you know them to be in the wrong. Contrary to popular belief the customer is not always right and good staff can be hard to get.

Honesty is of the utmost importance. It will only cause dissatisfaction if your establishment is not as advertised. Do not over-embellish or state things that are not accurate. This is the surest way of inviting complaints, and one dissatisfied customer can destroy the atmosphere for all the other guests. Should you still get a guest who is unhappy then it is best to refund the deposit if applicable and let the person find somewhere else. Even if you feel that you are in the right and the complaint is unjustified this is still the best course open to you. As the saying goes, 'one bad apple in the barrel . . .'.

In conclusion, it is really worthwhile to establish a successful hotel business, however small, and the sense of pride and achievement outweighs the work and worry involved.

Source: The authors are grateful to Stella and Paul Silver for providing the above commentary.

The nature of service industries

Hotel operations combine both a productive and a service element. However, although they are not pure service organisations, they exhibit many of the basic characteristics common to other service industries.[55]

Services may be viewed as displaying seven main characteristic features:

- the consumer as a participant in the process;
- simultaneous production and consumption;

- perishable capacity;
- site selection determined by customer demands;
- labour-intensive;
- intangibility;
- difficulty in measuring performance.[56]

The consumer as a participant in the process

Unlike physical production, where the environment of the 'factory' does not concern the eventual purchaser, the presence of the consumer requires attention to the surroundings and characteristics of the service facility. Customer satisfaction will be influenced by the location, furnishing and decoration of the establishment, and the environment in which the delivery of services takes place. The customer is part of the service process and can influence its operations. For example, hotel guests may make use of tea/coffee facilities in their own rooms and thus reduce the demand for room service or, as with the budget Formule 1[57] hotels, may even check themselves in using credit cards.

Simultaneous production and consumption

Services are created and consumed simultaneously. Unlike manufacturing, there can be no inventory of the service itself. For example, a receptionist giving assistance to a guest cannot be stored for future use. Services cannot be stockpiled to meet fluctuating demand. For the delivery of services to take place there must be direct, personal interaction with customers. The lack of an inventory can result in customers having to wait for attention or delivery of service.

Perishable capacity

Services cannot be stored and if they are not used they are likely to be wasted. Unlike manufacturing, services are time-perishable. High fixed costs will still occur during periods of low demand. The income lost from a hospitality room unsold on one day cannot be recouped later: it is lost forever. Additional hotel rooms may not be available to satisfy a higher than expected demand, resulting in a lost opportunity to generate additional income.

Site selection determined by customer demands

Unlike manufacturing, services do not move through distinct channels of distribution. The delivery of services and the customer must be brought together. Services cannot be provided at a single, centralised location for different geographical markets and it may not be possible to achieve economies of scale. Experience of hospitality services is dependent upon personal contact. As services are provided direct to the customer this may result in smaller-scale operations and limited geographical locations.

Labour-intensive

In service operations work, activity is people-orientated and labour is the important resource in determining organisational effectiveness. The personal nature of hospitality services places emphasis on the importance of direct interaction between employees and customers. The effective delivery of services is dependent upon the attention and attitudes of staff as well as their performance. The increased use of technology and automation may well lead to a demand for a higher level of personal attention and service.

Intangibility

Compared with physical products, the particular features of services are more difficult to explain or communicate. Promotion requires an understanding of consumer behaviour and needs to focus attention on the actual delivery of the service. Benefits derived from services are associated with feelings and emotions. The quality of service in a hotel is usually identified with its general culture and ambience, the disposition and attitudes of staff, and the nature of other customers. As Robin Shepherd points out (see above), the details of the experience may be hazy, but the emotional feeling stays sharply focused.

Difficulty in measuring performance

The measurement of output is difficult because there is unlikely to be a single, important criterion on which to evaluate effective performance. For example, profitability or the number of customers staying at a hospitality establishment is not necessarily a measure of the quality of service. The intangible nature of services, coupled with the heterogeneous nature of customers, means that the actual delivery of services will differ widely. It is difficult, therefore, to establish or to monitor objective standards of performance. Even within the same establishment the actual delivery of services to individual customers is likely to vary noticeably according to, for example, the reasons for the customers' presence and their particular requirements, together with the personalities and behaviour of both customers and members of staff.

Lack of ownership

Another feature of service operations is that, unlike manufacturers or suppliers of products, the purchase of services does not bestow ownership upon the customer. All the physical features remain in the ownership of the hotelier, and customers are only hirers of facilities for the duration of their stay.[58]

Are service industries different from other industries?

Hospitality organisations, then, exhibit many of the basic characteristics of service industries and may share many common features such as high fixed costs, labour-intensiveness, low wages and unsocial working hours. However, is a service industry any different from other industries? Not according to leading writers such as Levitt:

> Purveyors of service, for their part, think that they and their problems are fundamentally different from other businesses and their problems. They feel that service is people-intensive, while the rest of the economy is capital-intensive. But these distinctions are largely spurious. There are no such things as service industries. There are only industries whose service components are greater or less than those of other industries. Everybody is in service.[59]

However, Macdonald claims that there are substantial differences between manufacturing and services, and that service organisations have every right to claim that they are different. Internal contrasts between manufacturing and service include the following.

● *Manufacturing* – production is capital-or equipment-orientated; technical skills dominate; training will dominate; production results are variable.

● *Service* – production is people-orientated; interpersonal skills dominate; education will dominate; service results are subject to even more variation.[60]

The distinction between goods and services products is also demonstrated by Stamatis[61] (Figure 1.4).

Goods and Production-Centered Service Operations	Customer-Centered Service Operations
Customer involved in very few production processes	Customer involved in many production processes
Production and delivery processes are separate	Production and delivery processes overlap to: ● varying degrees and ● might even be identical
Production is independent of consumption	Production is frequently simultaneous with consumption
Product design is centered on the customer, and process design is centered on the employee	Both product design and process design are centered on the customer
Production results show less variability	Production results show more variability
More amenable to standards, measurements, inspection, and control	Less amenable to standards, measurements, inspection, and control
Technically more complex	Technically less complex
Employee–customer relationships are generally not complex	Employee–customer relationships are generally very complex
Technical skills dominate operations	Interpersonal skills dominate operations
Training is heavily physical	Training is heavily psychological
Most producers do not deal directly with the customer	Most producers deal directly with customer
Economies of scale are generally readily attainable	Economies of scale are less readily attainable

Source: Reproduced with permission from Stamatis, D. H., *Total Quality Service: Principles, Practices, and Implementation*, © CRC Press, Florida (1996), pp. 23–24.

Figure 1.4 Distinction between goods and services products

The nature of management

In addressing the question 'what is the nature of management in service industries?', Jones suggests that implicit in the question is the fundamental assumption that managers of services face different problems and act differently from other managers. However, Jones acknowledges that this assumption is contentious. Even where there is agreement that services are in some way different, there is no agreement on the cause or importance of this difference.[62]

A major characteristic of the hospitality industry is of course the role of people and the direct contact and interactions between staff and customers. The majority of hotel managers of the author's acquaintance stress the need for a high level of commitment to the job and the ability to be all things to all people. (As an example, the attributes of a hotel manager are discussed further in Chapter 5.)

Whatever one's view of service industries, they still have some functions and purpose to fulfil as part of their role within society. Service industries are in need of management in order to operate effectively in the same way as any other industry. People 1st[63] clearly identify the need for the development of good managers in the hospitality industry.

Service management

Hospitality organisations, while created to provide both service and hospitality, have not always managed service effectively. Today, other service organisations as well as the hospitality industry must recognise the need to manage service effectively and deliver high-quality products. Increased emphasis on quality, and increased customer demands, also mean an increased focus on customer service. As this refocusing takes place, management strategies referred to as 'service management' are being developed. Service management takes a market-orientated approach to service delivery, with an emphasis on long-term customer relationships. Albrecht defines service management as: 'a total organisational approach that makes quality of service, as perceived by the customer, the number one driving force for the operation of the business'.[64]

While traditional management approaches emphasise internal consequences and structure, service management emphasises external consequences and process. This change in focus requires changes in the work culture. The entire organisation needs to understand the emphasis on service and that the organisation can survive only if it meets the needs of the customer. The mission statement, along with company goals and objectives, emphasises the focus on customers. These statements clearly delineate the direction the company is taking. Employee goals are customer-orientated and reward systems are based on customer satisfaction.

Service strategy

The service strategy is the formal organisational link that delineates the focus on customer satisfaction. The strategy outlines what will be done for a certain customer segment, how this should be achieved, and with what kinds of resources. The service strategy reinforces the mission strategy of the organisation. Without a clear service strategy, inconsistent behaviour is evident. Strong service strategies not only aid in strengthening customer relationships, but they also aid in retention of employees. Service strategies can be a powerful management tool to sustain a competitive advantage in the marketplace.

For example, Chacko maintains that 'in an industry that is in the mature stage of its life cycle and where there is tremendous competition, hoteliers have realized that quality of service may be the most important competitive advantage'.[65]

Management focus

The focus of an organisation that utilises service management is different from that of a traditional organisation. The organisation will be structured so that it supports front-line workers and provides the resources that are necessary for them to serve the customers effectively. Decision-making, supervisory focus, reward systems and feedback mechanisms are also different. Decision-making is decentralised so that employees who are involved in the customer interaction are empowered to take action and do what is necessary to satisfy the customer. For example, if guest service representatives have an unhappy guest at the front desk, they have the authority to take care of the problem. Representatives have the authority to give a discount, offer a free meal or make arrangements with outside entities to satisfy the customer. However, long-term strategic decisions remain centralised.

Managers and supervisors focus on the encouragement and support of employees. Services by nature cannot be standardised, therefore the organisation needs to be flexible. Also, for employees to deliver quality service, some flexibility is needed to meet the special needs of every customer. The role of managers changes from that of 'order giver' and controller to 'facilitator', coach and team leader. The role of workers changes from merely being an 'order taker' to becoming an active participant in the creation of guest-satisfying values. Reward systems are based on customer satisfaction. Frequently, managers utilising a service management approach use 'moments of truth' as evaluation points. These moments of truth are the critical points of interaction between the customer and the service provider. Performance is measured against expectations at the critical moments. Customer feedback plays an instrumental role in this type of evaluation.

Berger and Brownell stress the importance of the manager in creating a service culture:

> The most important theme is the essential support of every single manager. When you encourage your subordinates, when you open channels of communication, and when you make sure that feedback regularly reaches members of your staff, you directly impact and improve your organization's service culture.[66]

Service culture

Service management strategies are successful only when they are accompanied by a corporate culture that can be labelled a service culture. The culture can be described as 'a culture where an appreciation for good service exists, and where giving good service to internal as well as ultimate external customers is considered a natural way of life and one of the most important norms by everyone'.[67]

Management, top executives and front-line employees all need to live the service culture. A service culture enhances the ability truly to meet the needs of the customers. The increasing recognition of a service culture, the delivery of high-quality products and the overriding

Thank you for choosing to stay with us. We hope you have a comfortable and enjoyable visit. We have tried to anticipate all your needs, but if there is anything we have overlooked which can make your stay more pleasurable, please do not hesitate to contact the manager on duty. Every effort will be made to assist you. Our staff is dedicated to making your stay trouble free.

Northwest Lodging Inc. prides itself on offering the best possible accommodations at a reasonable price. I welcome your comments or suggestions. You may drop this comment card in the mail or call me directly. We hope to see you again and again.

Dear Guest,

Just finished cleaning your room and wondered if you have any special needs such as extra linens or supplies during your stay. Let me know what it is that you need on the back side of this note and leave it on the table.

I want to help make your stay a comfortable one!

Your Housekeeper,

WELCOME

Dear Guest,

Hello, I'm Roxanne your room attendant. I cleaned your room today and trust that you will find everything to your satisfaction. If you have additional requests, please dial '0' for the Lodge Operator.

It has been our pleasure serving you and we wish you a most enjoyable stay.

THANK YOU FOR BEING OUR GUEST

Figure 1.5 Satisfaction of customer needs

importance of the customer (common in the US) is a growing feature of hospitality organisations. Some examples of attempts to provide a more customer(guest)-orientated environment and the satisfaction of their needs are given in Figure 1.5.

As Berger and Brownell, echoing Albrecht (above), point out, 'a service culture is created when the customer – either external or internal – is the most important focus of the organisation'.[68]

The open systems model of analysis

Earlier in this chapter we raised the debate about whether the hospitality industry is unique. For example, Riley suggests that 'looked at solely as a "managerial task", running a hotel, restaurant or institutional establishment can be seen as a set of systems and processes common to managing anything'.[69]

The approach of scientific management is greatly undervalued and unused by hospitality managers but this does not really contradict the case for uniqueness.[70]

The important questions, however, are:

● To what extent do the particular characteristics of the hospitality industry distinguish it From other industries?

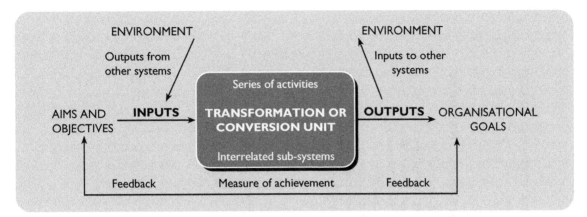

Figure 1.6 The open systems model of organisations

● To what extent do general principles of management theory and practice apply to hospitality organisations as work organisations?

The open systems model provides a useful basis of analysis.

All business organisations can be seen as open systems which take inputs such as people, finance, materials, and information from the external environment. Through a series of activities these inputs are transformed or converted and returned to the environment in various forms of outputs such as goods produced, services provided and completed processes or procedures. Outputs are intended to achieve certain goals such as profit, market standing/market share, level of sales or consumer satisfaction (Figure 1.6).

The open systems model applies in exactly the same way to hospitality organisations as to any other business organisation. By way of a representative example, Figure 1.7 shows the hotel as an open system. However, the same basis of analysis is equally applicable to other sectors of the hospitality industry.

The customer as the major throughput

Hospitality organisations are 'people-moulding' organisations and they are concerned with human beings as the basis of the nature of work carried out.[71] The major input is the customer seeking satisfaction of certain needs. The desired output is a satisfied customer. In order to achieve this output the transformation or conversion process will entail the customer being suitably rested/refreshed/entertained or undergoing a rewarding experience in a comfortable and safe environment. The customer is therefore also the major throughput of the system. It is the demands of the customer which will have the greatest influence on the series of activities involved in the transformation process. This customer involvement underlines the 'co-creation' model referred to earlier in the chapter.

Compared with most business organisations, the hotel is unusual in that customers as the main throughput are provided with and consume services within the establishment, and leave with no tangible product.[72] However, in terms of the open systems model, the hotel is no different from any other business organisation. It is subject to the same basic processes of:

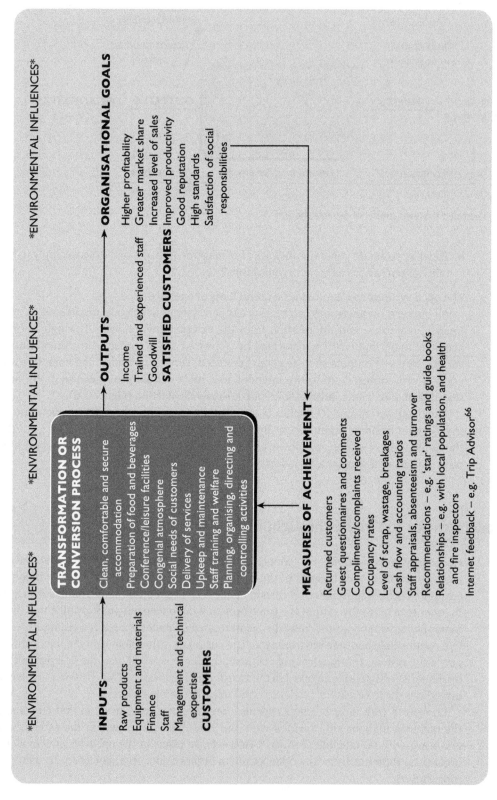

ENVIRONMENTAL INFLUENCES   *ENVIRONMENTAL INFLUENCES*   *ENVIRONMENTAL INFLUENCES*

INPUTS

Raw products
Equipment and materials
Finance
Staff
Management and technical
  expertise

CUSTOMERS

**TRANSFORMATION OR
CONVERSION PROCESS**

Clean, comfortable and secure
  accommodation
Preparation of food and beverages
Conference/leisure facilities
Congenial atmosphere
Social needs of customers
Delivery of services
Upkeep and maintenance
Staff training and welfare
Planning, organising, directing and
  controlling activities

OUTPUTS

Income
Trained and experienced staff
Goodwill

SATISFIED CUSTOMERS

ORGANISATIONAL GOALS

Higher profitability
Greater market share
Increased level of sales
Improved productivity
Good reputation
High standards
Satisfaction of social
  responsibilities

MEASURES OF ACHIEVEMENT

Returned customers
Guest questionnaires and comments
Compliments/complaints received
Occupancy rates
Level of scrap, wastage, breakages
Cash flow and accounting ratios
Staff appraisals, absenteeism and turnover
Recommendations – e.g. 'star' ratings and guide books
Relationships – e.g. with local population, and health
  and fire inspectors
Internet feedback – e.g. Trip Advisor[66]

Figure 1.7 The hotel as an open system

- organisational aims and objectives;
- inputs;
- series of activities as the transformation or conversion process;
- outputs;
- realisation of goals and measures of achievement.

Applications to hospitality management

Reservations about the application of management practices and techniques developed in other sectors of industry prompted Nailon to propose a model specifically related to elements of hospitality management.[74] This model was criticised heavily by Wood, however. The reasoning behind the attempt to create a model of management specifically suited to hospitality organisations was spurious considering the criticisms levelled at the 'blinkered' approaches of previous management theorists.[75]

Wood argues that Nailon's model could describe adequately the factors affecting the management of any organisation and follows closely the structure of the more general open systems theories which are themselves based on previous studies of manufacturing firms.

> There is nothing special about either management or hospitality management. A 'theoretical' understanding of 'management' can only be obtained through an appreciation of how management practices are produced within a framework of social and economic constraints, and how such practices interrelate at the societal level in respect of all social and economic institutions.[76]

Comparison with management elsewhere

Viewing the hospitality industry as unique, or as somehow special and different from other industries, will not improve the level of organisational performance. On the other hand, it may help to account for lack of progress and change in the industry. From his practical experience of hotel management, Venison comments on the striking similarity between the hotel industry and the retail industry. Venison believes hotel management students would benefit from a study of retailing.[77] Wood also challenges the myth of uniqueness in the hotel and catering industry which provides:

> for employers, managers and some workers a self-serving device for justifying the unjustifiable in terms of inadequate basic rewards, feudal management practices and the maintenance of a culture that discourages intervention in the affairs of the industry by others.[78]

We have seen, then, that the hospitality industry does differ in important respects from other industries. But this should not be seen as a convenient reason for disguising comparison with management procedures and practices elsewhere.

Common point of reference

A series of activities by which inputs are transformed into outputs is a common feature of any industry, and makes possible the application of general principles of organisation and management within the hospitality industry. A suitable form of structure must be designed. Essential administrative functions must be carried out. Legal requirements must be observed (for example, in respect of employment legislation). The common activities of management – clarification of objectives, planning, organising, directing and control – apply to a greater or lesser extent.

It is important to emphasise these common features. There are of course differences in the activities and methods of operation of organisations even of the same type, for example in relation to the nature, size and scale of activities of different establishments. The open systems approach provides not only for the critical analysis of the operations of a particular establishment but also a basis for comparison with other hospitality organisations, for example in highlighting similarities or variations in the nature of inputs, the series of activities in organisational processes and execution of work, environmental influences, organisational goals and measures of achievement.[79]

Such an approach will remind us yet again of the diverse nature of the industry but also that differences in the application and implementation of the common features are largely a matter only of degree and emphasis. Using the open systems model provides a common point of reference and enables us to take a general approach to the study of hospitality organisations, to analyse them, and to review applications of general management theory.[80]

Environmental influences

Hospitality organisations are in continual interaction with the external environment of which they are part. In order to be effective and maintain survival and development, they must respond to the opportunities and challenges, and risks and limitations, presented by changing circumstances. The open systems approach views the organisation within its total environment and emphasises the importance of multiple channels of interaction.

The increasing rate of change in major environmental factors has highlighted the need to study the establishment as a total organisation and to adopt a systems approach.

Beyond the control of the manager

Environmental influences are generally beyond the control of the individual manager. Consider how the functioning and operation of a hospitality organisation might be affected by such external environment influences as, for example(Figure 1.8):

- government actions on the rate of VAT, transport policies, health and safety regulations, drink-driving laws, banning of smoking inside buildings and need to provide external smoking areas; changes in Border Agency regulations;
- inflation, interest rates, levels of unemployment;
- international situations and foreign exchange rates;
- technological advances;
- activities of competitors;
- local business trade, or tourism or leisure attractions;

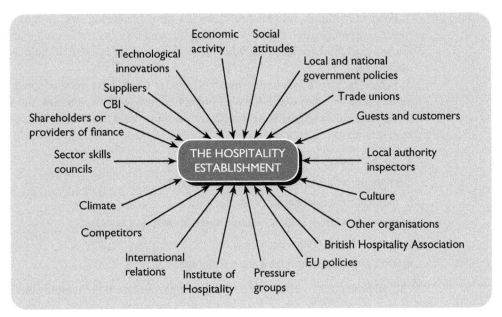

Figure 1.8 External environmental influences

- a major trend towards eating organically grown produce and buying fair trade products;
- increased leisure time for a wider range of the population;
- bankruptcy of, or a major strike at, an important supplier;
- a large increase in trade union activities and membership;
- the opening or closure of a local catering college;
- a long spell of particularly good or inclement weather or volcanic activity (2010);
- political uncertainty.

The effectiveness of hospitality operations will be determined not only by internal considerations and choices, but also by the successful management of the opportunities, challenges and risks presented by the external environment. Managers and their staff must therefore be readily adaptable to changes in the environment and the demands which are placed upon them.

Technological advances

Technology has played a crucial part in the hospitality as in any other industry and has affected the working environment. Indeed the BHA identifies this as an important area for staff development.[81]

Management control systems are becoming increasingly computerised. Internet bookings have revolutionised hotel reservations internationally. Customer expectations of service delivery are constantly changing. For example, mobile phones replace telephones in rooms, guests expect wifi links in rooms and public areas and may well book online, possibly through a comparison website. Guest feedback systems such as Trip Advisor play an important role in marketing hotels.

Food preparation systems are changing also. Increasing use of cook-chill and cook-freeze techniques can be used, particularly in mass catering. As a result many hospitals buy in cook-chill food prepared elsewhere, thereby reducing the size of their in-house catering operations.

People 1st identify six key areas of technology which have been adopted within the hospitality industry, and which have an impact on hospitality operations and the skills of the workforce, either requiring new skills, or, in some cases, de-skilling the operations. These key areas are:

1 online trading;
2 customer relationship management systems;
3 management information systems;
4 human resources (HR) functions and e/m learning systems;
5 front of house technologies;
6 food preparation and cooking technologies.[82]

This all provides new challenges and new opportunities in the working environment.

Exhibit 1.6 Morgans Hotel Group and In-room Technology

Morgans Hotel Group Expands In-room iPad Program featuring Intelity ICE Technology

Mondrian Soho New York Debuts with Virtual Access to Guest Services.

Thursday, March 3, 2011

Intelity, a pioneer in hospitality software, and Morgans Hotel Group have partnered to interactively bring the luxury hotel amenities of the newly opened Mondrian Soho to the fingertips of guests. Powered by Intelity's ICE Touch (Interactive Customer Experience™) software, all 270 guestrooms will feature an in-room iPad that will give guests the control to choose from 30 services and customize their experience.

With just the touch of a screen, guests can coordinate transportation; check flights; order room service; browse for local information such as maps and directions; make dinner reservations; and make housekeeping requests. To keep guests city-savvy, the Morgans Hotel Group iPad offers The List, a selection of local must-see attractions developed in collaboration with UrbanDaddy,

free music downloads curated by RCRD LBL, and current content on the most relevant events happening in New York City. The iPad even offers a customized playlist of ambient sleep sounds to provide guests with the ultimate sleeping experience. In addition, a service unique to Mondrian SoHo allows guests to order items from the iPad's virtual mini-bar service.

"This is the second Morgans Hotel property that we have equipped with our ICE technology," said Intelity CEO, David Adelson. 'We look forward to supporting the brand by providing cutting edge software that promotes overall operational efficiency by boosting on-property revenues, lowering operating costs and increasing guest satisfaction.'

In addition to providing a luxury service to guests, the innovative technology of ICE increases hotel efficiency and customer satisfaction with its backend management tool. Designed by and for hoteliers to reduce operational costs and increase guest satisfaction, ICE fully integrates with the hotel's property management systems and allows management to track and chart guest requests and response times. As a result, hotel managers can pinpoint how quickly needs are being met, staff strengths and weaknesses and which products and services are most in demand.

"The response from our guests at Royalton has been overwhelming and we are thrilled to be expanding this unique amenity to our newest hotel, Mondrian SoHo," said David Weidlich, Executive Vice President of Operations for Morgans Hotel Group. "As we are constantly challenging ourselves to push the envelope and reinvent the guest experience, we feel this offering continues to set us apart. Our newest feature will be our Minibar section – whereby a guest can order a wide arrange of curated items not typically available in a minibar such as Flip Video cameras, Rogan men's apparel and a limited edition Derringer bike upon which to discover New York City."

About Intelity

Intelity, headquartered in Orlando, Florida, is a hospitality software solution company focused on the self-service marketplace. Its ICE software with guest interface and "ICS" (ICE Control System) backend management has been recognized in a vote by hoteliers as the best guest interactive service technology available. Intelity designs its software/hardware products with a focus on generating higher hotel revenues, reducing operating costs and increasing guest satisfaction. Become acquainted with ICE and learn what Intelity's hotel partners are saying on the Intelity website. For more information please call 1-888-RevPAR-1 (1-888-738-7271) or follow us on Twitter.

For more information please visit http://www.morganshotelgroup.com/.[83]

Critical review and reflection

How significant is the Morgans Hotel development of iPad technology referred to above in enhancing the guest experience?

What might be the financial implications of this development to the hotel, in terms of costs, revenue and profitability?

Analysis of hospitality operations

By itself, the open systems model reveals little about the detailed activities undertaken within the hospitality establishment. To benefit from such an approach the system needs to be analysed in such a way that the total operations of the establishment as a unified whole can be reviewed and amended as necessary. Within the hospitality system as a whole each of the main transformation or conversion processes can be seen as separate sub-systems interacting with other sub-systems. For example, the analysis of the system could be based upon the traditional organisation structure with different departments or sections as sub-systems – such as front office, accommodation, food and beverage, conferences, accounting, human resources, security and maintenance. However, this form of analysis could lead to an investigation concentrating on blinkered, sectional interests rather than on the need to adopt a unified, corporate approach.

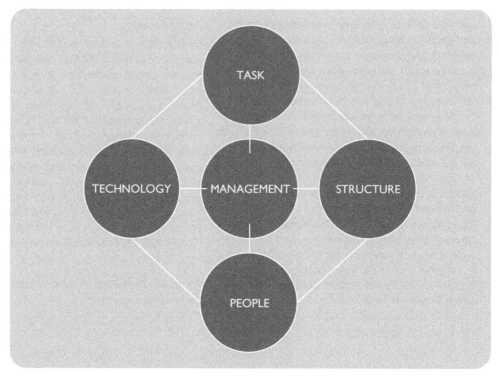

Figure 1.9 Interrelated sub-systems of hospitality operations

Interrelated sub-systems

However the sub-systems are identified, the task of management is to coordinate them and to ensure that the activities of the organisation as a whole are directed towards the accomplishment of its goals and objectives. We can therefore analyse hospitality operations in terms of five main interrelated sub-systems – task, technology, structure, people and management (Figure 1.9).

- *Task* – the goals and objectives of the establishment and the work to be carried out. This is the scale and nature of activities, and the range and quality of services provided, for example: the type of customers and their needs; family, conference or leisure facilities; nature of accommodation; speciality menus; standards of meals and service in the restaurant; opening hours of bars; porterage and room service.

- *Technology* – the manner in which the activities are carried out and the nature of work performance. The meaning of 'technology' is interpreted broadly and includes the physical aspects of equipment, machines, materials and work layout, and the methods, systems and procedures used in the transformation or conversion process, for example: the use of computers, microwaves and cook-chill; methods of food preparation; booking and reservation systems; procedures and methods for cleaning bedrooms. The technology of production in the kitchen is related to, for example, *table d'hôte, à la carte,* buffet or banquet service.

- *Structure* – patterns of organisation, lines of authority, and channels of communication among members of staff. This is the division of work and coordination of tasks by which the series of activities are carried out, for example: whether mechanistic or organic; the extent of centralisation; management and supervisory roles; the responsibilities of departmental managers; the informal organisation.

- *People* – the nature of the staff undertaking the series of activities, for example: training and qualifications; skills and abilities; loyalty; attitudes and interpersonal relationships; cultural influences; needs and expectations; group functioning and behaviour; styles of leadership.

- *Management* – coordination of task, technology, structure and people, and policies and procedures for the execution of the work of the hospitality establishment as a whole, for example: corporate strategy; decision-making; planning, organisation, direction and control of activities; systems and styles of management; interactions with the external environment; social responsibilities.

Overall effectiveness of hospitality operations

The overall effectiveness of hospitality organisations is dependent not only upon the products, services and facilities offered but very strongly on the social relationships which develop within each establishment. **The open systems approach is an attempt to view the organisation as a purposeful, unified whole in continual interaction with its external environment.** Consideration needs to be given to interactions between technical and social aspects of the organisation's operations. The five sub-systems are inextricably linked and changes in any one area will affect all other areas of the organisation's activities.

Critical review and reflection

'The traditional analysis of an organisation is usually based upon the structure and efficiency of individual departments. However, this leads to blinkered sectional interests rather than to the interrelationships and coordination of sub-systems of the organisation as an integrated whole.'

What do you see as the relevance of the traditional form of analysis?

Synopsis

- The hospitality industry has strong links with leisure, travel and tourism. Whilst the ownership of an organisation may suggest that it falls within a particular sector, this narrow view tends to overlook the extent to which the activities overlap. The industry has seen vast growth in recent years to become the fifth largest industry in the UK, directly employing over 2 million people in 2011.

- Managers in hotels and catering tend often to view the industry as unique. The hospitality industry does have a number of distinctive features but it also shares important features with other business organisations. Hospitality education and research is in need of further development, and attention should be given to potential applications of general management theory.

- Whilst defining hospitality is seen by some as problematic, by common consent the customer is central to the concept. The industry is about being hospitable, which leads to notions of respect and co-creation, with the customer contributing to the design and nature of the experience.

- The process of management takes place in the context of an organisational setting. The interrelationship of people, objectives, structure and management determines the effectiveness of hospitality operations. The nature of hotel operations and their organisational and staffing characteristics mean they are likely to embrace to a greater or lesser extent elements of associated sectors of the hospitality industry. Hospitality organisations need to give attention to the effective management of services.

- Applying the open systems model provides a common point of reference and a perspective for a meaningful comparison with other industries. We can analyse hospitality operations in terms of five interrelated sub-systems: task, technology, structure, people and management.

- Technology has a very significant influence on hospitality operations. It affects internal systems and ways of working and also the ways in which customers and guests interact with the organisation.

REVIEW AND DISCUSSION QUESTIONS

1 Explain what is meant by the organisational setting. What are the common factors that hospitality organisations share with other work organisations?

2 Summarise, with supporting practical examples, the important organisational and staffing characteristics of a hospitality organisation of your choice.

3 Identify clearly the main characteristic features of service industries. To what extent are service industries different from other industries?

4 Hospitality organisations were developed on the basis of service delivery. Does this mean that hospitality organisations by nature utilise service management? Provide examples to justify your answer.

5 Explain a hospitality organisation as an open system. How does the open systems model help in providing a basis for the analysis of hospitality operations?

6 Discuss the impact of technological advances on the working environment within the hospitality industry.

7 Consider the extent to which customer expectations have changed over the last decade.

8 The hospitality industry is often considered to be unique. Evaluate the factors that make the industry unique.

ASSIGNMENT 1

According to Venison there is a striking similarity between the hotel industry and the retail industry.

1 Investigate: (a) a hotel organisation; (b) a retail organisation; and (c) a different type of organisation.

2 Develop a comparative profile of the key characteristic features of each of your chosen organisations, together with a description of what is involved in their management.

3 Highlight common factors, similarities and significant differences across the three organisations.

4 What conclusions do you draw from your analysis?

ASSIGNMENT 2

With the aid of a diagram, depict an actual hospitality organisation of your choice in terms of the open systems model.

1 Explain the type and nature of the organisation including its size and location, and main characteristic features.

2 Give specific examples of how the functioning and operation of the organisation are affected by external environmental influences. How effective is the organisation in adapting to changes in its external environment?

3 Analyse, with supporting examples, the nature of the organisation's operations in terms of the main interrelated sub-systems: task, technology, structure, people and management. How effective are the interrelationships and interactions among these sub-systems?

4 Discuss critically the effectiveness of management in coordinating the sub-systems and directing the activities of the organisation as a unified whole towards the accomplishment of its goals and objectives.

ASSIGNMENT 3

The following commentary represents the personal views of the former General Manager of a Golf and Country House Hotel.

Attributes of the hotel manager

I will endeavour to list a few points on what in my opinion are the attributes of being a hotel manager and where we go wrong.

Firstly, degree students expect status but there is not any. Like a war, the best generals lead from the front, not the back. So you always put yourself in the firing line. Customers like to see the manager – not deputy manager, bar manager or restaurant manager. It might be a nod, shake of the hand or a wave, but they want recognition from the top. You should lead by example. Too many managers think that they have done all the hard work getting there, and then stop.

The hotel and leisure industry is too large to bracket. You cannot classify the Savoy or Hilton with a golf and country house hotel or night-club. So a manager needs different attributes. You need to have the ability to socialise with your customers. It may be a granny, newly-weds, a couple on their first date, a football supporter on a night out – the list is endless. You need to be able to converse with them in their language and put them at ease. So you need an ability to judge people very quickly.

Are we attracting people to the industry and giving them a false impression? It is not an easy way of earning a living. It is very hard work and stressful. You have to work split shifts, be up early, maybe in the middle of the night, and you work late at night. It is not a glamorous career where you just stand around in a dinner suit looking pretty. It is a people industry, full stop. You have to get on well with staff and customers and put on a smile even if your mother has died. Customers are not interested, in fact they could not give a damn, but the other way round is a totally different ball game.

As a manager you are there for when problems arise. If there are no problems you would not need a manager, so you are busy when there are difficulties. You need an ability to make quick decisions and you may not have the time to correct them so they must be right first time. You will have no social life because of the commitment needed for the job. You have to live, eat and breathe the establishment to be successful.

The hotel industry is unique. It should not be, but it is, in various ways – but then so are most industries. A good hotel manager may not be able to manage a circus or a coal pit. If hotel workers were rude to or ignored customers, as in some shops, I would be out of a job within a week. Very few people would complain when out shopping, but put them in a hotel and they change their character. So you have to have a thick skin and a long fuse. You must therefore have the ability to stay calm and composed when everything around you is burning to the ground.

I think it would be impossible to improve the standard of management without first tackling many major problems. In this country, hotel workers are always looked down upon. In France and Germany, for example, a restaurant waiter is a class job and held in high esteem. In this country, if you cannot get a job you can always work in the hotel and catering industry as a last choice.

We need more of a breakdown of what makes a successful manager. For example, making money, not receiving complaints, keeping staff, improving turnover, etc.? The job varies if it is company or privately owned. If you manage for a company you need no vision whatsoever as you get sent memos on everything from how to answer the telephone to the correct way of opening a can of beans, positioning the vegetables on a plate, serving a 2 oz portion of carrots. There is a standard for everything which cannot, and will not, be deviated from in any form.

So the only way to improve turnover is people-orientated again. You have to be nice to people. Large companies do not want managers but clones – they tell you how to do everything, full stop. And when you will not do it their way, you are replaced.

Large companies in their head offices have budget forecasters, company trainers, area managers, sales and marketing departments, planners, design consultants, auditors, stock-brokers, wage departments. In fact they have the lot. They tell you how to run a successful hotel, but they miss out the most important factor – life. When do I stop serving Mr Smith who is about to knife me? Or how do I deal with Mrs Jones who has just collapsed?

In the end it goes back to people. They can manage the whole show from 200 miles away, but they cannot control my tone of voice. You can say the word 'Hallo' in so many different ways – gruff, abrupt, sexy, quiet, pleasant, relaxing – the list is endless.

So you possibly need to define the word 'manager'. A manager of a café whose bosses are living in Spain probably has to be more of a 'manager' in some contexts than someone managing a 500-room chain hotel.

Do students who go into the trade know what they want from it? If you want to make decisions, then do not work for a company.

So far I have reached the conclusion that the most important attribute of a manager is the ability to carry out what you are told to do and not question people in authority. Maybe good hotel managers should be trained in either the police or the services because the only times you make decisions, or should make them, concern people again.

We are always given the guidelines or standards. We just have to adhere to them and this is probably the case for 95 per cent of managers. Perhaps you could categorise good managers as all yes-men?

So you need a totally new approach to the whole issue. Technical ability would be extremely high on the agenda while strategic-planning and decision-making skills are low down. If you do not know the technical side very well, you would not know if things were going amiss.

Now if we carry on this train of thought we come across a very big problem. Working for companies the amount of paperwork in triplicate is very high, so you have to spend a lot of time in the office. You have to rely on a second person or a third person, so good managers are only as good as the people around them. They therefore have to have the ability to choose a good team. And we are again back to people.

So when it comes down to the nitty gritty I do not think that you can generalise. Every case is individual. Yes, you have to mix with people. You have to give orders and clear instructions, have no social life, have an eye for detail. You take flak from all directions: from guests, staff, owners or directors. It can be a very lonely life because you are always on your own. You cannot get too close to people. You must never have a relationship with anyone you work with as this will cause you problems. You must try to stay aloof.

You must be cheerful, happy, honest, and above all fair. You must always be seen to look at both points of view and never go into conversation wearing blinkers. If you are a good listener it helps, as the hotel life varies so much. For many live-in workers, it is not a job – it is their life. Everything rolled into one. It is not a job where you clock off and go home on Friday forgetting everything until Monday morning.

At the end of the day you have to *love* the work and you are only as good as the weakest link in the chain. If you cannot stand the heat, get out of the kitchen, hotel, and grounds – because you will never make a successful manager.

TASKS

Meet in self-selecting groups of four to six.

1 Discuss critically what you see as the main points and issues which are raised in this commentary.

2 To what extent do you agree or disagree with the comments? Explain how these are borne out by your own experiences. How much agreement is there among members of your group?

3 Working as a group, suggest what actions you would propose in order to help overcome problem areas identified from the commentary.

CASE STUDY 1.1

Fred. Olsen cruise lines

An increasingly significant sector of the hospitality and leisure industry is that of cruise ships. In 2011, one in every eight package holidays booked was a cruise, and this accounted for 1.7 million UK holidaymakers.[84]

The successful management of a cruise ship is a complex and involved process, unlike that experienced in hardly any other area of the hospitality industry or other business organisation. Some particular factors to consider include, for example:

- Combination of travel agency, hotel and leisure activities, entertainment and organised tours
- Continual heavy occupancy and usage
- Rapid turnover, with mass entry and exit
- 'People logistics' – attending to the complex transportation needs of guests pre- and post cruise, as well as the logistics of a variety of shore excursions
- Wide range of activities and events throughout the day and night
- Purchasing and storage of large quantities of goods, often perishable
- Expectation of high-quality cuisine, design and mix of menus, especially for longer cruises. Attention to individual dietary requirements
- Relationships with Head Office, technical department, port authorities, pilots etc.
- Logistics and maintenance when at sea, and tender operations
- Chain of management command and empowerment
- Crew from a diverse range of cultures and backgrounds
- Health and hygiene, with large numbers of guests and crew in continual close contact
- Traditional formal dining and special 'theme' evenings, for example 'nautical' – props and 'scene-setting' requirements

- Crew resource deployment and rotation planning, including unexpected demands caused by (for example): sickness, rough weather, delayed tours, missed ports of call and need to rearrange daily schedule at short notice
- Unavailability of additional agency or temporary staff as with land-based hotels – requirement for crew to adopt flexible working practices in response to the demands of the business
- Crew with long periods away from home
- Accommodating annual leave requirements, including the necessity to arrange flights for some members of the crew, and managing opportunities for time on shore for crew
- Changeover of crew at the end of contracts – maintaining continuity within the business
- Ships with their own 'identities' – within Fred. Olsen Cruise Lines, each one of the four cruise ships has its own unique feel and 'personality'
- Need for 'continual improvement' to achieve the highest standards of safety – as defined in the International Safety Management ('ISM') Code, which provides an international standard for the safe management and operation of ships, preventing human injury or loss of life, and environmental damage, at sea
- Need for 'continual improvement' to achieve the highest standards of quality and conformance – as defined in the ISO9001 Quality Assurance standard 8.5.1: 'The organization shall continually improve the effectiveness of the quality management system through the use of the quality policy, quality objectives, audit results, analysis of data, corrective and preventive actions and management review.'

Within the structure of interrelated activities on board a cruise ship, by far the largest area of responsibility is that of hotel management, working hand-in-hand with the ship operation. For the majority of cruise guests, the two most important factors that determine the level of customer satisfaction are likely to relate to the standards

Case study 1.1 (*continued*)

of customer service delivered by the crew, and restaurant/dining facilities. **So how might the success and organisational performance of a cruise company, and its hotel management, be best judged?**

Fred. Olsen Cruise Lines: 'It's all about the people!'

In an ever-growing and continually-evolving cruise industry, the delivery of a memorable personal service experience is particularly significant as an integral part of organisational effectiveness. Goods and services are no longer enough and, in addition to providing a consistently high-quality product, cruise companies need to differentiate themselves by an emotional engagement with customers and the highest levels of customer service.[85]

Fred. Olsen Cruise Lines is the only family-run cruise line in the world, with sailing experience going back over 160 years. Unlike many of the vast floating cities of other cruise lines, Fred. Olsen has stylish, contemporary ships built 'on a human scale', with a capacity between 800 and 1,350 guests. They are large enough to provide the facilities desired by guests, but small enough to enable a close exploration of a wide range of exciting locations. Emphasis is on a comfortable, friendly atmosphere, with a 'country house hotel' feel delivered 'with a smile' by caring and attentive crew. Guests are welcomed as individuals in a relaxed, familiar ambience.

In September 2011 Fred. Olsen Cruise Lines was voted 'Cruise Line of the Year' in the first-ever Cruise International Awards.

Fred. Olsen Facts

- Operates a fleet of four smaller, more intimate cruise ships – *Balmoral*, *Braemar*, *Boudicca* and *Black Watch* – carrying nearly 100,000 guests per year.
- Is ideally suited to the traditional British cruise guest – well over 90 per cent of guests are British, and the target market is aged 55+.
- The Fred. Olsen ethos of 'It's all about the people!' underpins every aspect of the guest experience on board. The average crew-to-guest ratio across the fleet is 1:2.4.

- Offers a wide range of departures from convenient regional UK ports: Southampton, Dover, Portsmouth, Rosyth (for Edinburgh), Greenock (for Glasgow) and Newcastle.
- A wide range of destinations, including Europe, Norwegian fjords and Arctic, Canary Islands, Baltic, 'Around the World', 'Around South America', and Mediterranean.

For further information on Fred. Olsen Cruise Lines, visit the website at www.fredolsencruises.com.

Fred. Olsen prides itself on providing exceptional service by anticipating, meeting and exceeding its guests' expectations when they are on board its ships. As a result, the cruise line attracts a high level of 'repeat guests' – that is, loyal customers who have cruised with the company at least once before. Depending on their level of membership, these repeat guests receive a range of benefits and incentives to continue cruising with Fred. Olsen. On a typical Fred. Olsen cruise, more than half of the guests are repeat customers, which is one of the highest return rates of any major cruise line.

F riendliness
R espect
E xcellence
D eliver
O wn the problem
L ead by example
S ervice with a smile
E nglish
N eat & tidy

The Fred. Olsen Lines' 'Credo Card' is worn with pride by all crew on board its four cruise ships as an *aide mémoire* of the need for consistently high levels of customer service and guest satisfaction.

Case study 1.1 (*continued*)

Questions

1 What do you think are the most important factors that explain the high level of repeat guests on Fred. Olsen cruise ships?

2 Fred. Olsen has a particular attraction for more discerning, traditional guests. What particular additional considerations do you think this creates for the hotel management?

3 What do you think are the most appropriate measures of successful organisational performance and effectiveness for Fred. Olsen? Explain what additional and/or alternative measures you would suggest.

4 What measures of organisational performance and success do you think most appropriate for: (i) other cruise lines; and (ii) other sectors of the hospitality and leisure industry?

References

1 See, for example, Mullins L. J., 'Managerial Behaviour and Development in the Hospitality Industry', *Proceedings of The International Association of Hotel Management Schools Symposium,* Leeds Polytechnic, November 1988.

2 British Hospitality Association, 'Creating jobs in Britain – a hospitality economy proposition', November 2010, www.bha.org.uk

3 Davis, B., Lockwood, A. Pantedilis, I. and Alcott, P., *Food and Beverage Management*, 4th edn, Butterworth (2008).

4 www.people1st.co.uk., accessed 29.2.12

5 www.people1st.co.uk./about-us, accessed 20.4.12

6 Boella, M. and Goss-Turner, S., *Human Resource Management in the Hospitality Industry*, 8th edn, Elsevier Butterworth Heinemann (2005).

7 British Hospitality Association annual report 2010–11.

8 www.people1st.co.uk, accessed 6.3.12

9 See note 6.

10 Boella and Goss-Turner (2005), P.L. See note 6.

11 www.people1st.co.uk/webfiles/research/stateofthenationreport2011, accessed 20.4.12

12 See note 11.

13 King, C. A., 'What is Hospitality?', *International Journal of Hospitality Management*, vol. 14, nos. 3/4, 1995, 219–234.

14 Guerrier, Y., *Organizational Behaviour in Hotels and Restaurants: An International Perspective*, Wiley (1999).

15 Walker, J., *Introduction to Hospitality Management*, Pearson Prentice Hall (2004), p. 748.

16 Lashley, C. and Morrison, A. (eds) *In Search of Hospitality: Theoretical Perspectives and Debates*, Oxford: Butterworth Heinemann (2000).

17 Slattery, P., 'Finding the Hospitality Industry', *Journal of Hospitality, Leisure, Sport and Tourism Education*, vol. 1, no. 1, 2002, www.hlst.Itsn.ac.uk/johlste, accessed 22.4.12

18 Parasuraman, A., Zeithaml, V. and Berry, L., 'SERVQUAL: a multi-item scale for measuring consumer perceptions of service quality', *Journal of Retailing*, vol. 64, no. 1, 1988, 12–40.

19 Riley, M., Ladkin, A. and Szivas, E., *Tourism employment: planning and analysis,* Channel View, Clevedon (2002).

20 Turnbull, J., 'Customer experience and the human touch', in Todor J. I. and Todor, W. D. (eds), The importance of the customer experience in a down economy (electronic version), (International Thought Leader Report, 2008, pp. 17–19), Customer Future (2008).

21 Morgan, M., Elbe, J. and Curiel, J. E., 'Has the experience economy arrived? A comparison of three visitor-dependent areas' (2008), accessed April 5, 2011 from the Regional Studies Association website: http://www.regional-studies-assoc.ac.uk/events/2008/may-prague/papers/Morgan.pdf

22 Pine, B. J. and Gilmore, J. H., 'Welcome to the experience economy' (electronic version), *Harvard Business Review,* vol. 76, no. 4, 1998, 97–105.

23 see notes 21 and 22.

24 See note 21.

25 Hemmington, N., 2007. 'From service to experience: understanding and defining the hospitality business,' *The Service Industries Journal,* vol. 27, no. 6, 2007, 747–55, doi: 10.1080/02642060701453221

26 www.dinnerinthesky.com

27 www.icehotel.com

28 Toffler (1970), cited by Morgan *et al.* (2008). See note 21.

29 'Status Stones', 2008. Accessed 2 March 2011, from trendwatching website: http://trendwatching.com/trendo/statusstories.htm.

30 Prahalad, C. K. and Ramaswamy, Vo, 'Co-creating unique value with customers', *Strategy & headership,* Vol. 32, no. 3, 4–9.

31 http://www.saatchi.com/over_top_people/kevin_roberts, accessed 29 October 2012.

32 See note 20.

33 Ramaswamy, V., 'Leading the transformation to co-creation of value', *Strategy and Leadership,* vol. 37, no. 2, 2009, 32–7. DOI 10.1108/10878570910941208.

34 Erdly, M. and Kesterson-Townes, L., '"Experience rules": a scenario for the hospitality and leisure industry circa 2010 envisions transformation' (electronic version), *Strategy & Leadership,* vol. 31, no. 3, 2003, 12–18.

35 Gross, T. S., *Positively Outrageous Service,* 2nd edn, Dearborn Trade Publishing (2004). Heffernan, R. and LaValle, S., 'Emotional interactions: the frontier of the customer-focus enterprise', *Strategy & Leadership,* vol. 35, no. 3, 2007, 38–49, doi: 10.1108/10878570710745820.

36 Yoon, M. H., Beatty, S. E. and Suh, J., 'The effect of work climate on critical employee and customer outcomes: An employee-level analysis', *International Journal of Service Industry Management,* vol. 12, no. 5, 2001, 500–21.

37 Heffernan, R. and LaValle, S., 'Emotional interaction: the frontier & the customer focused interprise; *Strategy & Leadership,* vol. 35, no. 3, 38–49.

38 See note 35.

39 Amadeus, 'Hotels 2020: beyond segmentation', (2010) from http://www.amadeus.com/hotelit/beyond-segmentation.html, accessed March 7, 2011.

40 Scott-Halsell, S. A., Blum, S. C. and Huffman, L., 'A study of emotional intelligence levels in hospitality industry professionals' (electronic version), *Journal of Human Resources in Hospitality & Tourism,* vol. 7, no. 2, 2008, 135–52. 'Status stories' (2008). Accessed March 2, 2011, from Trendwatching website: http://trendwatching.com/trends/statusstories.htm.

41 Hornsey, T. and Dann, D., *Manpower Management in the Hotel and Catering Industry,* Batsford (1984).

42 Fearn, D. A., *The Practice of General Management: Catering Applications,* Macdonald (1971), p. 1.

43 Guerrier, Y. and Lockwood, A., 'Managers in hospitality: a review of current research', in Cooper, C. (ed.), *Progress in Tourism, Recreation and Hospitality Management*, vol. 2, Bellhaven Press (May 1990), pp. 151–67.

44 Medlik, S., *The Business of Hotels*, 3rd edn, Butterworth-Heinemann (1994), p. xvi.

45 Jones, P., 'Hospitality research – where have we got to?', *International Journal of Hospitality Management*, vol. 15, no. 1, 1996, 5–10.

46 www.youtube.com/watch?v=wcjSqGQQMUI Tom Baum.

47 Taylor, S. and Edgar, D., 'Hospitality research: the emperor's new clothes?', *International Journal of Hospitality Management*, vol. 15, no. 3, 1996, pp. 211–27.

48 Guerrier, Y. and Deery, M., 'Research in hospitality resource management and organizational behaviour', *International Journal of Hospitality Management*, vol. 17, 1998, 145–60.

49 See, for example, Riley M., *Human Resource Management in the Hospitality and Tourism Industry*, 2nd edn, Butterworth-Heinemann (1996).

50 Medlik, S., *The Business of Hotels*, 3rd edn, Butterworth-Heinemann (1994).

51 For example see Guerrier, Y. and Lockwood, A., 'Core and peripheral employees in hotel operations', *Personnel Review*, vol. 18, no. 1, 1989, 9–15.

52 See, for example, Mars, G., Bryant, D. and Mitchell, P., *Manpower Problems in the Hotel and Catering Industry*, Saxon House (1979).

53 See, for example, Ahmed, Z. U., Heller, V. L. and Hughes, K. A., 'South Africa's hotel industry', *Cornell HRA Quarterly*, February 1999, 74–85.

54 For a discussion on the small hotel, see, for example: Medlik, S., *The Business of Hotels*, 3rd edn, Butterworth-Heinemann (1994).

55 Jones, P. (ed.), *Management in Service Industries*, Pitman (1989).

56 Fitzsimmons, J. A. and Sullivan, R. S., *Service Operations Management*, McGraw-Hill (1982).

57 http://www.hotelformule1.com/gb/home/ibisfamily.shtml, accessed 21.3.12

58 Jones, P. and Lockwood, A., *The Management of Hotel Operations*, Cassell (1989).

59 Levitt, T., 'Production-Line Approach to Service', *Harvard Business Review*, September–October 1972, 41.

60 Macdonald, J., 'Service Is Different', *The TQM Magazine*, vol. 6, no. 1, 1994, 5–7.

61 Stamatis, D. H., *Total Quality Service*, St Lucie Press (1996).

62 See note 50.

63 www.people1st.co.uk/webfiles/research/stateofthenationreport2011, accessed 20.4.12

64 Albrecht, K., *At America's Service*, Dow Jones-Irwin (1988), p. 20.

65 Chacko, H. E., 'Designing a seamless hotel organization', *International Journal of Contemporary Hospitality Management*, vol. 10, no. 4, 1998, 134.

66 Berger, F. and Brownell, J., *Organizational Behavior for the Hospitality Industry*, Pearson Prentice Hall (2009).

67 Gronroos, C., *Service Management and Marketing*, Lexington Books (1990), p. 244.

68 See note 63.

69 Riley M., *Human Resource Management in the Hospitality and Tourism Industry*, 2nd edn, Butterworth-Heinemann (1996), p. 1.

70 See note 64.

71 Katz, D. and Kahn, R. L., *The Social Psychology of Organizations*, 2nd edn, Wiley (1978).

72 See, for example, Wachtel, J. M., 'Marketing or sales? Some confusion in the hospitality industry', *International Journal of Hospitality Management*, vol. 3, no. 1, 1984, 38–40.

73 www.tripadvisor.co.uk/Hotels, accessed 21.4.12

74 Nailon, P., 'Theory in hospitality management', *International Journal of Hospitality Management*, vol. 1, no. 3, 1982, pp. 135–143.

75 Wood, R. C., 'Theory, management and hospitality: A response to Philip Nailon', *International Journal of Hospitality Management*, vol. 2, no. 2, 1983, 103–4.

76 *Ibid.*, p. 104.

77 Venison, P., *Managing Hotels*, Heinemann (1983).

78 Wood, R. C., *Working in Hotels and Catering*, 3rd edn, International Thomson Business Press (1997), p. 74.

79 Mullins, L. J., 'Is the hotel and catering industry unique?', *Hospitality*, no. 21, September 1981, 30–3.

80 Mullins, L. J., 'The hotel and the open systems model of organisational analysis', *The Service Industries Journal*, vol. 13, no. 1, January 1993, 1–16.

81 www.people1st.co.uk, *Technology in the hospitality industry – adoption and skills needs*, accessed 3.10.11

82 See note 76.

83 http://www.hotelinteractive.com/article_print.aspx?articleID=19900, accessed 19.4.12

84 Passenger Shipping Association, 'The Cruise Review', published February 2012 – www.the-psa.co.uk

85 See, for example, Pine, J. and Gilmore, J. H., *The Experience Economy: Work is theatre & every business a stage*, Harvard Business School Press (1999), pp. 365–76.

Chapter 2

Understanding the nature of the workforce

Learning outcomes

After completing this chapter you should be able to:

- focus on valuing individual differences and factors affecting behaviour at work;
- apply aspects of personality theory to people within the hospitality industry;
- explain the particular relevance of emotional intelligence, and the requirement for emotional labour within the hospitality organisation;
- outline the nature of the perceptual process and its application within the hospitality industry;
- detail the nature and significance of attitudes to the workplace;
- explore the particular nature of hospitality employees and their psychological contracts.

Introduction

People interacting in order to achieve the organisational objectives form the basis of an organisation. As with any service industry, hospitality organisations rely upon the contribution of their people. If managers are to improve performance, they need knowledge and understanding of who they are employing, what influences the behaviour of these employees and why they are working within the industry.[1] This knowledge and understanding will enable hospitality managers to better meet the needs of the organisation and the people working in it.

Critical review and reflection

'People are not all made the same way. They are not all rounded. Some are angular, some are difficult, and you have to fit in with them and their personality.' (Charles Forte)[2]

'People are our asset.' (Vicky Williams H.R. Director, Compass Catering 2011)

How valid do you believe the above views are? Should managers make allowances for individual differences, and in your experience, do they?

The behaviour of people

A major characteristic of the hospitality industry is the role of people. Experience of service delivery is dependent upon the personal interaction between staff and customers. Effective management is therefore about working with people. Unlike physical resources, people are not owned by the organisation. People differ as individuals.

Members of staff will have their own perceptions of the hospitality organisation as a work organisation, and hold their own views on the systems and style of management. People bring their own feelings and attitudes towards their duties and responsibilities, and the conditions under which they are working.

Human behaviour is capricious and results from a multiplicity of influences which are difficult to identify or explain. Scientific methods or principles of behaviour cannot be applied with reliability. Tensions, conflicts and stress are almost inevitable, as are informal structures of organisation and unofficial working methods.[3]

Exhibit 2.1 The day a red-hot chef let his temper boil over

One of Britain's top young chefs has resigned from an exclusive restaurant after allegedly branding a trainee with a hot knife.

Tom Aikens is said to have 'turned on' 19-year-old Marcus Donaldson after he made a minor mistake in the kitchen of Pied à Terre, in London's West End.

The chef, the youngest in the country to be awarded two coveted Michelin stars, is claimed to have picked up a knife and held it under a blowtorch – normally used for putting a crisp top on crème brûlée desserts – until it was red-hot. He is then said to have pressed the knife against Mr Donaldson's arm, telling him: 'You don't have enough burns to work in this restaurant.'

Shocked staff in the basement kitchen were apparently told to 'get on with their work' and to 'forget' about the incident.

But yesterday, directors of the restaurant, in Charlotte Street, confirmed that fellow director Mr Aikens, 29, known for his fiery temperament, had been forced to resign as head chef. His wife Laura, who was assistant manager, also quit.

It is understood Mr Aikens faced disciplinary action if he had not agreed to leave immediately.

A source at the restaurant said: 'Aikens's resignation is directly linked to the incident last Friday night. We cannot have things like this going on in the kitchen. Even if it was in the heat of the moment it was a very stupid thing to do and gives Pied à Terre a very bad image. Behaviour like this cannot be tolerated, and it was the unanimous decision of the four other directors that he had to go.'

Restaurant senior partner David Moore added: 'Tom is a very talented chef who demands high standards from those around him. But in a hot kitchen, what people might accept as being normal is not always regarded as so in the cold light of day.' He predicted a bright future for Mr Aikens, but added: 'His temperament needs to be worked on.'

The incident at the Pied à Terre has not been reported to the police.

Mr Aikens's departure over his alleged behaviour is the latest in a long line of incidents involving leading London chefs in what is a lucrative but increasingly competitive business.

The trend for fiery chefs was set most notably by Marco Pierre White. More recently, former professional footballer Gordon Ramsay – who has a restaurant in Chelsea – has gained a reputation for his 'ranting and raving' in the kitchen. Mr Aikens and Mr Ramsay are themselves said to have become 'fierce rivals'.

'There can be a lot of aggravation'

Last night Mr Ramsay, who said he 'didn't have a problem' with being described as 'fiery or volatile' revealed he had heard about the alleged branding incident at Pied à Terre because one of his apprentices shared a flat with Mr Donaldson. He claimed the teenager's father Malcolm had come to London

from the family home in Sheffield 'looking for Tom Aikens'.

Last night neither Mr Aikens nor Mr Donaldson – who was back home in Yorkshire, but planned to return to Pied à Terre – was available for comment.

Mr Aikens, from Norwich, was awarded the Michelin stars for his 'brilliant and cutting edge' cuisine. He was 26 when he scooped the award only months after joining Pied à Terre. At the time, he said: 'I can't believe it. It's a dream come true. And being the youngest ever gives me an even greater buzz.' Mr Aikens, who has a twin brother, has spoken of 'nurturing' his ambition to become a top chef since the age of 12, and has worked up to 20 hours a day in pursuit of that goal.

He has also talked about 'violence' in restaurant kitchens, saying: 'There can be a lot of aggravation there. We all know the chefs who like to beat their staff up, but there is absolutely no need for it.' He was 'OK with giving someone a really good shouting at' but 'punching them and hitting them is totally out of order'.

He said of trainee staff: 'Some have talent, some don't. Those ones that don't, you've got to push them a bit more, and sometimes they still can't get it right.'

Source: Reproduced with kind permission from the *Daily Mail*, 17 December 1999, p. 8.

Exhibit 2.2 Cooking up a success

Chefs have a reputation for being quick-tempered and constantly shouting at incompetent staff. However, according to Gill Scott, chef and co-owner of the Bistro Montparnasse, Southsea, the chef's job does not have to be like that. She stresses that not all chefs are highly strung prima donnas and would recommend the job to anyone with the ambition to do it.

'If you are organised enough then you don't need to get into a panic. I have worked in places where the head chef would throw a pan along the floor at your ankles if you were talking or doing something you shouldn't. You can go to work in some kitchens and the head chef won't talk to you for two days. I have seen chefs sweep a whole batch of food on the floor because it hasn't been done the way he wants it. But I don't believe that is productive. I try not to lose my temper. It happens maybe once or twice a month. My two second chefs and I get on very well. It's a very happy environment and we enjoy what we do. The hours are long and unsociable. Hotel chefs have to work shifts, either late at night or very early in the morning. Some days you might have to do "back-to-back" shifts finishing at midnight and starting again at 5.30 the next morning. I start work at around 10 am and my two second chefs join me at 2 pm and work until midnight with one break between 6 pm and 6.45 pm. It's a long day and the wages are not very high but both my second chefs have been with me for a long time. They enjoy it. You have got to be determined and have ambition to succeed in chefing and in catering.'

Critical review and reflection

'The heat and pressure in the commercial kitchen environment inevitably leads to pressure and heated temperaments. However, the "macho" approach may not be acceptable in today's working environment.'

'Macho Head Chefs have passed their sell by date.'[4]

In general, how acceptable is the behaviour, as described? Are there factors in the commercial kitchen environment that make it more acceptable there?

Influences on behaviour

The behaviour of people at work cannot be studied in isolation. The hospitality organisation as a work organisation is a constantly changing network of interrelated activities. Using the open systems model discussed in Chapter 1 we can see that effective performance will be dependent upon interactions among people and the nature of the tasks to be undertaken, the technology employed and methods of carrying out work, patterns of organisation structure, the process of management, and the external environment.

These variables provide parameters which enable us to formulate a simple four-fold framework in which to view influences on behaviour: the individual, the group, the organisation and the environment.[5]

- *The individual* – for example, the personality, skills and attributes, values and attitudes, needs and expectations of individual members. The individual is the central feature of organisational behaviour, whether acting in isolation or as part of a group, in response to demands of the organisation or as a result of environmental influences.

- *The group* – for example, the structure and functioning of work groups, the informal organisation, role relationships. Groups are essential to effective working and everyone will be a member of one or more groups. People in groups influence each other in many ways, and groups may develop their own hierarchies and leaders. Group pressures can have a major influence on the behaviour and performance of individual members. (This will be examined in Chapter 8).

- *The organisation* – for example, objectives and policy, technology and methods of work, styles of leadership, methods of supervision and control. Individuals and groups interact within the formal organisation. The design of structure, patterns of management and organisational processes for the execution of work will impact on the behaviour of people.

- *The environment* – for example, technical and scientific developments, economic activity, social and cultural influences, governmental actions. The hospitality organisation functions as part of the wider environment of which it is part and must be responsive to the external demands placed upon it. Environmental factors are reflected in terms of the management of opportunities and risks, the operations of the organisation and the behaviour of people.

A behavioural science approach

Within the framework of individual, group, organisation and environment we can identify a number of interrelated dimensions which collectively influence the behaviour of people in the work situation. The framework presents a number of alternative approaches to the study of human behaviour which give rise to frequent debate and discussion.

It is possible, for example, to adopt a psychological approach with the main emphasis on the individual, or to adopt a sociological approach with the main emphasis on human behaviour in society. It is also possible to adopt an anthropological approach with emphasis on the study of culture and customs of human behaviour as a whole.

An interdisciplinary approach

All three areas are important, as are other related areas of the social sciences such as economics and political science. But our main concern here is not with finer details of specific academic disciplines, *per se*, but with the behaviour and management of people as human resources of the hospitality industry.

An understanding of people's behaviour at work cannot be achieved in terms of the study of a single discipline. It is more appropriate therefore to take an interdisciplinary, behavioural science approach by drawing upon relevant aspects of psychology, sociology and anthropology (see Figure 2.1).

- *Psychology* is concerned broadly with the study of human behaviour, with traits of the individual and membership of small social groups. The main focus of attention is on the 'personality system' and individual traits and properties such as perception, attitudes, motives and feelings.

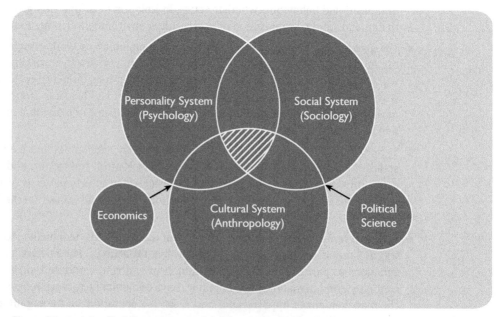

Figure 2.1 An interdisciplinary approach to the study of behaviour

- *Sociology* is concerned more with the study of social behaviour, and relationships among social groups and society. The main focus of attention is the 'social system' and the analysis of social structures and positions, for example the relationships between the behaviour of leaders and followers.
- *Anthropology* is concerned with the science of mankind and the study of human behaviour as a whole. A main focus of attention is on the 'cultural system' and the beliefs, customs, ideas and values within a society which affect the emphasis that individuals place on certain aspects of behaviour.

Applications of behavioural science

Once again, terminology is not always consistent and the wording 'behavioural science' has no strict scientific definition. It may be used in a generic sense for all the social sciences concerned with the study of human behaviour. But the term is now frequently applied in a more narrow and selective way to problems of organisation and management in the work environment. Behavioural science attempts to structure organisations in order to secure the optimum working environment. It is concerned with reconciling the needs of the organisation for the contribution of maximum productivity, with the needs of individuals and the realisation of their potential. Some applications of behavioural science to the hospitality industry are given by, for example, Atkinson,[6] Wood,[7] and Carmouche and Kelly.[8]

The role of social science

The nature of the hospitality industry as a people industry and the importance of the study of social science are widely recognised. For example, Slattery argues that the social sciences alone are able to offer theoretically grounded interpretations of people and social events in hospitality. The success of these interpretations depends upon:

- the selection of relevant theories;
- developing hospitality versions of the theories; and
- an evaluation of flaws and limitations, and value to the hospitality industry.[9]

Slattery suggests that although not all of the social sciences are useful or relevant, the range of theories which are useful is still vast. The selection of a theory depends upon the problems or issues in which we are interested. Theories of motivation, commitment and organisation are necessary bases.

The need for vocational relevance

In a critique of the role of social science subjects in hospitality management education, Wood suggests the need for a substantial reappraisal of social science education.[10] He questions the need to ensure vocational relevance and argues that such an approach could lead to dilution of the tenability of the subject matter. An alternative would be the grounding of specific components of social sciences – principally economics and sociology – with a theoretical and empirical base. However, as Wood himself states, 'whilst this approach *may* encourage intellectual integrity, it can promise nothing else'.

Such an approach as suggested by Wood would seem unlikely to gain much favour with either students or practitioners. The use of the social sciences should be seen as part of the tool kit of management, to be drawn upon and used as particular circumstances demand. The overriding objective must surely be how an understanding of the practical application of relevant aspects of social science can improve the people–organisation relationship.

In a study of the teaching of sociological subjects on vocational degree courses in hotel and catering management, Lennon and Wood also report on the claimed intellectual dilution of sociology and social scientific knowledge. Such dilution is seen as a result of a number of institutional pressures including the views of industrialists, and is characterised by a multi-disciplinary approach related to the criteria of relevance to the job of a manager and a 'learning to manage organisations' approach to social studies. Lennon and Wood conclude that 'there seems little danger of contradiction in asserting that (hotel and catering) management and business studies education is, in social scientific terms at least, intellectually weak and of dubious practical value'.[11]

Although one can perhaps understand Lennon and Wood's scepticism about the idea that the social sciences represent a unified body of knowledge, this should not detract from the advantages of an interdisciplinary, behavioural science approach to an understanding of the behaviour of people at work.

Problems of organisation and management

Sociological aspects can clearly be important but much of the argument tends to be presented in the abstract and is lacking in constructive ideas on how, in practical terms, action could be taken to improve organisational performance. A requirement for intellectual rigour is of course a commendable aim. But this should not be allowed to disguise the fact that an integral part of hospitality management and business studies education should rightly involve an emphasis on vocational relevance and attention to learning to manage organisations.

Our knowledge of human behaviour stems from different sources. In attempting to solve problems of organisation and management in the work environment it is necessary to cut across traditional academic disciplines.[12] It is for this reason that behavioural science has developed as a body of knowledge. There is now strong support for the belief that 'a knowledge and understanding of behavioural science, and the application of some of the key ideas about behaviour, can help improve both managerial and organisational performance'.[13]

The recognition of individuality

How do individuals differ?

Our sense of self is shaped by our inherited characteristics and by influences in our social environment. Most social scientists would agree that both inherited and environmental factors are important in our development, and it is the way in which these factors interact which is key to our adult personality. However, scientists differ with regards to the weight they place on these factors, some believing that our personality is most heavily influenced by our inherited characteristics, others that environmental factors are more important.

The differences among individuals include:

- personality traits and types
- intelligence and abilities

- perception
- attitudes
- motivation
- gender
- physique
- social and cultural factors
- ethnic origin
- national culture.

Some of these factors are shared with others such as individuals who are from the same ethnic group or who have the same ability levels. However, individual uniqueness stems from the dynamic ways in which these inherited and environmental factors combine and interact. Some of these factors may be analysed in more detail, as follows.

Personality

Personality may be viewed as consisting of stable characteristics that explain why a person behaves in a particular way. So, for instance, independence, conscientiousness, agreeableness and self-control would be examples of these personality characteristics. However, it is only when we see/hear/observe a person that we can gain an understanding of their personality. For example, a person who is independent may show that characteristic by displaying a strong sense of self-sufficiency. We would expect them to take the initiative and not to depend on other people. Furthermore, if the characteristic is 'stable' we can rely on this being a consistent part of the person's behaviour. We would be surprised if the person one day demonstrated autonomy and initiative and the next withdrew and delayed any decisions. We anticipate that individuals are generally consistent in the way in which they respond to situations.

There are times when we might be surprised by somebody's behaviour and we may feel they are 'acting out of character'. Of course this would be known only if we had an understanding of their 'typical behaviour' in the first place. Individuals may exaggerate or suppress certain personality traits, for example if they are under stress or influenced by drink/drugs. It is self-evident that managers need to learn the art of 'reading' people's behaviour in order to manage relationships effectively.

Employing people with a suitable personality is often quoted as particularly relevant in the hospitality industry. An understanding of personality theory can assist the manager in appropriate recruitment, selection and understanding of the workforce. For full discussion of theoretical approaches to personality, see Mullins.[14]

Nomothetic and idiographic approaches

Broadly speaking, personality studies can be divided into two main approaches – nomothetic and idiographic. Nomothetic approaches look at the identification of traits and personality as a collection of characteristics. These characteristics are ones that can be described, identified and measured and therefore can be subjected to observation and tests. Nomothetic approaches view personality as consistent, largely inherited and resistant to change. This resistance to change makes them good predictors of future personality, and by extension, behaviour, and for this reason they are seen as being particularly helpful in the selection, training and development of individuals.

The idiographic approach is, by comparison, a holistic and dynamic perspective, which insists that managers take into account a 'whole' understanding of the individual at work.

One of the most widely used nomothetic approaches is the so-called OCEAN approach. There is now a body of evidence which suggests that five dimensions capture distinct differences between people. These clusters of traits (not personality types) are known as the Big Five,[15] and sometimes expressed as the acronym OCEAN:

- Openness/closed-mindedness
- Conscientiousness/heedlessness
- Extraversion/introversion
- Agreeableness/hostility
- Neuroticism/stability

The Big Five form the basis of standard personality questionnaires that determine positive or negative scores for each dimension. Results from a wide number of studies have shown that these factors can be identified as being significant in measuring the variation between people.[16] Of these, conscientiousness has the highest positive link with high levels of job knowledge and performance across a range of occupations.[17] However, some researchers are critical of the descriptors used.[18] Bentall suggests they are 'tainted by the investigators' values' and continues: 'I suspect that most people will have a pretty clear idea of where they would like to find themselves on the dimensions of neuroticism, extraversion, openness, agreeableness and conscientiousness.' He questions the ethical and political nature of the scales.[19] The relationship between personality and work performance is also questioned by Robertson who suggests that the only two of the five dimensions linked consistently with high levels of performance are conscientiousness and emotional stability.[20]

Despite these reservations the strength and value of the Big Five model has been extolled in a review by Lord and Rust. They conclude that:

> Indeed, the five factor model has become the linchpin that holds personality assessment together, at least within the work context. Without it, how would we generalize with confidence from the validity of one work-based instrument to that of another? Furthermore, the model links the study of assessment instruments within the HR field to research in personality and related areas carried out within clinical and mainstream psychology fields in which the Big Five have also become dominant.[21]

Critical review and reflection

'Nowhere is an understanding of personality theory more important than in service industries. Workers are required to interact with customers and during this become a key part of the product.'[22]

Which of the personality traits identified in the Big Five would you say were important for front-line staff in the hospitality industry and why?

Personality profile of hospitality managers

A survey of general managers suggests that hotel managers tend to have particular personality profiles, distinguishing them from non-hotel managers. The survey suggested the following differences between the hotel managers and others to be that they are:

- calmer, more realistic and stable;
- more assertive, competitive and stubborn;
- more cheerful, active and enthusiastic;
- more realistic, independent and cynical;
- harder to fool, more deliberate and concerned with self;
- more concerned with practical matters and detail;
- socially bolder and more spontaneous.[23]

Other writers have suggested that personality is more important for hotel management than other factors.

Ineson[24] points out that 'Research has confirmed that personality is a key contributor to effective management especially in the service sector where well developed personal and interpersonal competencies are key to managerial success', whilst the general manager of the Four Seasons Hotel, Qatar indicates what he looks for in his hotel managers: 'if graduates are too academic they tend not to last'.[25]

Emotional labour

Until recently, workplaces were seen as rational, logical places where emotions were excluded or seen in a negative light. Hochschild's[26] research describes the way in which some jobs require a display of certain emotions, especially those in the service industries, where customer care is inextricably linked with making people feel good. Such work has been labelled as **emotional labour** and distinguishes between surface acting – displaying emotion without experiencing it, and deep acting – involving thinking, visualising to induce the emotion in the situation. Briner[27] challenges psychologists to broaden research to throw light on the complexities of emotions in the workplace. He notes that organisations specify the emotions they would like their employees to feel in the mission statements and, in more subtle ways, in terms of the rewards and career enhancements people receive, when they display appropriate emotions. However, he suggests that little is known about the incidence of emotion at work and the part it plays in work behaviours.

Emotional labour involves the acting of, or the hiding of, emotions. Mann[28] identifies three potential situations involving the match between emotions felt and emotions displayed in work roles:

- emotional harmony – where the individual actually feels the emotion required of the display rules and social expectations (this is not emotional labour because the individual is not hiding or faking emotions);

● emotional dissonance – when the emotions displayed for the purposes of the job role are not the emotions felt;

● emotional deviance – occurs when the person displays the emotions felt but these are not the ones that are expected to be displayed.[29]

Identifying the complex relations between emotional labour, Gursoy *et al.*[30] analyse the need to display particular emotions at work and the impact this has on the workforce: 'Unless they are dealing with a task of a negative nature, tourism and hospitality employees are expected to display positive and pleasant emotions, more specifically they are expected to be happy, jolly and cheerful.'

Many organisations such as Disney, Marriott and TGI Fridays openly ask their employees to consider themselves on stage when front of house.

A study by Chu *et al.*, 'When we are on stage we smile', points out that some degree of emotional labour is 'critical to the very nature of service and hospitality as the interaction between employees and customers is a significant component of the service encounter, which can affect the service quality'.

The study considers the emotional effect of 'surface acting' and 'deep acting' on the staff member and concludes that the emotional dissonance felt when an employee is required to display emotions which are not the real feelings (surface acting) leads to emotional exhaustion and a lack of job satisfaction. However, when an employee tries to feel the required emotion (deep acting), this tends to lead to increased job satisfaction.[31]

Critical review and reflection

'Some degree of emotional labour . . . is critical to the very nature of service and hospitality . . . as the interaction can affect the service quality.'

In the light of the comment by Chu et al., and their analysis in the previous paragraph, what do you think are the implications for hospitality workers and their managers?

Stress at work

Stress is a complex topic that involves personality and emotions. It is individually defined and is intrinsically tied into an individual's perceptual system. Everyone has a range of comfort within which they can feel steady and safe. Stress occurs when the individual feels that they are working outside of that comfort zone. Individuals will differ when they feel discomfort. The effects of stress will differ too: for some, the incidence of stress may energise and activate but for others it may immobilise.

The costs of stress at individual, organisational and national levels are well known. Cooper has indicated the high incidence of stress throughout organisations, irrespective of seniority. He suggests that every job has its own stress fingerprint.[32] Stress is a term that is commonly used and misused; some individuals may say that they are 'stressed-out' at the slightest amount of pressure and tension. It also contains a perverse sense of status; for instance, a librarian complained bitterly that her role was regarded as having low stress, implying that jobs given a 'high stress' position also ranked high in prestige.

Type A and Type B personalities

Two polar sets of behaviour that link with personality and health have been identified by medical students Friedman and Rosenman, who identified recurring patterns of personality in patients suffering from premature heart disease.[33] Individuals with a **Type A personality** are excessively competitive and thrive on hard work and long hours. They work under moderate to high levels of stress and exhibit characteristics such as:

- a high need for achievement;
- extreme competitiveness;
- impatience with obstacles to the completion of tasks;
- aggressiveness;
- a tendency to move and speak rapidly;
- an aversion to idleness;
- restlessness and urgency about time.

Individuals with a **Type B personality** are considered to exhibit the opposite characteristics from Type A. They may still have high levels of drive and ambition but are more relaxed, work at a steady pace and do not exhibit a sense of time urgency.

According to Friedman and Rosenman, Type A personalities are far more vulnerable to heart attacks than Type B personalities. Individuals who have a personality classified as Type A are more likely to suffer from heart disease under severe stress than individuals with a Type B personality.[34] Research also supports the link between stress and Type A personality.[35]

Type A people and team performance

Gratton reports on what happens when Type A people, for whom time urgency is crucial, get to work together with less time-urgent people. Type A people are likely to pay a great deal of attention to the passage of time, constantly check the time remaining and see time as their enemy. Typically they will be very efficient in their use of time, and will use deadlines to prioritise tasks and increase their work pace. Type A people have the potential to keep things moving and active but can have a detrimental impact.[36] A study by Waller et al.[37] found that where teams were responsible for completing creative tasks, Type A time-urgent people tended to impose strict, linear schedules on members and this reduced the innovative performance of the team.

(The implications of pressure and stress on people working within the hospitality industry will be considered in detail in Chapter 9.)

Intelligence

Individuals vary with regard to their mental abilities and the extent to which they apply them at work, and different occupations require different skills, competencies and abilities. The 'happy' scenario is one where a match occurs between the individual's abilities and their occupation, but reality suggests that this is not always the case. The extremes include employees bored rigid with a simple task who become careless and make a succession of mistakes and employees who have been promoted beyond their ability. Much work in the hospitality industry falls into the former category, being routine and monotonous and not challenging to the able person doing it. The opposite situation also occurs, where frequently employees have been promoted rapidly beyond their capability and/ or experience. Either situation can result in stress for the individual unable to cope with the job, or uninterested in it. The work colleagues are also likely to be adversely affected in each case.

In a similar vein to the studies of personality, different schools of thought have emerged with regard to the study of abilities. The research on intelligence has given rise to debates, similar to those around personality. The most obvious debate has been the perennial one about the extent to which intelligence is innate, or developed through life experience.

The **nativists** believe that intelligence is mostly inherited (nature), while the **empiricists** believe that our environment shapes our behaviour and mental abilities (nurture). Howe's[38] research tends to support the empiricists. He cites evidence from early intervention programmes such as Head Start initiatives to show that intervention can have an impact on IQ.

The nature of intelligence

There has been much debate over whether intelligence is a general ability, indicating that an individual's mental ability is more or less constant over a range of intellectual activities, or whether, as Thurstone suggests, there is a range of primary mental abilities, which he specifies as follows:

- spatial ability
- perceptual speed
- numerical reasoning
- verbal reasoning
- memory
- verbal fluency
- inductive reasoning.

This model suggests that an individual might be particularly able in one area, but not necessarily equally able in other areas.

Emotional intelligence

Individuals can be seen to be more, or less, intelligent in the accepted sense, and the degree of intelligence may be of interest when recruiting for the hospitality organisation. However, a measure that could be considered of greater relevance to hospitality, an industry that requires an understanding of a broad range of people and an ability to interact with them, is that of emotional intelligence.

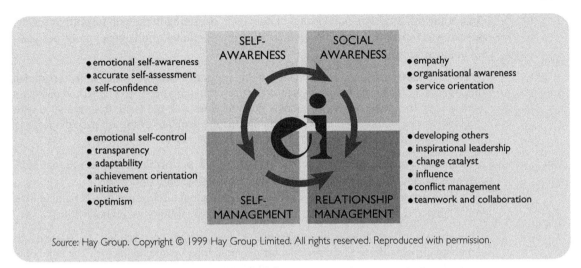

Figure 2.2 Emotional Intelligence Competence Model

Goleman considered that the classical view of intelligence was too narrow and extended the idea to emotional abilities. He identified the key characteristics of emotional intelligence as:

> abilities such as being able to motivate oneself and persist in the face of frustrations; to control impulse and delay gratification; to regulate one's moods and keep distress from swamping the ability to think; to empathise and to hope.[39]

Emotional intelligence (EI) has received considerable attention in recent years. The concept has been described as key to organisational success, with particular relevance in organisations like leisure services, where employee relations impact so directly on external customer experiences.[40]

The Hay Group, working with Goleman, have identified 18 specific competencies that make up the four components of emotional intelligence as shown in Figure 2.2. The Emotional Competence Inventory defines EI as 'the capacity for recognising our own feelings and those of others, for motivating ourselves and for managing emotions within ourselves and with others'.[41]

Significance of emotional intelligence

Those who are emotionally intelligent are said to have the following abilities:

- know their own emotions;
- manage their own emotions;
- motivate themselves;
- recognise emotions in others;
- handle relationships.

In an industry where the personal interaction with customers is so important, the abilities that comprise emotional intelligence are clearly crucial to both managers and employees: 'increasingly researchers are linking EI with successful hospitality management'.[42]

In a study by Langhorn[43] of a group of managers operating in the pub restaurant sector, evidence was found that there was a link between emotional intelligence, profit performance and team satisfaction.

> More profitable restaurants are managed by general managers with higher emotional intelligence . . . The ability to relate well to the team through a set of emotional competencies would seem to be beneficial in developing good relations with the team; this, combined with the ability to be adaptable in the face of the fluctuating demands of the job, would appear to be positive in developing the satisfaction of the team overall.

It was found that the main predictors of managerial performance are emotional self-awareness, social responsibility, interpersonal relationships and optimism.

In a study considering the effects of employees' emotional intelligence in a Korean de luxe hotel,[44] Jung and Yoon analysed the effects of emotional intelligence on behaviour.

> The importance of emotional intelligence is emphasised because human relations in organisations are affected by emotional factors more than by rational factors. The emotional quotient is as important as the intelligence quotient.

Critical review and reflection

'Many people do not consciously think about the person with whom they are interacting. They translate their model of the world from their own perceptions and assume that others are working from the same model. There is no way managers can cope with so many individual perspectives so they might just as well rely on their own judgement.'

What are your views?

The process of perception

A particularly significant aspect of individual differences, and a major determinant of behaviour within the hospitality industry, is the process of perception. People all 'see' things differently. Owners, managers, staff, union representatives, customers, guests, visitors, suppliers, health inspectors and local residents will all have their own perception of the functioning and operations of the particular establishment. And so will each person as an individual. All people have their own, unique picture or image of how they arbitrarily view what is to them the 'real' world. Consider the following example.

Exhibit 2.3 People perceive things differently

The general manager is preparing a human resource plan for the establishment and wishes to gather information which may help to improve future staffing levels. The manager requests section heads to provide details of agency and temporary staff employed within their section during the past six months and projections for the next six months.

- One section head may perceive the request as an unreasonable demand, intended only to enable management to exercise closer supervision and control over the activities of the section.

- Another section head may see the request only as increased bureaucracy and more paperwork, and believe that nothing positive will come of it anyway.

- A further section head may welcome the request and perceive this as a hopeful sign of an increase in permanent staffing levels for the section.

- But yet another section head is concerned that the manager is intending to put pressure on permanent staff to work harder and longer hours.

Stimuli from the environment

Why is it that the same request can provide such mixed reactions and why do people perceive things differently? We are faced constantly with a vast amount of information (stimuli) from the environment such as shapes, colours, movement, taste, sounds, touch, smells, pain, pressures and feelings. Perception is the process by which stimuli are screened and selected to provide meaning and significance to the individual. The manner in which stimuli are selected and organised gives rise to individual behavioural responses (Figure 2.3).

Individuals have their own 'mental' view of reality. Despite the fact that a group of people may 'physically' see or hear the same thing, each person has his or her own version of what is seen or heard. A person's pattern of behaviour is shaped in response to how that person perceives a particular situation. The process of perception is essential, therefore, to an understanding of human behaviour. Consider, for example, the shape in Figure 2.4.[45] Write down exactly what you see. Do this before reading further. We shall return to this later.

Perceptual ambiguity

A well-known example of what might be termed a perceptual ambiguity is the shape in Figure 2.5.[46] What do *you* see?

Most people will probably see a younger, well-dressed woman looking sideways. But other people will see an older, poor-looking woman facing more to the front. And some people will quickly see both. How can people who view the same thing 'see' something so different? This helps to explain the importance of perception.

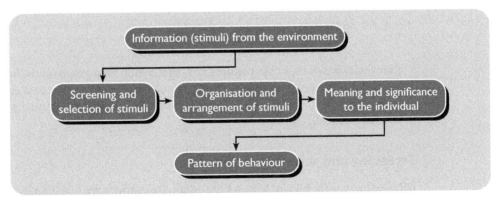

Figure 2.3 The process of perception

59

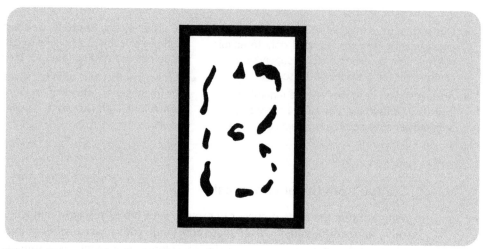

Figure 2.4 An example of incomplete stimuli

Figure 2.5 An example of perceptual ambiguity

Can you now see the other picture? If so this should help you to understand why other people have a different perception to your own. Also, once you have seen clearly both pictures your mental image may quickly jump from one to the other, causing some confusion as to what you really do see.

Screening and selection of stimuli

Because there is such a vast amount of stimuli, we cannot cope adequately with all of them so we focus on certain selected stimuli and screen or filter out others. This screening and

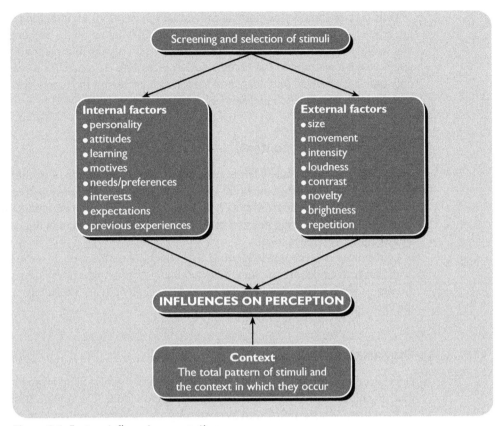

Figure 2.6 Factors influencing perception

selection of stimuli is based on a combination of internal and external factors, and the context in which the stimuli occur (see Figure 2.6).

Internal factors

Internal factors relate to the characteristics of the individual such as personality, attitudes, learning, motives, needs and preferences, interests, expectations and previous experiences. People usually perceive stimuli that are likely to satisfy their needs or prove pleasurable. People may also learn to ignore mildly disturbing stimuli but respond to more important ones. For example, a manager may screen out the constant movement of people, ringing telephones and other forms of activity, but respond quickly to a guest complaining to a receptionist.

External factors

External factors refer to the nature of the stimuli themselves. People will usually give more attention to stimuli which are, for example, large, moving, intense, loud, contrasted, bright, novel, repeated or standing out from the background. An example is the distinctive red and white 'pie-man' sign of Little Chef restaurants. As another example, a fire extinguisher should be immediately visible and stand out clearly from its surroundings.

Only certain stimuli enter into an individual's perception. An intending customer entering a hotel reception area sees a member of staff having an angry exchange with a guest and walks away without booking. The customer sees only the argument and disregards the many positive features of the hotel. Another intending customer for a restaurant notices only that it is crowded and noisy and leaves without seeing the empty spaces at the back, and unaware that the food and service are excellent.

The importance of context

Any number of stimuli may be present at a given time or situation. It is, therefore, the total pattern of stimuli and the context in which they occur that influence perception. The sight of a rack of muddy wellington boots is likely to be perceived quite differently in the entrance to a working farm offering bed and breakfast accommodation than in the reception area of a city-centre conference hotel.

Look now at the example in Figure 2.7.[47] Which centre black circle is the larger – A or B?

In fact both circles are the same size and many of you might have guessed this to be the answer. However, because circle B is framed by smaller circles it certainly *appears* larger to the vast majority of people.

Organisation and arrangement of stimuli

Once incoming stimuli have been screened, they are organised and arranged in such a way that provides meaning and significance to the individual. The organisation and arrangement of stimuli can be influenced by continuity, proximity or similarity, that is, the principle of grouping.

For example, in Figure 2.8(a) guests in a dining room are more likely to be perceived as 16 individuals, or possibly one large group. But in Figure 2.8(b) the guests are more likely to be perceived as four distinct sets or groups of people. And this perception may well influence the manner of the delivery of service.

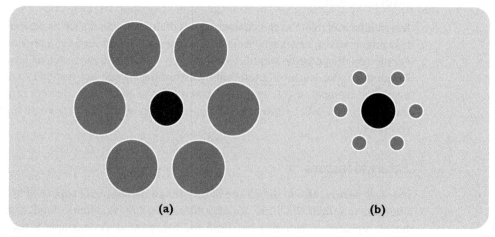

(a)   (b)

Figure 2.7 An example of context

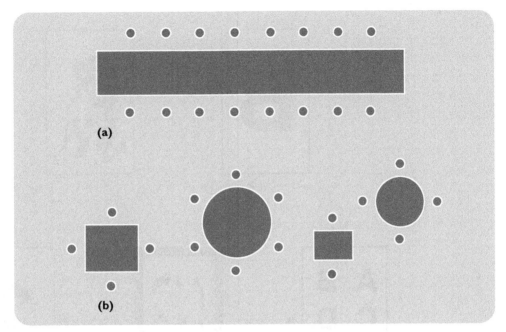

Figure 2.8 An example of the principle of grouping

The principle of closure

When people have incomplete or ambiguous stimuli there is a tendency to 'close' the information in order to complete the mental picture and create a meaningful image. Let us now return to Figure 2.4. It is probable that most people will perceive the shape either as an unconnected letter B or the unconnected number 13. However, some people may see the shape as no more than 11, or a series of, discrete blobs. For other people the shape may be perceived as some different meaningful object, for example a butterfly. Among responses from hotel and catering management degree students are a clown, a dog, a face, a series of letters of the alphabet, or a golf course (Figure 2.9). We may have difficulty in understanding how other people could possibly see such objects *but this is what they perceived the shape to be.*

The principle of closure is important as it applies not only to visual stimuli but to our other senses. We can probably all think of an example when we have 'got hold of the wrong end of the stick' as a result of our perception from overhearing only part of a conversation.

Applications within the hospitality industry

As people are selective in the stimuli which determine their responses and patterns of behaviour, it is important to be aware of those factors most likely to influence perception and create the desired image in the minds of customers. For example, many large hotel and catering groups adopt a standard colour scheme and layout for each of their individual establishments. This helps to influence customer perception through instant recognition and familiarity, and through helping the customer to know what to expect

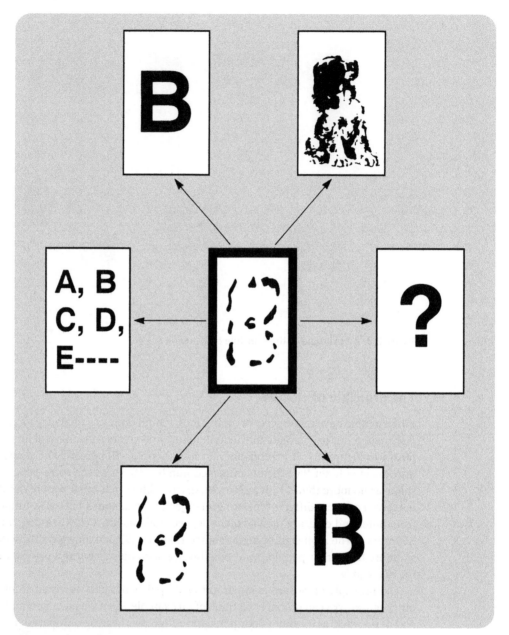

Figure 2.9 Examples of responses from the incomplete stimuli in Figure 2.4

and to feel at home. The aim is to reinforce identification with the group and to generate repeat business.

For example, with TGI Friday's, the distinctive wooden floors, tin ceilings, Tiffany lampshades, red striped tablecloths, traffic lights by the toilets and collection of badges worn by the waiters, in all restaurants wherever you are, help to create a unique corporate atmosphere.

Visual effects

Perception is influenced strongly by the appropriate use of visual effects which create a feeling of, for example, warmth or cold, intimacy or formality, large or small, cluttered or spacious. The design and layout and the lighting, patterns and colour schemes of premises, accommodation, restaurants and bars have a major impact on ambience and the atmosphere that is created.[48] Perception is also important in terms of how customers respond to the appearance and presentation of food, and to the arrangement, balance of colour and size as well as the aroma, texture and taste.

Importance of first impressions

First impressions are important. If a telephone enquiry from a potential new customer is received in a friendly, courteous and efficient manner by the receptionist the customer is likely to receive good 'vibes' and form a favourable perception of the establishment as a whole. Equally, the one curt, unhelpful receptionist can create an unfavourable perception of what is, in every other respect, a very friendly, pleasant and well-managed establishment.

A surprising number of people make a decision not to return to a hotel before they even enter the bedroom. This is linked to dissatisfaction arising from the arrival process: first impressions, the speed of check-in, the welcome, the smile, the acknowledgement, the porter service.[49]

Dress and appearance

Dress and appearance are important factors in perception, and again first impressions are important. The style of dress or uniform of the staff helps to create an image of the organisation and influences perception of the standards of service and staff–customer relationships. For example, the cleanliness of the chefs' whites influences perceptions of hygiene in the kitchen. The traditional black suits worn by the staff at Claridges convey an indication of high-class service and rather formal staff–customer relationships.

Perceiving other people

The hospitality industry is very much a people business. The way in which people perceive other people – that is, the process of interpersonal perception – is clearly of particular importance. It is essential that managers and staff have a highly developed sense of people perception and understand the reasons for perceptual distortions and errors discussed below.

An understanding of perception should help us to avoid making hasty decisions about other people before thinking fully about the situation. Snap judgements can impair the 'accuracy' of perception. For example, in Figure 2.5 above it often takes time to see both the old woman and the young woman in the same picture. Staff should be given proper guidance and training in social skills. They should be perceptually aware of customers' needs and expectations, and quick to recognise any indications that facilities or services are not up to the required standards.

Good customer care starts with good staff care.[50] It is equally important that managers also have a positive attitude towards caring for staff, and their needs and expectations at work. The manager's perception of the workforce is a major influence on the style of managerial behaviour which is adopted. (Managerial behaviour is discussed in Chapter 5.)

Interpersonal perception

The principles of perceptual differences, discussed above, reflect the way we perceive other people and are the source of many problems in the work situation. The process of interpersonal perception can influence both the manager–subordinate relationship and the staff–customer relationship. The perception of other people is a major determinant of behaviour and standards of service delivered.

Judgements about other people

Judgements made about other people can be influenced by perceptions of stimuli such as role or status, occupation, physical factors and appearance, and body language, for example eye contact, facial expression or tone of voice. For instance, the estimated height of a person may vary with that person's perceived status.

In a study with American college students, an unknown visitor from England was introduced briefly to five separate groups. The visitor was described with a different academic position to each group before leaving the room. Students were then asked to estimate the height of the visitor. As ascribed academic status increased, so did the group's estimate of the height of the visitor.[51]

Every person sees things in his or her own way and, as perception becomes a person's reality, this can lead to misunderstandings. There are three main factors which can create particular difficulties with interpersonal perception and cause problems in dealings with other people – selective perception, the halo effect and stereotyping.

Selective perception

Because of their own internal characteristics, people are selective about the information to which they pay particular attention. They see and hear only what they want to see and hear. This selectivity gives rise to perceptual defence. People may tend to select information which is supportive of their point of view and choose not to acknowledge contrary information. Consider the following example.

Exhibit 2.4 Selective perception

A manager has on a number of occasions expressed dissatisfaction with the head chef, with whom there have been a number of personality clashes. On leaving the restaurant the manager enquires of a regular guest who was entertaining some business colleagues whether they enjoyed the meal. The guest replies with a smile and pointing at a colleague says: 'Peter would have preferred his steak cooked a little less, he likes it really raw so he can put a piece on his black eye.' Then with a straight face, the guest continues: 'Apart from that it was an excellent meal and we all enjoyed it, thank you.'

The manager 'hears' only the comment that the steak could have been cooked a little less and does not 'see' the accompanying smile or gesture. The manager then reports back to the chef that there has been 'another' complaint and a customer's steak was overcooked.

Another manager who has experienced no difficulties with the chef, and who gets on well with him, could perceive the guest's comments quite differently. The comments about the steak could be seen simply as a joke against Peter. The manager is pleased to hear that it was an excellent and enjoyable meal and reports this back to the chef.

The halo effect

This arises when the judgements made about another person are formulated on the basis of particular characteristics or impressions that are readily available. The halo effect tends to influence perceptions of the rest of that person, either positively or negatively, and results in assumptions and generalisations from limited information.

A well-known example is with selection interviewing. A candidate arrives punctually, is smart in appearance, well-spoken and friendly. All positive characteristics–but these may well influence the perception of selectors of the candidate as a whole person. Because of the halo effect the selectors may tend to assume the candidate will perform well, and as a result place less emphasis on checking experience and technical ability.

The rusty halo effect

The process may also work in reverse (the rusty halo effect). This is where general judgements about a person are formulated from the perception of a negative characteristic. For example, a candidate is seen arriving late for an interview. There may be a very good reason for this and it may be completely out of character. But on the basis of that one particular event the person may be perceived as a poor timekeeper and unreliable.

Significance for managers

The halo effect has particular significance for managers and supervisors who may observe only a limited aspect of the behaviour or activities of staff. A single trait, such as good or bad timekeeping, may become the main, or even the sole, criterion for judging overall performance. A manager observing a member of staff performing a single task particularly well or badly may tend to see this as a judgement of that person's overall level of competence.

A danger associated with the halo effect is that the perceiver may become 'perceptually blind', and screen and shut out subsequent observations or information at variance with the original perception. For example, a manager who has recently refused to promote a member of staff despite the recommendations of the head of department may then tend to ignore favourable information about that member of staff and select only information which supports the decision not to agree to the promotion.

Another danger is that of projection. This is the tendency of people to project their own feelings, motives or characteristics to their perception of other people. A manager may make a more favourable judgement about members of staff who have characteristics largely in common with, and easily recognised by, the manager.

Stereotyping

This is the tendency to ascribe positive or negative characteristics to a person on the basis of a general categorisation and perceived similarities. Stereotyping is a form of typecasting. It is a means of simplifying the process of perception and making collective judgements of other people, rather than the recognition of each person as an individual.

Stereotyping results in the tendency to classify people according to easily recognisable characteristics and perceived common groupings and this may (perhaps subconsciously) influence the manner of the service delivery. For example, in a busy inner city four-star hotel the usual Monday to Thursday guest may be typecast as typically male, wearing a dark or grey suit, who prefers to dine alone, often reading, or makes frequent use of room service, makes little conversation, has a formal relationship with staff and whose company is paying the bills. This form of stereotyping contrasts with any individual Monday to Thursday guests who are private customers paying their own way or with families taking advantage of weekday leisure breaks. Without proper training it is possible that some staff may have difficulty in adjusting to the different patterns of behaviour and expectations of service of individual guests.

Typecasting may also be based on, for example: nationality, gender, age, skin colour, speech, appearance and style of dress. For example, in some hotels male guests are required to wear jackets and ties in the restaurant. Other establishments will not admit people wearing jeans or studded jackets. In each case there is a collective stereotyping of suitable or unsuitable clientele on the basis of their dress.

Perceiving each person as an individual

We all tend to make use of stereotypes. Indeed they may be helpful in enabling us to make quick predictions of likely patterns of behaviour, and reducing stress in dealing with people we do not know as individuals. However, although there is likely to be some truth in underlying stereotypes (this is why they exist), they are simplistic over-generalisations.

People of the same generalised 'grouping' do not necessarily fit into the stereotype. It is important, therefore, to be receptive to personal aspects of attitudes and behaviour. Initial perceptions based on stereotyping may need to be revised in order to perceive each person as an individual in his or her own right.

Sex stereotyping and gender

The (then) HCITB report on the image of hotel and catering work highlighted the importance of sex stereotyping, which is well established and persistent. Jobs are still perceived as being male or female and the distinction is seen as relevant in making a job choice which must be of the appropriate gender.

> The jobs which people consider suitable show substantial sex stereotyping, jobs in reception, accommodation services and the job of kitchen counter assistant being mentioned as suitable primarily by women, reception work also clearly being the most popular alternative overall. Men dominate responses concerned with management and portering. It may thus be desirable to counter established sex stereotyping and encourage women into training for management.[52]

The perception of women

Although the HCITB report demonstrated the existence of sex stereotyping, the image is grounded in reality. It is possible to predict who is most likely to be meeting customers at the reception desk, who will be cleaning their rooms and who will be cooking their meals. Typically, a woman will meet the customers, clean the rooms and serve the meals; and a man will cook the meals, repair any defects and manage the hotel.

> Statistics show that women dominate the industry, particularly at an operational level in part-time jobs. However, at a management level men outnumber women. Sex segregation can be seen in operation within some hotel departments; kitchens being almost exclusively male and housekeeping departments female.[53]

Why such distinct roles?

Why is it that men and women have such distinct roles within hotels? Is it that these roles suit their abilities or are there other explanations? Is it the women themselves who lack the ambition to become managers, or do the tradition and beliefs of the industry (the cultural milieu) exclude women? Are the ways in which management is perceived and the ways managers are developed the key to understanding the sex stereotyping of women in the industry?

In one respect it could perhaps be perceived that hotels typify the stereotype of 'women's work'. Hotels are temporary homes where staff have to anticipate and care for the physical needs of guests in terms of sleep, food and comfort. In such an environment it might be expected that women should be perceived to hold the necessary abilities, knowledge and understanding to perform well – and to attain managerial positions in large numbers.

Lack of women in management positions

For the past decade, 75 per cent of all students on higher-level hotel management courses have been female. Hence one might reasonably expect a greater proportion of women than men in management positions. However, a (then) HCITB report revealed that women are not well represented in general management positions but tend to opt for specialist career routes. Barriers exist for women, particularly with regard to differences in training opportunities.[54]

The research team also pointed out that barriers can exist 'within' women themselves and felt there was a lack of confidence shown both in their aspirations and in their career planning. However, it would seem that the study exaggerated the differences between men and women, at least in terms of their long-term ambitions, and tended to accept uncritically the 'fast' masculine route as being ideal.

Practical skills and personality

Hotel managers are expected to be multi-skilled and to be available at all times. A recurrent theme of the hotel industry is the 'traditional' style of operations characterised by a high level of activity linked to an emphasis on technical and craft skills.[55] Recent studies also confirm that hotel management is concerned primarily with the demonstration of practical skills and the personality to act as 'mine host'.[56]

If multi-skills are taken to refer to the skills of the kitchen rather than the housekeeping department, then clearly women would be disadvantaged. The food and beverage department has always held a key position in hotels, but women frequently do not receive experience or training in this section.[57] The notion of 'mine host' suggests connotations of a personality which in the past has always been associated with a male image. A number of studies have found personality to be the essential criterion in the selection and promotion of managers.[58]

The assessment of personality, however, is very subjective, it is open to interpretation and can be more concerned with whether the individual fits into the culture of the hotel. Career progression rests not only on the development of skills, or with a set of personality traits, but may be more related to whether the persona of an individual matches the culture of the hotel.

Kanter has shown that in this respect women are disadvantaged because they do not fit the conventional male profile.[59] Hicks, in her research, demonstrated that women were perceived in non-managerial terms, that management work was interpreted in a masculine framework and that not only was encouragement given predominantly to male trainees but females did not have an easy access to informal networks.[60]

Informal relationships and networks

Building alliances and networks are considered to be key factors in the career development and effectiveness of managers.[61] Career progression in the hotel industry is highly dependent on the managers of hotels assessing promising trainees and ensuring they receive the necessary guidance and experience. Using their own networks, hotel managers ensure the progression of trainees and reinforce the significance of the maxim 'it is not what you know, but who you know'. Research has indicated that managers expect their male trainees to be committed to a career in hotel management whereas they suspect that the females are more likely to leave the industry. Thus certain trainees, typically male, are pushed towards new opportunities and advancement.[62]

Action on employment practices

According to Jagger and Maxwell, many current employment practices discriminate covertly against women. Positive action is possible, however, to prevent such discrimination. This requires attention to practices and procedures relating to job evaluation, recruitment and selection, training, management development, career planning, appraisal systems, re-entry policies, tertiary education and childcare responsibilities.[63]

Concern is becoming more widespread about the 'cloning' of organisations and that typically a board of directors consists of white, middle-class, middle-aged males. Recent attention is being given to the idea that diversity is important for the success of organisations and hence women's contributions are regarded as being paramount.[64] Positive action can therefore be seen to lie with senior managers. There is no doubt that sexism is damaging for individuals and organisations. 'Until the more powerful own the responsibility for prejudice, it will continue to cripple us all.'[65]

Attitudes

Organisations consist of people working together but individuals offer different attitudes and perceptions towards their working life. Differences between people can be either a source of developing creativity or the root of potential conflict, frustration and organisational problems. It is possible to differentiate among individuals in terms of their types/traits, physique, gender, abilities, developmental aspects, attitudes, perception, motivation, and social and cultural environment. In order to help understand the behaviour of people, managers need to be aware of, and sensitive to, factors affecting individual differences and their own assumptions and attitudes.

Referring to a person's attitude is a common occurrence within the work situation, and especially within the hospitality industry where members of staff must cooperate closely with other people and may have direct contact with the customer. An understanding of the nature of attitudes and their relationships to behaviour is therefore an important aspect of the effective management of people. Attitudes can be defined as providing a state of 'readiness' or tendency to respond in a particular way.[66] Attitudes differ from opinions, beliefs (which are concerned with what is known about the world), and values (which are concerned with what is desirable and 'should be'). Gross suggests that 'to convert a belief into an attitude, a "value" ingredient is needed which, by definition, is to do with an individual's sense of what is desirable, good, valuable, worthwhile and so on'. Whereas adults may have thousands of beliefs, they may have only hundreds of attitudes and a few dozen values.[67]

Attitudes are learned throughout life and embodied within our socialisation process. There is no limit to the attitudes people hold. Some attitudes, such as religious beliefs or other cultural influences (discussed later), may be central to us – a core construct – and may be highly resistant to any change. Other, more peripheral attitudes may be subject to change more easily with new information or personal experiences. Specific events, particularly traumatic ones, for example unexpected redundancy, may have a dramatic effect on our attitudes.

Functions served by attitudes

Attitudes and motives are interlinked and, depending on an individual's motives, Katz has suggested that attitudes can serve four main functions.

- *Knowledge* – a basis for the interpretation and classification of new information. Attitudes provide a knowledge base and framework within which new information can be placed.
- *Expressive* – a means of expression. Attitudes enable individuals to indicate to others the values they hold and to express their self-concept and adopt or internalise the values of the group.
- *Instrumental* – held attitudes maximise rewards and minimise sanctions. Attitudes towards other people, or objects, might be held because of past positive (or negative) experiences. Knowledge or behaviour which has resulted in satisfaction of needs is more likely to result in a favourable attitude.
- *Ego-defensive* – attitudes may be held in order to protect the ego from an undesirable truth or reality.[68]

Important implications for the study of attitudes

It seems that people do not always behave in a way that is true to their beliefs: what they say and what they do may be very different. Attitudes can be revealed not only in behaviour but also by the individual's thoughts (although these may not be revealed in public) and by feelings, the strength of which demonstrates the extent to which the attitude is a core or peripheral construct.

This point is illustrated in a classic study by La Piere. Visiting American hotels and restaurants with a Chinese couple, La Piere found no apparent sign of prejudiced attitudes in face-to-face situations, but in the follow-up attitude survey there were marked racist attitudes. He found complete contradictions between public and private attitudes.[69]

There are two important issues in the study of attitudes for both the psychologist and the manager.

- *Attitudes cannot be seen; they can only be inferred* – heavy reliance is placed therefore on the accuracy of assessment. The attitudes held by members of staff are important for morale and organisational effectiveness so it is important to have confidence in the techniques used to assess the nature and strength of attitudes.

- *Attitudes are often shared within organisations* – they may be embodied in the culture of the organisation. Attitudes are not just formed individually but arise out of interaction with others (although not only just within the organisation but also within the wider community). Sharing the belief system of others, or not, can influence either positive or negative feelings about working in an organisation.

Attitude measurement

There are a number of different techniques which could be used to measure attitudes, the two most common being direct observation and self-reporting techniques. Direct observation relies on an informal, unsystematic approach based on assumptions and an understanding of social cues and body language. However, managers may be erroneous in their assumptions and beliefs. These may never have been tested – merely assumed to be correct – and they may be mistaken in their judgements.

Organisations which assess their employees' attitudes by questionnaires (self-reporting techniques) are attempting to systematically gauge and measure these assumptions and beliefs. Attitude questionnaires are used by many organisations as a barometer of attitudinal climate, and to enable managers to be in touch with employees' views and feelings.

However, attitude questionnaires are time-consuming to design and administer. The questions asked, their relevance, style and length are all important variables in the validity of the questionnaire. So, too, is the honest completion of questionnaires. Making people's private attitudes public may also have its dangers as expectations of change may be envisaged and if this does not occur, disappointment and low morale may result.[70]

Attitude change

Theories on attitude change stress the importance of balance and consistency in our psyche. For example, Heider suggests that, not only is it uncomfortable to hold two conflicting attitudes, but doing so motivates people to change one of the attitudes to reach a state of balance.[71] Festinger's theory of cognitive dissonance refers to the psychological discomfort felt when we hold inconsistent beliefs or act in a way that is inconsistent with our true beliefs. The theory suggests that we are motivated to reduce the impact of this discomfort by taking appropriate action and/or changing a belief.[72]

The process of attitude change is dependent on a number of key factors including: why an attitude is held in the first place; why it should change; what the benefits are and for whom; and the likely outcomes if it does not change. As mentioned previously, peripheral attitudes may change more easily upon receipt of new information or new personal experiences, whereas central attitudes tied to a core construct may be highly resistant to any change.

Awareness and understanding of the above factors can assist the manager in greater sensitivity and development of skills in the management of people. However, increased understanding can be developed through a knowledge and understanding of the likely workforce within the industry.

Critical review and reflection

'The hospitality industry has a reputation for long unsocial hours, poor pay and, in the UK, low status.'

To what extent is this reputation justified? Why do people work in the industry?

The nature of the workforce

The following factors seem to identify the workforce of the hospitality industry.
It is made up of, predominantly:

- young staff – particularly in the hotel sector, where they may often join organisations unskilled and require some training, although often the new recruit has skills in other areas;
- traditionally unskilled workers (90 per cent of the workforce have no formal qualifications);
- students – the flexibility of hospitality work often provides short-term and part-time employment for those studying for long-term careers elsewhere or for people yet to find permanent work after completing their studies;
- transient labour – labour turnover in the hospitality industry is high;
- a multinational, and multicultural, workforce, particularly in London and other large conurbations;
- a high proportion of illegal immigrants, or casual labour failing to declare earnings for tax and NI purposes (see Chapter 1);
- many live-in workers, in hotels.

Critical review and reflection

How might the nature and characteristics of the hospitality industry give rise to the workforce characteristics referred to above?

Kuşluvan *et al.*[73] provide a similar analysis of the nature of the workforce, suggesting that most jobs are unskilled, or semi-skilled and low paid, and the work is low status and has a poor image. There are high levels of labour turnover and frequent labour skills shortages.

He identifies that many employees are poorly educated and that there is a high proportion of disadvantaged workers, including itinerant and highly mobile labour, including migrant labour.

The British Hospitality Association (BHA) supports the above analysis, also identifying that despite there being a number of trade unions represented in the hospitality industry, there is low trade union membership, which might be expected to help workers achieve better terms and conditions. BHA also points out that there is a high proportion of part-time, female employees.

Critical review and reflection

'In times of economic recession people are forced to work in areas that they would not choose for preference.'

To what extent do you consider the hospitality industry is staffed by people in this position? Do you think it is worse than other industries such as manufacturing or other service industries?

Whatever the nature of the staff, good staff care is essential. This requires an understanding of the psychology and sociology of people.

Meaning of work in people's lives

Work holds a number of different meanings and values for people, and plays a variety of roles in their lives. Work helps to fulfil a range of diverse needs and expectations relating to, for example, economic rewards, intrinsic satisfaction and social relationships (see Chapter 7). People differ, therefore, in the extent and manner of their involvement with work. Goldthorpe *et al.*, for example, have identified three general sets of attitudes, or orientations, to work.[74]

- Some individuals may have only a calculative or economic involvement with work. This suggests an **instrumental orientation** with an attitude to work not as a central life issue but simply as a means to an end.

- For other individuals work may be seen more as a central life issue. There is a sense of obligation to the work of the organisation and a strong positive involvement in terms of a career structure. This suggests a **bureaucratic orientation**.

- Yet other individuals may view work primarily in terms of group activities and an ego involvement with work groups rather than the work of the organisation itself. This suggests a **solidaristic orientation** with a close link between work-related and social activities.

These different orientations will shape the individuals' attitudes towards work, and have a significant influence on the importance attached to those factors which affect their motivation and job satisfaction. Some people may have a set orientation to work whatever the nature of the work environment, while for other people different work situations may influence their orientation to work. For example, a perceived lack of opportunities for high economic rewards or job security may result in greater emphasis on a solidaristic orientation to work, and a primary concern for teamwork and satisfaction of social expectations.

Orientations to work in the hospitality industry

In a study of hospitality employees across four small independent restaurants Martin[75] identified four alternative orientations to work.

(a) **Instrumental** – the instrumental employees viewed work as a means to an end working to support a specific lifestyle outside the workplace. Examples include staff working to save for a specific event, women working to support children and requiring flexible working, students working to support study. Frequently the tips were a major factor.

(b) **Craft** – the craft-orientated employees viewed work as an end in itself. Preserving craft skills and the maintenance of prestige and reputation were important factors. For craft-orientated employees such as chefs or waiters there was a strong identity with work.

(c) **Solidaristic** – for the solidaristic-orientated employee, group activity and social relationships with others were rewarding. Lives and work were tightly bound.

(d) **Professional** – for the professionally orientated employees work was a mechanism for self-development and part of a career path.

In order to develop career paths, there was a need to move on to 'better' establishments and better positions.

Martin noted that commitment in all four orientations was towards self and not towards the business, an individualistic ideology. This influenced the decisions they made and their responses to working practices. The employment relationship was about managing work and life for personal satisfaction.

To what extent, then, does the nature of work in service industries and features such as low pay, poor working conditions, and the often routine and mundane nature of tasks give rise to a particular orientation or set of attitudes towards work? For example, Dodrill and Riley undertook a small research project in order to investigate the idea that hotel workers value variety and scope in their work.[76] The questionnaire project was expected to show that hotel workers display a positive attitude towards five characteristic factors – ambition, the desire for scope in the job, mobility, security and autonomy. However, the findings did not support this contention. Only ambition and desire for scope in the job were found as strong positive attitudes. From this admittedly small and limited study Dodrill and Riley conclude that hotel workers do not hold any unique orientation or distinctive attitudes towards work.

Critical review and reflection

Volunteers

The hospitality and tourism sectors often rely on volunteers (see Bourne Leisure case study).

Why do people work as volunteers, for example as guides of tourist sites? What is the meaning of this work in their lives?

The psychological contract

In addition to the formal contract between an employer and employees, there are additional unwritten expectations without which it would be difficult to ensure that all of the job requirements would be met.

The manager should attempt to mould elements of individual and group behaviour in order to avoid conflict and frustration. An important aspect of the effective management of people is this concept of the psychological contract. This is not a written document but implies a series of mutual expectations and satisfaction of needs between the individual and the hospitality organisation. The psychological contract covers a range of rights, privileges, behaviour, duties and obligations which are not part of a formal agreement but still have an important influence on the behaviour of people.[77]

The individual's expectations of the employer

Expectations of the individual, in the hospitality organisation, vary widely and may change over time but could include that the organisation will, for example:

- pay overtime rates or allow time off for additional hours worked in excess of the contract of employment;
- adopt equitable human resource management policies and procedures;
- provide a reasonable standard of live-in accommodation;
- respect the privacy of staff when not on duty;
- provide safe and hygienic working conditions and staff facilities;
- treat members of staff with consideration and respect;
- show an understanding and considerate attitude towards any personal problems;
- provide opportunities for training in new skills and career progression.

The hospitality organisation's expectations of the employee

Expectations of the hospitality organisation arise from the implicit attitudes and behaviour of its members. These expectations may include that members will, for example:

- accept the philosophy and ideology of the organisation and uphold its image;
- make every reasonable effort to satisfy customers' requirements;
- be prepared to work additional hours or undertake extra jobs, with, or without, appropriate recompense, when the need arises;
- show loyalty and honesty, and not betray positions of trust;
- work diligently in pursuit of objectives and accept the authority of senior members of staff;
- not abuse goodwill shown by customers or management;
- not abuse organisational facilities such as email or internet access;
- observe reasonable and acceptable standards of dress and appearance;
- show respect to customers and guests.

Implications for organisational strategy

The Chartered Institute of Personnel and Development (CIPD) suggests that the psychological contract may have implications for organisational strategy in a number of areas, for example:

- **process fairness** – people want to know their interests will be taken into account, and that they will be treated with respect and consulted about change;
- **communications** – an effective two-way dialogue between employer and employee;
- **management style** – adopting a more 'bottom-up' style and drawing on the strategic knowledge of employees;
- **managing expectations** – making clear what new recruits can expect and distinguishing rhetoric from reality;
- **measuring employees' attitudes** – regular monitoring of employee attitudes and acting on the results.[78]

These points are relevant throughout industry in general, including hospitality.

Bargaining and balancing

The hospitality organisation's side of the psychological contract may place emphasis on expectations, requirements and constraints which often differ from, and conflict with, the expectations of the individual. It is unlikely that all expectations of either side will be met fully. The nature of these expectations is not defined formally and there is a constant process of bargaining and balancing. Understanding the nature of the psychological contract is an important aspect of the socialisation of members of staff new to the organisation. The informal expectations serve as important determinants of behaviour and may have a major influence on an individual's subsequent attitudes, job satisfaction and work performance, and on the level of staff turnover.

Failure to honour the psychological contract

Unfortunately the hospitality industry in general does not have a good reputation for honouring the psychological contract towards its members. A prime example of this can be seen in respect of students on placement. Although not always the case, the following views expressed by a university degree student appear all too typical of their experiences:

> We go on placements and see staff being treated badly which is why I would not go into the hotel industry, unless things change. It's slave labour … I was working six days a week for 14 or 15 hours every day, receiving no training … When I went for my interview I was given a wonderful presentation about the training I would receive – but I was training others. I signed a contract to work 40 hours a week but when I raised the subject of overtime I was laughed at.

Situations such as these are clearly one reason why many degree and HND students turn their backs on the industry only to be snapped up by large retailing groups.[79]

However, Kelley-Patterson and George[80] in their study of expectations of placement students, graduates and managers commented that there is a mismatch of expectations: 'Graduates have a tendency to run before they can walk.'

Some interesting findings are shown, such as managers underestimating the importance to graduate employees of a number of fundamental hygiene factors including health and safety, pleasant working conditions, payment of expenses, holiday flexibility and fair pay (regular reviews, performance-related pay and overtime pay). In only one area did managers overestimate expectations: being able to work from home, and this is likely to be a projection of their own needs rather than a reflection of graduate expectations.

The research showed a clear mismatch between the expectations of the graduates and the management.

Changing nature of the hospitality contract

Hiltrop suggests that the increasing pressure for organisations to change has prompted growing disillusionment with the traditional psychological contract based on lifetime employment and steady promotion from within. Companies must develop new ways to increase the loyalty and commitment of employees. This includes attention to reward strategies based on recognition of contribution rather than status or position, systematic training and development including the skills for working in cross-functional teams, and the training of managers in counselling, coaching and leadership skills.[81]

According to Altman, restructuring and advances in technology mean it is time for a new psychological contract between employers and employees.

> How can employees continue to believe in any established, if unwritten, psychological contract based on previous secure employment, training and personal development? . . . Reducing layers of middle management is largely a consequence of technology and cutting down on bureaucracy. The more companies downsize, the more they are seen to be breaking the 'psychological contract' with employees. And once individuals perceive this to be the case, they will look after their own careers and their chief loyalty will be to themselves.[82]

According to CIPD, changes currently affecting the workplace have persuaded people to take the psychological contract seriously. These changes include more employees on part-time and temporary contracts and more jobs outsourced; de-layering and 'leanness' of organisations; more demanding customers and improved quality and service standards; the increasing importance of human capital as a source of competitive advantage, and more fluid organisation structures. The effect of these changes is that employees are increasingly recognised as the key business drivers. The psychological contract offers a framework for monitoring employee attitudes and priorities.[83]

If managers in the hospitality industry are to increase the willing commitment of staff to the aims and goals of the organisation, continual attention must be given to the importance of the psychological contract.

Critical review and reflection

'The mismatch of the psychological contract explains many dimensions of discontent within the hospitality industry.'

What unwritten expectations do you have of your employment? In your experience, how likely are employers to recognise these, and what additional expectations might they have in return?

Frustration-induced behaviour

The behaviour and actions of people at work result from the desire to achieve some goal in order to satisfy certain needs or expectations. This is the basis of a person's motivational driving force and a major influence on the nature of interpersonal relationships. Needs and expectations at work include the satisfaction of economic rewards, for example pay and security; intrinsic satisfaction, for example variety and an interesting job; and social relationships, for example comradeship and a feeling of belonging. (Motivation, and the needs and expectations of people at work, are discussed in Chapter 7.)

When a person's motivational driving force is blocked before reaching a desired goal there are two possible sets of outcomes: constructive behaviour or frustration (Figure 2.10). Even if a person engages in constructive behaviour it could be said that the person is sometimes 'frustrated', if only mildly or in the short term. The term 'frustration', however, is usually interpreted as applying to negative behavioural responses to a barrier or blockage which prevents satisfaction of a desired goal and results in a feeling of psychological discomfort.[84]

Constructive behaviour

This is a positive reaction to the blockage of a desired goal and can take two main forms: problem-solving or restructuring. These are not necessarily exclusive forms of reaction, and constructive behaviour may involve a combination of problem-solving and restructuring.

- *Problem-solving* entails removal of the barrier, for example: by-passing an uncooperative colleague; repairing broken equipment; undertaking training or gaining a qualification; persuading the manager to grant promotion; finding an alternative method of working.

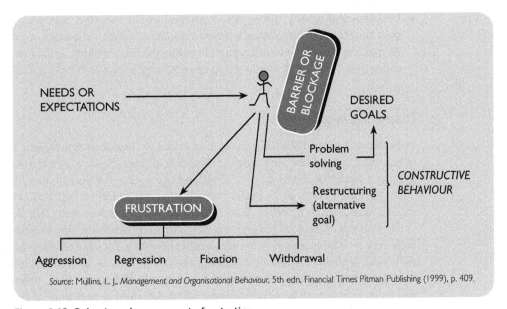

Source: Mullins, L. J., *Management and Organisational Behaviour*, 5th edn, Financial Times Pitman Publishing (1999), p. 409.

Figure 2.10 Behavioural responses to frustration

- *Restructuring* involves the substitution of an alternative goal, although such a goal may be of a lower order or priority. Restructuring may also entail compromise between the satisfaction of conflicting goals, for example: requesting a transfer to another department or to a different shift; taking an additional part-time job; accepting a less interesting job because the hours of work are more convenient.

Frustration

This is a negative response to the blockage of a desired goal and results in a defensive form of behaviour. There are many possible reactions to frustration but these can be summarised under four broad headings: aggression, regression, fixation and withdrawal.[85] Again, these categories are not mutually exclusive and most forms of frustration-induced behaviour at work are a combination of aggression, regression and fixation.

- *Aggression* is a physical or verbal attack on some person or object, for example: striking a supervisor, damaging equipment, destroying documents, shouting or using abusive language, spreading malicious gossip about a colleague. This form of behaviour may be directed against the person or object perceived as the actual blocking agent and the source of frustration.

- *Regression* is reverting to childish or a more primitive form of behaviour, for example: screaming, tantrums, crying, sulking, refusing to cooperate with colleagues or listen to reasoned arguments, constantly moaning, displaying neurotic behaviour, striking or kicking broken equipment or machinery.

- *Fixation* involves persisting in a form of behaviour which has no adaptive value and continuing to repeat actions which have no positive results, for example: continually trying to operate equipment which obviously will not work, insisting on applying for promotion to a position for which clearly not suited, being excessively critical, refusing to accept change or new ideas.

- *Withdrawal* is apathy, giving up or resignation, for example: losing interest in the job, poor timekeeping, increasing sickness and absenteeism, refusing to accept responsibility, passing work over to colleagues, avoiding decision-making, failing to give support to colleagues, refusing to join in group or social activities, leaving the job altogether.

Displaced aggression

Frustration-induced behaviour may often result in displaced aggression. This may occur when the source of the frustration is not clear or specific or where the source is feared, such as a powerful superior. With displaced aggression the person may find an easier or 'safer' person or object as an outlet of frustration, for example: being short-tempered with subordinates, slamming doors, kicking the waste-paper basket, being irritable with friends.

The concept of displaced aggression has particular significance in the hospitality industry Staff may well be expected to act in accordance with a doctrine of 'the customer is *always* right' and, however trying or demanding the circumstances, should not give vent to their frustration in public view of customers or guests. By the same token, however, managers and colleagues should be understanding when staff need to find some alternative outlet as a scapegoat for their frustration.

Factors influencing frustration

There are many factors which influence the feeling of frustration and an individual's reactions, for example the importance of the desired goal and strength of the need, cultural values, the perceived nature of the barrier or blocking agent, the pressure under which the individual is working, the personality characteristics and social skills of the individual.

It must also be remembered that most people do not necessarily separate their working lives from their domestic or social lives; neither is it reasonable to expect them to do so.[86] The behaviour and actions of people are influenced by problems and frustrations outside as well as inside the work organization. Managers have a social responsibility to recognise that people cannot always leave their personal difficulties behind when they come to work.

An understanding of human nature?

At the heart of successful management is the ability to relate well to other people.

> The fact is that management ultimately depends on an understanding of human nature. I suggest it goes much further than that. In the first place, good management depends on the acceptance of certain basic values. It cannot be achieved without honesty and integrity, or without consideration for the interests of others. Secondly, it is the understanding of human foibles that we all share, such as jealousy, envy, status, prejudice, perception, temperament, motivation and talent, which provides the greatest challenge to managers.
> (HRH The Duke of Edinburgh, Patron, Institute of Management)[87]

Understanding the feelings of staff, and their needs and expectations, together with a genuine concern for their welfare, goes a long way in encouraging them to perform well. Attention should be focused, therefore, on improving the people–organisation relationship and creating a climate in which people work willingly and effectively.

An understanding of human behaviour at work

Perception of 'self'

An important factor of interpersonal behaviour and relationships with other people is perception of self, or self-image. This is how people see and think of themselves, and their evaluation of themselves. People tend to have an ideal image of themselves and how they would like to be. This is the image that is projected in dealings with other people.

The responses of other people, and their approval or disapproval, influences the development of self-image. Approval from other people will serve to reinforce that image and will contribute to an individual's self-esteem. People tend to come to see themselves how other people come to know and expect them to be. Self-esteem is the extent to which people approve of and accept themselves, and their feelings of self-respect. Clearly, it is important for managers to appreciate what effect their reactions to, and attitudes towards, their staff will have upon those staff.

Role relationships

Self-image is influenced by the different roles that people play both inside and outside the work environment. A role is an expected pattern of behaviour and forms part of the network of activities and relationships with other people. Each individual will have a number of role relationships – a 'role-set' which comprises the range of associations or contacts with whom the individual has meaningful interactions.

The expected pattern of behaviour of a hospitality manager will influence the manager's self-image. And certain characteristic features associated with this self-image will tend to persist outside the work environment, for example smart appearance and courteous behaviour in dealings with other people.

Synopsis

- Effective management is all about working with people and this is particularly important in the hospitality industry. People differ in their attitudes and orientation to work. This is influenced by a broad range of interdisciplinary approaches.

- Individuals offer different attitudes and perceptions towards their working life. An understanding of attitudes and perceptions is a key feature of successful management of people in the hospitality industry.

- Organisations are made up of their individual members and the individual is a central feature of organisational behaviour. A distinguishing factor of successful managers is the recognition of individual differences and their ability to bring out the best in the people who work with them.

- A significant difference among individuals is in terms of their personality – those stable characteristics that explain why a person behaves in a particular way. Personality is often considered a particularly important dimension for consideration for successful employment in the hospitality industry.

- Individuals vary with regard to their mental abilities and application. Arguments rage over the nature of intelligence and the extent to which it is inherited. Emotional intelligence is the sum of a range of interpersonal skills that form the public persona and is often considered of particular relevance for employment within the hospitality industry.

- People have different orientations to work and different expectations of work. Understanding these different orientations can assist the manager in understanding the individual worker. An understanding of an individual's psychological contract can assist the manager in treating the employee in an appropriate manner.

- At the heart of successful management is the ability to relate well to other people. A high level of interpersonal skills is important for effective work performance.

REVIEW AND DISCUSSION QUESTIONS

1 What do you see as the main issues relating to the effective management of individuals at work?

2 Discuss the major ways in which individual differences are demonstrated at work.

3 What are the factors that influence attitudes to work within the hospitality industry?

4 Why do people work in the hospitality industry? To what extent can understanding the meaning of work in people's lives assist the manager to understand and, therefore, manage the workforce?

5 Explain what is meant by the psychological contract. Give practical examples of:

(a) expectations that might be held by individuals;

(b) expectations that might be held by managers within hospitality organisations. Give examples of your own expectations that you would hope to see covered by the psychological contract.

6 Why is the study of perception of particular importance within the hospitality industry? Explain what is meant by perceptual illusions, and the screening and selection of stimuli.

7 Discuss the factors which influence the judgements we make of other people. Explain the main sources of distortions and errors in interpersonal perception.

8 Why are attitudes difficult to measure and change? Design a simple questionnaire to administer to your colleagues on attitudes towards the meaning of work.

ASSIGNMENT 1

We all tend to be guilty of distortions and errors in interpersonal perception, and of making hasty decisions about the behaviour and actions of other people before thinking fully about the situation.

1 Consider honestly the biases, prejudices and attitudes that you have about certain people. Explain how you attempt to guard against these biases, prejudices and attitudes in order to make a fair and objective assessment of others.

2 Relate examples of judgements you have made about other people on the basis of:

(a) the halo effect;

(b) the rusty halo effect; and

(c) stereotyping.

3 Give a brief account of situations when you have:

(a) made a judgement about another person on the basis of *selective perception*; and

(b) assumed too much from *limited information* and when there was a reasonable, alternative interpretation which differed from your first reaction.

Be prepared to share and discuss your experiences in self-selecting groups of four to six. Make notes of what you feel has been learnt from undertaking this assignment.

ASSIGNMENT 2

From your own experience, provide a short account of an actual problem or difficulty you have encountered in working with other people in the hospitality industry. Explain clearly:

1 the exact nature of the problem or difficulty;

2 the behaviour/actions of the person(s) involved;

3 the steps taken to help overcome the situation and with what results *and/or* the actions you would now propose be taken.

Virgin Atlantic and Ryanair

Virgin Atlantic was founded by Richard Branson in 1984. Michael O'Leary became the Chief Executive of Ryanair in 1994. Both Branson and O'Leary are individuals with strong and distinctive personalities and frequently feature in the media.

Both airlines operate in the UK passenger air transport industry, using similar technology and systems, although the markets that they serve differ. Virgin Atlantic operates predominantly in the long haul market, and Ryanair in the budget short haul sector.

The nature and style of management in the two companies are very different, and so are their organisational cultures, which impacts on the way people in the respective organisations think, feel and behave. The brand image and the treatment of customers by each company also have a bearing on the nature of the organisational relationship with staff, and vice versa. At Virgin Atlantic, cabin crew are there to be helpful and welcoming; they are important projectors of the brand image and their job is partly to encourage customer loyalty (generating continuing profit). At Virgin Atlantic the importance of their staff as representatives of company values is reflected in their statements about the nature of work:

> Immaculate service and unrivalled quality are everything to us here at Virgin Atlantic. The high standards and experience of the people we hire has helped us become one of the world's most highly rated airlines. In fact, whether you join us in the air, on the ground or behind the scenes, you'll need to be totally focused on delivering everything our customers have come to expect of us.
>
> Because we're such a complex and rapidly evolving business, we expect all our people to be adaptable, quick thinking and people focused every day to contribute to our ongoing success. And in return, they get to share in the many benefits of working for one of the UK's favourite employers and one of the world's best-loved brands.

Ryanair is renowned as the most punctual 'on-time' airline in Europe and they say that:

> Our people have been at the forefront of our campaign to change European aviation by lowering fares, and fighting dinosaur flag carriers and high cost monopolies. This is a company where hard work and enthusiasm are rewarded and as we continue to grow we have a number of exciting roles available. It is always our preference to promote from within, so we offer excellent prospects for promotion and career progression. Ryanair does not operate seniority lists or other pointless restrictions that hold back talented people. We're straight talkers and have a strict no waffle policy. If you want a career that's challenging but rewarding then check out our vacancies listed below. As a minimum you need a good level of written and spoken English, a reasonable level of computer literacy and an EU passport.

Cabin crew recruitment

The recruitment process at Virgin Atlantic is lengthy and includes a group interview that acts as a filter for further tests before job offers are made. Training programmes for cabin crew are run from a dedicated training centre, and there is a wide range of benefits for staff.

At Ryanair cabin crew work for contracted supplier organisations (such as Crewlink), rather than Ryanair, and applications are made to these companies. Recruitment is through a three-step process. In the first step candidates must qualify by being:

- experienced in dealing with the public and comfortable in a selling role;
- physically fit with a good attendance record in their current position;
- hard working, flexible and willing to operate on a shift roster;
- over 18 years of age;
- over 5' 2" (1.57 m) in height, with weight in proportion;
- of normal vision (contact lenses acceptable);
- able to swim well;
- no visible tattoos when wearing uniform, including short-sleeve shirt/blouse;
- in possession of a valid European Union passport and have the right to work in both the UK and Ireland;

Case study 2.1 (*continued*)

- fluent in English (both written and spoken);
- prepared to live within one hour's travelling time of any Ryanair base;
- ready to meet the challenge of dealing with people and demanding situations;
- friendly and outgoing with a lively personality.

In the second step candidates must complete an approved training course, which they are required to pay for. The final step is when candidates are accepted for employment by one of the contract cabin crew agencies used by Ryanair. The company operates a rotational shift pattern and they also offer travel benefits to their staff.

Cabin crew role

The nature of the work for staff is different in short and long haul flights. Long haul flights are likely to have higher staffing levels and allow longer rest periods for staff at the destinations, whereas short haul flights do not require overnight stays and have fast turnaround times at airports (Ryanair aims for 20 minutes). However, the nature of customer service might be more demanding on long haul flights, where staff and customers are together for longer periods of time, and customer expectations may be more extensive.

Both organisations have been successful, but the company cultures and values could hardly be more different.

Questions

1 Review the careers sections for cabin crew at Virgin Atlantic and Ryanair. What are your impressions?

2 Identify the likely psychological contracts within each organisation.

Source: the authors are grateful to Nina Beckett for contributing this case study.

CASE STUDY 2.2

Managing volunteers at Warner Leisure Hotels

Warner Leisure Hotels, part of the Bourne Leisure group, own a range of hotels throughout Great Britain. Bourne Leisure can claim to be one of the best employers in the UK Hotel sector, having featured in the 'Times 20 Best Big Companies To Work For' survey in 2008, 2009 and 2010.

Warner Leisure Hotels aim at the older market. Their guest profile is in the 50–65 age group, relatively affluent, 'empty-nesters', pre-retired and retired. They specifically state that there are 'NO KIDS at any of our locations'.

The hotels offer a range of activities including ballroom dancing, fencing, and a range of sports such as rifle shooting, swimming, bowling, tennis, croquet and cycling together with other facilities such as saunas, beauty therapies, and art and craft activities. They offer themed weeks and short breaks, for example the 'Strictly Come Dancing'

break, and they can be considered as a form of activity hotel for the older guest.

Like most hotels, they tend to employ young staff. Unlike many hotels, however, staff turnover is relatively low. In line with the 'having fun' theme for their guests, there is an emphasis on their leisure staff running and joining in the leisure activities. One Leisure Manager suggested that the job consisted of '60 per cent cleaning and 40 per cent having fun', which may go some way to explaining the low staff turnover.

Recognising the disparity between the ages of the staff and the guests, they have introduced a new policy of encouraging older, unpaid, 'volunteers', who might be interested in working as leisure staff and/or leading leisure activities. In exchange for their time, these volunteers receive appropriate training as well as free Leisure Club membership

Case study 2.2 (*continued*)

(worth £500 per annum in 2011). In 2011, the organisation had 97 volunteers, who were expected to work set hours equivalent to one or two afternoons per week, depending on the activity and the particular hotel.

The company believes that this policy will broaden the range of leisure activities offered to guests, whose experience may be enriched as the volunteers are likely to have more in common with them.

Current leisure staff see this as a positive move, believing it will enable them to spend more time with the guests.

Questions

1 What do you see as the benefits of this arrangement to:
  (a) the volunteers
  (b) the organisation
  (c) current staff
  (d) guests?

2 What challenges can you identify for the managers of the departments in managing both the volunteers and the paid workforce?

Source: the authors are grateful to Gerard Ryan of Warner Leisure for this information.

References

1 See, for example, Arnold, J., Cooper, C. L. and Robertson, I. T., *Work Psychology*, 2nd edn, Pitman (1995).

2 Forte, Charles (Lord), *Forte: The Autobiography of Charles Forte*, Sidgwick & Jackson (1986), p. 123.

3 For example, see Wood R. C., *Working in Hotels and Catering*, 2nd edn, International Thomson Business Press (1997).

4 Midgely, D., 'Stay cool in the kitchen', *Management Today*, September 2005.

5 Mullins, L. J., 'The Organisation and the Individual', *Administrator*, vol. 7, no. 4, April 1987, 11–14.

6 Atkinson, P. E., 'Applications of the Behavioral Sciences Within the Hospitality Industry', *Hospitality*, September 1980, 7–13.

7 Wood, R. C., *Organizational Behaviour for Hospitality Management*, Butterworth-Heinemann (1994).

8 Carmouche, R. and Kelly, N., *Behavioural Studies in Hospitality Management*, Chapman & Hall (1995).

9 Slattery, P., 'Social science methodology and hospitality management', *International Journal of Hospitality Management*, vol. 2, no. 1, 1983, 9–14.

10 Wood, R. C., 'Against social science?', *International Journal of Hospitality Management*, vol. 7, no. 3, 1988, 239–50.

11 Lennon, J. J. and Wood, R. C., 'The teaching of industrial and other sociologies in higher education: the case of hotel and catering management studies', *International Journal of Hospitality Management*, vol. 11, no. 3, 1992, 239–53.

12 See, for example, Drake, R. and Smith, P., *Behavioural Science in Industry*, McGraw-Hill (1973).

13 Cowling, A. G. *et al.*, *Behavioural Sciences for Managers*, 2nd edn, Edward Arnold (1988), p. 1.

14 Mullins, L. J., *Management and Organisational Behaviour*, 9th edn, FT Prentice Hall (2010).

15 McCrae, R. R. and Costa, P. T., 'More reasons to adopt the Five-Factor Model', *American Psychologist*, vol. 44, no. 2, 1989, 451–2.

16 Bayne, R., 'The Big Five versus the Myers-Briggs', *The Psychologist*, January 1994, 14–17.

17 Barrick, M. R. and Mount, M. K., 'The Big Five personality dimensions and job performance: A meta-analysis', *Personnel Psychology*, Spring 1991, 1–26.

18 Mount, M. K., Barrick, M. R. and Strauss, J. P., 'Validity of observer ratings of the Big Five personality factors', *Journal of Applied Psychology*, April 1994, 272.

19 Bentall, R. P., 'Personality traits may be alive, they may even be well, but are they really useful?', *The Psychologist*, July 1993, 307.

20 Robertson, I. 'Undue diligence', *People Management*, no. 22, November 2001, 42–3.

21 Lord, W. and Rust, J., 'The Big Five revisited: where are we now? A brief review of the relevance of the Big Five for occupational assessment', *Selection and Development Review*, vol. 19, no. 4, August 2003, 15–18.

22 Lashley, C., and Lee-Ross, D., *Organization Behaviour for Leisure Services*, Elsevier (2003).

23 Stone, G., 'Personality and effective hospitality management', *Proceedings of the International Association of Hotel Management Schools Symposium'*, Leeds Polytechnic (1988).

24 Ineson, E., 'The contribution of personality to graduate managerial training', *International Journal of Hospitality Management*, vol. 30, 2011, 630–8.

25 'Education: hotel schools', *Caterer and Hotelkeeper*, August 10, 2006.

26 Hochschild, A. R., *The Managed Heart: Commercialization of Human Feeling*, University of California Press (1983).

27 Briner, R., 'Feeling and smiling', *The Psychologist*, vol. 12, no. 1, January 1999, 16–19.

28 Mann, S., *Hiding the way we feel, faking what we don't: understanding the role of emotions at work*, Element (1999).

29 Cited in Lashley, C. and Lee-Ross, D., *Organization Behaviour for Leisure Services*, Elsevier (2003).

30 Gursoy, D., Boylu, Y. and Avci, U., 'Identifying the complex relationships among emotional labour and its correlates, *International Journal of Hospitality Management*, vol. 30, 2011, 783–94.

31 Chu, K., Baker, M. and Murrmann, S., 'When we are on stage we smile: the effects of emotional labor on employee work outcomes', *International Journal of Hospitality Management*, vol. 31, no. 3, 2012, 906–15.

32 Cooper, C., 'Papering over the cracks: individual strategies or organizational intervention in dealing with stress at work', conference paper given at the British Psychological Society Occupational Psychology conference, University of Warwick, January 1995.

33 Friedman, M. and Rosenman, R., *Type A Behavior and Your Heart*, Knopf (1974).

34 Rosenman, R., Friedman, F. and Straus, R., 'A predictive study of CHD', *Journal of the American Medical Association*, vol. 89, 1964, 15–22; and Warr, P. and Wall, T., *Work and Well Being*, Penguin (1975).

35 See, for example, Jex, S. M., Adams, G. A., Elacqua, T. C. and Bachrach, D. G., 'Type "A" as a moderator of stressors and job complexity: a comparison of achievement strivings and impatience-irritability', *Journal of Applied Psychology*, vol. 32, no. 5, 2002, 977–96.

36 Gratton, L., *Hot Spots*, Financial Times Prentice Hall (2007).

37 Ibid., p. 83.

38 Howe, M. J. A., 'Can IQ Change?', *The Psychologist*, February 1998, 69–72.

39 Goleman, D., *Emotional Intelligence*, Bloomsbury (1996), p. 34.

40 Lashley, C. and Lee-Ross, D., *Organization Behaviour for Leisure Services*, Elsevier (2003).

41 Boyatzis, R., Goleman, D. and Hay/McBer, *Emotional Competence Inventory Feedback Report*, Hay Group (1999).

42 Ineson, E., 'The contribution of personality to graduate managerial training', *International Journal of Contemporary Hospitality Management*, vol. 30, 2011, 630–8.

43 Langhorn, S., 'How emotional intelligence can improve management performance', *International Journal of Contemporary Hospitality Management*, vol. 16, no. 4, 2004, 220–30.

44 Jung, H. and Yoon, H., 'The effects of emotional intelligence on counterproductive work behaviors and organizational citizen behaviours among food and beverage employees in a deluxe hotel', *International Journal of Hospitality Management*, vol. 31, 2012, 369–78.

45 Morgan, C. T. and King, R. A., *Introduction to Psychology*, 3rd edn, McGraw-Hill (1966), p. 343.

46 Hill, W. E., *Puck*, 6 November 1915.

47 Hellriegel, D., Slocum, J. W. and Woodman, R. W., *Organizational Behavior*, 8th edn, South Western College (1998), p. 76.

48 For example, see: Jones, P., *Food Service Operations*, Holt, Rinehart & Winston (1983).

49 Hubrecht, J. and Teare, R., 'A strategy for partnership in total quality service', *International Journal of Contemporary Hospitality Management*, vol. 5, no. 3, 1993, iii.

50 Klein, S., 'Customer care needs staff care', *Proceedings of The International Association of Hotel Management Schools Symposium*, Leeds Polytechnic, November (1988).

51 Wilson, P. R., 'Perceptual distortion of height as a function of ascribed academic status', *Journal of Social Psychology*, no. 74, 1968, 97–102.

52 Ellis, P., *The Image of Hotel and Catering Work*, HCITB (1981), p. 26.

53 *Women in the Hotel and Catering Industry*, HCITB (1987).

54 *Women's Path to Management in the Hotel and Catering Industry*, HCITB (1984).

55 Guerrier, Y. and Lockwood, A., 'Developing hotel managers – a reappraisal', *International Journal of Hospitality Management*, vol. 8, no. 2, 1989, 82–9.

56 Baum, T., 'Toward a new definition of hotel management', *Cornell HRA Quarterly*, Educators' Forum 1988, 36–9.

57 See note 54.

58 See, for example, Hicks, L., 'Excluded women: how can this happen in the hotel world?', *The Services Industries Journal*, vol. 10, no. 2, April 1990, pp. 348–63.

59 Kanter, R. B., *Men and Women of the Corporation*, Basic Books (1977).

60 Hicks, L., 'Gender and culture: a study of the attitudes displayed by managers in the hotel industry', Unpublished PhD dissertation, University of Surrey, 1991.

61 Kotter, J. P., 'What effective general managers really do', *Harvard Business Review*, vol. 60, no. 6, November-December 1982, 156–67.

62 See note 60.

63 Jagger, E. and Maxwell, G., 'Women in top jobs', *Proceedings of the International Association of Hotel Management Schools Symposium*, Leeds Polytechnic, November 1988.

64 Caulkin, S., 'Minorities get the vote', *The Observer*, Sunday 14 November 1993.

65 Quote by Gloria Steinem in Reardon, K., 'The memo every woman keeps in her desk', *Harvard Business Review*, March-April 1993, 16–22.

66 Ribeaux, P. and Poppleton, S. E., *Psychology and Work*, Macmillan (1978).

67 Gross, R. D., *Psychology: The Science of Mind and Behaviour*, Edward Arnold (1987).

68 Katz, D., 'The Functional Approach to the Study of Attitudes', *Public Opinion Quarterly*, vol. 21, 1960, 163–204.

69 La Piere, R. T., 'Attitudes versus action', *Social Forces*, vol. 13, 1934, 230–37.

70 For a simplified version of attitude measurement see Riley, M., *Human Resource Management in the Hospitality and Tourism Industry*, 2nd edn, Butterworth-Heinemann (1996).

71 Heider, F., 'Attitudes and cognitive organization', *Journal of Psychology*, vol. 21, 1946, 107–12.

72 Festinger, L. A., *A Theory of Cognitive Dissonance*, Row, Peterson and Co. (1957).

73 Kuşluvan, S., Kuşluvan, Z, Ilhan, I. and Buyruk, L., 'The Human Dimension: A review of Human Resource Management issues in the Tourism and Hospitality Industry', *Cornell Hospitality Quarterly*, vol. 51, 2010, 171–214.

74 Goldthorpe, J. H. *et al.* [Lokwood, D., Bechhofer, F. and Platt, J.], *The Affluent Worker: Industrial Attitudes and Behaviour*, Cambridge University Press (1968).

75 Martin, E., 'Who's kicking whom? Employees' orientations to work', *International Journal of Contemporary Hospitality*. vol. 16, no. 3, 2004, 182–88.

76 Dodrill, K. and Riley, M., 'Hotel workers' orientations to work: the question of autonomy and scope', *International Journal of Contemporary Hospitality Management*, vol. 4, no. 1, 1992, 23–5.

77 See, for example, Schein, E. H., *Organizational Psychology*, 3rd edn, Prentice-Hall (1988).

78 CIPD, *Managing the Psychological Contract*, Chartered Institute of Personnel and Development (December 2004).

79 Robinson, S., 'The learning curve', *Inside Hotels*, April/May 1992, 40–5.

80 Kelley-Patterson, D. and George, C., 'Securing graduate commitment: an exploration of the comparative expectations of placement students, graduate recruits and human resource managers within the hospitality, leisure and tourism industries', *International Journal of Hospitality Management*, vol. 20, 2001, 311–23.

81 Hiltrop, J. M., 'Managing the Changing Psychological Contract', *Employee Relations*, vol. 18, no. 1, 1996, 36–49.

82 Altman, W., Cooper, C. and Garner, A., 'New deal needed to secure commitment', *Professional Manager*, September 1999, 39.

83 CIPD, *Managing the Psychological Contract*, Chartered Institute of Personnel and Development (December 2004).

84 See, for example, Riley, M., *Managing People: A guide for managers in the hotel and catering industry*, Butterworth-Heinemann (1995).

85 Brown, J. A. C., *The Social Psychology of Industry*, Penguin (1954 and 1986).

86 See, for example, Hornsey, T. and Dann, D., *Manpower Management in the Hotel and Catering Industry*, Batsford (1984).

87 'In Celebration of the Feel-Good Factor', *Professional Manager*, March 1998, p. 6.

Chapter 3

Diversity management

Learning outcomes

After completing this chapter you should be able to:

- explain the importance and nature of managing diversity approaches;
- explore the nature and importance of diversity management and evaluate the business case for diversity;
- explain the theoretical approaches to understanding cultural differences and how they can assist the hospitality manager;
- explain the need for cultural sensitivity in the management of people in the hospitality industry;
- outline the keys stages of the communication process and how to be sensitive to the communication needs of different groups and individuals;
- detail the key issues in the management of migrant workers in the hospitality industry;
- Identify ways in which the hospitality manager can assist in the acculturation and assimilation of workers of differing cultures and ethnicity.

Introduction

Individual differences can foster creativity, enjoyment and satisfaction at work but can also be the root of conflict and frustration. Our unique bundle of different attributes and characteristics shapes our values, and what we plan to give and what we expect to receive from working. People are not homogeneous, and individual differences are the basis of diversity. This homogeneity also extends to the people who are the customers of the organisation. Effective managers therefore need to steer a course that matches the needs and expectations of the various individuals in order to meet the requirements of the organisation.

Critical review and reflection

'One of the major and most interesting challenges facing hospitality managers today is managing the multicultural, multi-ethnic workforce.'

What do you see as the most important and most interesting aspects of managing a multicultural, multi-ethnic workforce?

The impact of globalisation on the management of people in the hospitality industry

Globalisation is affecting all work organisations and this can be seen to be particularly true within the hospitality industry. Statistics, and the experience of anyone working within the industry, demonstrate that the workforce is strongly multinational, multicultural and diverse.

People working within the industry, for example managers, often move for experience and career opportunities, either within the same global organisation or to a different organisation. This is highly possible in hospitality as many of the skills they possess are generic.

It is also the case that, increasingly, unskilled economic migrants move from one country to another for economic, and other, reasons. These moves may be temporary or permanent. For those who are not fluent in the language of the new country, job opportunities are necessarily limited. In the UK, the hospitality industry offers many low-paid work opportunities for those who are relatively unskilled, or with poor language skills, who are unable to acquire better paid work elsewhere. Because of the nature of the industry, and the extreme mobility of the low-skilled staff working in hospitality, estimates of the number of migrants working in the industry vary widely. For example, People 1st estimated in 2011 that 21 per cent of the workforce were born overseas.[1] (This figure is massively higher for London; Mintel estimates placed it at 80 per cent in 2008.)

It is increasingly important for managers and staff to understand and be able to deal with the resulting cultural, nationality, ethnicity and communication issues. They will be considered in more detail later in this chapter.

Managing diversity

It is illegal for an employer to discriminate against employees, or candidates for employment, on the grounds of their membership, or non-membership, of a particular protected group. This equal opportunities legislation now applies to gender and marital status, race, religion, ethnic origin, physical disability, age and sexual orientation. Rehabilitated offenders are also offered protection from discrimination in employment (see The Clink case study in Chapter 9). The most recent development in this area is the creation of the Equality and Human Rights Commission, which replaces the various state agencies that formerly investigated different forms of alleged discrimination. The idea behind equal opportunities is 'the principle of sameness in which employees of one group (e.g. Black, Asian, gay, female, etc.) are not treated any differently to members of another social group'.[2]

The managing diversity approach differs from Equal Opportunities in a number of ways; notably, rather than seeking to prevent difference of treatment, it encourages the recognition of difference. Kandola and Fullerton[3] suggest that legislation deals with designated groups, diversity deals with all differences. They define diversity as follows:

> The basic concept of managing diversity accepts that the workforce consists of a diverse population of people. The diversity consists of visible and non-visible differences which will include sex, age, background, race, disability, personality and workstyle. It is founded on the premise that harnessing these differences will create a productive environment in which everybody feels valued, where their talents are being fully utilised, and in which organisational goals are met.

There is no universally agreed definition of managing diversity but guidance from the Chartered Management Institute (2008) suggests it is about 'valuing the differences between people and the ways in which those differences can contribute to a richer, more creative and more productive . . . (workforce)'[4].

A particular characteristic of the hospitality industry workforce is the marked diversity of people working independently or employed within hospitality and tourism organisations. The hospitality organisation will typically be a mixed gender, multi-ethnic and multicultural workforce.

Equality and diversity are issues that affect all workplaces and everyone in the workplace. The equality legislation has been brought in to protect vulnerable groups of people, to ensure that people are not discriminated against unfairly for reasons that are unconnected with their ability to do their job. The law is quite detailed and managers may feel that it is not possible for them to keep up to date with current developments in all areas. Each large organisation will, however, have human resource departments, part of whose role is to produce policies, procedures and guidelines for managers and staff to refer to and follow. Smaller organisations may find it helpful to refer to their trade organisation, or to the arbitration service ACAS which produces excellent advice in these areas.[5] Everyone should, however, be aware of the basic principles of not discriminating directly or indirectly against an individual because of his or her membership of a particular group. Neither should individuals be victimised because they seek to enforce their rights under the legislation.

A further problem is harassment, which is unwanted conduct that intimidates or humiliates an individual thereby affecting their dignity or causing a hostile atmosphere in the workplace. It is the responsibility of the manager to ensure that this inappropriate behaviour does not occur and when it does occur it is dealt with appropriately.

Managing diversity builds on the principles established by the various pieces of equal opportunities legislation in the late nineteenth and early twenty-first centuries. Diversity is about valuing differences between individuals including their values, background and preferences, not just their protected characteristics such as gender, age, sexual orientation, religion, ethnic group and country of origin. Whilst in the modern organisation it can be seen to be morally right to value diversity, there are also business benefits. Employing a diverse workforce gives employers access to applicants with a wider range of talents and attributes. Also, it is likely to lead to the employer becoming an employer of choice and, in the case of a hospitality organisation, through having a more diverse workforce attracting a more diverse range of customers.

The extent to which hospitality organisations embrace diversity is far from clear.

Business case for diversity

A joint report from the CBI and TUC, supported by the Equality and Human Rights Commission, suggests that promoting diversity in the workplace and employing people solely on the basis of their ability can bring many real business benefits. These include:

- increasing employee satisfaction, which helps attract new staff and retain those already there, reduces recruitment costs, and can increase productivity;
- understanding better how the company's diverse customers think and what drives their spending habits, or how they access markets they have not previously been able to tap into so effectively;
- finding enough workers to fill skills gaps in areas with tight labour markets, where there are not enough 'obvious candidates' for the vacancies they have.

The report also makes clear that diversity can be improved through positive action – such as encouraging applications from types of people who have not in the past applied for jobs, additional training, providing support networks or adapting work practices – but not positive discrimination.[6]

CIPD suggests a number of business benefits accrue from employing a diverse workforce, including helping to develop new or better products or services; new market opportunities; broadening the customer base; and improving market share.

Positive and negative propositions

A further report from the Chartered Institute of Personnel and Development refers to a central theme of diversity as 'valuing everyone as individuals' and suggests there is an increasing volume of evidence of a convincing link between valuing people and value creation in business. Diversity programmes require cultural and organisational changes that are difficult to manage. However, the benefits of a diverse workforce include customer focus, innovation, creativity and learning, business process improvement and the financial bottom line.

> There is no denying the mounting empirical and anecdotal evidence that good diversity management can lead to improved business performance where the business contexts and market conditions are taken into account appropriately. Conversely, poorly developed and poorly matched diversity practice can be detrimental to business, creating without gain, raising expectations without delivery, and increasing cost without benefit.[7]

The report introduces the idea of measuring diversity and suggests the adoption of a balanced scorecard approach to integrate diversity into business strategy and operational activities. The scorecard puts forward eight propositions that take into account both the positive and negative forces of diversity.

Positive forces of diversity are those that:

- promote cost-effective employment relations;
- enhance customer relations;

- enhance creativity, flexibility and innovation;
- promote sustainable development and business advantage.

    Negative forces of diversity are:

- diminishing cultural relatedness;
- the need for financial support to support flexibility;
- the jeopardising of workplace harmony;
- possible conflict between organisational slack and tight fit.

Exhibit 3.1 Diversity works

Our Diversity Initiatives at Hilton Hotels Corporation are designed to produce quantifiable and qualitative results which go beyond just establishing and maintaining a diverse workforce. We have incorporated diversity principles into all aspects of our business operations: employment, training and mentoring, marketing, community support, and management performance measurements.

While successful diversity programming can result in receiving awards, plaques and trophies (which look nice on our walls), at Hilton we're concerned with much more than an accumulation of hardware. Our achievements in diversity programming, and the priority we place on it, go to the very heart, soul and spirit of our organization ... who we are, and what we stand for.

Yes, we welcome and appreciate acknowledgements of our diversity accomplishments; and we'll find room for more plaques and trophies recognizing our good work. But far beyond the pride that goes with such recognition is our commitment to the belief that our Diversity Initiatives enhance our competitiveness and strengthen the business value of our corporation; for those reasons, we take pride in the fact that, at Hilton Hotels Corporation ... 'diversity works'.

(Stephen F. Bollenbach, President and CEO)[8]

Hilton Worldwide diversity and inclusion

Our diversity and inclusion approach is aligned with our mission to become the preeminent global hospitality company. We seek to leverage the unique cultures of our global communities, and to develop talent, workplace and marketplace strategies to cre-

ate a work environment of inclusiveness. As such, we hold ourselves and all of our Team Members to the highest standards of integrity, ethics and service excellence. We will achieve and maintain this status by living our core values; attracting the best and brightest talent; and valuing and leveraging the diversity of our Team Members, Guests, Suppliers, Partners and Owners.

Culture: we seek to understand our unique global cultures to ensure that all our Team Members are seen, heard, valued and respected. As a result, our senior leadership is committed to investing in programs that promote diversity, such as inclusion training and celebrations of international traditions and customs. We also aim to increase our presence in local communities through employee volunteerism, partnerships and giving programs.

One example of our commitment to foster appreciation of diversity is our company-wide information sharing and training initiative. As part of this effort, we highlight U.S. calendar months that recognize and celebrate diverse groups. We create internal newsletters detailing the purpose and history of each and Hilton Worldwide partnerships with related organizations. We also offer Team Members diversity training courses through Hilton Worldwide University, our internal online training platform.

Talent: An integral part of our Talent Management strategy is to create an inclusive work environment. Embracing diversity in thought, background and opinion not only adds to our talent pool but also provides significant value to our global business operations by fostering innovation and competition.

We value the diversity of our Team Members and strive to continue attracting strong talent by building local hiring pipelines and providing coaching, mentoring and leadership development opportunities for all Team Members. We have built relationships with select leading Historically Black Colleges and Universities (HBCUs) and Hispanic-Serving Institutions (HSIs) to recruit top talent within hospitality programs. In addition, our leadership team has taken positions on boards or councils for many professional associations.[9]

Critical review and reflection

What benefits can you see for Hilton Hotels from their diversity programme?

Are there any other specific benefits in employing foreign nationals in a city centre hotel, beyond those referred to by Bollenbach?

Is the concern with managing diversity a moral or social concern? To what extent is it more about benefits to business?

Diversity and age

A dimension of 'diversity' of particular significance to the hospitality industry is that of age. The hospitality industry has traditionally employed a 'younger' workforce due to the physical nature of much of the work. However, this is increasingly being seen as an area for consideration.

A BBC *Panorama* report, broadcast on 1 April 2011, made the point that *over-50s* make up less than 20 per cent of staff in hotels and leisure trade, suggesting that there is a culture of recruiting young people in their twenties and working them very hard for 10–15 years, when they leave to do something less demanding (and maybe more consistent with family life).

Approximately 49 per cent of hospitality workers are under 29 (compared with 18 per cent across the economy as a whole), while apparently in our sector you are an 'older worker' at the age of 25 . . . Yet . . . by 2020, almost a third of the workforce will be over the age of 50.[10]

In the UK, this generation of older people are living longer than previous generations and many are having to survive longer on inadequate pensions. The age at which the state retirement pension can be collected is planned to increase to 67 years by 2028,[11] and occupational pensions are also likely to be reduced. Thus where people are fit and able to work, many would like to carry on working for financial reasons. The recent removal of the default retirement age, previously set at 65 years, means that employers cannot compulsorily retire people at that time. This suggests that there is likely to be an increased pool of older people available for employment in future. J D Wetherspoon[12] stopped retiring people at 65, in 2006, to retain valuable skills and experience; as a result, they report improved customer satisfaction and staff retention levels well above the industry norm.

Exhibit 3.2 Older workers

Older workers are a key ingredient in the recipe for success[13]

Should the industry be doing more to attract and retain older workers? Lara Eade reports:

If you ask people to name their first ever job, the chances are that it had something to do with hospitality. Whether it was waiting tables, serving drinks or washing dishes at the local pub, the industry is traditionally seen as one that offers young people the opportunity for early employment, with flexible hours that fit around school and college.

In fact, it has become extremely reliant on its young workforce. People 1st's 'State of the Nation 2009' report shows that 16 per cent of workers (in the hospitality industry) are between the ages of 16 and 19, and a further 32 per cent are aged between 20 and 29. Across the whole economy, only five per cent of the total workforce is aged between 16 and 19, and 13 per cent between 20 and 29. But while the industry continues to push its revolving door of young workers, it is heading for problems later down the line.

As the media frequently reminds us, we now live in an ageing society. By 2033, 23 per cent of the UK's population will be aged 65 and over, up from 16 per cent in 2008, while those aged 16 or younger will have fallen from 19 to 18 per cent. Older workers are a constantly growing demographic, so why does hospitality continue to focus on a shrinking, younger workforce?

Staff retention is already a major issue in the hospitality industry, which has one of the highest rates of turnover of all UK sectors, and the failure to attract and utilise the older generation is one of the factors contributing to this. By positioning itself as an industry for the young, hospitality is missing out on a wealth of experience from later life workers who, despite having value to offer, may take a look and think "that's not for me."

One company that is bucking the trend, and reaping the benefits of employing older workers, is McDonald's. In August 2009, Lancaster University carried out a survey of over 400

McDonald's restaurants and found that customer satisfaction rose by 20 per cent in those employing staff over the age of 60. Around two fifths of restaurants currently employ staff in that age bracket.

Some of the strengths highlighted by the research included older workers' empathy, ability to connect with customers, and willingness to "go the extra mile" to deliver the best possible service. 44 per cent of respondents also valued the mentoring skills that later life workers offered to their younger counterparts, helping them to mature and grow within their roles.

It's clear that older workers have a lot to offer, often with essential skills that can only be learnt through experience but, like all other employees, they will continue to learn and grow with the business. In August 2009, a research project was conducted by the University of Stirling, which looked at how to sustain the employability of older workers in the hospitality sector through learning and training.

The findings suggest that older workers value an approach to training and development which recognises their previous experience and, in turn, acknowledges their diverse and individual learning needs and ambitions.

The research also showed that the traditionally perceived disadvantages of hospitality and tourism, such as low wages, unsocial hours, repetitive work and seasonal employment, were not entirely negative issues for older workers. Whereas younger workers may be put off by these factors and move on, older workers find compensation for them in being needed, valued, and maintaining a good work–life balance.

In an industry that traditionally suffers from high staff turnover, perhaps it is time for companies to look to this "new" pool of talent for some stability.

People 1st is looking at ways in which the research findings can be utilised, enabling more hospitality businesses to benefit from a more diverse workforce.

If more employers recognised the value of older workers, not only could they avoid the inevitable problems of over-reliance on a shrinking demographic, but they could also tap into a wealth of skills and experience that might broaden their customer appeal as a whole.

Critical review and reflection

'The hospitality industry is not suitable for workers over the age of 30. They cannot cope with the pace.'

Bearing in mind the experience of McDonald's and J D Wetherspoon referred to above, how might you justify the comment?

Diversity and stereotyping

Diversity also challenges many traditional stereotypes. Stereotyping implies that people within a particular perceived category are assumed to share the same traits or characteristics. Stereotypes are a means of making simplified judgements of other people instead of coping with a range of individual stimuli. Stereotyping attributes to all individuals the characteristics or tendencies of the categorisation as a whole. An important feature of managing diversity is an awareness of, and training in, overcoming inaccurate stereotyped perceptions and attributions. A greater understanding of cultural differences in non-verbal communications and body language will help improve interpersonal relationships.

There have been instances in my life, both at home and at work, when people have felt I'm a little crazy because I am pushy, outspoken, energetic, competitive, enthusiastic, driven and strong. Crazy, because that's not what's expected of an Asian woman. Crazy because it's not what the majority of people are like. And crazy, because they think they know me better than I know myself.

(Saira Khan – star of *The Apprentice* television series)[14]

Managers' attitudes, values and beliefs

If they are to be successful in managing diversity, managers need to have greater reserves of emotional intelligence (see Chapter 2). In turn this suggests that managers need to have an awareness of, and be able to get in touch with, their own attitudes, values and beliefs – what they are and where they come from. Clements and Jones recognise that the process can be uncomfortable:

A model of good diversity training will recognize that when people engage in an exploration of their attitudes, values, beliefs and prejudices, this may be an uncomfortable process. Some will find out things about themselves that will cause them emotional pain, and often the tension in learners will relate to how they should respond.[15]

In managing the diverse workforce, there can be a risk that managers and others will see individuals as being a member of a particular group, for example of a particular nationality, and expect them to follow the national stereotype, rather than seeing the particular individual characteristics. Managers need to be particularly aware of their own tendency to stereotype, positively or negatively, as well as the similar tendencies of staff.

Examples of common stereotyping may be based on:

- **nationality**, for example all Germans are orderly and industrious, all Australians like cricket;
- **occupation**, for example all accountants are boring, all librarians are serious and undemonstrative;
- **age**, for example all young people are unreliable, no old person wants to consider new ideas;
- **physical**, for example all people with red hair have a fiery temperament, all fat people are lazy;
- **education**, for example all graduates are intelligent;
- **social**, for example all unemployed people are lazy, immigrants do not want to learn English;
- **politics**, for example all Labour voters favour state intervention, all Conservative voters support reducing the size of the public sector.

A problem with stereotyping is that, although the stereotypes do not accurately portray the characteristics of all people in a group, there is usually truth in the portrayal if the group as a whole is considered. For example, 'men like football more than shopping and women like shopping more than football'. Few people would claim that all men like football or that all women like shopping but observations at a football ground or in a department store on a Saturday afternoon would confirm the general truth of the statement.

It would be helpful for the catering concession at the football ground to know who the customers will be, so that the right snacks can be available. The stereotype of the football supporter is used by the caterer in planning what food and drink to supply. In the same way that the above example of stereotypes is helpful, it can be helpful to appreciate the characteristics of national cultural stereotypes.

The nature of national culture

Working within and managing within a multicultural workforce can be enhanced through an understanding of culture and cultural values. It is possible to talk about the peculiar cultures of individual countries and, by extension, nationals of those countries. In attempting to understand particular organisational strategy, it is also useful to look at organisational culture, which will be looked at in Chapter 10.

There are many definitions of culture. Browaeys and Price[16] make the point that the attempts to define what culture is, all provide different and useful perspectives. However, although there does not seem to be any one ideal definition, one which may be useful for our purposes is that of Hofstede who refers to culture as 'the collective programming of the mind which distinguishes the members of one human group from another'.[17]

Hofstede elaborated with 'culture, in this sense, includes systems of values; and values are among the building blocks of culture'.

Bratton, Callinan, Forshaw and Sawchuck[18] build on this definition by suggesting that 'culture is the knowledge, languages, values, customs and material objects that are passed from person to person and from one generation to another in a human group or society'.

Trompenaars referred to the explicit observable aspects of culture such as language, preferred foods and diet, fashions, art and manners. Whilst one should be careful to avoid stereotyping individuals, it might be reasonable to suggest, for example, that the French are more interested in food and wines than the English.

In addition to the observable aspect of culture, he suggests that it is important to consider a country's norms and values, the mutual sense a group has of what is right and wrong.[19] The norms can be formal such as laws, or informal such as accepted ways of behaving, while values determine what a group considers to be good or bad.

Trompenaars' third layer of culture is the unseen part. It refers to deeply held assumptions about existence, a philosophy. Whilst this is less obvious to the observer than the other two layers, it can be extremely important in forming attitudes and subsequent behaviour.

Dimensions of culture: the contribution of Hofstede

Geert Hofstede is probably one of the most significant contributors to the study of culture.

Hofstede initially identified four dimensions of culture, to which he, with Bond, later added a fifth dimension:

- *Power distance* is essentially used to categorise accepted levels of inequality in organisations. Hofstede claims that this inequality depends on management style, willingness of subordinates to disagree with superiors as well as the education level and status accruing to particular roles. Countries which displayed a high level of power distance included Spain, Hong Kong and the Philippines. Countries as diverse as Germany, Italy, Australia and the USA were characterised as low power distance countries. Britain also emerged as low power distance.

- *Uncertainty avoidance* refers to the extent to which members of a society feel threatened by unusual situations. High uncertainty avoidance is said to be characteristic in France, Spain, Germany and many Latin American societies. Low to medium uncertainty avoidance is displayed in the Netherlands, the Scandinavian countries and Ireland. In this case Britain is said to be 'low to medium' together with the USA, Canada and Australia.

- *Individualism* describes the relatively individualistic or collectivist ethic evident in a particular society. Thus the USA and UK display high individualism. This contrasts with Hong Kong, India and Greece which are said to be low individualism societies. The UK is depicted as a high individualism society.

- *Masculinity*. This refers to the continuum between masculine characteristics such as assertiveness and competitiveness and feminine traits such as caring, a stress upon the quality of life and concern with the environment. High masculinity countries include the USA, Italy and Germany. More feminine (low masculinity) societies include the Netherlands and Scandinavian countries.

- The fifth dimension *long term/short term orientation* was originally labelled Confucian work dynamism. Countries which scored highly on this dimension exhibited a strong concern with time and investment payback periods. Thus, those with a short-term orientation would expect an early return on investment, whilst those with a long-term orientation would judge the success of the investment by calculating the potential return over a long period of time, maybe even over generations.

Hofstede has recently suggested a further dimension,[20] 'indulgence v restraint,[21] based on Minkov's analysis of the World Values Survey 2006, which looked at data from 93 different countries.

Indulgence stands for a society that allows relatively free gratification of basic and natural human drives related to enjoying life and having fun. Restraint stands for a society that suppresses gratification of needs and regulates it by means of strict social norms.[22]

Cultural diversity: the contribution of Trompenaars

Another significant contributor to this area of study is Fons Trompenaars whose later work is co-authored with Charles Hampden-Turner.[23] Whereas Hofstede explained differences in culture, Trompenaars was more concerned with practical managerial applications dealing with cross-cultural environment programmes. A questionnaire method comprised a significant part of his study. This involved requiring participants to consider their underlying norms, values and attitudes. His framework identified seven areas in which cultural differences could affect aspects of organisational behaviour.

These are:

- Relationships and rules. Here societies may be more or less **universal**, in which case there is relative rigidity in respect of rule-based behaviour, or **particular**, in which case the importance of relationships may lead to flexibility in the interpretation of situations.

- Societies may be more orientated to the **individual** or **collective**. The collective may take different forms, the corporation in Japan, the family in Italy or the Catholic Church in the Republic of Ireland. There may be implications here for such matters as individual responsibility or payment systems.

- It may also be true that societies differ in the extent to which it is thought appropriate for members to show emotion in public. **Neutral** societies favour the 'stiff upper lip', while overt displays of feeling are more likely in **emotional** societies. Trompenaars cites a survey in which 80 employees in each of various societies were asked whether they would think it wrong to express upset openly at work. The numbers who thought it wrong were 80 in Japan, 75 in Germany, 71 in the UK, 55 in Hong Kong, 40 in the USA and 29 in Italy.

- In **diffuse** cultures, the whole person would be involved in a business relationship and it would take time to build such relationships. In a **specific** culture, such as the USA, the basic relationship would be limited to the contractual. This distinction clearly has implications for those seeking to develop new international links.

- **Achievement-based** societies value recent success or an overall record of accomplishment. In contrast, in societies relying more on **ascription**, status could be bestowed on you through such factors as age, gender or educational record.

- Trompenaars suggests that societies view **time** in different ways which may in turn influence business activities. The American dream is the French nightmare. Americans generally start from zero and what matters is their present performance and their plan to 'make it' in the future. This is *nouveau riche* for the French, who prefer the *ancien pauvre*; they have an enormous sense of the past.

- Finally it is suggested that there are differences with regard to attitudes to the **environment**. In Western societies, individuals are typically masters of their fate. In other parts of the world, however, the world is more powerful than individuals.

Trompenaars' work is based on lengthy academic and field research. It is potentially useful in linking the dimensions of culture to aspects of organisational behaviour which are of direct relevance, particularly to people approaching a new culture for the first time.

The high and low context cultures framework (Hall and Hall)

This framework for understanding cultural difference has been formulated by Ed Hall; his work is in part co-authored with Mildred Reed Hall.[24] Hall conceptualises culture as comprising a series of 'languages', in particular:

- language of time;
- language of space;
- language of things;
- language of friendships;
- language of agreements.

In this model of culture Hall suggests that these 'languages', which resemble shared attitudes to the issues in question, are communicated in very different ways according to whether a society is classified as 'high' or 'low' context.

The features of 'high' context societies, which incorporate Asian, African and Latin American countries, include:

- a high proportion of information is 'uncoded' and internalised by the individual;
- indirect communication styles . . . words are less important;
- shared group understandings;
- importance attached to the past and tradition;
- 'diffuse' culture stressing importance of trust and personal relationships in business.

'Low' context societies, which include the USA, Australia and the Scandinavian countries, exhibit contrasting features including:

- a high proportion of communication is 'coded' and expressed;
- direct communication styles . . . words are paramount;
- past context is less important;
- 'specific' culture stressing importance of rules and contracts.

Other countries, for example France, Spain, Greece and several Middle Eastern societies, are classified as 'medium' context.

To take one example as an illustration: American managers visiting China may find that a business transaction in that country will take more time than at home. They may find it difficult to interpret the true feelings of their Chinese host and may need to decode non-verbal communication and other signals. They may seek to negotiate a rules-based contract whereas their Chinese counterpart may lay greater stress upon building a mutually beneficial reciprocal relationship. There is scope for potential miscommunication between the two cultures and interesting differences in interpersonal perception.

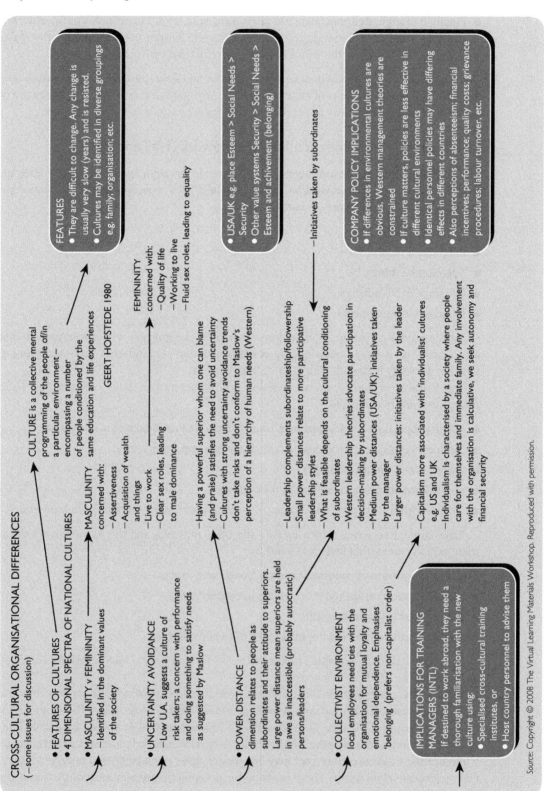

Figure 3.1 Concept map of cross-cultural organisational differences

As can be seen from the above example, there are likely to be differences between perceptions as well as communication styles due to people having different cultural backgrounds. The links between these areas will be considered in more detail later later in this chapter.

Implications for the hospitality manager

The theoretical approaches above can be used to help explain the differences in values, attitudes and behaviours of people of different nationalities. The following examples may help to illustrate this:

- Many foreign workers in the UK hospitality industry send their earnings home to their families in other countries, believing this is their responsibility. A **'collective'** approach – Trompenaars.

- Different nationalities and cultures place a differing emphasis on time and punctuality. The Germans are (to UK eyes) remarkably punctual – **'low context'**, whilst Caribbean countries are (again to UK eyes) remarkably relaxed about timekeeping – **'high context'** – Hall and Hall's framework.

- French managers would expect to be addressed formally. Staff would not address the manager by the first name and would expect a relatively autocratic management style – **'high power distance'**. This reflects an expectation of managerial style, which is different from the UK where staff may joke with managers and prefer to be consulted – **'low power distance'** – Hofstede.

The hospitality industry in the UK does not always seem consistent with the British cultural model. For example, British culture normally would be seen as **'specific'** (Trompenaars); this means that the employment relationship would be limited to the contract. In hospitality, however, it is necessary to adopt a **'diffuse'** approach, meaning that the employees need to put work first and work long additional hours, often without notice, to deliver the service that customers require. For example, in certain sectors of the hospitality industry in the UK, organisational culture requires much flexibility – a shift may end at 10 pm but if guests are still in the restaurant, staff must stay to serve them and may be expected to do this unpaid.

Another area where the general British cultural model often does not seem to fit is in the kitchen. The emotion often shown by chefs does not fit with the expected 'stiff upper lip' controlled British emotion. (Trompenaars would refer to this as **'neutral'**, rather than **'emotional'**.) Evidence of chefs losing tempers and behaving badly to kitchen staff seems to show this to be the norm. In kitchens, also, there does seem to be **'high power distance'** (Hofstede), with chefs behaving extremely autocratically, which is not generally seen as an appropriate management style in other industries.

Critical review and reflection

'Maybe, the international nature of the hotel and restaurant industry, with top chefs and hotel managers learning their trades with, and from, top professionals from other countries, has led to the industry adopting its own culture, which overrides the national culture.'

What are your views on the apparent disparity between the culture in the hospitality industry and the UK national culture?

A particularly significant aspect of individual difference and a major determinant of behaviour within the hospitality industry is perception, considered in the previous chapter. This process is closely linked with that of communication. It is of vital importance that managers understand these processes as a basis to understanding the people they manage. The processes of perception and communication are strongly influenced by background, individual difference and culture, and these links need to be explored.

It is well known that the workforce in the hospitality industry is very cosmopolitan and that staff are drawn from diverse ethnic backgrounds with many staff originating from overseas. With staff from so many different cultural and ethnic origins, it is becoming increasingly important for the enlightened manager to have an understanding and awareness of cultural difference. Movement of staff around the European Union requires management to be aware of, and sensitive to, differing expectations and cultural values.

Immigration from other parts of the world has also contributed to this multicultural workforce. Equally, trends in globalisation and the international nature of the industry are increasing the likelihood of hospitality managers and employees following international careers.

To manage this increasingly diverse workforce effectively, it is beneficial for managers to have an understanding and appreciation of cultural differences, including individuals' values and expectations. Similarly, it would help to establish harmonious working relations if staff also had an understanding of cultural differences and expectations. This would also contribute to understanding the international customers' needs and expectations. It could be argued that intercultural skills are crucial in the globalised society.

The importance of cultural influences

The hospitality industry is very cosmopolitan and it is therefore particularly important to recognise the significance of different cultural and ethnic values, and associated traditions, religious beliefs and customs. Understanding other people's views of the world will not only make for better customer and staff relations, but may also help to prevent possible allegations of discrimination.

Differences in culture may also help to explain the attitude of certain customers. Japanese businessmen who are accompanied by their wives may expect the best seats at the dining table. Americans often have a reputation for being particularly demanding and expecting a high level of personal attention. Such expectations might be better understood if managers and staff are aware of cultural differences, which in this case includes the high standards of customer service and concern for individual requirements which are customary in many parts of America.[25]

The different norms, rules and traditions of different cultures clearly affect behaviour. For example, managers also need to be aware of how cultural differences can influence the attitudes and motivations of staff, and their pace of work.

Behavioural differences

As an example of behavioural difference, German business people tend to expect business relationships to be conducted formally, in accordance with the relative positions of the people in the organisational hierarchy, and they would also tend to avoid familiarity in public. British business people would tend to be more relaxed about these matters. Some of the most important behavioural differences between different cultures would be religious observance, which can include dietary rules, dress, and communication.

Religious rules and observation

Alcohol is not acceptable to the majority of Muslims. If they have a large number of Muslim customers some hotels may remove alcoholic beverages from the minibars in their bedrooms. During Ramadan, Muslim members of staff may fast during daylight hours, eat meals only at certain times and not be prepared to work on certain days for religious reasons. The manager may therefore need to arrange holidays and shift working accordingly.

If there is a large number of Jewish customers, some restaurant managers will not put pork on the meat trolley. Airport hotels which receive many Jewish customers may even make special arrangements for the preparation and service of kosher food.

Culture and religion will also influence appearance and dress. One, of many, examples of this is Sikhs wearing their hair uncut and by tradition carrying a steel comb and bangle. Because of their culture many Muslim women will not wear clothes that show their legs, and will cover their heads and sometimes much of their faces with scarves. A further example is the dreadlocks hair style of Rastafarians.

The wearing of saris by Hindu women and the long flowing robes worn by Arabs need consideration by hospitality organisations when considering uniform and dress rules for staff.

Whilst some dietary rules, as above, are based on religion, others can be considered to be cultural preference, which leads some hospitality organisations to cater for the different tastes and preferences of their increasingly cosmopolitan customers and staff with a range of different cuisines. Tony Mullen, of Apex Hotels, speaking at the University of Portsmouth in March 2012, stressed the need to treat staff well and with respect, saying that good quality, varied food that suited all cultures was an important aspect of this.

Exhibit 3.3 An accusation of workplace discrimination

Muslim caterer accuses the Met of discrimination[26]

A Muslim catering manager has taken the Metropolitan Police to tribunal claiming he was racially abused and threatened with the sack for refusing to cook pork.

Hasanali Khoja, 60, said that when he called a meeting to discuss his objections to cooking pork for religious reasons, his line manager told him he could lose his job if he failed to follow instructions.

Khoja claimed he felt he was at risk of contact with pork products at his interview for a senior catering manager job with the Metropolitan Police Service, but was assured he would not have to handle food as it was a supervisory role.

He started work at a police training centre in 2005, but after being transferred to a kitchen at Heathrow airport in 2007, the chef was told he had to prepare, cook and serve all food products, including bacon and pork sausages.

Speaking at the tribunal about the meeting with his manager, Khoja said: 'The meeting was very threatening because I was reminded several times that if I refused to accept management instructions my job was at risk.'

He added that in a follow-up meeting, an HR manager pulled a face, making a gesture towards Khoja as if he was an alien.

'I was very humiliated and stressed out and was unable to continue', Khoja said. Khoja, who is now employed in another part of the Metropolitan Police catering structure, has alleged racial discrimination, religious discrimination and unlawful deduction of wages. The Met has declined to comment ahead of the trial's conclusion. The hearing continues.

(Daniel Thomas)

Critical review and reflection

How could the situation of the Muslim caterer with the Met have been handled more appropriately?

Exhibit 3.4 Accommodating religious beliefs

Clothing/appearance

If your workplace requires a certain uniform or 'look', make that clear right from the beginning, and discuss any conflicts that may arise. You must be able to show a tribunal you've been reasonable, taken any issues seriously and explored all options.

Handling food

How should you react if a chef or other employee says they cannot handle certain food, for instance pork, for religious reasons? Again, the answer is, unfortunately, 'it depends'. Depending on the role and seniority of the person, it may be possible to adjust how they work. But you do still have a business to run. If, assuming all avenues have been explored constructively and reasonably, and it's clear their religious beliefs now mean it's simply impossible for them to do their job, then you may have grounds for dismissal. One proviso is whether you were aware they had such strong beliefs, and so had implicitly accepted them as employable, when you hired them. Either way, it's probably worth taking advice before acting.

Hair

Health and safety regulations are clear on the issue that those handling food need to keep long hair tied back or otherwise restrained. For dreadlocks, a hygienic head covering may be considered reasonable, and for long beards, perhaps a net. The issue of whether you can force an employee to trim their locks or facial hair for appearance's sake is much less clear-cut and, again, worth taking advice on.

Time off/time to pray

Accommodating everyone's religious holidays – Eid, Ramadan, Divali, the Sabbath, Christmas, and so on – may seem like a nightmare juggling act, but can actually make good business sense. As long as you have fair warning, a good rota system, and everyone is prepared to be reasonable, it may not be too hard. Demanding regular time to pray is more of a problem. Allowing someone to disappear, say, five times a day could be disruptive and cause resentment. Again, it's a question of being reasonable. Can this demand be reasonably accommodated? If not, do you have a firm, business-based argument as to why not?[27]

Cultural differences in communication

Account must clearly be taken of differences in language, touching, gestures and mannerisms. For example, the English language is written from left to right but Hebrew is written from right to left, and Chinese is written downwards. There are many instances of different cultural gestures and mannerisms. A multicultural environment is a feature of the hotel industry. This demands effective systems of communication and attention to interpersonal relationships.[28]

It is clearly highly important to be aware of the cultural differences of overseas visitors, so as to avoid offence and misunderstandings. The same possibilities for poor communication exist with other staff members and it is therefore equally important to ensure that misunderstandings are avoided here also.

The communication process

An understanding of the process of communication, and exercising clear communication skills, are an integral part of good management. An extension of the development of good communication, particularly relevant to the hospitality organisation, is an understanding of the role that culture plays in communication.

Communication is the process of passing information from one, or more, individuals to one, or more, other individuals. This information can take many forms, for example it could be an instruction or a demand, a fact or opinion, an emotion or feeling.

The communication process used by the media is essentially one-way. That is, a message is broadcast and there is no facility for instant feedback from the receiver.

However, feedback is an integral part of the interpersonal communication process. In terms of the management of people this is the relevant model and the one which will be considered here.

The classic perception of interpersonal communication views it as a linear process comprising a series of steps (essentially: encoding, transmission, decoding and feedback), which, when completed, result in the successful transmission of a thought, emotion, or other message, from the sender(s) to the receiver(s).[29]

The elements within this linear model are thus:

- Sending: the person or group sending the message.
- Encoding: the sender translates the thought for transmission into a code which the receiver(s) can (hopefully) understand.

- The message: the result or output of encoding which is then transmitted.
- The medium of communication: the mode or modes of transmission (much communication relies on more than one medium. For example, face-to-face communication relies upon non-verbal communication as well as auditory communication.
- Decoding: the receiver interprets the meaning of the communication. This is a potential problem area as receivers may misinterpret for a number of perceptual or cultural reasons.
- The receiver: the person or group receiving the message.
- Feedback: the receiver at this point informs the sender that the message has been received and has been understood or not.

Another important factor in the process of communication is that of 'noise', which can be anything that hinders the clarity of the communication and includes perceptual filters.

As we all know, from our own experience, misunderstandings frequently arise when individuals communicate with each other. These misunderstandings can arise though problems at any stage of the communication process. For example, the sender may be unclear about the message being sent. The code chosen may not be shared with the receiver(s). The message may be awkwardly or ambiguously presented. The medium of communication may be inappropriate for the message. The receiver may incorrectly decode and interpret the meaning of the communication. Feedback may not be sent and, importantly, 'noise' or perceptual filters may stop or distort the message.

In the workplace much of the communication is face-to-face, oral, communication. There is written communication passing between managers and those whom they manage and there is clearly scope for misunderstandings here. Poor handwriting, inability to read, misinterpretation of technical and organisational jargon, as well as the more modern problem of excessive email communication, are all potential problems. However, the larger problem in the hospitality industry would be that of face-to-face communication.

Problems with face-to-face communication would include:

- misunderstanding and misinterpretation of non-verbal communication;
- psychological factors;
- interpersonal relationships; and
- differing interpretations of language used.

These problems can be considered to be accentuated by differing perceptions, cultural differences and status.

Critical review and reflection

'Communication is culture, culture is communication.'

From your own experience consider a situation when you were communicating with someone from another culture and a misunderstanding occurred. Consider the extent to which this was due to cultural difference.

The contribution of Lewis to understanding cross-cultural communication[30]

Effective communication is vital to effective management, and is frequently a source of misunderstanding in any context, but particularly when working with staff from other cultures.

The Lewis model can help the manager understand some of the different language styles. For example, Figure 3.2 shows how those of Germanic origin prefer clear direct language and may sometimes appear abrupt to the British ear.

If the language is not clear and the instruction is not clear, this can lead to genuine misunderstandings of what is required. The Lewis model shows how the courteous, 'listening' Chinese staff may not respond immediately or question the speaker, thus maybe seeming disinterested, whereas those of Mediterranean origin, trying to engage with the speaker, might sound, to a British ear, as if they are trying to overtalk and are more interested in their own views than in what the speaker is trying to say.

The Lewis model suggests that different nationalities have different language styles ranging from the 'cool and factual decisive planners' via 'the courteous amiable compromisers' to the 'warm and emotional, impulsive' types. For example, this model, begins to explain why typically those of Germanic origin prefer clear direct language and, sometimes, appear abrupt to the British national.

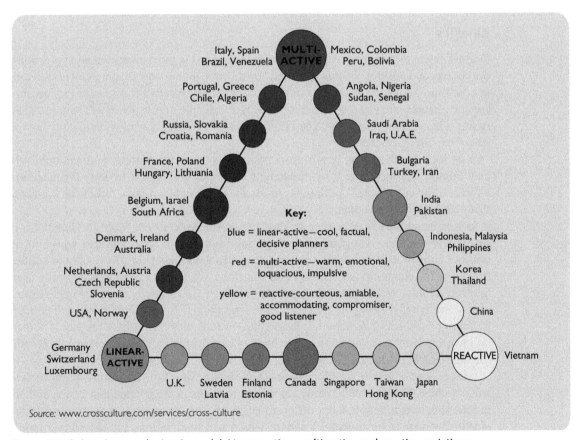

Source: www.crossculture.com/services/cross-culture

Figure 3.2 Cultural types: the Lewis model. Linear-active, multi-active and reactive variations

Non-verbal communication and body language

Non-verbal communication and body language is very significant in our communications with others. According to Mehrabian, in face-to-face communication, our feelings and attitudes are communicated less (only 7 percent) by the words we use than by our voice (38 per cent) and mostly (55 per cent) by non-verbal communication, including body language and facial expressions.

Bloisi[31] supports this contention: 'As much as 93 per cent of the meaning that is transmitted between two people in a face-to-face communication can come from non-verbal channels.'

What this means is that when people talk to others, they constantly look at and interpret, usually unconsciously, facial expressions, body posture, movement and gestures. At the same time they will be listening to and interpreting tone of voice and emphasis.

Where this non-verbal communication and body language confirms the meaning of the words, it is very usefuls; where this appears to contradict the words used, it indicates a problem. Often the non-verbal communication and body language amplifies the spoken message.

We can categorise non-verbal communication in a number of ways, including kinesics and proxemics.

Kinesics

Kinesics refers to gestures, hand and arm movements, leg movements, facial expressions, eye contact and posture.[32] Often hand and arm movements are used to complement or accent words. Thus, in one sense gestures can be considered to be verbal communication, because specific gestures often have a verbal meaning. For example, traffic police will stop traffic by raising a hand to indicate 'stop'. The fisherman might stretch his arms wide to illustrate the size of the fish that escaped!

A person's bodily stance, or posture, may also communicate feelings and emotions. We may think of an encouraging or threatening body posture. Norms in body language are influenced by culture and upbringing. In Japan, for example, a bow, rather than a handshake, is the formal greeting.

In Russia, smiling may be seen as showing lack of seriousness while in Thailand it is strongly encouraged. Laughing may show good humour in some cultures while in the Chinese culture it can signify embarrassment. Facial expressions, for example smiles, frowns, tears, communicate feelings and emotions. We would expect to see a smile used by a receptionist to show friendliness and politeness. For example, there are many examples of eye contact being an area for misunderstanding. In certain cultures eye contact is a sign of respect; it is impolite, even rude, to look away. In others respect is shown by lowering eyes and lowering one's head. Gaze avoidance shows respect in certain Afro-Caribbean cultures.

Other forms of formal or informal greeting vary across cultures: failure to appreciate when to hug, kiss or shake hands, or whom to greet in what way, can cause embarrassment between people from different cultures. For example, it is unacceptable for Muslim women to be touched by men, which has implications for the simple handshake.[33]

Proxemics

Proxemics refers to the use of space, including territoriality, which stands for the space that an individual claims temporarily or permanently.[34] Thus, proxemics is used to describe the use of personal space, as in how close to each other people stand, and the differences in meaning that are implied by any difference between the 'normal' distance and the distance chosen by one or both parties, on a particular occasion. Generally the closer the people are to each other the greater the degree of intimacy. Of course, there are crowded public areas, like the London Underground at rush hour, where people have no choice but to accept being squashed together; they cope with the discomfort by pretending that their personal space has not been invaded when, clearly, it has been.

The normal degree of proximity varies between cultures.[35] Arabs tend to stand very close when speaking to another person but most Americans when introduced to a new person will, after shaking hands, move backwards a couple of steps to place a comfortable space between themselves and the person they have just met.[36]

Effect of cultural differences on non-verbal communication

All of the above tends to be culturally derived: what is generally acceptable in one culture may not be in another. As with spoken communication, cultural differences can affect non-verbal communication. There are many cultural variations in non-verbal communications,in the extent of physical contact, and in the way body language is perceived and interpreted. For example, in many European countries it is customary to give three or four kisses on the cheek and pulling the head away may be taken as a sign of impoliteness.

Italians and South Americans tend to show their feelings through intense body language, while the Japanese tend to hide their feelings and have largely eliminated overt body language from interpersonal communication. When talking to another person, the British tend to look away spasmodically, but Norwegians typically look people steadily in the eyes without altering their gaze. In South Korea, women refrain from shaking hands. The Japanese often have a weak handshake whereas in Britain a firm handshake is encouraged. When the Dutch point a forefinger at their temples this is likely to be a sign of congratulations for a good idea, but with other cultures the gesture has a less complimentary implication. All cultures have specific values related to personal space and 'comfort zone'.

> All things are not what they seem. The ability to work out what is really happening with a person is simple – not easy, but simple. It's about matching what you see and hear to the environment in which it all happens and drawing possible conclusions. Most people, however, only see the things they think they are seeing.[37]

Critical review and reflection

'There are so many forms of non-verbal communication cues, either intentional or unintentional, that can be interpreted in a number of ways. There are also wide variations in cultural norms that influence the essential meaning and context of interactions. Attempting to make valid inferences from body language is of little real value and its use should be discouraged.'

How would you argue against this assertion?

It is clear that non-verbal communication is a difficult area, when dealing with people of other nationalities and cultures. There are many similarities and shared meanings, for example most people would easily distinguish between a happy face and a sad face. But, perhaps because we feel that we know what we would mean by an expression, a bodily posture, a touch or a gesture, it is easy to misinterpret others, particularly those of different cultures.

Critical review and reflection

In Muslim cultures men and women must not touch. A standard Western gesture such as shaking hands becomes an issue.

To what extent do you consider tensions between cultures are based on misunderstanding and lack of knowledge?

Migrant workers

Whilst it is difficult to establish an exact analysis of the hospitality workforce within the UK, it is clear that the industry has become increasingly multicultural in recent years. One London firm stated their workforce spoke around 30 languages in total.[38] Much has been written of the influx of workers from the EU accession states, particularly Poland, contributing to the varied and diverse nature of staff in the hospitality industry. Without the Polish workforce certain sectors of the hospitality industry could be seriously understaffed, and indeed at the time of writing some observers are worried about the effects of the recent recession on the availability of such workers.

Janta[39] found that the profile of Polish workers working in the UK hospitality industry was 'predominantly young, female and highly qualified'.

The typical employment pattern for these workers would be to begin working for an organisation in low-paid, relatively unskilled positions and, as managers develop an appreciation of their abilities, gradually to move to supervisory and front-of-house positions. Janta cites People 1st research from 2008, which indicated that 43 per cent of migrants working in London pubs originated from Poland.

Their reasons for working in the UK included the lack of job opportunities in Poland combined with EU accession, which meant that as EU citizens, Polish people had the right to live and work anywhere in the EU. Hospitality organisations in the UK could recruit highly qualified and able staff, who were willing to work under terms and conditions that equally qualified British people would not be happy with; this was particularly true in London.

Janta suggests that firms in the hospitality sector were pleased to benefit from this overqualified migrant workforce. These migrants typically entered at unskilled levels, such as kitchen porter, before moving to better jobs in the industry or elsewhere: 'perhaps their university degrees enable migrants to learn faster and adapt quickly'.

The research indicated that more than half of the respondents working in hospitality had plans to stay in the UK. However, many aimed to move from the hospitality industry as a result of the poor image and poor working conditions.

Migration from Commonwealth countries has given rise to a substantial number of ethnic restaurants such as those serving Indian and Chinese cuisine. The latter are experiencing staffing shortage issues as the second generation take advantage of the British education system and follow more lucrative careers, instead of entering the hospitality industry. Students, particularly international students, now play an important role in the staffing of hospitality and catering organisations, providing a substantial proportion of the part-time flexible seasonal workforce needed.

To the extent that there is increasing upward mobility for the British ethnic minorities, there is likely to be a migration from low-paid to higher-paid jobs, and from jobs offering long hours to jobs offering better terms and conditions. The same problems would seem to apply to migrant workers and British -born ethnic minorities.

Some ethnic minorities will also be migrants, but migrants may or may not be ethnic minorities as Tessa Wright[40] points out: 'the ethnic minority and migrant workers categories . . . are complex, changing and overlapping'.

It may be that non-British-born ethnic minorities and migrants may lack fluency in English, which seems, in some cases, to lead to discrimination. Discrimination may also be racism based on skin colour. Whatever the cause, it is clear that, if organisations are to benefit from a multicultural, diverse workforce, managers need to support these employees and ensure that they are treated with respect by all members of staff and also customers.

Tessa Wright points out that ethnic minorities share experiences with migrant workers. There are shared experiences unfortunately not of a good kind:

> There was evidence of employers expressing preferences for white staff: an employers' organisation representative told how employers welcomed the availability of Eastern European workers, partly on the grounds that 'they are good-looking people' which may be related to their 'whiteness'.

In other cases 'bloody foreigner' had been used as a term of abuse by chefs to waiters and waitresses. A Portuguese waitress, working in a hotel in the south-west of England, felt this was a common experience: 'The only thing I always noticed since I arrive in England was the racism against other people, foreign people. And I was a victim of that.' This does seem to be different from the experience of the Polish workers referred to above; however, Janta's research is not altogether positive, pointing out that some of her respondents were leaving the industry for a range of reasons, including low pay and mistreatment from management.

Alberti[41] discusses some of the problems of the migrant workers in London. Much work is subcontracted to agencies. Staff are paid at or below minimum wage, there is high labour turnover and low union presence. Longer-term migrants fear losing jobs to newer cheaper migrants.

A 2008 Mintel report estimated that about 40 per cent of workers in the industry are migrant workers; in some businesses this is as high as 80 per cent. It is seen to be relatively easy to recruit the labour required in the form of migrant workers, and their work ethic is seen as a key benefit. This contrasts with the perception that UK workers regard working in restaurants as 'beneath them' or too poorly paid to bother.[42]

A problem area?

Research suggests that in some organisations there is scope for improvement in the management of the diverse workforce. The experiences encountered by the ethnic minority workforce in the UK are reputed to be below an ideal standard. Wright in 2007[43] talks of the ethnic minority workforce as making up 59 per cent of the London workforce.

Working conditions in the hospitality industry have a reputation for being low paid and low status with the exploitation of employees and lack of unionization.[44] Much of the work, and therefore the workforce, is unskilled. However, research suggests that the ethnic minority groups in some cases are subject to more intense bullying, expectations to work long hours, exploitation, not being paid correct wages or receiving fair shares of tips than other staff.

Critical review and reflection

'The difficulties that some hospitality organisations have in attracting British workers is the perception that the work is beneath them and is too poorly paid.' (Chris Dreyfus)

How might the management style of some managers contribute to the industry's recruitment problems and to what extent is the problem, as Dreyfus suggests, due to the attitude of the potential recruit?

Culture shock and cultural adjustment

The term culture shock refers to the feelings of disorientation and anxiety that may be experienced when entering a new culture. Perkins and Shortland[45] claim that:

> It is . . . expected that most people will experience culture surprise when interacting with other cultures, and culture shock, to some degree, particularly when living and working in another country. Culture shock is a normal and predictable phenomenon, although those experiencing it may feel they are inadequate or weak, even believing they are suffering some form of mental illness.

Whenever people move to a new culture, they will need to learn to adapt to a new cultural environment. Acculturation refers to the changes that people undergo as they encounter these aspects. These changes may be physical or psychological. However, whether it is someone embarking on employment within an overseas branch of an organisation, or an employee moving from a different environment, they will all undergo some form of adjustment process. An understanding of this process can help the individual encountering these changes, while an appreciation of what the individual may be encountering will be useful to management in helping the new staff to adjust.

Berry[46] identified four coping strategies that individuals use in the acculturation process:

- assimilation (interaction with individuals from the host culture and devaluation of one's own culture);

- integration (maintenance of one's culture as well as interaction with individuals from the host culture);

- marginalisation (rejection of one's culture of origin as well as avoidance of individuals from the host culture);

- separation (maintenance of one's culture of origin and minimal interaction with other groups, especially individuals from the host culture).

While it is possible that the acculturation process will proceed without any problems, it may also be stressful and result in adaptation difficulties.[47]

Integration is seen as the most positive coping strategy and implies that individuals adapt and mix with the local population, whilst also keeping in touch with nationals from their own culture or country.

The process of culture shock consists of four phases starting with:

- the honeymoon period – refers to the initial euphoria and optimism, felt when new to the job;
- confusion and frustration – felt when people fail to comprehend their environment as quickly as they would expect to, and when their previous ways of behaving are challenged;
- the fight or flight symptoms – these occur when people complain about local customs, withdraw into their own cultural group, or into themselves, and become completely isolated;
- settled adjustment – occurs finally (for those who survive the previous phases). At this point the individual is much more confident.

A point to note is that, if and when the expatriates return to their home culture, the process may well be repeated as the individuals find that everything they once knew has changed. Frequently, however, it is the individuals who have changed and must begin to adapt, in order to settle back into the home culture.

Critical review and reflection

'Adjusting to a new culture is solely the responsible of the individual.'

Discuss the extent to which it is:

(a) the responsibility of the individual to find adaptation methods to overcome culture shock;

(b) the responsibility of the supervisor/manager to assist this process.

Acculturation, assimilation and retention of international workers

In their research considering the acculturation, assimilation and retention of international workers in the United States, Taylor and Finley[48] comment:

> On a global basis, a majority of the workers who travel to other countries to obtain work are unskilled. The motivation for these workers is generally economic as the wage gap for unskilled workers between rich and poor countries is larger than the wage gap for skilled workers.

They cite a study by Magnini[49] related to hospitality organisations where he presented recommendations for human resource managers to consider when managing a multicultural work force. These can also be used as a basis for working with guest workers. These recommendations include:

- adjust training starting points to account for prior service orientation of the trainee;
- understand that forms of motivation may vary based on home culture;
- (be aware that) different styles of verbal and non-verbal communication have a cultural basis;
- instil employees with diversity-related values; and
- do not use cultural background bias or ethnocentrism as a basis for making decisions.

Other studies, for example Perry,[50] stress the need for managers to consider the language barriers and be aware of motivational differences due to cultural backgrounds. Reference is also made to the need to:

> speak slowly and clearly, look for signs of confusion, reinforce verbal instructions with visual cues. When considering differences due to cultural backgrounds, managers should recognize a respect for authority and establish policies and procedures that encourage the importance of family.

In a study of managing cultural diversity in Northern Ireland, Devine *et al.* identify three main challenges, namely communication, discrimination and training.

Training includes the need to ensure local employees understand the needs of multicultural workers: 'the management of diversity should really be as much about changing of attitudes, mindsets, and cultures as about regulations and procedures'.

Devine *et al.* recommend increasing employee teamwork among culturally- diverse employees and improving cross-cultural skills. They also suggest providing English language training, translating skills-training manuals into a range of languages, providing a 'simple guide to understanding Irish cultural cues for use by employers and employees' as well as developing and piloting an introductory welcome workshop, which would include 'Irish culture, customer care, health, safety and hygiene and . . . teamwork'.[51]

Critical review and reflection

Now that such a large percentage of the workforce originate from other countries it is essential that provision is made to assist the assimilation of these staff.

From your own experience, suggest suitable methods to assist the integration of the multicultural workforce into the organisation.

The importance of face and respect

Whilst everyone, regardless of cultural background, is entitled to be treated with respect for their personal dignity, this can be a more serious issue for some cultures. It is important for managers and staff to be aware of the cultural concept of 'face'. 'Face can loosely be defined as personal dignity.'[52]

Brooks links the concept of 'face' to the Confucian philosophy underpinning much of Chinese and Asian behaviour, as well as being significant in Arab countries and South America.[53] French cites Gao who distinguishes between the two components of 'face' in

Chinese culture, which are 'lian' and 'mian'. The former refers to a person's sense of integrity and moral character, whilst the latter refers to projected public image.[54] It is about maintaining the relationship, showing respect for the elder or superior, avoiding confrontation and promoting harmony.[55] A certain amount of teasing and joking about others is quite normal in British society, but some cultures would find anything that damages their self-image, including criticism, severely embarrassing and humiliating.

Reynolds and Valentine point out that: 'to those from Confucian cultures, losing face can be devastating and not only involves embarrassment but profound shame'.[56]

Those from 'collectivist' cultures are also more likely to speak as a group or team member, rather than to express a personal viewpoint. This can extend to reluctance to contradict a superior, even where they know that the superior is wrong. British managers can find this irritating, since they may welcome their subordinates' input, which shows a willingness to become involved. There is often an expectation of a more directive management style.

Improving cross-cultural skills

Research indicates a range of skills and attitudes required to manage, or work within, a multicultural workforce. Key attributes include being open-minded, self-aware, resourceful and showing empathy. Lewis identifies tact, politeness, calm, patience, and generally being sensitive to others as key attributes to enhance communication across cultures.[57] Berger and Brownell also refer to the need to develop empathy:

> Understanding and relating to the experiences and feelings that individuals encounter as they become acclimatised to a new work environment . . . Empathy implies that managers closely listen to their employees and anticipate the difficulties they will encounter.[58]

On a practical basis, they identify that managers and organisations need to ensure staff are given appropriate orientation/induction programmes. They also suggest educating all workers and supervisors regarding cultural difference, and the provision of language classes.

Exhibit 3.5 Language training in hotels

'Speaking the lingo':[58] examples of good practice

The Savoy way

Jutta Asta, executive housekeeper at London's Savoy hotel, has taken up the challenge of improving the assimilation of her staff. Of her staff, 34 per cent are Lithuanians, 11 per cent are Mongolians and 9 per cent are Poles, with a further 23 nations represented among her housekeeping team.

For newly hired staff with a basic grasp of English, Asta gives a language-free visual presentation explaining servicing methods and standards expected at the hotel. The programme is something that Asta and her team created themselves, setting up rooms, staff and equipment and taking digital images to compose the bespoke training. After that, new staff learn housekeeping procedures through demonstrations, practice and working with experienced staff.

In addition, for two hours a week, Savoy staff can learn English on a website funded by the Learning and Skills Council. For staff wishing to learn more, a qualified tutor from Kensington and Chelsea Further Education College provides tuition over 20 weeks, at no cost to the employee, towards the Cambridge Certificate for the more able and the Individual Learning Plan Certificate for the complete beginner.

The Hilton way

At the Hilton Coylumbridge hotel, in Scotland's scenic Aviemore resort, Marie McKenna heads up the housekeeping department of 35 staff, plus 40 casual staff for the RCI timeshare lodges. The dominant language groups are the Poles and Latvians, who together comprise 60 per cent of her staff. McKenna deploys one of the Polish staff with good English to translate for her as she trains. Some parts of the training manual have also been translated into Polish.

At Hilton hotels, new employees take the Spirit of Hilton induction course, which introduces them to development opportunities available through the 'Hilton University'. Each hotel has a 'learning zone', with computers and course books available. As well as a wide range of courses from operations to management level, there is a one-year course in English as a foreign language available through the website of GlobalEnglish. Employees use the language programme at their own pace and are assessed as they go along.

The American experience

Throughout its history the USA has absorbed immigrants into its society and workforce. The majority of these did not speak English on arrival.

Audrey Goh, executive housekeeper at the 455-bedroom Halekulani Resort Hotel on Waikiki Beach, Hawaii, has 20 years' experience at executive housekeeper level. In the course of managing housekeeping in a series of large five-star hotels in Singapore, Hong Kong, Hawaii and the USA, she has acquired extensive experience in dealing with non-English-speaking employees. 'In Dallas and Los Angeles my housekeeping employees were mostly Spanish-speaking. Especially

for five-diamond or five-star hotel settings, we believe it is essential to conduct the interview in English and have the application form filled in on our premises and not taken home to fill in. By so doing, you can gauge their level of English proficiency.'

When Goh recruits immigrants not conversant in English and with no clue about hotel vocabulary and terms, training sessions involve the more visual 'show and tell' method. But Goh will also work on their English by listing words for items and amenities, which they have to learn to spell and say for homework.

She feels it's important that the employees master some simple phrases right away and try to relate to the guests. Even if they make some mistakes, the guests appreciate a sincere effort. 'Our global clientele finds it charming if an employee says a simple greeting such as "Good morning, sir, how are you today?" in their own language and follows it up in English,' she says. 'This is especially attractive here in Hawaii, where the people have a natural giving-and-caring aloha spirit.'

In Goh's view, the hotel's management has a responsibility to encourage and, ideally, facilitate language acquisition in staff. In most hotels, management realises it must invest in its employees to ensure consistent standards and services. She believes English classes should be readily accessible, and if an employee completes a course themselves, the fee should be reimbursed by the hotel. Management should also make a genuine effort to learn about the culture and language of its immigrant employees, as this shows respect.

'In some hotels I have worked in, the employees' dining room would celebrate Chinese New Year, Cinco de Mayo or Filipino Independence Day by serving ethnic foods, which shows the employees their ethnic diversity is valued. From this, mutual respect for co-workers from different cultures is enhanced', she says.

Berger and Brownell have developed the following 'Create It' model as a simple guide for people working in situations that require cultural sensitivity, which, of course, applies to any hospitality manager, or worker, who interacts with people of different ethnicity or culture.

Exhibit 3.6 The 'Create It' model

CREATE IT (Harmony within Diversity)

Curiosity	to learn about other cultures
Recognition	of your own biases and stereotypes
Empathy	put yourself in your employees' shoes and understand how they feel
Acceptance	of individual differences
Team building	create synergy among employees, who are different from one another
Explain	make sure everyone understands the company's goals
Invest	In people
Training	constantly[60]

Working overseas

Increasingly, individual members of staff and managers are being offered short-term and sometimes longer-term international assignments. This could be for a range of reasons, including their own personal development or, maybe in some cases, so that they can pass on skills to colleagues operating in another country. This could be initiated by the employing organisation, or by the individuals themselves who may feel that periods elsewhere will broaden their skills and marketability, or who may be offered lucrative contracts with other organisations. 'The importance of well trained and motivated hospitality expatriates is universally recognised as key for success in international business endeavours.'[61]

In any event, the expatriate will need to be able to perform successfully in a foreign country, with foreign colleagues and in a foreign culture. This will require adjustment and understanding, without which the individual is unlikely to be competent. The considerations referred to throughout this chapter, in dealing with migrants and people from differing cultures, apply equally to the expatriates, who will be operating in what, to them, are foreign cultures with added complications, not least of which will be foreign laws and maybe company rules.

Synopsis

- As a result of globalisation, there is a need for hospitality managers to develop an understanding of, and increased sensitivity to, issues of diversity, as well as cultural difference and communication.

- The managing diversity approach accepts that the workforce consists of a diverse population of people. It is founded on the premise that harnessing the differences of sex, age, race and ability/disability produces a productive environment with substantial business benefits.

- Theoretical models such as those of Hofstede, Trompenaars and Hall can provide a framework for analysis and understanding of cultural difference.

- Good communication skills are essential for any manager. In the case of hospitality managers, oral and non-verbal communication is particularly valuable. Cultural difference can be a contributor to difficulties in communication; frameworks, such as that of Lewis, can present guidance and understanding of requirements of the people involved in the communication process.

- Movement between nations involves adjustment. Understanding of the adjustment process can facilitate integration. Management and employees need to appreciate the need to understand different cultural values and consequent behaviours.

- The multi-ethnic nature of the hospitality workforce brings with it problems that may not be peculiar to those of ethnic minorities, but are compounded by their difficulties in understanding. Enlightened hospitality managers should be aware of potential problems, to ensure they are reduced, including serious efforts to improve individuals' language skills.

- Managers need to develop sensitivity to the problems faced by ethnic minorities, people of different cultures and migrant workers. By displaying understanding, managers can help workers to overcome culture shock and thereby help the assimilation, acculturation and retention of valuable workers.

REVIEW AND DISCUSSION QUESTIONS

1 What are the distinctive features of Hofstede's model of culture? Show how his model can be applied to work situations.

2 Discuss the extent to which the multicultural, multi-ethnic workforce in the British hospitality industry can be a positive enhancement to the working environment and business success.

3 Outline ideas for the creation of a multicultural awareness programme for staff within a large city-centre hospitality establishment.

4 Identify some typical barriers to effective communication in the hospitality industry and explain how they can be overcome.

5 What might be the advantages and disadvantages of a hospitality organisation employing older workers?

6 What steps could you take as a manager to ensure staff who are new to the country are helped to adjust to a new country and work culture?

7 Evaluate how the communication triangle developed by Lewis can assist managers and staff understand differences in communication and therefore communicate more effectively within the hospitality industry.

8 To what extent do you feel that diversity awareness is vitally important in the hospitality industry?

ASSIGNMENT 1

Taking one country as an example (for example Poland), using Hofstede's dimensions of culture suggest the likely differences that a migrant from that country might encounter when first working in the UK.

ASSIGNMENT 2

Hospitality Across Cultures[62]

'The Hospitality Etiquette Training courses provide personnel within the hospitality industry, such as managers and front of house staff, with key cross cultural skills to enable them to deal effectively with foreign guests.

Etiquette is perhaps one of the most fundamental skills hospitality staff must acquire. Meeting the cultural needs of foreign guests, dignitaries and/or V.I.P.s ensures that offense or costly cross cultural blunders do not occur and helps raise the profile of an establishment.

Our bespoke training courses are tailored to meet the requirements of each of our select clients.

Courses cover a number of areas in relation to culture and/or nationality including:

- Meeting & Greeting
- Use of names and titles
- Body language
- Touching
- Proxemics
- Eye contact
- Dining/Serving etiquette
- Foods
- Conversation
- Hospitality & Customer service expectations
- Conflict resolution'

The above details are taken from the Kwintessential web page. The focus of the information is dealing with international customers. However, many points could also apply to understanding staff and the differences they may be encountering.

1 Taking a country of your choice, make notes on how your chosen country differs from the UK.

2 Prepare an information pack for managers on key areas of communication differences.

CASE STUDY 3.1

Milly's placement experience

Milly was an international student from Hong Kong who was studying for a degree in Hospitality Management at a university in the south of England. She was bright and intelligent and spoke good English. She had achieved good grades in the first two years of her course and was expected to achieve a 2.2 degree and possibly a 2.1 degree. Although she had experienced a little culture shock on first arrival in the UK, she had settled in well and made friends on the course. She was eager to embark on a career in the hospitality industry and to learn more about the industry in the UK.

She was therefore delighted to be offered a placement opportunity in a four-star hotel in a famous and popular international tourist destination in central England. She was interviewed and offered a placement programme for a year. This was going to provide her with a varied experience

Case study 3.1 (*continued*)

in many departments. She already had some experience of the industry back in Hong Kong so had a good idea of the nature of work in the industry.

She was a long way from home, and needed staff accommodation. This was provided in a staff house a few minutes from the hotel, where she lived with other hotel staff. It was a little basic but she soon made it feel like home.

She started work in the housekeeping department. The work was very physical, as is expected when cleaning rooms, making beds and cleaning bathrooms. She appreciated this was all part of learning about the industry. She worked alone as a room maid, again recognising this as normal practice.

What she was not expecting was that the majority of staff were from an eastern European country and spoke very little English. They also formed a large group and all sat together at coffee break. Milly sat alone. In the evenings she went back to her accommodation and was again alone. On one occasion, she was asked if she would like to go to the pub with a few British staff. She did not like to drink alcohol, wanted to save her money for the final year of study and was anxious about visiting pubs having been warned about them by her parents. She had also been a little embarrassed by some of the comments that another member of staff had made to her when they returned from the pub after a few drinks one evening. Wanting to save her money, in order to take the pressure off her parents, who were

supporting her through the degree, she preferred to stay in her room rather than spend her money on socialising.

She felt desperately homesick. In her days off she occasionally went down to London, where she visited a few friends, also from Hong Kong. She became so unhappy she wanted to leave her placement and, if necessary, change her course but did not want to let her parents down and bring shame to her family.

Eventually her period in housekeeping ended and she moved to the restaurant. Here she worked with staff who spoke English. She also worked in the evenings, so felt less alone. At last she could begin to enjoy her placement experience.

Questions

1 Using Hofstede's and Trompenaars' models, identify the dimensions of cultural difference that Milly was encountering.

2 Identify the different features of culture that the example displays.

3 To what extent do you consider a manager or supervisor has responsibility to ensure their live-in staff are happy?

4 What would you do as a manager to avoid such a situation occurring?

5 Identify the steps the hotel should take to ensure a better integration of international staff in future.

References

1 www.People1st.co.uk, State of the Nation Report 2011, accessed 14 April 2012.
2 Dundon, T. and Rollinson. R., *Understanding Employment Relations*, 2nd edn, McGraw-Hill (2011).
3 Kandola, R. and Fullerton, J., *Diversity in Action: Managing the Mosaic*, 2nd edn, IPD (1998).
4 Devine, F., Baum, T. and Hearns, N., *Resource Guide: Cultural Awareness for Hospitality and Tourism*, The HE Academy Hospitality Leisure Sport and Tourism Network (2009).
5 www.acas.org.uk
6 'Talent not tokenism: the business benefits of workforce diversity', CBI and TUC, June 2008.
7 'Managing diversity: linking theory and practice to business performance', CIPD, May 2005.
8 From http://hiltonworldwide.hilton.com, accessed 1 March 2006.
9 From http://hiltonworldwide.hilton.com, accessed 9 March 2012.

10 Kent, M. C., 'Is going grey a solution to industry retention issues?', *EP Business in Hospitality*, vol. 37, April 2011, 44.

11 Pensions-service.direct.gov.uk/en/state-pensions, accessed 14 April 2012.

12 See note 10.

13 http://www.epmagazine.co.uk/older-workers-are-a-key-ingredient-in-the-recipe-for-success/

14 Khan, S., *P.U.S.H. for Success*, Vermilion (2006), p. 230.

15 Clements, P. and Jones, J., *The Diversity Training Handbook*, Kogan Page (2002), p. 45.

16 Browaeys, M. and Price, R., *Understanding Cross Cultural Management,* FT Prentice Hall (2008).

17 Hofstede cited in Browaeys, M.-J. and Price, R., *Understanding Cross Cultural Management,* FT Prentice Hall (2011), p. 10.

18 Bratton., J., Callinan, M., Forshaw, C. and Sawchuck, P., *Work and Organizational Behaviour*, Palgrave Macmillan (2007).

19 Hampden-Turner, C. and Trompenaars, F., *Riding the Waves of Culture*, McGraw-Hill (1998), p. 222.

20 Hofstede, G., Hofstede, G-J. and Minkov, M., *Cultures and Organisations: Software of the Mind*, McGraw-Hill (2010).

21 Minkov, M., *What makes us different and similar,* Classic (2007).

22 http://www.geerthofstede.com/culture/dimensions-of-national-cultures.aspx, accessed 11.5.11.

23 Trompenaars, F. and Hampden-Turner, C., *Riding the Waves of Culture*, 2nd edn., Nicholas Brealey (1999).

24 Hall, E. T. and Hall, M. R., *Understanding Cultural Differences*, Intercultural Press (1990).

25 See, for example, Weaver, P. A. and Oh, H. C., 'Do American business travellers have different hotel service requirements?', *International Journal of Contemporary Hospitality Management*, vol. 5, no. 3, 1993, 16–21.

26 Thomas, D., 'Muslim caterer accuses the Met of discrimination', www.caterersearch.com, 12 May 2009.

27 Paton, N., 'Religious discrimination', www.caterersearch.com, 15 March 2005, retrieved 14.4.12.

28 For example, see Hornsey, T. and Dann, D., *Manpower Management in the Hotel and Catering Industry*, Batsford (1984).

29 French, R., *Cross Cultural Management,* 2nd edn, CIPD (2010), p. 137.

30 Lewis, R., *When Cultures Collide: Managing Successfully across cultures*, Nicholas Brealey (2004).

31 Bloisi, W., Cook, C. and Hunsaker, P., *Management and Organisational Behaviour*, 2nd European edn, McGraw-Hill (2003), p. 332.

32 Liu, S., Volcic, Z. and Gallois, C., *Introducing Intercultural Communication*, Sage (2011), p. 144.

33 See note 21.

34 See note 32.

35 French, R., *Cross Cultural Management,* 2nd edn, CIPD (2010), p. 141.

36 For other examples of cultural differences, see Schneider, S. C. and Barsoux, J., *Managing Across Cultures*, 2nd edn, Financial Times Prentice Hall (2003).

37 Pease, A. and Pease, B., *The Definitive Book of Body Language*, Orion (2005), p. 2.

38 Greencore sandwiches, http://www.rln-london.com/Business/casestudies.aspx

39 Janta, H., 'Polish migrant workers in the UK hospitality industry: profiles, work experience and methods for accessing employment', *International Journal of Contemporary Hospitality Management*, vol. 23, no. 6, 2011, 803–819.

40 Wright, T., 'The problems and experiences of ethnic minority and migrant workers in hotels and restaurants in England', *Just Labour: A Canadian Journal of Work and Society*, vol. 10, Spring 2007, 14–84.

41 Alberti, G., 'Transient Labour in London Hotels working lives', research institute paper presented July 2011.

42 Dreyfus, C., 'Where are the British workers?', *Caterer and Hotelkeeper,* 17 June 2011, accessed from www.caterersearch.com/Articles/17/06/2011

43 Wright, T., 'The problems and experiences of ethnic minorities and migrant workers in hotels and restaurants in England', *Just Labour: A Canadian Journal of Work and Society*, vol. 10, Spring 2007.

44 e.g. Head and Lucas (2004) cited in Wright, T., 'The problems and experiences of ethnic minorities and migrant workers in hotels and restaurants in England', *Just Labour: A Canadian Journal of Work and Society,* vol. 10, Spring (2007).

45 Cited in French, R., *Cross Cultural Management in Work Organisations,* 2nd edn, CIPD (2010) p. 223.

46 Berry, 1980, 1990 cited in Liu, S., Volcic, Z. and Gallois, C., *Introducing Intercultural Communication,* Sage (2011).

47 Berry (1990). See note 46.

48 Taylor, M. and Finley, D., 'Acculturation assimilation and retention of international workers in resorts', *International Journal of Contemporary Hospitality Management,* vol. 22, no. 5, 2010, 681–92.

49 Magnini, V. P., 'A look at the changing acculturation patterns in the United States and implications for the hospitality industry', *Journal of Human Resources in hospitality and tourism,* vol. 2, no. 2, 2004, 57–74.

50 Perry, P. M., 'Culture clash', *Restaurant Hospitality,* vol. 90, no. 8, 74–6.

51 Devine, F., Baum, T., Hearns, N. and Devine, A., 'Managing Cultural Diversity: opportunities and challenges for Northern Ireland Hoteliers', *International Journal of Contemporary Hospitality Management,* vol. 19, no. 2, 2007, 120–32.

52 Reynolds, S. and Valentine, D., *Guide to Cross Cultural Communication,* Prentice Hall (2004).

53 Brooks, I., *Organisational Behaviour: Individuals, Groups and Organisation,* FT Prentice Hall (2009), p. 310.

54 French, R., *Cross-cultural Management in Work Organisations,* 2nd edn, CIPD (2010).

55 Browaeys, M., and Price, R., *Understanding Cross Cultural Management,* FT Prentice Hall (2008), p. 235.

56 See note 52.

57 Lewis, R., *When Cultures Collide: Managing successfully across cultures,* Nicholas Brealey (2004).

58 Berger, F. and Brownell, J., *Organizational Behavior for the Hospitality Industry,* Pearson Prentice Hall (2009).

59 'Training: Speaking the lingo', www.caterersearch.com, 9 April 2006, accessed 18.4.12

60 See note 58.

61 Causin, G., and Ayuon, B., 'Packing for the trip: A model of competencies for successful expatriate hospitality assignment', *International Journal of Hospitality Management,* vol. 30, no. 4, December 2011, 795–802.

62 'Hospitality across cultures', www.kwintessential.co.uk/cross-cultural/hospitality-training.html, accessed 3.8.11.

Chapter 4

Organisational goals and structure

Learning outcomes

After completing this chapter you should be able to:

- explain the importance of organisational goals, objectives and policy;
- detail an awareness and understanding of corporate social responsibility and ethical considerations;
- review the dimensions and underlying concepts of organisation structures;
- identify traditional approaches to structure and organisational design;
- explore the influence of structure on the management of people;
- examine the context of the organisation in terms of its focus, goals and structure.

Introduction

The management of people in the hospitality industry obviously takes place within the context of the organisation. Every organisation has a purpose. To fulfil its purpose, both long- and short-term goals will need to be set, and organisational goals formulated. These determine the more specific objectives and related policy, leading to the strategies that the organisation intends to adopt followed by the activities decided on which will hopefully lead to the achievement of its goals. Outputs are measured against the goals set and new goals formulated.

The organisation is affected by external, environmental, influences of all kinds and, in its turn, this influences the organisational structure, which is developed to ensure the effective coordination of all activities and functions. The image that the organisation presents to the world will obviously be an important influence on how people react to it.

Purpose (goals)

All organisations need clear aims and objectives which will determine the nature of the inputs, and series of activities undertaken, to achieve outputs and realisation of goals. The goals of an organisation are the reason for its existence.

The meaning of **goal** is subject to different interpretations. It can be used in a very broad sense to refer to the overall purpose of the hospitality establishment, for example to make profit. A goal may also refer to more specific desired achievements, such as to provide a given level of facilities or standard of service, within a particular part of the organisation.

Integration of goals

Organisational goals are established by people, either individually or, more usually, by a number of individuals cooperating together (Figure 4.1). Strictly, organisations do not have goals; only people do, so organisational goals are set by senior (or strategic) management as targets that the organisation should achieve, for example to achieve a £10 million profit. Stakeholders, any person or group of people with an interest in the organisation, have different and often conflicting goals. Owners may have a particular concern with high profits

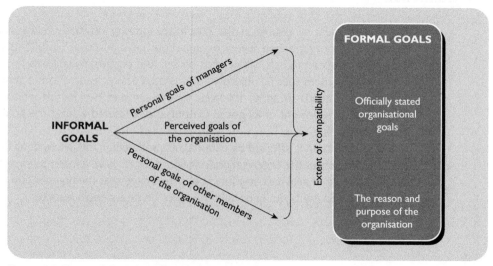

Figure 4.1 Compatibility of goals within an organisation

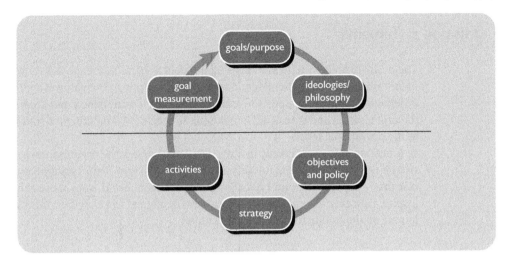

and return on their investment; customers a concern with the cost and quality of their experience; and employees with security of employment, high wages and good working conditions. Members of the organisation and customers will also have their own perception of the organisational goals which may, or may not, be consistent with their own requirements.

If organisational goals and personal goals differ, conflict will arise and performance is likely to suffer. It is the responsibility of management to clarify organisational goals and to reconcile conflicting interests. This demands the formulation of clear lines of direction for the establishment as a whole and its subsequent activities and operations. Staff need to know what senior management expects the organisation to achieve, if they are to be committed to achieving the organisational goals and to contribute to the achievement.

Organisational ideologies and philosophy

The goals of the organisation may be pursued in accordance with an underlying ideology or philosophy based on beliefs, values and attitudes. Company philosophy determines the common doctrine or codes of behaviour which guide the establishment in the conduct of its operations and its dealings with others. In recent years it has become increasing popular for an organisation to produce a *mission statement* and/or its vision that sets out its overall philosophy and objectives, the general direction for the organisation to follow, and its guiding values and principles. There is sometimes an apparent uncertainty over the distinction between the terms 'mission' and 'vision'. It seems generally accepted that the vision provides the overall frame of reference within which mission statements are written and goals selected. 'If vision is ill formed, mission statements will be vague and goal achievement hard to measure.'[1]

Certain aspects of an organisation's philosophy may be so dominant that they become the hallmark of the organisation, place constraints on other areas of activity and determine the culture of the organisation and its overall conduct and management. Examples could include the Walt Disney Company, where quality service and the focus on individual and mutual effort are embedded deeply within its corporate culture, and Starbucks for its concentration on good staff care.

Mission statements

The desire to identify with as many stakeholders as possible means that many mission statements are all-embracing with bland and abstract wording. The value of a mission statement is dependent, however, upon the extent to which it is understood and accepted throughout the organisation and translated in meaningful terms to all members of staff including those at the operational level.

A mission statement is only likely to be of any value if the organisation actually practises what it preaches. Reeves maintains that the problem with vision statements is that they are just that – statements, and typically they are disconnected from those they are meant to inspire. However, when mission and values are aligned to behaviour, this has an enormous impact on the productivity of organisations.[2]

Exhibit 4.1 Red Carnation Hotels

About the Red Carnation Collection

At **RCH** our mission statement is:

'To provide exceptional, memorable hospitality by meeting or exceeding guest expectations and creating an environment in our hotels where our guests, as well as our employees, refer to our hotels as their "home away from home".'

This applies to every aspect of what we do. We never lose sight of our core purpose: to make every guest's stay as enjoyable and trouble free as we possibly can, and to address and put right any problems they might encounter during their visit. In short, RCH is all about 'service, service, service!'

Core values

Our core values reflect what is really important and matters to us as a company and group of individuals. They are the solid foundation and main principles of our company culture. By consistently working hard to maintain our values, we endeavour to preserve what makes Red Carnation Hotels so special – a sincere and deep commitment to each other, our guests whom we serve every day and the communities within which we work and live.

Our Core Values are:

To give personalised, warm and consistently exceptional service

We appreciate the myriad of choices and alternatives our customers have to choose from, and therefore set the bar high for ourselves, to provide the highest quality services and products we possibly can. We constantly challenge ourselves to update and enhance. Innovation, constant training and refurbishment help create an environment whereby our guests and our employees refer to our properties as their home from home.

To value, respect and support each other

We believe that care comes from caring and so provide a level of care for our team members that inspires by example, generates trust, respect, open and honest communication and appreciation.

To create positive, memorable experiences for every guest

We work hard to meet or exceed our customers' expectations on every visit or touch point they have with us. By delighting and satisfying our customers, we ensure the longevity of our business and employment for our team. By serving our customers with very personable, proficient, friendly, competent service, and listening to their needs we create memorable and distinctive experiences as well as loyal, returning guests.

To care about and give back to our local communities

We recognize and appreciate our responsibility to be active participants in our local communities. We believe in trying to also give of our time to community and service organizations. We believe that it is important to give something back and make a difference. In a world of shrinking natural resources, we must endeavour to conserve, reuse and care about those around us.

So all of our hotels make it an ongoing priority to support and contribute positively to a variety of charitable organizations within their respective communities. The charities we support in England include The Starlight Foundation, Great Ormond Street Children's Hospital, Action Against Hunger, the National Autistic Society and the Cystic Fibrosis Trust. In Geneva we have provided help for The Red Cross and in South Africa we support the Nelson Mandela Children's Fund, and our bath amenities are purchased from Charlotte Rhys, a Founding Member of the Proudly South African Organisation, dedicated to the support of disadvantaged women and men in South Africa. Recycling efforts continue to be reviewed and improved upon wherever possible.

Our guests, staff, and suppliers have been wonderfully sympathetic to our aims, assisting us with their wholehearted support, and we would like to send a sincere 'thank you' to every one of them. While we believe our collective contributions do make a difference we are not content to sit back, and constantly challenge ourselves to increase our involvement with the global community. We welcome ideas and input from our customers, staff and suppliers.

(Jonathan Raggett, Managing Director, Red Carnation Hotels)[3]

Red Carnation Hotel Collection is listed in the 'Sunday Times Top 100 Companies to Work For' for the first time

The **Red Carnation Hotel Collection** is very proud to announce that it has been listed in the **Sunday Times Top 100 Companies (to work for) 2012** for the first time in its history. The results of this prestigious and highly sought after accolade were announced at an award ceremony in Battersea, London and are officially released today. The Red Carnation Hotel Collection is delighted to have been named for the first time in the list, not only as it **debuts at number 71** but also because it is the only privately-owned, family-run hotel collection in the top 100 list.

The prestigious list is compiled annually and thousands of companies apply from a huge cross section of industries in the UK. This year the final list was derived from a Sunday Times survey of over 246,000 employee opinion polls and an evaluation of each organisation's key statistics, processes and policies.

Jonathan Raggett, Managing Director of Red Carnation Hotel Collection says: 'Being a **family run hotel collection**, our employees are at the heart of our whole operation. Every effort is made from our wonderful Human Resources team through to all our dedicated managers to ensure we have the **best training and development available** for the whole staff, which ensures their career progress and objectives are being met and most importantly that they are happy and feel fulfilled in their respective roles.

'Our staff's satisfaction is what ensures we live up to and embody our guest philosophy of **"no request is too large, no detail too small"** and their happiness and motivation is paramount. So, it is with great pride that we have been acknowledged not only by the *Sunday Times* but also by our loyal staff.'

Objectives and policy

Goals are translated into **objectives** and **policy**, whilst remaining true to the organisation's **philosophy** in order to provide corporate guidelines for the operations of the establishment. Objectives and policy provide a focus for management decisions and actions. Terminology varies in the literature but objectives can be seen as the 'what', and policies as the 'how', 'where' and 'when', the means that follow the objectives.

● Objectives set out more specifically the goals of the organisation, the aims to be achieved and desired end results.

- Policy is developed within the framework of objectives. It provides the basis for decision-making and courses of action to follow in order to achieve objectives.

Objectives and policy are an essential part of the decision-making process and form a basis for the process of management. Objectives and policy may be formulated within the framework of an underlying philosophy of sets of beliefs, attitudes and conventions. These may not always be incorporated into formal policies but still influence the overall conduct of the establishment, and the behaviour and performance of staff.

> ### Critical review and reflection
>
> 'In large-scale organisations, the goals and objectives of the organisation, management and the workforce are never likely to be fully compatible. Attempts at harmonisation are not worth the effort and may cause further friction. It is easier just to accept the inevitability of organisational conflict.'
>
> *To what extent do you agree? How would you attempt to achieve compatibility of goals and objectives?*

Corporate strategy

Increased business competitiveness and the dynamic external environment have placed important emphasis on corporate **strategy** and the competencies of managers. According to Kanter, for example, 'Managing means managing an entire context. If you strip out one element and apply one methodology, it won't work.'[4] Effective management therefore takes place within the total corporate context and involves clearly established relationships and coordination among all levels of the organisation. Objectives and policy are formulated within the framework of a corporate strategy. Some form of corporate strategy is necessary for all organisations, particularly for large ones – and this includes service organisations.[5] Organisational performance is dependent upon the process of matching structure, strategy and the environment.[6]

From research at Swallow Hotels, Webster draws attention to the importance of strategic management in a hospitality context:

> In outline, strategic management entails a stream of decisions and actions which lead to the development and implementation of effective strategy. Strategic decisions determine the future direction and competitive position of an organisation and thus have fundamental effects on it. Strategies such as growth, consolidation and diversification are general programmes of action which have an implied commitment of resources.[7]

Strategic planning stages

Strategic planning can be approached in a number of ways. Keiser, for example, suggests the following seven specific steps to accomplish strategic planning in the hospitality industry.[8]

- *Assess the current position of the organisation* – what are the present strengths and weaknesses, competition and market, challenges and opportunities?
- *Assess the current and future environments* – what is happening in the external and internal environment, what changes will affect present business or create possible new opportunities?

- *Assess the impact of projected changes* – what impact will the changes be likely to have on present operations, will they provide threats or opportunities?
- *Identify possible opportunities and evaluate possible risks* – identify possible opportunities from changes in the environment, and estimate the risks including cost, different markets and effects on present business.
- *Select feasible goals or objectives* – expanding current business or developing into new opportunities.
- *Establish priorities and allocate resources* – decide on selection of objectives and ensure supply of necessary resources.
- *Provide operational guidelines* – implement detailed operational and tactical plans.

SWOT analysis

An important aspect of strategic planning and strategic change is the analysis of the internal strengths and weaknesses of the hospitality organisation following the formulation of objectives, and the opportunities and threats presented by its external environment.[9] SWOT is an acronym for the analysis of these Strengths, Weaknesses, Opportunities and Threats. The use of SWOT analysis can also assist the evaluation of hospitality operations and performance.

- *Strengths* are the distinctive attributes and positive aspects which provide a significant market advantage, or upon which the hospitality organisation can build and develop, for example present market position, size and structure of operations, physical and financial resources, managerial expertise, staffing, image and reputation.
- *Weaknesses* are those deficiencies in the present skills and expertise or resources of the hospitality organisation, or its image or reputation, which need to be corrected and for which action needs to be taken to minimise their effect. Weaknesses may stand in the way of achieving particular goals or objectives. Examples of weaknesses could include a high cost structure compared with competitors or a high level of customer complaints.
- *Opportunities* are favourable situations which arise from the nature of environmental change. The hospitality organisation needs to be responsive to changes which will provide an opportunity to offer new, or develop existing, facilities and services. Opportunities may arise from, for example, improved economic factors, greater leisure time, failure of competitors, new markets or products, or technological advances.
- *Threats* are the converse of opportunities. Threats refer to unfavourable situations which arise from environmental change and which are likely to endanger the operations of the organisation. Examples could include government legislation, new competitors, or demographic changes.

Identification of opportunities and risks

Costa *et al.* refer to the pace of change in the business environment, the fierce competition faced by hospitality organisations, and the need for better identification of opportunities and risks. Managers need to understand the importance of formal environmental scanning in order to provide decision-makers with the support information for their managerial activities. Hospitality organisations would explore opportunities and avoid threats better if these could be identified at an early stage.[10]

People and strategy

Johnson *et al.* draw attention to the importance of the relationship between people and successful strategies. The people dimension of strategy is concerned with three related issues:

● *people as a resource* – personal and organisational competences, and performance management;
● *people and behaviour* – personal behaviours and collective behaviour;
● *organising people* – HR function, line managers, structures and processes.

The ability to change behaviours may be the key ingredient for success. Creating a climate where people strive to achieve success and the motivation of individuals are crucial roles of any manager and are a central part of their involvement in their organisation's strategy.[11]

Ethical aspects

Ethics is concerned with the study of morality: practices and activities that are considered to be importantly right or wrong, together with the rules that govern those activities and the values to which those activities relate. Company philosophy can be based on both an ethical foundation and an operational foundation.[12]

● The **ethical foundation** embodies basic principles which govern the external and internal relations of the establishment and concern standards of behaviour in all dealings with, for example, customers, suppliers, competitors, representatives, health or fire inspectors, educational establishments, staff and union representatives.

● The **operational foundation** relates to the nature, operation and conduct of hospitality activities, for example methods of production, use of equipment, hygiene and cleanliness, dress and appearance, systems and styles of management and supervision.

The underlying philosophy of the establishment will also have a bearing on the nature of the psychological contract (see Chapter 2).

Upchurch suggests that:

In general, hospitality researchers have determined that management is confronted with ethical issues surrounding guest rights, empowerment, sexual harassment, equal opportunity, departmental relations, vendor relations, yield management, community and public relations, and the balance of personal and organisational values . . . Overall, these studies have reflected on profiling ethical situations and in understanding management's role in resolving ethical situations within a service based setting.[13]

Objectives are sometimes only implied, but the formal, explicit definition of objectives will help to highlight the activities which the establishment needs to undertake and the comparative importance of its various functions. Objectives should not be stated in such a way that they detract from the recognition of possible new opportunities, potential danger areas, the initiative of staff, or the need for innovation or change. However, a clear, explicit statement of objectives may assist communications, reduce misunderstandings and provide meaningful criteria for evaluating performance.

Many anecdotal accounts indicate practice that may be considered dubious, such as payment of staff below the legal minimum,[14] selling products that do not conform to standards or overcharging customers to ensure the required profit percentages are achieved.

General and sectional policy

Policy is translated into rules, directives, plans and procedures; it relates to all activities of, and to all levels in, the establishment. General policy is determined by top management (directors, owners or senior managers) and provides broad guidelines for the operations as a whole.

Certain aspects of general policy may be so dominant that they become the overriding image or 'hallmark' of the establishment and place constraints on other policy areas. The desire to create a unique corporate image and experience, such as for instance with all TGI Friday's restaurants wherever you are in the world, is an example of a dominant aspect of general policy. Another example could be a country and golf hotel that wants to see itself as a high-class establishment, and goes out of its way to show that it is not a family hotel and does not provide for children under five years of age.

Sectional policy flows from general policy and provides, in more specific operational terms, guiding principles for particular aspects and activities of operations. Specific policies have more defined areas of application and time limits.

For example, specific policy relating to **customer relations** could include areas of decision-making and delegation relating to types of customers, facilities provided, pricing and discounts, customer care and standards of service, attitudes and behaviour of staff, and handling of grievances and complaints.

Specific policies may also be formulated for other areas of relationships such as employees and suppliers, for main areas of activity such as accommodation and food and beverages, and areas of functional support such as accounting and marketing.

Exhibit 4.2 Ethical dilemma in hospitality

'I just read this story about how a U.S. Senator says the Chinese government is ordering foreign-owned hotels to install software so that authorities can monitor the Internet activity of guests.

My first reaction as a red-blooded, apple-pie-eating, baseball-watching American was to say, 'Well, too bad! American companies should put their foot down. If I had an exten-sion of my company in China, I wouldn't bend my ethics.'

But then I remember that this is the hospitality industry. Governmental spying, (while becoming more popular), is frowned upon in this country, but that is how China operates. And the hospitality industry is founded on being just that – hospitable. So, if you build a hotel in another country, it is only right to abide by their social mores and laws. It's not like they made you build a hotel there.

I just think it's an interesting ethical dilemma. Could you run your business in a manner counter to your own ethics? Are there even alternatives since the government says there will be punishment for non-compliance? Am I making too big of a deal out of this?[15]

Critical review and reflection

Consider the above situation.

Is this an ethical dilemma or purely cultural difference? Do you feel that the organisations should help the authorities monitor the guests or not?

What are the arguments for, and against, your recommendation?

The profit motive

The hospitality industry involves an economic activity and its aims and objectives are of a commercial nature. To be successful the primary objectives may be seen as: to survive as a business and continue in existence, to maintain growth and development, and to make a profit. If we accept survival as the ultimate objective of the hospitality establishment, this involves the need for a steady and continuous profit. The establishment must be prepared to accept the possibility of a reduction in short-term profitability in order to provide for future investments.

Other considerations and motivations

Although the objective of profit maximisation is undoubtedly of great importance, it is not, by itself, a sufficient criterion for the effective day-to-day management of hospitality operations. This view is supported by Fearn, who suggests a somewhat different interpretation of the role of profit in the objectives of hospitality management.

Why are we in business?' The favourite answer to this question, and one often thought to be the correct one, is 'to make a profit'. This is indeed important, but it is hardly an adequate basic approach to the administration of a business. To consider profit as the sole reason for the existence of a company is certainly an attractive idea, but it is more logical to consider profit as the reward for serving others well. It is therefore the things that are done to obtain profit which are the subject of objectives.[16]

In practice, there are many other considerations and motivations which affect the desire for the greatest profit or maximum economic efficiency. Attention needs to be given to multiple areas of objective-setting, including the importance of social responsibilities.

Multiple performance objectives

Any business organisation has a number of important areas of performance and results which require the setting of objectives. Drucker has referred to the 'fallacy of the single objective' of a business. The search for the one, right objective is not only unlikely to be productive, but is certain to harm and misdirect the business enterprise.

> To emphasise only profit, for instance, misdirects managers to the point where they may endanger the survival of the business. To obtain profit today they tend to undermine the future . . . To manage a business is to balance a variety of needs and goals . . . the very nature of business enterprise requires multiple objectives which are needed in every area where performance and results directly and vitally affect the survival and prosperity of the business.[17]

Drucker lists eight key areas in which objectives should be set in terms of performance and results. This list provides a useful framework in which to review objectives of hospitality organisation.[18]

- *Market standing* – for example, type of customers and their requirements as the principal source of business, nature of facilities and services offered, distinctions from main competitors.
- *Innovation* – for example, need for flexibility in a dynamic environment, opportunities to reach new customers, developments arising from technological advances, new processes and procedures.
- *Productivity* – higher productivity distinguished from higher production or output; for example, more advanced equipment, optimum use of resources, decision-making techniques, improved methods, systems and procedures.
- *Physical and financial resources* – for example, location, size and nature of premises; equipment and facilities; supply of capital and budgeting; financial planning; provision of supplies.
- *Profitability* – for example, capital investment policy, profitability forecasts and planning, sales objectives such as for accommodation, food and beverages, measurements of profitability such as return on capital employed and food costs to sales.
- *Manager performance and development* – for example, the direction of managers' work, areas of responsibility, results achieved by subordinate staff, achievement of objectives, staff relationships, strengthening the management team, management succession planning.
- *Worker performance and attitudes* – for example, organisation and execution of work, standards of performance, control systems, staff appraisals, customer relations, personnel policies, employee relations, respect for authority, loyalty.
- *Public responsibility* (commonly referred to as social responsibilities) – demands made upon the organisation internally and by the external environment, for example by customers and staff, by law or public opinion, or by responsibilities to society and the public interest. The importance of the social responsibilities of management is considered more fully in a separate section below.

Constraints and limitations

We can see, therefore, that although the profit objective is clearly of importance, it is not, by itself, a sufficient criterion for the effective management of hospitality operations. Individuals in the hotel are not necessarily guided at all times by the profit objective. This is only one of a number of constraints.

> Profit may not enter directly into the decision-making of most members of a business organisation. Again, this does not mean that it is improper or meaningless to regard profit as a principal goal of a business. It simply means that the decision-making mechanism is a loosely coupled system in which the profit constraint is only one among a number of constraints and enters into most sub-systems only in indirect ways.[19]

The key areas of performance and results draw attention to the many constraints which may affect the satisfactory attainment of objectives, for example the failure to innovate, low productivity, lack of physical and financial resources, poor management development or staff training. Other limiting factors may arise as a result of general policy decisions or environmental pressures.

Realistic level of objectives

It is important, therefore, to take account of constraints and to set limitations and objectives at a realistically attainable level. Objectives set at too low a level do not stretch staff or provide a sufficient challenge or sense of achievement. This can result in a lost opportunity for higher performance and results.

However, if objectives are set at too high a level this will be counter-productive. Staff may feel that undue pressure is put upon them and will again fail to gain a sense of achievement or personal satisfaction. If objectives are not seen to be in reasonable reach this is likely to result in the loss of positive motivation and a lower-than-possible level of performance.

Corporate social responsibility

In striving to satisfy their goals and achieve their objectives, hospitality organisations cannot operate in isolation from the environment of which they are part. Such organisations require the use of factors of production and other facilities of society. Economic efficiency is affected by governmental, social, technical and cultural variables. In return, society is in need of the products and services supplied by the organisation, including the creation and distribution of wealth.

Economic survival and performance are dependent upon a series of activities between the hospitality organisation and its environment. These exchanges and the continual interaction with the environment give rise to a number of broader obligations to society in general. These broader obligations are both internal and external and are usually referred to as social responsibilities. In recent years there has been a growing awareness of the social and environmental consequences of human activity, particularly in business operations, the hospitality industry included.

Exhibit 4.3 Corporate responsibility: Compass Catering

'Compass Group is a people business and we cultivate an environment of mutual respect, where everyone is highly motivated by their work.

The Board of Compass Group PLC is fully engaged in delivering a holistic approach to corporate responsibility and has a sub-committee to oversee the implementation of a global strategy and regularly review key performance indicators and targets.

Within our UK & Ireland business the Executive Committee as a whole is responsible for corporate responsibility. The directors are responsible for ensuring compliance with Compass Group's corporate values and standards. Going forward, we will be setting up a forum to consider and review environmental, ethical and social issues relevant to our business and this will report regularly to the Executive Committee. Its role will be to promote awareness of this Framework across the business, including training and communication. I will chair the forum and will have specific responsibility for our corporate responsibility policies and leading the development of new initiatives and targets.

All employees have a responsibility to abide by our policies and procedures which have been developed to guide colleagues and, therefore, monitor and regulate the conduct of the day-to-day operations of the business. These policies and procedures include our health, safety and environmental policy and are available to all employees through a web-based information system. Everyone is encouraged to make suggestions to improve the way we work.'

(Ian Sarson, Group Managing Director, Compass Group UK & Ireland)[20]

Broad range of responsibilities

The potential range of social responsibilities is very broad and concerns different groups of people. Social responsibilities may be considered under a number of different headings such as, for example, employees, shareholders, customers, community, the government, and suppliers, business associates and competitors.

- *Employees and employment quality* – responsibilities extend beyond formal treatment, consultation and participation, effective personnel and employee relations policies, equal opportunities employment, good working conditions and live-in accommodation, training in new skills and technologies, job satisfaction, observance of the psychological contract and, more recently, work–life balance issues and providing employee assistance programmes.

- *Shareholders or other providers of capital* – shareholders are drawn from a wide range of the population, including private individuals. Many people also subscribe indirectly as shareholders through pension funds and insurance companies. Responsibilities to shareholders extend beyond a purely financial reward for risk-taking and include the safeguarding of investments, the opportunity to exercise rights as owners, participation in policy decisions, the opportunity to question top management on the affairs of the company and the provision of full information in a clearly understood format.

- *Customers* – responsibilities to customers may arguably be seen as no more than a natural outcome of good business, especially in the hospitality industry. There are, however, broader social responsibilities including fair standards of advertising and promotions, good value for money, a positive approach to customer satisfaction, honesty and full information on all costs and charges, prompt and courteous attention to queries or complaints, safety and security.

- *Community* – it is in the area of concern for the community at large that social responsibilities can usually be seen most clearly. The hospitality organisation has a responsibility to society and to take care of amenities. Examples under this heading include: the effects and potential nuisance of the siting and appearance of new buildings, noise, and disposal of waste, the use of biodegradable materials and aerosol sprays which do not contain chlorofluorocarbons (CFCs), concern for the welfare of the local community. Some larger organisations extend the range of social responsibilities further, for example by donations to, or sponsorship of, the arts, educational or sporting organisations, or charities.

- *Environment* – an area of increasing awareness and concern is that of environmental considerations such as mitigation of climate change, energy conservation, renewable energy use and clean energy production, water conservation, waste reduction and recycling water, and soil pollution reduction.[21]

- *Government* – hospitality management should, of course, respect and obey the law relating to the conduct of business operations even if it is not regarded as in their best interests. What is debatable is the extent to which top management should also cooperate voluntarily with actions requested by the government, for example attempts to avoid inflation, acceptance of controls over imports, employment of staff under government training schemes, control of potential social problems such as the sale of tobacco, alcohol or accidents at work. More recently issues such as obesity have been subject to debate with pressure on fast-food restaurants to offer healthy options.

- *Suppliers, business associates and competitors* – examples under this heading include: fair standards of trading, honouring terms and conditions of purchase and settlement dates for payment of accounts, assistance to small organisations, engaging in only fair competition and not disparaging competitors. The use of Fair Trade[22] products is an increasingly popular approach.

A question of balance

The distinction between the exercise of social responsibilities for genuine philanthropic reasons, and actions taken in pursuit of what is seen as no more than good business practice and enlightened self-interest, is not always easy to determine. In practice it is a question of degree and balance, of combining sound economic operations with an appropriate concern for broader responsibilities to society.

The recognition of social responsibilities should form part of strategic planning, and the formulation of objectives and policy. It is up to top management to determine the extent to which, and the manner in which, the hospitality organisation will attempt to satisfy its social responsibilities.

Exhibit 4.4 Community service award

The cast of the **Walt Disney World Swan and Dolphin Resort** recently received the Community Service Award from Starwood Hotels and Resorts for the tremendous amount of support and charity they have given to the community. Hearts for Humanity, the resort's humanitarian committee, comprised of caring associates from various departments throughout the property, organizes, coordinates, and participates in all the charitable work done on behalf of the **Walt Disney World Swan and Dolphin**. This includes

➡

both charity drives and volunteer events. Below is a sample of what our Disney hotel accomplished with Hearts for Humanity in 2007:

- Approximately 200 cell phones were donated to Secure the Call
- Quarterly blood drive
- Over 400 books were collected and donated for Head Start
- Over 600 pounds of clothes donated to Mustard Seed
- School Supplies collected and delivered to an 'adopted' school
- Over 190 Thanksgiving Day Food Baskets donated
- Over 125 'Christmas Angels' adopted and given gifts for the holidays
- Over 500 duvets donated to many different organizations
- *Disney resort* room nights to over 20 charitable organizations
- High Chairs donated to Shepherd's Promise

- Invited workers from Children's Home Society to eat at one of the resort's signature restaurants for the good work they do
- Organized Fins & Feathers Fun Run – all money went to Hearts for Humanity
- Participated in the Charity Challenge to benefit local charities
- Invited families staying at the Shepherd's Promise Transitional Home to the Hotel Children's Party
- Had holiday party for children at Children's Home Society where they received gifts from Santa and entertainment from a magician, a DJ and craft station
- Sent Volunteers from our Disney hotel to work at Give Kids the World
- Approximately 103,000 pounds of food donated to The Orlando Bridge
- Donated approximately $28,000 this year to United Way
- Donated over $2,000 worth of new clothes and toiletries to Children's Home Society[23]

Corporate social responsibility and the hospitality industry

In a study evaluating corporate social responsibility reporting practice among the largest hotel companies in the world, de Grosbois[24] found that the most popular environmental concerns were waste reduction, recycling, reduction of water consumption and the mitigation of climate change.

Tsai,[25] in a study of hotels in Hong Kong, discussed the importance of staff commitment to corporate social responsibility. It was found that staff had a relatively low awareness of environmental influences.

Critical review and reflection

'An organisation that shows a positive concern for the environment will be an employer of preferred choice.'

Why might that be and to what extent would you believe the statement to be true?

According to Reeves a few well-chosen aims in goal-setting can sharpen focus and boost productivity but too many can lead to stress and even disaster. Clear objectives expressed as specific goals should improve performance, but measurement should not be confused with target-setting, and problems occur when there are too many targets and they are closely attached to individual performance.

> The more freedom an individual has over the way their job is done, the higher the productivity and the bigger the rewards reaped by the firm for which they work. People need to know the objectives of their organisation and how their performance contributes to them. Employee engagement is much more likely to follow from autonomy than from a battery of management-dictated targets.[26]

Realistic level of objectives

It is important to take account of constraints and to set limitations and objectives at a realistically attainable level. Objectives set at too low a level do not stretch staff, or provide a sufficient challenge or sense of achievement. This can result in a lost opportunity for higher performance and results. (See also Chapter 9.)

However, if objectives are set at too high a level this will be counter-productive. Staff may feel that undue pressure is put upon them and will again fail to gain a sense of achievement or personal satisfaction. If objectives are not seen to be in reasonable reach this is likely to result in the loss of positive motivation and in under-performance.

Organisational structure

The importance of organisational structure

There is a close relationship between organisation structure and corporate strategy. Richardson and Evans[27] refer to a number of authors who have emphasised the importance of structure following the organisation's strategy, not only in supporting but in driving the objectives and plan. However, Lynch suggests that the nature of the relationship, and whether structure follows strategy or strategy follows structure, is not clear.[28]

The application of the process of management and the execution of work take place within the structure of the hospitality establishment. Structure is the pattern of relationships among positions in the establishment and among members of the staff. Structure creates a framework of order and command through which the work activities are planned, organised, directed and controlled.

It is structure, therefore, that gives shape to the establishment, and provides the basis for organisational processes and the execution of work. The purpose of structure is to define:

- the division of work;
- tasks and responsibilities;
- work roles and relationships; and
- channels of communication.

In very small establishments there are likely to be fewer problems with structure. The distribution of tasks, the definition of authority and responsibility, and relationships among members of staff can be built on a personal and informal basis. But all establishments, of whatever type or size, require some form of structure by which people's interactions and efforts are channelled and coordinated. With larger establishments there is a greater need for a carefully designed and purposeful form of structure.

An outline of typical key activities and division of work is given in Figure 4.2.

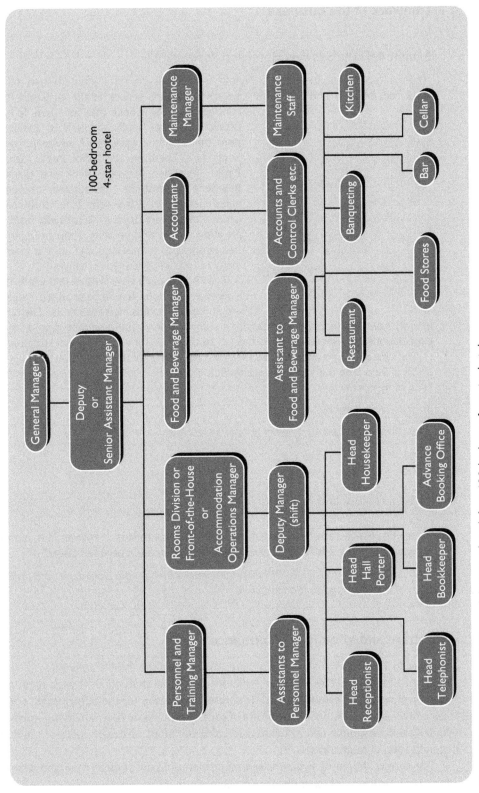

Figure 4.2 Typical key activities and division of work for a 100-bedroom four-star hotel

Framework of the business

Exhibit 4.5 The Seaview Hotel and Restaurant

'There is no organisation chart. People work in teams (as illustrated) that have to work cooperatively and flexibly to provide a seamless service to the customer. This is controlled by log books that are used to record issues, comments, faults, suggestions and instructions that ensure continuity of service across shift boundaries. These are the **Office Book**, **Manager's Book**, **Telephone Message Book** and diaries for **Bedroom Reservations, Restaurants, Conferences** and **Functions**. They are contributed to by all staff and are read every day by the partners, team leaders and staff coming on shift. They are referred to frequently at team meetings and are the source for many process improvement initiatives.'

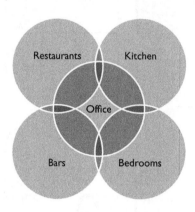

The above points were written in the late 1990s. However, the hotel has since changed hands and the number of rooms increased to 29. The number of staff have also increased to 40 with a combination of full- and part-time, and guest expectations have increased. This has led to the need for a more formal structure.

The restaurant and kitchen have their own departmental managers. The message book is still utilised. There is now an organisation chart. They hold regular meetings with the head of department.

http://www.seaviewhotel.co.uk/

Source: The authors are grateful to Andrew Morgan, manager of the Seaview Hotel, for this information.

Critical review and reflection

'It may be possible to avoid a formal structure in a small concern. However, it is impossible to manage without a formal structure when the organisation becomes larger.'

To what extent do you agree with this statement? What are the advantages and disadvantages of a formal organisation structure?

Structure and effective performance

In order to achieve its goals and objectives the work of the establishment has to be divided among its members. The resulting structure should be that which is most appropriate to the objectives of the establishment. Structure is necessary for the effective performance of key activities and to support the efforts of staff. It provides accountability for areas of work undertaken by groups and individual members of staff. Structure therefore involves the organisation of human assets.[29]

The correct design of structure is a major determinant of effective organisational performance. Drucker, for example, makes the point that:

Good organisation structure does not by itself produce good performance. But a poor organisation structure makes good performance impossible, no matter how good individual managers may be. To improve organisation structure . . . will therefore always improve performance.[30]

There is also a need for the continual review of structure to ensure that it is the most appropriate form for the particular establishment, and is in keeping with its change and development. The quality of structure will affect the grouping of functions, the allocation of responsibilities, decision-making, coordination, control and reward. These are all fundamental requirements for the continued operation of an organisation.[31]

Structure will affect not only economic efficiency and performance, but also the morale and job satisfaction of the staff. Managers need to consider how structural design and methods of work organisation influence the behaviour and performance of members of the establishment. Structure is also a major component of an effective corporate strategy.[32]

Approaches to organisation, structure and management

Organisation structure, the process of management and the behaviour of people at work are inextricably linked. Underlying the development of management theory and practice are contrasting ideas on structural design and attitudes towards people. Identification of major trends in the study of organisations and management will help to provide a perspective on concepts and ideas discussed in subsequent chapters.

Much has been written about different approaches to improving the effectiveness of work organisations. It is usual, therefore, to categorise the work and ideas of writers into various 'approaches' based on their views of structure and management. This provides a framework in which to direct study and focus attention.

It is important, however, to emphasise that no single approach provides all the answers. It is the comparative study of different approaches which yields benefits for the manager. The skill of organisational design lies in taking from the different approaches those ideas which suit best the particular situation and requirements.

Categorisation of approaches

There are many different ways of attempting to categorise these various approaches. For example, Gullen and Rhodes refer to the traditional, empirical, human relations, decision theory and formalism approaches.[33] On the other hand, Keiser identifies the classical scientific, classical organisation, human relations, management science, contingency and Japanese approaches.[34]

Whatever the broad classification of main approaches it is possible to identify a number of possible cross-groupings and sub-groupings. Some of these sub-groupings might be seen as mutually exclusive while others might be viewed as sub-divisions of broader approaches.[35]

In order to provide a convenient framework as a basis for our discussion we will use a broad four-fold categorisation of:

- the classical approach – including scientific management and bureaucracy;
- the human relations approach – including the structuralists;
- the systems approach; and
- the contingency approach (Figure 4.3).

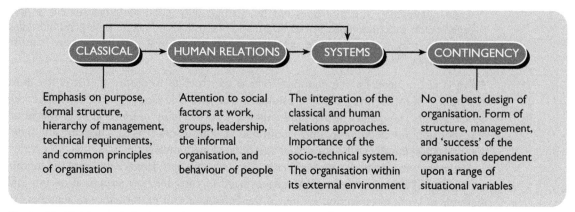

Figure 4.3 Main approaches to organisation, structure and management

The classical approach

The classical approach is associated with work carried out initially in the early part of the twentieth century. Classical writers placed emphasis on purpose and structure, and on the technical requirements of the organisation. Identification of general objectives would lead to clarification of purposes and responsibilities at all levels of the organisation, and to the most effective structure.

Attention is focused on the division of work, reporting relationships, the clear definition of duties and responsibilities, and maintaining specialisation and coordination. The emphasis is on structure based upon a hierarchy of management and formal organisational relationships.

Principles of organisation

The classical writers were concerned with improving the process of management and organisation structure as a means of increasing efficiency. Emphasis was placed on the importance of a common set of principles for the design of a logical structure. Most classical writers had their own set of principles but probably the leading authority was Urwick, who specified ten principles of organisation.[36]

1 *The principle of the objective*:

   'Every organisation and every part of the organisation must be an expression of the purpose of the undertaking concerned, or it is meaningless and therefore redundant.'

2 *The principle of specialisation*:

   'The activities of every member of any organised group should be confined, as far as possible, to the performance of a single function.'

3 *The principle of coordination*:

   'The purpose of organising per se, as distinguished from the purpose of the undertaking, is to facilitate coordination and unity of effort.'

4 *The principle of authority*:

   'In every organised group the supreme authority must rest somewhere. There should be a clear line of authority to every individual in the group.'

5 *The principle of responsibility*:

'The responsibility of the superior for the acts of the subordinate is absolute.'

6 *The principle of definition*:

'The content of each position, both the duties involved, the authority and responsibility contemplated and the relationships with other persons should be clearly defined in writing and published to all concerned.'

7 *The principle of correspondence*:

'In every position, the responsibility and the authority should correspond.'

8 *The principle of span of control*:

'No person should supervise more than five, or at the most, six direct subordinates whose work interlocks.'

9 *The principle of balance*:

'It is essential that the various units of an organisation should be kept in balance.'

10 *The principle of continuity*:

'Re-organisation is a continuous process: in every undertaking specific provision should be made for it.'

The definition of responsibilities

Another major contributor to the classical approach, Brech, attempts to provide a practical approach to organisation structure based on tried general principles as opposed to concentrating on specific cases or complex generalisations.[37] Brech emphasises the importance of formal relationships, written definition of responsibilities and the value of job descriptions as an aid to effective structure and delegation. His work builds on the ideas of earlier writers and therefore provides a comprehensive view of the classical approach.

Relevance and applications

The classical writers have been criticised generally for not taking sufficient account of personality factors, and of creating an organisation structure in which people can exercise only limited control over their work environment. Research studies have also expressed doubts about the effectiveness of the classical approach when applied in practice.[38]

However, although the work of the classical writers is sometimes regarded as an out-of-date approach, it does focus attention on important factors in the study of organisational design.[39] Good structure is necessary for efficiency and an essential factor in improving performance.

The idea of common sets of principles has been subject to much criticism. Simon, for example, states that:

> Organisational design is not unlike architectural design. It involves creating large, complex systems having multiple goals. It is illusory to suppose that good designs can be created by using so-called 'principles' of classical organisation theory.[40]

Many of the principles are expressed as bland statements in non-operational terms and give little basis for specific managerial action. Nevertheless, the principles are still relevant and they do provide general guidelines on the design and structuring of organisations. It is also of interest to note that, despite the criticisms, many of the more recent writings on the subject appear to be based on the original work of the classical writers.

The basic concepts can be of value to the hospitality manager if modified to suit the demands of the particular situation. The application of these principles needs to take account of:

- the particular situational variables of the establishment; and

- the psychological and social factors relating to the people who work within the structure.

Two major 'sub-groupings' of the classical approach of particular importance for organisational design and structure are:

- scientific management; and

- bureaucracy.

Scientific management

Scientific management places emphasis on obtaining increased productivity from individual workers through the technical structuring of the work organisation. The major contributor to this approach was F. W. Taylor (1856–1917), who believed that in the same way that there is a best machine for each job, so there is a best working method by which people should undertake their jobs.[41]

Taylor was concerned with finding more efficient methods and procedures for the coordination and control of work. He also believed in the rational-economic needs concept of motivation. The provision of monetary incentives was the primary motivator for higher levels of output. Workers would be motivated by obtaining the highest possible wages through working in the most efficient and productive way.

Principles of scientific management

Scientific management was based on the principles of:

- the scientific selection, training and development of workers;

- the clear division of work and responsibilities between management and workers; and

- close management control over the actual processes of work.

Taylor considered that all work processes could be analysed into discrete tasks and that by scientific methods it was possible to find the 'one best way' to perform each task. Each job was broken down into component parts, each part timed, and the parts rearranged into the most efficient method of working.

Criticisms of scientific management

Scientific management is often referred to as a machine theory model. It adopts an instrumental view of human behaviour together with the application of specialisation and standard procedures of work. Workers were viewed less as isolated individuals and more as units of production to be handled in much the same way as machines. The scientific study of work can lead to jobs becoming repetitive, boring and requiring little skill.

The ideas behind scientific management have been largely discredited by subsequent management writers. There has been strong criticism of scientific management as representing close management control over workers. By removing decisions about how their work is carried out, by division of labour, and by dictating precise stages and methods for every aspect of work performance, management could gain control of the actual process of work. The rationalisation of production processes and division of labour tend to result in the de-skilling of work, and this may be a main strategy of management.[42]

The question of de-skilling would appear to have particular significance in hotel and catering where in recent years there have been many examples of the de-skilling of work.[43] (See also the discussion on the shamrock organisation later in this chapter.)

Relevance to the hospitality industry

Despite the criticisms, the underlying approach of scientific management still has some relevance to the hospitality industry. Taylor and his followers introduced the concept of a systematic approach to management. They have left to modern management the legacy of practices such as job analysis, systematic selection and training, work study, payment by results, production control and management by exception. The adoption of such practices has a significant effect on hospitality management.

Managers need to find the most efficient and productive methods of work. In particular, the efficiency of 'production' areas, such as food preparation and service and housekeeping, is likely to benefit from a clear division of work and responsibilities, prescribed methods of working and labour-saving approaches.

Standard recipes and performance standard manuals including photographs of finished dish presentations are widely used in the industry. With chain hotels in particular, it is common to have a prescribed standard layout for each room with training based on procedure manuals and the one best way. Staff are expected to clean a given number of rooms per shift with financial incentives for additional rooms. However, the context and manner in which such practices are put into effect are important, as is whether there is any scope for personal initiative.

Critical review and reflection

'Although the approach of scientific management is often criticised as outdated and inappropriate, many argue that, today, work practices in fast food operations are pure scientific management.'

'In what ways do you think that scientific management principles are helpful and unhelpful in organising fast food ways of working?

Bureaucracy

A common form of structure, especially in large-scale establishments, is bureaucracy, though today the term has common connotations of rigidity and red tape. However, in the study of organisation and management it is important that the term is seen not *necessarily* in a negative way, but as applying to certain structural features of formal organisation.

The German sociologist, Max Weber, showed particular concern for what he called 'bureaucratic structures'. He argued that the decisive reason for the growth of bureaucratic organisation was its purely technical superiority over any other form of organisation.[44] Although Weber did not actually define bureaucracy, he did attempt to identify the main characteristics of this type of organisation.

Main features of bureaucracy

Bureaucracy is characterised by:

- clear role definitions of duties and responsibilities;
- division of labour and a high level of specialisation;
- a hierarchical structure of authority;
- uniformity of decisions;
- an elaborate system of rules, procedures and regulations;
- employment based on technical qualifications and formally attested merit;
- impartiality in undertaking duties and responsibilities.

Four main features of bureaucracy are summarised by Stewart as: specialisation, hierarchy of authority, a system of rules, and impersonality.[45]

- *Specialisation* applies more to the job than to the person undertaking the job. This makes for continuity, as the job usually continues if the present job holder leaves.
- *Hierarchy of authority* makes for a sharp distinction between management and workers. Within the management ranks there are clearly defined levels of authority.
- *A system of rules* aims to provide for an efficient and impersonal operation. The system of rules is generally stable, although some rules may be changed or modified over time. Knowledge of the rules is a requisite of holding a job in a bureaucracy.
- *Impersonality* means that allocation of privileges and the exercise of authority are in accordance with the laid-down system of rules. In more highly developed bureaucracies there may be carefully defined procedures for appealing against certain types of decisions. According to Stewart, the characteristic of impersonality is the feature of bureaucracy which most distinguishes it from other types of organisation. A bureaucracy should not only be impersonal but it should be seen to be impersonal.

Criticisms of bureaucracy

These features provide an accurate account of how many organisations actually do function. However, bureaucratic structures have a number of potential disadvantages and are subject to severe criticisms, including the following.

- The over-emphasis on rules and procedures. Record-keeping and paperwork may become more important in their own right rather than as a means to an end.
- Members may develop a dependence upon bureaucratic status, symbols and rules.
- Initiative may be stifled and there is lack of flexibility or adaptation to changing circumstances.

- Hierarchical position and responsibilities in the organisation can lead to officious bureaucratic behaviour.
- Impersonal relationships can lead to stereotyped behaviour and a lack of responsiveness to individual situations or problems.

Among the strongest critics of bureaucratic organisation, and the demands it makes on the worker, is Argyris. He claims that the formal, bureaucratic organisation restricts the pyschological growth of the individual. It causes feelings of failure, frustration and conflict. Argyris argues that the organisation should provide a more 'authentic' relationship with its members and provide:

- a significant degree of individual responsibility and self-control;
- commitment to the goals of the organisation;
- productiveness and work; and
- an opportunity for individuals to apply their full abilities.[46]

Hotels as bureaucracies

The growth of bureaucracy has come about through the increasing size and complexity of modern work organisations and the associated demand for effective operations. Greater emphasis has been placed on the careful design of structure, and the definition of individual duties and responsibilities. Greater specialisation and expertise, and applications of technical knowledge, have highlighted the need for laid-down procedures.

As a result, many hotels, especially large-scale ones, reflect – at least in part – similar characteristics to a bureaucratic form of organisation. This view is supported by Lockwood and Jones:

> On looking at organisation structures within hotels, we find an emphasis on a mechanistic or bureaucratic format, such as the classical kitchen brigade. This structure is based on tradition, with a breakdown of the operations into specialist occupational areas. It is also influenced by the need for a formal framework within which the uncertainty and instability of the guest input can be handled – all staff know their respective roles and positions and therefore the basis of their reactions to customers' requests.[47]

There appears therefore to be a particular dilemma for management between the underlying characteristics of bureaucracy and the inherent nature of the hospitality industry. The concept of personal service delivery requires a flexible approach, and a responsiveness to individual requirements and problems of guests. This demands that staff should have a broad definition of their duties and responsibilities and the opportunity to use their initiative and inventiveness.

Raub, in a study based on Swiss hotels,[48] suggests that too much bureaucracy kills individual initiative. He discusses the need for staff to be able to 'break away from regular duties and address and resolve the issue . . . whoever receives a complaint, owns it'.

In practice, however, few organisations fit neatly into any particular model of organisational design and structure. Most are hybrid and will lie somewhere on a continuum between bureaucracy and more organic forms of structure. The hotel organisation in particular seems unlikely to fit fully into the bureaucratic model of structure.[49]

Much of the criticism of bureaucracy is undoubtedly valid, but much also appears to be unfair comment. In any case, many staff working in the hotel industry are generally conservative by nature. They feel more comfortable working within a rigid structure and 'knowing where they stand'. The main point, however, is that whatever the validity of the criticisms it is difficult to envisage how modern large-scale hotels could function effectively without exhibiting at least some of the features of a bureaucratic structure.

The human relations approach

The main emphasis of the classical approach was on structure and the formal organisation as the basis for achieving high levels of work performance. But during the 1920s greater attention began to be given to the social factors at work and to the behaviour of people in the organisation – that is, to human relations. Whereas the classical approach adopted more of a managerial perspective, the human relations approach strove for a greater understanding of people's psychological and social needs at work as well as improving the process of management. It is usually regarded as the first major approach to organisation and management to show concern for industrial sociology. The major impetus to the human relations approach came with the famous Hawthorne studies at the Western Electric Company in America (1924–1932).

There were four main phases to the Hawthorne studies: the illumination experiment, the relay assembly test room, the interviewing programme and the bank wiring observation room.

The illumination experiment

This investigation was conducted to test the belief that improvements in physical working conditions, such as the intensity of lighting, would improve productivity. The results of the tests were inconclusive as production varied with no apparent relationship to the level of lighting, but actually increased when conditions were made worse. Production also increased in the control group although the lighting remained unchanged. Clearly other factors influenced the level of production and this prompted a series of further experiments.

The relay assembly test room

This experiment involved six women workers who assembled telephone relays by hand. The work was boring and repetitive. The researchers selected two assemblers who were friends with each other, and they chose three other assemblers and a layout operator. The six workers were moved to a room by themselves but with the same general environmental conditions as the main assembly area. The workers were subjected to a series of planned and controlled changes such as hours of work, rest pauses, and refreshment breaks. During the experiment the observer adopted a friendly manner, consulting with the workers, keeping them informed and listening to their complaints. Following all but one of the changes there was a continuous rise in the level of production. Also, sickness and absenteeism dropped, and morale appeared to improve. The researchers formed the conclusion that the main reasons were small group working, the extra attention given to workers, and the apparent interest in them shown by management.

The interviewing programme

In an attempt to find out more about the workers' feelings towards their supervisors and conditions of work, a large interviewing programme was introduced. Initially the interviewers approached their tasks using a set of prepared questions related mainly to how workers felt about their jobs. However, this method produced only limited information, so the style of interviewing was changed to be more non-directive and open-ended. Workers were free to talk about any aspect of their work. Everything was confidential, no identification was given and no personal details were revealed to management.

The interviewers set out to be friendly and sympathetic. They adopted an impartial, non-judgemental approach and did not take sides or offer opinions. If necessary they would explain company policy and details of, for example, benefit schemes but they concentrated on listening. Using this approach the interviewers found out far more about the workers' true feelings towards the company, working conditions, supervision and management, group relations and matters outside work.

Many workers appeared to welcome the opportunity to have someone who would listen to their feelings and problems, and to whom they could 'let off steam' in a friendly atmosphere. The interviewing programme was significant in giving an impetus to present-day personnel management and the use of counselling interviews. It also highlights the importance of managers actively listening to the workers.[50] Given the nature of the hospitality industry and the importance of good employee relations, the lessons learnt from the interviewing programme have particular significance for the manager.

The bank wiring observation room

This experiment involved the observation of a group of 14 men working in the bank wiring observation room. It was noted that the men formed their own informal organisation with sub-groups and cliques, and with natural leaders emerging with the consent of members. The group developed its own pattern of informal social relations with 'norms' of what constituted 'acceptable' behaviour together with a system of sanctions against those members who did not conform with the group norms. Group pressures on individual workers restricted the level of work achieved despite financial incentive schemes offered by management. The importance of informal working practices and group 'norms' is discussed further in Chapter 8.

Evaluation of the human relations approach

The Hawthorne studies have been subject to criticism and to a number of different interpretations.[51] But, however the results are regarded, the studies have important implications for organisational structure. They generated new ideas on social interaction, output restrictions and individuals within work groups. As Nailon, for example, points out: 'Most managers have experienced antagonism when any suggestion is made for the composition of groups to be changed.'[52]

The human relations approach marked a change in emphasis away from the precision of scientific management and led to ideas on increasing productivity by humanising the work organisation. The classical approach sought to increase production through means of formal structure and rationalisation of the work organisation. With the human relations approach, recognition was given to the importance of the informal organisation which will always be present within the formal structure. Workers were seen as individuals and members of a social group, with their behaviour and attitudes as the key to effectiveness.[53]

Neo-human relations

The results of the Hawthorne studies and the subsequent attention given to social organisation gave rise in the 1950s and 1960s to a group of writers who are usually categorised under the heading of neo-human relations. The major focus of concern was the personal adjustment of the individual within the structure of the work organisation, the effects of group relationships and leadership styles. Writers under this heading include Maslow, Argyris, Herzberg, McGregor and Likert. The works of these writers are examined in more detail in subsequent chapters.

A radical perspective

Sometimes the work of Weber is associated with the ideas of writers such as Karl Marx under the sub-heading of the structuralist approach, which is a synthesis of the classical (or formal) school and the human relations (or informal) school.[54] A major line of thought was that the earlier approaches were incomplete. The structuralist approach provides a radical perspective of social and organisational behaviour. Greater attention should be given to the relationships between the formal and informal aspects of the organisation, and the study of conflict between the needs of the individual and the organisation, and between workers and management.

The systems approach

The classical approach emphasised the formal structure as a major mechanism in optimising organisational performance. The human relations approach emphasised the social needs of people at work and the importance of the informal organisation. The systems approach attempts to reconcile these two earlier approaches. Attention is focused on the total work organisation and the interrelationships of structure and behaviour. The systems approach views the organisation within its broader external environment and with multiple channels of interaction.

The systems approach draws attention to the importance of the socio-technical system. This directs attention to viewing the organisation as a whole and the relationships between technical and social variables. Changes in one part, technical or social, will affect other parts and thus the whole organisation as a system. An analysis of the hotel as an open system was discussed in Chapter 1.

The contingency approach

The contingency approach, which can be viewed as an extension of the systems approach, highlights possible means of differentiating between alternative forms of organisation structure and systems of management. There is no one optimum state. The structure of the organisation and its 'success' are dependent upon a range of situational factors.

The contingency approach takes the view that there are a large number of variables or situational factors which influence organisational design and performance. There is therefore no one, best, universal structure. The most appropriate structure is dependent upon the contingencies of the situation for each individual hotel. It is these situational factors which account for variations in the structure of different hotels.

Although contingency models have not involved the hospitality industry directly, their relevance and potential applications should be readily apparent. Managers can use these models to compare and contrast the structure and functioning of their own hotel, and to take from them those ideas which suit best their particular requirements.

An 'if-then' relationship

Contingency models can be seen as a form of 'if–then' matrix relationship.[55] If certain situational factors exist, then certain variables in organisational structure and systems of management are most appropriate. A simplified illustration of contingency relationships is given in Figure 4.4.

Situational variables may be identified in a number of different ways. Some obvious bases for comparison are the type and nature of the establishment, the range and standard of services and facilities offered, and the nature of the customers and characteristics of the staff. Other important variables include size, technology and the environment (see Figure 4.5).

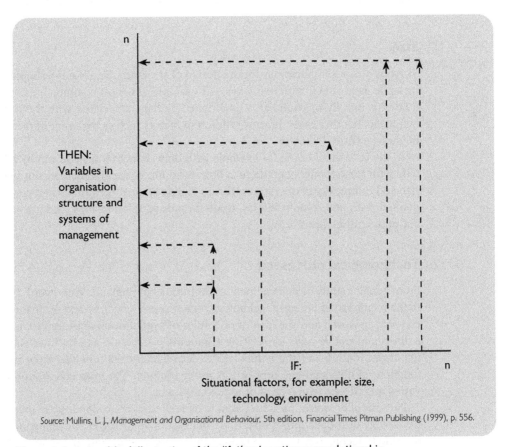

Source: Mullins, L. J., *Management and Organisational Behaviour*, 5th edition, Financial Times Pitman Publishing (1999), p. 556.

Figure 4.4 A simplified illustration of the 'if-then' contingency relationship

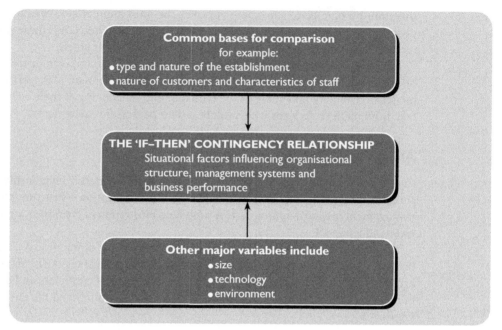

Figure 4.5 The contingency approach – main influences on organisation and management

Size

Size has obvious implications for the design of structure. Size is not a simple variable, and it can be measured in different ways. For example, the most common indication of size for a hotel is usually the number of bedrooms, perhaps associated with the number of staff employed. In other cases, however, different factors such as the range of facilities provided might be a better indicator.

In the very small hotel, for example with only six bedrooms and run by a husband and wife with some family help, there is little need for a formal structure. But with increasing size and complexity of operations, the hotel may be divided into distinct departments with defined tasks and responsibilities, more formalised relationships, and greater use of rules and standardised procedures.

Technological processes

From a major study of management organisations in England, Woodward draws attention to the relationships between technology, organisation structure and business success.[56] The classical approach and the idea of principles of organisation appeared to fail in providing a direct and simple basis for relating organisation structure and business success. Another important finding was the nature of the actual relationship between the three key 'task' functions of development, production and marketing. The most critical of these functions varied according to the type of production system.

Patterns of organisation were found to be related more to similarity of objectives and the technology of production. Among the organisational characteristics showing a direct relationship to technology were the ratio of managers to total staff, the shape of the structure, the span of control and the number of levels of authority. One might consider how the nature of the 'production technology' process accounts for differences in the patterns of structure and systems of management of different hospitality organisations – between for example a fast-food burger chain, a large hotel concentrating on conference and leisure facilities, a public house attracting largely family customers, a small country club hotel and a very expensive up-market restaurant.

Environment influences

Two important studies have focused on the effects of uncertainty and a changing environment on the organisation and on its management and structure. These are:

- Burns and Stalker – mechanistic and organic organisations; and
- Lawrence and Lorsch – differentiation and integration.

Mechanistic and organic organisations

Burns and Stalker investigated the relationship between the pattern of structure, the nature of the external environment and economic performance.[57] They identified two ideal types of organisation at opposite extremes of a continuum – the 'mechanistic' organisation and the 'organic' organisation. These represented the polar extremes of the form which organisations could take when adapted to technical and commercial change. In practice, most organisations are likely to be a mix of both mechanistic and organic structures.

The mechanistic organisation

The mechanistic organisation resembles a bureaucracy and has a rigid, hierarchical structure. It is characterised by closely defined duties, responsibilities and technical method, the specialisation of tasks, knowledge centred at the top of the hierarchy, instructions from superiors and vertical interaction between superior and subordinates. The mechanistic organisation is unable to deal adequately with rapid change. It is therefore more appropriate for stable environmental conditions. An example might be a traditional, high-class and expensive hotel operating along classical lines and with an established reputation and type of customer.

The organic organisation

The organic organisation is more flexible and has a fluid structure. It is characterised by a network structure of control and authority, lateral communications based on information and advice, the contribution of special knowledge and expertise throughout the organisation, the continual redefinition of tasks, and commitment to the common task of the organisation.

The organic organisation is required when new problems and unforeseen circumstances arise constantly. It is therefore more appropriate for uncertainty and changing environmental

Mechanistic		Organic
High, many and sharp differentiations	SPECIALISATION	Low, no hard boundaries, relatively few different jobs
High, methods spelled out	STANDARDISATION	Low, individuals decide own methods
Means	ORIENTATION OF MEMBERS	Goals
By superior	CONFLICT RESOLUTION	Interaction
Hierarchical based on implied contractual relation	PATTERN OF AUTHORITY CONTROL AND COMMUNICATION	Wide net based upon common commitment
At top of organisation	LOCUS OF SUPERIOR COMPETENCE	Wherever there is skill and competence
Vertical	INTERACTION	Lateral
Directions, orders	COMMUNICATION CONTENT	Advice, information
To organisation	LOYALTY	To project and group
From organisational position	PRESTIGE	From personal contribution

(*Source*: © Joseph A. Litterer, 1973 reprinted with permission of the author, Litterer, Joseph A. *The Analysis of Organizations*, 2nd edn, John Wiley & Sons (1973), p. 339.)

Figure 4.6 Characteristics of mechanistic and organic organisations

conditions. An example could be a holiday or tourist hotel with an unpredictable demand and many different types of customer. Another example could be a country club hotel specialising in a range of different functions, such as wedding receptions and corporate sports days, which require the erection of marquees and provision of other facilities according to particular requirements.

A summary of the main characteristics of mechanistic and organic systems is provided by Litterer (Figure 4.6) and this provides a helpful basis for reviewing the structure and management of a particular hospitality organisation.

Differentiation and integration

Lawrence and Lorsch undertook a study of a number of firms, including two in the consumer food industry, and analysed the structure of organisation in terms of 'differentiation' and 'integration'.[58] They attempted to extend the work of Burns and Stalker and examined not only the overall structure, but also the way in which specific departments were organised to meet different aspects of the external environment.

Differentiation

Differentiation refers to differences among departments of the organisation in terms of their goals, timespans, interpersonal relations and formality of structure. It was recognised that different departments could have their own distinctive forms of structure according to the nature of their tasks, the different demands of the environment and the different levels of uncertainty.

Integration

Integration refers not to the minimising of differences between departments but to the degree of coordination and cooperation between different departments and attempts to achieve unity of effort. The mechanisms to achieve integration include: policies, rules and procedures; teamwork and mutual cooperation; formal lateral relations, committees and project teams; and assigned 'integrators' or liaison officers.

Demands of the environment

Lawrence and Lorsch suggest that the extent of differentiation and integration in effective organisations will vary according to the demands of the environment. In an unstable and dynamic environment the more effective organisation would be highly differentiated and highly integrated. This study would seem to have particular relevance to the hotel industry because of the different orientations and demands among departments such as the kitchen, front office, conference and banqueting, security and maintenance.

The relevance of contingency models

Contingency models of organisation draw attention to the situation factors which account for variations in structural design. They are more concerned with differences among organisations than with similarities. The contingency approach tends to assume, however, that organisational performance is dependent upon the extent to which the structure of the organisation matches prevailing contingencies.

As with other approaches to organisation and management, contingency theory has been subject to a number of criticisms.[59] It does run the risk of concluding that 'it all depends on everything' and there is the danger of over-emphasis on differences between organisations and the exclusion of similarities. There must be a balance.

Greater understanding of organisation and structure

Despite the criticisms and limitations, contingency theory has provided a further insight into our understanding of relationships among factors influencing the structure, management and operations of organisations. It can help our thinking about how hotels should be organised.

Based on the distinction between mechanistic and organic organisations, Shamir suggests that hotels tend to resolve the conflict between the demands for bureaucracy and hospitality service by a mixture of informal, organic systems of control and a lateral pattern of communication which lies behind the façade of a formal, mechanistic structure. Apart from those managers who have responsibility for coordinating the work of a number of different departments, most large hotels appear to lack formal integrating mechanisms at the organisational level.[60]

Contingency models draw attention to the importance of different structures for different organisations and for different activities of the organisation. Nailon, for example, feels that most theories have helped to provide a greater understanding of the catering industry and that: 'choosing the appropriate form of organisation will prevent the problems created by inappropriate structures'.[61]

Social action theory

Social action represents a contribution from sociologists to the study of organisations. Social action writers attempt to view the organisation from the standpoint of individual members (actors) who will each have their own goals, and interpretation of their work situation in terms of the satisfaction sought and the meaning that work has for them. Social action looks to the individual's own definition of the situation as a basis for explaining behaviour. Conflict of interests is seen as normal behaviour and part of organisational life.

Action theory of hotel and catering

A particular theory of human behaviour from an 'action approach' to hotel and catering is presented by Bowey.[62] She suggests that it would be possible to take the best parts of systems theory and contingency theory and combine them into a theory that would model empirical behaviour and also facilitate the analysis of large numbers of people in organisations.

Bowey gives four basic concepts taken from systems theory and redefined in accordance with an action approach.

● *Role* – this is needed for the analysis of behaviour in organisations. It explains the similar action of different people in similar situations within the organisation, and the expectations held by other people.

● *Relationships* – this is needed to explain the pattern of interaction among people and the behaviours displayed towards one another.

● *Structure* – the relationship among members of an organisation give rise to patterns of action which can be identified as a 'transitory social structure'. The social factors and non-social factors, such as payment systems, methods of production and physical layout, together form the behavioural structure.

● *Process* – human behaviour can be analysed in terms of processes, defined as 'continuous interdependent sequences of actions'. The concept of process is necessary to account for the manner in which organisations exhibit changes in structure.

Bowey goes on to illustrate her theory by case studies of five different types of organisations, all in the restaurant industry.

The flexible organisation

Increasingly organisations are becoming flatter and leaner with a need for flexibility in terms of staff numbers and staff roles. In addition to this there is a greater demand from the workforce to work flexible hours. This is featuring regularly in hospitality organisations. Two approaches to the flexible organisation are suggested by Handy and by Atkinson.

The shamrock organisation

Handy's concept of 'shamrock' organisation has interesting applications for the hospitality industry.[63] The three leaves to each stem of the shamrock are symbolic of the organisation which is seen as made up of three distinct groups of people who are managed, organised and paid differently, and who have different expectations: the professional core, the contractual fringe and the flexible labour force (see Figure 4.7).

- *The professional core* comprises qualified professionals, technicians and managers essential to the existence and effective performance of the organisation. Collectively these people own the knowledge which distinguishes the organisation. The professional core are expensive and the tendency has been for organisations to restructure in order to reduce their numbers.

- *The contractual fringe* comprises those people, or other organisations, outside of the organisation who provide specialist services and undertake all non-essential work which can be done by somebody else, and in theory are able to do it better for less. It is wise for the shamrock organisation to put boring and repetitive work out to contract, specifying the results expected and then paying the fee.

- *The flexible labour force* represents all those part-time and temporary workers which are the fastest-growing group in the pattern of employment. It provides for flexibility in human resourcing. People are brought in as occasional extra part-time labour or temporary staff as changing work situations demand.

- *Customers* are sometimes referred to as the fourth leaf in that many more organisations now provide facilities for customers to 'serve themselves'.

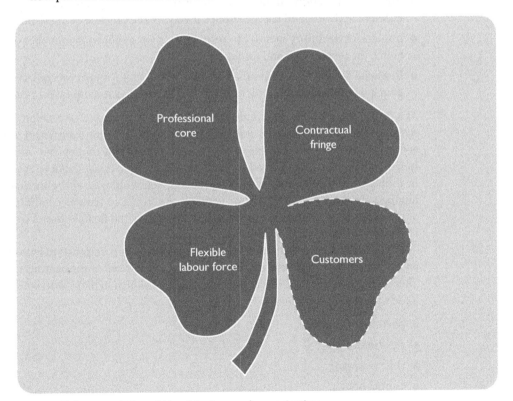

Figure 4.7 Representation of Handy's shamrock organisation

According to Handy, organisations now have three significant workforces, each with a different kind of commitment to the organisation and a different set of expectations, and each workforce needs to be managed in different ways.

Customers as the fourth leaf?

Handy also refers to the growing practice of saving labour in the core by introducing another, informal and unpaid, form of subcontracting – that of getting customers to do some of the work of the organisation. In the hospitality industry there are many examples of this 'serve yourself' philosophy. Examples are the provision of shoe-cleaning equipment or machines, hotel guests making their own tea and coffee in their rooms, restaurant self-service breakfast and buffet meals, standard meals and beverages in fast food outlets with help-yourself condiments and customers expected to clear their own meal tables, the provision of vending machines for snacks and beverages. In addition to this, chains such as Formule 1 requires guests to (normally) book ahead via the internet, check in using a code and pay by card, never actually seeing a member of staff.

Atkinson and the flexible firm

A further significant approach was Atkinson's idea of the flexible firm.[64] He suggests that firms are really looking for three kinds of flexibility:

- **functional flexibility** in order to permit the rapid redeployment of employees among different activities and tasks (perhaps involving the practice of multi-skilling);
- **numerical flexibility** in order to restructure so as to adjust the number of employees to match the level of demand for labour;
- **financial flexibility** in order that pay and other employment costs reflect the supply and demand of labour and in order to shift to new pay and remuneration systems.

As a result, Atkinson suggests that flexible firms have attempted to develop an organisation structure based on a central, stable 'core' group of full-time permanent career employees who undertake the organisation's key, firm-specific activities and with emphasis on functional flexibility, supported by peripheral and numerically flexible groups of workers including agency temporaries, subcontracting, self-employed and part-time staff, whose numbers, in theory, can expand or contract according to market conditions. Some have argued that in some sectors of the hospitality industry the flexible casual workforce is core to the operation.

Flexible working arrangements are a range of options designed to help employees balance work and home life and can describe the place of work or the contract of employment. There is a wide range of flexible working practices, which in many instances can be used in a wide variety of workplaces:

- part-time working;
- flexitime;
- shift swapping;
- annual hours;
- work at or from home;

- term-time working;
- staggered hours;
- self-rostering;
- career breaks from work;
- mobile working/teleworking;
- compressed working hours;
- time off in lieu;
- job sharing.

These approaches are being adopted increasingly in the hospitality industry.

Implications for the hospitality industry

Economic pressures, rapid developments in information technology and the need for review of structural design have highlighted the significance of these different groups. Organisations have reduced the size of their workforce, especially full-time staff, and have flatter structures with fewer levels of authority. The concept of the shamrock organisation can encourage hospitality managers to question the operation of their organisations. It gives rise to important decisions concerning what activities and which people should belong to the core, to the management and control of subcontracting and to the flexible workforce.

The increasing tendency to make use of subcontracting and the buying-in of convenience or standardised food products raises important questions of management control over performance and results. Contracting-out can arguably lead to a reduction in the range of customer choice and the potential de-skilling of jobs. For example, many hotels and restaurants now buy in their pastry products and as a result no longer have the need for their own specialist pastry chef as part of the core.

A number of American motels also have microwaves for guests to heat popcorn or other snacks purchased from the vending machines. Other American restaurants invite customers to purchase their steak or seafood in the restaurant but then cook their meal themselves.

Managing the flexible labour force

The increase in the flexible labour force is particularly noticeable with the growth of service industries. Services are created and consumed simultaneously. Unlike manufacturing, services are time-perishable and cannot be stored. The flexible labour force has increasingly been used as a cheaper and more convenient means of dealing with the peaks and troughs of demands, and as a means of adjusting the level of service to match changing customer requirements.

Although casual and part-time staff are unlikely to have the same degree of commitment or ambition as the core, it is important that they are taken seriously and regarded as a valuable part of the organisation. The flexible workforce should be treated with respect, given fair and equitable treatment, adequate training and status, and decent pay and conditions. If casual and part-time staff are to respond in a positive way and provide a high standard of service then they have to be managed in a considerate and effective manner.

Exhibit 4.6 McDonald's agrees shift-swapping 'family contract'

McDonald's has begun a trial of a 'family contract', which enables two people from the same family working in the same restaurant to cover each other's shifts with no prior notice.

About 1,000 people out of McDonald's 67,000-strong workforce are family members. Pairs made up of married couples, parents, children, siblings, grandparents, step-families, adopted families, co-habiting partners and same-sex partners are all eligible to apply for the contract.

David Fairhurst, vice-president for people at McDonald's, said: 'By giving our employees the freedom to manage their shift commitments, we will increase their motivation and enjoyment of work. That is fundamental to our business because it is a simple fact that happy employees mean happy customers.'

If the family contract proves successful, McDonald's will look to widen the scheme, Fairhurst said. 'In the future we may even look to extend it beyond the family to include friends and extended family members, such as cousins,' he said.[65]

Critical review and reflection

What benefits does flexible working bring to the employer and the employee?

What might be the negative aspects of the increasing use of flexible working in the hospitality industry?

The relationship between structure and people

Whatever the overall shape of the organisation, its effectiveness will be influenced both by sound structural design and by the individuals filling the various positions within the structure. The views of the human relations writers remind us of the importance of the human element in the design of structure. Managers need to consider how structural design and methods of work organisation influence the behaviour and performance of staff.

The functions of the formal structure, and the activities and defined relationships within it, exist independently of the members of staff who carry out the work. Personalities, however, are an important aspect of the working environment. The actual operation of the establishment and success in meeting its objectives will be dependent upon the behaviour of people who work within the structure, and who give shape and personality to the framework. 'Organisational structure is but a simplification of complex patterns of human behaviour.'[66]

Maintaining the socio-technical system

Earlier we referred to the importance of the relationships between technical efficiency and social considerations. Structure must be designed, therefore, to maintain the effectiveness of the socio-technical system and of the establishment as a whole. Attention must be given to the interactions between both the structural and technological requirements, and human factors and the needs and demands of people.

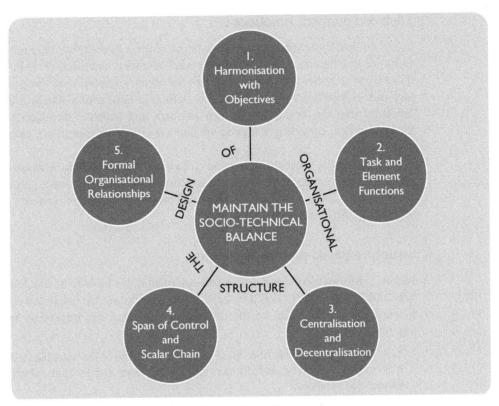

Figure 4.8 Basic considerations in the design of structure

Design of structure

In the final analysis, however, there is an underlying need to establish a framework of order and command by which the activities of the establishment are accomplished successfully. This demands that attention be given to certain basic considerations in the design of structure (Figure 4.8).

Harmonisation with objectives

Structure must harmonise with the goals and objectives of the establishment. Only when the objectives have been clearly stated and agreed can alternative forms of structure be analysed and compared. A clear definition of goals and objectives provides a basis for the division of work and grouping of activities into sub-units. The objectives for these sub-units must be related to the overall strategy of the hotel in order that an appropriate pattern of organisation structure is established.

For example, Schaffer emphasises the importance of lodging organisations continuously engaging in the process of matching their competitive strategies and organisation structures to changes in the environment. In order to achieve effective performance, strategy must be adjusted to suit the environment. Organisation structure and processes must then be created that properly support that strategy.[67]

Task and element functions

In her study of the management organisation of firms in the United Kingdom, Woodward distinguishes between 'task' functions and 'element' functions.[68] Task functions are those basic activities which are related to the actual completion of the 'productive' process, and directed towards specific and definable end-results. These are the essential functions that the organisation must perform and involve: developing the product/facility/service, providing the product/facility/service, marketing it, and financing the organisation.

Element functions are those activities which are not directed towards specific and definable ends but are supportive of the task functions and form an intrinsic part of the management process. These include, for example, planning, management services, administrative support, quality control and maintenance.

Structure based on task functions

Within the formal structure, duties and responsibilities have to be divided among members and different jobs related to each other. The difference between task and element functions forms the basis for the division of work and has important implications for organisation:

> Organisation is a function of purpose and the complexity of the hotel business arises because it is concerned with several distinct products, services and facilities, which are offered in various combinations.[69]

Structure should therefore be centred around the key activities which relate directly to the products, services and facilities offered by the establishment. These task functions are likely to relate to such activities as front office and reception, food and beverage, accommodation, conferences and banqueting, marketing or sales, and other direct customer facilities or services, for example leisure facilities or laundry and valeting. Support services are likely to include, for example, accounting, security, works and maintenance, and administration.

Need to distinguish task and element functions

Failure to distinguish between task and element functions can lead to confusion and difficulties in relationships among members. Woodward comments on the bad relationships between management accountants and other managers. The accountants tended to assume responsibility for end-results that were not properly theirs. They saw their role as a controlling and sanctioning one, rather than as a servicing and supportive one. Activities concerned with raising funds for the business, keeping accounts and determination of financial policy are task functions. But management accounting is an element function. Relationships seemed better when the two functions were organisationally separate.

The human resource function

The human resource function is generally identified as one of the key functions of an organisation. But in the hospitality industry the importance of staff contact to customer satisfaction means that personnel can be seen as associated closely with a task function.

Centralisation and decentralisation

The division of work and grouping together of activities raises the question of the extent of centralisation or decentralisation. This arises at two levels:

- the authority of individual managers within a chain or group, for example the extent of authority for local purchasing, or to recruit or dismiss staff; and
- specific delegation to sub-units, departments or sections within the individual establishment, for example a central kitchen, or decentralisation of some of the food preparation.

The underlying issue is the measure of devolved autonomy, independence and freedom of action enjoyed by the hospitality manager or by the individual sub-units.

Advantages and disadvantages

The general advantages claimed for centralisation usually include identification of a corporate image, better decision-making, easier implementation of a common policy for the chain/group or the hotel as a whole, improved coordination and control, economies of scale and reduction in overhead costs, and use of specialisation, including better facilities and equipment.

There are, however, a number of arguments against centralisation. It creates a more bureaucratic structure and may result in a longer chain of command. The decision-making process may be cumbersome when needing to be cleared through top, and perhaps distant, management. Too much centralisation can stifle initiative and the sense of responsibility.

In addition, there are positive arguments in favour of decentralisation. It enables decisions to be made closer to the operational level of work and according to immediate needs. Support services are more likely to be effective if provided closer to the activities they serve. Decentralisation provides greater opportunities for management training and development. Also, it usually has a positive effect on the motivation and morale of staff. The extent of centralisation or decentralisation should be considered in terms of the size and nature of the establishment, geographical location and particular circumstances, and the quality of staff. It is a question of balance and managerial choice. The growth of international hospitality organisations has drawn particular attention to the question of the extent and manner of decentralisation and empowerment related to design of structure and management control.[70]

Span of control and scalar chain

Two of the most specific, and related, principles of good organisational design are: (a) the span of control; and (b) the scalar chain. The span of control arises in line authority and refers to the number of subordinates who report *directly* to a given manager or supervisor. It does not refer to the total number of subordinate operating staff. Hence the term 'span of responsibility' or 'span of supervision' is sometimes preferred.

Limits to span of control

The classical writers placed emphasis on the span of control but tended to suggest that this should be limited to a definite figure (normally between four and eight).

Importance of span of control

If the span of control is too narrow it increases the number of levels of authority. A narrow span of control can result in too close a level of supervision and failure to make best use of potential managerial talent. But with too wide a span of control it becomes difficult to supervise subordinates effectively. Sub-groups or cliques and informal leaders may evolve. A wide span of control places more demands on the manager with less time to carry out all activities properly. It may also limit opportunities for promotion.

In discussing the span of control, Venison comments that:

> The hotel general manager has an impossible task to perform because it is generally beyond the behavioural range of most human beings and the sufferer has been the hotel guest – since guest contact and, to a large degree, staff contact have often been lost in the process.[71]

This observation illustrates the importance of good organisation structure including attention to span of control.

Practical considerations

In practice, however, it is not feasible to lay down a single, ideal, span of control: there are many situational variables which influence the limit of how many subordinates one person can control successfully. These include the nature of the establishment and facilities/ services offered, standardisation of methods and procedures, the ability of the manager, the quality, training and motivation of subordinates, communication and control systems, geographical or physical location, and length of the scalar chain.

The scalar chain

The 'scalar chain' refers to the number of different levels in the structure, the chain of hierarchical command. The scalar chain establishes the vertical graduation of authority and responsibility, and the framework for superior–subordinate relationships. The very act of creating structure introduces the concept of the scalar chain.

All members of staff must know their position within the structure. A clear line of authority and responsibility is necessary for the effective operation of the organisation. It is generally accepted, however, that there should be as few levels as possible. Too long a scalar chain can have an adverse effect on morale, decision-making and communications.

Need for balance

There is a general movement towards flatter organisation structures. However, if efforts are made to reduce the number of levels, this may bring about an increase in the span of control. The design of structure therefore necessitates maintaining a balance between span of control and scalar chain. It is the combination of span of control and scalar chain which determines the overall pyramid shape of the organisation and whether the hierarchical structure is 'flat' or 'tall'. (See Figure 4.9.)

The inverted organisation

Greater awareness of the importance of service delivery, total quality management and the continual search for competitive advantage has resulted in the concept of an inversion of the

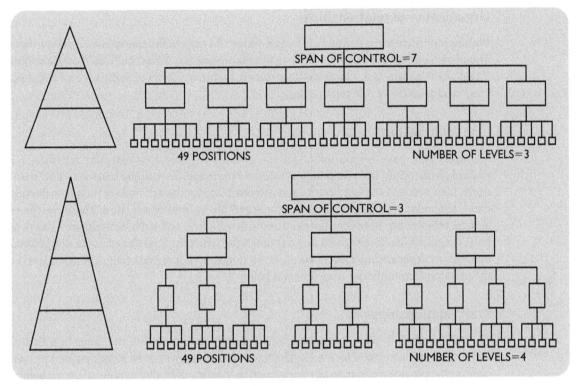

Figure 4.9 Effects of span of control and scalar chain

traditional hierarchical structure with customers at the summit and top management at the base. This will be accompanied by the devolution of power and delegation to the empowered, self-managing workers near the top of the inverted pyramid.[72]

In inverted organizations the line hierarchy becomes a support structure. The function of line managers becomes bottleneck-breaking, culture development, consulting on request, expediting resource movements and providing service economies of scale. Generally, what was line management now performs essentially staff activities. The inverted organization poses certain unique challenges. The apparent loss of formal authority can be very traumatic for former line managers.[73]

Critical review and reflection

'Advancement through the hierarchy is seen as an indicator of career progression, recognition of merit and a reward for hard work. Organisations are a form of social stratification. Removing the hierarchy will only cause lack of ambition and dissatisfaction.'

How do you feel about working in an organisation with little or no hierarchy? How would your answer differ, if you intended to work in the organisation over a long period or if you expected a short-term contract?

Organisational relationships

Within the structure the defined pattern of duties and responsibilities creates certain formal organisational relationships between individual members. These *individual* relationships establish the nature of the superior–subordinate hierarchy, flows of authority and responsibility, and patterns of role relationships.

Line relationships

Managers who have responsibility for the primary objectives or essential activities, for example front office, accommodation, food and beverage, are usually known as 'line' managers. Line managers have authority and responsibility for the activities of their own department. Line relationships are the most simple and direct form of structure. There is a direct vertical relationship between superiors and subordinates, and each subordinate reports to only one person. Authority flows down through the structure from, for example, the general manager to departmental (line) managers, section supervisors and other staff. Each level of the hierarchy has authority over the level below it.

Staff relationships

As establishments develop in size and work becomes more complex, the range of activities and functions undertaken increases. The line structure may then be supplemented by specialists who provide a common advisory function, horizontally, throughout all departments. Such specialist advisory functions are often known as 'staff'. They should serve to support the primary activities and work of the line managers. Staff functions include, for example, personnel, management accounting, marketing, maintenance and administration.

People in a 'staff' relationship have little or no direct authority over employees in other departments: this is the responsibility of the line manager. However, as the role and responsibilities of the staff positions would have been established by top management, line managers might be expected to accept the specialist advice which is given. Staff managers may also be assigned a specific responsibility which gives direct authority over other workers, for example if the personnel manager is appointed as health and safety officer for the establishment as a whole. And within their own group there is still a line relationship between functional specialists and their own subordinates and superior.

Line and staff structure

When staff positions are created they have to be integrated into the managerial structure. A 'line and staff' structure attempts to make full use of specialists while maintaining the concept of line authority (Figure 4.10). But this form of structure can present potential difficulties, and friction often occurs between line and staff managers. A major source of difficulty is often to persuade line managers to accept, and to act upon, the advice and recommendations which are offered by staff managers.

Line managers may feel that staff managers have an easier and less demanding job because they have no direct responsibility for providing facilities or services to the customer. Staff managers are often criticised for unnecessary interference in the work of the line manager, and for attempting to impose their views and advice. Line managers are often criticised for resisting the attempts of staff managers to provide assistance and coordination, and for

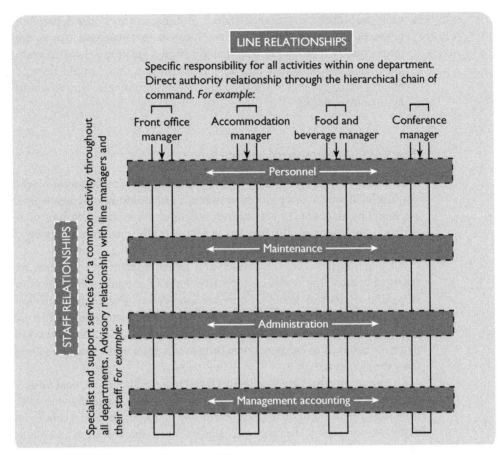

Figure 4.10 Representation of line and staff structure

making unnecessary demands for departmental independence. Staff managers may also feel that their own difficulties and work problems are not appreciated fully by the line manager.

Need for effective cooperation

It is not always easy to distinguish clearly between what is directly essential to the operation of the establishment, and what might be regarded only as a support function. The distinction between a line manager and a staff manager is not absolute. The important thing is that both line and staff recognise fully the purpose and role of the other. To be successful, line and staff need to work together and establish effective cooperation. The more staff managers can demonstrate the practical benefits of their specialist advice to line managers, the more such advice is likely to be heeded – and actively sought in the future.

Matrix structures

The matrix organisation is a combination of:

- functional departments which provide a stable base for specialised activities, for example housekeeping, or food and beverage;

- units that integrate various activities of different functional departments on a project team, product, programme, geographical or systems basis. An example might in a large country house hotel which might have a small multi-skilled team seconded to a geographically separated annexe. The barperson there would be accountable to the annexe manager, and to the food and beverage manager, who would be located in the main hotel building.

The value of organisation charts

It is usual for the structure to be depicted in the form of an organisation chart. This can be very useful in providing a pictorial presentation of the structural framework of the establishment and its main area of activities. It is helpful, for example, as part of a staff induction manual. The chart may also be used as a basis for the analysis and review of structure, for training and management succession, and for formulating changes.

An organisation chart may show, at a given moment in time, how work is divided, spans of control, the levels of authority, lines of communication, and formal relationships. But charts vary greatly. Some are intended to give a minimal amount of information, perhaps for example only an outline of the management structure of the hotel. Others give a range of additional detail – for example, all main positions in the structure, names of senior post holders, and a broad indication of the duties and responsibilities of the various sections.

Organisation charts are usually displayed in a traditional, vertical form. They can, however, be displayed in other ways, for example either horizontally with the details reading from left to right,[74] or concentrically with top management at the centre. Some charts add a rider, for example: 'The chart indicates lines of communication and not necessarily lines of authority.'

Limitations

There are a number of limitations with most organisation charts. They depict only a static view of the establishment and what the structure should be. They do not show, for example, comparative authority of positions on the same level, lateral contacts, personal delegation from superior to subordinates, or relationships between line and staff positions. A chart does not show the informal structure, how an organisation actually works, or the behaviour of people.

The seamless organisation structure

Chacko suggests that although the pyramid has been the framework of organisational structure for a very long time, this structure does not support front-line workers as well as it controls them. As hospitality customers become more seasoned, well travelled and quality conscious, a hotel's organisation structure must facilitate the implementation of strategies designed to provide higher levels of service quality. The need is for the development of a seamless hotel organisation. The structure is designed to be circular, flat and dynamic: *circular*, so that all boundaries of the hotel where employees serve customers are equally accessible; *flat*, to reduce the number of

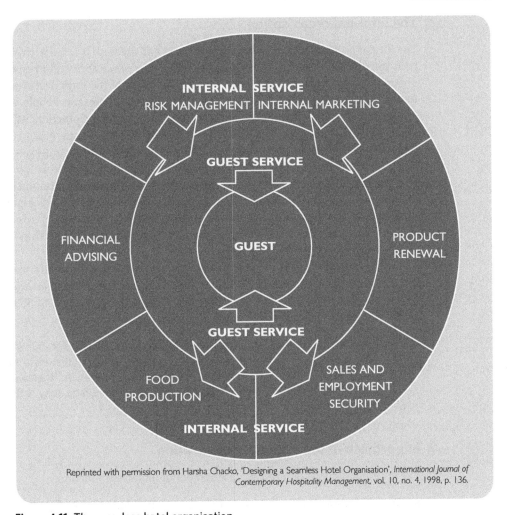

Reprinted with permission from Harsha Chacko, 'Designing a Seamless Hotel Organisation', International Journal of Contemporary Hospitality Management, vol. 10, no. 4, 1998, p. 136.

Figure 4.11 The seamless hotel organisation

hierarchical levels within the hotel; and *dynamic*, to create the flexibility to serve the changing needs of guests. In this seamless design there will be no departments, as exist currently, but rather just two job categories. The first is named Guest Service and the second is Internal Service.

Guest Service employees take care of all guest needs in the hotel and must be trained to be truly multi-skilled and prepared to work in cross-functional teams. The first and most important skill is the ability to satisfy each guest's unique needs. Internal Service, traditionally called staff functions, comprises certain specialised skills, apart from guest service, necessary for the effective functioning of the hotel. Employees have the primary responsibility of supporting guest service employees. These are traditionally called staff functions but in the new organisation the purpose of each group will be redefined as: internal marketing (human resource management); financial advising (accounting); risk management (security); product renewal (housekeeping and maintenance); sales and employment security (sales and marketing); and food production (if necessary).[75] (Figure 4.11.)

The informal organisation

The formal organisation is deliberately planned and created. It is hierarchically structured with the division of tasks, and defined relationships of authority and responsibilities. An organisation chart, for example, gives a representation of the formal structure. Within the formal structure an informal organisation will always be present. People will modify the formal organisation, methods of operations and actual working practices. What happens in practice will vary from the formal structure. See for example Figure 4.12.

The hospitality establishment is not only a work organisation, it is also a social organisation. Members of staff will establish their own social groupings and relationships, irrespective of those defined within the formal structure. The informal organisation arises from the interactions of people, their psychological and social needs, and the development of groups with their own relationships and norms of behaviour. The informal organisation is flexible and loosely structured. Relationships may be left undefined. Membership is spontaneous and with varying degrees of involvement.[76]

The style of management, the personality of members and the informal organisation will influence the operation of the establishment and actual working arrangements. What happens in practice may differ from the formal structure. According to Stewart there is a reciprocal relationship between people and the organisation.

> People modify the working of the formal organisation, but their behaviour is also influenced by it. The method of work organisation can determine how people relate to one another, which may affect both their productivity and morale. Managers, therefore, need to be conscious of the ways in which methods of work organisation may influence people's attitudes and action.[77]

Importance of the informal organisation

The informal organisation can serve a number of important functions.

- The satisfaction of members' social needs at work, and a sense of personal identity and belonging.

- A means of motivation, for example through status, social interaction, variety in routine or tedious jobs, and informal methods of work.

- Additional channels of communication. For example, through the 'grapevine' information of importance to members is communicated directly and quickly.

- A feeling of stability and security. Through informal 'norms' of behaviour a form of control is exercised over members.

- A means of highlighting deficiencies or weaknesses in the formal organisation, for example areas of responsibilities not covered in job descriptions, or outdated systems and procedures. The informal organisation may also be used when formal procedures would not be appropriate to deal with an unusual or unforeseen situation.

The informal organisation, therefore, has an important influence on the behaviour of people. It affects morale, motivation, job satisfaction and work performance. The informal organisation can provide members with greater opportunity to use their initiative and creativity in both personal and organisational development. People will view the hospitality organisation through the values and attitudes of their colleagues.

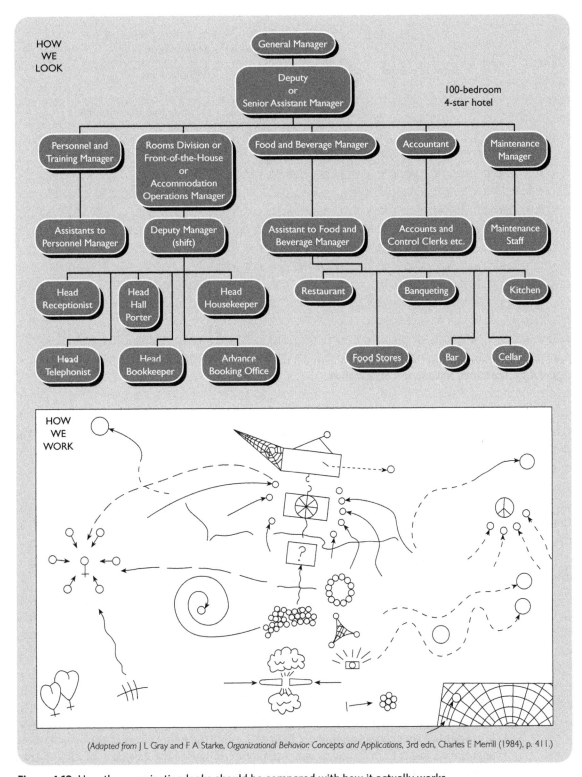

(*Adapted from* J L Gray and F A Starke, *Organizational Behavior: Concepts and Applications*, 3rd edn, Charles E Merrill (1984), p. 411.)

Figure 4.12 How the organisation looks should be compared with how it actually works

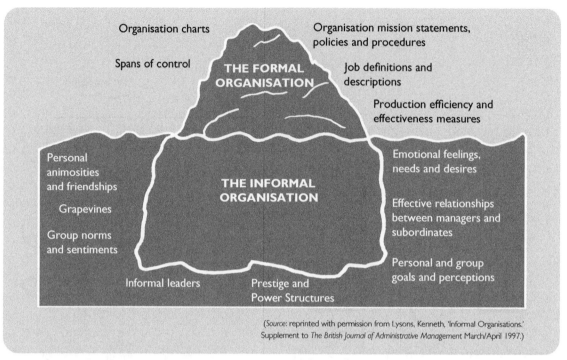

Figure 4.13 The formal and informal organisation

An illustration of the formal and informal organisation is given in Figure 4.13. (The importance and nature of informal groups is discussed in more detail in Chapter 8.)

Critical review and reflection

'Buying a coffee machine and water cooler could be the most important investments a company ever makes in its future. For it's at these social hubs of office life that the real business often gets done, as part of a casual chat or chance meeting.'[78]

In your experience, is this the case or do people waste a lot of time, standing around chatting, and how about smokers timing quick breaks to go out at the same time? To what extent are they wasting time or solving problems?

Managing through the informal organisation

It is necessary for managers to recognise the existence, and importance, of the informal organisation. They should attempt to manage through the informal organisation and where appropriate use it to their advantage. Attempting to ignore the existence of the informal organisation is likely to lead only to frustration and potential conflict.

Synopsis

- All organisations need clear goals, objectives and policy which provide a focus for management decisions and actions. Organisational goals should be integrated with the needs of individual members. Objectives and policy may be formulated within the framework of an underlying company philosophy which influences the overall conduct of the hospitality organisation, and the behaviour and performance of staff.

- Although undoubtedly of great importance, the profit motive is not by itself a sufficient criterion for the effective management of hospitality operations. Attention needs to be given to multiple areas of objective- and performance-setting, including social responsibilities. Organisational performance is dependent upon the process of matching organisational structure, strategy and the environment.

- Structure provides the basis for organisational processes and the execution of work. The structure of the organisation will affect both economic performance and the morale and job satisfaction of staff. Underlying the development of management theory are contrasting ideas on organisation and structural design.

- The classical approach places emphasis on purpose, technical structure and hierarchy of management, and includes scientific management and bureaucracy. The human relations approach gives attention to social factors and human behaviour at work, including the informal organisation. The systems approach attempts to integrate these two earlier approaches and views the organisation with multiple channels of interaction.

- The contingency approach highlights variations in structure and management, and the influence of situational variables. One particular approach to structural design is the concept of the shamrock organisation. This draws attention to the constitution of the professional core, and to the management and control of subcontracting and the flexible labour force.

- It is important to remember the human element and to consider how structural design can influence the behaviour and performance of staff. Attention must be given to maintaining the socio-technical system and to the interactions between structure and technological requirements, and to the needs and demands of people.

- In order to establish a system of order and command it is also important to give attention to certain basic considerations in the design of structure: harmonisation with objectives, task and element functions, centralisation and decentralisation, the span of control and scalar chain, and formal organisational relationships. The formal structure of the organisation will also be modified by the informal structure.

REVIEW AND DISCUSSION QUESTIONS

1 What do you see as the importance of organisational ideology or philosophy? Explain the extent to which there is a clear ideology or set of principles that govern the overall conduct of your organisation.

2 To what extent do you believe that profit maximisation is a sufficient criterion for effective management of a hospitality organisation? What other indicators might be applied in terms of organisational performance and results?

3 Discuss critically the extent to which you accept the concept of corporate social responsibilities when applied to the hospitality industry.

4 How would you attempt to explain the meaning and significance of organisational values and business ethics in the hospitality industry?

5 How does structure relate to the overall effectiveness of an organisation? Explain the main factors to be considered in the design of an organisation structure in the hospitality sector. Discuss critically the continuing importance of hierarchy.

6 Despite the criticisms of bureaucracy, it is difficult to envisage how modern large-scale establishments could function effectively without exhibiting at least some of the features of bureaucratic structure. Discuss critically the validity of this contention.

7 Discuss critically the questions that are raised by the increased demand for flexibility and greater freedom for individuals.

8 To what extent would you agree with the contention that a logical structure for organisation is better for efficiency and morale than a structure allowed to develop around personalities? What are the likely consequences of a poorly designed structure?

ASSIGNMENT 1

Conduct a study of the corporate social responsibility of three hospitality organisations.

(a) Analyse the area of focus in terms of environmental focus, employment quality, diversity and accessibility, community well-being, economic prosperity.

(b) What conclusions do you draw from the findings?

ASSIGNMENT 2

Investigate a hospitality organisation of your choice and obtain, or prepare, a chart depicting the structural design of the organisation.

(a) Comment critically on:

- the relationships between task and element functions;

- the extent of centralisation and decentralisation;

- span of control and scalar chain; and

- formal organisational relationships.

(b) Applying your knowledge of contingency models, comment on the apparent effectiveness of the structure of the organisation and/or particular departments of the organisation.

(c) Identify and explain what you believe to be good and poor examples of structural design.

(d) Explain, with supporting reasons, the changes you would recommend to the organisation structure. Where appropriate, prepare a revised organisation chart.

(e) Give practical examples of the influence and importance of the *informal* organisation.

CASE STUDY 4.1

Lexington Catering

Lexington are a successful contract catering company based in London. Their mission statement says that the company is 'super people providing great food, having fun and enjoying success'. They provide delicious food and drink for people at work and they are passionate about creating the best dining experiences for their customers and a highly valued catering management service to their clients. Lexington takes a responsible approach to every aspect of their business and recognises their responsibilities to all of their stakeholders.

The importance of their people is seen as vital to the continuing success of the company and they create a culture that encourages inclusivity and values individuality. They are committed to being an employer of choice offering an environment that is both rewarding and enjoyable. The company was awarded Gold status from Investors in People in 2010, the highest accolade possible from the UK's leading people management standard, and they were listed as one of the Sunday Times 'best 100 companies to work for' in 2009 and 2011.

Questions

1 Who would be the stakeholders of Lexington and what responsibilities would the company have for these different stakeholders?
2 Using Handy's shamrock model or Atkinson's flexible firm as a model, how would you describe the situation of the Lexington employees who worked at one of the clearing bank head offices?
3 Why would a major corporation employ the services of a firm like Lexington?
4 What areas of corporate responsibility could Lexington be engaged with?
5 What might be included in staff benefits in a company such as Lexington that is committed to valuing its employees?
6 What are the potential benefits to Lexington and their employees of the Investors in People and Sunday Times best 100 companies to work for awards?

Source: The authors are grateful to Nina Beckett for this contribution.

CASE STUDY 4.2

Hazel Wood Court

Introduction

Hazel Wood Court was built in 1958, when its owners claimed that it was one of the first motels to be opened in Britain. The motel is situated in south-east England on the outskirts of a large seaport and within easy reach of a major trunk road and the motorway system. It lies about five miles north of a busy cross-Channel ferry service terminal and is also within four miles of an expanding industrial estate. Hazel Wood Court stands on the site of a ruined sixteenth-century inn, where the original tavern known as the King's Retreat still remains, and is still in everyday use as a public bar. The bar is very popular because of its authentic period character which is derived from a large open fireplace, wooden settees, and low ceilings supported by thick oak beams. Such is its attraction that the local people who use the bar still refer to it as The Retreat

Case study 4.2 (*continued*)

nearly 30 years after it started trading under the name of Hazel Wood Court.

Other facilities

As well as the popular King's Retreat public bar, the motel's other facilities include 51 bedrooms, a conference suite with seating for 40 delegates, a restaurant capable of serving up to 160 covers, and an attractive cocktail bar with seating for 55 persons. Hazel Wood Court is surrounded by extensive, well-kept gardens on three sides and there is a large free car park at the rear of the motel.

The motel is AA and RAC appointed with a three-star classification.

Accommodation

Only 25 bedrooms were included in the original design of the motel, but as the reputation of the Hazel Wood Court grew this total was increased to 40 rooms in 1968, and a new wing was built in 1976. The 51 bedrooms include 31 twin-bedded, 12 double, and eight rooms with three beds in each which can be converted into 'quads' if required.

All the rooms have private bathrooms, colour television, radio and tea- and coffee-making facilities. It should be noted that despite the company's attempts to 'standardise' the accommodation units, the management has had to contend with numerous complaints, mainly from regular customers, since soon after the final extension was completed in 1976. The substance of most of these complaints is that the tariff charges do not reflect the allegedly different standards of accommodation provided by the motel.

Sources of revenue

Revenue is obtained from the following main sources:
(a) *Local business trade* – uses the restaurant to entertain guests for lunch and dinner, makes frequent use of the conference suite, and provides a steady flow of reservations for overnight accommodation.
(b) *Tour operators* – accommodation is also provided for various tour operators, on a dinner, room and breakfast basis, and several groups of 30–60 people (mainly American, Dutch, Australian and German) arrive at the motel each week during the summer season.
(c) *Visiting business trade* – close proximity to the motorway system makes the motel an ideal stopping-off point for visiting business people, and 'regulars' stay at the motel at least one night every week, booking accommodation many months in advance.
(d) *Casual trade* – because of the easy access to a cross-Channel ferry terminal there is a regular demand during the high season for overnight visitors travelling to and from the continent. Special arrangements are made for the service of early breakfasts for these visitors if required.
(e) *Wedding receptions/functions* – a steady trade has been developed mostly at weekends.
(f) *Bar trade* – the cocktail bar provides steady revenue from resident guests and diners in the restaurant, in contrast to the King's Retreat which derives most of its sales from the local inhabitants and chance trade. Snack-bar meals are a popular feature.

Fluctuations in trade

Apart from a general seasonal fall in demand for the motel's services outside the June–September period, there are also weekly fluctuations in demand which result in services being well utilised from Monday through to Friday morning throughout the rest of the year. Various attempts have been made to increase trade in the motel on Friday and Saturday nights, and on Sundays during the off-season period. Sustained local advertising has created a heavy demand for dinner on Saturday evenings and luncheon on Sundays.

Sunday nights, however, continue to be regarded as what are known in the trade as 'dead nights'. Despite these difficulties an annual guest occupancy of between 70 and 75 per cent is generally achieved in Hazel Wood Court and none of these fluctuations affects trade in the King's Retreat.

Group structure

The Hazel Wood Court is owned by a large group of companies. The group's interests are split into

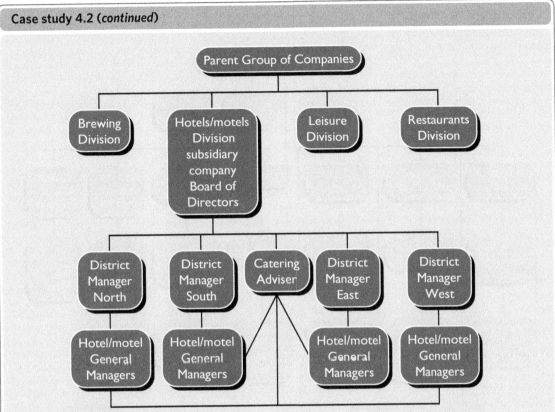

Figure 4.14 Group structure

different divisions which are controlled by numerous subsidiary companies, most of which are also based in London. The relationship between hotels and motels like Hazel Wood Court and the parent company is shown in Figure 4.14.

The subsidiary company has its own board of directors and is run by a managing director, who is directly responsible to the board of directors of the parent company. The subsidiary company consists of hotels and motels throughout Britain which are divided into four areas. The general manager of a hotel/motel in any one of these areas is responsible to the catering adviser for all food and beverage operations and to a district manager for the overall profitability of the hotel.

Communication between the hotel/motel general manager and these district executives is normally confined to one visit per month in the case of the catering adviser, and to one visit per week from the district manager.

Hazel Wood Court organisational structure

The staff at the Hazel Wood Court consists of 50 full- or part-time personnel, all of whom are ultimately responsible to the motel general manager, as shown in Figure 4.15.

A new general manager is appointed

Mid-way through 1987 Mr Jack Cox, who had been general manager of Hazel Wood, was promoted to the position of catering adviser for all the hotels and motels operating under the subsidiary company's banner. Numerous applications were received when Mr Cox's position was advertised in the trade press and the board eventually decided to appoint Mr Pat Squires as the new general manager of the motel from August onwards.

Mr Squires possessed nearly 32 years' experience in the hotel and catering industry, including six years as an officer of field rank in the Army

Case study 4.2 (*continued*)

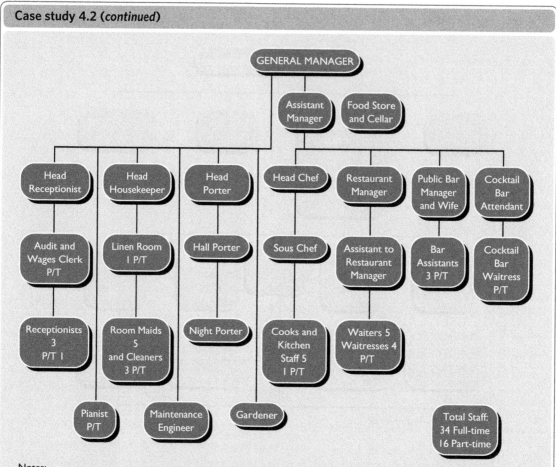

Notes:
(a) The general manager's wife was not employed but assisted him socially and provided all the floral decor.
(b) Trainee managers were often attached for periods up to six months on instructions from Head Office.
(c) Additional part-time waitresses were employed if required.

Figure 4.15 Organisation structure of Hazel Wood Court

Catering Corps. He had previously been general manager of a small chain of three motels in south-west England, but had decided to accept what was on paper a less demanding position at the Hazel Wood Court, after his doctor had advised him to reduce his workload.

Mr Squires was appointed by the managing director of the subsidiary company who informed him that, as general manager, he would be jointly responsible to the newly appointed catering adviser for food and beverage operations and to the district manager for the overall profitability of the motel.

Mr Squires' remuneration included a substantial salary, plus a 5 per cent commission on net profitability, which would be progressively reduced to 2 per cent as net profits increased beyond agreed targets. Accommodation for Mr Squires and his family would also be provided above the King's Retreat public bar.

The managing director forewarned Mr Squires that the restaurant manager, Mr Ray Welsh, and head housekeeper, Mrs Brenda Cox, might find it difficult to adjust to his appointment, as both employees were inclined to be temperamental and had enjoyed considerable privileges under the previous

Case study 4.2 (*continued*)

general manager. The managing director added that Mrs Brenda Cox was, in fact, the wife of Mr Jack Cox, the newly appointed catering adviser. He urged Mr Squires to do what he could to develop a new team spirit, but stressed that if this proved to be impossible, disciplinary action was not to be taken against either employee without his prior permission.

Other key positions at Hazel Wood Court

When Mr Pat Squires took up his position as general manager of Hazel Wood Court the key positions were filled by the following personnel:

(a) *Assistant general manager* – Mr Ted Gascoigne, a local man in his early 20s with limited experience, whose wife, Frances, was employed as head receptionist.

(b) *Head chef* – this position was held by Mr John Drury, aged 45, who had been with the motel for six years, and was regarded as a very conscientious member of staff.

(c) *Public bar management* – this was jointly held by another husband and wife team, Lee and Beryl Marks, who had only recently taken up the appointment.

Mr Squires' first year as general manager

This was considered to be an unqualified success. Revenue was increased above the budgeted figure on both accommodation and food and beverage sales by over 15 per cent.

Several ways of increasing revenue over weekends during the off-peak season were also introduced. Mr Squires worked particularly hard at maintaining high morale amongst the motel staff and, although he had found it necessary tactfully to censure Mrs Cox's behaviour on various occasions during the year, he was quietly optimistic about the relationships he had built up with Mr Welsh, the restaurant manager, and the rest of the staff at the motel.

An unhappy second year

Things began to go wrong for Mr Squires during his second year as general manager. At first the problems seemed to be small ones which could

quickly be corrected. They began when the district manager drew Mr Squires' attention to the fact that although revenue continued to rise, profitability could have been even higher if the labour costs at the motel were reduced to the same level as those at other hotels and motels in the district manager's area.

Mr Squires was unsure that like was being compared with like, but he conceded that labour costs could be reduced if both Mrs Cox and Mr Welsh reduced their staff levels, especially with regard to part-time employees. Mr Squires was requested to submit a report on the situation which the district manager promised to raise in confidence with the managing director.

Summary of confidential report on Mrs Cox's performance

Attention was drawn to the following problems:

(a) Mrs Cox had always taken every Saturday and Sunday off since she joined the company, and was never available to supervise her staff during weekends.

(b) Her department had always been overstaffed by at least two operatives.

(c) Overtime was offered to her staff on an indiscriminate basis and often when double-time rates had to be paid.

(d) She was inefficient in checking rooms and this had resulted in guests complaining on several occasions about the standard of cleanliness, etc.

(e) She ordered cleaning materials and other cleaning equipment without prior approval and authorisation from the manager.

In conclusion, Mr Squires expressed the view that, had he not been specifically advised by the managing director to retain Mrs Cox's services, it would not have been necessary to write a report on her performance as she would have been replaced soon after his appointment because of her general inefficiency.

Summary of confidential report on Mr Welsh's performance

With regard to the restaurant manager, Mr Squires stated that in his opinion Mr Welsh had recently adopted an arrogant approach to the management, his own staff and visitors alike.

Other main problems were as follows:

(a) Mr Welsh, having been employed at the motel since it had opened, was apparently of the opinion that he could run his department as he wished, irrespective of demand. The restaurant was overstaffed at most times; however, when staff were needed at peak periods they were not all available.

(b) Mr Welsh's unfavourable attitude to guests, other than regular well-liked customers, was becoming more obvious and in some cases it had brought complaints from diners about some of his remarks which appeared to be bordering on the offensive.

Mr Squires was fully prepared to resolve these difficulties with Mr Welsh, but was of the opinion that he could no longer entirely count on his loyalty.

Bar problems

Bar and cellar stocktaking was carried out at agreed intervals of approximately six weeks by a firm from London which had been appointed by the parent company. Normally this took place on a Monday afternoon with two representatives commencing work at 2 pm and finishing at approximately 5 pm. They obtained all the sales figures and 'goods inwards' information from the weekly returns sent to Head Office by the motel. Their results were received approximately two to three weeks after each stocktake. The cocktail bar and wine cellar produced excellent figures, indicating that they were being run in accordance with good commercial practice.

The public bar results caused Mr Squires considerable concern because deficiencies occurred on the cellar reconciliation figures, and the external stocktakers concluded that these shortages mainly concerned the public bar.

It was decided that all goods were delivered to the main cellar, and that each bar requisitioned from the food and beverage manager, who issued the items daily. These requisitions were then aggregated over the stocktaking period and were added to the stocks for each bar. For total cellar stocks to be reconciled, the opening cellar stock

with all the purchases added, less the total of all the requisitions, etc., had to equal the closing stock of each item in the cellar, and it was these discrepancies, amounting to nearly 3 per cent of turnover, which were serious and could never be explained adequately by either the bar manager or his wife.

As the refrigerated cold room, which housed all the beers, was within the cellar compound, there had to be access for deliveries, maintenance, cleaning of the pipes and the replacement of kegs, etc.

The bar manager therefore had a set of keys for this purpose, but not to the section housing the spirits, liqueurs, aperitifs, etc., which were stored in a separate cage in the main cellar. Mr Squires and his assistant manager shared the view that the entrance to the main cellar was too easily accessible, being located behind the service counter of the public bar.

Between them they devised a tactful system of monitoring staff movements, and were disturbed to notice that Mr Welsh, the restaurant manager, who was on very friendly terms with Mr Marks and his wife, made regular visits to this part of the motel outside normal working hours. Mr Squires reported his concern to both the district manager and the catering adviser as, even though the case against Mr Welsh was purely circumstantial and far from proven, they should be aware of the situation in case corrective action eventually had to be taken.

The response of the district manager

After discussing Mr Squires' complaints with the managing director, the district manager informed him that two courses of action would be taken:

(a) Mrs Cox would be interviewed by the district manager in the presence of Mr Squires and, unless she provided a satisfactory explanation for her behaviour, would receive a verbal disciplinary warning from the company.

(b) No action would be taken against Mr Welsh for the time being, but stocktaking in the public bar and cellar would be carried out at more regular intervals, possibly unannounced.

Case study 4.2 (*continued*)

Disciplinary proceedings against the head housekeeper

The district manager kept his word, and Mrs Cox was requested to attend disciplinary proceedings in the presence of Mr Squires. The meeting was well conducted by the district manager, who kept proceedings at a low key, raised each complaint calmly, allowed Mrs Cox the opportunity to defend herself, and remained impartial throughout. Mrs Cox was denied the opportunity to turn the meeting into an angry debate and ended up by admitting responsibility for all of the criticisms raised against her by Mr Squires.

The meeting closed with the district manager quietly insisting that a change of attitude was called for from Mrs Cox, who should communicate more frequently and in a more cooperative way with Mr Squires in the future; she should also introduce a more effective system of supervision to cover weekend work.

Additional public bar and main cellar stocktake by external auditors

Within three weeks of the previous stocktake a further audit was carried out by the same two representatives. The surprise element of the check was lost when the firm telephoned the public bar manager on the day before to enquire if an afternoon visit would be acceptable. The stocktake was completed in under two hours and the senior auditor advised Mr Squires that no significant discrepancy had been discovered. Mr Squires enquired how it was possible to carry out a detailed audit of this proportion in such a short time and draw such conclusions, but his question was received in embarrassed silence.

He later communicated his dissatisfaction to the district manager at Head Office, but was informed that the additional audit had been accepted by the board and the complaints against Mr Welsh would be dropped and the matter closed. By persisting, Mr Squires did receive a begrudging acceptance from the outside firm of stocktakers that he or his assistant should be present at all audits in the future.

Complaints from the catering adviser

During the months that followed, the catering adviser, who had previously been satisfied with the improvements that Mr Squires had introduced, began complaining about unacceptable profit margins on the food sales at the motel.

Normal procedure was for the catering adviser to call once a month for a meeting with Mr Squires, but he suddenly began appearing every week at unconventional hours. An unpleasant situation occurred when he arrived at the motel at 7 o'clock one Saturday evening and remonstrated with Mr Squires because he was not on duty. The explanation that Mr Squires had only shortly left the motel for a rest after officiating at a large wedding reception all afternoon, leaving his assistant on duty, was not accepted. Mr Cox insisted that as Saturday evenings were extremely busy he should have been there personally to see that everything was progressing satisfactorily.

He also broadened his criticism of Mr Squires for complaining to Head Office about the newly introduced 'Country Style' menu, before this experiment had been given a fair chance to prove itself. Mr Squires denied this allegation by pointing out that in the past Hazel Wood Court had enjoyed a very good reputation for its à la carte menu. He had tried to enhance this reputation during his time as the manager. The 'Country Style' menu experiment, which entailed prepacked frozen foods being despatched from London for reprocessing and serving to the motel's clientele, had not been successful. The meals were reasonably priced, but the choice was extremely limited and every regular customer had complained about this change in policy. All Mr Squires had done was to pass these complaints on to the district manager in the usual way. The catering adviser again refused to accept this explanation and left the motel in an angry mood.

The restaurant manager's response

Relations between the restaurant manager and the general manager deteriorated thereafter and Mr Squires formed the opinion that Mr Welsh took every opportunity to 'fan the flames' of the growing conflict between the motel manager and the catering adviser.

Matters came to a head between Christmas and the New Year when the motel advertised a Christmas

Case study 4.2 (*continued*)

luncheon at a fixed charge, to which Mr Welsh added a 10 per cent service charge while Mr Squires was indisposed with flu. This caused numerous complaints and Mr Squires had to rise from his sick bed to calm the situation and authorise the necessary refunds.

During the following week when Mr Squires had recovered and was entertaining some prominent members of the local business community to dinner, a *flambé* dish was ordered by several guests, but this was presented so far below the accepted standard by the restaurant manager that Mr Squires' party suffered considerable embarrassment.

Mr Squires decides to resign

Mr Squires informed his wife soon afterwards that he had decided to seek another position. His wife was relieved as she had never settled in the limited accommodation provided, and she was of the opinion that a flat above a public bar was no place to raise a teenage daughter.

Quite fortunately, Mr Squires met an old army colleague at a hotel and catering exhibition in London a few weeks later, who was now employed as chief catering officer for a large county council in the Midlands. A vacancy as catering consultant had arisen at the county's largest teacher training college, and Mr Squires was urged to apply.

Mr Squires' application and interviews were successful and he was offered the appointment, subject to a satisfactory medical which took another two months to arrange.

Although Mr Squires was in sound health, he decided not to hand in his notice until after the medical. Somehow word of this intended move leaked out, and about 10 days later he was surprised by an unexpected visit from the district manager, who mentioned that word had been received that Mr Squires wished to leave, and a decision had been taken by the managing director that he should depart in four weeks' time. Mr Squires responded by pointing out that he was entitled to four weeks' holiday by the company which he would take and leave at the end of that week. He left with a letter from the district manager confirming that he had been given four weeks' notice 'because of staff re-organisation'.

The following week Mr Squires signed on as unemployed and received benefit for three weeks before this was stopped by the Department of Employment because his former employers had stated that he had resigned from his position. Mr Squires produced the letter stating that he had been asked to leave and was able to obtain unemployment benefit for a further five weeks until he could take up his new appointment.

Postscript

Mr Squires is still employed in a catering consultancy role by a higher education institution in the Midlands and he has since taken on more responsibility.

He was replaced at Hazel Wood Court by a young graduate who, before taking up his appointment, telephoned Mr Squires at home to ask his advice about running the motel. As a consequence the new manager insisted that the head housekeeper should be transferred or dismissed before he would accept the appointment, and that he would also be given a free hand to make any decision he felt was necessary regarding the running of the restaurant and public bar. These requests were granted.

The head housekeeper decided to resign to concentrate more on her home life, during the week before the new manager arrived, and the restaurant manager took an early retirement a few months later. Shortly after these changes, the parent company were taken over by an international organisation and both the district manager and the catering adviser left the company.

Source: McEwan, T. and Mullins, L. J., *Horae*, Portsmouth Business School, *Hotel and Catering Research Unit Review*, vol. 1, no. 1, Summer 1989, pp. 3–13.

TASKS

1 Identify clearly the main issues of organisation and management raised in this case study.

2 Suggest how the situation at Hazel Wood Court could be improved.

References

1 Mills, D. Q. and Frieson, G. B., 'Empowerment', in Crainer, S. and Dearlove, D., *Financial Times Handbook of Management*, 2nd edn, Financial Times Prentice Hall (2001), p. 334.

2 Reeves, C., 'Making vision statements meaningful', *Manager, British Journal of Administrative Management*, April/May, 2006.

3 www.Redcarnationhotels.com, accessed March 2012.

4 Merriden, T., 'The Gurus: Rosabeth Moss Kanter', *Management Today*, February 1997, 56.

5 Jones, P. (ed.), *Management in Service Industries*, Pitman (1989).

6 Schaffer, J. D., 'Structure and Strategy: Two Sides of Success', in Rutherford, D. G. (ed.), *Hotel Management and Operations*, Van Nostrand Reinhold (1990).

7 Webster, M. W., 'Strategic Management in Context at Swallow Hotels', *International Journal of Contemporary Hospitality Management*, vol. 6, no. 5, 1994, 3–8.

8 Keiser, J. R., *Principles and Practices of Management in the Hospitality Industry*, 2nd edn, Van Nostrand Reinhold (1989).

9 Ansoff, H. I., *Corporate Strategy*, rev. edn, Penguin (1987).

10 Costa, J., Eccles, G. and Teare, R., 'Trends in Hospitality: Academic and industry perceptions', *International Journal of Contemporary Hospitality Management*, vol. 9, no. 7, 1997, 285–94.

11 Johnson, G., Scholes, K. and Whittington, R., *Exploring Corporate Strategy*, 7th edn, Financial Times Prentice Hall (2005), p. 448.

12 Brech, E. F. L. (ed.), *The Principles and Practice of Management*, 3rd edn, Longman (1975).

13 Upchurch, R. S., 'Ethics in the hospitality industry: an applied model', *International Journal of Contemporary Hospitality Management*, vol. 10, no. 6, 1998, 227.

14 Alberti, G., 'Transient labour in London's hotels: an ethnography of migrant's experiences at work and challenges for union organising', accessed from www.keele.ac.uk/media/keeele university/ri/risocsci/events/esrcmigrantlabour, 7 April 2012.

15 http://questexhoteltalk.blogspot.com/2008/08/ethical-dilemma-in-hospitality.html

16 Fearn, D. A., *The Practice of General Management: Catering Applications*, Macdonald (1971), p. 17.

17 Drucker, P. F., *The Practice of Management*, Pan Books (1968), pp. 82–3.

18 For a more detailed account, see Gullen, H. V. and Rhodes, G. E., *Management in the Hotel and Catering Industry*, Batsford (1983).

19 Simon, H. A., 'On the concept of organisational goal', *Administrative Science Quarterly*, vol. 10, June 1984, 21.

20 http://www.Compass-uk.com, accessed 5 November 2011.

21 De Grosbois, D., Corporate social responsibility reporting by the global hotel industry: commitment, initiatives and performance, *International Journal of Hospitality Management*, vol. 31, no. 3, 2012, 896–905.

22 http://www.fairtrade.org.uk/, accessed March 2012.

23 http://www.swandolphin.com/aboutus/staff.html, accessed 12 March 2012.

24 See note 21.

25 Tsai, H., Tsang, N. and Cheng, S., 'Hotel employees' perceptions on corporate social responsibility: the case of Hong Kong', *International Journal of Hospitality Management*, vol. 31, no. 4, 2012, 1143–54.

26 Reeves, R., 'The Trouble with Targets', *Management Today*, January 2008, 29.

27 Richardson, M. and Evans, C., 'Strategy in action', *The British Journal of Administrative Management*, April 2008 and July 2008.

28 Lynch, R., *Corporate Strategy*, 4th edn, Financial Times Prentice Hall (2006).

29 See, for example, Boella, M. J. and Goss-Turner, S., *Human Resource Management in the Hospitality Industry: An introductory guide*, Elsevier (2005).

30 Drucker, P. F., *The Practice of Management*, Pan Books (1968), p. 273.

31 Child, J., *Organisation: A Guide to Problems and Practice*, 2nd edn, Harper & Row (1984).

32 Schaffer, J. D., 'Structure and strategy: two sides of success', in Rutherford, D. G. (ed.), *Hotel Management and Operations*, Van Nostrand Reinhold (1990).

33 Gullen, H. V. and Rhodes, G. E., *Management in the Hotel and Catering Industry*, Batsford (1983).

34 Keiser, J. R., *Principles and Practices of Management in the Hospitality Industry*, 2nd edn, Van Nostrand Reinhold (1989).

35 For a detailed account, see Mullins, L. J., *Management and Organisational Behaviour*, 9th edn, Pearson (2010).

36 Urwick, L., *The Elements of Administration*, 2nd edn, Pitman (1974).

37 Brech, E. F. L., *Organisation: The Framework of Management*, 2nd edn, Longman (1965).

38 Woodward, J., *Industrial Organization: Theory and Practice*, 2nd edn, Oxford University Press (1980).

39 See, for example, 'Managing in the 21st century', *Manager, The Institute of Administrative Management*, January/February 2000, 8–10.

40 Simon, H. A., *Administrative Behavior*, 3rd edn, Free Press (1976), p. xxii.

41 Taylor, F. W., *Scientific Management*, Harper & Row (1947).

42 See, for example, Gospel, H. F. and Littler, C. R. (eds), *Managerial Strategies and Industrial Relations*, Heinemann (1983).

43 For an interesting debate on de-skilling and work flexibility, see Wood, R. C., *Working in Hotels and Catering*, 2nd edn, International Thomson Business Press (1997).

44 Weber, M., *The Theory of Social and Economic Organization*, Collier Macmillan (1964).

45 Stewart, R., *The Reality of Management*, 2nd edn, Pan Books (1986).

46 Argyris, C., *Integrating the Individual and the Organization*, Wiley (1964).

47 Lockwood, A. and Jones, P., *People and the Hotel and Catering Industry*, Holt, Rinehart & Winston (1984), p. 173.

48 Raub, S., 'Does bureaucracy kill individual initiative? The impact of structure on organizational citizenship behaviour in the hospitality industry', *International Journal of Hospitality Management*, vol. 27, 2008, 174–86.

49 Shamir, B., 'Between bureaucracy and hospitality: some organisational characteristics of hotels', *Journal of Management Studies*, vol. 15, no. 3, October 1978, 285–307.

50 See, for example, Fletcher, W., 'Good listener, better manager', *Management Today*, January 2000, 30.

51 See, for example, Rose, M., *Industrial Behaviour*, 2nd edn, Penguin (1988).

52 Nailon, P., 'A theory of organisation in the catering industry', *HCIMA Journal*, vol. 61, 1977, 7.

53 Torrington, D., Weightman, J. and Johns, K., *Effective Management: People and Organisation*, Prentice-Hall (1989).

54 See, for example, Etzioni, A., *Modern Organizations*, Prentice-Hall (1964).

55 See, for example, Luthans, F., *Organizational Behavior*, 5th edn, McGraw-Hill (1989).

56 Woodward, J., *Industrial Organization: Theory and Practice*, 2nd edn, Oxford University Press (1980).

57 Burns, T. and Stalker, G. M., The *Management of Innovation*, Tavistock (1966).

58 Lawrence, P. R. and Lorsch, J. W., *Organization and Environment*, Irwin (1969).

59 See, for example, Child, J., *Organization: A Guide to Problems and Practice*, 2nd edn, Harper & Row (1984).

60 Shamir, B., 'Between bureaucracy and hospitality: some organizational characteristics of hotels', *Journal of Management Studies*, vol. 15, no. 3, October 1978, 285–307.

61 Nailon, P., 'A theory of organisation in the catering industry', *HCIMA Journal*, vol. 61, 1977, 9.

62 Bowey, A. M., *The Sociology of Organisations*, Hodder & Stoughton (1976).

63 Handy, C. B., *The Age of Unreason*, Business Books (1989).

64 Atkinson, J., 'Manpower strategies for flexible organisations', *Personnel Management*, vol. 16, no. 8, August 1984, 28–31.

65 www.personnel today.com, 6 September 2007, accessed 3.6.11

66 Meyer, M. W., *Theory of Organizational Structure*, Bobbs-Merrill (1977), p. 44.

67 Schaffer, J. D., 'Structure and strategy: two sides of success', in Rutherford, D. G. (ed.), *Hotel Management and Operations*, Van Nostrand Reinhold (1990).

68 See note 56.

69 Medlik, S., *The Business of Hotels*, 2nd edn, Heinemann (1989), p. 74.

70 See, for example, Goss-Turner, S., 'Human Resource Management', in Jones, P. and Pizam, A. (eds), *The International Hospitality Industry: Organizational and Operational Issues*, Pitman (1993), pp. 152–64.

71 Venison, P., *Managing Hotels*, Heinemann (1983), p. 33.

72 Heller, R., 'The Manager's Dilemma', *Management Today*, January 1994, 42–7.

73 Quinn, J. B., Anderson, P. and Finkelstein, S., 'Leveraging Intellect', in Crainer, S. and Dearlove, D. (eds), *Financial Times Handbook of Management*, 2nd edn, Financial Times Prentice Hall (2001), p. 592.

74 For an example, see Medlik, S., *The Business of Hotels*, 3rd edn, Butterworth-Heinemann (1994), p. 81.

75 Chacko, H. E., 'Designing a seamless hotel organization', *International Journal of Contemporary Hospitality Management*, vol. 10, no. 4, 1998, 133–8.

76 For a detailed account of the informal organisation, see Gray, J. L. and Starke, F. A., *Organizational Behavior: Concepts and Applications*, 4th edn, Charles E. Merrill (1988).

77 Stewart, R., *The Reality of Management*, 2nd edn, Pan Books (1986), p. 127.

78 Law, S., 'Beyond the water cooler', *Professional Manager*, January 2005, 26.

Defining management

Introduction

Organisations achieve their goals and objectives through the coordination of activities and efforts of their members. It is through the process of management and the execution of work that the activities of the hospitality organisation are carried out. Management is essentially an integrating activity that permeates every facet of the operations of the organisation. The actions and behaviour of managers and their style of management will influence the effort expended and level of performance achieved by members of staff and the ultimate effectiveness of the organisation.

Critical review and reflection

'Junior staff who complain that a good manager should not sit in an office all day doing paperwork and drinking coffee fail to understand the nature and role of successful management.'

To what extent do you believe this is a valid point of view?

The meaning of management

Management is a generic term and subject to many possible interpretations. A number of contrasting ideas are attributed to the meaning of management and to the work of the manager.[1]

In certain respects everyone can be regarded as a manager. We all manage our own time and everyone has some choice whether or not they do something. For our purposes, however, we are concerned with management as:

- taking place within a structured work organisation and with prescribed roles;
- directed towards the attainment of goals and objectives;
- achieved through the efforts of other people; and
- using systems and procedures.

The setting of objectives and formulation of policy takes place at different levels in an organisation but as part of the same process. The board of directors or their equivalent establish objectives and formulate policy for the organisation as a whole. Management is responsible for the implementation of policy decisions and for the execution of work designed to meet these objectives.

> Management is active, not theoretical. It is about changing behaviour and making things happen. It is about developing people, working with them, reaching objectives and achieving results. Indeed, all the research into how managers spend their time reveals that they are creatures of the moment, perpetually immersed in the nitty-gritty of making things happen.[2]

Management may be viewed as 'making things happen' through other people.

Manager as a job title

Within hospitality organisations you cannot identify a manager necessarily by what a person is called or their job title. In some organisations there is a liberal use of the title 'manager' in an apparent attempt to enhance the status and morale of staff. As a result there are a number of people whose job title includes the term manager but who, in reality, are not performing the full activities of a manager. For example, it might be questionable whether a 'storekeeping manager' responsible for ordering and monitoring the stores with the assistance of one kitchen porter may be truly a manager. Yet there are many people whose job title does not include the term manager, such as executive chef, head receptionist, team leader, maitre d', but who, in terms of the activities they undertake and the authority and responsibility they exercise, may be very much a manager.

The role of supervisors

Supervisors may too often be regarded primarily as 'doers' or as technicians rather than managers. However, supervisors, especially in the hospitality industry, are an integral part of the process of management. They are usually very much in the front line of management and are increasingly called line managers. They have a prime responsibility for seeing that work gets done by others. Supervisors can be seen as having a particular concern with the directing, guiding and controlling performance activities of management. They need to have the required skills to motivate staff to perform well, deal first-hand with problems of production or service, handle difficulties or complaints diplomatically, and perhaps discipline staff.

Supervisors are required to act in a fair and sensitive manner, and to provide a pivotal role as both the link and the buffer between the opposing expectations of senior management and operatives.[3] The general movement towards flatter organisation structures and fewer levels of management has highlighted the importance of the role of the supervisor or team leader.

There are also opportunities to recruit high-level hospitality managers from the ranks of existing supervisory staff,[4] a frequent occurrence in the industry.

Management and leadership

What is the relationship between leadership and management? Although the two terms are often used interchangeably, management is more usually viewed as getting things done through other people in order to achieve stated organisational objectives. Management is regarded as relating to people working within a structured organisation and with prescribed roles. To people outside the organisation the manager might not necessarily be seen as a leadership role. The emphasis of leadership is on interpersonal behaviour in a broader context. (Chapter 6 considers the nature of leadership.)

The importance of management

The responsibility and importance of management are widely, and rightly, recognised. Among the leading writers emphasising this is Drucker:

> The responsibility of management in our society is decisive not only for the enterprise itself but for management's public standing, its success and status, for the very future of our economic and social system and the survival of the enterprise as an autonomous institution.[5]

The importance of management within the hospitality industry is also widely acknowledged:

> Effective management is one of the most important factors in the success or failure of any business. This applies to hotel, catering and institutional services as much as any other industry particularly as their managers need a balance of technical and management knowledge and skills acquired through a blend of education and experience.[6]

Management relates to all activities of the organisation and is not a separate and discrete function. It cannot be departmentalised or centralised. With the possible exception of the board of directors, or similar, an organisation cannot have a department of management in the same way as it can have a department for other functions, such a food and beverage, marketing or human resources. Management is seen best, therefore, as a process common to all other functions carried out within the organisation. Through the execution of work, the central focus of management is on achieving the goals and objectives of the organisation and satisfying the needs and expectations of its members (see Figure 5.1). Management is essentially an integrating activity.

It is not easy to find agreement on what the process of management involves. Management takes place in different ways and is undertaken at all levels of the organisation. It is difficult to think of any aspect of the functioning of a hospitality organisation that does not in some way link back to management; for example, a personality clash amongst staff may result from inappropriate recruitment, while poor work standards may be due to lack of training.

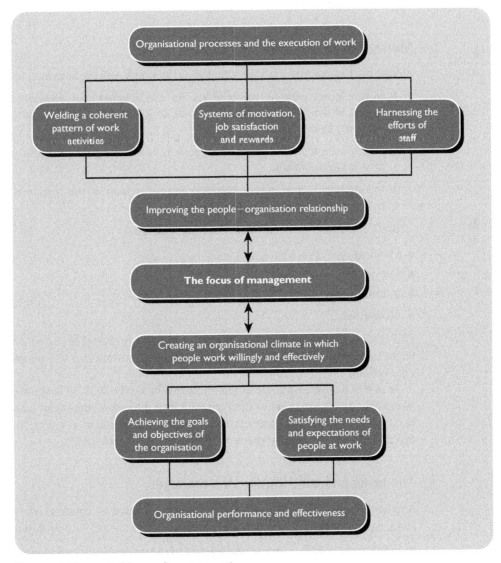

Figure 5.1 The central focus of management

The principles and processes of management

People–organisation relationship

It is generally accepted that at the heart of successful management is the ability to relate well to other people. Managers spend much of their time in meeting and talking with other people and this is especially the case in the hospitality industry. A high level of interpersonal skills is clearly important therefore for effective work performance and effective management of people. The objective is to create the optimum working environment and reconcile the demands of the organisation for effective performance and productivity, while satisfying the needs and expectations of people at work. It is frequently stated that good customer care begins with good staff care. Part of management is therefore a social process.

Management as a social process

Among the best-known analyses is that given by Brech, who defines management as:

> A social process entailing responsibility for the effective and economical planning and regulation of the operation of an enterprise, in fulfilment of given purposes or tasks, such responsibility involving:
>
> (a) judgement and decision in determining plans, and in using data to control performance and progress against plans;
>
> (b) the guidance, integration, motivation and supervision of the personnel composing the enterprise and carrying out its operations.[7]

Brech identifies four main elements of management:

- Planning
- Control
- Coordination
- Motivation.

This is a useful definition in that it draws attention to management as a 'social process', to the responsibilities of a manager and to the importance of the people–organisation relationship.

As part of a debate on the need for a framework for the study of hospitality management Wood also draws attention to the recognition of the essentially **social** nature of management. The social and therefore variable nature of management as an activity precludes the evolution of any 'systematic' theory or theories of such activities.[8]

The tasks and contribution of a manager

Another approach to describing management is provided by Drucker, who identifies three tasks, equally important but essentially different, that have to be performed:

- fulfilling the specific purpose and mission of the institution, whether business enterprise, hospital or university (and we can add 'or hospitality organisation');

- making work productive and the worker achieving; and
- managing social impacts and social responsibilities.[9]

The work of the manager requires a combination of analytical ability, synthesising ability, integrity, human perception and insight, and social skill.

Drucker also suggests that managers can be defined by their function and by the contribution they are expected to make:

> The function that distinguishes the manager above all others is the function no one but the manager can perform. The one contribution a manager is uniquely expected to make is to give others vision and ability to perform. It is vision and moral responsibility that, in the last analysis, define the manager.[10]

Exhibit 5.1 Unlikely managers

Restaurateur: Le Gavroche restaurant, London
Name: Silvano Giraldin

When did you become a manager? In 1973, when Le Gavroche was in Chelsea and I was 26. I was one of the youngest restaurant managers in the country.

What does management mean to you? Full control of Le Gavroche – except the food, which is done by Michel (Roux) – so all the beverages and the front of house. The restaurant has to look nice, the team has to be there and if someone's missing, positions have to be filled without customers noticing. There has to be a good atmosphere – if a restaurant's chefs and waiters are yelling at each other, it's a badly run place. My job is to act as a go-between and ensure these situations never arise – a happy staff means happy customers. It's no secret I also have to deal with difficult customers. We insist on a jacket and tie and one man refused to keep his jacket on. When I said, 'Sir, you have to keep it on', his wife took her skirt off and asked 'Now what will you do?' I said 'Nothing madam, you look very pretty like that, but your husband still has to keep his jacket on.'

What do you love/hate about it? I love the quality of the guests. It brings me into contact with everyone, from pop stars to politicians and from the bottom of society to the top. The only thing I don't like is the long hours.

Source: Reprinted with permission from *Management Today*, October 1999.

If you look at how staff actually spend their time you should be able to see a difference between those whose main occupation is carrying out discrete tasks and actually doing work themselves; and those who spend proportionally more of their time in deciding what is to be done, determining the work to be undertaken by others, planning and organising their work, issuing them with instructions and giving advice, and checking on their performance.

From a study of 65 Irish hotels, Baum found that managers were actively involved in supervision, and frequently in the operation of such areas as front office, restaurant, bar and kitchen. Time was spent on tasks that craft or semi-skilled employees could perform and this suggested little awareness or concern for cost-effective use of time. However, central to the operational focus of the managers was the 'mine host' concept. More than half the managers defined their job as being essentially concerned with satisfying the needs of guests.[11]

As previously stated, the nature of management is variable. The particular nature of the hospitality industry, including the frequently perceived need for managers to demonstrate proficiency in technical and craft skills, means that certain managers might be seen to be spending somewhat more time actually doing work themselves rather than deciding work to be done. However, the basis of the distinction between managing and actively 'doing' still applies and enables a study of the main activities of management.

Typically the managerial activity is divided into five elements of management which can be defined as:

- **Clarification of objectives and policy** – Objectives are the aims to be achieved and the desired end results. Policy provides guidelines for the operations of the hospitality organisation and determines the course of action to follow. The clarification of objectives and policy is a prerequisite if the process of management and execution of work is to be effective. If not, the manager has no secure basis for decision-making and the management of subordinate staff.

- **Planning of work** – Planning sets out the courses of action to be followed in order to meet objectives and achieve desired end results, for example in relation to occupancy rates, financial measures or sales performance. Good forward planning is essential if staff are to know what to do and what is expected of them, for example the timing and sequencing of operations, methods by which the operations are to be carried out and standards of performance.

- **Organising** – The work of the establishment has to be divided among its members. Organising involves the structuring of related areas of work activities such as reception, accommodation, kitchen and restaurant. Organisation provides the framework within which the process of management takes place. It makes possible the execution of work and involves the allocation of tasks and responsibilities, levels of hierarchical authority, formal relationships and coordination among individuals, groups and departments.

- **Directing subordinate staff (command)** – It is the responsibility of managers to encourage staff to work willingly and effectively. This is often referred to as motivation. It is certainly part of a manager's job to motivate staff and to provide them with job satisfaction, but it involves more than this. Subordinate staff also need development and guidance. They need to be motivated to *perform well in the right areas*. Their efforts should be directed towards the achievement of given objectives within stated policy guidelines. The manager has a responsibility to see that staff are effective as well as efficient in what they do.

- **Controlling performance**
  - Control is a necessary part of the process of management. It involves gauging the measure of success in achieving objectives and planned targets. Management control involves far more than a means of restricting behaviour or the exercise of authority over others. It should not be seen therefore only in a negative sense; it can have many positive effects.
  - Effective control systems are a means of monitoring performance and progress, providing feedback to staff and a guide to future operations and personal development. Control completes the cycle of managerial activities and is an important part of the process of management.

Common activities of management

One of the first, and most widely quoted, analyses of the activities of management is that given by Henri Fayol, in the 1920s.

Fayol describes these elements as:

- *Planning* – examining the future, deciding what needs to be achieved, and developing a plan of action.
- *Organising* – providing the material and human resources and building the structure to carry out the activities of the organisation.
- *Commanding* – maintaining activity among personnel, getting the optimum return from all employees in the interests of the whole organisation.
- *Coordinating* – unifying and harmonising all activities and effort of the organisation.
- *Controlling* – verifying that everything occurs in accordance with plans, instructions, established principles and expressed command.

Principles of management

Despite the variable nature of management, Fayol has suggested a set of 14 well-established principles to help concentrate discussion on management theory:[12]

1 *Division of work* – the advantages of specialisation and the division of work. However, there are limits to division of work which experience and a sense of proportion suggest should not be exceeded.

2 *Authority and responsibility* – responsibility is the corollary of authority. Wherever authority is exercised, responsibility arises. The application of sanctions is essential to good management, and is needed to encourage useful actions and to discourage their opposite. The best safeguard against abuse of authority is the personal integrity of the manager.

3 *Discipline* – this is essential for the efficient operation of an organisation, and is in essence the outward mark of respect for agreements between the organisation and its members. The manager must decide on the most appropriate form of sanctions for offences against discipline.

4 *Unity of command* – in any action an employee should receive orders from one superior only; if not, authority is undermined and discipline, order and stability threatened. Dual command is a perpetual source of conflicts.

5 *Unity of direction* – in order to provide for unity of action, coordination and focusing of effort, there should be one head and one plan for any group of activities with the same objective.

6 *Subordination of individual interests to general interest* – the interest of the organisation should dominate individual or group interests.

7 *Remuneration of personnel* – remuneration should as far as possible satisfy both employee and employer. Methods of payment can influence organisational performance and the methods should be fair and encourage keenness by rewarding well-directed effort, but should not lead to over-payment.

8 *Centralisation* – is always present to some extent in any organisation. The degree of centralisation is a question of proportion and will vary among particular organisations.

9 *Scalar chain* – the chain of superiors from the ultimate authority to the lowest ranks. Respect for line authority must be reconciled with activities which require urgent action, and with the need to provide for some measure of initiative at all levels of authority.

10 *Order* – this includes material order and social order. The objective of material order is avoidance of loss. There should be an appointed place for each thing, and each thing in its appointed place. Social order involves an appointed place for each employee, and each employee in his or her appointed place. Social order requires good organisation and good selection.

11 *Equity* – the desire for equity and for equality of treatment are aspirations to be taken into account in dealing with employees at all levels.

12 *Stability of tenure of personnel* – generally, prosperous organisations have a stable managerial personnel. But changes of personnel are inevitable and stability of tenure is a question of proportion.

13 *Initiative* – this represents a source of strength for the organisation and should be encouraged and developed. Tact and integrity are required to promote initiative and to retain respect for authority and discipline.

14 *Esprit de corps* – this should be fostered as harmony and unity among members of an organisation are a great strength. The principle of unity of command should be observed. It is necessary to avoid the dangers of 'divide and rule' of one's own team, and the abuse of formal communication. Wherever possible, verbal contacts should be used.

A number of these principles relate directly to, or are influenced by, the organisation structure in which the process of management takes place.

Relevance today

Inevitably there are doubts about the relevance of these activities and principles today but it is hard to argue against their continuing underlying importance.

Hamell suggests there would be little argument about Fayol's description of the work of the manager but puts forward his own synthesis of what the practice of management entails:

- setting and programming objectives;
- motivating and aligning effort;
- coordinating and controlling activities;
- developing and assigning talent;
- accumulating and applying knowledge;
- amassing and allocating resources;
- building and nurturing relationships;
- balancing and meeting stakeholder demands.[13]

Although there are variations, the basic principles of management proposed by Fayol are confirmed as having relevance to management approaches today.

Managerial roles

The classical view of the manager as someone who organises, coordinates, plans and controls is not always easy to relate to what we see of the work of the manager. Mintzberg, for example, believes that the classical view tells us little about what managers actually do. It is more meaningful to describe the manager's job in terms of various 'roles' or organised sets of behaviour identified with a position.[14]

Based on a study of the work of five chief executives in medium-to-large organisations, Mintzberg classifies the essential functions of a top manager's job into ten interrelated roles. These roles are divided into three main groups: (i) interpersonal roles; (ii) informational roles; and (iii) decisional roles.[15]

The manager's formal status and authority give rise to the importance of interpersonal relationships. As a result of the interpersonal roles the manager is the focus for the collection and processing of information. The informational roles provide the basis for decision-making (Figure 5.2).

Interpersonal roles

Interpersonal roles are relations with other people and arise from the manager's status and authority.

1 *The figurehead role* is the most basic and simple of managerial roles. The manager is a symbol and represents the organisation in formal matters such as signing documents, at important social occasions or welcoming distinguished guests such as royalty. The manager is also available for people who insist on access to the 'top', for example a guest with a serious complaint or a member of staff with a major grievance.

2 *The leader role* is among the most significant of roles and permeates all activities of a manager. This role involves a responsibility for staffing, and the motivation and guidance of subordinate staff.

3 *The liaison role* involves the manager in relationships with individuals and groups outside their own unit, for example other managers, or outside the organisation, for example conference organisers. This role provides a link between the organisation and its environment.

Informational roles

Informational roles relate to the sources and communication of information arising from the manager's interpersonal roles.

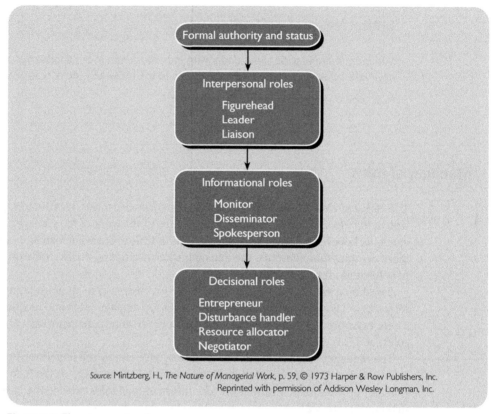

Source: Mintzberg, H., *The Nature of Managerial Work*, p. 59, © 1973 Harper & Row Publishers, Inc. Reprinted with permission of Addison Wesley Longman, Inc.

Figure 5.2 The manager's roles

4 *The monitor role* identifies the manager in seeking and receiving information in order to develop an understanding of the working of the organisation and its environment. This could include, for example, information on occupancy rates, future bookings, levels of staff turnover or weekly wage percentages.

5 *The disseminator role* involves the manager in the transmission of external and internal information. External information, for example the results of a meeting with another manager, is passed through the liaison role. Internal information, for example a request to comply with new instructions, is passed through the leader role between subordinates.

6 *The spokesperson role* involves the manager as formal authority in transmitting information to people outside the unit, for example the board of directors, or to people outside the organisation such as suppliers, guests, government departments or the press.

Decisional roles

Decisional roles involve making strategic organisational decisions on the basis of the manager's status and authority, and access to information.

7 *The entrepreneurial role* is the manager's function to initiate and plan controlled change through exploiting opportunities or solving problems, and taking action to improve the

existing situation, for example by introducing a wider range of low-season offers or improving productivity.

8 *The disturbance handler role* involves the manager in reacting to involuntary situations and unpredictable events. When an unexpected disturbance occurs, for example the sudden and unexplained breakdown of kitchen equipment, the manager must take action to correct the situation.

9 *The resource allocator role* involves the manager in using formal authority to decide where effort will be expended, and making choices on the allocation of resources such as money, time, materials and staffing; for example, a choice might be required between enlarging the leisure facilities and improving conference facilities.

10 *The negotiator role* involves the manager in negotiation activity with other individuals or organisations, for example a new wages agreement with staff representatives or a trade union, or negotiations with a potential new supplier.

An integrated whole

Mintzberg emphasises that the set of ten roles is a somewhat arbitrary division of the manager's activities. It presents one of many possible ways for categorising the view of managerial roles. The ten roles are not easily isolated in practice but form an integrated whole. If any role is removed this affects the effectiveness of the manager's overall performance.

The ten roles suggest that the manager is in fact a specialist required to perform a particular set of specialist roles. Mintzberg argues that empirical evidence supports the contention that this set of roles is common to the work of all managers.

Applications to the hotel manager

Among the studies of the application of Mintzberg's work to the hotel manager are those by Ley, Arnaldo and Shortt.

Head office rating of managerial effectiveness

Ley undertook a detailed observation of general managers in seven medium-sized Holiday Inn hotels in America. The study was concerned with time spent on different managerial roles related to head office ratings of the managers' effectiveness.[16] After classifying the functions of the managers' jobs in terms of Mintzberg's roles, the managers were then rated by their corporate superiors.

- Two managers were rated highly effective,
- Three were rated effective and,
- Two were rated less than effective.

Effective managers appeared to allocate their time among the roles in a manner different from less effective managers. Those managers who devoted a high proportion of their time to the **entrepreneurial** role were judged to be more effective. But managers who worked the longest hours were also rated most effective by head offices and this raises doubts about the validity of the rating system. Although all managers saw the **leadership** role as important, there appeared to be no direct relationship between time spent on this role and ratings of effectiveness. The two highly effective managers actually allocated less time to the leadership role than the two less effective managers.

Time and importance assigned to roles

Arnaldo surveyed 194 American hotel general managers who were asked to classify their activities in terms of Mintzberg's ten managerial roles, and to indicate the amount of time and importance assigned to each of the roles.[17] The study asked the managers to provide a relative ranking of time and importance to the various functions within each of the three main groupings.

- Of the interpersonal roles that of **leader** clearly absorbed most time (71.7 per cent) and was considered of most importance (86.1 per cent).

- With the informational roles, both **monitoring** and **disseminating** were said to be relatively time-absorbing and important. The spokesperson role took up less time and was considered less important.

- Of the decisional roles, all apart from negotiating absorbed roughly equal time. The **entrepreneurial** role was clearly judged to be the most important (55.2 per cent), although a lesser proportion of time (35.6 per cent) was spent on this role.

From the results of this study Arnaldo suggests that the development of training programmes might emphasise the crucial activities of leader, monitor, disseminator and entrepreneur.

A similar study undertaken by Shortt concerned 62 general managers of inns in Northern Ireland.[18] The most important roles were identified as **disturbance handler**, **leader** and **entrepreneur**. The least important roles were identified as **figurehead**, **disseminator** and **negotiator**.

Behaviour patterns of managers

Another way of analysing the role of management is by considering what managers actually do and here the work of Kotter can be considered.

From a detailed study of 15 successful American general managers involved in a broad range of industries, Kotter found that although their jobs differed and the managers undertook their jobs in a different manner, they all spent most of their time interacting with other people and meetings provided exchanges of information over a wide range of topics in a short period of time. Managers had two significant activities in common: agenda-setting and network-building.[19]

- *Agenda-setting* is a constant activity of managers. This is a set of items, or series of agendas, involving aims and objectives, plans, strategies, ideas, decisions to be made and priorities of action in order to bring about desired end results.

- *Network-building* involves the managers interacting with other people and establishing a network of cooperative relations. These networks are outside of the formal structure and often include a large number of people, many of whom are in addition to their boss or direct subordinates and also include individuals and groups outside the organisation. A major feature of network building is to establish and maintain contacts that could assist in the successful achievement of agenda items.

The diversity of management in the hospitality industry

It is frequently suggested that management in the hospitality industry has differences.

For example, from a review of the literature on the nature of managerial work in the hospitality industry, which has focused primarily on hotel management, Wood summarises six principal characteristics of management work:[20]

- People enter hotel management careers via a range of routes including: formal hotel school training, training for management within the industry and late entry after an earlier career in another industry. The last appears most typical of the owner-manager but in general all three routes seem typical of career paths in the industry.

- Hotel management, like other occupations and the industry itself, is very insular. Students are usually separated from general business studies students and their industrial placement training serves as a means of pre-entry socialisation. There is a perceived need for an emphasis on technical skills and competence, particularly in food and beverage management.

- Most senior hotel managers obtain their appointment at a relatively early age. Formal qualifications do not appear to influence either entry position or career patterns or promotion prospects. Vocational education or time spent gaining experience of the industry are alternatives that make little difference to long-term prospects.

- Hotel management positions are gained as a result of substantial mobility. Hotel and catering managers change their jobs more frequently than managers in other industrial sectors. Experience of both front of house and food and beverage is usually essential to promotion. Experience may be gained from frequent lateral moves between hotels within the same company or from moves involving a change of company. Pay appears to be generally linked to size of hotel and this therefore provides another incentive to mobility.

- The degree of latitude given to individual managers in the running of their units is reflected in the conduct of hotel management work. Particular importance is attached to leadership and entrepreneurial roles. Hotel management is dominated by operational demands and time spent in supervision of staff and contact with customers. Managers have a preference for active management and, rather than sitting behind a desk, emphasise the 'being there' aspect of the job. The attitudes of management at unit level evidence a unitary outlook as opposed to a pluralistic perspective.

- Managers' basic remuneration, like the rest of the hotel and catering workforce, is relatively poor. Average salaries for hotel and catering managers are below those in other industrial sectors. Although hotel management careers are easier for some, the work is usually hard and the rewards are perceived, to outsiders at least, as somewhat limited.

The managerial wheel

Addressing the issue of the relationship between expected and actual behaviour, Hales and Nightingale studied managers in a wide range of organisations in the hospitality industry.[21] They identified a 'role set' – that is, the set of people with whom the manager has contacts and the demands made upon the manager from a variety of role senders. In addition to the manager's own perception of his or her role, each member of the role set was asked to identify the demands, requirements and expectations of the manager under study. These were recorded in a 'managerial wheel', as depicted in Figure 5.3. (The nature of role relationships and the role set are discussed in more detail in Chapter 8.)

As might be anticipated, the study found that the unit manager's job is subject to a range of competing and conflicting demands from a wide range of sources, both internal and external. The range of expectation of the manager varied between different sectors and different members of the role set. A main conclusion was that the character of unit management is determined as much by the kind of unit and what is being managed as by the general characteristics of the management process.

How restaurant managers spend their time

Using a similar methodology to Kotter, a study of nine restaurant managers was undertaken by Ferguson and Berger. From observation and documentation of the activities of the managers, their time was categorised as being used in the following five ways:

- desk sessions   17%
- telephone calls   13%

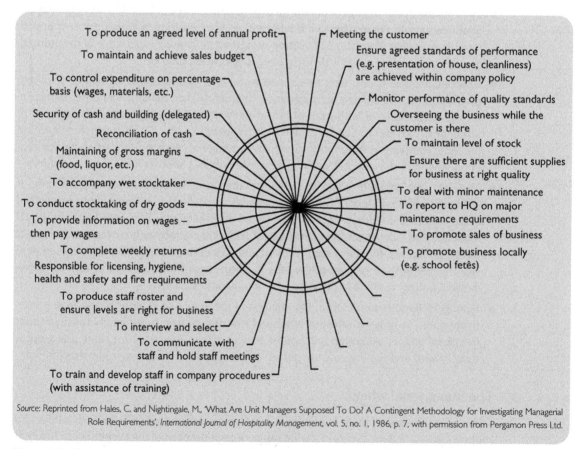

Source: Reprinted from Hales, C. and Nightingale, M., 'What Are Unit Managers Supposed To Do? A Contingent Methodology for Investigating Managerial Role Requirements', International Journal of Hospitality Management, vol. 5, no. 1, 1986, p. 7, with permission from Pergamon Press Ltd.

Figure 5.3 A managerial wheel: expectations of unit manager by regional general manager

- scheduled meetings   29%
- unscheduled meetings   35%
- tours   6%

Ferguson and Berger see the two categories of desk sessions and scheduled meetings as suggesting a reasonable level of structure and organisation, and conducive to organising, planning and deciding. However, from their study, the activities of the restaurant managers seemed far removed from textbook descriptions of planner, organiser, coordinator and controller.

> Mintzberg described executives' activities as brief, fragmented and reactive. The restaurant operators' activities in this study seem even further removed from the textbook description of a planner, organiser, coordinator and controller than did those in the Mintzberg sample. Planning seems to have been eclipsed by reacting; organizing might be better described as simply carrying on; coordination appears more like juggling; and controlling seems reduced to full time watching.[22]

Management by walking about

A key aspect of effective management is visibility.[23] This is particularly important in the hospitality industry, as is confirmed by Ferguson and Berger. Managers need to balance time for themselves with their availability for consultation with staff and customers, and ensuring effective processes of communication.[24]

The approach of management by walking about (MBWA), together with informal communication processes, is often heralded as a positive management practice – and indeed it may well be. However, it is only likely to be effective if perceived by staff as part of a genuine belief by management in listening to and understanding the actual working conditions, feelings and problems of staff; and not with the suspicion of management snooping.[25]

Administrative or mobile type of manager

The approach of 'management by walking about' has arguably always been a feature of hospitality managers, work patterns.[26]

For example, Venison refers to the use of a simple ten-point scale which distinguishes between an excessively administrative type of manager and an excessively mobile and promotions-orientated manager.[27]

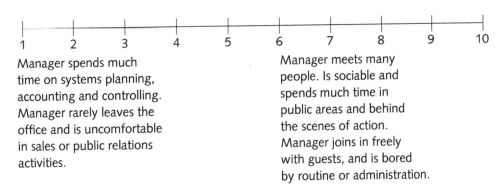

Manager spends much time on systems planning, accounting and controlling. Manager rarely leaves the office and is uncomfortable in sales or public relations activities.

Manager meets many people. Is sociable and spends much time in public areas and behind the scenes of action. Manager joins in freely with guests, and is bored by routine or administration.

Applicants for hotel management positions are asked to indicate their own management style. The majority place themselves between points 3 and 4 or between points 6 and 7. This suggests that the two distinct ends of the scale are recognised clearly and that most potential hotel managers have a natural leaning towards one direction or the other.

Venison draws attention to the importance of the manager being at the 'front' of the hotel and of 'being there'. The manager is then in a position to see employees at work and to get to know them, to check standards of service, and quickly to see trouble spots and to take corrective action.

The ideal hotel manager, however, does not sit permanently at any one point of the scale but is able to move freely from one end to the other as particular situations demand. The 'perfect' hotel manager needs to be comfortable at all positions on the scale. Success in extending the range of comfortable behaviour is an important aspect of the manager's personal development.

The influence of management style

From a further examination of several well-performing organisations in America, Waterman draws attention to meeting the needs of their staff so that they attract better people, who are more motivated to do a superior job and satisfy the needs of their customers. The conclusion is 'people first'. Treat your own people and your customers well and good results will follow.[28] From case histories of hospitality organisations, Lockwood *et al.* refer to the importance of management style linked to the subjects of control, corporate culture and motivation.[29]

The 'being there' style of management and a directive approach to staff is one of the principal characteristic features of hospitality management.[30] In a study of five seasonal seaside hotels, all privately owned and operated and with between 30 and 65 bedrooms, Lee-Ross investigated the influence of management style on employee job perceptions and job satisfaction.[31]

The investigation contrasted a 'hands-on' style of management (whereby managers worked for most of the time alongside operatives and undertook similar tasks), with a 'coordinative' style of management (where for most of the time managers delegated tasks to operatives). It was suggested that, given the nature of hotel jobs, the hands-on managers who work alongside their staff may be expected to have similar job perceptions, be more aware of operational problems and therefore be more effective in engendering job satisfaction than coordinative managers.

Little effect on employee job perception

In practice, however, the concepts of hands-on and coordinative styles of management were often not clearly definable. Management style appeared to result from the demands of the customers, the employment policy of the hotel and the manager's departmental expertise. Managers occupied both roles and were involved at the operative level in certain departments while leaving other departments unsupervised. The study also indicated that although employees who experience a hands-on management approach are more likely to share the managers' perception of their jobs, management style has little significant effect on the way employees perceive their jobs.

Critical review and reflection

'The traditional training of hospitality managers working in different departments as operators, as well as supervisors, is a distraction from developing their main role of attaining the aims and objectives of the organisation.'

To what extent do you think this is a valid criticism of the hospitality industry?

The differing styles and approaches of management

Managerial behaviour

The task of management is to make the best use of staff and to ensure that they satisfactorily meet the standards required of them. It is the responsibility of management to manage. But it is people who are being managed and people should be considered in human terms. The efficiency of staff and their commitment to the aims and philosophy of the establishment are fostered by good human relationships and by the nature of managerial behaviour.

> The majority of staff come to work eager to do a good job and with the desire to perform to the best of their abilities. Where actual behaviour fails to match the ideal this is largely the result of the manner in which staff are treated by management and the perception they have of the managerial function. This places a heavy responsibility on managers.[32]

It is generally accepted that attention should be focused on improving the people–organisation relationship and in creating a climate in which members of staff work willingly and effectively. At the heart of successful management is the ability to relate well to other people. The manager's perceptions of the workforce are a major influence on the style of managerial behaviour which is adopted. **Management style can be as important as management competence.** The general movement towards flatter organisation structures, flexible working arrangements and greater employee empowerment places greater emphasis on an integrating rather than a traditional controlling style of management.

Managers' attitudes towards people

The way in which managers approach their jobs and the behaviour they display towards subordinate staff are likely to be conditioned by predispositions about people, human nature and work. The style of management adopted is a function of the manager's attitude towards people.

McGregor put forward two sets of suppositions based on polar assumptions about the attitudes of managers towards people at work: Theory X and Theory Y.[33]

The Theory X assumptions

Theory X represents the assumptions on which traditional organisations are based and was widely accepted and practised before the development of the human relations approach.

The assumptions are that:

- the average person is lazy and has an inherent dislike of work;
- most people must be coerced, controlled, directed and threatened with punishment if the organisation is to achieve its objectives;
- the average person avoids responsibility, prefers to be directed, lacks ambition and values security most of all;
- motivation occurs only at the physiological and security levels.

The central principle of Theory X is direction and control through a centralised system of organisation and the exercise of authority. Assumptions based on a Theory X approach, and the traditional use of rewards and sanctions exercised by the nature of the manager's position and authority, are likely to result in an exploitative or authoritarian style of management.

The Theory Y assumptions

At the other extreme to Theory X is Theory Y, which represents assumptions consistent with more recent approaches to human nature and behaviour. The assumptions are that:

- for most people work is as natural as play or rest;
- people will exercise self-direction and self-control in the service of objectives to which they are committed;
- commitment to objectives is a function of rewards associated with their achievement;
- if given the right conditions, the average worker can learn to accept and to seek responsibility;
- the capacity for creativity in solving organisational problems is distributed widely;
- the intellectual potential of the average person is only partially utilised;
- motivation occurs at the affiliation, esteem and self-actualisation levels as well as the physiological and security levels.

The central principle of Theory Y is the integration of individual and organisational goals. It is the task of management to create the conditions in which individuals may satisfy their motivational needs, and in which they achieve their own goals through meeting the goals of the organisation. McGregor develops an analysis of the implications of accepting Theory Y in regard to performance appraisal, administration of salaries and promotions, participation, staff–line relationships, leadership, management development and the managerial team.

The manager–subordinate relationship

Although possibly simplistic, Theory X and Theory Y do represent identifiable philosophies which influence the nature of the manager–subordinate relationship. The two views tend to represent extremes of the natural inclination of managers towards a particular style of behaviour.

Assumptions based on the traditional use of rewards and sanctions, close supervision and control, and the nature of the manager's power are likely to result in an exploitative or authoritarian style of management.

Most people, however, have the potential to be self-motivating. They can best achieve their personal goals through self-direction of their efforts towards meeting the goals of the organisation. Broadening educational standards and changing social values mean that people today have wider expectations of the quality of working life, including opportunities for consultation and participation in decisions which affect them.

McGregor implies that a Theory Y approach is the best way to elicit cooperation from members of an organisation. Based on practical experience of hotel management this view is supported by Venison.

> I have personally always tried to manage more in accordance with the assumptions of Theory Y than those of Theory X and my experience seems to concur with much research which indicates that Theory Y assumptions about people's attitudes are closer to the truth. Theory Y, however, does not involve abdication of management, absence of leadership or the lowering of standards. It is not a 'soft' approach to management. It is, in fact, more difficult to achieve but potentially more successful.[34]

This approach is becoming more prevalent, according to Alexakis: 'Theory X managers and leaders are fast becoming a relic of the past in the tourism and hospitality industry. They are being replaced by theory Y types.'[35]

Demands of the situation

Regardless of the inclinations of managers towards Theory X or Theory Y, in practice, the actual style of management adopted will be influenced by the demands of the situation. Even when a manager has a basic belief in Theory Y assumptions, and in the self-motivation and self-direction of subordinate staff, there may be occasions when it is necessary or more appropriate to adopt a modified approach.

When the nature of the job itself offers little intrinsic satisfaction or limited opportunities to satisfy higher-level needs, a more authoritative and controlling style of management might work best. Some jobs are designed narrowly, with highly predictable tasks and output measured precisely. With these types of jobs, a Theory X approach may be needed if an adequate level of performance is to be maintained.

Emergency situations, or where there is a shortage of time or other overriding factors, may demand a greater use of management authority and control in directing the tasks in hand. Consider, for example, the hustle, heat and noise of a busy kitchen where a range of fresh meals needs to be prepared for a large banquet. Many tasks must be coordinated over very short timescales and a more forceful and directed style of management may therefore be appropriate. And while such conditions persist, this form of managerial behaviour appears also to be understood by the kitchen staff.

Where both the manager and subordinates share the Theory Y assumptions this style of management is likely to be effective. However, it must be recognised that given the staffing characteristics of the hospitality industry (discussed in Chapter 2), there are many staff who do not wish to exercise self-direction or accept responsibility at work and may have little commitment to organisational objectives. They have an instrumental attitude to work and seem to prefer, and respond better to, a more directive style of management. There are times, therefore, when the manager may be justified in adopting Theory X assumptions about staff.

Theory Z

An extension of Theory X and Y has been developed by Ouchi, in Japan. Theory Z emphasises trust, less hierarchy and bureaucracy and higher levels of involvement, all of which are frequently seen as more up-to-date approaches to management style.

However, other dimensions of this approach, such as long-term, often lifelong employment, although traditional of Japan, are increasingly less common in Western organisations and even changing in Japan.

Critical review and reflection

'The underlying culture and nature of the hospitality industry workforce makes the adoption of a Theory Y or Z approach impractical. Theory X is much more likely to be successful.'

How would you attempt to challenge this point of view?

Blake and Mouton Managerial Grid

One means of identifying and evaluating different styles of management is the Blake and Mouton Managerial Grid®, republished as the Leadership Grid® in 1991.[36] The Grid provides a basis for comparison of managerial styles in terms of two principal dimensions:

1 concern for production; and

2 concern for people.

Concern for production is the amount of emphasis which the manager places on accomplishing the tasks in hand, achieving a high level of production, and getting results or profits. This is represented along the horizontal axis of the Grid. *Concern for people* is the amount of emphasis which the manager gives to colleagues and subordinates as individuals, and to their needs and expectations. This is represented along the vertical axis of the Grid.

Each axis is on a scale of 1–9 indicating varying degrees of concern that the manager has either for production or for people. The manner in which these two concerns are linked together depends upon the use of the hierarchy, the 'boss' aspect, and assumptions that the manager makes about the use of power and how to achieve production.

Five basic combinations

With a nine-point scale on each axis there is a total of 81 different combinations (see Figure 5.4). The four quadrants of the Grid provide five basic combinations of concern for production coupled with concern for people. These five combinations represent the extremes of managerial behaviour.

● *Impoverished managers* (1,1 rating) tend to be remote from their subordinates and believe in the minimum movement from their present position. They do as little as they can with production or with people. Too much attention to one will cause difficulties with the other.

● *Authority-compliance managers* (9,1 rating) are autocratic and tend to rely on a centralised system and the use of authority. Staff are regarded as a means of production. If staff challenge an instruction or standard procedure they are likely to be viewed as uncooperative.

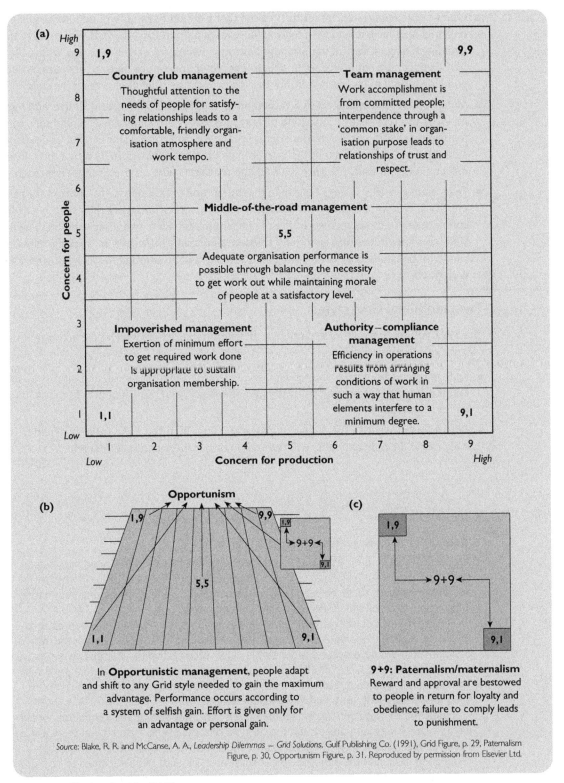

Figure 5.4 The Leadership Grid®

Source: Blake, R. R. and McCanse, A. A., *Leadership Dilemmas – Grid Solutions*, Gulf Publishing Co. (1991), Grid Figure, p. 29, Paternalism Figure, p. 30, Opportunism Figure, p. 31. Reproduced by permission from Elsevier Ltd.

- *Country club managers* (1,9 rating) believe that a contented staff will undertake what is required of them and achieve a reasonable level of output. Production is secondary to the avoidance of conflict and maintaining harmony among the staff. Managers will seek to find compromise solutions acceptable to everyone. Innovation may be encouraged but good ideas tend to be rejected if they are likely to cause difficulties among the staff.

- *Middle-of-the-road managers* (5,5 rating) adopt an approach of 'live and let live' and tend to avoid the real issues. This style of management is the 'dampened pendulum', with managers swinging between concern for production and concern for people. Under pressure this style of management tends to become task management (9,1) but, if this causes resentment from staff, pressure is eased and managers adopt a compromise approach.

- *Team managers* (9,9 rating) believe in the integration of task needs and concern for people. They believe in creating a situation whereby people can satisfy their own needs by commitment to the objectives of the organisation. Managers will discuss problems with staff, seek their ideas and give them freedom of action. Difficulties in working relationships will be handled by confronting staff directly and attempting to work out solutions with them.

Two additional Grid styles

The 1991 edition of the Grid also refers to two additional styles, which take account of the reaction of subordinates:

- *9+9 paternalistic 'father knows best' management* where reward and approval are granted to people in return for loyalty and obedience, and punishment is threatened for failure to comply.

- *Opportunistic 'what's in it for me' management* in which the style utilised depends on which style the manager feels will return him or her the greatest self-benefit.

Critical review and reflection

'Country Club' management at the sailing club

A private sailing club on the south coast was being run for, and by, paying members. A catering manager and catering staff were employed to run a restaurant for the benefit of the club members. These employees were accountable to the club catering committee, which comprised volunteers elected by the club members.

The committee's objectives were for the restaurant to be seen by the members as an attractive facility that they would enjoy and use for occasional meals, as well as for the formal occasions that would provide a focus to the club's social activities. Members were to be encouraged to bring guests, so that the restaurant would be busy and therefore profitable. The committee wanted a relaxed atmosphere around the restaurant, which would encourage members to enjoy, and therefore use, the facility.

Whilst the demand for occasional meals was not as strong as the committee would have wished, it was fairly steady and the calendar of social events ensured that there was a strong demand for meals on these occasions. The meals were perceived by the members as being good value and the atmosphere as being convivial. Staff morale seemed to be high, and though pay was not particularly high, there was low staff turnover.

Unfortunately, although the restaurant seemed to be fairly busy, the accounts showed that the restaurant was producing a financial loss. As a result of this the Club Treasurer asked a catering consultant to investigate and produce a report.

The consultant found that:

- for much of the time, the staff were underemployed;
- staff seemed to be very happy with the working environment;
- stock control was relatively poor and there was a suspicion that staff were helping themselves to food;
- the manager was seen to care for the staff and was well liked by them;
- the portions were too big and the meals were not only good value, but seemed to be too cheap.

In line with these findings, the report suggested that:

- the manager be required to implement proper stock control;
- staff should be made to work flexible shifts to match demand;
- staff numbers should be reviewed, and redundancies made, so that retained staff would be more productive.

When put to the committee they rejected the recommendations, not wishing to upset the happy staff team or the club members.

How do you think the committee should have reacted to the report?

How would you have handled the situation if you were the manager?

If the recommendations were implemented, how would the staff have reacted?

To what extent is this relaxed 'country club' style management appropriate for this type of organisation?

Management by objectives (MBO)

One major, participative approach to management, which directly concerns the involvement and motivation of staff, is management by objectives (MBO). The phrase 'management by objectives' appears to have been introduced by Drucker in 1954.[37] The approach was taken up by McGregor who advocated its use as a preferred means of goal-setting, appraisal of managerial performance and self-assessment. MBO attempts to relate the achievement of organisational goals to individual performance and development.

MBO involves a continuous cycle of interrelated activities (see Figure 5.5) and its basis is the *involvement and participation* of subordinates through:

- The clarification of organisational goals and objectives. These should be communicated clearly to, and understood fully by, all members of staff.
- Review of organisation structure. The need is for a flexible structure and systems of management that make for effective communications, quick decision-making and timely feedback information.
- Participation with subordinates in order to gain their willing acceptance of objectives and targets, key results areas and standards and measurements of performance.

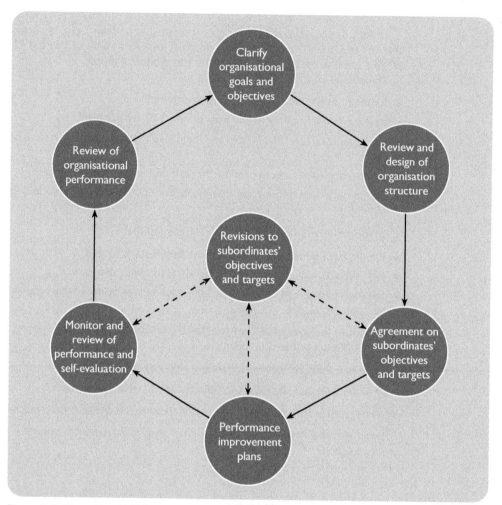

Figure 5.5 The cycle of MBO activities

- Agreement on performance improvement plans that will enable subordinates to make the optimum contribution to meeting their own objectives and targets and improved organisational performance.
- Establishment of an effective monitoring and review system for appraisal of progress and performance, including self-checking and evaluation.
- Undertaking any necessary revisions to, or restatement of, subordinates' objectives and targets, review of organisational performance against stated goals and objectives.
- Review of organisational performance.

Applications to service operations

Some writers also refer to MBO as a technique but it is much broader than this. MBO is more correctly described as a style or system of management. It can take a number of different forms and can be adapted to the demands of different organisations, including smaller hospitality organisations.

MBO appears particularly suited to service activities when it is not always easy to discern clear-cut quantified standards. In hospitality operations objectives and targets could, for example, be related to the following key result areas: (i) ensuring customer satisfaction; (ii) maintaining employee performance; and (iii) protection of assets.[38]

Some obvious areas in which specific MBO targets could be agreed for a stated time period could include:

- an increase in general occupancy rates or in a specific area such as return guests, conference business, restaurant trade;
- reduction in staff turnover or incidence of bad debts;
- control of costs, stock levels, breakages, wastage;
- increase in sales or spend per head in the bars or on other customer services;
- reduction in staff absence, accidents or injuries;
- increase in favourable guest comments/reduction in number of complaints;
- improved profit related to turnover or costs of purchases.

MBO is potentially an attractive system. It provides an opportunity for staff to accept greater responsibility and to make a higher level of personal contribution. Properly installed, and as part of a general participative style of management, there is much to recommend it to both the hospitality organisation and individual members of staff.

Boella and Goss-Turner suggest that MBO is an approach to management which, if operated effectively, influences all levels and activities of an organisation. Although in concept it is typical of a democratic style of management, in practice it is often introduced by other types of managers.

> Where MBO concepts have been used in hotels and catering to set standards, generally speaking it is found that the performance standards of operative staff are 'guest-centred', that is they are concerned with identifying standards of service to be provided to the guest. The performance standards of heads of departments, on the other hand, are 'profit-centred', that is, they identify the cost criteria for producing the services to the guest. Heads of departments are, however, directly responsible for ensuring that the operational performance standards are met by departmental staff, so their performance standards may incorporate quality management standards as well as the 'profit-centred' standards.[39]

MBO has been criticised in recent years for being rather too narrow, in that the objectives set are deliberately quantitative, so that they can be measured. As Boella and Goss-Turner observe in the above quotation, the hospitality organisation performance standards need to incorporate quality as well as profit. A more modern approach that does attempt to combine the qualitative with the quantitative is Kaplan and Norton's balanced scorecard.

The balanced scorecard

The **balanced scorecard** (BS) is an attempt to combine a range of both qualitative and quantitative indicators of performance which recognises the expectations of various stakeholders and relates performance to a choice of strategy as a basis for evaluating organisational effectiveness. Citing the work of Kaplan and Norton,[40] Anita van de Vliet refers to the approach of a 'balanced scorecard' and the belief that:

relying primarily on financial accounting measures was leading to short-term decision-making, over-investment in easily valued assets (through mergers and acquisitions) with readily measurable returns, and under-investment in intangible assets, such as product and process innovation, employee skills or customer satisfaction, whose short-term returns are more difficult to measure.

Van de Vliet suggests that in the information era, there is a growing consensus that financial indicators on their own are not an adequate measure of company competitiveness or performance and there is a need to promote a broader view.

The balanced scorecard does still include the hard financial indicators, but it balances these with other, so-called soft measures, such as customer acquisition, retention, profitability and satisfaction; product development cycle times; employee satisfaction; intellectual assets and organisational learning.[41]

According to Bourne and Bourne most people think about the balanced scorecard in terms of key performance indicators (KPIs) and target-setting, but it is about aligning actions to strategy and showing people what is important. A well-constructed scorecard tells everyone in the organisation where it is going and what they are trying to achieve. It clarifies objectives and communicates them widely.[42]

Thus, the balanced scorecard needs to be designed to meet the needs of the organisation by first identifying what the organisation is trying to achieve and how each person's actions relate to these objectives. In the hospitality organisation, for example, greater emphasis would need to be placed on guest-centred activities and behaviours as suggested by Boella and Goss-Turner.[43]

Management style and international culture

It is recognised that organisations within the hospitality industry tend to be more multi-cultural and multinational than in many other industry sectors. As the UK is becoming an increasingly multicultural society, clearly managers are increasingly required to lead and manage diverse and multicultural teams.

One aspect of cultural difference is differing expectations that workers from different cultures bring to the workplace. This extends to the expectations that these workers have of their managers and their preferred management styles. Similarly, the managers' preferred styles may be seen to be due to their particular culture. It is therefore important that managers recognise and take account of these differences in the ways that they manage their staff.

The work of Hofstede (covered in more detail in Chapter 3) provides a useful model to draw attention to these factors. Four of Hofstede's dimensions that are important when looking at management style are:

- power distance
- uncertainty avoidance
- individualism
- masculinity–femininity.

In a practical context, in some cultures staff prefer and expect clear guidance with consultation being considered inappropriate, in others consultation and participation in decision-making is expected.[44] Some cultures expect supervisors and managers to be close to staff, others expect them to be more distant. In some cultures masculinity and assertiveness are valued, in others care and compassion are more respected.[45]

Increasingly, globalisation and the development of international hospitality companies are providing opportunities for staff to move internationally. If international managers are to perform successfully, they need to understand the effects of different cultures on behaviour and expectations within organisations and be capable of moderating their approaches accordingly. Equally, managers in their home countries need also to take into account the cultures of any foreign subordinates. Reliance on theories developed in one culture is not sufficient.[46]

Table 5.1 indicates some of the cultural differences that will be reflected in individuals' expectations of appropriate management style. For example, the UK worker would expect the manager to be relatively flexible with regard to observance of rules (due to low uncertainty avoidance), and reasonably friendly and approachable (low power distance). The Scandinavian countries expect a caring approach from their managers and recognition that a personal life may be more important to an individual than their work (low masculinity).

Table 5.1 Expectations of appropriate management style

Cultural dimension	High	Low
Power distance	China, Malaysia	UK, USA
Uncertainty avoidance	Germany, Portugal	China, UK
Individualism	UK, USA	Bangladesh, China
Masculinity	Japan, Austria	Denmark, Sweden

Critical review and reflection

'Staff originating from different cultures or ethnic backgrounds require different styles of management.'

How would you suggest this theory be applied in practice in a hospitality organisation?

The attributes and skills of hospitality managers

Attributes and personality

The pressurised nature of the work of a hospitality manager does make certain demands, and to be successful it is certainly helpful, if not absolutely essential, that the manager possesses certain attributes. We have already looked at the desired personality (in Chapter 2). Another and arguably more constructive approach is to concentrate on the general attributes required of the successful manager.[47]

In order to carry out the process of management and execution of work the manager requires a combination of technical competence, social and human skills, and conceptual ability. Although a simplistic approach, it does provide a useful and pragmatic framework within which to examine the attributes of the successful hospitality manager.

- *Technical competence* relates to the application of specific knowledge, methods and skills to discrete tasks, the actual 'doing' of work and day-to-day operations concerned with the provision of services.

- *Social and human skills* refer to interpersonal relationships in working with other people, teamwork, and direction and leadership of staff to achieve coordinated effort and high levels of performance.

- *Conceptual ability* is required in order to view the complexities of the operations of the organisation as a whole, including external environmental influences. It also involves strategic planning and decision-making skills.

Hard and soft skills of management

It is increasingly common to distinguish between 'hard' skills and 'soft' skills.[48] Hard skills are the technical skills required to undertake work and to accomplish jobs. Soft skills concern interpersonal relationships with other people and team-building. (Hard and soft skills can be related to the idea of group task and group-building and maintenance roles discussed in Chapter 8.) Green refers to the importance of the ability to conceptualise how to manage other people. The managerial activity operates along a continuum of hard skills and soft skills. Examples at the extremities of the continuum would be the hard skills of conducting serious disciplinary matters or fighting your corner in a debate about allocation of budgets; and the soft skills of counselling or a member of staff looking for support, advice and empathy. Effective managers need the sensitivity and ability to move along the continuum, and to adjust their attitude and approach as each occasion demands.[49]

Social and human skills

Social and human skills reflect the ability to get along with other people and are, therefore, important attributes at all stages and levels of management, and in the development of staff. The ability to make the best use of people is a distinctive feature of management.

Drucker, for example, makes the point that:

> The function that distinguishes the manager above all others is the function no one but the manager can perform. The one contribution a manager is uniquely expected to make is to give others vision and ability to perform.[50]

The importance of people as a major resource of the hospitality industry is also well recognised.

> The only resources within an organisation capable of transformation are human resources. Money and materials are depleted. Meals are consumed, beds are slept in. Equipment is subject to wear and tear; it can be used well or badly, but can never perform more efficiently than it was originally designed to do. Humans only can grow and develop. Therefore, it is this resource in industry which is both the most complex to deal with and the most rewarding.[51]

The hospitality industry is very much a 'people industry'. Many members of the workforce have direct contact with the customer and people are an essential ingredient of effective operations: they are part of the finished product that the customer is paying for. Customer satisfaction is likely to be affected as much by the attitudes and behaviour of staff as by the standard of accommodation, food and beverages, and other services provided. This emphasises the importance of the effective management of human resources. Interpersonal skills are an especially important feature of hospitality management.[52]

Creative skills

Lashley talks of the need to develop creative skills in managers[53] and the importance of encouraging innovative processes. He proposes managers should occupy three innovative roles:

- *Ideas champion* – a person who generates or believes in the value of new ideas and supports it despite possible problems;
- *Sponsor* – a middle manager who recognises the significance of an idea, and helps find resources for its development and implementation;
- *Orchestrator* – a top manager who explains the need for innovation, provides funding and creates incentives and protects 'new ideas people'.

People a common factor

Jones makes the point that the principal factor that underpins his assertion that services and managing services are different is the role of people.[54] This may be true, but at the same time it also illustrates that people are a common factor in any form of work organisation. The perceived role of people within the hospitality industry serves to emphasise the importance of the social and human skills of its managers.

Managers achieve results through the efforts of other people. An understanding of the pervasive influences which determine the behaviour of people within the work organisation should therefore form a central focus of the education and development of managers.

Theory and practice are both important. For example, using accumulated knowledge of management theory, Mullins and Aldrich have constructed an integrated model of managerial behaviour and development which applies as much to the hospitality industry as to any other business organisation.[55]

The effective management of people

Whatever the debate on the personality characteristics or attributes of an effective hospitality manager, one central requirement is abundantly clear – competence in dealing with people. The one essential ingredient of any successful manager is the ability to manage people effectively. Popular books on managerial behaviour appear to take a positive view of human nature, and support an approach which gives encouragement for people to work willingly and to perform to the best of their ability.[56] However, as many of us will have witnessed for ourselves, an understanding, people-centred approach to management seems often to be lacking in practice.

The culture of management is important. For example, Freemantle suggests that a festering deficiency in management culture is that managers are not really concerned about people until they become a problem. According to Freemantle, the perception of 'people as costs' leads to relatively little weight being given to people management and leadership skills when appointing managers. Many companies tend to appoint technical specialists to managerial positions, neglecting the vital task of managing people.[57]

Despite the particular importance of people within the hospitality industry, it does not have a good reputation for adopting a caring and positive approach to the management of people.

As an industry looking after people, we seem to make an absolute dog's breakfast of caring for employees.[58]

Management in the hospitality industry pays considerable lip service to the notion that human resources constitute a major organisational asset . . . Although the contribution and importance of human resource decisions are often acknowledged abstractedly (i.e. 'our people are our most important asset'), the day-to-day decisions of line and top management often belie this sentiment.[59]

As suggested here, the alternative approach to looking at people 'as costs' to be minimised is to consider them as 'resources' to be cherished and developed.

Basic managerial philosophies

A positive policy of investment in people and an interpersonal relationship approach to management is, in the longer term, worth the effort. It is important that managers have a highly developed sense of 'people perception' and understand the feelings of staff, and their needs and expectations. It is people who are being managed and people should be considered in human terms. A genuine concern for staff and their welfare goes a long way in enhancing organisational performance and effectiveness. In the belief of the author there are a number of basic, underlying philosophies which are likely to make for the successful management of people *and* lead to improved work performance (Figure 5.6).

Consideration, respect and trust

People generally respond according to the way they are treated.[60] If you give a little you will invariably get a lot back. Make people feel important and give them a sense of personal worth. The majority of staff will respond constructively if treated with consideration and respect, and as responsible individuals who wish to serve the organisation

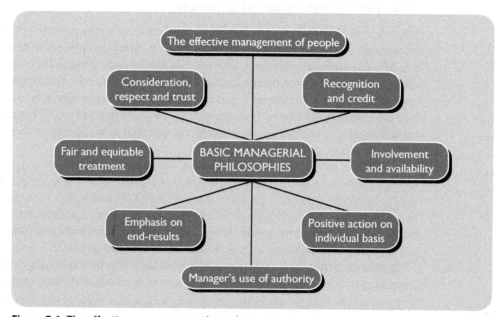

Figure 5.6 The effective management of people

well. 'If people feel trusted they will make extraordinary efforts to show the trust to be warranted.'[61]

From their research of outstandingly successful American companies, Peters and Waterman make the following comment on the fundamental lesson of achieving productivity through people:

> Treat people as adults. Treat them as partners; treat them with dignity; treat them with respect. Treat *them* – not capital spending and automation – as the primary source of productivity gains.[62]

While Gratton makes the point:

> Treat people with politeness, respect and dignity and in doing so create a strong role model for others to follow. Building a reputation of fairness gives you a buffer against the times when the policy is wrong, or you behave badly.[63]

A similar point is made by Lloyd:

> A good people manager believes in the value of people, treats them fairly and with respect: hence that vital element of trust is established and grown. But how often does this happen in practice? Management, of course, involves a combination of what you do and the way it is done.[64]

However, how can members of staff show that they can be trusted unless trust is first put in them? A report from the Chartered Management Institute found that a manager's relationship with their line manager had a powerful impact on job satisfaction and related issues. A high level of reciprocal trust was related strongly to reported levels of motivation and productivity.[65]

Charles Handy writes of the *Trust – Control* equation in the superior – subordinate relationship in which the sum of trust plus control is a constant amount.

$$[T + C = Y]$$

where

T = the trust a superior has in the subordinate and the trust which the subordinate feels the superior has in him

C = the degree of control exercised by the superior over the subordinate

Y = a constant unchanging value

So any increase in control leads to a decrease in trust. If the superior retains more control the subordinate will recognise this, probably show less initiative, and avoid work when possible. If the employee believes he/she is trusted through, for example, delegation or reduced supervision, the employee is likely to show more initiative and take more responsibility.[66]

Critical review and reflection

'The nature of employees in the hospitality industry is such that they cannot be trusted and must be closely monitored at all times. Managers have to exercise a high degree of control over members of their staff.'

How would you attempt to challenge this statement?

Recognition and credit

People can be praised on to success. Give full recognition and credit when it is due and let people know you appreciate them. Managers are often unresponsive to good performance, and appear to take this for granted; but they are quick to criticise the few occasions when performance falls below expectations. Positive feedback on good performance is a strong motivator, *and* staff are then more likely to accept and respond to constructive criticism.

Experience from visits to hospitality management degree students during their training placement year has emphasised the importance of feedback on their performance. One of the most common enquiries is the desire for more information on how well they are doing. If staff are to take a pride in their work they need to know when they are performing well and to receive appropriate recognition for their efforts.

Involvement and availability

Involve yourself with the work of the staff, and make sure you fully understand the difficulties and distastes of their duties and responsibilities. Ensure an open flow of communications, and encourage participation and feedback. Take an active interest in the work of staff but without excessive supervision or inhibiting their freedom of action. Wherever possible be available to staff as a priority, rather than to administration, and remember the importance of giving time to listen to the feelings and problems of staff. It is important to remember what Fletcher reminds us: 'Hearing is not listening. Listening is not a passive activity. It is hard work. It demands attention and concentration.'[67]

Fair and equitable treatment

Treat people fairly but according to merit. Ensure justice in treatment, equitable systems of motivation and rewards, clear personnel policies and procedures, and full observance of all laws and codes of conduct relating to employment. People expect certain outcomes in exchange for certain contributions or inputs. A feeling of inequality causes tension and

If You Catch Someone Doing Something Right, Let Us Know!

Employee Name: _____

Date: _____

(Brief Description On Back)

BEST WESTERN HOTEL, USA

motivates the person to indulge in certain forms of behaviour in order to remove or to reduce the perceived inequity. Equity theory of motivation is discussed in Chapter 7.

Positive action on an individual basis

Treat members of staff as individuals. Deal with individual situations on an individual basis and avoid the 'blanket' approach. For example, it has come to the manager's attention that a couple of members of staff on the same shift have been late in arriving for work. The manager's reaction is to send a circular to *all* members of the department reminding them of the need for, and importance of, good timekeeping. This may appear to be an easy way out to the manager. But what is likely to be the reaction of staff in the department?

The two members of staff concerned might shield behind the generality of the circular and even persuade themselves that it does not apply particularly to them. They might even choose to believe that the manager must be referring to staff on a different shift, and take little notice of the circular. In contrast, the majority of staff in the department who do have a good record of timekeeping might well be annoyed or upset by the circular.

There could, for example, be some staff who, despite pressing personal difficulties, have taken great pride in their work and made special efforts to maintain an excellent record of timekeeping – quite possibly without any previous positive recognition from management. Again, it would be understandable if the reaction of these staff was one of resentment and disillusionment, with a possible adverse effect on their future attitude to work. The manager has more to lose than to gain from adopting a 'blanket' approach to a particular problem and from failing to take selective, positive action on an individual basis.

Emphasis on end results

Good timekeeping can be an important part of the job and especially in a service industry such as hospitality. However, if 'always being there' is not an absolute requirement *per se* for effective performance, what is to be gained by insisting on rigid times of attendance? The increasing movement to flexible working patterns is placing growing attention on what staff actually achieve rather than just time spent at work. The important criteria are the level and quality of service and performance. Even where 'being there' is an essential requirement of the job, managers should place emphasis on end results, and levels of actual performance and achievement, rather than just hours in attendance or compliance with detailed instructions, rules or regulations.

The manager's use of authority

Some might argue that these philosophies are too idealistic and that, given the harsh realities of the hospitality industry, managers need to adopt a more dominant stance. But it is not suggested that managers should in any way give up the right to manage: it is a question of *how* they manage and how they use their authority.

An interesting example is provided by the German hotelier, Klaus Kobjoll, whose hotel has a 92 per cent occupancy and a long waiting list of applicants to join an already highly motivated workforce.

Modern times require a basic shift in the management/employee relationship. There are three types of authority: the God-given sort of Louis XIV which many company presidents assume — but it means nothing to the guy on the shopfloor, authority gained through the exercise of professional skills, and finally authority by 'human sympathy' where you show that you care as much for employees privately as you do professionally. That's the best and highest form of authority . . . If a hotel owner says his staff are working poorly, it's him that needs to change his style.[68]

A caring attitude towards staff

Managers need to adopt a positive attitude towards staff and to develop a spirit of mutual cooperation. Staff should feel that they are working with the manager rather than for the manager.

As an overriding principle on which to guide managerial behaviour, it is difficult to argue against putting people first and a philosophy based on the Golden Rule of life – **manage others as you would like to be managed yourself**. Venison draws a striking comparison between the hotel industry and the retail industry,[69] and interesting and enlightened examples of a people approach to management are provided by Marks & Spencer and John Lewis Partnership.

Make all staff part of the management team

- Virgin pays some of the lowest salaries in the industry yet its staff are very talented and loyal.
- The company's success in this field is down to Sir Richard (Branson)'s management philosophy where all staff feel valued and Branson is just as interested in a flight stewardess's opinion as he is in his marketing director's.
- Successful people management is about inclusion and Branson works on making all his staff like a team where each is valued not only for fulfilling their job remit but for contributing to the development of the business as a whole.

(The Virgin Factor)[70]

Managerial effectiveness

The importance of managerial performance and effectiveness has long been recognised by major writers such as Drucker who propounded that: 'the manager is the dynamic, life-giving element in every business. Without their leadership the resources of production remain resources and never become production'.[71]

The importance of management performance has also more recently been emphasised by Foppen:

Management is of pivotal importance for modern society. It is for this reason that no matter what, thinking about management is of great relevance to management practice. So apart from the question of whether management's claim that it is indispensable is really valid or not, the fact that practically everyone believes it is, is what counts.[72]

The overall responsibility of management can be seen as the attainment of the given objectives of the organisation, upon which rest the success and ultimate survival of the organisation. There is therefore a clear and important need for effective management. However, managerial effectiveness in any organisation is a difficult concept both to define and measure.

Efficiency and effectiveness

Managerial effectiveness can be distinguished from managerial efficiency.

- **Efficiency** is concerned with 'doing things right' and relates to inputs and what the manager does.
- **Effectiveness** is concerned with 'doing the right things' and relates to outputs of the job, and what the manager actually achieves.[73]

To be efficient the manager must attend to the input requirements of the job – to clarification of objectives, planning, organisation direction and control. To be effective the manager must give attention to **outputs of the job** – to performance in terms of obtaining best possible results in the important areas of the organisation, optimising use of resources, increasing profitability, and attainment of aims and objectives of the organisation.

Effectiveness should also be distinguished from activity. Rees, for example, distinguishes between those managers who define what has to be done and get on with it, and those who seek to justify their positions by creating a flurry of activity rather than by the results they achieve.

> The great danger is that, if managers spend too much time simply justifying themselves, they may fail actually to diagnose what they should be doing and therefore fail to do it. Ultimately managers are much more likely to be judged by results than by anything else. Activity-centred behaviour is in any case much more likely to spring from incompetence and/or insecurity rather than adroit political behaviour. This type of behaviour is likely to aggravate the position of the manager in the long run rather than ameliorate it.[74]

Measurements of effectiveness

Managerial effectiveness should be related to the performance of the process of management and the execution of work, and measured in terms of the results that the manager is expected to achieve and the quality of decision-making.[75] But managerial effectiveness is not easy to measure objectively. Managers are judged not just on their own performance but also on results achieved by subordinate staff. The manager's effectiveness may be assessed in part, therefore, by such criteria as:

- the strength of motivation and morale of staff;
- the success of their training and development, and the quality of their work performance (Figure 5.7);
- the creation of an organisational environment in which staff work willingly and effectively.

The difficulty is determining objective measures of such criteria. Some possible indicators might be given by, for example:

- the level of staff turnover;
- the incidence of sickness;
- absenteeism;
- poor timekeeping;
- accidents at work including breakages and the amount of waste.

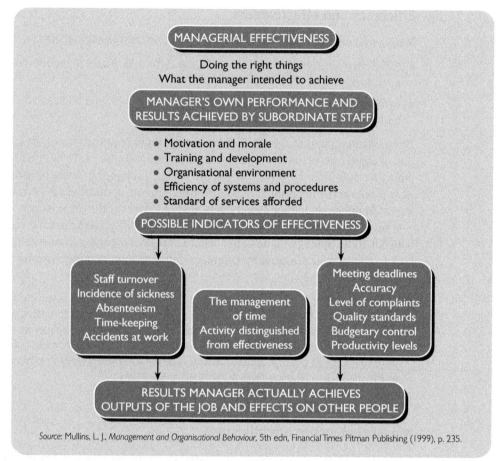

Figure 5.7 Possible indicators of managerial effectiveness

The added difficulty in applying such measures is that figures are likely to be influenced also by broader organisational or environmental factors outside the control of an individual manager, for example: the type, size and location of the establishment, the competitive level of the market, the general economic climate giving a feeling of poor job security or otherwise, company philosophy or general policy directives. In any case there is the general question of the extent to which such figures bear a direct relationship to the actual perform-ance of subordinate staff.

Outputs of the job

To be effective the manager must give attention to the outputs of the job – to performance – in terms of factors such as obtaining the best possible results in the key areas of operations, optimal use of resources, increasing profitability, and attainment of the aims and objectives of the hospitality organisation.

Criteria which *may* give some indication of managerial effectiveness include:

● the efficiency of systems and procedures;

● the standard of service afforded to other departments, and to customers;

- meeting important deadlines;
- adherence to quality standards, the number of recorded errors or complaints;
- keeping within agreed budget limits and productivity such as wage percentage to sales, food gross profit, room occupancy, increase on turnover.

Again, however, there is the question of how to determine objective measurement of such criteria and the extent to which they are under the control of the manager.[76]

Other broad qualitative criteria of increasing significance today are in terms of perceived social accountability, the ethical behaviour of individual managers and the organisation as a whole.

Measuring the performance of managers in the hospitality industry is not easy due to the diverse and varied nature of the work and organisational expectations.

Critical review and reflection

'Disgruntled members of staff are too eager to complain about poor and ineffective management and put the blame on managers for their failure to provide job security or acceptable financial rewards.'

To what extent do you believe this is a valid criticism of hospitality management?

The world of work and management in 2018

A major study ('Management Futures') by the Chartered Management Institute, including a survey of 1,000 senior executives, has investigated how the world of work and management will look in 2018. Among the key findings are that:

The working population will be more diverse. Changing expectations of work and the impact of new technologies will require managers and leaders to develop a range of skills that focus on emotional and spiritual intelligence, judgement and the ability to stimulate creative thinking to improve productivity.

Among the recommendations to leaders and managers are the necessity to focus on individual employees and their needs when developing new technologies; make organisations more human; and motivate people creatively.

A greater degree of emotional intelligence will be required by managers so that they can understand how people work and their likely reactions to change. They will also benefit from having the humility to accept that they are not always the ones with the best or most appropriate ideas.[77]

Critical review and reflection

'The majority of hospitality managers lack the range of personal skills necessary to meet the changing expectations of work, the impact of new technologies and required changes in management styles.'

How would you attempt to justify the truth of this statement?

Synopsis

- Management is a generic term and is subject to many interpretations. The concern in this text is with management approaches within the hospitality industry. This involves structured organisational setting and the exercise of a formal relationship over the work of other people. Management is not homogenous but takes place in different ways at different levels.

- By distinguishing managing from doing we can summarise the nature of managerial work as clarification of objectives, planning, organising, directing and controlling. General principles of management provide helpful guidelines for the process of management.

- In order to carry out the process of management and execution of work the manager requires a combination of technical competence, social and human skills and conceptual ability. Increasing attention is attached to interpersonal relationships, emotional intelligence creativity and the manager as a coach.

- A key aspect of management within the hospitality industry is visibility. The approach of 'management by walking about' is a feature of hospitality management. Interpersonal skills are especially important in the hospitality industry.

- It is the responsibility of managers to achieve results through the efforts of other people. Management style and behaviour displayed towards subordinate staff may be analysed adopting the approaches of Theory X and Theory Y predispositions about people, human nature and work and be described using the Managerial/Leadership Grid.

- Management today takes place in multicultural organisations. Managers therefore need to understand staff expectations in order to adopt appropriate managerial style.

- A major determinant of an individual manager's job is the internal and external environment in which the manager is working. Managerial effectiveness needs to be distinguished from managerial efficiency. Criteria for assessing the effectiveness of a manager should be related to the output measures of the job, which are partly quantitative but should also relate to qualitative criteria related to the management and development of people, as well as the quality of the customer experience.

REVIEW AND DISCUSSION QUESTIONS

1 How would you summarise the essential nature of managerial work? In what ways does the job of a manager differ from any other job in a work organisation?

2 Why do organisations need managers? Give your own views of the importance of management in the hospitality industry.

3 To what extent do you consider the role of the manager in the hospitality organisation may be similar to or differ from management in other organisations?

4 Distinguish between different sets of attitudes and assumptions about people at work that managers within the hospitality industry might hold. Suggest how these different attitudes and assumptions might influence actual managerial behaviour.

5 Discuss how the cultural background of members of staff might influence their perception of preferred management style.

6 Explain the leadership grid as means of comparing managerial styles. What is the importance of team management in the hospitality industry? Explain fully, and with supporting reasons, what you see as the most important attributes or qualities required of a successful manager in the hospitality industry. To what extent do these attributes and qualities differ according to the sector of the industry?

7 How would you attempt to distinguish between an effective and ineffective manager in the hospitality industry? Give specific examples of criteria you would apply to assess the effectiveness of a particular managerial job of your choice.

ASSIGNMENT 1

Select a particular hospitality managerial job and observe the manager in action, preferably over an extended period of time.

1 Make notes of how much of the manager's work and time is spent on:
   (a) the carrying out of discrete tasks and the actual 'doing' work personally; and
   (b) deciding what work is to be done and planning, organising, directing or controlling the work of other people.

2 Identify clearly those factors which determine the demands, constraints and choices of the job. Comment critically on how those factors determined the flexibility in the manager's job.

3 Analyse particular ways in which features of the internal and external environment influence the job of the manager.

4 Suggest the managerial styles that you observe the manager adopting.

5 Summarise the conclusions you draw from your observations.

ASSIGNMENT 2

From your own experience:

1 Explain fully a situation which you believe demonstrates an effective and/or an ineffective way of dealing with subordinate staff. Comment critically on the behaviour, actions and decisions of the manager or supervisor concerned.

2 Explain to what extent you can relate this situation to the application of theories and/or principles of managerial behaviour.

3 Meet in groups of four to six to share and discuss your observations. Make notes of your colleagues' perceptions of the situation and ways in which they support, or differ from, your own observations.

4 Prepare a summary of your discussions to share with other groups in the class.

CASE STUDY 5.1

Jamie Oliver: The Naked Manager?

It would seem that the British are media food junkies. The last decade has seen an apparently unstoppable growth in the number and type of television shows (generally with accompanying recipe books) by and about celebrity chefs. Scarcely any weekend newspaper is complete without its food and cookery section, and almost every possible type of cuisine and food-related angle is covered from domestic goddess to obsessive restaurateur, from food technologist to wilderness survivalist. Websites abound, and there are heated discussions about the quality and ethical provenance of our food. And yet, despite this obsession with reading about it, the British generally don't seem to like cooking and show very limited concern about the quality of what they, and perhaps more importantly their children, actually eat.[1] The catering industry remains one dominated by low pay, stressful working conditions and very limited prestige. Jamie Oliver (christened the 'Naked Chef' in an early series) is a British celebrity chef, and one who has spent his whole career in kitchens, albeit occasionally kitchens full of camera crew. In 2005 he became a campaigner for the provision of better-quality food in British schools after a startling series on Channel 4, *Jamie's School Dinners*.[2] This was followed in 2008 by a further attempt to get the British public weaned off ready meals and fast food through his 'Ministry of Food' initiative. But his approach to the recruitment, training and motivation of the first group of 15 young people to work in his new London restaurant gives a lively example of effective, if sometimes unconventional, managerial behaviour.

Jamie's Kitchen: the project

Jamie himself went into the catering business at 16 after leaving school with no qualifications. His 2002 attempt to inspire some similarly unqualified young people to launch themselves into a career as chefs was followed by a Channel 4 documentary team.[3] The scheme itself was ambitious and required Jamie to fulfil several roles, first being the entrepreneur, as he was investing a substantial amount of his own money in the creation of a new restaurant (to be named 'Fifteen' for the 15 trainees who would work there). Secondly, he was the professional chef at the heart of the enterprise and his name, reputation and style of cooking would provide the basis of the business. And finally, he became a very public manager of people. The series shows his involvement in the recruitment and selection of the trainees, and his contributions to the design of the overall training programme which was in part sponsored by the UK government under the New Deal initiative, but also heavily reliant on Jamie's contacts in the industry to obtain access to work experience placements in some of London's top restaurants. It also shows him monitoring the trainees' development and follows his attempts to inspire and motivate them to achieve standards of performance which would

match his own professional reputation and make the business successful. In other words, the series records a microcosm of management in a highly competitive and pressured business context.

Jamie's management style

The Oliver image is that of a tousled, cheeky but hugely enthusiastic cockney lad-made-good; and at a boyish 28 when the series was shot, not perhaps the stereotypical manager. The events of the series, however, show him very clearly in a managerial role, and some of the incidents illustrate significant managerial skill. Some of his trainees are what would generally be classed as 'difficult' staff; they are unskilled, at times some of them are seriously de-motivated and disruptive, and none of them has had successful experience of holding down a permanent job. What are the key components of Oliver's managerial approach to the trainees?

Vision

There is no doubt that Oliver has a very clear vision of what the business itself should be. His particular style of cooking is based around fresh ingredients, and he has an almost evangelical enthusiasm for the authenticity of produce and its 'traceability' (he emphasises the importance of knowing exactly where things come from, and building long-term relationships with growers and suppliers who share his values). He takes the trainees, many of whom have never really thought about the source of raw ingredients, on field visits to suppliers, farms and markets in order to communicate this vision. He has an equally clear goal, and one which is much harder to reach, of helping unemployed and unskilled people to launch themselves into a career as chefs. This is the people side of the vision: 'It's about training unemployed people to a really professional level. I want them to be employable.'[4]

The early episodes of the series show the recruitment of the initial fifteen potential trainees. A high profile, media-friendly project such as this attracted large numbers of applicants; but the selection process could not be based on more usual criteria such as knowledge, skills or experience since the whole purpose of the project was to offer opportunities for training to young people without these things. Instead, the selectors had to gauge potential and trainability, so a series of tests were constructed as a form of assessment centre, each stage taking place within a few days. At an open day, all applicants were asked to talk about food on camera; the purpose was to identify what Jamie considered an essential quality, enthusiasm or passion about food. The initial shortlist was largely based on these recordings. The next stage was an elimination day when the 60 chosen candidates were put through a 'taste test'. Jamie and three fellow chefs prepared two items for the candidates to taste: a butternut squash ravioli, and a tempura fried oyster. He deliberately chose items which he believed the candidates would not have tasted before, then challenged them to describe what they were eating in terms of textures and flavours. This was designed to find out how well candidates could use important sensory information. Very few were able to go beyond 'like' or 'don't like' and do what he asked, even when prompted. Students were then discussed and the four selectors finally agreed on 30 who would be put forward for a second test. This was a more detailed attempt to assess their ability to observe the method of preparing a simple dish of fried salmon and mixed vegetables, and then reproduce it in the kitchen. Having demonstrated and explained all the elements of the process, Jamie and the assessors were concerned to see how observant the candidates were, and also to watch the degree to which they took control of the process and reacted to the way the food was cooking. As they worked, the observers questioned them about what they were doing, often prompting them to remember the details of the process. The final selection was made on the basis of their approach to the work as much as on the quality of the finished dish.

Having recruited the trainees, Jamie participated in the training process. The trainees received instruction in basic skills at college, but as they progressed he began the attempt to shape them to the needs of his particular style and the standards which would be necessary in the restaurant. This involved classes and demonstrations followed by practical activity (for instance, in bread making) which additionally gave him the opportunity to pay

Case study 5.1 (*continued*)

detailed attention to each individual's ability to do the job. As the trainees began to realise the amount of work and mental effort which is involved in being a chef, some of them became de-motivated and failed to attend college. His approach to the weaker students was personal and supportive; he talked to them individually, paid for travel expenses to ensure they could attend college on time, and even visited some of them at home to discuss their problems. But he expected them to respond and so he also gave them some tough assignments to check their commitment. At one stage he sent them to work the night shift in a bakery for a week, a shift which he shared with them and used as a way to observe their growing skill and determination. Additionally, he was concerned to create a strong team spirit because of the importance of cooperation in a commercial kitchen environment. He took the group to spend a week camping (and of course catering for themselves as a group) on a Cumbrian farm, where they got to know about the business of livestock farming and observe first hand how to evaluate the quality of meat. This too would be important in the restaurant; chefs are responsible for ordering, and checking and assessing the quality of the goods being delivered. They also learned how to make sausages, including a chance to experiment and design their own.

Technical knowledge and understanding

As a chef, Oliver is both trained and experienced. His technical knowledge and ability is very important to the whole enterprise, as it provides him with part of his credibility amongst the young trainees as well as forming the basis for much of their training. The series shows him demonstrating basic techniques such as cutting and food preparation, as well as devising menus and improvising his way around the occasional disaster experienced by the trainees. The second half of Episode 5 shows Oliver putting the trainees together in a kitchen for the first time, with the task of cooking a set menu for 50 guests. He watches them carefully during prep (the hours prior to service), coaching individuals in the application of simple techniques they are learning at college, but which they forget under pressure: which knife to use for vegetables, how to shave parmesan, not to waste egg whites, even how to boil water efficiently

to cook pasta to time. He then supervises with growing horror as service continues and many of the trainees fail to cope, but at the same time observing and praising those who are doing well, or who ask for the help they need to get things right. The orders pile up, some of the trainees become confused and prepare partial orders rather than complete ones, others forget key components so that dishes have to be sent back and re-done; and the time they take to prepare the main course runs to over 45 minutes. One or two become increasingly bad-tempered which causes them to make further mistakes; they argue with Jamie and waste more time. As the whole project descends into chaos, Oliver calls a halt; it was in fact only a simulation and there are no guests in the restaurant. However, the point of this training exercise was to create a real sense of urgency and not only to give the trainees a chance to practise their recently acquired technical skills, but also to give them a sense of the importance of teamwork. It underlined the need to stay calm under pressure, to concentrate on what they are doing and achieve the standards required and, most importantly for their future careers, to show respect for the chef. It is an important lesson for them to learn because the working culture of a restaurant kitchen is one of absolute respect and obedience; perhaps because the work is fast, dangerous in itself and potentially harmful to customers in a way which can cause a business to fold overnight.

Delegation and standards

Whilst he is very 'hands-on' in the management of the kitchen side of the enterprise, the series also shows that Jamie knows he can't do it all. The business side of the project involves accountants, project managers and builders, and the frustrations and problems involved in the actual creation of the premises clearly give Oliver serious headaches. We see the building project going over budget, and experience technical delays and setbacks; and at times it looks as if it will fail to hit schedule or even open at all. Oliver's personality often appears to be the only thing which keeps the project running, and he is not afraid to make unusual demands on his team to achieve the objective (he takes a similarly demanding approach with some of the school dinner ladies

Case study 5.1 (*continued*)

in the *Jamie's School Dinners* series). This is, in part, a reflection of the standards which he sets both by example and in his interactions with other professional members of the team and, indeed, with the trainees. However, he also knows he is a hard taskmaster, and when he gets that extra effort or sees a positive response, he acknowledges and praises the students. This 'hands-on' style shows the value of knowing what is going on as the result of personal observation and attention to detail. In Episode 6, he debriefs the students after they have delivered a successful charity dinner, a challenge which involved them having to cook in a tent in a field outside a stately home, in the rain. He thanks them for their effort, encouraging them to feel proud of what they have achieved as a group. He also evaluates each of them individually, singling out both strengths and weaknesses in their technique and attitude.

Trust, respect and discipline

His technical knowledge aside, another important aspect of Oliver's credibility with this difficult group derives from his own experience as a young unqualified person and his natural empathy with some of the trainees' problems and circumstances. However, he does not let this empathy blind him to their faults and failings, or prevent him from dealing quickly and firmly with poor standards or breaches of discipline. He makes it clear that trust and respect have to run both ways: he bestows considerable trust upon the employees; in return he asks that they trust his judgement and do what he wants. Similarly he respects them as individuals and encourages them to respect each other – for instance by making sure that they all greet each other at the start of service and say goodbye at the end of the day.

If their behaviour is unacceptable then he does not hesitate to tell them so; nevertheless his emphasis is always on their behaviour, and what they need to do differently in the future in order to meet the required standards. One of the technically better students is eventually suspended from the course after aggressive and violent behaviour at college; this cannot be accepted in an already potentially dangerous working environment. In Episode 6 Oliver carries out a disciplinary interview which is in effect a final warning for another two of the trainees who

have been absenting themselves without reason from both college and the kitchens where they have been doing their practical experience placement. His language is colourful but in essence he spells out the problem, explains how it affects all concerned and makes very clear what they need to do next. He explains that their absence not only causes him to waste time on unnecessary phone calls, but, and using the sort of language they will understand, that:

> If you treat them (the chefs hosting the trainees in their kitchens) like shit and you're unprofessional, one, they think I'm a wanker, two, they think the charity is a load of bollocks and three, they ain't going to take on another student. So you're not only disrespecting yourselves, you're disrespecting me and you're disrespecting the students who are going to come on this course for evermore. So this is what is going to happen; three strikes and you're out . . . You've got to behave like an adult, and in return I'll give you my time and I'll give you the connections . . . If you're not going to do that, then go away.

His approach to discipline is quick and consistent; when someone makes a mistake he points out what they have done, explains why it caused a problem, and tells them what to do to remedy the situation; after that it is over and forgotten – at least as far as he is concerned.

Success or failure?

Not all of the original 15 students completed the course successfully; however, some were able to retake exams and continue in the profession, and the scheme resulted in some real success stories for those who did achieve qualifications and subsequently pursued new careers as chefs. One of the successful students, Elisa Roche, has written about kitchen culture and the difficulty, particularly for women, of adapting to an aggressive, macho world.[5] On the other hand, the restaurant itself was a success, and established itself on the London food scene very quickly. The whole idea behind the restaurant and the training project attracted a certain amount of criticism in the press; it was accused of being a publicity stunt and essentially self-promotion by Oliver. The creation of a permanent foundation

Case study 5.1 (continued)

(originally called Cheeky Chops) to recruit disadvantaged young people into the industry clearly shows this was more than a one-off stunt for the cameras. In 2004 Cheeky Chops was relaunched as The Fifteen Foundation[6] when Oliver and Liam Black, an experienced social entrepreneur, went into partnership to extend the programme. The majority of the money to run the Foundation came initially from fundraising events featuring Oliver, but by 2005 the profits from the original restaurant in London made a significant contribution to the Foundation.[7] Franchised versions of the restaurant, together with the associated training programme, form the nodes of the Foundation's activity, and the franchises are expected to make increasing contributions to its revenues in the future. The first franchise opened in Amsterdam in December 2004,[8] the second in Cornwall in May 2006; and an Australian branch in Melbourne was recruiting in September of that year.[9] A further venture in the UK is an online shop (**www.fifteenshop.net**), the profits from sales going to the Foundation. Far from being a one-off, Fifteen is becoming a serious global brand of social entrepreneurship.

Questions

1 Using Mintzberg's classification, analyse the roles played by Jamie Oliver as a manager in the 'Fifteen' enterprise.

2 Critically evaluate the idea that managers can be regarded as Theory X, Theory Y or Theory Z. Which is Jamie? Find evidence from the case to support your view.

3 Carry out an analysis of the manager in this case using the framework provided in Figure 5.6 above.

4 How does Jamie 'make things happen' through the activities of the people he recruits?

Notes and references

1 Blythman, J., *Bad Food Britain*, Fourth Estate (2006).
2 See www. feedmebetter.com.
3 *Jamie's Kitchen*, Channel 4. Available on DVD.
4 *Jamie's Kitchen*, episode 3.
5 Roche, E., 'If You Can't Stand the Heat ... Get Some Balls', *The Guardian*, 28 January 2004.
6 The Fifteen Foundation website is at www.fifteen.net (accessed 5 August 2009).
7 Benjamin, A., 'Recipe for Success', *The Guardian*, 10 May 2006.
8 www.fifteen.nl.
9 www.fifteenfoundation.org.au.

References

1 See for example: Magretta, J., *What Management Is: How It Works and Why It's Everyone's Business*, Harper Collins (2002).

2 Crainer, S., *Key Management Ideas: Thinkers that Changed the Management World*, 3rd edn, Financial Times Prentice Hall (1998), p. 11.

3 See, for example, Wentworth, F., 'It's time we took supervisors seriously', *Professional Manager*, January 1993, 15–17.

4 Williams, P. W., 'Supervisory hotel employee perceptions of management careers and professional development requirements', *International Journal of Hospitality Management*, vol. 11, no. 4, 1992, 347–58.

5 Drucker, P. F., *The Practice of Management*, Pan Books (1968), p. 455.

6 *The Profile of Professional Management*, results from research into the Corpus of Knowledge, HCIMA (1977), p. 20.

7 Brech, E. F. L. (ed.), *Principles and Practice of Management*, 3rd edn, Longman (1975), p. 19.

8 Wood, R. C., 'Theory, Management and Hospitality: A Response to Philip Nailon', *International Journal of Hospitality Management*, vol. 2, no. 2, 1983, 103–4.

9 Drucker, P. F., *People and Performance*, Heinemann (1977), p. 28.

10 *Ibid.*, 59, 28, 29.

11 Baum, T., 'Toward a New Definition of Hotel Management', *Cornell HRA Quarterly*, Educators' Forum, August 1988, 36–9.

12 Fayol, H., *General and Industrial Management*, rev. edn by Gray, I., Pitman (1988).

13 Hamel, G., with Breen, B., *The Future of Management*, Harvard Business School Press (2007) p. 20.

14 Mintzberg, H., 'The Manager's Job: Folklore and fact', *Harvard Business Review Classic*, March–April 1990, 163–75.

15 Mintzberg, H., *The Nature of Managerial Work*, Harper & Row (1973).

16 Ley, D. A., 'The Effective GM: Leader or entrepreneur?', *Cornell HRA Quarterly*, November 1980, 66–7.

17 Arnaldo, M. J., 'Hotel General Managers: A profile', *Cornell HRA Quarterly*, November 1981, 53–6.

18 Shortt, G., 'Work activities of hotel managers in Northern Ireland: A Mintzbergian analysis', *International Journal of Hospitality Management*, vol. 8, no. 2, 1989, 121–30.

19 Kotter, J. P., 'What effective general managers really do', *Harvard Business Review*, vol. 60, no. 6, November–December 1982, 156–67.

20 Wood, R. C., *Working in Hotels and Catering*, 2nd edn, International Thomson Business Press (1997).

21 Hales, C. and Nightingale, M., 'What are unit managers supposed to do? A contingent methodology for investigating managerial role requirements', *International Journal of Hospitality Management*, vol. 5, no. 1, 1986, 3–11.

22 Ferguson, D. H. and Berger, F., 'Restaurant Managers: What Do They *Really* Do?', *Cornell HRA Quarterly*, May 1984, 30.

23 See, for example, Sieff, M. (Lord Sieff of Brimpton), *Management the Marks & Spencer Way*, Fontana Collins (1991).

24 See, for example, Coates, J., 'It is legitimate to be unavailable?', *Industrial and Commercial Training*, vol. 22, no. 5, 1990, 8–11.

25 For a fuller account of MBWA, see Peters, T. J. and Austin, N. K., *A Passion for Excellence*, William Collins (1985).

26 See, for example, Wood, R. C., *Organizational Behaviour for Hospitality Management*, Butterworth-Heinemann (1994).

27 Venison, P., *Managing Hotels*, Heinemann (1983), p. 32.

28 Waterman, R., *The Frontiers of Excellence*, Nicholas Brealey (1994).

29 Lockwood, A., Baker, M. and Ghillyer, A. (eds), *Quality Management in Hospitality*, Cassell (1996).

30 Wood, R. C., *Working in Hotels and Catering*, 2nd edn, International Thomson Business Press (1997).

31 Lee-Ross, D., 'Two styles of hotel manager, two styles of worker', *International Journal of Contemporary Hospitality Management*, vol. 5, no. 4, 1993, 20–24.

32 Mullins, L. J., 'Management and managerial behaviour', *International Journal of Hospitality Management*, vol. 4, no. 1, 1985, 39.

33 McGregor, D., *The Human Side of Enterprise*, Penguin (1987).

34 Venison, P., *Managing Hotels*, Heinemann (1983), p. 56.

35 Alexakis, G., 'Transcendental leadership: the progressive hospitality leader's silver bullet', *International Journal of Contemporary Hospitality Management*, vol. 30, no. 3, 2011, 708–13.

36 Blake, R. R. and McCanse, A. A., *Leadership Dilemmas – Grid Solutions*, Gulf Publishing Company (1991).

37 Drucker, P. F., *The Practice of Management*, Heinemann Professional (1989).

38 Jones, P. J. and Lockwood, A., *The Management of Hotel Operations*, Cassell (1989).

39 Boella, M. J. and Goss-Turner, S., *Human Resource Management in The Hospitality Industry*, Elsevier (2005), pp. 51–3.

40 Kaplan, R. S. and Norton, D. P., *The Balanced Scorecard: Translating Strategy into Action*, Harvard Business School Press (1996).

41 Van de Vliet, A., 'The New Balancing Act', *Management Today*, July 1997, 78–80.

42 Mann, S., in conversation with Bourne, M. and Bourne, P., 'Insights into Using Strategy Tool', *Professional Manager*, vol. 16, no. 6, November 2007, 30–33.

43 Boella, M. J. and Goss-Turner, S., *Human Resource Management in the Hospitality Industry*, Elsevier (2005), pp. 51–3.

44 Browaeys, M. J. and Price, R., *Understanding Cross Cultural Management*, FT Prentice Hall (2011).

45 See note 43.

46 Francesco, A. M and Gold, B. A., *International Organisational Behaviour*, 2nd edn, Prentice Hall (2005).

47 Mullins, L. J. and Davies, I., 'What makes for an effective hotel manager?', *International Journal of Contemporary Hospitality Management*, vol. 3, no. 1, 1991, 22–5.

48 See, for example, Handy, C., *The Empty Raincoat*, Hutchinson (1994).

49 Green, J., 'When was your management style last applauded?', *Chartered Secretary*, December 1998, 28–9.

50 Drucker, P. F., *People and Performance*, Heinemann (1977), p. 59.

51 Mercer, K., 'Psychology at Work in the Hotel and Catering Industry', *HCIMA Review*, 4, 1978, 212.

52 See, for example, Clark, M., *Interpersonal Skills for Hospitality Management*, Chapman & Hall (1995).

53 Lashley, C. and Lee Ross, D., *Organization Behaviour for Leisure Services*, Elsevier (2003).

54 Jones, P. (ed.), *Management in Service Industries*, Pitman (1989).

55 Mullins, L. J. and Aldrich, P., 'An Integrated Model of Management and Managerial Development', *Journal of Management Development*, vol. 7, no. 3, 1988, 29–39.

56 See, for example, Blanchard, K. and Johnson, S., *The One Minute Manager*, Willow Books (1983).

57 Freemantle, D., 'The People Factor', *Management Today*, December 1985, 68–71.

58 Gunn, B., 'Are educationalists and employers in harmony on hotel management training?', *Master Innholders' Forum*, London, June 1990. Reported in *Caterer & Hotelkeeper*, 14 June 1990, 14.

59 Maher, A., 'Accounting for human resources in UK hotels', *Proceedings of CHME Research Conference*, Manchester: Metropolitan University, April 1993.

60 See, for example, Freemantle, D., 'The people factor', *Management Today*, December 1985, 68–71.

61 Martin, P. and Nicholls, J., *Creating a Committed Workforce*, Institute of Personnel Management (1987), p. 97.

62 Peters, T. J. and Waterman, R. H., *In Search of Excellence*, Harper & Row (1982), p. 238.

63 Gratton, L., *Living Strategy: Putting People at the Heart of Corporate Purpose*, Financial Times Prentice Hall (2000), p. 206.

64 Lloyd, B., 'Words, meaning and management-speak', *Professional Manager*, vol. 13, no. 5, September 2004, 37.

65 'The Quality of Working Life 2007: Managers' Health Motivation and Productivity', Chartered Management Institute, October 2007.

66 BPP Publishing Business Basics, *Organisational Behaviour* (1997).

67 Fletcher, W., 'Good listener, better manager', *Management Today*, January 2000, 30.

68 Tarpey, D., 'Handling With Care', *Caterer & Hotelkeeper*, 12 July 1990, 52.

69 Venison, P., *Managing Hotels*, Heinemann (1983).

70 'Management Insights, The Virgin Factor', *Management Today*, May 2000.

71 Drucker, P., *The Practice of Management*, Heinemann Professional (1989) p. 3.

72 Foppen, J. W., 'Knowledge Leadership', in Chowdhury, S., *Management*, Financial Times Prentice Hall (2000) pp. 160–1.

73 See, for example, Drucker, P. F., *People and Performance*, Heinemann (1977).

74 Rees, W. D., *The Skills of Management*, 4th edn, International Thomson Business Press (1996), p. 26.

75 Gore, J., 'Hotel managers' decision making: can psychology help?', *International Journal of Contemporary Hospitality Management*, vol. 7, nos. 2/3, 1995, 19–23.

76 See, for example, Morey, R. C. and Dittman, D. A., 'Evaluating a Hotel GM's Performance', *Cornell HRA Quarterly*, October 1995, 30–35.

77 'Management Futures: The World in 2018', Chartered Management Institute, March 2008. See also Mann, S. 'Looking Forward to a Decade of Change', *Professional Manager*, vol. 17, no. 3, May 2008, 24–5.

Chapter 6

Nature of leadership

Learning outcomes

After completing this chapter you should be able to:

- explain the meaning and importance of leadership in hospitality organisations;
- contrast the main approaches to and studies of leadership;
- examine leadership as an aspect of behaviour, and different styles of leadership;
- explain the leadership relationship and the exercise of leadership power and influence;
- review the variables which determine effective leadership;
- explore the effects that cultural differences have on people's preferred leadership styles;
- evaluate the nature and main components of transformational leadership and inspirational leadership;
- explain the practical application of transcendental or servant leadership.

Introduction

An essential part of the process of management is coordinating the activities of people and guiding their efforts towards the goals and objectives of the organisation. This involves the process of leadership and the choice of an appropriate form of behaviour and action. Leadership is a central feature of organisational performance. The manager needs to understand the nature of leadership influence, factors that determine relationships with other people and the effectiveness of the leadership relationship.

Never before has leadership been a more central concern than in the current decade. Recent events have demonstrated beyond a doubt that not only does leadership matter, but the character of the leader matters. We have vividly witnessed how a leader's actions, values, and ethical standards can affect our global economy and the quality of life for citizens worldwide. Global hospitality organizations, in particular, are profoundly affected by a leader's behaviors and personal characteristics and especially the manner in which the leader relates to and influences followers.

Brownell[1]

The meaning of leadership

There are many ways of looking at **leadership** and many interpretations of its meaning. Leadership might be interpreted in simple terms, such as 'getting others to follow' or 'getting people to do things willingly', or interpreted more specifically, for example as 'the use of authority in decision-making'. It may be exercised as an attribute of position, or because of personal knowledge or wisdom. Leadership might be based on a function of personality or it can be seen as a behavioural category. It may also be viewed in terms of the role of the leaders and their ability to achieve effective performance from others. Leadership can also be discussed in terms of a form of persuasion or power relationship.

From a comprehensive review of leadership theory and research, Bass concludes that: 'There are almost as many different definitions of leadership as there are persons who have attempted to define the concept.'[2] According to Crainer there are over 400 definitions of leadership and 'it is a veritable minefield of misunderstanding and difference through which theorists and practitioners must tread warily'.[3] It is difficult, therefore, to generalise about leadership, but essentially it is a **relationship through which one person influences the behaviour or actions of other people**. This means that the process of leadership cannot be separated from the activities of groups and effective team-building (see Chapter 8).

Changing nature of the work organisation

The changing nature of work organisations involves moving away from an emphasis on getting results by the close control of the workforce and towards an environment of coaching, support and empowerment (see Chapter 7). This places an ever-growing importance on leadership. The leader–follower relationship is reciprocal and effective leadership is a two-way process that influences both individual and organisational performance. Leadership is related to motivation and interpersonal behaviour.[4] A major report from the Advanced Institute of Management Research refers to the dual role of leadership.

Leaders both motivate employees and design effective organisations. There are two broad conceptions of what leaders do – they motivate their followers and they design organisational contexts to enable their followers to function effectively.[5]

Teamwork and inspiration

Leadership today is increasingly associated not with command and control but with the concept of teamwork, getting along with other people, inspiration and creating a vision with which others can identify. According to Levine, leaders need to focus on moving people and organisations forward by increasing the competency of staff and the cooperation of teams in order to improve the organisation. A leader's job is constantly to challenge the bureaucracy that smothers individual enthusiasm and the desire to contribute to an organisation. Leaders will create an environment that encourages the development of skills, learning and openness so that those on their team can participate in the deployment of financial and human resources.[6] A CBI report makes the point that 'effective leaders, who can inspire their people to realise their personal and collective potential, are often the deciding factor between a company being good at what it does and achieving greatness'.[7]

Critical review and reflection

'Leadership is all about determination, personality and innate ability at the right time for a particular competitive situation. Many effective leaders have no formal academic qualifications and each has their own individual leadership style.'

Does this suggest that successful leaders are more likely born to be so rather than trained? To what extent is this particularly true in the hospitality industry?

Leadership in the hospitality industry

Leadership is a central feature of the effective management of people. It is related to motivation, interpersonal behaviour and patterns of communication.[8] It is leadership which gives direction and guidance to the efforts created by motivation. The manager's style of leadership also affects employee job satisfaction and performance.[9] Leadership is important in attempting to reduce employee dissatisfaction.[10] And effective leadership is never more sought after than in times of change and uncertainty.[11]

From a survey of managers in the hospitality industry which asked how leadership should be, it was described as 'the ability to stimulate people to understand for themselves what they should do and be motivated to do it'.[12]

From a study of leadership research in the hospitality industry, Pittaway *et al.* refer to the importance of effective leadership for all hospitality organisations as increasing demands are made to improve their performance, anticipate change and develop new structures. The labour-intensive nature of the industry also emphasises the importance of leadership skills. Although the nature of leadership is a dominant area of study in organisation and management, 'leadership' remains an ambiguous word that is difficult to define with any degree of precision. Pittaway *et al.* found only a few studies of research into leadership in the hospitality industry and suggest that a conceptual understanding of leadership is needed to help to improve the application of leadership research.[13]

Leadership or management

Sometimes management and leadership are seen as synonymous, but there is a difference. Whereas effective management involves leadership, it does not follow that every leader is necessarily a manager. In Chapter 5 it was identified that the primary concern of managers is the achievement of organisational objectives through the use of systems and procedures. Management relates to people working within a hierarchy, and with prescribed positions and roles within the formal structure of the organisation. Hollingsworth, for example, poses, and answers, the question: 'How many managers consider themselves, first and foremost, to be leaders, thereby relegating "manager" simply to their job title? Not many I think.'[14] The confusion between leader and manager is underlined by Cutler, in the critical review and reflection exercise.

Critical review and reflection

'As an industry, we have great management ... We are over-managed in places ... There are too many people in our industry who think that they are leaders, but actually are managers.' (Alan Cutler[15])

*From your own experience, to what extent do you believe members of staff would identify with these statements? How would **you** distinguish between a leader and a manager?*

The changing nature of business, including hospitality organisations, such as downsizing, flatter structures and greater attention to the efficient use of human resources, places growing importance on leadership and an environment of coaching, teamwork and empowerment.[16] However, despite all the attention to, and writing about, leadership, Taffinder suggests that although we know quite a lot about management, we know less about leadership.[17]

Summarising the views of scholars who have attempted to differentiate between leading and managing, Kent draws attention to the following characteristics:

- Managers do things right; leaders do the right things.
- Managing is an authority relationship; leading is an influencing relationship.
- Managing creates stability; leading creates change.

Kent suggests that although the ideas are provocative and stimulating, they provide a basis for a deeper understanding of the dynamics behind two processes.[18]

Critical review and reflection

'Management is a role involving a set of tasks. Leadership is how a person conducts themselves in carrying out those tasks.'

To what extent do you agree?

The leadership process

The emphasis of the leadership process is on interpersonal behaviour in a broader context. It is often associated with the willing and enthusiastic behaviour of followers. A leader often has sufficient influence to bring about long-term changes in people's attitudes and to make change more acceptable. Leadership therefore can be seen primarily as an inspirational process.[19] It does not necessarily take place only within the hierarchical structure. Many people operate as leaders without their role being formally established or defined.

Managers are more concerned with the 'hard' 'S's of strategy, structure and systems. Leaders have an inherent inclination for utilisation of the 'soft' 'S's of style, staff, skills and shared goals.[20] Managers also tend to adopt impersonal or passive attitudes towards goals. They maintain a low level of emotional involvement in their relationships with other people. Leaders adopt a more personal and active attitude towards goals. They have empathy with other people and give attention to what events and actions mean.[21]

Leadership skills and the management of people

Despite the differences, there is a close relationship between management and leadership, and it is not easy to separate them as distinct activities. For example, a Theory X or Theory Y style of managerial behaviour will have a significant influence on the nature of leadership. Many methods of management training can also be used as a means of measuring leadership style. For example, the Leadership Grid the previous was formerly known as the Managerial Grid.

Being an effective manager involves the successful management of people. To be an effective manager it is necessary to exercise the role of leadership. You may recall, for example, that one of the interpersonal roles of a manager identified by Mintzberg (discussed in Chapter 5) is that of leader. The leader role permeates all activities of a manager and includes a responsibility for the motivation and guidance of subordinate staff.[22] Leadership is therefore a part of managerial behaviour, although it is a special attribute which can be distinguished from other elements of management.

The leadership relationship

A leader may be imposed, or formally appointed or elected. The leader exercises authority as an attribute of position or because of a stated position within the hierarchical structure of the organisation. Leadership, however, is more than just adherence to a formal role prescription or a superior–subordinate relationship, as John Adair memorably points out: 'Remember that you can be appointed a manager but you are not a leader until your appointment is ratified in the hearts and minds of those who work for you'.[23]

A leader may also be chosen informally, or emerge through the wishes of the group or the demands of the situation.[24] Leadership may be exercised because of accepted knowledge, wisdom or expertise, or by reputation. It may also be based on the personal qualities, or charisma, of the leader and the manner in which authority is exercised. This view of leadership gives rise to the debate over 'born' or 'natural' leaders.

Leadership is therefore a dynamic form of behaviour. McGregor, for example, suggests that leadership is not a property of the individual but a complex relationship among a number of variables. The leadership relationship is affected by:

- the characteristics of the leader;
- the attitude, needs and other personal characteristics of the followers;
- the nature of the organisation, such as its purpose, structure and tasks to be performed; and
- the social, economic and political environment.[25]

Leadership power and influence

The nature of the leadership relationship can arise in a number of different ways. Leadership influence will be dependent upon the type of 'power' that the leader can exercise over other people. The exercise of power is a social process which helps to explain how different people are able to influence the behaviour and actions of others.

French and Raven have identified five main sources of power upon which the influence of the leader is based.[26] It is important to note that these sources of power are based on the **perception** of the influence of the leader, whether it is real or not. The leader may exercise different types of power in particular circumstances and at different times. We can consider these in terms of the work situation of the hospitality organisation.

- *Reward power* is based on the perception that the leader has the ability and resources to obtain rewards for those who comply with directives, for example pay, promotion, allocation of tasks, responsibilities and hours of work, granting of privileges, praise, recognition.

- *Coercive power* is based on fear and the perception that the leader has the ability to bring about punishment or undesirable outcomes for those who do not comply with directives. This is in effect the opposite of reward power. Examples include withholding pay rises, promotion or privileges, allocating undesirable duties or responsibilities, withdrawal of friendship or support, formal reprimands or possibly dismissal.

- *Legitimate power* is based on the perception that the leader has a right to exercise influence because of role or position. Legitimate power is based on formal authority, for example that of managers and supervisors within the hierarchical structure. The leader's influence arises from 'position' power and not from the nature of personal relationships.

- *Referent power* is based on a feeling of identification with the leader. Influence over others arises because of the perceived reputation, personal characteristics or 'charisma' of the leader. For example, a particular member of staff may not be in a position to influence rewards or punishments but may still exercise power through commanding respect or esteem.

- *Expert power* is based on the perception of the leader as someone who is competent and who has some special knowledge or expertise in a given area. Expert power is based on credibility and is usually limited to narrow, well-defined areas of activity or specialisms, for example the technical expertise of the head chef or catering manager, or the professional knowledge of the accountant or personnel manager.

The five sources of power are interrelated. The use of one type of power, for example coercive, may affect the ability to use another type, for example referent power, in this case adversely.

Critical review and reflection

'The Gordon Ramsay effect'

'The media in recent years has frequently shown the nature of "leaders" within commercial kitchens as being strong, authoritarian and even to some extent involve what might be termed "bullying" yet young people clamour to work for these celebrity chefs.'

Why do you consider this to be so? Referring to French and Raven's work, what is the attraction of working for a celebrity chef?

The study of leadership

Because of its complex and variable nature there are many ways of analysing leadership. It is helpful therefore to have some framework in which to approach further study of the subject area (Figure 6.1). We can examine leadership in terms of:

- the qualities or traits theories;
- the functional or group approach;
- leadership as a behavioural category;
- styles of leadership;
- the situational approach and contingency models;
- transactional or transformational leadership;
- Inspirational or visionary; and
- transcendental, or servant, leadership.

The qualities or traits theories

The qualities or traits approach is based on the belief that leadership consists of certain inherited characteristics, or personality traits, which distinguish leaders from their followers. This is the so-called 'Great Person' theory of leadership and leads to the suggestion that leaders are born and not made. Drucker, for example (writing originally in 1955), makes the point that 'leadership is of utmost importance. Indeed there is no substitute for it. But leadership cannot be created or promoted. It cannot be taught or learned.'[27]

The qualities approach focuses attention on the man or woman in the job and not on the job itself. It suggests that people with certain personality traits or characteristics would be successful leaders whatever the situation. Attention is given to the selection of leaders rather than to the training for leadership.

Limitations

Despite many research studies, attempts to find common personality, physical or mental characteristics of 'good' or 'successful' leaders have met with little success.[28] Investigations have identified lists of traits which tend to be overlapping, contradictory or with little correlation for most features. The lists of possible traits tend to be very long

241

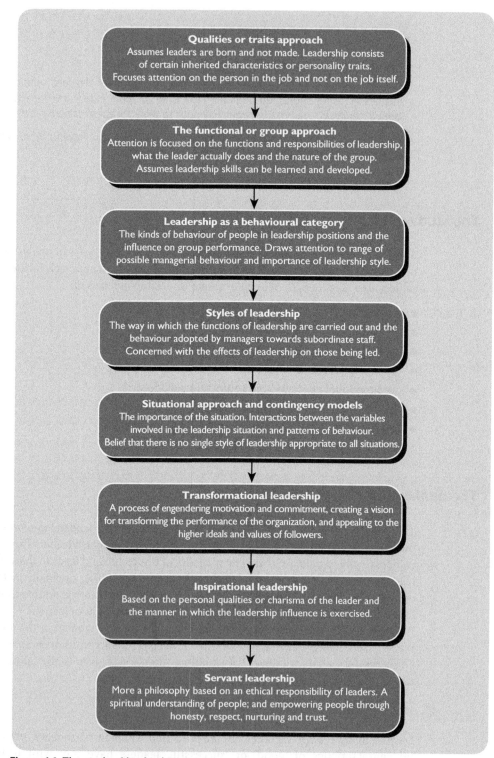

Figure 6.1 The study of leadership

and there is not always agreement on the most important. It is noticeable, however, that such characteristics as individuality or originality usually feature in these lists of traits. This suggests that there is little in common between specific personality traits of different leaders.

There is, in any case, bound to be some subjective judgement in agreeing who is regarded as a good or successful leader. Even if it were possible to identify an agreed list of more specific qualities this would provide little explanation of the nature of leadership. It would do little to help in the training and development of future managers.

Another, major limitation of this approach is that it ignores the situational factors.

Early developments in the hospitality industry

In the early development of the hospitality industry many organisations were based upon the family unit and leadership was closely associated with ownership. Attempts to maintain the dynasty were based on the acceptance of a natural leader with the 'right' of leadership passing down to departmental levels.[29] However, as hospitality organisations have grown in size and complexity, increasing attention has been given to the need for a more broadly based approach to the appointment and development of leaders.

Leadership characteristics of hospitality managers

Attempting to find a common list of those characteristics which make for an effective leader is likely to encounter the same limitations as the qualities approach. Based on the perceptions of a group of catering students who were asked about effective leaders they had encountered, Jacob presents a 'simplistic' profile of a good leader as a person who: has a positive manner; is respected and liked; knows the job; is a proven problem solver; is a communicator; is a persuader; is dedicated to the job; has drive, enthusiasm and initiative; has confidence in own ability; gives praise when due; motivates others to act; does not hold grudges; listens; relaxes under stress; has the strength of character to admit weaknesses; and has the ability to empathise.[30]

Writing in the *Cornell HRA*, Walker however suggests that excellent leadership is not just a matter of talent. The real key to leadership involves developing appropriate personality characteristics and the talents of other members of the organisation.[31]

Experienced managers have generally developed an intuitive ability to evaluate the leadership potential of others. The objective of screening for managerial potential is to locate the individuals whose past experience and temperament show a pattern typical of successful leaders. Walker identifies the following as some of the most important indicators of the appropriate temperament for leadership.

- *Self-control* – potential leaders should be above-average in their ability to exercise self-control as this ability will be most frequently called upon.
- *Sense of values* – the greatest leaders are those who downplay materialistic values and status symbols, and instead respect the intangible, spiritual side of life.
- *Drive* – a strong drive is an advantage in any assignment and a 'doer' is preferred to the person who procrastinates.
- *Moodiness* – the manager should not be prone to inconsistency in personality but be optimistic, cheerful and generally capable of maintaining morale and team spirit.

- *Sensitivity* – people who are sensitive themselves are generally sensitive to others and have a high potential for managerial success.
- *Defence of ideas* – successful managers must be willing and able to support and defend their own ideas while remaining receptive to the ideas of others.
- *Self-awareness* – everyone needs a certain amount of appreciation from others but the person needing less recognition for *individual* contribution is generally more successful as a manager.
- *Balance* – the best managers seem to have the ability to defend their ideas and a low degree of self-consciousness, coupled with a high degree of sensitivity to other people.

Are leaders born or made?

Despite the limitations of the qualities (or traits) approach, there is still a frequent debate about whether leaders are born or made, or whether leadership is an art or a science. The important point, however, is that these should not be viewed as mutually exclusive alternatives. Even if there are certain inborn qualities which make for a good leader, these natural talents need encouragement and further development. Even if leadership is an art, it still requires knowledge and application of special skills or techniques.

There is, then, still some interest in the qualities (or trait) approach but increasing attention has been directed to other approaches to leadership. The focus now is more on what the leader does and how the functions of leadership are carried out.

The importance of the situation

A variety of people with different personalities and from varying backgrounds have emerged as effective leaders in different situations. The person who becomes the leader is regarded as most appropriately qualified, who knows best what to do and who is seen as the most suitable leader in the particular set of circumstances. This gives rise to the influence of situational factors in analysing the nature of leadership. The importance of situational factors is discussed later in this chapter.

The functional or group approach

This approach is based on the process and content of leadership. Attention is focused on the functions and responsibilities of leadership, what the leader actually does and the nature of the group. Leadership is always present in any group engaged in a task. Greater attention can be given to the successful training of leaders by concentrating on those functions which lead to effective performance by the work group.

The functional approach believes that the skills of leadership can be learned, developed and perfected. In contrast to the view of Drucker (referred to above), Kotter, for example, makes the point that successful companies do not wait for leaders to come along.

> They actively seek out people with leadership potential and expose them to career experiences designed to develop that potential. Indeed, with careful selection, nurturing and encouragement, dozens of people can play important leadership roles in a business organisation.[32]

A similar point is made by Whitehead.

> There has been a dramatic change in how management thinkers regard leadership today. Leaders are not born, they say, but made. And the good news is everyone can do it. You don't have to be promoted to a management position. You can be a leader whatever job you do. You don't have to be the boss to be a leader.[33]

The functions and responsibilities of leadership

In order to help understand the process of leadership it is necessary to analyse the role of the leader. The functions and responsibilities of leadership require varying emphasis in different situations according to the nature of the group. It is possible, however, to identify a range of general functions which are served by the leadership position. For example, Krech provides a useful summary of 14 functions:[34]

- *The leader as executive* – coordinating group activities and overseeing the execution of policies.
- *The leader as planner* – deciding the ways and means by which the group achieves its objectives.
- *The leader as policy-maker* – establishing group goals, objectives and policies.
- *The leader as expert* – acting as a source of readily available information and skills, although there will be some reliance on technical expertise and advice from other members of the group.
- *The leader as external representative* – acting as official spokesperson for the group, representative of the group and the channel for communications.
- *The leader as controller of internal relations* – determining specific aspects of the group structure and functioning.
- *The leader as purveyor of rewards and punishment* – controlling group members by the use of reward power and coercive power.
- *The leader as arbitrator and mediator* – controlling interpersonal conflict among members of the group.
- *The leader as exemplar* – acting as a model of behaviour for members of the group and setting an example of what is expected.
- *The leader as symbol of the group* – enhancing the group unit by providing a cognitive focus and establishing the group as a distinct entity.
- *The leader as substitute for individual responsibility* – relieving individual members from the necessity of, and responsibility for, personal decisions.
- *The leader as ideologist* – serving as the source of beliefs, values and standards of behaviour for individual members of the group.
- *The leader as father figure* – serving as focus for the positive emotional feelings of individual members, and the object for identification and transference.
- *The leader as scapegoat* – serving as a target for aggression and hostility of the group, and accepting blame in the case of failure.

These 14 functions help illustrate the range of roles and responsibilities that the leader might be expected to fulfil. Leadership resides in the functions and not a particular person and can be shared among members of the group. When a member fulfils a particular activity which is accepted by members as relevant to the needs of the group, then this could become a leadership function.

Cutler identifies differences between team leaders, operational leaders and strategic leaders, suggesting their functions will vary according to their level within the organisation. He sees the functions as follows:

- *Team leaders* – planning, briefing, monitoring, supporting, setting an example and reviewing.
- *Operational leaders* – informing, interpreting, initiating, implementing, networking, influencing and succession planning.
- *Strategic leaders* – providing direction for the organisation, strategic planning, exercising executive responsibility, balancing the whole with its constituent parts, releasing the corporate spirit and building relationships with all stakeholders and future leadership provision.[35]

Needs and leadership functions

A major contribution to the functional approach to leadership is the work of John Adair, and his ideas on action-centred leadership and the 'three circles' model.[36] The effectiveness of the leader is dependent upon meeting three key functions, or areas of need, within the work group:

- the need to *achieve the common task*;
- the need for *building and maintaining the team*; and
- the need for *developing the individual*.

These areas of need are symbolised by three overlapping circles in Figure 6.2.

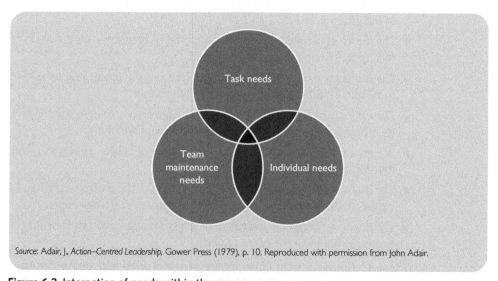

Source: Adair, J., *Action–Centred Leadership*, Gower Press (1979), p. 10. Reproduced with permission from John Adair.

Figure 6.2 Interaction of needs within the group

Task needs involve:

- achieving the objectives of the group;
- defining group tasks and planning the work;
- allocation of resources;
- organisation of duties and responsibilities;
- controlling quality, checking performance and reviewing progress.

Team maintenance needs involve:

- maintaining morale and building team spirit;
- the cohesiveness of the group as a working unit;
- setting standards and maintaining discipline;
- systems of communication within the group;
- training the group;
- appointment of sub-leaders.

Individual needs involve:

- meeting the needs of individual members of the group;
- attending to personal problems;
- giving praise and status;
- reconciling conflicts between group needs and needs of the individual;
- training the individual.

The action by the leader in any one area of need will affect one or both of the other areas of need. The ideal position is where complete integration of the three areas of need is achieved. In any work group the most effective leader is the person who sees that the task needs, the needs of the group and those of the individual are all adequately met. The effective leader elicits the contribution of members of the group and draws out other leadership from the group to satisfy the three interrelated areas of need. The list of leadership functions can be connected with Henri Fayol's classic list of common management activities.[37] Building the team and satisfying individual needs would include leadership. Achieving the common task clearly involves the process of management.

Part of group functions and activities

The characteristics of the hospitality industry, and the nature of the delivery of services, place emphasis on a leadership style which should result in managers and supervisors being an integral part of the functions and activities of work groups.

Adair, however, makes the point that a leader is not there to dominate a group of people or simply to coordinate functions. The leader strengthens unity of a common purpose through the complementary and enhanced efforts of individuals.

> In industry, as in every other sphere where free and able people need to cooperate, effective leadership is founded upon respect and trust, not fear and submission. Respect and trust help to inspire whole-hearted commitment in a team; fear and submission merely produce compliance. Leadership involves focusing the efforts of a group towards a common goal and enabling them to work together as a team. A leader should be directive in a democratic way.[38]

Leadership as a behavioural category

This approach draws attention to the kinds of behaviour of people in leadership situations. One of the most extensive research studies on behavioural categories of leadership was the Ohio State Leadership Studies undertaken by the Bureau of Business Research at Ohio State University. The focus was on the effects of leadership styles on group performance. Results indicated two major dimensions of leadership behaviour, labelled 'consideration' and 'initiating structure'.[39]

- **Consideration** reflects the extent to which the leader establishes trust, mutual respect and rapport with the group and shows concern, warmth, support and consideration for subordinates. This dimension is associated with two-way communication, participation and the human relations approach to leadership.

- **Initiating structure** reflects the extent to which the leader defines and structures group interactions towards attainment of formal goals and organises group activities. This dimension is associated with efforts to achieve organisational goals.

Consideration and initiating structure can be seen as the same as the maintenance function (building and maintaining the group as a working unit and relationships among group members) and task function (accomplishment of specific tasks of the groups and achievement of goals). They were found to be uncorrelated and independent dimensions. Leadership behaviour could, therefore, be shown on two separate axes. A high-consideration, high-structure style appears to be generally more effective in terms of subordinate satisfaction and group performance, but the evidence is not conclusive and much seems to depend upon situational factors. However, later findings suggest that the best leadership style entails high levels of both people-centred and task-centred dimensions.[40]

Employee-or production-centred supervisors

Another major research study was carried out at the University of Michigan Institute for Social Research at the same time as the Ohio State studies. Effective supervisors (measured along dimensions of group morale, productivity and cost reduction) appeared to display four common characteristics:

- delegation of authority and avoidance of close supervision;
- an interest and concern in their subordinates as individuals;
- participative problem-solving; and
- high standards of performance.

Likert, who has summarised the findings of the University of Michigan studies, used the terms **employee-centred** and **production-centred** supervisors.[41] These terms are similar to the dimensions of consideration and structure. The first three of these supervisory characteristics are examples of consideration. The fourth characteristic exemplifies structure. Like consideration and structure, employee-centred and production-centred supervision need to be balanced.

Likert concluded that employee-centred supervisors who get best results tend to recognise that one of their main responsibilities is production. Both the Ohio State and the University of Michigan studies appear to support the idea that there is no single behavioural

Group interaction analysis	Task functions	Maintenance functions
Ohio State leadership study	Initiating structure	Consideration
University of Michigan study	Production-centred supervision	Employee-centred supervision
McGregor, assumptions about people and work	Theory X	Theory Y
Blake and McCanse, Leadership Grid®	Concern for production	Concern for people

Figure 6.3 Two major dimensions of managerial leadership

category of leadership that is superior. There are many types of leadership behaviour and their effectiveness depends upon the variables in any given situation.

Major dimensions of managerial leadership

Despite the many types of actual leadership behaviour, we have seen that there appears to be general agreement on two major dimensions of managerial leadership, a concentration on production (task-orientation) or on employees (people-orientation). This can be extended to include the works of McGregor and of Blake and McCanse (formerly Blake and Mouton), discussed as part of managerial behaviour in Chapter 5 (see Figure 6.3).

Leadership in hotels

Using the dimensions of consideration and initiating structure, Worsfold studied the leadership style of 31 general managers of a major UK hotel group.[42] The managers obtained a relatively high mean score for both dimensions. This indicates good interpersonal relationships with subordinates and an active role in directing group activities through planning and trying out new ideas.

Worsfold refers to the image of the hotel and catering industry as being people orientated with a need to maintain good interpersonal relations. This suggests the need for high scores on consideration. But it is also necessary to maintain high standards, and to establish rules and procedures to which staff adhere. This suggests the need for effective hotel managers to demonstrate high levels of initiating structure.

Styles of leadership

Attention to leadership as a behavioural category has drawn attention to the importance of leadership style. In the work situation it has become increasingly clear that managers can no longer rely solely on the use of their position in the hierarchical structure as a means of exercising the functions of leadership. In order to get the best results from subordinates the manager must also have regard for the need to encourage high morale, a spirit of involvement and cooperation, and a willingness to work. This gives rise to consideration of the style of leadership and provides another heading under which to analyse leadership behaviour.

Leadership style is the way in which the functions of leadership are carried out, the way in which the manager typically behaves towards members of the group. The attention given to leadership style is based on the assumption that subordinates are more likely to work effectively for managers who adopt a certain style of leadership than for managers who adopt alternative styles. Attention to the manager's style of leadership has come about because of a greater understanding of the needs and expectations of people at work. It has also been influenced by such factors as:

- increasing business competitiveness and recognition of efficient use of human resources;
- changes in the value-system of society;
- broader standards of education and training;
- advances in scientific and technical knowledge;
- changes in the nature of work organisation;
- pressure for a greater social responsibility towards employees, for example through schemes of participation in decision-making and work–life balance; and
- government legislation, for example in the areas of employment protection and the influence of the European Union.

All of these factors have combined to create resistance against purely autocratic styles of leadership.

Broad framework of leadership style

There are many dimensions to leadership and many possible ways of describing leadership style, such as dictatorial, unitary, bureaucratic, benevolent, charismatic, consultative, participative and abdicatorial. With so many potential descriptions of leadership styles it is useful to have a broad framework in which to focus attention and study. The style of managerial leadership towards subordinate staff and the focus of power can therefore be considered within a simplified three-fold heading.

- The **authoritarian (autocratic) style** is where the focus of power is with the manager and all interactions within the group move towards the manager. The manager alone exercises decision-making and authority for determining policy, procedures for achieving goals, work tasks and relationships, control of rewards or punishments.

- The **democratic style** is where the focus of power is more with the group as a whole and there is greater interaction within the group. The leadership functions are shared with members of the group and the manager is more part of a team. The group members have a greater say in decision-making, determination of policy, implementation of systems and procedures.

- A **laissez-faire (genuine) style** is where the manager observes that members of the group are working well on their own. The manager consciously makes a decision to pass the focus of power to members, to allow them freedom of action 'to do as they think best', and not to interfere; but is readily available if help is needed. There is often confusion over this style of leadership behaviour. The word 'genuine' is emphasised because this is to be contrasted with the manager who could not care, who deliberately keeps away from the trouble spots and does not want to get involved. This type of manager just lets members of the group get on with the work in hand. Members are left to face decisions that rightly belong with the manager. This is more a non-style of leadership or it could perhaps be labelled as abdication.

Continuum of leadership behaviour

One of the best-known works on leadership style is that by Tannenbaum and Schmidt (see Figure 6.4).[43] Originally written in 1958 and updated in 1973, their work suggests a continuum of possible leadership behaviour available to a manager and along which various styles of leadership may be placed. The continuum presents a range of action related to the degree of authority used by the manager and to the area of freedom available to non-managers in arriving at decisions. The Tannenbaum and Schmidt continuum can be related to McGregor's supposition of Theory X and Theory Y (discussed in Chapter 5). Boss-centred leadership is towards Theory X and subordinate-centred leadership is towards Theory Y.

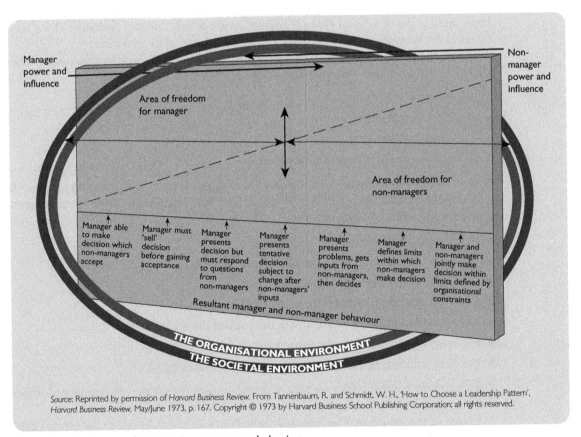

Figure 6.4 Continuum of manager–non-manager behaviour

Four main styles of leadership

Moving along the continuum, the manager may be characterised according to the degree of control that is maintained. Neither extreme of the continuum is absolute as there is always some limitation on authority and on freedom. This approach can be seen as identifying four main styles of leadership by the manager: tells, sells, consults, joins.

- **Tells** – the manager identifies a problem, makes a decision and announces this to subordinates, expecting them to implement it without an opportunity for participation.
- **Sells** – the manager still makes a decision but recognises the possibility of some resistance from those faced with the decision and attempts to persuade subordinates to accept it.
- **Consults** – the manager identifies the problem but does not make a decision until the problem is presented to the group, and the manager has listened to the advice and solutions suggested by subordinates.
- **Joins** – the manager defines the problem and the limits within which the decision must be made and then passes to the group, with the manager as a member, the right to make decisions.

Three main forces

Tannenbaum and Schmidt suggest that there are three factors, or forces, of particular importance in deciding what types of leadership are practicable and desirable. These are: forces in the manager, forces in the subordinate and forces in the situation.

Forces in the manager. The manager's behaviour will be influenced by their personality, background, knowledge and experiences. These internal forces will include:

- value systems;
- confidence in subordinates;
- leadership inclinations;
- feelings of security in an uncertain situation.

Forces in the subordinate. Subordinates are influenced by many personality variables and their individual set of expectations about their relationship with the manager. Characteristics of the subordinate are:

- the strength of the need for independence;
- readiness to assume responsibility for decision-making;
- the degree of tolerance for ambiguity;
- interest in the problem and feelings as to its importance;
- understanding and identification with the goals of the organisation;
- necessary knowledge and experience to deal with the problem;
- the extent of learning to expect to share in decision-making.

The greater the positive response to these characteristics, the greater the freedom of action that can be allowed by the manager.

Forces in the situation. The manager's behaviour will be influenced by the general situation and environmental pressures. Characteristics in the situation include:

- type of organisation;
- group effectiveness;
- nature of the problem;
- pressure of time.

Tannenbaum and Schmidt conclude that successful leaders are keenly aware of those forces which are most relevant to their behaviour at a particular time. They are able to behave appropriately in terms of their understanding of themselves, the individuals and the group, the organisation, and environmental influences. Successful managers are both perceptive and flexible. Forces lying outside the organisation are also included. Tannenbaum and Schmidt suggest a new continuum of patterns of leadership behaviour in which the total area of freedom shared between managers and non-managers is redefined constantly by interactions between them and the forces in the environment.

Critical review and reflection

'The Tannenbaum and Schmidt continuum is probably the single most important and relevant study of leadership. Successful managers clearly need to be both consistent in personality and behaviour, yet adaptable to the three forces that continually influence their leadership style and decision-making along the various points of the continuum.'

To what extent can you argue against this assertion? What do you think is the single most important study of leadership?

Solo leader and team leader

Belbin distinguishes between two broad contrasting or diverging styles of leadership in industry: the solo leader and the team leader.[44] The solo leader enjoys free range, and rules as if absolutely. The leader takes no risks with other people, adopts a directive approach, prefers specific tasks and goals, expects compliance and acts as a model for others to follow. In times of crisis or urgency the talented solo leaders have been effective in overcoming departmental barriers and obstacles, and implementing decisions quickly. However, when the solo leaders fail, they are discarded.

By contrast, the team leader declines to rule as if absolutely and deliberately limits his or her role. The leader creates a sense of mission, expresses greater respect for and trust in subordinates, recognises the skills and strengths of others, and is more inclined to delegate. Belbin suggests that solo leadership is familiar to most people because part of crowd psychology is to seek to be led and to have faith in the leader. However, increasing uncertainty and continuous change together with societal pressure for the sharing of power have led to increasing attention to team leadership.

Attention to styles of leadership

The development of behavioural science has drawn attention to the processes of interpersonal behaviour in the work situation and to the effects of leadership on those being led. The attention given to leadership style is based on the assumption that subordinates are more likely to work willingly and effectively for managers who adopt a certain style of leadership than for those managers who adopt alternative styles.

Attention to the manager's style of leadership has come about because of a greater understanding of individual motivation, and the needs and expectations of people at work. It has also been influenced by broader standards of education and training, changes in the value system of society, pressure for a greater social responsibility towards employees, the concept of the quality of working life and the nature of the multicultural, multi-ethnic workforce. These have all combined to create resistance against purely dictatorial styles of leadership. For example, the demands for organisational change and creating an empowerment culture require employees who are self-managed, and leadership existing not only at the top of the hospitality organisation.[45]

The situational approach and contingency models

The continuum of leadership behaviour draws attention to forces in the situation as one of the main forces influencing the nature of managerial behaviour. The **situational approach** emphasises the situation as the dominant feature in considering the characteristics of effective leadership. There are, however, limitations to the situational approach. There are people who possess the appropriate knowledge and skills and appear to be the most suitable leaders in a given situation, but who do not emerge as effective leaders. Another limitation is that it does not explain fully the interpersonal behaviour or the different styles of leadership and their effect on members of the group. Finally, in the work organisation, it is not usually practicable to allow the situation continually to determine who should act as the leader.

Despite the limitations of the situational approach, situational factors are important in considering the characteristics of leadership. More recent studies focus on the interactions between the variables involved in a leadership situation and patterns of leadership behaviour, and provide another general approach to the study of leadership – contingency theory. Contingency theories are based on the belief that there is no single style of leadership appropriate to all situations. Major contingency models of leadership include:

- **favourability of leadership situation** – Fiedler;
- **path–goal theory** – House, and House and Dessler;
- **readiness (or maturity level) of followers** – Hersey and Blanchard.

Fiedler's contingency model

One of the first leader–situation models was developed by Fiedler in his contingency theory of leadership effectiveness.[46] Fiedler's contingency model was based on studies of a wide range of group situations and concentrated on the relationship between leadership and organisational performance. In order to measure the attitudes of the leader, Fiedler developed a 'least preferred co-worker' (LPC) scale. This measures the rating given by leaders about the person with whom they could work least well. The questionnaire contains up to 20 items. Examples of items in the LPC scale are pleasant/unpleasant, friendly/unfriendly, helpful/frustrating, distant/close, cooperative/uncooperative, boring/interesting, self-assured/hesitant, open/guarded.

Each item is given a single ranking of between one and eight points, with eight points indicating the most favourable rating. For example:

Pleasant	:	:	:	:	:	:	:	:	Unpleasant
	8	7	6	5	4	3	2	1	

The LPC score is the sum of the numerical ratings on all the items for the 'least preferred co-worker'. The original interpretation of the LPC scale was that the leader with a high LPC score derived most satisfaction from interpersonal relationships and, when relationships with subordinates need to be improved, is motivated to act in a supportive, considerate manner. The leader with a low LPC score derived most satisfaction from performance of the task and achieving objectives. Establishing good relationships with subordinates is a secondary motivation. It was thought that high LPC scores would be associated with effective performance by the group. However, the interpretation of LPC has changed a number of times and there is still uncertainty about its actual meaning.

Favourability of leadership situation

Fiedler suggests that leadership behaviour is dependent upon the favourability of the leadership situation. There are three major variables which determine the favourability of the situation and which affect the leader's role and influence:

- **Leader–member relations** – the degree to which the leader is trusted and liked by group members, and their willingness to follow the leader's guidance.
- **The task structure** – the degree to which the task is clearly defined for the group and the extent to which it can be carried out by detailed instructions or standard procedures.
- **Position power** – the power of the leader by virtue of position in the organisation, and the degree to which the leader can exercise authority to influence (for example) rewards and punishments, or promotions and demotions.

From these three variables, Fiedler constructed eight combinations of group–task situations through which to relate leadership style (see Figure 6.5).
When the situation is

- **very favourable** (good leader–member relations, structured task, strong position power), or
- **very unfavourable** (poor leader–member relations, unstructured task, weak position power),
- then a **task-oriented leader** (low LPC score) with a directive, controlling style will be more effective.

When the situation is

- **moderately favourable** and the variables are mixed, then the leader with an interpersonal relationship orientation (high LPC score) and a **participative approach** will be more effective.

Fiedler is suggesting, therefore, that leadership style will vary as the favourability of the leadership situation varies.

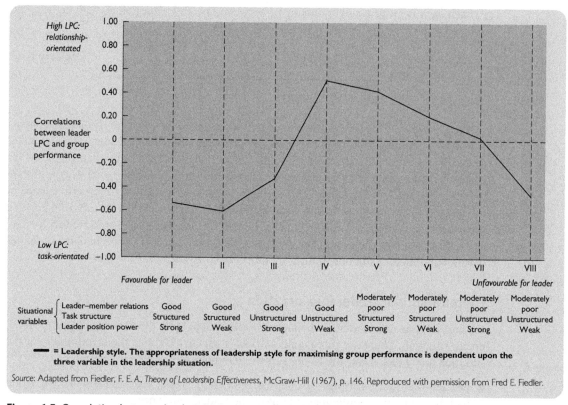

Situational variables		I	II	III	IV	V	VI	VII	VIII
	Leader–member relations	Good	Good	Good	Good	Moderately poor	Moderately poor	Moderately poor	Moderately poor
	Task structure	Structured	Structured	Unstructured	Unstructured	Structured	Structured	Unstructured	Unstructured
	Leader position power	Strong	Weak	Strong	Weak	Strong	Weak	Strong	Weak

▬▬ = **Leadership style. The appropriateness of leadership style for maximising group performance is dependent upon the three variable in the leadership situation.**

Source: Adapted from Fiedler, F. E. A., *Theory of Leadership Effectiveness*, McGraw-Hill (1967), p. 146. Reproduced with permission from Fred E. Fiedler.

Figure 6.5 Correlation between leader's LPC scores and group effectiveness

Applications to the hospitality industry

Although there appears to be some uncertainty about the interpretation of the LPC scale, and Fiedler's work may at first appear somewhat complex, it does provide a further dimension to the study of leadership. Consideration is given to the importance of organisational variables which affect leadership effectiveness.

As discussed previously, the nature of the hospitality industry does make particular demands upon its managers. The nature of managerial behaviour and style of leadership is a significant factor in both staff and customer satisfaction.

> The industry provides the manager, in most situations, with a multiplicity of tasks and very complex interrelationships between staff and customers. Together with this the nature of demand in hotels is highly fluctuating. These factors mean that the hotel manager must be highly adaptable to prevailing circumstances.[47]

Fiedler's contingency model draws attention to the importance of situational variables and leadership style, and to matching changes in the leader–member relations, task structure and position power to the characteristics of the leader. The model would therefore appear to have particular significance for the hospitality manager.

Path–goal theory of leadership

The importance of the path–goal theory for the hospitality manager is that it attempts to explain the influence of leadership behaviour on the performance and job satisfaction of subordinates. The model is based on the expectancy theory of motivation (discussed in Chapter 7). The main work in this field has been undertaken by House[48] and House and Dessler.[49]

The theory suggests that the performance of subordinates is affected by the extent to which the manager satisfies their expectations. Subordinates will see leadership behaviour as a motivating influence to the extent that it means:

1 satisfaction of their needs is dependent upon effective performance; and

2 the necessary direction, guidance, training and support, which would otherwise be lacking, are provided.

House identifies four main types of leadership behaviour.[50]

- *Directive leadership* involves letting subordinates know exactly what is expected of them and giving specific directions. Subordinates are expected to follow rules and regulations. This type of behaviour is similar to 'initiating structure'.

- *Supportive leadership* involves a friendly and approachable manner, and displaying concern for the needs and welfare of subordinates. This type of behaviour is similar to 'consideration'.

- *Participative leadership* involves consulting with subordinates, and the evaluation of their opinions and suggestions before the manager makes the decision.

- *Achievement-orientated leadership* involves setting challenging goals for subordinates, seeking improvement in their performance and showing confidence in their ability to perform well.

Two main situational factors

According to path–goal theory, the effect of leadership behaviour is determined by two main situational factors: the personality characteristics of subordinates; and the nature of the task (Figure 6.6).

- **The personal characteristics** of subordinates determine how they will react to the manager's behaviour and the extent to which they perceive such behaviour as an immediate or potential source of need satisfaction.

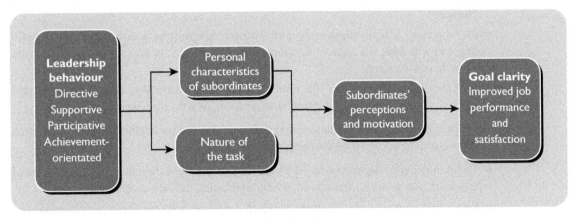

Figure 6.6 Representation of the path–goal theory of leadership

- **The nature of the task** relates to the extent that it is routine and structured, or non-routine and unstructured.

These situational factors determine the subordinates' perceptions and motivation, which in turn lead to improved goal clarity, performance and job satisfaction. The situational factors also influence the subordinates' preferences for a particular style of managerial behaviour. For example, when a task is highly structured, the goals are readily apparent and subordinates are confident, then a directive style of leadership may not be welcomed. However, when a task is highly unstructured, the nature of the goals is not clear and subordinates lack experience, then a more directive style of leadership may be welcomed.

Different types of behaviour can be practised by the same person at different times in varying situations. By using one of the four styles of leadership the manager attempts to influence subordinates' perceptions and motivation, and smooth the path to their goals. Effective leadership is based on both the willingness of the manager to help subordinates, and the needs of subordinates for help. Leadership behaviour will be motivational to the extent that it provides necessary direction, guidance and support, helps clarify path–goal relationships and removes any obstacles which hinder the attainment of goals.

Readiness (or maturity level) of followers

A major variable in the style of leadership adopted by the hospitality manager is the nature of subordinate staff. This leads to consideration of another important contingency model – the **situational leadership model** presented by **Hersey and Blanchard**.[51] The model is based on the 'readiness' level of the people the leader is attempting to influence. Readiness (formerly called 'maturity') is the extent to which followers have the ability and willingness to accomplish a specific task. It is not a characteristic of the individual, but how ready the individual is to perform a particular task.

Readiness (R) is divided into a continuum of four levels: R1 (low), R2 and R3 (moderate), and R4 (high).

- *R1 – low follower readiness.* This refers to followers who are both unable and unwilling, and who lack commitment and motivation, or who are unable and insecure.

- *R2 – low to moderate follower readiness.* This refers to followers who are unable but willing, and who lack ability but are motivated to make an effort, or who are unable but confident.

- *R3 – moderate to high follower readiness.* This refers to followers who are able but unwilling, and who have the ability to perform but are unwilling to apply their ability, or who are able but insecure.

- *R4 – high follower readiness.* This refers to followers who are both able and willing, and who have the ability and commitment to perform, or who are able and confident.

For each of the four levels of readiness, the appropriate style of leadership is a combination of task behaviour and relationship behaviour (Figure 6.7).

- *Task behaviour* is the extent to which the leader provides directions for the actions of followers, sets goals for them, and defines their roles and how to undertake them.

- *Relationship behaviour* is the extent to which the leader engages in two-way communications with followers, listens to them, and provides support and encouragement.

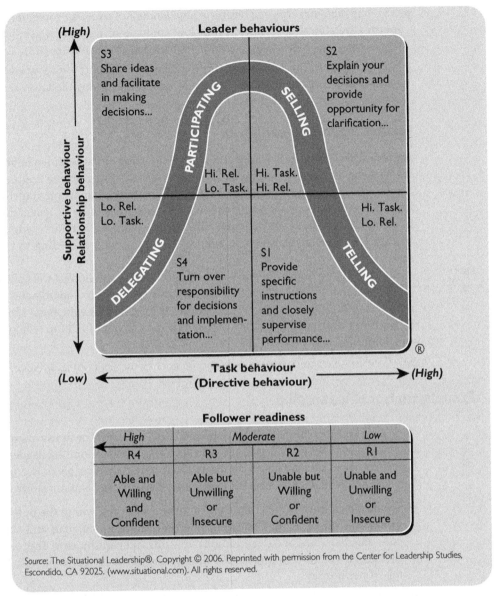

Figure 6.7 Situational Leadership® model

Four leadership styles

The combination of task behaviour and relationship behaviour produces four leadership styles (S): telling, selling, participating and delegating.

- *S1 – telling*. This emphasises high amounts of guidance (task behaviour) but limited supportive (relationship) behaviour. This style is most appropriate for low follower readiness (R1).

- *S2 – selling*. This emphasises high amounts of both directive (task) and relationship behaviour. This style is most appropriate for low to moderate follower readiness (R2).

- *S3 – participating.* This emphasises a high amount of two-way communication and supportive (relationship) behaviour but low amounts of guidance (task behaviour). This style is most appropriate for moderate to high follower readiness (R3).
- *S4 – delegating.* This emphasises little direction or support with low levels of task and relationship behaviour. This style is most appropriate for high follower readiness (R4).

Flexible leadership behaviour

According to Hersey and Blanchard, the key to using situational leadership is that any leader behaviour may be more or less effective depending on the readiness of the followers whom the leader is attempting to influence. An important contribution for the hospitality manager is therefore the need for a flexible style of leadership behaviour. It is important to treat subordinates differently according to their 'readiness' (or maturity level), and to treat the same subordinate differently according to changes in the situation.

The model also draws attention to the importance of developing the ability, confidence and commitment of subordinates. The manager should help subordinates to develop in readiness to the extent that they are able and willing. This development should take place by adjusting leadership behaviour through the four styles of telling, selling, participating and delegating.

Transformational leadership

Increasing business competition and the need for the most efficient use of human resources have resulted in writers on management focusing attention on how leaders revitalise or transform organisations. Based on the work of Burns, this has given rise to a distinction between two fundamental forms of leadership: transactional and transformational.[52]

- *Transactional leadership* is based on legitimate authority within the bureaucratic structure of the organisation. The emphasis is on clarification of goals and objectives, work tasks and outcomes, and organisational rewards and punishments. Transactional leadership appeals to the self-interest of followers and an exchange process of: 'I will give you this, if you do that.'
- *Transformational leadership* is a process of engendering higher levels of motivation and commitment among followers. The emphasis is on generating a vision for the organisation and the leader's ability to appeal to higher ideals and values of followers, and creating a feeling of justice, loyalty and trust. In the organisational sense, transformational leadership is about transforming the performance or fortunes of a business.

Components of transformational leadership

According to Bass, the transformational leader motivates followers to do more than originally expected and the extent of transformation is measured in terms of the leader's effects on followers. Bass proposed a theory of transformational leadership which argues that the leader transforms and motivates followers by:

1 generating greater awareness of the importance of the purpose of the organisation and task outcomes;

2 inducing them to transcend their own self-interests for the sake of the organisation or team; and

3 activating their higher-order needs.[53]

Transformational leadership is comprised of four basic components:

- *idealised influence* – the charisma of the leader and the respect and admiration of the followers;

- *inspirational motivation* – the behaviour of the leader which provides meaning and challenge to the work of the followers;

- *intellectual stimulation* – leaders who solicit new and novel approaches for the performance of work and creative problem solutions from followers; and

- *individualised consideration* – leaders who listen and give special concern to the growth and developmental needs of followers.[54]

Yukl provides a set of guidelines for transformational leadership:

- **Articulate a clear and appealing vision** of what the organisation could accomplish or become to help people understand the purpose, objectives and priorities of the organisation, and to help guide the actions and decisions of members.

- **Explain how the vision can be attained** and establish a clear link between the vision and a credible conventional yet straightforward strategy for attaining it.

- **Act confident and optimistic** about likely success, demonstrate self-confidence and conviction, and emphasise positive aspects of the vision rather than the obstacles and dangers.

- **Express confidence in followers** and their ability to carry out the strategy for accomplishing the vision, especially when the task is difficult or dangerous, or when members lack confidence in themselves.

- **Use dramatic, symbolic actions to emphasise key values** and demonstrate leadership behaviour through dramatic, highly visible actions including risking personal loss, self-sacrifice or acting unconventionally.

- **Lead by example** by recognising that actions speak louder than words, through exemplary behaviour in day-to-day interactions with subordinates and by demonstrating consistency in daily behaviour.[55]

Transformational leadership in the hospitality industry

A number of articles have drawn attention to the increasing complexity of, and dramatic changes that have occurred within, the hospitality industry, and to the importance and benefits of transformational leadership.[56]

From their study of 291 managers in 47 US lodging properties, Tracey and Hinkin conclude that:

> It is unlikely that the hospitality industry will become any more stable or less complex in future. As such, transformational leadership, exemplified by the ability to create and communicate a vision and adapt the organisation to a rapidly changing environment, may be the most crucial type of leadership in the years to come.[57]

261

Clark, Hartline and Jones suggest that a transformational leadership style is likely to be most appropriate when managing front-line hotel employees.[58] However, Brown and Arendt in their study of transformational leadership behaviours and subordinates' performance in hotels found there was no significant relationship between supervisors' transformational leadership dimensions and employees' performance. [59]

Inspirational (or visionary) leadership

> Now the big question is whether you are born with **charisma** or whether you can develop it. I believe you can develop elements of it. For example, you can take courses to improve your speaking skills. You can learn to stage events that send powerful messages. You can learn to think more critically about the status quo and its shortcomings. You can do more on a daily basis to motivate your team. What you simply cannot learn is how to be passionate about what you do. You have to discover that for yourself, and passion is a big part of what drives a charismatic leader. It is also what motivates and inspires those who work for the charismatic leader.[60]

Many writers see transformational leadership as the same thing as charismatic, visionary or inspirational leadership. Kreitner *et al.* refer to **charismatic** leadership as **transforming** employees to pursue organisational goals over self-interests:

> Charismatic leaders transform followers by creating changes in their goals, values, needs, beliefs, and aspirations. They accomplish this transformation by appealing to followers' self-concepts – namely, their values and personal identity.[61]

On the other hand, Hunt suggests that while charismatic leaders can have a tremendous effect on members of an organisation there is no guarantee that this will be positive. What really matters is the nature of outputs and that the leadership mobilises power to change social systems and reform organisations.[62] Similarly, writers such as Burns and Bass identified leaders by their actions and the impact those actions have on other people.

Successful transformational leaders are usually identified in terms of providing a strong vision and sense of mission, arousing strong emotions in followers and a sense of identification with the leader. As mentioned at the start of this chapter, leadership today is increasingly associated with the concept of creating a vision with which others can identify, getting along with other people and providing inspiration. This might be considered as part of transformational leadership or, arguably, a new approach to leadership – that of **inspirational** or **visionary leadership**. Inspirational leadership is concerned not so much with the theory of leadership but more with the skills of motivating and inspiring people.

The importance of vision

Effective transformational leaders are those who inspire people and create a vision for the organisation and its future direction. According to Whitehead:

> The big word now associated with leadership is vision. The ability to see the bigger picture. To take the long-term view. What the ultimate objectives of the organisation are and how people can work together to achieve them ... Perhaps the most important attribute is that a

good leader inspires people by creating a climate where it is OK for people to make mistakes and learn from them, rather than what happened in the past which was to blame and punish them. Leading from this position, they gain a higher level of commitment from their people than mere compliance.[63]

Kahan sees visionary leadership as transformative. It involves greatness, penetrating the ordinary, and requires total involvement. Among the qualities visionary leaders cultivate are imagination, engagement, tangible results and penetrating self-reflection. They engage society with its competitive, divergent viewpoints. Visionary leadership is ultimately about increasing performance but also brings the rewards of tangible results to your membership and deep personal satisfaction.[64]

Leadership is not about the leader, it is about how he or she builds the confidence of everyone else. Leaders are responsible for both the big structures that serve as the cornerstone of confidence, and for the human touches that shape a positive emotional climate to inspire and motivate people . . . Leaders deliver confidence by espousing high standards in their messages, exemplifying these standards in the conduct they model and establishing formal mechanisms to provide a structure for acting on those standards.[65]

Critical review and reflection

'Charisma and the ability truly to inspire and move loyal followers in the desired direction is one of the most controversial and elusive leadership qualities.'

Do you believe charismatic leadership brings about improved individual and organisational performance? Can you relate personal experience(s) of charismatic leadership that has truly inspired? Do you possess charisma?

Personal qualities or charisma

Leadership may be based on the personal qualities, or charisma, of the leader and the manner in which influence is exercised. The concept of charismatic or inspirational leadership is not new and has been applied in the organisational context by writers such as Max Weber.[66] The importance of charisma for effective leadership today is emphasised by Conger, who also believes that many of the traits that make a successful leader can be taught, including charisma.

Berger and Brownell refer to the power of speech as being a dimension of charisma. They point out that 'hotel or restaurant managers cannot indulge in high level oratory',[67] but that it is important for managers to communicate clearly and confidently and those who are sure of their own beliefs are more likely to inspire confidence in their leadership.

Is charisma enough?

However, the extent to which charismatic or inspirational leadership helps bring about improvement in organisational performance is open to much debate. Conger also draws attention to the danger that the leader's vision, dynamism and inspirational nature are highly attractive to followers, which leads to a natural dependence. Staff see this extraordinary figure as a model to be emulated and the leader's abilities become the yardstick by which they measure their own performance. This is a potential source of leadership derailment. Dependence makes the followers more susceptible to deception.[68]

Dearlove draws attention to the increasing focus on leaders as real people managing in a consensus-seeking manner. 'While traditional views of leadership tend eventually to concentrate on vision and charisma, the message now seems to be that charisma is no longer enough to carry leaders through.'[69] Bloomfield also refers to the cult of the individual, supposedly charismatic leader and the danger that this leads businesses into deep water far more often than the application of rational leadership. Too often the charismatic leader, aided and abetted by the language of current management fashion, attempts to 'inspire', to delight with their vision and to produce a mission statement of where the business might be – at the expense of real substance.[70]

Adair argues that to be a truly inspirational leader one must understand the spirit within. All people have the potential for greatness. The inspirational leader connects with the led, appreciates the capabilities of others and through trust will unlock the powers in others. Adair refers to 'the inspired moment' – a recognition and seizure of a brief window of opportunity that can act as a powerful catalyst that inspires both the leader and the led.[71]

Cutler points out the dangers of charismatic leadership: 'They . . . (charismatic leaders). . . believe in themselves so highly that they can easily be persuaded they are infallible and will ignore advice and warnings.'[72] He also points out that the charismatic leader with an influential position, who has been intolerant of challenge and reliant on the power of his/her personality, will be difficult to replace. In these cases it is likely that there will be no obvious successor.

He suggests that a leader need not be charismatic 'to be an effective even an inspirational leader' and he notes that some great American companies have had leaders who were 'self effacing individuals who did not seek the spotlight in any way'.[73] They were ambitious but the ambition was for the institution not for themselves.

Critical review and reflection

'The hospitality industry, being so people-centred and customer-driven, needs more inspirational leadership in all its sectors.' (John Adair)[74]

To what extent do you agree? Identify examples where you or others have been inspired by the leader. How would you attempt to inspire others?

Need for visionary leadership

Many writers are calling for leaders at all levels with vision and who can inspire with passion and emotion, as well as deliver bottom-line results. For example, during the American presidential election of 2008 there was considerable debate over the comparative appeal between the experience of Hillary Clinton and the charisma of Barack Obama.

In her discussion of the creation of the democratic enterprise (organisations that can flourish economically and can also be places of excitement and stimulation, fulfilment and tranquillity), Gratton maintains that it is the creation of a shared purpose and the role of the leadership team that are most vital. The role of the leader as visionary is fundamental to creating the broad philosophical context of democracy and as the architect of shared purpose.[75]

Referring to the work of Goffee and Jones, Witzel suggests: 'leadership is one of the most vital and yet elusive ingredients in modern business. Leaders provide vision, direction, inspiration, give the business a sense of purpose and at the same time act as a moral compass.'[76]

Goffee and Jones point out that the need for visionary leadership is becoming increasingly important. Traditional business hierarchies gave managers and workers a sense of their own position and what was expected of them. Now, as these hierarchies break down, it is leaders themselves who must fill the void, helping subordinates to understand their place and purpose. Personal leadership is beginning to replace organisational structure.[77]

> What sets great leaders apart is their ability to engage those around them in a shared vision of the future. By making the right decisions, they demonstrate their commitment to turning that vision into reality; and by doing so successfully, they instil in others the confidence to trust in their leadership.
>
> (Sir Bryan Nicholson)[78]

The inspirational gap

According to a survey by the Chartered Management Institute, the power to inspire is rated highest among desirable leadership qualities. A detailed survey of almost 1,500 practising managers in a broad cross-section of organisations found that the key characteristic that leaders should ideally possess, inspiration, was identified by 55 per cent of managers. However, most leaders appeared to lack this characteristic, with only 11 per cent of respondents saying they experienced this in reality.[79]

The survey from the Chartered Management Institute highlighted a significant 'inspirational gap' in leadership across UK organisations. The Department of Trade and Industry (now BERR) undertook a research project to explore how to start closing this critical leadership inspiration gap.[80]

> It is now accepted that for the UK to maintain its competitiveness there is a growing need for companies to adopt strategies that will enable a greater level of innovation and the provision of higher value and services.

The report is based on a study of 568 followers at different management levels working in a wide variety of organisations. It confirms that today's workforce is more diverse, informed and sophisticated than ever before. Ultimately people are still looking for something different and better in organisational leadership.

Key conclusions of the report include:

- For the past 30 years there have been increasing amounts of data to suggest that leadership has a lot more to do with inspiration and vision than with straightforward technical competence. Leadership is now recognised as a transferable skill, and it can be developed by continued learning and development throughout a person's career.

- Managers demand visionary leaders who win not only results but also the trust and respect of their teams. It is the relationship between people that results in action.

● In order to keep followers motivated and committed in an era of unrelenting change, leaders must be able to create organisation cultures that foster not only performance but also a sense of pride and fun.

The leadership jigsaw

Cutler believes that the principles of inspirational leadership have not changed greatly over recent years. He states:

● A leader is a visionary
● A leader sets an example
● A leader understands what motivates each team member
● A leader builds supportive relationships
● A leader empowers others to reach their potential
● A leader understands the power of communications.[81]

In his 2005 work, he designed a 'jigsaw' of best practice. He identifies the same six interlinking pieces: vision, example, motivation, relationships, empowerment and communications as a guide to the measurement and development of leadership skills. Cutler believes that leadership is not such a difficult role if condensed to these essential elements, and has devised a set of questions to help aspiring leaders to find out if they have all the necessary pieces of the jigsaw (*see* Figure 6.8).[82]

Transcendental (servant) leadership

More recent writing considers the terms 'transcendental' and 'servant' leadership. Alexakis talks of transcendental leadership as an emerging perspective, 'interested in aligning the motivations of associates and organizations for extraordinary results'.[83] The concept of transcendental leadership is based on the idea that the leader can move beyond the limits of ordinary behaviour to peak performance, and through his/her example, encourage others to do the same, thereby leading to satisfying or exceeding organisational goals. Transcendental leaders are concerned with people. They encourage staff to be motivated to do things for others.

The idea is that if a transcendental leader does the right things, everything will fall into place. It was suggested by Nicolaides[84] that the transcendental type of leader is generally more desirable in a tourism or hospitality enterprise.

The emphasis of this approach is that leader should, through his/her own attitudes and behaviour, create an appropriate environment for the workforce to be empowered and motivated (see Chapter 7).

Servant leadership in the hospitality industry

The next step in leadership evolution is servant leadership, in which the leader seeks to support and empower followers. The implications are considerable for the hospitality industry,

VISION–Do you:
1 Work hard at communicating your vision for the organisation to all staff at all levels?
2 Understand that your vision must appeal to your staff at both an emotional and practical level if they are to join you on your journey?
3 Understand the culture and values of your organisation and their impact on its future development?
4 Recognise blind alleys?

MOTIVATION–Do you:
1 Understand that every member has a different set of motivational stimuli?
2 Explain your decisions in terms of their benefit to the organisation and its members?
3 Celebrate and reward individual and team achievements?
4 Prefer to offer carrots, rather than wield sticks?

EXAMPLE–Do you:
1 Match your words with your actions?
2 Take full responsibility for organisational problems, even if you were not directly responsible?
3 Occasionally muck in when your staff are under pressure at work?
4 Regularly consider what you see in the bathroom mirror?

EMPOWERMENT–Do you:
1 Believe that people generally respond well when given greater responsibility for their own performance?
2 Allocate sufficient resources to training and development?
3 Get a buzz when staff set and achieve their own goals?
4 Realise that the organisation would still function if you were not there?

RELATIONSHIPS–Do you:
1 Work hard at countering a 'them and us' culture within your organisation?
2 Set clear codes of acceptable conduct and take action against breaches of them?
3 Stress that everyone contributes to the success of the team(s) they belong to?
4 Admit when you make a mistake?

COMMUNICATIONS–Do you:
1 Use your influence to encourage two-way communications at all levels in your organisation?
2 Encourage personal contact rather than written, mechanical or technological alternatives?
3 Encourage a diversity of opinion and constructive criticism?
4 Walk the talk?

Source: Cutler, A. 'A Good Fit Is Essential', Professional Manager, vol. 15, no. 3, May 2005, p. 38. Reproduced with permission from Chartered Management Institute and Alan Cutler.

Figure 6.8 The leadership 'jigsaw'

since it is based on the concept of leadership through service. Hospitality educators could take steps to instil servant leadership principles in students to equip them for this increasingly relevant leadership style.[85]

Brownell further comments that global hospitality organisations are 'profoundly affected by a leader's behaviours and personal characteristics and especially the manner in which the leader relates to and influences followers'.[86] She identifies that the emphasis of the idea of 'servant leadership' is focusing on the support and development of staff, 'the essence of servant leadership is that the leader is motivated by a desire to serve and empower followers: influence is achieved through the act of service itself'.[87]

Hale and Fields, cited by Alexakis,[88] defined servant leadership as placing the good of those led over the self-interest of the leader. They emphasise 'leader behaviours that focus on follower development and de-emphasizing glorification of the leader'.[89] This is very much in line with what Brownell considers to be the important behaviours of servant leaders.

- Listening intently to others combined with personal reflection on what is heard.
- Empathy: assuming the good intentions of colleagues.
- Awareness: understanding issues involving ethics and values.
- Persuasion: rather than relying on authority or coercion.
- Conceptualisation: servant leaders dream great dreams and are also operationally skilled.
- Foresight: the ability to foresee the likely outcome of a situation.
- Stewardship: holding institutions in trust for the greater good of society.
- Commitment to the personal and professional growth of all employees.
- Building community within the organisation.[90]

Brownell comments that building a culture of trust and respect and fostering ethical practices in a global workplace are particularly relevant to the hospitality manager.

The essence of servant leadership is serving the employee by meeting his/her needs with trust and respect, thereby empowering him/her. As a result of being so served by the leader, the employee is likely, in turn, to better serve the guest. The nature of the hospitality industry makes this a particularly desirable outcome.[91]

Gary Miles of the Roffey Institute also suggests that servant leadership is a particularly relevant model for today's leaders in the hospitality industry: 'great leaders inspire people to do more than they believe they're capable of'.[92]

According to Miles a leader is someone who:

- challenges the process;
- inspires a shared vision;
- enables others to act;
- leads by example;
- is prepared to make personal sacrifices for the sake of the common good.

He points out that in modern leadership:

> Today's leader is often a servant to their team. Leadership is not just about vision and bravado but whether the leader is prepared to deal with the hard discussions and tasks on behalf of their team. So often the need to make sacrifices is ignored when talking about the traits of great leadership.
>
> To counter this view, there is a darker point too – great leaders often succeed as they allow others the opportunity for advancement and to become powerful.[93]

Leadership effectiveness

Goleman reports that the most effective executives use a collection of distinct leadership styles, each in the right measure, at just the right time. Although the authoritative style of leadership can be occasionally overbearing, it was found to be most effective and can motivate and inspire commitment to the goals of the organisation. The affiliative style has potential to create harmony within teams and can be used in conjunction with the authoritative style. The democratic approach was seen as positive, and encourages input from staff and helps build consensus through participation. The coaching style, although the least frequently used, can help staff identify their strengths and encourage long-term development goals. The study concludes that the most effective leaders rely on more than one leadership style, and were able to master a mixture of authoritative, democratic, affiliative and coaching styles. Leaders with the best results use most of the styles in a given week – seamlessly and in different measure – depending on the business situation.[94]

Goleman also reminds us that whatever a leader is wanting to achieve it is all done with people and from his recent research identifies six leadership styles. Each style springs from different components of emotional intelligence, and helps build commitment and improve the emotional climate. They are:

1 **visionary** – provides long-term vision;

2 **coaching** – develops people long-term;

3 **affiliative** – creates harmony in work;

4 **democratic** – commitment through consultation;

5 **pace-setter** – pushes to accomplish tasks;

6 **commanding** – demands compliance.

Goleman cautions that the last two styles are easily misused. The more of all these styles deployed the better: research suggests that mastery of four or more fosters improved performance and a better working environment.[95]

Cross-cultural dimensions of leadership

Cross-cultural dimensions of organisational behaviour have been considered in earlier chapters, identifying some potentially important differences in attitudes and behaviour between different cultural groups. In particular, it was suggested that people's perceptions of authority, independence and uncertain situations could vary according to cultural background and experience and their perception of 'good leadership' will also be subject to national cultural variation. The multicultural nature of the hospitality industry requires the enlightened manager/leader to be aware of different cultural expectations.

Tannenbaum and Schmidt identify leaders' own value-systems as factors that influence their chosen style. They also highlight subordinates' – or non-managers' – needs for independence and tolerance of ambiguity as relevant variables in the choice of style.[96] These factors vary according to the cultural context in which the leadership relationship takes place. One should be wary of stereotyping the behaviour of leaders or subordinates, and many myths appear to have grown around notions of 'orderly' German, 'undisciplined' Italian and even 'obstructive' British workers. However, there are reasons to suggest that there may indeed be national cultural differences that are relevant to an understanding of leadership.

Culture as a contingent factor in leadership

The contribution of contingency approaches to understanding leadership suggests that contrasting types and styles of leadership may be more or less appropriate in different situations. Tayeb draws attention to cross-cultural leadership and points out that in a global business landscape, national culture affects leadership styles and behaviours. It is clear that people living in different parts of the world have different expectations from those in a leadership position. The way in which employees perceive their leaders, as employee-oriented or task-oriented, appears to vary from culture to culture.[97]

Global Leadership and Organisational Behaviour Effectiveness (GLOBE)

Project GLOBE, the full name of which is the Global Leadership and Organisational Behaviour Effectiveness research programme, is a very large-scale research project which sought to identify those leader behaviours and attributes which would be accepted and therefore effective in all societies and, contrastingly, those which would only be accepted and effective in some cultural contexts. This study was conducted by an international team of researchers led by Robert House and encompassed 62 countries across the world, including some which had not always featured in cross-cultural study – for example newly capitalist states in Eastern Europe. The GLOBE study commenced in 1991 and has led to a series of publications in the early twenty-first century.[98]

The GLOBE study conceived leadership as essentially reciprocal, in that leadership must be endorsed by followers, which endorsement, the authors claim, will be subject to cultural variation. At the same time, leaders will themselves have been immersed in a particular culture and consequently influenced by the norms and values surrounding leadership within that culture.

The results, according to the GLOBE researchers, are some significant variations in leadership style, attributes and behaviour. In the GLOBE study, charismatic and team-orientated leaders were shown to be globally endorsed – and hence universally effective. Leaders who displayed high levels of trust, integrity and vision were supported by subordinates in all societies.

It was also found that there were so-called universal impediments to success; for example, self-protective leaders characterised by malevolence and 'face-saving' were viewed negatively by subordinates in all cultures.

There were, finally, some aspects of leadership which varied between societies. In common with Hofstede (see Chapter 3), the GLOBE study identifies clusters of societies with important points of commonality. To take one example, in a situation which might imply a directive style of leadership, subordinates in the 'Anglo' cluster of societies (in effect the main English-speaking countries) would prefer some degree of informality on the part of the leader and as much of a participative style as the situation allowed.

The GLOBE study recognises that strategic organisational contingencies such as the sector an organisation operates in will affect leadership style and behaviour; however, the GLOBE researchers concluded that such factors would be moderated by the national cultural context. Leader effectiveness will be influenced by the interaction between leaders and subordinates, which is dependent on the nature of power relations within the particular culture, and organisational contingencies applying in all societies.

As previously noted, leaders managing a multicultural, multi-ethnic workforce as in the hospitality industry may consider adapting their style to suit the different cultural backgrounds of staff.

Best leadership style in the hospitality industry

We have seen that there are many alternative styles of managerial leadership. And contingency models demonstrate the importance of situational variables. Different types of leadership may also be most appropriate at different stages in the development of a business organisation.[99] Clearly, there is no simple answer to what is the best style of leadership.

Cutler provides a checklist of behaviours that should be adopted by successful twenty-first-century leaders in the hospitality industry:

- Promote the organisation as a good company to join.
- Encourage staff to see their long-term future with the organisation.
- Address the industry's negative reputation.
- Create a positive multicultural working environment.
- Change from being boss to being a team player and to coach team members.
- React to the impact of external influences.
- Empower front-line staff to exceed customer expectations.
- Share business goals with employees.
- Introduce corporate social responsibility.[100]

Studies on leadership in the hospitality industry appear to yield conflicting results. For example, using Fiedler's contingency model, Nebel and Stearns conducted a survey of first-line supervisors in the American hotel and restaurant industry. Their findings contradict Cutler and indicate that a task-orientated style of management leadership would be most effective.[101]

In contrast, however, is the survey by Keegan of managers in the hotel and restaurant industry. The managers identified effective leadership as being neither autocratic/dictatorial nor as creating followers out of fear or patronising dedication. Rather, they were aware of the need for, and the trend towards, a more human relations style of leadership. Changing social values have increased the demands of employees for a 'good' job and it is the style of managerial leadership which contributes most to their satisfaction and motivation.

Keegan presents a strongly argued case for the adoption of a more supportive, behavioural approach to managerial leadership and draws the following conclusion.

> The challenge for us is not so much to change the job, but to provide the managerial leadership that would create an environment in which the employee's real needs are satisfied. Such a leadership is characterised as being personal, supportive and participative, and is firmly based on a solid relationship between the manager and employees. This managerial leadership

should be an integral part of the hospitality environment, a behavioural model as it were, of how best to behave with people in general whether they be guests or employees. Such a leadership style is in many ways in direct opposition to the leadership traditionally associated with our industry. We must change and change dramatically, so let our goal be then to develop this new leadership for our industry.[102]

More recent writings suggest that the newer approaches such as transformational and transcendental (servant) leadership, which aim to empower and trust the employee, are the way forward.[103]

Exhibit 6.1 Managerial leadership – a personal perspective

Many of those who work within hospitality, and therefore know the industry, comment upon the quality of service (and the attitude of those they see working) when they themselves are customers of a hospitality outlet. The comments generally centre on the attitudes of people working together and the treatment of staff by managers.

What is this problem that so many managers appear to have with the treatment of their staff? Quality of service and managerial leadership are inextricably linked in an industry where people – be they guests, customers or staff – and their treatment are paramount to organisational performance and success.

The hospitality industry is a people industry. This is what attracted me to the industry. I like people and I enjoy making people feel welcome, at home and valued. The industry works hard to project this welcoming message to its customers, and all forward-looking organisations, in their own way, tell customers how they can ease their burdens. They offer positive and life-enhancing, relaxing experiences based upon levels of service and attention to the details, which make life so special. Each tries to outdo its nearest competitor in terms of facilities and guest comforts – gyms, beauty salons, IT, conference facilities, baby-sitting services, play areas, etc., solely to say we care about our customers' needs and meet them at all times.

The problem with the image of this 'caring' industry is the horror stories that both employees and customers can tell of situations where staff have been maltreated, or instances of management actions or decisions that destroyed a pleasant atmosphere.

Recently I had a discussion with students who had been on their industrial placement and also held jobs within the industry. One of the salient comments was that managers in a variety of different scenarios did not appear to have any training or skills in the effective management of people. Too many individual managers treated staff very poorly. There was little or no regard for personal issues or even for systems and policies which previously had worked well but were now abandoned either by the individual or, more seriously, by a policy decision of the organisation. Both on an individual manager and organisational level, teamwork and leadership skills were often poor to non-existent.

There are a number of basic underlying factors which relate to people management. First, the hospitality industry has always attracted people at all levels of the social scale. It is considered an easy option by many and the practical nature of the work is also appealing to a section of the population who enjoy 'doing' rather than the outcomes of more academic pursuits.

The hospitality industry is seen as one where employment is easy – service staff are always required and the transient nature of staff almost an accepted characteristic of the trade. People move from job to job within a town or an area, a country or various countries, something that attracts many students to hospitality courses.

In recent years and partly in line with government-led trends, organisations large and small have tried to keep their staff by offering company benefits and additional training as an incentive to staff to stay and develop. This does work, but why does the transient nature of the business remain? Is there a link between transience and staff handling?

Hospitality is not known as a high-paying industry at an operative or even supervisory level. Certain managers can be very well paid but also many are very badly paid. Financial benefits as a whole are few. Accommodation for staff may be provided but it is often basic to poor in standard. The conditions of the job involve unsocial hours with few opportunities to socialise out of the working colleague circle. Food is often of a low standard with staff being offered leftovers from the main restaurant. Larger organisations may offer greater benefits but they make up a relatively small percentage of hospitality employers. Most hospitality employees work for medium to small organisations, run on low overheads.

That being the case, it seems clear that all members of an organisation's staff should support their fellow employees and use all their self-awareness, people management and managerial skills to create a working environment which is happy, successful and profitable for the organisation. This does happen, but not always, and apparently not often enough.

The following scenarios heard through a variety of people in many walks of the industry are legion. They serve to illustrate general patterns and types of managerial behaviour.

1 The new broom. Often a young manager comes to an outlet and immediately begins to make changes which are not announced previously or are communicated badly. Staff become upset and anxious and begin to leave. The drift may start very quickly or start slowly and build in momentum. Sometimes this is for the good, if things have been badly run and changes have to be made, but the failure is that the effect on staff is not calculated. A variation on this scenario is where a manager has been moved by the organisation from one outlet to another. Whether or not there is a reputation to precede that person, the damage that can be done will be the same.

2 The weak manager who can be bullied by certain members of staff and/or will not challenge problems or bad working practices. This is usually in the name of ensuring a happy environment but staff will become resentful. If someone is perceived to be a manager, then people want that person to manage.

3 The manager whose *raison d'être* is ensuring profitability. The profit and loss sheet is this person's bible and new practices will be introduced or systems will be abandoned if he or she feels that profit margins are being affected. This type of manager is uninterested in the staff as a whole and on an individual level, seeing them as truly an 'economic resource' to be exploited at will. Again staff react badly to this form of management. They feel that they do not know where they stand and that any personal touches or influences they bring to the situation are unappreciated and ignored.

4 The manager who wishes to stamp his or her authority on the staff (most often, again, new staff) by disciplining at the first opportunity a subordinate to 'show them who's boss'. This sad ploy is all too often used as a management tool. Initially, it may appear to work for the manager and problems may seemingly remain few: but more likely the manager loses credibility in the eyes of staff, who would have worked happily and well anyway without this unnecessary show of strength.

All these scenarios can be transferred to the organisational level and can be seen in all types of industry. Why the problem is exacerbated in the hospitality industry is that our staff work in an industry that is completely people-focused – at least, 'customer'-focused. They are expected to treat those whom they serve with respect and grace, but they are highly aware that their employers do not have the same feelings towards them. The sad fact is, however, that the loss of staff in these scenarios is put down to a variety of 'personnel'-based excuses – the old staff not being able to take change, or 'well, it is expected that people move on in this industry'.

So we have a set of problems which stem from poor team-building and leadership, but their cause goes undetected because the results – staff dissatisfaction and staff turnover – are blamed on the industry rather than on bad management practices.

Considering the question 'Did these managers have any training in the skills of people management, and if so what happened?', various thoughts come to mind:

● Does profit have to affect the way staff are treated?

● Do staffing limitations and the busy environments typical of the hospitality industry mean that good leadership and team-building techniques are ignored or abandoned?

- In training people to be leaders and team-builder, should self-confidence and trust be highlighted to a greater degree than theoretical learning?

- Should both managers and organisations be more aware of the psychology of leadership and team-building in terms of motivation?

If we continue to blame poor terms and conditions of employment – which appear to be an accepted part of the hospitality industry – for the transient nature of a disinterested staff, we overlook a far greater evil. Unless managers exhibit confidence and ability in successful team-building and leadership skills at a practical level, the industry is unlikely ever to solve labour shortages or improve the motivation of staff.

Source: The authors are grateful to Nigel Maggs-Oosterhagen, Department of Catering and Hospitality Studies, Highbury College, Portsmouth, for providing this contribution.

Synopsis

- There are many ways of looking at leadership and many interpretations of its meaning, but essentially it is a relationship through which one person influences the behaviour or actions of other people. The leader–follower relationship is reciprocal and effective leadership is a two-way process. Leadership is related to motivation, the process of communication, the activities of groups and the process of empowerment. The labour-intensive nature of the hospitality industry emphasises the importance of leadership skills.

- There is arguably a close relationship between leadership and management, especially in hospitality organisations. However, there is much to suggest that there are differences between the two, and it does not follow that every leader is a manager. Leadership occurs at many different levels and in many different ways. It may be viewed in more general terms, with emphasis on interpersonal behaviour in a broader context.

- Due to its complex nature there are many alternative ways of analysing leadership. Leadership may be examined in terms of the qualities or traits approach; the functional or group approach; as a behavioural category; styles of leadership; through the situational approach and contingency models; the distinction between transactional or transformational leadership; and inspirational or visionary leadership.

- Contingency theories draw attention to the interactions between the variables involved in a leadership situation and patterns of leadership behaviour. The most appropriate form of leadership is dependent upon the variables in a particular leadership situation. Different contingency theories have concentrated on different situational variables. These include favourability of the leadership situation, decision acceptance and decision quality, path–goal theory, and the 'readiness' of followers.

- The attention given to transformational, transcendental and servant leadership as well as the importance of charisma has given rise to an increasing focus on the concept of leaders creating a vision with which others can identify and inspiring followers to improve organisational performance. There is, however, doubt about the extent to which leaders possess these personal qualities. Leadership is a dynamic form of behaviour and the leader's influence is dependent upon the type of power exercised over other people.

- Attention needs to be given to the criteria for leadership effectiveness. Leaders of the future will face new expectations and will need to learn new sets of skills. There are many variables that underlie the effectiveness of leadership, including dimensions of national culture. There is no one best form or style of leadership and there are many variables which underlie the effectiveness of managerial leadership in the hospitality industry. The most successful form of leadership behaviour is a product of the total leadership situation. Leaders of the future will need to work within less hierarchical systems of command and control.

REVIEW AND DISCUSSION QUESTIONS

1 Explain the meaning and nature of leadership. How would you attempt to distinguish leadership from management?

2 What is meant by the leadership relationship? Give practical examples of the different sources of leadership power and influence within the hospitality industry.

3 Critically assess the relevance of the qualities or trait theories of leadership. Suggest what you believe to be the most important characteristics of an effective leader in the work situation.

4 Explain your understanding of the functional approach to leadership. Discuss the main areas of need which constitute the core responsibility of the leader.

5 Explain the meaning and importance of leadership style. Suggest ways in which leadership styles can be classified. Why do you think greater attention is being given to more participative styles of managerial leadership?

6 Discuss critically the practical value of contingency models of leadership. What are the main factors which are likely to influence the most appropriate form of managerial leadership in the hospitality industry?

7 Contrast transactional and transformational forms of leadership. Discuss critically the relevance and applications of transformational leadership within the hospitality industry.

8 Using examples, from your own experience if possible, state in what circumstances, if any, would a task-orientated approach to leadership be appropriate in today's hospitality organisation?

ASSIGNMENT 1

Assume you are a departmental manager in a hospitality organisation of your choice.

1 Using the Tannenbaum and Schmidt continuum, identify your *preferred* style of leadership. Explain fully the rationale for your preference.

2 Detail fully, and preferably from actual experience, an example of a particular situation when you believe a different form of managerial leadership is likely to be most effective.

ASSIGNMENT 2

Three months ago you were appointed head housekeeper at ABC Hotel. A member of your staff, several years older than yourself and with five years' service, and who you understand was very popular with colleagues, has in recent weeks had a poor record of punctuality and sickness absence, and often a below-expected standard of work. Despite speaking about it informally and attempts to find out what might be the cause, the member of staff has been reluctant to say anything. Other members of the group have been covering for their colleague but now the strain is showing and morale is beginning to suffer. The general manager has expressed concern at the situation. You are given clear instructions as 'leader of the group' to sort out the problem as quickly as possible. If not, action will have to be taken at a higher level.

Explain fully and with supporting reasons the actions you would propose to take.

ASSIGNMENT 3

Your leadership style

For each of the following ten pairs of statements, divide five points between the two according to your beliefs, perceptions of yourself, or according to which of the two statements characterises you better. The five points may be divided between the A and B statements in any way you wish with the constraint that only whole positive integers may be used (i.e. you may not split the points equally between the two). Weigh your choices between the two according to the one that better characterises you or your beliefs.

1   A   As leader I have a primary mission of maintaining stability. _____

   B   As leader I have a primary mission of change. _____

2   A   As leader I must cause events. _____

   B   As leader I must facilitate events. _____

3   A   I am concerned that my followers are rewarded equitably for their work. _____

   B   I am concerned about what my followers want in life. _____

4   A   My preference is to think long-range: 'what might be'. _____

   B   My preference is to think short-range: 'what is realistic'. _____

5   A   As leader I spend considerable energy in managing separate but related goals. _____

   B   As leader I spend considerable energy in arousing hopes, expectations, and aspiration among my followers. _____

6   A   While not in a formal classroom sense, I believe that a significant part of my leadership is that of a teacher. _____

   B   I believe that a significant part of my leadership is that of a facilitator. _____

7   A   As leader I must engage with followers at an equal level of morality. _____

   B   As leader I must represent a higher morality. _____

8   A   I enjoy stimulating followers to want to do more. _____

   B   I enjoy rewarding followers for a job well done. _____

9 A Leadership should be practical. _____

B Leadership should be inspirational. _____

10 A What power I have to influence others comes primarily from my ability _____
to get people to identify with me and my ideas.

B What power I have to influence others comes primarily from my status _____
and position.

Details of scoring and interpretation will be provided by your tutor.

Source: From Schermerhorn, J. R., Jr., *et al.*, *Managing Organizational Behaviour*, 4th ed, John Wiley & Sons (1991), p. 484. Reproduced with permission from John Wiley & Sons Inc.

CASE STUDY 6.1

The Promenade Hotel

The Promenade Hotel was developed from a Georgian mansion into a 117-bedroomed hotel in the 1930s. It sits on the promenade of a south coast resort, where it holds an imposing position. Since that time it has seen many ups and downs. In recent years it has been taken over by a small hotel group specialising in resort-type hotels at the three-star level.

The manager, Peter Crane, has been at the hotel for two years – his first general manager position. He and his wife live in a pleasant purpose-built flat within the building. Jill Crane began her career as a receptionist at a hotel in Bournemouth. She and Peter began dating when Peter was a duty manager at the same hotel. When they married, eight years ago, Jill was a head receptionist and decided that she would not work as she felt it might lead to conflicts of interests if she and Peter worked in the same establishment. Now in their early thirties, they enjoy running a large, prestigious hotel on the front.

The deputy manager is Duncan Williams. He joined the hotel eighteen months ago. He has known Jill Crane from their college days together. Duncan also knew the Cranes because he worked in Bournemouth, although at a different hotel when they were there.

The restaurant/duty manager is Jamie Lloyd. He joined the staff three months ago. Jamie comes from a family of hoteliers on the Isle of Wight and this job is a promotion for him, from being a restaurant supervisor at a five-star hotel in Buckinghamshire.

The whole complement of staff numbers twenty-five full- and part-timers. Few of the staff have been with the hotel very long. When the hotel was taken over by its present owners many of the old-timers took the opportunity to retire, as they were unsure of what to expect from the new situation.

The general atmosphere of the hotel is good. The arrival of the Cranes was greeted with interest. Peter's reputation was as a switched-on chap who knew his stuff. This reputation has puzzled the staff, as he appears quite ineffectual. He is perfectly pleasant for most of the time but has a fierce temper, which is displayed at the oddest times. The staff have begun to ignore him somewhat. He often passes responsibility on to Duncan, leaving him with decisions to be made while he concentrates on the paperwork.

Duncan is a strange man. A good-looking chap in his late twenties, he is always well turned out and good with guests. To the staff, though, he is known as 'the Fish'. This nickname has been bestowed upon him as he is a very cold man. He shows little emotion and is quite happy to be unpleasant to staff in order to get his way. This has made most of the staff very wary of him; they don't like his sharp tongue and they don't feel valued by him. The consensus is that he enjoys being unpleasant. This would certainly appear to be true. In conversation Duncan will say that he is there to be the deputy manager and not to be liked by the staff. He doesn't actually care what people say about him – in fact it appears to amuse him. A few of the staff find it stimulating to try to get into his less-acerbic books but they are in a minority and even they are tiring of his constant cold demeanour.

Jamie's first months have been a complete eye opener; a larger hotel with more room has been a dream of his to work in. He is in his mid-twenties and this is his second job since gaining an HND in Hotel, Catering and Institutional Management. Jamie's parents run a fifty-bed hotel on the Isle of Wight that was run by Jamie's grandparents before that. He has served at table and prepared rooms for use since he was a boy.

The Promenade came at an ideal time for Jamie. Since he went to college he had been working at the same mainland hotel where he had worked his way through all the departments and he was fed up with the place. He was ready for a change but wanted to keep his interests in F&B alive while progressing his career. The job at the Promenade was exactly right for him.

It is part of Jamie's plan to take over the family's hotel eventually, but he is in no hurry to push his parents out so he wants to get as much experience as he can in order to open a small establishment of his own. He is not sure what form this place will take but he is keen to get his ideas off the ground.

Jamie has become popular with the staff in the short time that he has been at the hotel. He is always cheerful and acknowledges all the staff of the hotel both at work and outside work. He obviously enjoys what he does and is always happy to help a member of staff achieve the task in hand. The restaurant has eighty covers and the staff is made up of three full-time staff who cover the whole day from breakfast to dinner with ten part-timers who spread their time throughout the day. Many of these staff are students at the local college who need to earn money and wish to gain as much experience as they can. They like Jamie because he encourages their project work and helps them with problems when he can.

In the time that Jamie has been with the hotel, Jill Crane's standing has fallen in the eyes of the reception staff. They have always found Jill to be aloof, although she is happy to give them instructions about what to do and what instructions they need to leave for her husband when she is

going out. She has, in fact, become something of a laughing stock with them and when she comes towards the desk they take it in turns to serve her and enjoy talking about the experience during their breaks.

The staff overall appear to be on the move. The head housekeeper was the first to leave and the reservations manager has recently announced his departure. In an unusual meeting of the senior staff of Peter, Duncan and Jamie the problem has been discussed. Peter is concerned that the trend may spread. Business has been all right over the past eight months but not as good as he was expecting and the area manager questioned the figures Peter presented at his last meeting with him.

Duncan feels that there is nothing to worry about. He feels that the staff are malleable and that there is nothing to be concerned about. Jamie is quite nervous of this meeting. It is his first meeting of this sort at the Promenade. He finds Duncan quite an intimidating man and tends to agree with the staff that Peter is pleasant but ineffectual. Jamie actually feels that there are some pretty big problems on the horizon. The word in the staff room is that every one is fed up with working there. Picking the bones out of the usual mixture of scare talk, Jamie has discovered that the head housekeeper has moved to another large hotel in the next resort and is busy encouraging the best of the housekeeping staff to join her.

The restaurant team is about to undertake some changes as many of the students are going on placement and they need to train new staff fairly quickly to deal with the start of the season.

There was also an incident a month ago when a management student from another college asked to leave because she was not getting the training promised and Peter paid her off using the petty cash out of the safe. The student took the money but told Peter within earshot of the kitchens that she thought he was an idiot and the sooner he realised what a mess the hotel was in, the sooner things might improve. This has been the talk of the hotel staff since then and the Cranes' name now holds little respect.

The receptionists are beginning to get a little irked by Jill's antics and their gossip about her is now being passed on to regular guests.

TASKS

1 Explain the managerial leadership styles in operation in this case.

2 Do you think that these leadership styles will ultimately help or hinder the problems the hotel is experiencing?

3 Suggest what steps might be taken to help to improve the situation.

Source: The copyright of this case study rests with the authors' former colleague, Nigel Maggs-Oosterhagen, Highbury College, Portsmouth. The case is reprinted with permission.

References

1 Brownell, J., 'Leadership in the Service of Hospitality', *Cornell Quarterly*, vol. 51, no. 3 (2010), 363.

2 Bass, B. M., *Handbook of Leadership: Theory, Research and Managerial Applications*, 3rd edn, The Free Press (1990), p. 11.

3 Crainer, S., 'Have the corporate superheroes had their day?', *Professional Manager*, March 1995, 8–12.

4 See, for example, Adair, J., *Leadership and Motivation*, Kogan Page (2006).

5 'Leadership for Innovation', Advanced Institute of Management Research (2005).

6 Levine, S. R., 'The value-based edu-leader', in Chowdhury, S. (ed.), *Management 21C*, Financial Times Prentice Hall (2000), p. 90.

7 CBI, 'The path to leadership: developing a sustainable model within organisations', Caspian Publishing (2005), p. 4.

8 Tack, A., *Motivational Leadership*, Gower (1984).

9 See, for example, Mill, R. C., *Managing for Productivity in the Hospitality Industry*, Van Nostrand Reinhold (1989).

10 Crow, S. M. and Hartman, S. J., 'Can't Get No Satisfaction', *Leadership and Organization Development Journal*, vol. 16, no. 4, 1995, 34–8.

11 Hooper, A. and Potter, J., 'Take it from the top', *People Management*, 19 August 1999, 46–9.

12 Keegan, B. M., 'Leadership in the hospitality industry', in Cassee, E. and Reuland, R. (eds), *The Management of Hospitality*, Pergamon (1983), p. 78.

13 Pittaway, L., Carmouche, R. and Chell, E., 'The way forward: leadership research in the hospitality industry', *International Journal of Hospitality Management*, vol. 17, 1998, 407–26.

14 Hollingsworth, M. J., 'Leadership: purpose and values', *Manager, The British Journal of Administrative Management*, January/February 1999, 22.

15 Statements made by managers in research by Cutler, A., *Aspire to Inspire*, Hospitality Leadership Ltd (2010).

16 See, for example, Gretton, I., 'Taking the Lead in Leadership', *Professional Manager*, January 1995, 20–22.

17 Taffinder, P., *The New Leaders: Achieving Corporate Transformation Through Dynamic Leadership*, Kogan Page (1995).

18 Kent, T. W., 'Leading and Managing: it takes two to tango', *Management Decision*, vol. 43, nos. 7/8, 2005, 1010–17.

19 Hunt, J. W., *Managing People at Work*, 2nd edn, McGraw-Hill (1986).

20 Watson, C. M., 'Leadership, management and the seven keys', *Business Horizons*, March–April 1983, 8–13.

21 Zaleznik, A., 'Managers and leaders: are they different?', *Harvard Business Review*, May–June 1977, 67–78.

22 Mintzberg, H., *The Nature of Managerial Work*, Harper & Row (1973).

23 Adair, J., *Effective Teambuilding*, Gower (1986), p. 123.

24 For an example, see Riley, M., *Human Resource Management in the Hospitality and Tourism Industry*, 2nd edn, Butterworth-Heinemann (1996).

25 McGregor, D., *The Human Side of Enterprise*, Penguin (1987), p. 182.

26 French, J. R. P. and Raven, B., 'The basis of social power', in Cartwright, D. and Zander, A. F. (eds), *Group Dynamics: Research and Theory*, 3rd edn, Harper & Row (1968).

27 Drucker, P. F., *The Practice of Management*, Pan Books (1968), p. 194.

28 See, for example, Jennings, E. E., 'The Anatomy of Leadership', *Management of Personnel Quarterly*, vol. 1, no. 1, Autumn 1961, 2–9.

29 Hornsey, T. and Dann, D., *Manpower Management in the Hotel and Catering Industry*, Batsford (1984).

30 Jacob, J., 'Towards a Simplistic Theory of Leadership', *Hospitality*, June 1980, 40–1.

31 Walker, R. G., 'Wellsprings of Managerial Leadership', *Cornell HRA Quarterly*, vol. 27, no. 2, August 1986, 14–16.

32 Kotter, J. P., 'What leaders really do', *Harvard Business Review*, May–June 1990, 103.

33 Whitehead, M., 'Everyone's a Leader Now', *Supply Management*, 25 April 2002, 22–4.

34 Krech, D., Crutchfield, R. S. and Ballachey, E. L., *Individual in Society*, McGraw-Hill (1962).

35 Cutler, A., *Aspire to Inspire*, Hospitality Leadership Ltd (2010).

36 Cutler, A., *Aspire to Inspire* (2010), also Adair, J., *The Skills of Leadership*, Gower (1984).

37 Adair, J., *Leadership and Motivation*, Kogan Page (2006).

38 Adair, J., *Effective Teambuilding*, Gower (1986), p. 116.

39 Fleishman, E. A., 'Leadership climate, human relations training and supervisory behavior', in Fleishman, E. A. and Bass, A. R., *Studies in Personnel and Industrial Psychology*, 3rd edn, Dorsey (1974).

40 Bryman, A., 'Leadership in Organisations', in Clegg, S., Hardy, C. and Nord, W. (eds), *Managing Organisations: Current Issues*, Sage (1999), pp. 26–62.

41 Likert, R., *New Patterns of Management*, McGraw-Hill (1961).

42 Worsfold, P., 'Leadership and managerial effectiveness in the hospitality industry', *International Journal of Hospitality Management*, vol. 8, no. 2, 1989, 145–55.

43 Tannenbaum, R. and Schmidt, W. H., 'How to choose a leadership pattern', *Harvard Business Review*, May–June 1973, 162–75, 178–80.

44 Belbin, R. M., *Team Roles at Work*, Butterworth-Heinemann (1993).

45 Erstad, M., 'Empowerment and Organizational Change', *International Journal of Contemporary Hospitality Management*, vol. 9, no. 7, 1997, 325–33.

46 Fiedler, F. E., *A Theory of Leadership Effectiveness*, McGraw-Hill (1967).

47 Hornsey, T. and Dann, D., *Manpower Management in the Hotel and Catering Industry*, Batsford (1984), p. 108.

48 House, R. J., 'A Path–Goal Theory of Leadership Effectiveness', *Administrative Science Quarterly*, vol. 16, September 1971, 321–38.

49 House, R. I. and Dessler, G., 'The path–goal theory of leadership', in Hunt, J. G. and Larson, L. L. (eds), *Contingency Approaches to Leadership*, Southern Illinois University Press (1974).

50 House, R. I. and Mitchell, T. R., 'Path–goal theory of leadership', *Journal of Contemporary Business*, vol. 3, Autumn 1974, 81–97.

51 Hersey, P. and Blanchard, K., *Management of Organizational Behavior*, 6th edn, Prentice-Hall (1993).

52 Burns, J. M., *Leadership*, Harper & Row (1978).

53 Bass, B. M., *Leadership and Performance Beyond Expectations*, Free Press (1985).

54 Bass, B. M. and Avolio, B. J., *Improving Organizational Effectiveness Through Transformational Leadership*, Sage Publications (1994).

55 Yukl, G., *Leadership in Organizations*, 6th edn, Pearson Prentice Hall (2006).

56 See, for example, Hinkin, T. R. and Tracey, J. B., 'Transformational Leadership in the Hospitality Industry', *Hospitality Research Journal*, vol. 18, no. 1, 1994, 49–63.

57 Tracey, J. B. and Hinkin, T. R., 'How transformational leaders lead in the hospitality industry', *International Journal of Hospitality Management*, vol. 15, no. 2, 1996, 174.

58 Clark, R., Hartline, M. and Jones, K., 'The effects of leadership style on hotel employees' commitment to service Quality', *Cornell Quarterly*, vol. 50, no. 2, 2009, 209–31.

59 Brown, E. and Arendt, S., 'Perceptions of transformational leadership behaviours and subordinates' performance in hotels', *Journal of Human Resources in Hospitality and Tourism*, vol. 10, 2011, 45–59.

60 Conger, J., 'Charisma and how to grow it', *Management Today*, December 1999, 81.

61 Kreitner, R., Kinicki, A. and Buelens, M., *Organizational Behaviour*, 1st European edn, McGraw-Hill (1999), p. 487.

62 Hunt, J. W., *Managing People at Work*, 3rd edn, McGraw-Hill (1992), p. 255.

63 Whitehead, M., 'Everyone's a leader now', *Supply Management*, vol. 25, April 2002, 22–4.

64 Kahan, S., 'Visionary Leadership', *The Great Washington Society of Association Executives*, www.leader-values.com, accessed 28 January 2006.

65 Kanter, R. M., *Confidence: Leadership and the Psychology of Turnarounds*, Random House (2004), pp. 325–6.

66 Weber, M., *The Theory of Social and Economic Organization*, Oxford University Press (1947).

67 Berger, F. and Brownell, J., *Organizational Behavior for the Hospitality Industry*, Pearson Prentice Hall (2009).

68 Conger, J., 'The Danger of Delusion', *Financial Times*, 29 November 2002.

69 Dearlove, D., 'Reinventing Leadership', in Crainer, S. and Dearlove, D. (eds), *Financial Times Handbook of Management*, 2nd edn, Financial Times Prentice Hall (2001), p. 538.

70 Bloomfield, S., 'Charismatic leaders are passé', *Professional Manager*, vol. 12, no. 1, January 2003, 37.

71 Adair, J., *The Inspirational Leader: How to motivate, encourage and achieve success*, Kogan Page (2003).

72 Cutler, A., *Aspire to Inspire*, Hospitality Leadership Ltd (2010).

73 See note 72.

74 See note 71.

75 Gratton, L., *The Democratic Enterprise*, Financial Times Prentice Hall (2004).

76 Witzel, M., 'Book review: A rewarding read if you want to lead', www.ft.com, accessed 31 January 2006.

77 Goffee, R. and Jones, G., *Why Should Anyone Be Led By You?*, Harvard Business School Press (2006).

78 Nicholson, (Sir) B., 'In My Opinion', *Management Today*, January 2006, 10.

79 Horne, M. and Jones, D. S., *Leadership: The Challenge for All?*, Chartered Management Institute (2001).

80 'Inspired Leadership: Insights into People Who Inspire Exceptional Performance', Department of Trade and Industry, August 2004.

81 See note 72.

82 Cutler, A., 'A good fit Is essential', *Professional Manager*, vol. 14, no. 3, May 2005, 38.

83 Alexakis, G., 'Transcendental leadership: The progressive hospitality leader's silver bullet', *International Journal of Hospitality Management*, vol. 30, no. 3, 2011, 708–13.

84 Nicolaides, A., 'Transcendental leadership versus management in the South African hospitality industry: a recipe for success', in *The Eighth International Conference on Knowledge, Culture and Change in Organisations*, Cambridge University, United Kingdom, 5–8 August 2008.

85 Brownell, J., 'Leadership in the service of hospitality', *Cornell Hospitality Quarterly*, vol. 51, no. 3, 2010, 363–78.

86 See note 85.

87 See note 85.

88 See note 83.

89 Hale, J. R. and Fields, D. L., 'Exploring servant leadership across cultures: a study of followers in Ghana and the USA', *Leadership,* vol. 3, no. 4, 2007, 397–417.

90 See note 85.

91 See also Berger, F. and Brownell, J., *Organizational Behavior for the Hospitality Industry*, Pearson Prentice Hall (2009).

92 Tobin, A., 'The Mark of a Leader', *EP Business in Hospitality*, issue 36, January 2011, 34–5.

93 See note 92.

94 Goleman, D., 'Leadership that gets results', *Harvard Business Review*, vol. 78, no. 2, March–April 2000, 78–90.

95 Goleman, D., reported in 'Leaders in London: fifth annual International Leadership Summit', *Manager: The British Journal of Administrative Management,* Winter 2009, 17–21.

96 Tannenbaum, R. and Schmidt, W. H., 'How to Choose a Leadership Pattern', *Harvard Business Review*, May–June 1973, 162–75, 178–80.

97 Tayeb, M., 'Cross-Cultural Leadership', in CBI, *The Path to Leadership: Developing a Sustainable Model within Organisations*, Caspian Publishing (2005), pp. 14–20.

98 House, R. J., Hanges, P. J., Javidan, M., Dorfman, P. J. and Gupta, V. (eds), *Culture, Leadership and Organisations: The GLOBE Study of 62 Societies*, Sage (2004).

99 See, for example, Clarke, C. and Pratt, S., 'Leadership's four-part progress', *Management Today*, March 1985, 84–6.

100 See note 72.

101 Nebel, E. C. and Stearns, K., 'Leadership in the hospitality industry', *Cornell HRA Quarterly*, vol. 18, no. 3, November 1977, 69–76.

102 Keegan, B. M., 'Leadership in the Hospitality Industry', in Cassee, E. and Reuland, R. (eds), *The Management of Hospitality*, Pergamon (1983), pp. 69–93.

103 See note 83.

Workforce motivation and involvement

Introduction

Previous chapters have considered the nature of management and leadership and how this may be applied to the hospitality industry. Current trends in approaches to leadership tend to emphasise the need to allow staff greater freedom in their ways of working: styles of leadership and design and content of jobs can have a significant effect on the satisfaction of staff and levels of performance. Managers need to know how best to elicit the cooperation of staff, and encourage their efforts to achieve the goals and objectives of the hospitality organisation.

Critical review and reflection

'All work should be fun.' (Tom Peters)
Many people work in the hospitality industry because it is 'fun'.

What are your views? To what extent do you agree with the above points?

In recent years, a more strategic approach to HRM has been applied, in which employees are viewed as strategic and valuable assets to be invested in and developed, rather than costs to be controlled. In that regard, a highly committed, capable, empowered, involved, and motivated workforce was seen as the way to competitive advantage and sustained business success.

(Kuşlevan et al.)[1]

Managers achieve results through the efforts and performance of other people. Thus, the ability to encourage staff to work willingly and effectively is an essential ingredient of successful management; this requires understanding of what motivates staff to work and the satisfaction they derive from their work, also how staff may be encouraged to become more **committed, empowered and involved**. A factor in the motivation of staff is clearly the nature of the job they are given to perform. Increasingly providing more interesting and stimulating work through 'empowering staff' is considered to be a component of both staff and customer satisfaction.

The nature of motivation

The management of people is influenced by the attitudes which are brought to bear on relationships with them and the problems which affect them. Attention should be given to the feelings of staff and to appropriate systems of motivation and reward, which may affect job satisfaction. This is clearly important in any work organisation but especially so in labour-intensive service organisations such as those in the hospitality industry.[2] As Riley, for example, suggests, 'Hotel and catering management has a real investment in motivation because most of its jobs require input where effort and personal character actually matter.'[3]

The study of motivation is concerned with why people behave in a certain way, and with what determines the direction and persistence of their actions. Levels of work performance are determined not only by the ability of staff but also by the strength of their motivation. If staff are to perform to the best of their abilities, attention must also be given to the nature of work motivation and job satisfaction.

The underlying concept of motivation is a driving force within individuals by which they attempt to achieve some goal in order to satisfy a need or expectation. This gives rise to the basic motivational model, illustrated in Figure 7.1.

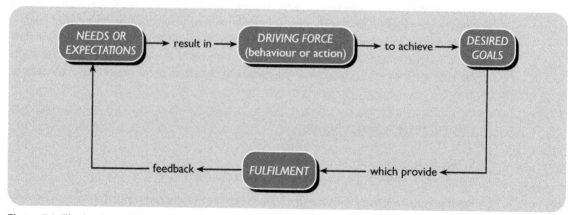

Figure 7.1 The basic motivational model

The Chartered Management Institute gives the following definition of motivation:

> Motivation is the creation of stimuli, incentives and working environments that enable people to perform to the best of their ability. The heart of motivation is to give people what they really want most from work. In return managers should expect more in the form of productivity, quality and service.[4]

The opportunity to perform

If the manager is to improve the work of the organisation, attention must be given to the level of motivation of its members. The manager must encourage staff to direct their efforts (their driving force) towards the successful attainment of the goals and objectives of the organisation.

Performance is a function of both ability level and the motivation to use ability,[5] as well as the opportunity to perform.[6]

Performance = function (**ability** $\times$ **motivation** to use ability $\times$ **opportunity** to perform)

You cannot motivate someone to do something that they do not have the ability to do. This emphasises the importance of training to motivation. The desire to perform well must be encouraged and supported by the opportunity for staff to perform and to realise their full potential.

People should be able to experience a sense of achievement and personal growth in a purposeful and meaningful job. Staff are then more likely to feel motivated to perform to the best of their abilities. Motivation is derived from the fulfilment of an individual's needs and expectations.[7]

Needs and expectations at work

People's behaviour and actions are directed towards the satisfaction of certain needs and expectations which form the basis of their motivational driving force. Motivation is a complex subject, it is a very personal thing, it is multifaceted and influenced by many variables. Farren reminds us of the 12 human needs that have been around since the beginning of recorded history: family, health and well-being, work/career, economic, learning, home/shelter, social relationships, spirituality, community, leisure, mobility and environment/safety. 'Work and private life in the new millennium will continue to revolve around the 12 human needs.'[8]

Individuals have a variety of changing, and often conflicting, needs and expectations at work which they seek to satisfy in a number of different ways. These various needs and expectations can be categorised in various ways. One basic form of categorisation is into the simple division of extrinsic and intrinsic motivation.

- Extrinsic motivation – relates to 'tangible' rewards such as pay and fringe benefits, subsidised accommodation or meals, job security, promotion, contract of service, the work environment and conditions of work.

- Intrinsic motivation – relates to 'psychological' rewards and internal feelings such as a sense of personal satisfaction from the job, the opportunity for challenge and achievement, receiving appreciation, positive recognition, and being treated in a caring and considerate manner.

Higher set of motivational needs

According to Kets de Vries, the best-performing companies possess a set of values that creates the right conditions for high performance; he questions whether in such companies there is something more going on that touches upon a deeper layer of human functioning, causing people to make an extra effort. The emphasis is on widening choice that enables people to choose more freely, instead of being led by forces of which they are unaware; and it is a motivational needs system on which such choice is based. Kets de Vries suggests that in addition to the motivation needs system for physiological needs, sensual and enjoyment needs, and the need to respond to threatening situations, companies that get the best out of their people are characterised by a system based on a higher set of motivational needs:

- **attachment/affiliation** – concerning the need for engagement and sharing, a feeling of community and a sense of belonging to the company; and
- **exploration/assertion** – concerning the ability to play and work, a sense of fun and enjoyment, the need for self-assertion and the ability to choose.[9]

A broad, three-fold framework

Because of the diverse and complex nature of motivation it is helpful to have some initial framework of analysis. The following broad, three-fold framework provides a convenient starting point as a focus on work motivation and job satisfaction.

- *Economic rewards* – such as pay, perks and fringe benefits, material goods, job security and pension rights. The provision of live-in accommodation and meals at work could also be included under this heading.
- *Intrinsic satisfaction* – which is derived from the nature of the work itself and includes an interesting and challenging job, variety, a sense of involvement and achievement, and scope for personal development and use of initiative.
- *Social relationships* – such as the nature of the work environment, comradeship, friendship, group membership, the desire for affiliation, and a feeling of status, support or belonging.

Comparative importance

Motivation, job satisfaction and work performance will be determined by the comparative importance of these sets of needs and expectations, and the extent to which they are fulfilled (Figure 7.2).

Economic rewards are clearly a motivating factor to a greater or lesser extent for all staff. But given the generally low levels of pay for the majority of staff within the hospitality industry, other motivating influences would seem to be of particular significance. Pay as a motivator is discussed later in this chapter.

Intrinsic satisfaction will vary from job to job and often between different parts of the same job. Most of us would probably perceive a distinction between the intrinsic satisfaction

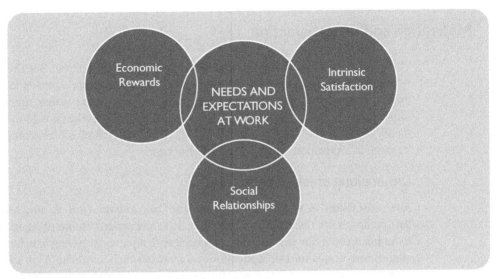

Figure 7.2 Needs and expectations of people at work

of the head chef compared with a kitchen porter, or between that of serving in the bar compared with cleaning or porterage. It is difficult to generalise, however. Intrinsic satisfaction is a personal attitude which varies according to the individual and according to particular circumstances.

Social relationships would appear to be an important feature for many staff. The characteristics of the hospitality industry as a service industry, the role of people, interactions with others, and the importance of good teamwork and supportive working relationships can be strong motivators at work. Many staff are attracted to work in the hospitality and leisure industries as much for the enjoyment and 'fun' of the work which they perceive as compensating for the long hours and low pay.

Combination and balance

Motivation at work is a very personal thing. Each individual will seek to achieve the desired combination and balance of economic rewards, intrinsic satisfaction and social relationships. For some hospitality workers the potential for tips, and subsidised live-in accommodation and meals, may be important considerations. For others, a low level of pay, although obviously not welcomed, may be accepted because of the strong motivating influence of an interesting job and rewarding social relationships. The comparative importance of the three sets of needs and expectations is liable to change according to the particular situation in which individuals find themselves.

The motivation to work is also influenced by the 'psychological contract' (discussed in Chapter 2). Although not defined formally, the psychological contract implies a series of mutual expectations and satisfaction of needs between the individual and the organisation. It covers a range of rights, privileges, behaviours, duties and obligations which have an important influence on the behaviour and actions of people at work.

Motivation and job satisfaction

The motivation to work well is usually related to job satisfaction. But the nature of this relationship is not clear. Satisfaction with the job may motivate a person to achieve a high level of performance. The content theories of motivation, in particular, are related more to satisfaction. For example, Herzberg's two-factor theory (discussed below) is essentially a theory of job satisfaction. However, although the level of job satisfaction may well affect the strength of motivation, this is not always the case.

Dimensions of job satisfaction

Job satisfaction is a complex concept and not always easy to measure objectively. Satisfaction is not the same as motivation. Job satisfaction is more of an attitude, an internal state. It could, for example, be associated with a personal feeling of achievement, either quantitative or qualitative. Motivation is a process which may lead to job satisfaction.

It is not clear whether job satisfaction consists of a single dimension or a number of separate dimensions. There does appear to be a positive correlation between satisfaction and different areas of work. But some workers may be satisfied with certain aspects of their work and dissatisfied with other aspects.[10] What is clear is that the level of job satisfaction is affected by a wide range of variables related to individual, social, cultural, organisational and environmental factors. These factors all influence job satisfaction of individuals in a given set of circumstances, but not necessarily in others.

Early approaches to motivation and job satisfaction

Early approaches to motivation were based on the simple premise of the satisfaction of economic needs. You may recall that an underlying principle of scientific management was a belief in the rational-economic concept of motivation. (See Chapter 4.) Workers would be motivated primarily by the satisfaction of the highest possible wages. Emphasis was placed on the content of a 'fair day's work' and on optimising the level of workers' productivity. However, the definition of a fair day's work is very subjective and, if individuals work hard to increase their earnings, management might redefine the target for a fair day's work.

A range of different needs

The findings of the Hawthorne experiments and the human relations writers demonstrated that people are motivated to work in order to satisfy a range of different, complex needs; not simply monetary reward. Emphasis was given to the importance of the satisfaction of the psychological and social needs of individuals; group values and norms; and styles of leadership. This in turn gave rise to the work of the neo-human relations writers and to theories of motivation based on the personal adjustment of the individual, and the content and meaning of work.

Reeves draws attention to the relationship between accomplishment at work and the need to 'work harder'.

> All this busy-ness and stress is creating more heat than light. It is a sign not of work being too hard but too shallow. Human nature is driven by a desire to accomplish things, and so the fewer opportunities for accomplishment a job contains, the more likely we are to fill the void by tearing around in a frenzy in an effort to persuade ourselves and others that our work has a purpose, that it is important.[11]

Theories of motivation

Unfortunately there is no single or simple answer to the question of what motivates people to work well. Motivation is by its nature a complex subject and is influenced by a wide range of individual, social, cultural and situational variables. Motivation also varies over time and according to circumstances. It is often most acute for people at a mid-career position and especially for those who find opportunities for further advancement or promotion are limited.[12] Factors such as commitment to the organisation may also influence the older employees' motivation and performance.[13]

The complex and variable nature of work motivation has given rise to many competing ideas and theories. *But these theories are not conclusive.* They are all subject to criticism or alternative findings. It is always easy to quote an example which appears to contradict any generalised observation on what motivates people to work well (Figure 7.3).

These theories, however, help to highlight the many motives which influence people's behaviour and performance. Collectively, the different theories provide a framework within which the manager can direct attention to the problem of how best to motivate staff to work willingly and effectively. Anything which aids an understanding of how best to motivate

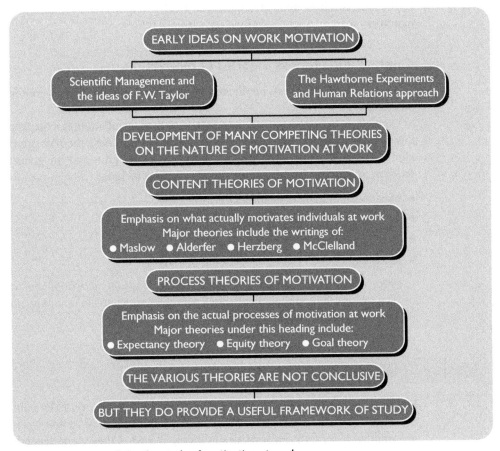

Figure 7.3 Framework for the study of motivation at work

staff must be useful. *'All managers have a duty to motivate their teams. Motivated people take more pride in their jobs and work better. But many managers don't know how to motivate their staff.'*[14]

Motivation in the service sector

Willman refers to the particular difficulties of motivating non-career staff in the service sector. These staff are often female, part-time non-graduates, who work in important customer contact roles, and infrequently move up into managerial ranks.

> Their attachment to the organisation is fleeting, their pay often low, their job content often routine. However, the problem for service businesses is that, frequently, they are all the customer sees. They define the quality of service the organisation can offer. This matters more in businesses where the service itself is the product, than where poor service may be offset by good products . . . The motivation, skills and knowledge of these staff is a key issue for the quality of service offered by an organisation.[15]

Managers can learn from the different theories and approaches to motivation. If a hospitality manager can identify different motivating factors within staff, this is likely to lead to improved attitudes to work, lower turnover and improved customer relations. The manager can judge the relevance of the different theories, how best to draw upon them and how they might successfully be applied in particular work situations. This is part of being an effective manager.

Content and process theories of motivation

Theories of motivation can be divided into two broad approaches – content theories and process theories.

Content theories place emphasis on *what motivates* and attempt to explain those specific things which actually motivate the individual at work. These theories are concerned with identification of people's needs and their relative strengths, and the goals they pursue in order to satisfy these needs. Major content theories include:

- Maslow's hierarchy of needs model;
- Alderfer's continuum of needs model (ERG theory);
- Herzberg's two-factor theory; and
- McClelland's theory of achievement motivation.

Process theories place emphasis on the actual *process of motivation* and attempt to identify the relationships among the dynamic variables which make up motivation. These theories are discussed later in this chapter.

Maslow's hierarchy of needs

Maslow's theory of individual development and motivation, originally published in 1943, provides a useful starting point.[16] The basic proposition of Maslow's work is that people are wanting beings; they always desire more, and what they want depends on what they already have. He suggests that human needs are arranged in a series of levels – a hierarchy of importance. At the lowest level are physiological needs, then safety needs, love (or social) needs, esteem needs – to, at the highest level, the need for self-actualisation (Figure 7.4).

The basic premise of Maslow's theory is that once a lower-level need has been satisfied it no longer acts as a strong motivator. The needs of the next highest level in the hierarchy demand satisfaction and become the primary motivating influence. Only the unsatisfied needs motivate a person. Thus Maslow asserts that 'a satisfied need is no longer a motivator'.

It is important to note, however, that Maslow points out that a particular need at one level does not necessarily have to be satisfied fully before a subsequent need arises. There is a gradual emergence of a higher-level need as lower-level needs become 'largely' satisfied.

Not necessarily a fixed order

The hierarchy is not necessarily a fixed order and for some people there will be more dominant needs and a reversal of the hierarchy. To some people, for example, self-esteem may seem to be more important than love or social needs. For some innately creative people the desire to satisfy esteem needs or self-actualisation may be the prime motivating influence. This might be true for some chefs, for example.

A report of the former HCITB highlights the image of the job of the chef as very definitely seen as important, skilled and responsible. It is a challenging rather than an easy job. Although it is seen as secure, a number would prefer a more adventurous job rather than

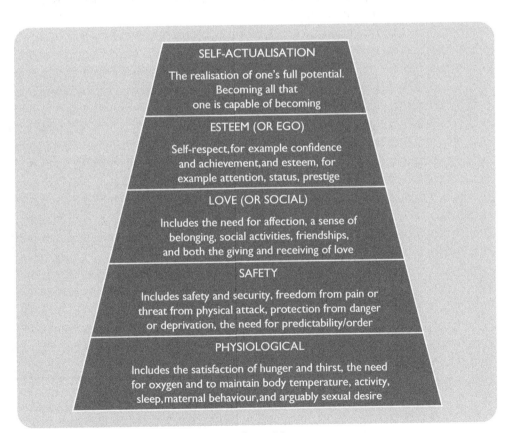

Figure 7.4 Maslow's hierarchy of human needs model

security. The most satisfying aspects of its image are that the job is seen as well respected and offering good opportunities for promotion.[17]

Relevance of Maslow's theory

Maslow's work is open to doubts and criticisms.[18] The theory is difficult to test empirically and has been subject to various interpretations by different writers. There are also a number of problems in relating Maslow's theory to the work situation.

People do not necessarily satisfy their needs, especially higher-level needs, just through the work situation. The manager would require a complete understanding of people's private and social lives, not just their behaviour at work. Also, some rewards or outcomes at work may satisfy more than one level of need. For example, higher salary or promotion can be applied to all levels of the hierarchy.[19]

However, despite the rather simplistic nature of the need hierarchy model, it does provide a convenient framework for viewing the different needs and expectations of people at work. The position of individual members of staff in the hierarchy will help determine the most appropriate motivators. For example, if a person's physiological and safety needs have been satisfied, giving more of the same does not provide motivation. In order to provide motivation for a change in behaviour, the manager would need to direct attention to the next highest level and the satisfaction of social needs. Steers and Porter suggest a list of general rewards and organisational factors used to satisfy different needs[20] (Figure 7.5).

Needs levels	General rewards	Organisational factors
1 Physiological	Food, water, sex, sleep	a Pay b Pleasant working conditions c Cafeteria
2 Safety	Safety, security, stability, protection	a Safe working conditions b Company benefits c Job security
3 Social	Love, affection, belongingness	a Cohesive work group b Friendly supervision c Professional associations
4 Esteem	Self-esteem, self-respect, prestige, status	a Social recognition b Job title c High status job d Feedback from the job itself
5 Self-actualisation	Growth, advancement, creativity	a Challenging job b Opportunities for creativity c Achievement in work d Advancement in the organisation

Source: Reproduced with permission from Steers, R. M. and Porter, L. W., *Motivation and Work Behavior*, 5th edn, McGraw-Hill (1991), p. 35.

Figure 7.5 Applying Maslow's need hierarchy

It should be remembered that Maslow's theory relates to individual development and motivation in life and not just to the behaviour of people at work. The hierarchy of needs model, therefore, can also be applied to the satisfaction of the needs and expectations of hotel customers as well as to members of staff.[21]

Saunders contends that despite the time that has elapsed, Maslow's theory remains watertight.

> When prehistoric man first took shelter in a cave and lit a fire, he was satisfying his lowest – physiological and safety – needs. When a Buddhist achieves a state of nirvana, she is satisfying the fifth and highest – self-actualisation . . . The cave these days might be a three-bedroom semi with garden and off-street parking, but the fact remains that once we've got enough to feed, clothe and house our families money is a low-level motivator for most people. The dash for cash is soon replaced by the desire for recognition, status and ultimately (although Maslow reckoned that a lot of us never get this far) the need to express yourself through your work.[22]

Critical review and reflection

'John Adair points out that presenting Maslow's hierarchy as a pyramid model gives the impression that the greatest needs are in the lower levels. Adair suggests that the pyramid should be inverted as physiological needs, for example, are limited but there are fewer limitations the further up you go.'[23]

How would you best explain and present Maslow's hierarchy of human needs?

Alderfer's continuum of needs model

A modified need hierarchy model, applied to the organisational setting, has been presented by Alderfer. This model condenses Maslow's five levels of need into a continuum based on three core sets of needs: existence, relatedness and growth (ERG theory).[24]

- *Existence needs* are concerned with sustaining human existence and survival. They cover physiological and safety needs of a material nature.
- *Relatedness needs* are concerned with relationships to the social environment. They cover love or belonging, affiliation and meaningful interpersonal relationships of a safety or esteem nature.
- *Growth needs* are concerned with the development of potential. They cover self-esteem and self-actualisation.

A continuum of needs

Alderfer suggests that although individuals normally progress through the different levels of needs, they are more of a continuum than a hierarchy. ERG theory states that an individual may be motivated to satisfy more than one basic set of needs. Individuals may also move down to a lower-level need. For example, if an individual is continually frustrated in attempting to satisfy growth needs, then relatedness needs may reassume importance as a motivating influence and become the main focus of the individual's efforts.

The results of Alderfer's work support the idea that lower-level needs decrease in strength as they become satisfied. However, lower-level needs do not have to be satisfied before a higher-level need emerges. The order of the sets of needs and their relative importance varies from individual to individual. Some people will be motivated by a strong desire to satisfy their existence needs, while others will have a high desire for satisfaction of relatedness and/or growth needs.

Flexible strategies of motivation

ERG theory appears to provide for a practical and more flexible approach to motivation. One set of needs does not operate to the exclusion of others. Therefore, if a person's needs at a particular level are blocked, then the manager should focus attention on the satisfaction of other sets of needs. Alternative strategies of motivation may be more appropriate for different departments and for different types of staff. For example, if waiters feel their growth needs are blocked through lack of opportunity for personal development, the manager should attempt to provide increased opportunities to satisfy existence and relatedness needs (for example TGI Friday's 'fun' working environment).

Herzberg's two-factor theory

Herzberg's two-factor theory is essentially a theory of job satisfaction related to motivation at work.[25] The original study consisted of interviews with 203 accountants and engineers in America. They were asked to relate: (i) times when they felt exceptionally 'good' about their present job or a previous job, and (ii) times when they felt exceptionally 'bad' about their job.

From the responses to the interviews Herzberg revealed two distinct sets of factors affecting motivation and work: the two-factor theory of motivation and job satisfaction, and the motivation-hygiene theory (Figure 7.6).

Hygiene factors or dissatisfiers

One set of factors, known as the 'hygiene' or 'maintenance' factors (hygiene being used in the medical concept of 'preventive and environmental'), serve to prevent dissatisfaction. These factors are related to job context and include salary, job security, working conditions, level and quality of supervision, company policy and administration, and interpersonal relations. The hygiene factors are concerned with how people are treated at work.

If the hygiene factors are absent, or inadequate, they cause dissatisfaction. Proper attention to the hygiene factors will tend to overcome dissatisfaction and bring motivation back to normal – a zero – state. But the hygiene factors do not, by themselves, create a positive attitude or increase the motivation to work. Accordingly, **the opposite of dissatisfaction is not satisfaction but rather no dissatisfaction.**

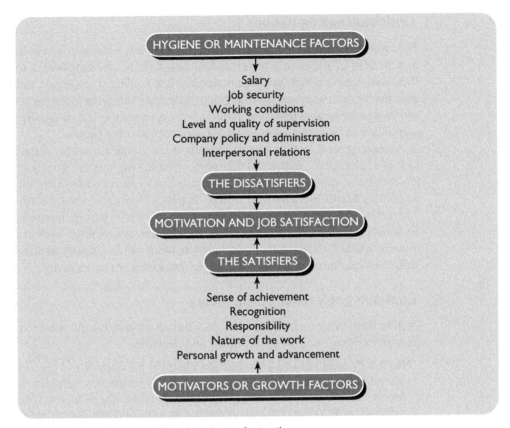

Figure 7.6 Representation of Herzberg's two-factor theory

Motivating factors or satisfiers

To motivate workers to give of their best and to sustain higher levels of performance, the manager must give attention to a second set of factors – the 'motivators' or 'growth' factors. These factors are related to job content and include a sense of achievement, recognition, responsibility, the nature of the work itself, and personal growth and advancement. The motivating factors are concerned with what people are able to do at work. The strength of the motivators will affect feelings of satisfaction or no satisfaction, but not dissatisfaction.

Herzberg emphasises that both sets of factors are important, but for different reasons. Hygiene factors are not a 'second-class citizen system'. They are as important as the motivators and necessary to avoid unpleasantness at work, and to deny unfair treatment by management. The motivating factors relate to what people are allowed to do at work. They are the variables which actually motivate people.

Applications to guest satisfaction

In addition to its normal application to employee motivation, Herzberg's theory and the importance of hygiene and motivating factors can also be applied to the area of guest satisfaction.[26]

Criticisms and limitations

The two-factor theory is a source of frequent debate and controversy. It is also subject to a number of different interpretations. One general criticism relates to methodology. Describing events which gave rise to good or bad feelings is subjective and likely to influence the results. People are more inclined to attribute satisfying incidents at work, the motivators, as a favourable reflection on their own performance. The dissatisfying incidents are more likely to be attributed to external factors and to other people.

Another general, major, area of criticism is the simplistic nature of the theory and the lack of allowance for individual differences. Not all workers are greatly interested in the job content of their work, or with motivators or growth factors. (See the discussion on motivating hourly workers later in this chapter.) Some staff appear content to adopt an 'instrumental' view – that is, work as a means to an end. They are motivated almost solely by financial rewards and security rather than by the nature of the work or the satisfaction of social needs.[27] Other staff appear happy to work within a tightly structured framework, with closely defined work tasks and limited autonomy or responsibility.

Continuing relevance of the theory

Despite these criticisms there is still evidence of support for the continuing relevance of Herzberg's theory. According to Crainer and Dearlove:

> Herzberg's work has had a considerable effect on the rewards and remuneration packages offered by corporations. Increasingly, there is a trend towards 'cafeteria' benefits in which people can choose from a range of options. In effect, they can select the elements they recognise as providing their own motivation to work. Similarly, the current emphasis on self-development, career management and self-managed learning can be seen as having evolved from Herzberg's insights.[28]

Whatever the validity of the two-factor theory, much of the criticism comes with the benefit of hindsight. Herzberg did, at least, attempt an empirical approach to the study of motivation at work and job satisfaction. Furthermore, his work has drawn attention to the importance of job design in the 'quality of work life'.

Applications to hospitality staff

It is often claimed that the theory has only limited application to 'manual' workers, or to people with unskilled jobs, or whose work is limited in scope. Yet these are the people who often present management with the biggest problem of motivation. For example, in considering the application of Herzberg's work to hospitality staff, MacQueen comments: 'the trouble with Herzberg's motivation-hygiene theory of motivation is that it applies least to the people management most want to motivate – those with monotonous, repetitive, uninteresting jobs'.[29]

Hygiene factors are more likely to be significant in the hospitality industry than in other industries. Workers who live in, or take meals when on duty, are more likely to be concerned with the workplace and the quality of their working conditions. It might also be that some workers have a low expectation of satisfying higher-level needs and, therefore, place greater emphasis on the hygiene factors.

This view would seem to be supported from a study by Chitiris on the application of Herzberg's theory to workers in the Greek hotel industry. From the results of questionnaire interviews on levels of job satisfaction and the importance of certain job factors, Chitiris found that in general workers were more interested in the hygiene factors than in the motivators.[30]

Critical review and reflection

In 2012, Tony Mullen, Human Resources Director of Apex Hotels, stated that staff wanted to be treated properly and shown respect, to be given decent meals, decent staff facilities including clean toilets and changing rooms, and to be paid on time.

To what extent do you agree that, because it is not possible for all jobs in the hospitality industry to be interesting and stimulating, providing the benefits that Mullen suggests must be the main focus of management?

The importance of job design

Despite doubts concerning the two-factor theory, Herzberg's work has drawn attention to wider issues which may influence motivation and job satisfaction. If managers are to provide positive motivation and improve job satisfaction, then attention must be given to both the hygiene and the motivating factors.

A particular feature of Herzberg's theory is that it drew attention to the importance of job design and the structuring of hospitality jobs. This point is acknowledged by MacQueen: 'the value of Herzberg's approach lies in its emphasis on the need for the re-design of jobs in order to bring the motivators to bear'.[31] We return to the importance of job design later in this chapter.

McClelland's achievement motivation

The need for achievement underlies the higher levels of Maslow's hierarchy and is also one of Herzberg's motivating factors. The importance of achievement is emphasised by McClelland, who has developed a theory of motivation which is rooted in culture.[32] The work of McClelland is based on the concept of four main sets of needs and socially developed motives:

- the need for **affiliation**;
- the need for **achievement**;
- the need for **power**;
- the need for **avoidance**.

People possess all four of these important needs but the relative intensity of these motives varies among individuals and different occupations. McClelland's research concentrates mainly on how managers can develop the need for achievement in subordinate staff.

Variations among individuals

The extent of individuals' achievement motivation is dependent upon cultural influences, occupational experiences and the type of organisation in which they work. Some people are highly motivated by achievement, they are challenged by opportunities and work hard to achieve a goal, whilst to others achievement is not very important.

Characteristics of high achievers

For high achievers money may seem to be important, but it is valued more as symbolising successful goal achievement. Money may serve as a means of giving feedback on performance. For this reason, people with high achievement motivation seem unlikely to remain long with an organisation that does not pay them well for good performance. For people with low achievement motivation, money may serve more as a direct financial incentive for performance.

Although it is difficult to apply objective measures, McClelland has identified four common characteristics of people with high achievement needs: the preference for personal responsibility, the setting of moderate but achievable goals, the desire for specific feedback and being innovative.

Personal satisfaction is derived from the accomplishment of the task itself and recognition need not come from other people. They prefer situations in which they can assume *personal responsibility* for solving problems. They like to attain success through their own efforts, rather than by teamwork or by chance factors outside their control.

They tend to set *moderate achievement goals* with an intermediate level of difficulty, and to take calculated risks. If a task is too difficult or too risky it would reduce the chances of success and of gaining need satisfaction. If the course of action is too easy or too simple, there is little challenge in accomplishing the task and little satisfaction from successful performance.

They want *clear and unambiguous feedback* on how well they are performing. A knowledge of results within a reasonable time is necessary for self-evaluation. Feedback enables them to determine success or failure in the accomplishment of their goals, and satisfaction from their activities.

They are *more innovative* and tend always to be moving on to something a little more challenging. There is a constant search for variety, and for information to help find new ways of doing things.

Development of achievement drive

McClelland has attempted to understand the characteristics of high achievers. He suggests that n-Ach (need for achievement) is not hereditary but results from environmental influences. McClelland has investigated the possibility of training people to develop a greater motivation to achieve and suggests four steps in attempting to develop achievement drive:

1 Striving to attain feedback on performance. Reinforcement of success serves to strengthen the desire to achieve higher performance.

2 Developing models of achievement by seeking to emulate people who have performed well.

3 Attempting to modify the self-image, so as to see themselves as needing challenges and success.

4 Controlling day-dreaming and to think about themselves in more positive terms.[33]

Applications to the hospitality industry

There are, of course, potential benefits to any business organisation from the efforts and performance of high achievers. However, McClelland's theory implies an individualistic approach to the motivation of staff, whilst the hospitality industry is characterised by the need for close cooperation and effective teamwork in order to provide customer satisfaction. In hospitality, the behaviour and performance of work groups is as important as individual motivation. Attempts to satisfy the needs of higher achievers must be matched with the requirements of the industry and this may not be an easy task.

Paying and motivating hourly workers

The content theories of motivation place emphasis on the importance of psychological rewards, and personal growth and achievement. According to Weaver, however, such theories have little meaning for hourly workers in the hotel and restaurant industry.[34] The work of, for example, cooks, dishwashers and waiting or housekeeping staff does not change much among different companies, so such staff feel little attachment to a particular company. Where there is little pleasure in the work itself or the job offers little opportunity for career advancement, personal challenge or growth, hourly workers are working for their pay cheque.

Motivating with money

Weaver proposes a 'Theory M' programme of motivation based on direct cash rewards for above-average productivity. A percentage base is calculated from the average performance of workers on the staff. Workers then receive a percentage of any *increase* in sales or savings to the company generated by their efforts. Although particularly suited to food and beverage operations, Weaver suggests that the programme could be extended to other hotel employees, for example a bonus payment to night-desk staff for selling as many vacant rooms as possible or a wage incentive to housekeeping staff for cleaning an above-average number of rooms in a shift.

Note, however, that on a more general level, a survey of human resource managers responding to *Personnel Journal* found that it is often difficult to attract, retain and motivate minimum wage workers through pay alone. The survey uncovered that 62 per cent of respondents had a problem retaining minimum wage workers strictly because of pay. Many employers must provide other incentives, such as bonuses or prizes, on top of pay to keep workers on the job.[35]

> Work is about letting people know they are important, their hard work and efforts matter, and they're doing a good job. And this kind of recognition, in fact, can sometimes be more important than money.
>
> (Gary Kusin, CEO, FedEx Kinko's)[36]

Process theories of motivation

Process theories attempt to identify relationships among the dynamic variables which make up motivation. They provide a further contribution to our understanding of behaviour and performance at work, and the complex nature of motivation. Process theories are concerned with how behaviour is initiated, directed and sustained. There are a number of different process theories but major approaches under this heading include:

- Expectancy theory
- Equity theory
- Goal theory.

The basis of expectancy theory

Expectancy theory provides a dominant framework in which to view motivation at work. The basis of expectancy theory is that people are influenced by the expected results of their actions. Motivation is a function of the relationship between:

1 effort expended and the perceived likely outcomes; and

2 the expectation that reward will be related to performance.

There must also be

3 the expectation that rewards (desired outcomes) are available (Figure 7.7).

An example of how the level of performance depends upon the perceived expectations regarding effort expended and the desired outcome could be a sous chef desiring higher status and seeking promotion to head chef. This desire will lead to a high level of performance only if the sous chef believes that the opportunity for promotion is available, and that higher performance is likely to lead to promotion, and that promotion will result in a satisfactory increase in status.

As another example, a human resources assistant, who is unqualified, desires a higher salary but believes this is not possible in the present job. The assistant also believes that promotion would be most unlikely without an examination qualification. In this case there is likely to be a lack of positive motivation to achieve a high level of performance.

In broader terms, however, the generally high levels of staff turnover in the industry may well mean that good performance is perceived as very likely to lead to greater opportunities for rapid promotion.

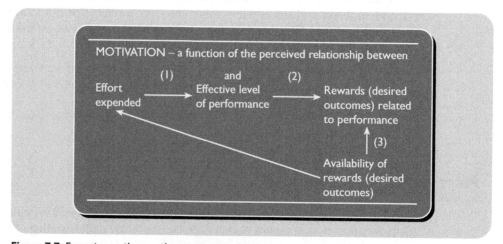

Figure 7.7 Expectancy theory: the motivational link

Effort, performance and rewards

The underlying premise of expectancy theory, therefore, is that motivation is determined by the perceived strength of the link between:

Effort expended – Performance achieved – Rewards obtained

A person's behaviour reflects a conscious choice between the comparative evaluation of alternative behaviours. The choice of behaviour is based on the expectancy of the most favourable consequences, and expectancy is based on the person's **perception** of the situation, irrespective of whether, or not, this is *de facto* the situation.

Vroom's expectancy theory

Vroom's expectancy model is aimed specifically at the work situation. It is centred on three key variables: valence, instrumentality and expectancy (VIE theory). On the basis of Vroom's work it is possible to depict a general model of expectancy theory[37] (Figure 7.8).

● *Valence*. This is the feeling that individuals have about specific outcomes. It is a measure of the attractiveness or preference, to the individual, for a particular outcome. Valence is not the same as value. Valence is *the anticipated satisfaction provided by*

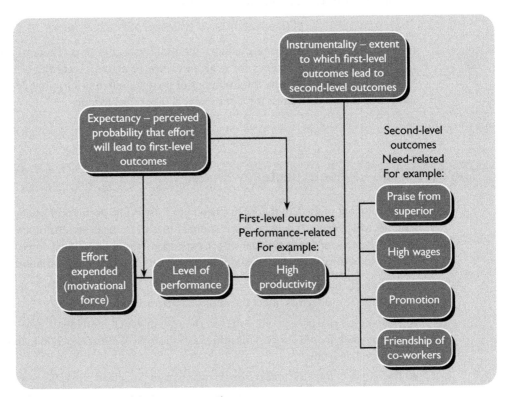

Figure 7.8 A basic model of expectancy theory

an outcome. This may differ from value, which is the actual satisfaction derived by an outcome.

● *Instrumentality*. This is the extent to which performance-related (first-level) outcomes lead to the satisfaction of need-related (second-level) outcomes. Some people may seek to achieve a high level of performance 'for its own sake' and without thought to further expectations. Usually, however, good performance achieves valence because this will be *instrumental* in leading to the satisfaction of second-level outcomes, for example the need for higher wages, promotion or status.

● *Expectancy*. This is the perceived degree of probability that the choice of a particular action will actually lead to the desired outcome. When a person chooses between alternative forms of behaviour which have uncertain outcomes, the choice is affected not only by preference (valence), but also by the probability that such an outcome will be achieved. Expectancy is the relationship between a chosen course of action and its predicted outcome.

Motivational force

The assumption of expectancy theory is that an individual considers in a rational manner the comparative advantages of alternative choices of action and the likelihood of attaining the desired outcome from that action. It is the combination of valence and expectancy which determines a person's motivation for a given form of behaviour. This is the motivational force. Expressed as an equation, this is:

$$M \text{ (motivation)} = V \text{ (valence)} \times E \text{ (expectancy)}$$

If either valence or expectancy is zero, then motivation is zero. There are likely to be a number of different outcomes for a given choice of action. Accordingly the measure of $V \times E$ is summed across the total number of possible outcomes to provide a single figure indicating the attractiveness for a particular choice of behaviour.

The Porter and Lawler expectancy model

A development of the VIE theory has been put forward by Porter and Lawler. They present a model which extends beyond motivational force and considers performance as a whole.[38] Porter and Lawler maintain that effort expended (the motivational force) does not lead directly to performance. It is mediated by three sets of intervening variables:

● *Individual abilities and traits* – such as intelligence, skills, knowledge, training and personality. These factors affect the ability to perform a given activity.

● *The person's role perceptions* – that is, the way in which individuals view their work and the role they should adopt. This influences the type of effort expended, and the direction and level of action.

● *The nature of intrinsic and extrinsic rewards*, and perceived equitable rewards.

A representation of the Porter and Lawler model is given in Figure 7.9.

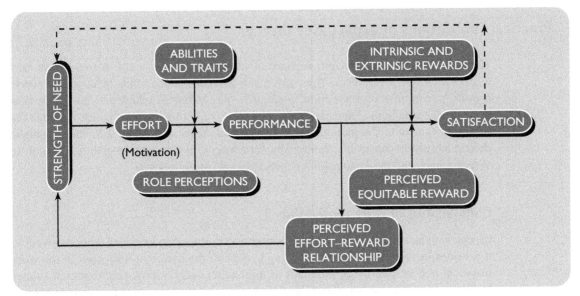

Figure 7.9 Representation of the Porter and Lawler motivation model

Intrinsic and extrinsic rewards

Rewards are desirable outcomes and both intrinsic and extrinsic rewards are important. Intrinsic rewards derive from the individuals themselves and include personal satisfaction, a sense of achievement, a feeling of responsibility and recognition. Extrinsic rewards derive from the organisation and the actions of others, and include salary, working conditions and supervision. The proportion of intrinsic and extrinsic will vary among individuals and different work situations, but there must be a minimum of both. However, Porter and Lawler suggest that intrinsic rewards are more likely to produce job satisfaction related to performance than are extrinsic rewards.

Most people have an implicit perception about the level of rewards, intrinsic and extrinsic, they should receive commensurate with the requirements and demands of the job, and the contribution expected of them. Perceived equitable reward is the level of rewards people feel they should fairly receive for a given standard of performance. The experience of satisfaction derives from actual rewards which meet or exceed the perceived equitable rewards.

Motivation, satisfaction and performance

Porter and Lawler see motivation, satisfaction and performance as separate variables, and attempt to explain the complex relationships among them. The effort, or amount of energy, a person exerts on a given activity is associated more with motivation than with performance. It does not relate to how successful a person is in carrying out an activity.

The human relations approach tended to assume that job satisfaction leads to improved performance. In contrast, Porter and Lawler suggest that job satisfaction is an effect rather than a cause of performance. Job satisfaction is more dependent upon performance, than performance is upon job satisfaction.

Practical applications of expectancy theory

There are a number of different versions of expectancy theory and it is not always easy to understand or apply them. There are many variables which affect behaviour at work. A problem can arise in attempting to identify those variables which are most important in particular situations. Expectancy theory applies only to behaviour which is under the voluntary control of the individual. Individuals may have only limited freedom to make choices because of constraints imposed by, for example, policies and procedures, the nature of technology, and the organisation structure or role prescriptions.

Complexities of work motivation

Expectancy theory does, however, draw attention to the complexities of work motivation. It provides further information in helping to explain the nature of behaviour in the work situation, and in identifying problems in motivation and performance. Research studies highlight difficulties with some of the concepts involved but do appear to provide general support for the theory.[39]

Porter *et al.* emphasise that the expectancy model is just a model. People rarely sit down and consciously list their expected outcomes, expectancies and valences. But they do consider the likely outcomes of their actions and the attractiveness of various alternatives in deciding what they will do. The expectancy model provides a means of mirroring the process and predicting its outcome.[40]

Attention by management

Expectancy theory indicates that, in order to improve the motivation and performance of staff, the manager should give attention to a number of factors including the following:

- Attempt to establish clear relationships and strong links between effort and performance, and performance and rewards.

- Review appropriateness of rewards in terms of individual performance rather than on a more general basis. Outcomes with a high valence for the individual should be used as an incentive for improved performance.

- Establish clear procedures for the monitoring and evaluation of individual levels of performance.

- Ensure subordinates have the required understanding, knowledge and skills to enable them to achieve a high level of performance.

- Give attention to intervening variables such as company policies, organisational procedures and support facilities which, although not direct motivational factors, may still affect performance.

- Minimise undesirable outcomes which may be perceived to result from a high level of performance, for example accidents, sanctions from co-workers or the imposition of increased targets. Also minimise those undesirable outcomes which result despite a high level of performance, such as a reduction in bonus payments.

Equity theory of motivation

One of the variables identified in the Porter and Lawler expectancy model is perceived equitable rewards. This leads to consideration of another process theory of motivation – equity theory – which adds further to our understanding of the behaviour of people at work. *Equity theory focuses on people's feelings of how fairly they have been treated in comparison with the treatment received by others.* Applied to the work situation, equity theory is usually associated with the work of Adams.[41]

People evaluate their social relationships in the same way as buying or selling an item. Social relationships involve an exchange process. People expect certain outcomes in exchange for certain contributions or inputs. Equity theory is based on this concept of exchange theory. For example, a person may expect promotion as an outcome of (and in exchange for) a high level of contribution in helping to achieve an important organisational objective (input).

Comparison of outcomes and inputs

People also compare their own position with that of others. They determine the *perceived* equity of their own position. Feelings about the equity of the exchange are affected by the treatment they receive when compared with what happens to other people. Most exchanges involve a multiple of inputs and outcomes. According to equity theory, people place a weighting on these various inputs and outcomes according to how they perceive their importance.

If the ratio of a person's total outcomes to total inputs equals the perceived ratio of other people's outcomes and inputs, there is equity. But when there is an unequal comparison of ratios the person experiences a sense of inequity. The feeling of inequity might arise when an individual's ratio of outcomes to inputs is either greater than or, more usually, less than that of other people.

Behavioural consequences of inequity

The feeling of inequity causes tension. This motivates the person to take action to restore equity. The magnitude of perceived inequity determines the level of tension, and the level of tension determines the strength of motivation. Adams identifies six broad types of behaviour which arise as a consequence of inequity (Figure 7.10).

1 *Changes to inputs* – for example, through the amount or quality of work, timekeeping or absenteeism.

2 *Changes to outputs* – for example, attempting to improve pay, working conditions, fringe benefits or perks, status and recognition, without changes to inputs.

3 *Cognitive distortion of inputs or outcomes* – for example, the belief about how hard a person is really working, the value of examination qualifications, or what can be achieved with a given level of pay.

4 *Leaving the field* – for example, through absenteeism, lack of interest or involvement with the work, request for transfer, or resignation from a job or the organisation.

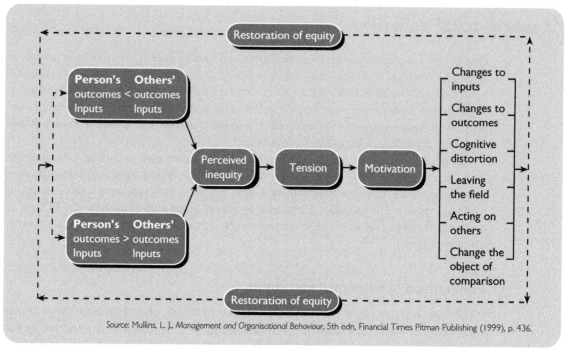

Source: Mullins, L. J., *Management and Organisational Behaviour*, 5th edn, Financial Times Pitman Publishing (1999), p. 436.

Figure 7.10 Representation of Adams's equity theory of motivation

5 *Acting on others* – for example, tempting others to increase their inputs or lower their outcomes, or trying to force others to leave the field.

6 *Changing the object of comparison* – for example, viewing people with whom comparisons have previously been made as now belonging to a different level in the organisation, and finding a new reference group with whom comparison is made.

Managers need to recognise such forms of behaviour as possible consequences of perceived inequity, and need to take appropriate action to reduce tension and restore a sense of equity.

Goal theory

Another theory sometimes considered under the heading of motivation to work is goal theory, or the theory of goal-setting. This theory is based mainly on the work of Locke.[42] The basic premise of goal theory is that people's goals or intentions play an important part in determining behaviour. Locke accepts the importance of perceived value, as indicated in expectancy theories of motivation, and suggests that these values give rise to the experience of emotions and desires. People strive to achieve goals in order to satisfy their emotions and desires. Goals guide people's responses and actions. Goals direct work behaviour and performance, and lead to certain consequences or feedback.

Goal-setting and performance

The combination of goal difficulty and the extent of the person's commitment to achieving the goal regulates the level of effort expended. People with specific quantitative goals, such as a defined level of performance, or a given deadline for completion of a task, will perform better than people with no set goal or only a vague goal such as 'do the best you can'. People who have difficult goals will perform better than people with easier goals.

A number of research studies have attempted to examine the relationship between goal-setting and performance. Although, almost inevitably, there are some contrary findings, the majority of evidence suggests strong support for the theory, and its effects on motivation.[43] Locke subsequently pointed out that 'goal-setting is more appropriately viewed as a motivational technique rather than as a formal theory of motivation'.[44] However it is viewed, the theory of goal-setting provides a useful approach to work motivation and performance.

Practical implications for the manager

Goal theory has a number of practical implications for the manager.

- Specific performance goals should systematically be identified and set in order to direct behaviour and maintain motivation.
- Goals should be set at a challenging but realistic level. Difficult goals lead to higher performance. However, if goals are set at too high a level, or are regarded as impossible to achieve, performance will suffer, especially over a longer period.
- Complete, accurate and timely feedback and knowledge of results is usually associated with high performance. Feedback provides a means of checking progress on goal attainment and forms the basis for any revision of goals.
- Goals can be determined either by a superior or by individuals themselves. Goals set by other people are more likely to be accepted when there is participation. Employee participation in the setting of goals may lead to higher performance.[45]

Applications of motivational theories

The application of motivational theories, and a greater understanding of job satisfaction and work performance, has led to increasing interest in job design. Redesigning the nature of the work organisation and the structure of jobs can have a significant effect on the attitudes and satisfaction of staff, and their level of performance.

A major contribution of Herzberg's two-factor theory lies in the emphasis on the redesign of jobs in order to bring the motivators to bear. His belief is that people should have the opportunity to use their talents and abilities, and to exercise more self-control over the job. Inherent in the job should be a learning and growth experience.[46] Expectancy theory suggests that improving the effort–performance–reward link through job design will have a powerful motivating influence on people, especially those who place a high value on intrinsic rewards.

Alienation at work

One common approach to job satisfaction and work performance is in terms of frustration and alienation at work. Alienation refers to the feeling of detachment of individuals from their work roles. Four major dimensions of alienation are powerlessness, meaninglessness, isolation and self-estrangement.[47]

1 *Powerlessness* denotes the workers' lack of control over management policy, their immediate work processes or conditions of employment.

2 *Meaninglessness* stems from standardisation and the division of labour. It denotes the inability to see the purpose of work done, or to identify with the total process or completed product or service.

3 *Isolation* is the feeling of not belonging to an integrated work group or to the social work organisation, or not being guided by group norms of behaviour.

4 *Self-estrangement* arises from the failure to see work as an end in itself or as a central life issue. Workers experience a depersonalised detachment and work is seen solely as a means to an end.

In order to help overcome alienation, management should attempt to develop within individuals a feeling of attachment to the organisation and to the work situation. The attachment of individuals and the satisfaction derived from their jobs are influenced by the formal structure, managerial style, and the nature of technology and work organisation.

The impact of information technology can also have a significant influence on the feelings of attachment to the job. Information technology will demand new patterns of work. It can affect the nature and content of individual jobs; the function and structure of work groups; changes in the nature of supervision; the hierarchical structure of jobs and responsibilities; and the nature of the management tasks.

The nature of hospitality work

Unlike many manufacturing or administrative situations, the hospitality industry offers potentially high levels of attachment to the work.[48] As mentioned previously, workers who live in or take meals on duty are especially likely to feel closely involved with their workplace. For many live-in workers, it is not a job – it is their life.

Conflicting opinions

However, there appear to be conflicting opinions as to the nature of work in the hospitality industry. One view is that many jobs are monotonous, basic and routine in nature, performed under difficult working conditions and with added harassment from customers. Job enrichment may be difficult to achieve and in any case many workers do not seem greatly interested.

According to a report by what was then the HCITB, low status and the servile nature of jobs are a feature of work in the industry. Jobs such as those of cashier, kitchen staff and (surprisingly) receptionists lack variety and job satisfaction. The nature of the working environment deters substantial numbers of job seekers from accepting kitchen jobs.[49]

In contrast, a later HCTC publication suggests an alternative and more positive view, that the industry offers great potential for job satisfaction. Many jobs provide satisfying contact with the customer and allow individual flair and creativity. Staff usually have close and frequent contact with their manager or supervisor, unlike the 'anonymous' nature of some factory or office situations.[50] These positive features should be built upon and developed through the restructuring of work and job design.

Likes and dislikes about working in the industry

A study of 442 recent graduates from 11 American hospitality management colleges highlighted the importance of job challenge and career advancement as a key factor of job satisfaction.[51] Responses to an open-ended question on what was liked and disliked about working in the hospitality industry were categorised into five groups of likes and six groups of dislikes (Figure 7.11).

The most frequent response on what was liked best about the job or career referred to the challenge and direct involvement in their work. The second most frequent set of liked factors referred to interactions with others and people-related responses. Other attractions related to the nature of the work environment, including opportunities for learning and the physical surroundings, the fast pace of the industry, and for a relatively small group, benefits, travel and prestige. Women were more likely to mention likes relating to people and the public than were men, who were more likely to mention challenges and the work environment.

Likes:
1. Challenge, direct involvement, autonomy, independence, rewarding work
2. People, the public, and professional contacts
3. Working environment, opportunity for growth and advancement
4. Fast pace, change
5. Benefits, travel, prestige

Dislikes:
1. Long hours, nights and weekend schedule
2. Low pay
3. Stress, demanding supervisors and duties, no personal time, quality of life
4. Routine, no advancement or growth, no import or recognition
5. Company politics, management
6. Labor shortages, poor staff, lack of employee motivation, employees' and co-workers' attitudes

Note: Each list is presented in descending order of frequency.

Source: reprinted by permission of Elsevier Science Inc. from 'Job Satisfaction: What's Happening to the Young Managers?' by Pavesic, D. V. and Brymer, R. A., *Cornell Hotel and Restaurant Administration Quarterly*, vol. 30, no. 4, February 1990, p. 95, Copyright 1990 by Cornell University.

Figure 7.11 Hospitality jobs: likes and dislikes

Exhibit 7.1 Positive aspects of the hospitality industry – a personal view

I started working in hotels full-time from the age of 17, and over the next 10 years I was fortunate to work in a variety of hotels and gain valuable experience. Very few industries offer the same opportunities with regard to career advancement and responsibility as the hospitality industry. From my personal experience by the age of 20, having worked in hotels in Blackpool and Oxford, I applied for my first post as head receptionist in a three-star 120-bedroom hotel. This was my first management position and the responsibility was enormous; my salary with the benefits was far higher than most people of my age in other industries.

The image is still a conflicting one and many of the benefits of the industry are over-looked. Although research shows that money is not the most important aspect of the job, most would agree that a reasonable wage is essential. What most people fail to realise is that additional benefits are incorporated within the salary.

- Accommodation is often provided for hotel workers either as part of the package, or for a minimum amount of rent.
- Accommodation is often either on the premises or close by, reducing or eliminating the cost of travel to and from work.
- Heating, lighting, water and other amenities are provided free of charge.
- Meals on and off duty are provided for live-in staff.
- Uniforms are often part of the package, saving on the cost of work clothes.
- Use of on site laundry facilities is often available to live-in staff.
- The social activities often centre around the live-in staff.

Taking all of the above into account means that hotel staff often earn far more than they think, so, although the salaries are low in comparison with other sectors of the industry the benefits are worth a great deal. It is, however, difficult to appreciate these benefits, and they are often taken for granted. So it is up to the employers to make this clear to future employees.

I spent ten years working and living in hotels, generally in pleasant furnished flats, with no expenses, so my salary was 'pocket money'. It also gave me the opportunity to move within the industry without having the added problem of looking for somewhere to live. It was an invaluable education and one which I enjoyed enormously. It also had great social benefits, and many of the people I worked with over 15 years ago are still great friends.

Source: The authors are grateful to Sandra Cartwright for providing this contribution.

The most disliked factors related to the long hours involved in hotel and food-service work, particularly hours worked at evenings and weekends. Many respondents also referred to not being paid enough for working the odd hours. Other dislikes referred to the stress of the job and the demands of supervisors and their duties, the routine nature of jobs and lack of recognition, especially with lower-level jobs, company politics and management, staffing shortages and the nature of the staff. Women were more likely to mention low pay and management politics than men were. But both men and women were equally likely to refer to long hours and low pay as the features most disliked about their jobs.

What hotel employees want from their work

Simons and Enz undertook a study of 278 employees in 12 different hotels in the United States and Canada to learn what employees want from their work.[52] In order to understand how hotel workers might differ from other workers, the hotel employees were asked to rank the same 10 job-reward work factors used in an earlier major study of industrial workers by Kovach.[53] Only a single factor was to be ranked in any order.

The responses from the hotel workers showed a marked difference from those described in the earlier studies of workers in manufacturing industries (Figure 7.12). Overall, the three things most wanted by hotel employees were: (1) good wages; (2) job security; and (3) opportunities for advancement and development.

Simons and Enz also found that the job factors were ranked differently by workers in different hotel departments (Figure 7.13) and they suggest that: 'the adept manager should take these differences into account when considering what kinds of incentives and rewards to offer for high performance'.

Cross-cultural dimensions of motivation

Whatever the popularity of different theories of motivation, doubts are raised about their universality on the ground that they have not adequately addressed the factor of culture.[54] Are theories of motivation universally applicable or are there meaningful differences in motivation at work, or in life more generally, in different societies? The multicultural nature of the hospitality workforce emphasises the need for awareness of differing factors of motivation. A number of writers have questioned whether motivational theories and models originating in one culture are amenable to transference to other cultures.

Work Factor	Hospitality Workers	Industrial Workers
Good wages	1	5
Security	2	4
Opportunity	3	6
Good working conditions	4	7
Interesting work	5	1
Appreciation	6	2
Loyalty to employees	7	8
Feeling of being in on things	8	3
Tactful discipline	9	9
Sympathetic personal help	10	10

Source: reprinted by permission of Elsevier Science, Inc. from 'Motivating Hotel Employees: Beyond the carrot and the stick', by Simons, T. and Enz, C. A., Cornell Hotel and Restaurant Administration Quarterly, vol. 35, February 1995, p. 23. Copyright 1995 by Cornell University.

Figure 7.12 Work factors ranked by hospitality and industrial workers

Work Factor	F&B Servers	Rooms, Front desk	House-keeping	Accounting, Control	Sales, Marketing	Back of House F&B	Human Resources
Good wages	1	1	2	1	2	1	3
Security	3	4	1	4.5	4	5	6
Opportunity	2	2	5	2	1	4	1
Good working conditions	4	5.5	3	4.5	5	2	4
Interesting work	6	5.5	4	3	3	3	2
Appreciation	5	3	6	6	6	6	5
Loyalty to employees	7	7	7	8	8	7	7
Feeling of being in on things	9	8	8	7	7	8	8
Tactful discipline	8	9	9	9	9	9	9
Sympathetic personal help	10	10	10	10	10	10	10

(Source: As for Figure 7.12.)

Figure 7.13 Work factors ranked by employees in different hotel departments

Francesco and Gold devote a substantial proportion of a discussion of motivation to examining the extent to which American motivation theories are applicable outside the United States.

When discussing Maslow's contribution to this topic and, in particular, the concept of a hierarchy of needs, Francesco and Gold suggest: 'In an international context the circumstances and values of a particular culture can influence the ordering and importance of needs. The values of individualism and collectivism can make the hierarchy more or less relevant.'[55] In evaluating McClelland's work, Francesco and Gold question whether the meaning of an underlying concept, in this case achievement, can even be understood worldwide in the sense it was intended. A study of motivation and job satisfaction among hotel workers in Brazil found that a number of Herzberg's hygiene and motivating factors did not affect job satisfaction or dissatisfaction. A main cause of this difference appeared to be the influence of organisational culture.[56]

It has already been suggested that one criticism of content theories of motivation centres on how applicable they are in different circumstances, and the suggestion that there may be variations across cultures falls within this line of reasoning. However, perhaps less obviously, process theories of motivation have also been criticised for being culture-bound. As they focus on process rather than content, such theories may appear to be more applicable in diverse cultural contexts. Nonetheless it has been suggested that process theories of motivation contain certain inbuilt assumptions that are themselves culturally derived.

Adler reminds us that expectancy models of motivation assume that individuals believe that they can, to some extent, control their environment and influence their fate. If, as in the cases of more fatalistic cultures such as China, people do not have the same sense of internal attribution, the expectancy model may have less force and therefore less applicability. When Adams's equity theory is applied across the world, differences in interpretation have been recorded.[57] Chen suggests that while individualistic cultures place a high regard on equity, collectivist cultures value equality more than equity. Again we see here the possibility that while a theory of motivation may be essentially valid in principle, it is legitimate to think about the ways in which national culture can intervene in terms of its interpretation in different societies.[58]

Job satisfaction and job design

'If you want people to do a good job for you, give them a good job to do'(Herzberg).[59]

Critical review and reflection

Organisations should provide their staff with interesting work. But how do you make bed-making and cleaning bathrooms appear interesting?

What do you consider are the key motivators of staff carrying out mundane routine work?

To make the best use of people as a valuable resource, attention must be given to the relationship between staff and the nature and content of their jobs. The work organisation and the design of jobs can have a significant effect on the behaviour and performance of staff.

Job design is concerned with the relationship between workers and the nature and content of jobs, and their task functions. It attempts to meet people's personal and social needs at work through the reorganisation or restructuring of work. There are two major, inter-related reasons for attention to job design:

- to enhance the personal satisfaction that people derive from their work; and
- to make the best use of people as a valuable resource and to help overcome obstacles to their effective performance.

There are many broader ways of viewing job design. For example, Boella and Goss-Turner relate job design to five sets of expectations:

- employer's expectations;
- employee's expectations;
- customer's expectations;
- colleagues' expectations;
- society's expectations.[60]

There are then many possible aspects of job design. We can view attention to job design in terms of two broad, related approaches (Figure 7.14):

- the restructuring of individual jobs; and
- broader approaches concerned with the wider organisational context.

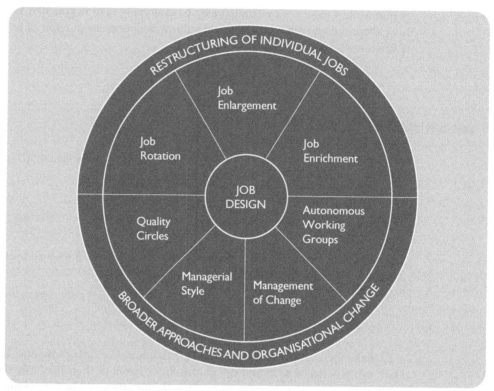

Figure 7.14 Main aspects of job design

Restructuring of individual jobs

Earlier approaches to job design concentrated on the restructuring of individual jobs and the application of three main methods: (i) job rotation, (ii) job enlargement and (iii) job enrichment.

The extent of centralisation/decentralisation (discussed in Chapter 4) can also be seen as a feature of job design.

Job rotation

Although usually included under this heading, job rotation is not strictly job design because neither the nature of the task nor the method of working is restructured. Job rotation involves moving a person from one job or task to another, for example rotating staff from kitchen work to waiting and to reception, normally in order to gain some understanding and experience of the work of other departments, or to introduce some variety to the work. This can benefit the hotel by increasing flexibility in staffing and reducing differences in occupational status.

Job rotation may lead to the acquisition of additional skills and can be applied as a form of training. A planned programme of job rotation is often used, for example, for hospitality management students on their industrial training placements. There is also growing attention to cross-training as a means of enhancing employees' knowledge of a wider range of jobs. Job rotation should help the person to identify more with the total work of the establishment and with the completed delivery of service. It may help remove monotony and boredom. Under normal circumstances, however, job rotation is often positively resisted by some staff. If the tasks involved are all very similar and routine, then once the person is familiar with new tasks the work may quickly prove boring again.

Job enlargement

This involves increasing the scope of the job and the range of tasks that the person is responsible for carrying out. It is usually achieved by combining a number of related jobs at the same level. Job enlargement is *horizontal job design*. It makes the job structurally larger. It lengthens the time-cycle of operations and may give the person greater variety – for example, allowing commis chefs to undertake a wider range of food preparation. A group of banquet waiters, who each set only part of the placement for each guest, could undertake the entire setting for a smaller number of guests.

Job enlargement, however, is not always very popular and may even be resisted by workers. Although it may give the person added variety and a wider range of tasks, it does little to improve intrinsic satisfaction or the development of skills. Workers may see job enlargement as simply increasing the number of routine, boring tasks they have to perform.

Job enrichment

This attempts to enrich the job by incorporating motivating or growth factors such as increased responsibility and involvement, opportunities for personal development and a sense of achievement. Job enrichment involves *vertical job enlargement*. It aims to give the person greater autonomy and authority over the planning, execution and control of their own work. Job enrichment should help provide the person with a more meaningful and challenging job, and focuses attention on intrinsic satisfaction.

Methods of achieving job enrichment can include allowing workers to undertake a full task-cycle or provide a more complete delivery of service, providing opportunities for more direct contact with the customers, giving workers greater freedom over the scheduling and pacing of their own work, reducing the level of direct supervision, and giving workers increased responsibility for the monitoring and control of their own work.[61]

For example, receptionists could be encouraged to monitor guest comment cards, and to handle complaints and develop solutions to problems rather than bringing every concern to management. Room attendants could be given greater autonomy for complying with the checklists and inspection of rooms instead of relying on a supervisor to find mistakes. Holiday Inn, for instance, introduced a system of self-checking attendants who are responsible for supervision of their own work. Supervisors now check only a sample number of rooms to monitor the overall standard of performance. Kitchen staff could be given greater responsibility for their own budget, including ordering supplies and controlling the costs of wastage and breakages.

Stages of a job

Magurn views every job as consisting of three separate stages:

- planning and organising the job, such as use of people and equipment, standards of quality, quantities needed, and work layout;
- doing the job, such as cooking meals, waiting at tables, serving drinks and cleaning;
- control, such as evaluating what is done, inspecting, measuring and adjusting, and correcting.[62]

Most jobs in the hospitality industry are concerned only with the 'doing' stage. Attention to job design would involve exploring ways in which people could have increased autonomy and responsibility for the planning and organising, and the control stages, of their jobs.

Job enrichment and core job dimensions

A popular and comprehensive model of job enrichment has been developed by Hackman and Oldham. The model views job enrichment in terms of increasing five core job dimensions: skill variety, task identity, task significance, autonomy and feedback (Figure 7.15). These core job characteristics create three psychological states:

- experienced meaningfulness of the work;
- experienced responsibility for outcomes of the work; and
- knowledge of the actual results of work activities.

Five core dimensions can be summarised as follows:

- *Skill variety* – the extent to which a job entails different activities and involves a range of skills and talents.
- *Task identity* – the extent to which a job involves completion of a whole piece of work with a visible outcome.
- *Task significance* – the extent to which a job has a meaningful impact on other people either inside or outside the organisation.
- *Autonomy* – the extent to which a job provides freedom, independence and discretion in planning the work and determining how it is undertaken.
- *Feedback* – the extent to which work activities result in direct and clear information on the effectiveness of job performance.

An example of a job with little enrichment could be that of a kitchen porter, where all five factors are likely to rate low. An example of an enriched job could be that of a hospital dietician who draws upon a range of skills involving theoretical knowledge and understanding and also social skills in dealing with patients. This tends to give the job clear and important meaning and significance. There is a relatively high level of autonomy as well as the likelihood of direct and clear feedback.

Motivating potential score

From these five core job dimensions, Hackman and Oldham have developed an equation which gives a single index of a person's job profile. By answering a questionnaire – the Job Diagnostic

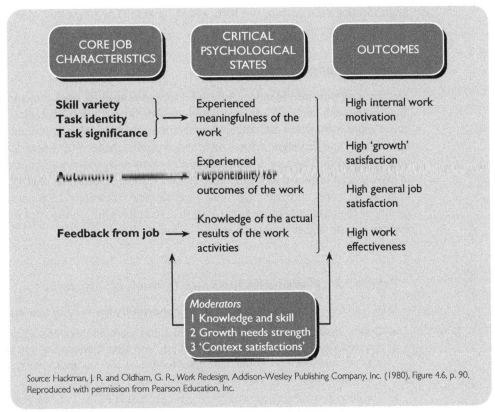

Figure 7.15 A job characteristics model of work motivation

Survey (JDS) – and by giving a score (between 1 and 7) to each job dimension, the person can calculate an overall measure of job enrichment, called the motivating potential score (MPS).

Examples of questions from the JDS are:

- How much variety is there in your job?
- To what extent does your job involve doing a whole and identifiable piece of work?
- In general, how significant or important is your job?
- How much autonomy is there in your job?
- To what extent does doing the job itself provide you with information about your work performance?

$$\text{MPS} = \frac{(\text{Skill variety} + \text{Task identity} + \text{Task significance})}{3} \times \text{Autonomy} \times \text{Feedback}$$

The first three job dimensions of skill variety, task identity and task significance are averaged, since it is the combination of these dimensions which contributes to experienced meaningfulness of work. The remaining two job dimensions, autonomy and feedback, stand on their own. Since scores for skill variety, task identity and task significance are additive, this means that the absence of one dimension can be partially offset by the presence of the other dimensions. However, if either autonomy or feedback is absent then, because of the multiplicative relationship, the MPS would be zero. The job would offer no potential to motivate the person.

Empirical support for the model

Empirical support for the model is mixed. From their studies, Hackman and Oldham claim that people with enriched jobs and high score levels on the Job Diagnostic Survey experienced more satisfaction and internal motivation. The core job dimensions of skill variety, task identity and task significance combined to predict the level of experienced meaningfulness of the work. The core dimensions of autonomy and feedback did not relate so clearly to experienced responsibility and knowledge of results. Some of the other dimensions were as good, or better, in predicting these psychological conditions. In general, however, the results of their studies showed that jobs that scored higher on the core dimensions were associated with higher levels of personal and work outcomes.

Exhibit 7.2 UK graduates frustrated by levels of responsibility

people 1st **New survey finds lack of opportunity holds back new employees**

- Over a third (36 per cent) of recent graduates were disappointed with the levels of responsibility given to them in their first job, and almost one in five (18 per cent) feel they've never been given the right opportunities to take on responsibility, according to a new survey by UKSP, part of People 1st.

- The survey, which interviewed those who graduated in the last five years, also found that almost 45 per cent believe they could have progressed quicker in their chosen career if given the right opportunities, with 22 per cent feeling they have less responsibility now than they thought they'd have at this career stage. As a result, 45 per cent said that the lack of responsibility they are given has made them question whether or not they are in the right job.

- Lesley Potter from UKSP said of the findings: 'At a time of high graduate unemployment, it's disappointing to also see that many employers are not making the most of the graduates they do take on – frustrating them by not giving them opportunity and leading them to become disillusioned with their jobs. For young people currently considering career options, as our recent State of the Nation report shows, managers in the hospitality, leisure, travel and tourism industries are often younger than average – especially those working in pubs, bars and nightclubs, restaurants and events. There's a wealth of opportunity – both at graduate and non-graduate level – within the sector for those who want to experience managing a business at an early age.'[63]

Critical review and reflection

'All staff welcome responsibility and challenge.'

To what extent do you agree with this statement when considering staff employed within the hospitality industry?

The concept of empowerment

Discussion of management and leadership styles and particularly more recent concepts of servant leadership (see Chapter 6) draws attention to the importance of empowerment. Discussion on motivation, job satisfaction and job enrichment also leads to consideration of empowerment.

Increasing business competitiveness demands that hospitality organisations have to offer the best quality products and services to meet the demands of customers. At the same time, organisations need to control wage costs, which has led to many downsizing and de-layering.

This requires that organisations develop, and harness, the talents and commitment of their remaining employees so that performance standards are maintained or improved. Developments in attitudes towards social democracy is another factor that may affect the way in which employees are managed.

In this changing business environment, close managerial control would seem neither effective nor possible, and empowerment of employees is the way in which many organisations seek to achieve the required business performance. Empowered employees are particularly valuable in the hospitality industry where, frequently, customers' first, or only, point of contact is with relatively junior staff. In addition to this, many believe that employee empowerment is also closely linked with employee satisfaction. Gill et al.[64] comment on the close relationship between transformational leadership and employee desire for empowerment. (See Chapter 6.)

The meaning of empowerment

Empowerment is generally explained in terms of allowing employees greater freedom, autonomy and self-control over their work, and responsibility for decision-making. However, there are differences in the meaning and interpretation of the term. Wilkinson refers to problems with the existing prescriptive literature on empowerment. The term 'empowerment' can be seen as flexible and even elastic, and has been used very loosely by both practitioners and academics. Wilkinson suggests that it is important to see empowerment in a wider context. It needs to be recognised that it has different forms and should be analysed in the context of broader organisational practice.[65]

The concept of empowerment also gives rise to a number of questions and doubts. For example, how does it differ in any meaningful way from other earlier forms of employee involvement? Is the primary concern of empowerment getting the most out of the workforce? Is empowerment just another, somewhat more fanciful, term for delegation? Some writers see the two as quite separate concepts while other writers suggest empowerment is a more proactive form of delegation.

According to Mills and Friesen, 'empowerment can be succinctly defined as the authority of subordinates to decide and act'.

> It describes a management style. The term is often confused with delegation but, if strictly defined, empowerment goes much further in granting subordinates authority to decide and act. Indeed, within a context of broad limits defined by executives, empowered individuals may even become self-managing.[66]

> ### Critical review and reflection
>
> It is essential to 'empower front-line staff to exceed customer expectations'.[67]
>
> *To what extent do you agree with this statement?*

Empowerment and delegation

Attempting to distinguish clearly between empowerment and delegation is not easy. However, there appears to be general agreement that empowerment describes a management style and the granting of genuine additional power and responsibility to other members of staff. Empowerment is viewed as the more embracing process. Arguably, it is the process of empowerment that gives rise to the act of delegation. According to Tulgan, for example, 'the key to empowerment is effective delegation; giving individual contributors ownership of tangible results.'[68]

Delegation

At the individual (or personal) level, **delegation** is the process of entrusting authority and responsibility to others throughout the various levels of the organisation, whilst still retaining accountability. It is the authorisation to undertake activities that would otherwise be carried out by someone in a more senior position. Downsizing and de-layering have arguably limited the opportunities for delegation, although this may be offset by demands for greater flexibility and empowerment. In any event, delegation is still an essential process of management. As Crainer points out, in the age of empowerment, the ability to delegate effectively is critical.

> Delegation has always been recognized as a key ingredient of successful management and leadership. But, in the 1980s delegation underwent a crisis of confidence . . . The 1990s saw a shift in attitudes. No longer was delegation an occasional managerial indulgence. Instead it became a necessity. This has continued to be the case.[69]

Extreme forms of behaviour

The concept of delegation may appear to be straightforward. However, anyone with experience of a work situation is likely to be aware of the importance of delegation and the consequences of badly managed delegation. Successful delegation is a social skill. Where managers lack this skill, or do not have a sufficient awareness of people-perception, there are two extreme forms of behaviour that can result.

- At one extreme is the almost total lack of meaningful delegation. Subordinate staff are only permitted to operate within closely defined and often routine areas of work, with detailed supervision. Staff are treated as if they are incapable of thinking for themselves and given little or no opportunity to exercise initiative or responsibility.

- At the other extreme there can be an excessive zeal for so-called delegation when a manager leaves subordinates to their own resources, often with only minimal guidance or training, and expects them to take the consequences for their own actions or decisions. These 'super-delegators' misuse the practice of delegation and are often like the Artful Dodger, somehow contriving not to be around when difficult situations arise. Such a form of behaviour is not delegation; it is an abdication of the manager's responsibility.

Either of these two extreme forms of behaviour can be frustrating and potentially stressful for subordinate staff, and unlikely to lead to improved organisational effectiveness. The nature of delegation can have a significant effect on the morale, motivation and work performance of staff. In all but the smallest organisation the only way to get work done effectively is through delegation, but even such an important practice as delegation can be misused or over-applied.

The manager – subordinate relationship

Delegation is not just the arbitrary shedding of work. It is not just the issuing and following of orders or carrying out of specified tasks in accordance with detailed instructions. Within the formal structure of the organisation, delegation creates a special manager–subordinate relationship. It is founded on the concept of:

- authority;
- responsibility; and
- accountability (ultimate responsibility).

> Delegation means the conferring of a specified authority by a higher authority. In its essence it involves a dual responsibility. The one to whom authority is delegated becomes responsible to the superior for doing the job, but the superior remains responsible for getting the job done. This principle of delegation is the centre of all processes in formal organization.
>
> (J. D. Mooney, *The Principles of Organization*)[70]

- *Authority* is the right to take action or make decisions that the manager would otherwise have done. Authority legitimises the exercise of empowerment within the structure and rules of the organisation. It enables the subordinate to issue valid instructions for others to follow.
- *Responsibility* involves an obligation by the subordinate to perform certain duties or make certain decisions and having to accept possible reprimand from the manager for unsatisfactory performance. The meaning of the term 'responsibility' is, however, subject to possible confusion: although delegation embraces both authority and responsibility, effective delegation is not abdication of responsibility.
- *Accountability* is interpreted as meaning ultimate responsibility and cannot be delegated. Managers have to accept 'responsibility' for the control of their staff, for the performance of all duties allocated to their department/section within the structure of the organisation, and for the standard of results achieved. That is, 'the buck stops here'.

The manager is in turn responsible to higher management. This is the essence of the nature of the 'dual responsibility' of delegation. The manager is answerable to a superior and cannot shift responsibility back to subordinates. The responsibility of the superior for the acts of subordinates is absolute.[71] In order to help clarify the significance of 'dual responsibility' in delegation, it might be better expressed as: **the subordinate is responsible to the manager for doing the job, while the manager is responsible for seeing that the job gets done. The manager is accountable to a superior for the actions of subordinates.**

Authority commensurate with responsibility

Delegation, therefore, embraces both authority and responsibility. It is not practical to delegate one without the other (see Figure 7.16). Responsibility must be supported by

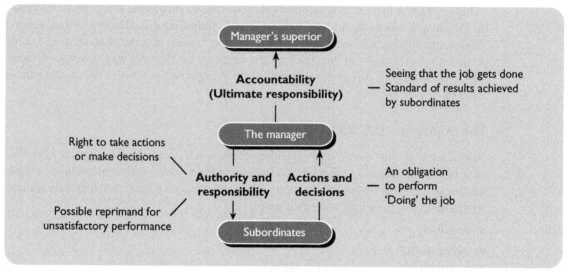

Figure 7.16 The basis of delegation

authority and by the power to influence the areas of performance for which the subordinate is to be held responsible. Authority can be delegated readily, but many problems of delegation stem from failure to delegate sufficient authority to enable subordinates to fulfil their responsibilities. For example, if a section head is held responsible to a departmental manager for the performance of junior staff but is not empowered (given authority) to influence their selection and appointment, their motivation, the allocation of their duties, their training and development, or their sanctions and rewards, then the section leader can hardly be held responsible for unsatisfactory performance of the junior staff. To hold subordinates responsible for certain areas of performance without also conferring on them the necessary authority within the structure of the organisation to take action and make decisions within the limits of that responsibility is an abuse of delegation.

The manager should accept the blame as the person **accountable** for the performance of the department/section, and obliged to see that the task was completed satisfactorily. It is necessary to maintain the organisational hierarchy and structure of command. Managers should protect and support subordinate staff and accept, personally, any reprimand for unsatisfactory performance. It is then up to managers to sort things out in their own department/section, to counsel members of staff concerned and to review their system of delegation.

Critical review and reflection

'The idea of empowerment and helping people accept a feeling of ownership and personal responsibility for their actions and to exercise a high level of self-control is all right in theory. But as I am held accountable for the performance of staff in my department and have to accept any adverse consequences of their behaviour it is only right that I should exercise close control and supervision over them.'

What is your point of view?

Benefits of delegation

It is a principle of delegation that decisions should be made at the lowest level in the organisation compatible with efficiency. It is a question of opportunity cost. If decisions are made at a higher level than necessary, they are being made at greater cost than necessary. Delegation is therefore a matter of sound economics as well as good organisation. Properly handled, delegation offers many potential benefits to both managers and staff. Delegation should lead to the optimum use of human resources and improved organisational performance. Studies of successful organisations lend support to the advantages to be gained from effective delegation.[72]

Best use of time

Time is one of the most valuable, but limited, resources and it is important that the manager utilises time to the maximum advantage. Delegation leaves the manager free to make profitable use of time, to concentrate on the more important tasks and to spend more time in managing and less in doing. This should enable the manager to be more accessible for consultation and improve the process of communications.

Training and development

Delegation provides a means of training and development, and of testing the subordinate's suitability for promotion. It can be used as a means of assessing the likely performance of a subordinate at a higher level of authority and responsibility. Delegation thereby helps to avoid the 'Peter Principle' – that is, 'in a hierarchy every employee tends to rise to his level of incompetence'. If managers have trained competent subordinates this will not only aid organisational progress but should also enhance their own prospects for further advancement.

Strength of the workforce

Delegation should lead to an improvement in the strength of the workforce. It should give subordinates greater scope for action and opportunities to develop their aptitudes and abilities. Delegation is a form of participation and can lead to improved morale by increasing motivation and job satisfaction. If empowerment focuses attention on 'motivators' or 'growth' factors it can help satisfy the employee's higher-level needs. Delegation creates a climate in which subordinates can become more involved in the planning and decision-making processes of the organisation.

Reasons for lack of delegation

With so many good reasons for delegation, why is it that managers often fail to delegate or do not delegate successfully? Delegation is influenced by the manager's perception of subordinate staff. It is also influenced by the subordinate's perception of the manager's reasons for delegation. Failure to delegate often results from the manager's fear. The manager may fear that the subordinate is not capable of doing a sufficiently good job. Also, the manager may fear being blamed for the subordinate's mistakes. Conversely, the manager may fear that the subordinate will do too good a job and show the manager in a bad light.

The manager should, of course, remember that the task of management is to get work done through the efforts of other people. If the subordinate does a particularly good job this should reflect favourably on the manager.

Critical review and reflection

It has been said that the nature of staff in the industry requires close controls being placed on them and close monitoring otherwise they will not work.

Can you present a counter-argument to this contention?

The art of delegation

Empowering other people is a matter of judgement and involves the question of discretion. Delegation is not an easy task. It involves behavioural as well as organisational and economic considerations, and it is subject to a number of possible abuses. Effective delegation is a social skill. It requires a clear understanding of people-perception, reliance on other people, confidence and trust, and courage. It is important that the manager knows what to delegate, when and to whom. Matters of policy and disciplinary power, for example, usually rest with the manager and cannot legitimately be delegated.

Training and learning experience

Delegation involves subordinates making decisions. For example, as Guirdham points out: 'a strict separation of manager and subordinate roles sends the message to workers that they are only responsible for what they are specifically told to do. Managers who neglect to, or cannot, delegate are failing to develop the human resources for which they have responsibility.'[73]

Mistakes will inevitably occur and the subordinate will need to be supported by the manager, and protected against unwarranted criticism. The acceptance of ultimate responsibility highlights the educational aspect of the manager's job. The manager should view mistakes as part of the subordinate's training and learning experience, and an opportunity for further development. 'Even if mistakes occur, good managers are judged as much by their ability to manage them as by their successes.'[74]

The need for control

Authority, responsibility and accountability must be kept in parity throughout the organisation. This is essential in order to maintain effective coordination and control, and to maintain the chain of command. The manager must remain in control. The manager must be on the lookout for subordinates who are more concerned with personal empire-building than with meeting stated organisational objectives and should prevent a strong personality exceeding the limits of formal delegation. We have said that delegation creates a special manager–subordinate relationship and this involves both the giving of trust and the retention of control. Control is, therefore, an integral part of the system of delegation. However, control should not be so close as to inhibit the effective operation or benefits of delegation. It is a question of balance.

A systematic approach to empowerment and delegation

In order to realise the full benefits of empowerment and delegation without loss of control, it is necessary to adopt a planned and systematic approach. Setting up a successful system of delegation involves the manager examining four basic questions:

1 What tasks could be performed better by other staff?
2 What opportunities are there for staff to learn and develop by undertaking delegated tasks and responsibilities?
3 How should the increased responsibilities be implemented and to whom should they be given?
4 What forms of monitoring control system would be most appropriate?

In order to set up an effective system of delegation, subordinates should know exactly what is expected of them, what has to be achieved, the boundaries within which they have freedom of action, and how far they can exercise independent decision-making. It is possible to identify six main stages in a planned and systematic approach to delegation (see Figure 7.17).

- **Clarification of objectives and suitable patterns of organisation.** Policies and procedures must be established and defined in order to provide a framework for the exercise of authority and the acceptance of responsibility.

- **Agreement on terms of reference and acceptance of authority and responsibility.** The manager can then negotiate and agree the subordinate's role prescription and terms

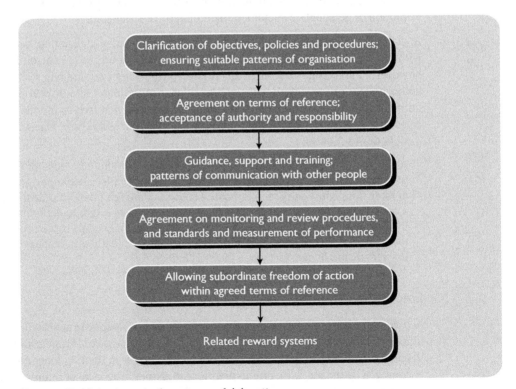

Figure 7.17 Main stages in the process of delegation

of reference. Those areas of work in which the subordinate is responsible for achieving results should be identified clearly. Emphasis should generally be placed on end-results rather than a set of detailed instructions.

- **Guidance, support and training, and patterns of communication.** When subordinates have agreed and accepted the delegation, they should be properly briefed, given guidance and support and any necessary training. They should be advised where, and to whom, they could go for further advice or help.

- **Effective monitoring and review procedures.** The manager should agree time limits for delegation (such as a target date for completion of a specific task or a specified time period). It is necessary to agree the level and nature of supervision, and to establish a system to monitor progress and provide feedback. **Delegation is not an irrevocable act; it can always be withdrawn.** It is also important to make clear expected levels of achievement and agree on performance standards (wherever practically possible in quantitative terms), and how performance in each area is to be measured and evaluated.

- **Freedom of action within agreed terms of reference.** The subordinate should then be left alone to get on with the job. One of the most frustrating aspects of delegation is the manager who passes on authority but stays close behind the subordinates' shoulders keeping a constant watch over their actions. This is contrary to the nature of delegation. The true nature of successful delegation means that the subordinate is given freedom of action within the boundaries established and agreed in the previous stages.

- **Related reward system.** Wherever possible, the process of delegation should be related to some form of associated 'reward' system. Examples could include bonus payments, improved job satisfaction, reduction of work stress and enhanced opportunities for promotion or personal development, including further delegation.

A planned and systematic approach means that effective delegation can be achieved within the formal structure of the organisation and without loss of control. It is important, however, to make sure that subordinates accept the extent of, and any restrictions on, the authority and responsibility delegated to them. Subordinates should feel a sense of commitment to their new tasks or assignments and should feel free to discuss any doubts or concerns. Delegation involves the acceptance theory of authority. Davis and Newstrom explain this as follows:

> Although authority gives people power to act officially within the scope of their delegation, this power becomes somewhat meaningless unless those affected accept it and respond to it. In most cases when delegation is made, a subordinate is left free to choose a response within a certain range of behaviour. But even when an employee is told to perform one certain act, the employee still has the choice of doing it or not doing it and taking the consequences. It is, therefore, the subordinate who controls the response to authority. Managers cannot afford to overlook this human fact when they use authority.[75]

Empowerment in hospitality services

According to Jones and Davies, evidence suggests that empowerment will become a significant factor in how hotel and food service firms are managed. From a study of attitudes to empowerment by general managers of four-star hotels in the UK, Jones and Davies were encouraged by the response rate to their investigations. The level of interest displayed suggests a great deal of interest over the issue of empowerment in the hotel industry.[76]

From a discussion of the benefits and problems of empowerment and a review of its operation in a number of companies, Pickard concludes that empowerment does appear to be having an effect on the way people work. As an example, Pickard describes improved job satisfaction and the changing attitudes of staff arising from the introduction of empowerment in Harvester restaurants. Within a framework handed down from head office, staff work in teams which are responsible for making their own decisions on the running of individual restaurants.[77]

In a study of staff in hotels in Turkey, Pelit *et al.* found that although staff were dissatisfied with the levels of pay, there was a significant effect of empowerment on job satisfaction.[78] They also noted that job enrichment and rotation, important components of empowerment, should be given more importance. Empowerment will contribute to the morale and motivation of employees and in turn to customer satisfaction. 'Empowerment changes not only employees' rights and responsibilities but those of the leader as well. It requires that leaders put their trust in their staff and respect their judgment.'[79]

Managerial meanings and initiatives

Lashley argues that interest in employee empowerment in hospitality operations has been associated chiefly with interest in gaining competitive advantage through service quality and the paramount importance which is placed on the performance of front-line staff.[80]

By employing and adapting terms used in the wider literature on empowerment, Lashley suggests it is possible to summarise four managerial initiatives and meanings which claim to be empowering:

1 *Empowerment through participation* – for example, the delegation for decision-making which in a traditional organisation would be the domain of management.

2 *Empowerment through involvement* – for example, when management concern is to gain from employees' experiences, ideas and suggestions.

3 *Empowerment through commitment* – for example, through greater commitment to the organisation's goals and through improvement in employees' job satisfaction.

4 *Empowerment through de-layering* – for example, through reducing the number of tiers of management in the organisation structure.

Empowerment takes a variety of forms. Managers frequently have different intentions and organisations differ in the degree of discretion with which they can empower employees. Lashley concludes therefore that the success of a particular initiative will be judged ultimately by the extent to which the empowered employees feel personally effective, able to determine outcomes and have a degree of control over significant aspects of their working life.

Managerial perceptions of empowerment

Based on a further cluster of research projects into employee participation in services, Lashley concludes that although, on face value, empowerment has much to offer organisations' operating services, employees will react more quickly to customer needs and to rectifying complaints, take personal pride in successful service encounters, and feel pride and concern for the customer experience. However, account needs to be taken of different definitions and meanings used by managers; and different perceptions of business problems and motives for introducing empowerment.

The term 'empowerment' is used to describe a wide variety of practice in service delivery. There is considerable overlap between employee empowerment, employee participation, employee involvement and even employee commitment, yet these terms are often used interchangeably. Ultimately, the success of a particular initiative will be dependent in the first instance on the empowered being given the authority and freedom to make decisions which they themselves consider to be valuable, significant and important. Whatever the intentions of managers, the effects of empowerment will be mediated by the feelings and experiences of the supposedly empowered. Hence any consideration of the various forms which empowerment takes must be sensitive to the potential tensions between managerial meanings and employees' experiences.[81]

Empowerment and organisational change

According to Erstad, among the many fashionable management terms, empowerment refers to a change strategy with the objective of improving both the individual's and the organisation's ability to act. In the service sector, and more specifically the hotel industry, empowerment is often seen as a way to gain competitive advantage but the true potential is broader. From the context of articles specialising in this area, Erstad concludes that empowerment is a complex process. In order to be successful it requires a clear vision, a learning environment both for management and employees, and participation and implementation tools and techniques. In order to achieve a truly entrepreneurial culture the hospitality industry can learn many lessons from research and experience in other business sectors.[82]

An essential ingredient of effective management is the ability to put your trust in others and to let go of some of the workload. Empowerment is also a matter of confidence and trust – both in subordinates and in the manager's own performance and system of delegation. In allowing freedom of action to subordinates within agreed terms of reference and limits of authority, managers must accept that subordinates may undertake delegated activities in a different manner from themselves. This is at the basis of the true nature of trust. However, learning to put trust in other people is one of the most difficult aspects of successful delegation for many managers, and some never learn it.

As Stewart points out, managers who think about what can be done only in terms of what they can do, cannot be effective. Managing is not a solo activity.

> Managers must learn to accept their dependence upon people. A key part of being a good manager is managing that dependence. Managers who say that they cannot delegate because they have poor staff may genuinely be unfortunate in the calibre of the staff that they have inherited or been given. More often this view is a criticism of themselves: a criticism either of their unwillingness to delegate when they could and should do so, or a criticism of their selection, training and development of their staff.[83]

The process of empowerment entails the removal of constraints and the granting of autonomy for independent actions. As part of her discussion on the democratic enterprise, Gratton refers to the importance of trust and power.

> The re-appropriation of choice from senior members of the organization to individuals themselves implies trust on both parts, but particularly on the part of senior members. It is they who have to cede power to individual employees and to trust them to behave in an autonomous manner and make decisions and take action that serve their personal good and the good of the organization. Democracy implies the giving of authority to individuals to

make choices within the context of obligations and accountabilities. Authority, obligations and accountability are deeply bound up with trust. Trust without accountability and obligation is likely to become one-sided, that is, to slide into dependence. Accountability without trust is impossible because it would mean the continual scrutiny of the motives and actions of individuals.[84]

According to Watson, there has been a growing trend of questioning the extent to which social science study of work behaviour and managerial practice has been sufficiently critical.

> The crux of the problem that all writers and researchers interested in managerial issues have to face up to is the fact that managerial activities are always and inevitably implicated in issues of power and relative advantage and disadvantage between human groups and human individuals . . . Helping make work organisations more efficient or more effective is not a politically neutral matter.[85]

Trust is clearly a two-way process. Kim *et al.* suggest that employees cannot be empowered unless they have trust in their managers. Similarly, managers can empower their employees by showing that they trust their staff, value them and show an interest in their career development. Management trustworthiness is a core element. If management trust and empower their staff this can lead to increased job satisfaction for the employees.[86]

Does empowerment deliver?

Effectively managed, empowerment can offer a number of potential benefits throughout all levels of the organisation. But does empowerment promote greater motivation and increase job satisfaction and work performance? Does empowerment deliver?

Although there is a continuing debate about the real benefits of empowerment there appears to be a general assumption that 'empowerment programmes will result in motivated staff, quality customer service and improved profits'.[87] From a discussion of the benefits and problems of empowerment and a review of its operation in a number of companies, Pickard concludes that empowerment does appear to be having a radical effect on the way people work. As an example, Pickard describes improved job satisfaction and the changing attitude of staff arising from the introduction of empowerment at Harvester restaurants. Within a framework handed down from head office, staff work in teams which are responsible for making decisions on the running of individual restaurants.[88]

Peiperi poses the question 'Does empowerment deliver the goods?' and concludes:

> Empowerment says that employees at all levels of an organization are responsible for their own actions and should be given authority to make decisions about their work. Its popularity has been driven by the need to respond quickly to customer needs, to develop cross-functional links to take advantage of opportunities that are too local or too fleeting to be determined centrally. Better morale and compensation for limited career paths are other advantages. Potential difficulties include the scope for chaos and conflict, a lack of clarity about where responsibility lies, the breakdown of hierarchical control, and demoralization on the part of those who do not want additional authority. Successful empowerment will typically require feedback on performance from a variety of sources, rewards with some group component, an environment which is tolerant of mistakes, widely distributed information, and generalist managers and employees. The paradox is that the greater the need for empowerment in an organization, the less likelihood of success. It has to be allowed to develop over time through the beliefs/attitudes of participants.[89]

Potential benefits of empowerment

Empowerment makes greater use of the knowledge, skills and abilities of the workforce; it encourages teamworking; and if there is meaningful participation, it can aid the successful implementation of change programmes.[90] Wall and Wood suggest that although few manufacturing companies empower their staff, research shows that empowerment can be one of the most effective tools in raising both productivity and profit. Empowerment improves performance because of the opportunities empowerment provides for them to do their work more effectively. It develops an individual's knowledge so they take a broader and more proactive orientation towards their job and are more willing to suggest new ways of doing things and to engage in meaningful teamworking.[91] Findings from a Whitehall II study of over 10,000 civil servants on work-related stress suggests that giving people more control over their jobs can greatly benefit their health.[92]

Critical review and reflection

'Trust is a two-way process. In order for the concept of empowerment to work effectively within hospitality organisations, staff must have confidence a trust in their managers and managers must trust their staff.'

Discuss the points for and against this statement.

Organisational citizenship

Taking the concept of empowerment further, it may be useful to consider the idea of organisational citizenship. Organ defines organisational citizenship behaviours as: 'the discretionary behaviours that are not directly or explicitly recognized by the formal reward system and that, in the aggregate promote the effective functioning of the organisation'.[93]

Baum[94] discusses the aspects of organisational citizenship and suggests this includes points on civic virtue, altruism and courtesy. There is evidence that if the culture of an organisation fosters good organisational citizenship, this can encourage excellent customer service.[95]

Synopsis

- Good management is concerned with understanding the needs and expectations of individuals. The study of motivation is concerned basically with why people behave in a certain way. The underlying concept of motivation is some driving force within individuals, by which they attempt to achieve some goal, in order to fulfil some need or expectation.

- Attempting to understand the nature of job satisfaction and its links with work performance is not easy. Although the level of job satisfaction may well affect the strength of motivation, this is not always the case. Job satisfaction is more of an internal state and could be associated, for example, with a feeling of personal achievement. Job satisfaction is a complex concept and is difficult to measure objectively. The level of job satisfaction is affected by a wide range of individual, social, organisational and cultural variables.

- Broader approaches to satisfaction aim to give the person improved empowerment and job enrichment, through greater autonomy and control over their work. Attention has also been given to a comprehensive model of job enrichment and five core dimensions. Moves towards greater flexibility may have noticeable effects on job satisfaction and performance of staff. There have been many studies and resultant theories but, as yet, no definitive conclusions as to how best to manage an organisation so that staff have both high job satisfaction and productivity.

- For the hospitality organisation to function effectively there must be processes of delegation, supervision and control. Delegation embraces both authority and responsibility but managers retain accountability for actions and decisions of subordinates. Delegation creates a special manager–subordinate relationship.

- The balance between control and autonomy draws attention to the importance of empowerment and allowing employees greater freedom. This is considered of particular importance in the hospitality industry, where empowerment is considered to enable members of staff to cater more appropriately for guest needs.

REVIEW AND DISCUSSION QUESTIONS

1 Explain what you understand by the underlying concept of motivation. Summarise the main needs and expectations to be taken into account in considering the motivation of people to work.

2 Critically assess the practical value of Maslow's hierarchy of needs model to improving the motivation of people to work in the hospitality industry.

3 Discuss the extent to which you consider the modern workforce expects to be trusted or controlled.

4 Compare and contrast the terms *delegation* and *empowerment*. Give examples from the hospitality industry to illustrate your answer.

5 Discuss the extent to which the maximisation of profit and minimisation of costs causes managers to empower, or not empower, their staff.

6 Explain what is meant by job design. Suggest with supporting examples how the various approaches might be applied within the hospitality industry.

7 What exactly do you understand by the term job satisfaction? What are the main dimensions of job satisfaction? Give specific examples of causes of both job satisfaction and job dissatisfaction that you have experienced in the hospitality industry.

8 What motivational factors will empowerment at work satisfy? To what extent might the concept of empowerment be inappropriate for a multicultural workforce in the hospitality industry?

ASSIGNMENT

1 Interview at least three people with different jobs in any aspect of the hospitality industry. Identify as clearly as possible, together with reasons and supporting examples:

- those aspects of the job which the person feels to be of particular importance and/or significance;
- what aspects of the job the person likes most and those aspects disliked the most;
- what motivates the person to work well and perform to the best of his or her ability.

2 Select a particular department within a hospitality organisation and investigate specific causes of job dissatisfaction. Suggest how these particular problems of dissatisfaction could be tackled in a positive and practical way.

3 Explain what conclusions you draw from your observations and the extent to which you can relate your findings to different theories/studies of motivation and job satisfaction.

CASE STUDY 7.1

The Southsea Hotel

During my last period of industrial placement at the Southsea Hotel, I spent some time as a supervisor in the wash-up area. I had worked at the hotel on previous occasions as a grill chef and as a commis waiter.

The wash-up was part of the back of house department, which also took in back of house cleaning, porterage, stores receipt and issue, and the linen room. The department had a staff of 16, some of whom had been with the hotel for quite a while. However, the work in the wash-up was seen as particularly boring and it was hard to get any of the regular staff to work there.

At the time I worked as a supervisor, the wash-up was staffed with teams of school children doing holiday jobs. I had four lads aged between 16 and 18 working for me. Two worked the morning and lunchtime shift and two in the afternoon and evening.

From the start I had trouble getting the boys to work well. The morning shift consisted of Alan and Tom. Alan, aged 17, was the son of one of the chefs and always showing off. Tom, who was 16, was a friend of Alan's who modelled his own behaviour after him. I spent considerable effort coaxing and prodding these lads to work hard but they were slow workers and were always disappearing for a smoke outside. Consequently a backlog of dishes used to pile up.

The afternoon shift of Neil and Patrick had a more systematic approach to work and their output was better. In dealing with the morning shift, I often pointed out that the boys in the afternoon had a better attitude and got more work done. This was supposed to improve their efforts, but mainly it caused resentment and certainly not more work output. Actually, I did not feel that either shift was doing a good job. The boys were fully aware of my disappointment in their performance.

This was my first supervisory position and I was unsure of myself in how to handle the leadership role. I asked Alan's father, the chef, to speak to his son, which he said he had done, but I did not notice any change in Alan's attitude or performance.

Questions

1 With reference to your understanding of motivation theories, suggest how you might improve the situation if employed as the supervisor.

2 What recommendations would you make to senior management to improve the situation in the future?

Source: Adapted from THF hotels graduate recruitment programme selection exercise.

References

1   Kuşluvan, S., Kuşluvan, Z. and Ilhan, I., 'The human dimension: a review of human resources management issues in the tourism and hospitality Industry', *Cornell Hospitality Quarterly*, vol. 51, no. 2, 2010, 171–214.

2   Mullins, L. J., 'Management and Managerial Behaviour', *The International Journal of Hospitality Management*, vol. 4, no. 1, 1985, 39–41.

3   Riley, M., *Human Resource Management in The Hospitality and Tourism Industry*, 2nd edn, Butterworth-Heinemann (1996), p. 44.

4   'Motivating Your Staff in a Time of Change', Checklist 068, Chartered Management Institute, March 2006.

5   See, for example, Vroom, V. H. and Deci, E. L. (eds), *Management and Motivation*, Penguin (1970).

6   Boxall, P. and Purcell, J., *Strategy and Human Resource Management*, Palgrave (2003).

7   See, for example, Rudolph, P. A. and Kleiner, B. H., 'The Art of Motivating Employees', *Journal of Managerial Psychology*, vol. 4, no. 5, 1989, i–iv.

8   Farren, C., 'Mastery: The Critical Advantage', in Chowdhury, S. (ed.), *Management 21C*, Financial Times Prentice Hall (2000), p. 95.

9   Kets de Vries, M., 'Beyond Sloan: trust is at the core of corporate values', in Pickford, J. (ed.), *Financial Times Mastering Management 2.0*, Financial Times Prentice Hall (2001), pp. 267–70.

10 Ellis, P., *The Image of Hotel and Catering Work*, HCITB Research Report (1981).

11 Reeves, R., 'Reality Bites', *Management Today*, May 2003, 37.

12 Hunt, J. W., *Managing People at Work; A Manager's Guide to Behaviour in Organizations*, 3rd edn, McGraw-Hill (1992).

13 Lun, J. and Huang, Xu., 'How to motivate your older employees to excel? The impact of commitment on older employees' performance in the hospitality industry', *International Journal of Hospitality Management*, vol. 26, no. 4, 2007, 793–806.

14 British Institute of Management, *Management News*, no. 64, February 1990, p. 6.

15 Willman, I., 'Human Resource Management in the Service Sector', in Jones, P.(ed.), *Management in Service Industries*, Pitman (1989), p. 217.

16 Maslow, A. H., 'A Theory of Human Motivation', *Psychological Review*, vol. 50, no. 4, July 1943, 370–96, and Maslow, A. H., *Motivation and Personality*, 3rd edn, Harper & Row (1987).

17 Ellis, P., *The Image of Hotel and Catering Work*, HCITB Research Report (1981).

18 See, for example, Hornsey, T. and Dann, D., *Manpower Management in the Hotel and Catering Industry*, Batsford (1984), and Mullins, L. J., *Management and Organisational Behaviour*, 5th edn, Financial Times Pitman Publishing (1999).

19 For example, see Robertson, I. T., Smith, M. and Cooper, D., *Motivation: Strategies, Theory and Practice*, 2nd edn, Institute of Personnel and Development (1992).

20 Steers, R. M. and Porter, L. W., *Motivation and Work Behavior*, 5th edn, McGraw-Hill (1991).

21 For a more detailed account of Maslow's model applied to guest behaviour, see Venison, P., *Managing Hotels*, Heinemann (1983).

22 Saunders, A., 'Keep Staff Sweet', *Management Today*, June 2003, 75.

23 Adair, J., *Leadership and Motivation*, Kogan Page (2006).

24 Alderfer, C. P., *Existence, Relatedness and Growth*, Collier Macmillan (1972).

25 Herzberg, F., Mausner, B. and Snyderman, B. B., *The Motivation to Work*, 2nd edn, Chapman & Hall (1959).

26 Balmer, S. and Baum, T., 'Applying Herzberg's Hygiene Factors to the Changing Accommodation Environment', *International Journal of Contemporary Hospitality Management*, vol. 5, no. 2, 1993, 32–5.

27 See, for example, Goldthorpe, J. H. *et al.*, *The Affluent Worker: Industrial Attitudes and Behaviour*, Cambridge University Press (1968).

28 Crainer, S. and Dearlove, D. (eds), *Financial Times Handbook of Management*, 2nd edn, Financial Times Prentice Hall (2001), p. 361.

29 MacQueen, N., 'What Happened to Herzberg: Is Motivation Theory Out of Date?' *Hospitality*, no. 29, May 1982, 16.

30 Chitiris, L., 'Herzberg's Proposals and Their Applicability to The Hotel Industry', *Hospitality Education and Research Journal*, vol. 12, 1988, 67–79.

31 See note 29.

32 McClelland, D. C., *The Achieving Society*, Van Nostrand Reinhold (1961) (also published by Irvington, 1976), and *Human Motivation*, Cambridge University Press (1988).

33 McClelland, D. C., 'Business Drive and National Achievement', *Harvard Business Review*, vol. 40, July–August 1962, 99–112.

34 Weaver, T., 'Theory M: Motivating with Money', *Cornell HRA Quarterly*, vol. 29, no. 3, November 1988, 40–45.

35 'What you thought: motivating minimum-wage workers', *Personnel Journal*, vol. 75, no. 3, March 1996, 16.

36 Kusin, G., 'A 360-Degree Spin', *Hemisphere United*, October 2005, 76.

37 Vroom, V. H., *Work and Motivation*, Wiley (1964) (also published by Krieger, 1982).

38 Porter, L. W. and Lawler, E. E., *Managerial Attitudes and Performance*, Irwin (1968).

39 See, for example, Graen, G., 'Instrumentality Theory of Work Motivation', *Journal of Applied Psychology Monograph*, vol. 53, no. 2, 1969, Part 2.

40 Porter, L. W., Lawler, E. E. and Hackman, J. R., *Behavior in Organizations*, McGraw-Hill (1975).

41 Adams, J. S., 'Injustice in Social Exchange', abridged in Steers, R. M. and Porter, L. W., *Motivation and Work Behaviour*, 2nd edn, McGraw-Hill (1979), pp. 107–24.

42 Locke, E. A., 'Towards a Theory of Task Motivation and Incentives', *Organizational Behavior and Human Performance*, vol. 3, 1968, 157–89.

43 For examples, see: (i) Latham, G. P. and Yukl, G. A., 'A Review of the Research on the Applications of Goal Setting in Organizations', *Academy of Management Journal*, vol. 18, 1975, 824–45; (ii) Latham, G. P. and Locke, E. A., 'Goal Setting: A Motivational Technique that Works', *Organisational Dynamics*, Autumn 1979, 28–80.

44 Locke, E. A., 'Personal Attitudes and Motivation', *Annual Review of Psychology*, vol. 26, 1975, 457–80.

45 For a summary of research supporting these conclusions, see Miner, J. B., *Theories of Organizational Behavior*, Holt, Rinehart & Winston (1980).

46 Herzberg, F., 'One more time: how do you motivate employees?', *Harvard Business Review*, vol. 46, 1968, 3–62.

47 Blauner, R., *Alienation and Freedom*, University of Chicago Press (1964).

48 See, for example, Riley, M., *Human Resource Management: A guide to personnel practice in the hotel and catering industry*, Butterworth-Heinemann (1991).

49 Ellis, P., *The Image of Hotel and Catering Work*, HCITB Research Report (1981).

50 *Employee Relations for the Hotel and Catering Industry*, 7th edn, HCTC (1990).

51 Pavesic, D. V. and Brymer, R. A., 'Job satisfaction: what's happening to the young managers?' *Cornell HRA Quarterly*, vol. 30, no. 4, February 1990, 90–6.

52 Simons, T. and Enz, C. A., 'Motivating hotel employees: beyond the carrot and the stick', *Cornell HRA Quarterly*, February 1995, 20–7.

53 Kovach, K., 'What motivates employees? Workers and supervisors give different answers', *Business Horizons*, September–October 1987, 58–65.

54 See, for example, Cheng, T., Sculli, D. and Chan, F. S., 'Relationship dominance – rethinking management theories from the perspective of methodological relationalism', *Journal of Managerial Psychology*, vol. 16, no. 2, 2001, 97–105.

55 Francesco, A. M. and Gold, B. A., *International Organizational Behavior*, 2nd edn, Pearson Prentice Hall (2005), p. 126.

56 Sledge, S., Miles, A. K. and Coppage, S., 'What role does culture play? A look at motivation and job satisfaction among hotel workers in Brazil', *International Journal of Human Resource Management*, vol. 19, no. 2, September 2008, 1667–82.

57 Adler, N. J., *International Aspects of Organizational Behaviour*, 3rd edn, South Western College Publishing (1997).

58 Chen, C. C., 'New trends in reward allocation preferences: a Sino-US comparison', *The Academy of Management Journal*, vol. 38, no. 2, 1995, 402–28.

59 Herzberg, F., *Jumping for the Jelly Beans*, (film) BBC (1973).

60 Boella, M. J. and Goss-Turner, S., *Human Resource Management in the Hospitality Industry*, Elsevier (2005), p. 40.

61 See, for example, Mill, R. C., *Managing for Productivity in the Hospitality Industry*, Van Nostrand Reinhold (1989).

62 Magurn, J. P., *A Manual of Staff Management in the Hotel and Catering Industry*, Heinemann (1983).

63 People 1st, www.peoplelst.co.uk

64 Gill, A., Bhutani, S., Mand, H. and Sharma, S., 'The relationship between transformational leadership and employee desire for empowerment', *International Journal of Contemporary Hospitality Management*, vol. 22, no. 2, 2010, 263–73.

65 Wilkinson, A., 'Empowerment: theory and practice', *Personnel Review*, vol. 27, no. 1, 1998, 40–56.

66 Mills, D. Q. and Friesen, G. B., 'Empowerment', in Crainer, S. and Dearlove, D. (eds), *Financial Times Handbook of Management*, 2nd edn, Financial Times Prentice Hall (2001), p. 323.

67 Cutler, A., *Aspire to inspire*, Hospitality Leadership(2010).

68 Tulgan, B., 'Winning the talent wars', in Crainer, S. and Dearlove, D., *Financial Times Handbook of Management*, 2nd edn, Financial Times Prentice Hall (2001), p. 348.

69 Crainer, S., *Key Management Ideas: Thinkers That Changed the Management World*, 3rd edn, Financial Times Prentice Hall (1998), p. 126.

70 Mooney, J. D., *The Principles of Organization*, rev. edn, Harper & Row (1947), p. 17.

71 Urwick, J. F., *Notes on the Theory of Organization*, American Management Association (1952).

72 See, for example, Waterman, R. H., *The Frontiers of Excellence*, Nicholas Brealey (1994); and Yukl, G. and Fu, P., 'Determinants of delegation and consultation by managers', *Journal of Organizational Behavior*, vol. 20, 1999, 219–32.

73 Guirdham, M., *Interactive Behaviour at Work*, 3rd edn, Financial Times Prentice Hall (2002), p. 569.

74 Gracie, S., 'Delegate Don't Abdicate', *Management Today*, March 1999, 94.

75 Davis, K. and Newstrom, J. W., *Human Behaviour at Work*, 8th edn, McGraw-Hill (1989), pp. 336–7.

76 Jones, P. and Davies, A., 'Empowerment: a study of general managers of four-star hotel properties in the UK', *International Journal of Hospitality Management*, vol. 10, no. 3, 1991, 211–17.

77 Pickard, J., 'The real meaning of empowerment', *Personnel Management*, vol. 25, no. 11, November 1993, 28–33.

78 Pelit, E., Ozturk, Y. and Arslanturk, Y., 'The effects of employee empowerment on employee job satisfaction: a study on hotels in Turkey', *International Journal of Contemporary Hospitality Management*, vol. 23, no. 6, 2011, 784–802.

79 Brownell, J., 'Leadership in the service of hospitality', *Cornell Hospitality Quarterly*, vol. 51, no. 3, May 2010, 363–78.

80 Lashley, C., 'Towards an Understanding of Employee Empowerment Hospitality services', *International Journal of Contemporary Hospitality Management*, vol. 7, no. 1, 1995, 27–32.

81 Lashley, C., 'Employee empowerment in services: a framework for analysis', *Personnel Review*, vol. 28, no. 3, 1999, 169–91.

82 Erstad, M., 'Empowerment and Organizational Change', *International Journal of Contemporary Hospitality Management*, vol. 9, no. 7, 1997, 325–33.

83 Stewart, R., *The Reality of Management*, 3rd edn, Butterworth Heinemann (1999), p. 180.

84 Gratton, L., *The Democratic Enterprise*, Financial Times Prentice Hall (2004), pp. 188–9.

85 Watson, T. J., *Organising and Managing Work*, 2nd edn, Financial Times Prentice Hall (2006), p. 12.

86 Kim, B., Lee, G., Murrmann, S. and George, T., 'Motivational effects of empowerment on employees organizational commitment: a mediating role of management trustworthiness', *Cornell Hospitality Quarterly*, vol. 53, no. 1, 2012, 10–19.

87 Jamison, C., 'Top 10 myths of customer service', *The British Journal of Administrative Management*, July/August 1999, 20.

88 Pickard, J., 'The real meaning of empowerment', *Personnel Management*, vol. 25, no. 11, November 1993, 28–33.

89 Peiperi, M., 'Does empowerment deliver the goods?', *Mastering Management*, FT/Pitman Publishing (1997), p. 287.

90 See, for example, Sell, R., 'Empowerment', *QWL News and Abstracts*, ACAS, no. 133, Winter 1998, 7–11.

91 Wall, T. and Wood, S., 'Delegation's a powerful tool', *Professional Manager*, November 2002, 37.

92 Wheatley, R., 'Stress and Delegation', *Professional Manager*, vol. 12, no. 3, May 2003, 22 (The Whitehall II Study, HSE Contract Research, Report 422/2002).

93 Organ, D. W., *Organizational Citizenship Behaviour: The good soldier syndrome*, Lexington Books (1988).

94 Baum, T., *Human Resource Management for Tourism, Hospitality and Leisure*, Thomson (2006).

95 Cheung, C., 'The impact of employees' behaviour and the implementation of total quality management on service quality a case study in the hotel industry', unpublished PhD thesis, University of Strathclyde, cited in Baum (2006).

Chapter 8

Managing through groups and teams

Learning outcomes

After completing this chapter you should be able to:

- explain the meaning and importance of work groups and teams;
- distinguish between groups and teams and between formal and informal groups;
- detail the main reasons for the formation of groups and teams;
- examine factors that influence group cohesiveness and performance;
- analyse the nature of role relationships;
- explore the changing nature of teams such as multicultural and virtual teams;
- review the importance of and influences on successful teamworking.

Introduction

Groups are an essential feature of the structure of any hospitality organisation. Individuals seldom work in isolation from others and almost all staff in the hospitality industry will be a member of one or more groups. If effective performance is to be achieved, the activities of staff require coordination through the operation of effective groups and teamwork. Increasingly, as organisation structures become flatter, the manager needs to be aware of the interactions and operations of groups and teams and their effects on organisational performance. To operate successfully, a group must function as a team and a manager should be aware of the approaches that may be adopted to develop cohesive team action.

Critical review and reflection

'But let's be honest. A good operation is about the team, the people. They need to bond together, work as a unit, and too often not enough focus is given to this. Managers must let their teams have freedom but within very clear guidelines.' (Stuart Everson of Compass)

Do you agree with this statement? What sort of 'guidelines' do you consider should be given?

The nature of work groups

The structure of most hospitality organisations is made up of groups of people working together. Members of a group must cooperate together in order that activities are carried out. Groups have a major influence on behaviour and the work pattern of the organisation. The manager must use groups in order to achieve a high standard of work and improve the effectiveness of hospitality operations. This requires an understanding of the functioning and processes of groups, and their influence on the behaviour and performance of people at work.[1]

What is a group?

Most people will readily understand what constitutes a group although there appears to be no single, accepted definition. The central feature of a group is that its members regard themselves as belonging to the group. One way of defining a work group is a collection of people who share most if not all of the following characteristics:

- a definable membership;
- group consciousness;
- a sense of shared purpose;
- interdependence;
- interaction; and
- ability to act in a unitary manner.[2]

It is important to consider both the structure and processes of the group, and its effects on the behaviour of individual members.

Another useful definition of the group, in psychological terms, is any number of people who:

1 interact with one another;

2 are psychologically aware of one another; and

3 perceive themselves to be a group.[3]

Differences between groups and teams

The use of the word 'teams' has become increasingly fashionable in recent years. Crainer refers to the use of 'teamworking' as a side effect of increasing concentration on working across functional divides. It fits neatly with the trend towards empowerment. However, despite the extensive literature about teams and teamworking, the basic dynamics of teamworking often remain clouded and uncertain.

> Teams occur when a number of people have a common goal and recognise that their personal success is dependent on the success of others. They are all interdependent. In practice, this means that in most teams people will contribute individual skills many of which will be different. It also means that the full tensions and counter-balance of human behaviour will need to be demonstrated in the team.[4]

In common usage and literature, including to some extent in this book, there is a tendency for the terms 'groups' and 'teams' to be used interchangeably. It is not easy to distinguish clearly between a group and a team. According to ACAS: 'the term "team" is used loosely to describe many different groupings and a variety of labels are given to the types of teams.

It is doubtful whether any definitions of types of teams would be universally acceptable.'[5]

According to Holpp, while many people are still paying homage to teams, teamwork, empowerment and self-management, others have become disillusioned. Holpp poses the question: 'What are teams?'

> It's a simple enough question, but one that's seldom asked. We all think we know intuitively what teams are. Guess again. Here are some questions to help define team configurations.

- Are teams going to be natural work groups, or project-and-task oriented?
- Will they be self-managed or directed?
- How many people will be on the teams; who's in charge?
- How will the teams fit into the organisation's structure if it shows only boxes and not circles or other new organisational forms?

Holpp also poses the question: 'why do you want teams?'

> If teams are just a convenient way to group, under one manager, a lot of people who used to work for several downsized supervisors, don't bother. But if teams can truly take ownership of work areas and provide the kind of up-close knowledge that's unavailable elsewhere, then full speed ahead.[6]

Exhibit 8.1 Ad-hoc teams

Contracting catering companies in the world of major international events face interesting and complex challenges when teams are put together just for the duration of the event.

Consider this scenario: a large British caterer has secured contracts to provide food and beverage services to a number of exhibiting organisations at the Paris Air Show. The event organiser provides temporary, luxurious chalets – complete with heavy kitchen equipment and furniture. The caterer provides the staff, light equipment, and food and drink.

One of the caterer's contracts is with an internationally respected company manufacturing electronic components – let's call it 'ABC Aviation'. This organisation has high hopes of securing orders worth in excess of £10 million at the show. Their clients visiting their chalet will include senior representatives of aircraft manufacturers, and government ministers. They will expect first class standards of hospitality, and are paying handsomely for this.

Menus are prepared by the caterer's Executive Chef, and will be common to all their clients at the show.

The caterer's Human Resource Department puts together a team to run the chalet for ABC Aviation. The team will be managed by a lecturer in Food and Beverage Operations from a leading catering college. He has considerable experience of this sort of work, and is on his summer vacation. There will be two chefs – one a very experienced Warrant Officer Chef in the British Army, currently on leave after a tour of active service in Afghanistan. The other is a young but well-qualified chef, recently made redundant when an up-market restaurant business went into receivership. A team of ten students from a small provincial catering college will share the duties of food service, bar service and wash-up. Their average age is 18. Most have had some part-time experience in pubs and restaurants.

Apart from the ten students who know each other quite well, no members of the team have met before.

The show lasts for a week, and there are plans for two days of preparation prior to the opening. *The problem is – how can the caterer be confident that the team will coalesce rapidly, so that from the outset the client will receive the standard of service that is expected under the terms of the contract? Each member of the team is principally there to earn money over a very short time period. Why should they buy into notions of quality?*

Possible key issues here are:

1 The two preparation days are crucial. Once operations begin, the pace will be frenetic and opportunities to adjust anything will be minimal.

2 Presenting and clarifying the required standards is the first step to ensuring delivery. Demonstrations, a simple clear manual, photographic illustrations, videos, role plays, all help – especially participative activities – we learn more by 'doing' than by anything else.

3 Team-building can be developed amazingly quickly. Tasks that require multiple participants, 'blind man's buff' for example, develop a sense of confidence in colleagues, and a knowledge and understanding of character traits.

4 Early team-building gives the opportunity to recognise the strengths that exist, which should be exploited, and the weaknesses that exist, which must be remedied. There is no time for generic basic training – it has to be specific and focused. For example, the chefs will recognise technical menu terms (salpicon, coulis, jus, etc.) but the students may need training.

5 Simple techniques of identification of team members can be very powerful. The well-known motivational feeling of pulling on the team jersey in an international match can be replicated – even when all company staff are wearing a standard uniform. Even pin badges can produce this effect as McDonald's have famously proven.

6 The clear announcement of rewards available has been shown to have a major impact. Whilst this strategy may be considered divisive, and nothing short of bribery, the principles of expectancy, defined by Vroom and Deci (1983)[7] will apply to many employees. They see the real potential of a target to work towards, which will give them clear benefit.

7 A few employees may be identified as being 'self-starters' with a high level of skills, and these individuals can usually be easily recognised. They are often suitable for supervisory roles because they will not let inferior work of others impact on their own performance. It must be noted, however, that such individuals are rare in the world of 'mercenary' workers.

8 The award of prizes – both individual and corporate – is often used as a competitive motivational tool. 'Chalet of the Show' with prizes for ALL team members can encourage the team to pull together, and any team member's poor performance will be admonished by their peers. This lightens the manager's quality control responsibility considerably.

9 Prizes for individual performance can provide a reward for outstanding individual effort, and may be most usefully used with workers in a relatively individual role – say with the chefs for quality of food presentation, or a cocktail barman for artistry or innovation.

Thoughtful planning can ensure that some mix of these and similar strategies will provide a service which will be of such quality that the client will be totally unaware that the team providing the service were strangers just 48 hours earlier.

Source: The authors are grateful to Gerry Banks for this contribution.

Teamwork as a fashionable term

Cane suggests that organisations are sometimes unsure whether they have teams or simply groups of people working together.

It is certainly true to say that any group of people who do not know they are a team cannot be one. To become a team, a group of individuals needs to have a strong common purpose and to work towards that purpose rather than working individually. Also, they need to believe that they will achieve more by cooperation than by working individually.[8]

Whereas all teams are, by definition, groups, it does not necessarily follow that all groups are teams.

Belbin points out that, to the extent that teamwork was becoming a fashionable term, it began to replace the more usual reference to groups and every group activity was being

	Team	Group
Size	Limited	Medium or large
Selection	Crucial	Immaterial
Leadership	Shared or rotating	Solo
Perception	Mutual knowledge understanding	Focus on leader
Style	Role spread co-ordination	Convergence conformism
Spirit	Dynamic interaction	Togetherness persecution of opponents

Source: Belbin, R. M., *Beyong the Team*, Butterworth-Heinemann (2000). Copyright © 2000. Reproduced with permission from Elsevier Ltd.

Figure 8.1 Differences between a team and a group

described as 'teamwork'. He questions whether it matters if one is talking about groups or teams, and maintains that the confusion in vocabulary should be addressed, if the principles of good teamwork are to be retained. Belbin also suggests that there are several factors that characterise the difference between groups and teams (see Figure 8.1). The best differentiator is size: groups can comprise any number of people but teams are smaller with a membership between (ideally) four and six. The quintessential feature of a small, well-balanced team is that leadership is shared or rotates whereas large groups typically throw up solo leaders.[9]

While acknowledging the work of Belbin it appears that the term 'group' is often used in a more general sense and 'team' in a more specific context. We continue to refer to 'group' or 'team' according to the particular focus of attention and the vocabulary of the quoted authors.

Reasons for formation of groups or teams

Individuals have varying expectations of the benefits from group membership (formal and/or informal) relating to both social processes and work performance.

- Groups provide companionship and a source of mutual understanding and support from colleagues. This can help in solving work problems or mitigate stressful, or demanding, working conditions.
- Membership of the group can provide the individual with a sense of belonging. The group provides a feeling of identity, and the chance to acquire role recognition and status within the group.

- The group provides guidelines on generally acceptable behaviour. It helps to clarify ambiguous situations such as, for example, the extent to which official rules and regulations are expected to be adhered to in practice. Group allegiance can serve as a means of determining norms of behaviour.

- The combined efforts of members of a group can have a synergistic effect. The collective knowledge and expertise of members can help in problem-solving and in the performance of complex or difficult tasks.

- Groups may encourage the modification of formal working arrangements, to become more to the liking of members, for example by sharing or rotating unpopular tasks. Group membership can provide opportunities for initiative and creativity.

- The group may provide mutual support and protection for its members, for example by collaborating to safeguard their interests from outside pressures or threats.

Morale and work performance

Groups are, therefore, a potential source of motivation and job satisfaction, and also a major determinant of effective organisational performance. Membership of a cohesive group can be a rewarding experience for the individual and can contribute to the promotion of morale. Members of a high-morale group are more likely to think of themselves as a group and to work together effectively.

Groups are a characteristic feature of all social situations. The working of groups, and the influence they exert over their membership, is a major feature of human behaviour and group processes. People in groups influence each other in many ways, and groups develop their own hierarchies and leaders. Group pressures to conform with 'norms' and social conventions can have a significant influence over the behaviour of individual members and their work performance.

Group values and norms of behaviour

The classical approach to organisation and management tended to ignore the importance of groups and the social factors of work.

One experiment (in the Hawthorne Studies) involved the observation of a group of 14 men working in the bank wiring room. It was noted that the men formed their own informal organisation with sub-groups and cliques, and with natural leaders emerging with the consent of members. They would often help each other with the work and, contrary to management instructions, members would often exchange jobs.

The group developed its own pattern of informal social relations, and codes and practices ('norms') of what constituted 'proper' group behaviour:

- *not to be a 'rate buster'* – not to produce at too high a rate of output compared with other members or to exceed the production restriction of the group;

- *not to be a 'chiseller'* – not to shirk production or to produce at too low a rate of output compared with other members of the group;

- *not to be a 'squealer'* – not to say anything to the supervisor or management which might be harmful to other members of the group;

- *not to be 'officious'* – people with authority over members of the group, for example inspectors, should neither take advantage of their seniority nor maintain a social distance from the group.

Despite a financial incentive scheme where workers could receive more money the more units they produced, the group decided on 6,000 units a day as a fair level of output. This was well below the level they were capable of producing but group pressure was stronger than the financial incentives offered by management.

It was also company policy that the supervisor should report daily on each man's output. However, the workers preferred to do their own reporting. On some days the men would actually produce more than reported in order to 'build up' extra units for days when they produced less than reported. In order to remain in favour with the group, the supervisor did nothing to stop this practice.

System of sanctions

If individual members did not conform to these norms of behaviour the group had its own system of sanctions. These included ostracising members, sarcasm and verbal abuse, damaging completed work, hiding tools, and playing tricks on inspectors. Threats of physical violence were also made. The group developed a system of 'binging' which involved striking someone a fairly hard blow on the upper part of the arm. The process of 'binging' also became a recognised method of controlling conflict within the group.

According to Riches one way to improve team performance is to establish agreed norms or rules for how the team is to operate and rigorously stick to them. Norms could address the obligations of individual members to the team, how it will assess its performance, how it will work together, what motivation systems will be used, and how it will relate to customers. They would also include the mechanisms to facilitate an honest exchange about the team norms and behaviour.[10]

Critical review and reflection

'People value their individuality and enjoy the right of self-expression. Membership of a group means giving up some of that personal identity. The real skill of management is therefore to make full use of people's individuality for the mutual benefit of the group as a whole.'

If you were a manager in the hospitality industry, how would you attempt to achieve this balance?

Developing effective groups

Cooperation among members is likely to be greater in a united, cohesive group. The manager's main concern is that members of a work group cooperate in order to achieve the results expected of them. The work of a hospitality organisation entails a wide range of operations, many of which are undertaken simultaneously, and depend upon a high degree

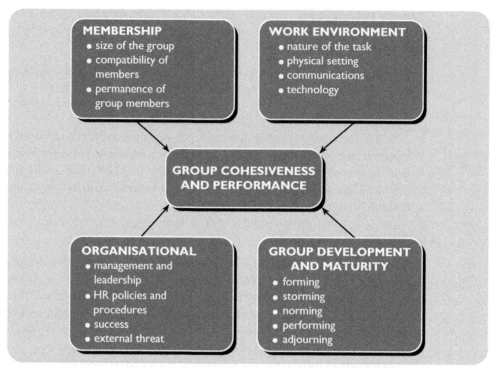

MEMBERSHIP
- size of the group
- compatibility of members
- permanence of group members

WORK ENVIRONMENT
- nature of the task
- physical setting
- communications
- technology

GROUP COHESIVENESS AND PERFORMANCE

ORGANISATIONAL
- management and leadership
- HR policies and procedures
- success
- external threat

GROUP DEVELOPMENT AND MATURITY
- forming
- storming
- norming
- performing
- adjourning

Figure 8.2 Factors contributing to group cohesiveness and performance

of coordination and teamwork. This calls for good working relationships among staff and effective group activities.[11]

In order to develop the effectiveness of work groups, the manager will be concerned with those factors that contribute to group cohesiveness, or that may cause frustration or disruption to the operation and performance of the group. The manager needs to consider, therefore, both the needs of individual members of the group and the promotion of a high level of group identity and cohesion.

Many factors contribute to group cohesiveness and performance.[12] These can be summarised under four broad headings: membership, work environment, organisational, and group development and maturity (Figure 8.2).

Membership of the group

- *Size of the group* – it is difficult to put a figure on the ideal size of a work group and much will depend upon other variables. However, it seems to be generally accepted that cohesiveness becomes more difficult to achieve when a group exceeds 10–12 members. Berger and Vanger, for example, suggest that team-building is most successful in groups of six to ten people.[13] As a group increases in size, problems arise with communications and coordination. Large groups are more difficult to handle and require a higher level of supervision. Absenteeism also tends to be higher in larger groups. When a group becomes too large, it may split into smaller units and friction may develop between sub-groups.

- *Compatibility of the members* – the more homogeneous the members of a group in terms of, for example, shared backgrounds, interests, attitudes and values, the easier it is to promote cohesiveness. Differences between individual members such as personality and skills can serve to complement each other and help make for a cohesive group. However, such differences may also be the cause of disruption and conflict.
- *Permanence of membership* – group spirit and relationships take time to develop. Cohesiveness is more likely to be achieved when members of a group are together for a reasonable length of time and changes occur only slowly. A frequent turnover of members is likely to have an adverse effect on morale and social satisfaction, and on the cohesiveness of the group. The high labour turnover encountered in many sectors of the hospitality industry is a typical factor here.

The work environment

- *The nature of the task* – where individuals are involved in similar work, share a common task or face the same problems, this may assist cohesiveness. The nature of the task may serve to bring people together. An example could be receptionists working in a large and busy international hotel.
- *Physical setting and communications* – where members of a group work in the same location or in close physical proximity to each other, this will often help cohesiveness. The more easily members can communicate freely with each other, the greater the likelihood of group cohesion. Members of the maintenance staff working on their own in different parts of a hotel may experience a lack of group identity. However, isolation from other workers may also tend to build cohesiveness. This may apply, for example, to a smaller number of workers on the night rota.
- *Technology and the manner in which work is carried out* – where the nature of the work process involves a craft- or skill-based 'technology' there is a higher likelihood of cohesiveness. For example, in a small, high-class hotel particularly noted for the standard of its cuisine, members of the kitchen brigade need to interact and work closely with each other for effective performance. (You could compare this, for instance, with the mass production technology of fast- food chains.)

Groups in organisations

- *Managerial style* – the activities of groups cannot be separated from management and the process of leadership. The style of leadership adopted will influence the relationship between the group and management, and is a major determinant of group cohesiveness. In general terms, cohesiveness will be affected by the manner in which the manager gives guidance, encouragement and support to the group, provides opportunities for participation, attempts to resolve difficulties and conflicts, and adopts a Theory Y approach.
- *Success and positive motivation* – the more successful the group, the more cohesive it is likely to be, and cohesive groups are more likely to be successful. Success is usually a

strong and positive motivational influence on the level of work performance. Success or reward as a positive motivator, for example the satisfactory completion of a difficult task through cooperative action, recognition and praise from management, a feeling of high status or esteem, high wage payments from a group-based bonus scheme, can be perceived by group members in a number of ways.

- *Human resource management policies and procedures* – attention should be given to the effects that systems of appraisal, transfers, promotion and discipline, and opportunities for training and personal development have on members of the group. Harmony within the group is more likely to be achieved if human resource policies and procedures are perceived to be equitable, and all members receive what they believe is fair treatment by management.

- *External threat* – cohesiveness may be enhanced by members cooperating with one another when faced with a common external threat, for example the introduction of new technology or changes in their method of work, or the appointment of a new supervisor. Even if the threat is subsequently removed, the group may still continue to have a greater degree of cohesion than before the threat arose. Conflict between groups will also tend to increase the cohesiveness of each group and the boundaries of the groups become drawn more closely.

Group development and maturity

Cohesiveness is affected by the manner in which groups progress through the various stages of development and maturity. Tuckman, for example, identifies five main successive stages of group development and relationships: forming, storming, norming, performing and adjourning.[14]

- *Stage 1: Forming* – the initial formation of the group. This involves the bringing together of a number of individuals and the tentative identification of the purpose of the group, its composition and terms of reference. Consideration is given to the hierarchical structure of the group, pattern of leadership, individual roles and responsibilities, and codes of conduct. At this stage there is likely to be considerable anxiety as members attempt to create an impression, to test each other and to establish their personal identity within the group.

- *Stage 2: Storming* – as members of the group get to know each other better, they will put forward their views more openly and forcefully. Disagreements will be expressed and challenges offered on the nature of the task and the arrangements made during the forming stage. The storming stage is important because, if it is successful, there will be discussions on reforming the working and operation of the group, and agreement on more meaningful structures and procedures.

- *Stage 3: Norming* – as conflict and hostility start to be controlled, members of the group will establish guidelines and standards, and develop their own norms of acceptable behaviour. The norming stage is important in establishing the need for members to cooperate together in order to plan, agree standards of performance and fulfil the purpose of the group.

- *Stage 4: Performing* – when the group has progressed successfully through the earlier three stages it will have created structure and cohesiveness to work effectively as a team.

At this stage the group can concentrate on the attainment of its purpose, and performance of the common task is likely to be at its most effective.

- *Stage 5: Adjourning* – this refers to the adjourning or disbanding of the group because of, for example, completion of the task, or members leaving the organisation, or members moving on to other tasks. Some members may feel a compelling sense of loss at the end of a major or lengthy group project and their return to independence is characterised by sadness and anxiety. Managers may need to prepare for future group tasks and engendering team effort.

Characteristics of a successful group

Bass and Ryterband also identify four distinct stages in effective group development:

- mutual acceptance and membership;
- communication and decision-making;
- motivation and productivity; and
- control and organisation.[15]

Another writer suggests that new groups go through the following stages:

- the polite stage;
- the 'why are we here, what are we doing?' stage;
- which dominant will emerge? – the power stage;
- the constructive stage, when sharing beings; and
- the unity stage – which often takes weeks, eating together and talking together.[16]

The characteristics of a successful work group are not always easy to isolate clearly. The underlying feature is a spirit of cooperation in which members work well together as a united team, and with harmonious and supportive relationships. This may be evidenced when members of a group exhibit:

- a belief in shared objectives;
- a sense of commitment to the group;
- acceptance of group values and norms;
- a feeling of mutual trust and dependency;
- full participation by all members and decision-making by consensus;
- a free flow of information and communications;
- the open expression of feelings and disagreements; and
- the resolution of conflict by the members themselves.[17]

Creative leadership and group development

In an examination of creative leadership and team effectiveness, Rickards and Moger propose a modification to the Tuckman model and suggest a two-barrier model of group development. Creative leadership is suggested as producing new routines or protocols designed as **benign structures** which help teams progress through the first barrier at Tuckman's **storm(ing)** stage (a behavioural barrier), and beyond a second barrier at the **norm(ing)** stage (a norm-breaking barrier). From empirical studies of small groups and project teams Rickards and Moger put forward two challenges to the prevailing model of team development:

1 Weak teams posed the question 'what is happening if a team fails to develop beyond the storm(ing) stage?'

2 The exceptional teams posed the question 'what happens if a team breaks out of the performance norms developed?'

The suggestion is that the teams are differentiated by two barriers to performance. The weak barrier is behavioural and defeated a minority of teams; the strong barrier was a block to creativity or innovation, and defeated the majority of those teams who passed through the weak barrier. The two-barrier model provides a starting point for exploring the impact and influence of a team leader on the performance of teams. Rickards and Moger suggest seven factors through which a leader might influence effective team development:

1 building a platform of understanding;

2 creating a shared vision;

3 a creative climate;

4 a commitment to idea ownership;

5 resilience to setbacks;

6 developing networking skills;

7 learning from experience.[18]

Critical review and reflection

'The most important factor influencing group cohesiveness and performance is the style of leadership. Leaders are the role models who set the culture and values for the organisation and the group. It is therefore the leaders who make a group become a team.'

What are your views? How do you think a group becomes a team?

Formal and informal groups

Groups are deliberately planned and created by management as part of organisational design. An organisation chart, for example, gives a representation of the formal structure of the hotel. But groups also arise from social processes and the informal organisation. The informal organisation arises from the interactions of people working within the hospitality organisation and the development of groups with their own relationships and norms of behaviour, irrespective of those defined within the formal structure. This leads to a major distinction between formal groups and informal groups.

Formal groups

Formal groups are concerned with the achievement of specific organisational objectives and with the coordination of work activities. They are created by management with established rules, relationships and norms of behaviour. The nature of the tasks to be undertaken is a predominant feature of the formal group. People are brought together on the basis of defined roles within the structure of the establishment. Formal groups tend to be relatively permanent although there may be changes in actual membership. However, temporary formal groups may also be established by management, for example to undertake a specific task such as preparations for a special banquet.

Informal groups

Within the formal structure there will always be an informal structure. The formal structure, and system of role relationships, rules and procedures, will be augmented by interpretation and development at the informal level. Informal groups are based more on personal relationships and agreement of group members than on defined role relationships. They serve to satisfy psychological and social needs which are not necessarily related to the tasks to be undertaken.[19]

Informal groups may arise from the same horizontal level, but they also arise vertically or diagonally (Figure 8.3). The membership of informal groups therefore cuts across the formal structure. They may comprise individuals from different parts of the establishment and/or from different levels. An informal group could also be the same as the formal group or it might comprise a part only of the formal group.

Characteristics of informal groups

Informal groups develop their own characteristics. They may have their own culture, status values and symbols, and their own system of communications through the 'grapevine'. Informal groups are also agents of social satisfaction and control. As a result there is often strong resistance to changes which threaten the status quo, or the environment or working practices of the group.[20]

It is possible for the leader of an informal group to be the same person as the formal leader appointed officially by management. It is more usual, however, for the group to have its own informal leader who exercises authority by the consent of the members themselves. The informal leader may be chosen as the person who reflects the attitudes and values of the members, helps to resolve conflict, leads the group in satisfying its goals, or liaises with management or other people outside the group.

You may recall the discussion on the importance of cultural influences in Chapter 3. A multicultural work environment may lead to the emergence of informal groups and cliques based on common nationality, religion or shared ethnic values, and with their own leaders and spokespersons. Such informal groups are not necessarily harmful to the operations of the establishment but it is important that the manager emphasises the need for effective cooperation and teamwork.

Major functions of informal groups

Lysons suggests four main reasons for informal groups:

1 **The perpetuation of the informal group 'culture'.** Culture in this context means a set of values, norms and beliefs which form a guide to group acceptance and group behaviour. Unless you broadly subscribe to the group culture, you will not belong and will be an 'outsider' or 'isolate'.

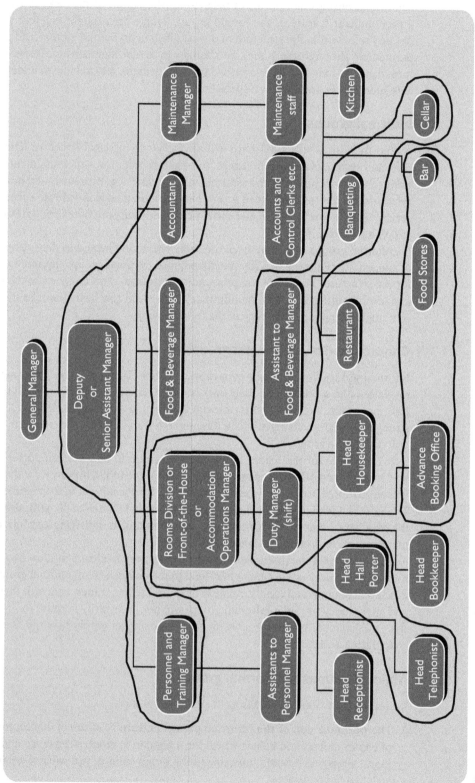

Figure 8.3 Possible examples of informal groups within the formal structure

2 **The maintenance of a communication system.** Groups want all the information that affects their welfare, either negatively or positively. If groups are not apprised of policies and motives behind actions, they will seek to tap into formal communication channels and spread information among group members.

3 **The implementation of social control.** Conformity to group culture is enforced by such techniques as ridicule, ostracism and violence. This is illustrated, for example, by the enforcement of group norms in the bank wiring room discussed in the previous section.

4 **The provision of interest and fun in work life.** Many jobs are monotonous and fail to hold workers' attention. Work may also offer few prospects. Workers may try to compensate by interpersonal relations provided by the group and in such activities as time-wasting by talking, gambling, practical joking and drinking.[21]

> We humans are a gregarious lot. We like to gather together and establish our own social networks, which are often the real key to creativity and innovation in organisations . . . But many managers are unaware that, seemingly pointless, social networking does, in fact, play a crucial part in the way people interact with each other and get work done.
>
> (Sue Law)[22]

Individuals have varying expectations of the benefits from group membership, relating to both work performance and social processes. However, working in groups may mean that members spend too much time talking among themselves rather than doing. Groups may also compete against each other in a non-productive manner. It is a question of balance. It is important, therefore, that the manager understands the reasons for the formation of groups and is able to recognise likely advantageous or adverse consequences for the organisation.

The need for teamwork

Work is a group-based activity and especially so in hospitality operations. How people behave and perform as a member of a group is as important as their behaviour or performance as individuals. If the hotel, for example, is to operate effectively it requires good teamwork.[23] Simmons and Teare draw attention to the emphasis on teamwork at every level of Scott's Hotels and to the importance of group working, quality improvement teams and action teams as part of a total quality management approach to improved quality and performance.[24]

Not only must members of a group work well as a team but each group must also work well with other groups. It is important to reduce conflict between different groups, and especially between front-of-house staff such as receptionists and back-of-house staff such as housekeepers.[25]

Groups and teams

Whereas all teams are, by definition, groups it does not necessarily follow that all groups are teams. A team, therefore, involves something extra such as high levels of morale and group cohesiveness, mutual trust and goodwill among members, and commitment to group goals and objectives.[26]

'A team is always a group, but a group is NOT always a team.'
'A hotel is a team of people, not a collection of individuals.'

To what extent do you agree with these statements? What do you consider is the difference between a group and a team when working within the hospitality industry?

It is not easy to distinguish clearly between a 'group' and a 'team'. Riley, for example, offers the following observation:

> Managers like to talk of teams and teamwork but these words are both difficult to define, let alone achieve. Giving a set of individuals group tasks to do will not, of itself, form them into groups. Putting on a coloured shirt and running onto a field with others similarly attired won't make them a team! Yet teamwork can be seen and felt – it is a tangible thing. The real problem is that we organise people into groups, call them teams, but don't look to see if they are actually behaving like groups or teams. The words 'group' and 'team' tend to be used coterminously, but one expression is central to both concepts and that is 'common identity'.[27]

Harmonious working relationships and good teamwork help make for a high level of both staff morale and customer satisfaction. An example of the importance placed on teamwork is the extract from the introductory pages of Foxhills' staff induction manual.

The importance of teamwork

Exhibit 8.2 Teamwork

What is teamwork?

When a group of people communicate well and clearly, work closely together and help each other with instruction and/or actual labour during work, teamwork is achieved. This means HELPING your colleagues WHENEVER and WHEREVER they need it.

Why is teamwork important?

Teamwork makes everyone's job easier and makes the department a better place to work in. It also allows and promotes friendship and caring. When you help another colleague get their job done, you are helping yourself. If the customer is served by a person with a confident attitude everyone benefits. This means the cooperation of all staff is essential. It is very obvious that the waiting and barstaff are contributing to customer service and satisfaction. There are others who will ensure a customer is comfortable and happy. The kitchen staff doing their job well is of the highest importance. There are good food waiters and waitresses but you cannot be good without a good product. Think about it!

THE NUMBER ONE RULE IS TO COMMUNICATE CLEARLY AND EFFECTIVELY WITH YOUR COLLEAGUES.

If you expect and receive instructions and help, return the favour. Before you know it everyone is not only doing their job well, but also helping others and working as part of the team.

Remember to tell people you appreciate what they are doing for you. Thank each person that helps you do your job. We all play a role in customer satisfaction.

Watch your attitude – no one wants to work with a grump or worse, if you are down you spread it around and nobody needs that.

Teamwork at Foxhills is essential to everyone's morale. Try it. Help out a fellow employee and watch it come back to you in the form of appreciation. Teamwork means helping each other and solving problems together. It is mutual respect and open communications on all levels, employee to employee, employee to manager, manager to manager.

TEAMWORK IS WORK

BUT IT IS WORTH IT.

Source: Extract from staff induction manual, Foxhills Golf and Country Club; reproduced with permission.

Creating team effectiveness

The importance of people's ability to work together in the hospitality industry and the many potential benefits from successful team-building are emphasised by Berger and Vanger.

A successful team-building effort will improve your employees' productivity. They will be better able to handle complex operations; they will respond more quickly to new situations; they will be more motivated and will make better decisions.[28]

Berger and Vanger suggest six main steps in the team-building cycle.

- Identify the problem you wish to solve and define the objective for team-building. An example would be to encourage a competent team to work together even more successfully or to assemble a new team for a special project. It is important to secure the willingness and commitment of staff to the team-building process.

- Gather information about the problem. This can be achieved through: (i) an open 'clear the air' meeting to discuss grievances; (ii) conducting a survey to establish the conflicts and difficulties the group might face; or (iii) bringing in an outside consultant.

- Communication with group members. Sufficient time should be allowed so that the discussion can focus on each item in turn and be free-ranging. The group leader should participate and encourage group members to join the discussion, and to elaborate their views on each topic.

- Plan for change. Group members should be able to work together and establish plans for eliminating blockages to the operation's effectiveness. Each member must be willing to compromise. The team should establish group objectives, the decision-making process and strategies for overcoming conflict.

- Implement the plans. The team should continue to function according to the guidelines it has established for itself. Other members of staff who have not been involved in the team-building sessions should be kept fully informed and involved in the plans.

- Evaluate the group's ability as a team. One way of measuring success is for the group to establish its own charter of procedures and to survey team members to find out how well the charter is being adhered to. Negative feedback should be addressed to the group as a whole and balanced with complimentary remarks. Reassurance and appreciation should be given when overall performance is acceptable.

Berger and Vanger claim that one of the greatest blocks to teamwork is a failure of communications. If members of staff feel isolated, they avoid talking with each other. This can result in a number of individuals, each operating according to their own concept of customer service. Such an attitude means that functioning as a team is extremely difficult and it makes for an erratic service to customers.

From a study of three TGI Friday's restaurants, Gardner and Wood found that team-building was the result of practical measures, especially the careful selection of employees, and identified six key features which contributed to the achievement of teamwork:

- careful selection of employees;
- substantial training;
- regular formal meetings of service personnel;
- a small number of explicit articulated rules of behaviour and procedure;
- emphasis on relationships with customers;
- clear and open systems of performance rewards in addition to formal remuneration.[29]

Happy teams at Heineken

Included in a study of top European companies, 'making teamwork work', Heller refers to the happy teams at Heineken. As part of the cultural strength of Heineken is a realisation that the best culture for an organisation is a strong team culture, and that people who have to work together as a team must also think together as a team, the team-thinking at Heineken demonstrates 'the power of decentralised team management'. The essence of teamworking is that all members are responsible for the results of the team – but this principle in no way absolves leadership in cases of disaster.[30] (Leadership is discussed in Chapter 6.)

According to ACAS, teams have been around for as long as anyone can remember and there can be few organisations that have not used the term in one sense or another. In a general sense, people talk of teamwork when they want to emphasise the virtues of cooperation and the need to make use of the various strengths of employees. Using the term more specifically, teamworking involves a reorganisation of the way work is carried out. Teamwork can increase competitiveness by:

- improving productivity;
- improving quality and encouraging innovation;
- taking advantage of the opportunities provided by technological advances;
- improving employee motivation and commitment.[31]

The general movement towards flatter structures of organisation, wider spans of control and reducing layers of middle management, together with increasing empowerment of employees, all involve greater emphasis on the importance of teamworking. 'There's no doubt that effective teamwork is crucial to an organisation's efforts to perform better, faster and more profitably than their competitors.'[32]

This view on the importance of teamwork is supported by Adams.

> The point is that teamwork is not an option for a successful organisation; it is a necessity. Teamwork can lead to achievement, creativity and energy levels that someone working alone, or perhaps with just one other person, could hardly imagine.[33]

Cutler refers to the developing role of management and stresses that the modern manager must change from being boss to being a team player and to coaching team members.[34]

Social identity theory

Within work organisations there will be a number of different but overlapping groups representing a variety of functions, departments, occupations, technologies, project teams, locations or hierarchical levels. Organisational effectiveness will be dependent upon the extent to which these groups cooperate together, but often the different groupings are part of a network of complex relationships resulting in competitiveness and conflict. A feature of the importance and significance of group membership is the concept of social identity theory. Tajfel and Turner originally developed the idea of **social identity theory** as a means of understanding the psychological basis of intergroup discrimination.[35] Individuals are perceived as having not just one 'personal self' but a number of 'selves' derived from different social contexts and membership of groups.

Because of the need for a clear sense of personal identity, the groups or social categories with which we associate are an integral part of our self-concept (social identity). A natural process of human interaction is social categorisation by which we classify both ourselves and other people through reference to our own social identity. For example, membership of high-status groups can increase a person's perceived self-esteem. According to Guirdham 'self-categorisation is the process that transforms a number of individuals into a group.'[36] See Figure 8.4.

Haslam refers to the relationship between individuals and groups in an understanding of organisational behaviour, and argues that:

> in order to understand perception and interaction in organizational contexts we must do more than just study the psychology of individuals as **individuals**. Instead, we need to understand how social interaction is bound up with individuals' **social identities** – their definition of themselves in terms of group memberships.[37]

We identify ourselves in terms of membership of certain social groupings and differentiate ourselves from other social groupings. This leads to minimising differences between members of our own groupings (in-groups) and maximising differences from other groupings (out-groups). Over time the sense of shared identity with the in-group increases a feeling of what is right and proper and highlights differences from the out-groups.[38] As a result, this reinforces both social identity with our own category and the projection of negative perceptions and stereotypes towards out-groups. Stereotyping can lead to shared attitudes to out-groups and to increased conflict amongst work groups. The examples of group stereotyping discussed in Chapter 6 are associated with social identity theory. Tajfel and Turner suggest that the mere act of individuals categorising themselves as group members leads them to exhibit in-group favouritism. Hewstone *et al.* suggest that even without realising it, we tend usually to favour the groupings we belong to more than denigrate out-groups. Successful inter-group bias enhances self-esteem.[39]

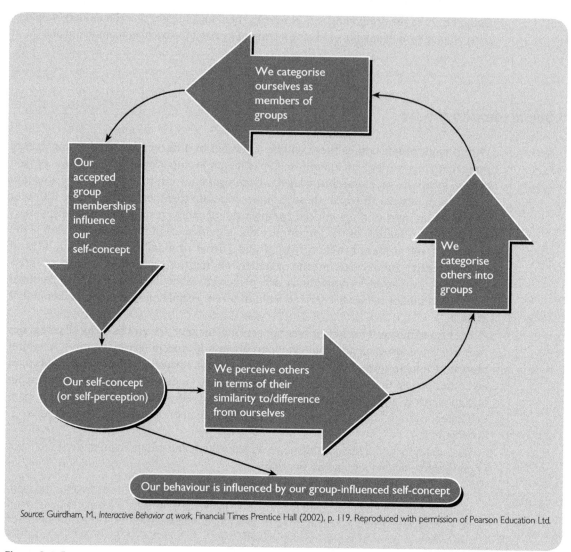

Source: Guirdham, M., *Interactive Behavior at work*, Financial Times Prentice Hall (2002), p. 119. Reproduced with permission of Pearson Education Ltd.

Figure 8.4 Processes of social and self-categorisation

Potential disadvantages of cohesive groups

In order to develop effective working groups the manager should give attention to those factors which influence the creation of group identity and cohesiveness. But strong, cohesive groups also present potential disadvantages for management. Cohesive groups do not necessarily produce a higher level of output. Performance varies with the extent to which the group accepts or rejects the goals of the organisation. The level of output is likely to respond to a standard acceptable as a norm by the group.[40] It may be remembered, for example, that in the bank wiring room experiment group norms and pressures on individual members led to unofficial working methods, and restrictions on the level of output. But cohesive groups may result in greater interaction, lower turnover and absenteeism, and higher output.[41]

It is important, therefore, that the manager attempts to influence the group during the norming stage when members are establishing guidelines and standards and their own norms of acceptable behaviour. Once a group has become fully developed, become cohesive, and established its own culture, it is more difficult for the manager to change successfully the attitudes and behaviour of the group.[42]

Inter-group conflict

Strong, cohesive groups may develop a critical or even hostile attitude towards people outside the group or members of other groups. This can be the case, for example, when group cohesiveness is based on common status, social background, qualifications or technical expertise. Strong, cohesive groups might cause difficulties for the socialisation and effective assimilation of new members of staff and add to the induction crisis and high staff turnover. For example, Bowey reports a case of high staff turnover among waitresses in a restaurant where in order to protect their own interests the established waiting staff adopted an unpleasant demeanour to new members of staff.[43]

Group cohesiveness may result in a lack of cooperation with other groups. Resentment and inter-group conflict may arise, to the detriment of the organisation as a whole. A classic example is Whyte's study of the American restaurant industry and the social interactions between two groups of workers – the chefs and the waiting staff.[44] The chefs, who regarded themselves to be of high status and generally recognised as such by the staff, resented being 'told' what to do by the waitresses, who were generally regarded to be of lower status. As a result arguments resulted, disrupting performance. The conflict in status was resolved by the introduction of an ordering process by which the chefs received customers' orders without the appearance of taking instructions from the 'lower-status' waitresses.

In order to help prevent, or overcome, unconstructive inter-group conflict, the manager should attempt to stimulate a high level of communication and interaction between the groups, and attempt to maintain harmony. Where appropriate, rotation of members among different groups should be encouraged.

However, inter-group rivalry may sometimes be encouraged as a means of helping to build stronger within-group cohesiveness.[45] The idea is that a competitive element may help to promote unity within a group. But inter-group rivalry and competition need to be carefully handled by the manager. Groups should not normally be put in a situation where they have to compete for resources, status or approval.[46] The manager should attempt to avoid the development of 'win–lose' situations. Emphasis should be placed on broader objectives of the organisation which are over and above the issues at conflict and which, if they are to be achieved, require effective cooperation of the competing groups.

Inter-departmental conflict

Dann and Hornsey draw attention to the prevalence of inter-departmental conflict as a distinctive feature of hotel operations. They suggest four main reasons which, either in isolation or collectively, may heighten inter-departmental conflicts:

- interdependence and the relationships between departments;
- the hotel environment and the framework within which activities occur;
- rewards and the nature of the total payment package;
- status and stigma, and the perceptions of workers within the industry.[47]

Interdependence

Interdependence arises from the nature of work flows in the industry, and the requirement for close and often immediate cooperation between two or more departments, for example the kitchen and the restaurant. A fundamental conflict may arise between the desire for autonomy and independence, and the necessity for interdependence and reliance on other people. If one department feels that the other has acted unfairly or has not reciprocated a favour, there is potential for conflict. An important reason for inter-departmental conflict is different goals, for example between the chef's concern for quality and that of the service staff for speed.

Social environment

The social environment of the hotel industry has a number of distinctive features which are potential sources of conflict. Departments which have direct contact with the customers adapt their attitudes and work behaviour to the situation, and this emphasises differences from other departments. The speed of operations and need for quick decisions put stress and pressure on staff. The industry is typified by authoritarian leadership styles and formal patterns of organisation. There are often strong territorial perspectives about the place of work, for example in the kitchen or the front office desk.

Reward structure

The structure of the reward system can cause perceived inequity and result in conflict between departments. The presence of tips can lead to a distorted view of differences in earnings, and different attitudes towards the customers and management. The perceived opportunities for fiddles can also be a source of conflict between departments. Another source of conflict is perceived inequity in the allocation of scarce resources to different departments.

Perceived status or stigma

Rigid organisational hierarchies have resulted in a highly differentiated and established status system in the industry. This is based on the perception of different positions and job titles. For example, receptionists see themselves as a high-status group whilst other positions such as kitchen porters are low-status. The status system is established by tradition and myth, and reinforced through group pressure. Perceived differences in status can also arise between different nationalities or between men and women. (You may recall the discussion on sex stereotyping and gender in Chapter 3.)

The performance of groups

We have seen the importance of groups to the working life of the hospitality industry, and of creating effective teamwork. But is group performance better than individual performance? It is difficult to draw any firm conclusions. An example is the process of decision-making. Certain groups, such as management teams, may be concerned more specifically with decision-making, but all groups must make some decisions. Group decision-making can be costly, time-consuming and possibly frustrating for members but it would appear to offer a number of advantages.

- Groups bring together a range of complementary knowledge, skills and experience.
- Interaction among members can have a 'snowball' effect, and provide an impetus for further thoughts and ideas in the minds of others.
- Group discussion leads to the evaluation and revision of possible decisions.
- Provided full participation has been facilitated, decisions will have the acceptance of all, or most, members. They are then more likely to be committed to decisions made, and to their implementation.

Given these advantages, one might expect a higher standard of decision-making to result from group discussion. However, there is the danger of compromise and decisions being made in line with the 'highest common view'. There is also the phenomenon of the so-called 'risky-shift', and the concept of 'groupthink'.

The 'risky-shift' phenomenon

This suggests that instead of the group taking fewer risks and making safer or more conservative decisions, the reverse is often the case. There is a tendency for groups to make more risky decisions than would be taken by members of the group as individuals.[48]

It is perhaps understandable that members of a group do not feel the same sense of responsibility for decisions of the group or their possible outcomes. This seems to be summed up in the belief that: 'a decision which is everyone's is the responsibility of no one'. Other possible explanations for the risk-shift phenomenon include:

- people who are inclined to be more adventurous and take more risks may be more influential in group discussions;
- the group may generate a greater range of possible solutions including those that carry greater risk; and
- risk-taking may be perceived as a desirable cultural characteristic which is more likely to be expressed in a social situation such as group discussion.

Groups do, however, appear to work well in the evaluation of ideas. They are more effective than individuals for problem-solving tasks requiring a range of knowledge and expertise. Research evidence appears to support the view that, compared with individuals, groups produce more solutions, and better solutions, to problems.[49]

Groupthink

The effectiveness of group behaviour and performance can be adversely affected by the idea of 'groupthink'. From an examination of some well-known government policy-making groups, Janis concluded that decisions can be characterised by groupthink which he defines as: 'a deterioration of mental efficiency, reality testing, and moral judgement that results from in-group pressures'. The idea of groupthink is not, however, limited to government policy-making groups but it is a generalised feature and can be apparent in any organisational situation where groups are relied upon to make important decisions.[50]

Janis identifies a number of specific symptoms of groupthink, including the following:

- There is an illusion of invulnerability with excessive optimism and risk-taking.
- Pressures on individual members to conform and reach consensus mean that minority or unpopular ideas may be suppressed. Members who oppose the group are stereotyped as evil, weak or stupid.

- The search for group consensus can result in collective rationalisation by members to discount warnings and there is an illusion of unanimity. There is self-censorship of any deviation from group norms or apparent group consensus.

- An unquestioned belief in the inherent morality of the group which leads members to be convinced of the logical correctness of what it is doing and to ignore ethical or moral consequences of decisions.

The effects of groupthink often occur in committees and working parties with a tendency towards decisions which may be inappropriate or which are not questioned fully.[51]

Critical review and reflection

'Groupthink is a dangerous dimension of group working. It leads to incorrect and inappropriate decision-making.'

How far do you agree with this statement?

Brainstorming

One method of attempting to evoke full group discussion and to generate possible solutions to problems is through a 'brainstorming' approach (sometimes now called 'thought showers' or 'cloud bursting'). Brainstorming is based on the assumption that creative thinking is achieved best by encouraging the natural inclinations of group members and the free association of ideas. The quantity of ideas is supposed to lead to quality of ideas. A brainstorming approach involves the group adopting a 'free-wheeling' attitude and generating as many ideas as possible. The more wild or apparently far-fetched the ideas, the better.[52]

There are a number of basic procedures for a brainstorming approach.

- Emphasis is placed initially on the quantity of ideas generated, and not the quality of ideas.

- No matter how wild or fanciful they may appear, no individual ideas are criticised or rejected at this stage.

- Members are encouraged to elaborate or build on the ideas of others and to bounce suggestions off one another.

- There is no evaluation of any particular idea or suggestion until all possibilities have been generated.

Channels of communication in groups

The level of interaction among members of a group is influenced by the structuring of channels of communication. Laboratory research by Bavelas[53] and subsequent studies by other researchers such as Leavitt[54] have resulted in the design of a series of communication networks.

There are five main types of communication networks: wheel, circle, all-channel, Y and chains (see Figure 8.5).

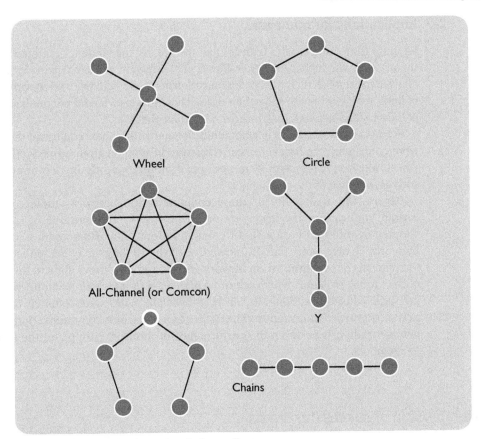

Figure 8.5 Communication networks in small groups

- The **wheel**, also sometimes known as the star, is the most centralised network. This network is most efficient for simple tasks. Problems are solved more quickly with fewer mistakes and with fewer information flows. The link person is at the centre of the network and acts as the focus of activities and information flows, and the coordinator of group tasks. The central person is perceived as leader of the group and experiences a high level of satisfaction. However, for members on the periphery, the wheel is the least satisfying network.

- The **circle** is a more decentralised network. Overall it is less efficient. The group is unorganised, with low leadership predictability. Performance tends to be slow and erratic. However, the circle is quicker than the wheel in solving complex problems, and also copes with change or new tasks more efficiently. The circle network is most satisfying for all the members. Decision-making is likely to involve some degree of participation.

- The **all-channel network** involves full discussion and participation. This network appears to work best where a high level of interaction is required among all members of the group in order to solve complex problems. Leadership predictability is very low. There is a fairly high level of satisfaction for members. The all-channel network may not stand up well under pressure, in which case it will either disintegrate or reform into a wheel network.

- A Y or **chain network** might be appropriate for simpler problem-solving tasks, requiring little interaction among members of the group. These networks are more centralised, with information flows along a predetermined channel. Leadership predictability is high to moderate. There is a low to moderate level of satisfaction for members.

Implications for managers

Findings from these studies indicate that the greater the amount of interconnectedness of the network, the higher the general level of satisfaction of members in the group. Groups allowed to establish their own communication networks, and who did so with the minimum of links, took less time to solve their tasks. Those groups who did not minimise the number of links in their network took more time to solve the tasks.

From a review of studies in communication networks, Shaw confirmed that simple tasks were consistently undertaken most efficiently in more centralised networks such as the wheel. More complex tasks were performed more efficiently by decentralised networks such as the circle or the all-channel.[55]

Despite the artificiality of these communication network studies, they do have certain implications for managers who can observe the patterns of communication adopted by different groups in different situations, and also note how communication networks change over time. A knowledge of the findings may be applied to influence the patterns of communication in work groups and how they relate to the performance of the group. Problems which require a high level of interaction among members of the group may not be handled efficiently if there are inadequate channels of communication or sharing of information. The choice of a particular communication network may involve trade-offs between the performance of the work group and the satisfaction of its members.

Membership of successful teams

What factors should be considered in deciding the membership of a management team? Based on years of research and empirical study, Belbin concludes that the most consistently successful teams comprise a range of roles undertaken by various members.[56] The constitution of the team itself is an important variable in its success. Teams composed entirely of clever people, or of people with similar personalities, display a number of negative results and lack creativity.

Key team roles

In his original work on teams, Belbin described 'team role' as a pattern of behaviour characteristic of the way in which one team member interacts with another where performance serves to facilitate the progress of the team as a whole. Eight useful types of contribution were proposed:

- Company worker (CW)
- Shaper (SH)
- Resource investigator (RI)
- Team worker (TW)
- Chairman (CH)
- Plant (PL)
- Monitor–evaluator (ME)
- Completer–finisher (CF)

An explanation of these team roles is given in Figure 8.6. The eight types of people identified are useful team members and form a comprehensive list. These are the key team roles and the primary characters for successful teams. Creative teams require a balance of all these roles and comprise members who have characteristics complementary to one another. Belbin claimed that good examples of the eight types would prove adequate for any challenge, although all eight types were not necessarily needed. Other members might be welcome for their personal qualities, for example a sense of humour, but experience suggested that there was no other team role that it would be useful to add.

Back-up team roles and functional roles

The most consistently successful teams were 'mixed' with a balance of team roles. The role that a person undertook in a group was not fixed and might change according to circumstances. Individuals could have a 'back-up team role' with which they had some affinity other than their primary team role. If certain roles were missing, members would call upon their back-up roles. Team roles differed from what Belbin called 'functional roles'. These are the roles that members of a team perform in terms of the specifically technical demands placed upon them. Team members were typically chosen for functional roles on the basis of experience and not personal characteristics or aptitudes.

Revised list of nine team roles

In a follow-up publication Belbin discusses the continued evolution of team roles which now differ in a few respects from those identified in earlier research.[57] Two roles are renamed, largely for reasons of acceptability: 'coordinator' replaces chairman, and 'implementer' replaces company worker. The most significant change is the addition of a ninth role, that of 'specialist'. This role was added because of the significance of the importance of a given form of professional expertise in much project work and its recurring importance as an issue in career development. A description of the evolved nine team roles is given in Figure 8.6.

A summary outline of effective work groups is given in Figure 8.7.

Constructing the perfect team

Referring to the research of Belbin, White suggests that a team, in the true sense of the word, is only a team if it achieves more than the sum of the individual contributions. He suggests that there is a collective spirit, a managerial alchemy that causes this. If business people are happy to accept that group effort is always better than individuals working in isolation, the research of Belbin may help in constructing the perfect team. White suggests that, in the end, it is all about trust. The dream team is probably out there, sitting opposite you or just around the corner; all you have to do is fit them into Belbin's nine defined roles.[58]

Role relationships

In order that the organisation can achieve its goals and objectives, the work of individual members must be linked into coherent patterns of activities and relationships. This is achieved through the role structure. A 'role' is the expected pattern of behaviours associated with

Roles and descriptions – team-role contribution	Allowable weaknesses
Plant: Creative, imaginative, unorthodox. Solves difficult problems.	Ignores details. Too pre-occupied to communicate effectively.
Resources investigator: Extrovert, enthusiastic, communicative. Explores opportunities. Develops contacts.	Overoptimistic. Loses interest once initial enthusiasm has passed.
Co-ordinator: Mature, confident, a good chairperson. Clarifies goals, promotes decision-making, delegates well.	Can be seen as manipulative. Delegates personal work.
Shaper: Challenging, dynamic, thrives on pressure. Has the drive and courage to overcome obstacles.	Can provoke others. Hurts people's feelings.
Monitor evaluator: Sober, strategic and discerning. Sees all options. Judges accurately.	Lacks drive and ability to inspire others. Overly critical.
Teamworker: Co-operative, mild, perceptive and diplomatic. Listens, builds, averts friction, calms the waters.	Indecisive in crunch situations. Can be easily influenced.
Implementer: Disciplined, reliable, conservative and efficient. Turns ideas into practical actions.	Somewhat inflexible. Slow to respond to new possibilities.
Completer: Painstaking, conscientious, anxious. Searches out errors and omissions. Delivers on time.	Inclined to worry unduly. Reluctant to delegate. Can be a nit-picker.
Specialist: Single-minded, self-starting, dedicated. Provides knowledge and skills in rare supply.	Contributes on only a narrow front. Dwells on technicalities. Overlooks the 'big picture'.

Strength of contribution in any one of the roles is commonly associated with particular weaknesses. These are called allowable weaknesses. Executives are seldom strong in all nine team roles.

Source: reprinted, with permission, from Belbin, R. M., *Team Roles at Work*, Butterworth-Heinemann (1933), p. 23.

Figure 8.6 Revised list of nine team roles

members occupying a particular position within the organisation structure. (The formal organisational relationships discussed in Chapter 6 can also be seen as types of role relationships.)

The concept of 'role' is important to the functioning of groups, and for an understanding of group processes and behaviour. It is through role differentiation that the structure

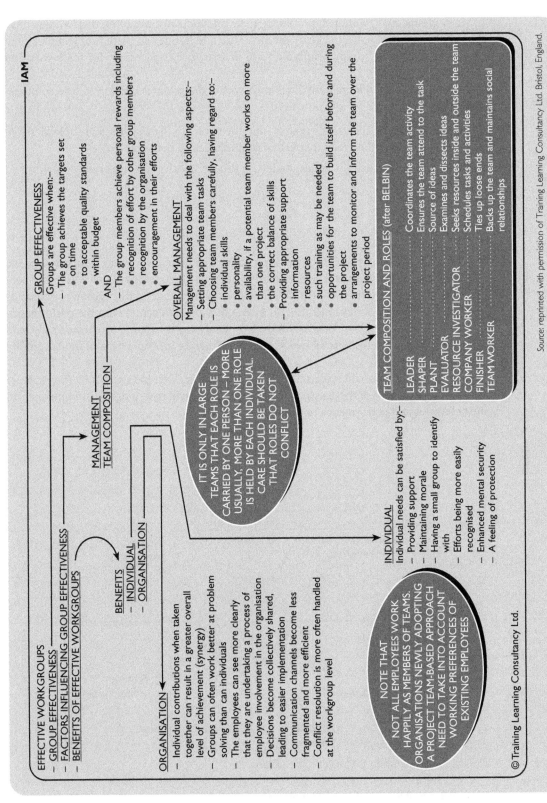

Figure 8.7 Summary outline of effective workgroups

of work groups and relationships among their members are established. The identification of distinct roles helps to clarify the structure and define the pattern of complex relationships within the group. A suitable form of structure is necessary for teamwork and cooperation.

The role, or roles, that an individual plays within the group is influenced by a combination of:

- situational factors, such as the type of unit, the nature of the task, the style of leadership, other members of the group, pattern of communication network; and
- personal factors, such as values, beliefs, attitudes, motivation, experience, ability and personality.

A role set

In addition to the role relationships with members of their own group – superior, peers, subordinates – individuals will have a number of role-related relationships with other people. This is a person's 'role set'. A role set comprises the range of associations or contacts with whom individuals have meaningful interactions in connection with the performance of their role. A role set provides a useful basis for analysing the nature of a person's job, and associated duties and responsibilities, within the structure and operation of the hospitality organisation.[59]

An example of a possible role set for a receptionist is given in Figure 8.8. The range of different expectations of these associations and contacts will have a significant influence on the behaviour and performance of the receptionist.

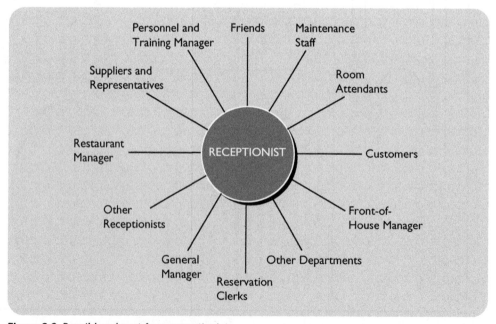

Figure 8.8 Possible role set for a receptionist

Role expectations

The role that a person plays in one work group may be quite different from the role that person plays in other work groups. However, everyone within a group is expected to behave in a particular manner and to fulfil certain role expectations. These role expectations may be established formally, or be informal, or they may be self-established.

- Formal role expectations indicate what the person is expected to do, and the duties and obligations. Formal role prescriptions provide guidelines for expected behaviour. Examples are a written contract of employment, rules and regulations, policy decisions or standards, compliance with legal requirements, job descriptions or directives from superiors.

- Informal role expectations are not prescribed formally but nevertheless are expected patterns of behaviour. These informal role expectations may be imposed by the group itself. Examples include general conduct, mutual support to co-members, attitudes towards superiors, means of communication, dress and appearance. Members may not always be consciously aware of these informal expectations, yet they still serve as important determinants of behaviour. Under this heading could be included the psychological contract, discussed in Chapter 2.

- Self-established role expectations arise when members have formal expectations which are specified loosely or only in very general terms. This allows members to determine their own role expectations and patterns of behaviour. Opportunities for self-established roles are more likely in senior positions, for example the general manager or senior departmental managers. They may also arise within certain professional or technical groups or where there is a demand for creativity or artistic flair, for example the head chef.

Role conflict

Patterns of behaviour result from both the role and the personality. The concept of role focuses attention on aspects of behaviour existing independently of an individual's personality. A personality clash arises from incompatibility between two or more people as individuals, even though their roles may be defined clearly and understood fully. Role conflict, however, arises from inadequate or inappropriate role definition. A classic example is the conflict in status between chefs and waiting staff.

In practice, the manner in which a person actually behaves may not be consistent with their expected pattern of behaviour. This inconsistency may be a result of role conflict. As a generic term, role conflict may include role incompatibility, role ambiguity, role overload and role underload. These are all areas associated with the creation of role expectations (Figure 8.9).

Role incompatibility

This occurs when a person faces a situation in which simultaneous different or contradictory expectations create inconsistency. Compliance with one set of expectations makes it difficult or impossible to comply with other expectations. The two incompatible sets of expectations are in conflict. A typical example concerns the person 'in the middle', such as the supervisor or section head who faces opposing expectations from subordinates and from senior

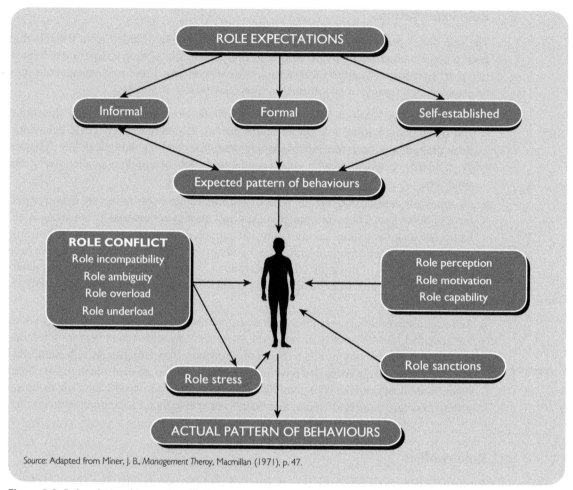

Figure 8.9 Role relationships and conflicts

management. For example, the subordinates may expect a relaxed, Theory Y approach and good working relationships, but management may expect the supervisor to adopt a more directive, Theory X approach with emphasis on achieving maximum output. (See Chapter 5.)

Role incompatibility may also be used to describe situations in which the person is expected to fulfil a role for which they are not suited.[60] This may arise when the values, attitudes, personality, skills or interests of the person do not equate with the demands of the role. An obvious example is a person with an introverted personality occupying a role that demands frequent dealings with people. Role incompatibility may also arise when a person accepts promotion without taking account of the different expectations of the new position. Revised working practices may result in changes to the nature and expectations of a person's role, for example from the introduction of computers or the appointment of a new manager.

Role ambiguity

This occurs when there is lack of clarity as to the precise requirements of the role and the person is unsure what to do. The person's own perception of the role may differ from the expectations of others. The person is uncertain about the expected pattern of behaviour.

This implies that insufficient information is available for adequate performance of the role. The characteristic nature of service industries, discussed in Chapter 1, gives rise to a high potential for ambiguity. Role ambiguity may result from a lack of formally prescribed expectations and often arises at times of constant change. Uncertainty may relate to such matters as the range of duties and responsibilities, the method of performing tasks, standards of work, or the evaluation and appraisal of performance.

Common examples of role ambiguity concern management trainees who may be uncertain as to how much authority they are expected to exercise over other members of staff. Management degree students on their industrial placement training may suffer from role ambiguity. It may be unclear to what extent they are expected to be involved in practical working experience at the operator level, or in gaining exposure to supervisory responsibilities. Another example could be a person appointed to a newly created position, perhaps because of the expansion or reorganisation of the establishment, where the person may be uncertain about the exact nature of the new job or the authority and responsibility it involves.

Role overload

This is where a person faces too many separate roles or too great a variety of expectations. The person is unable to meet, satisfactorily, all expectations and some must be neglected to satisfy others. This leads to a conflict of priorities. Role overload can be distinguished from work overload. Role overload is seen in terms of the total role set and implies that the person has too many separate roles to handle at the same time. Where there are too many expectations of a single role, i.e. it is a problem of quantity rather than variety, this is work overload.[61]

An example of role overload for a hotel assistant manager is given by Lockwood and Jones. The manager is already responsible for personnel and training, but is now asked to act as duty manager, and in addition becomes health and safety officer, security officer and chairs the staff social committee.[62]

Role underload

This can arise when the prescribed role expectations fall short of the person's own perception of their role. The person may feel the role is not demanding enough or that it lacks variety, responsibility or challenge. It is possible, however, that the person could still suffer from work overload. Role underload may arise, for example, from the initial effects of delegation or from the appointment of an over-qualified member of staff. It may also arise from examples mentioned above such as the cases of management trainees, students on their industrial training, or members of staff appointed to a new position.

Role stress

Role conflict can result in role stress. Although work may be a source of satisfaction it is also increasingly a potential source of stress. Given the nature of service industries discussed in Chapter 1, stress is arguably a prevailing feature of hospitality organisations. According to Wood, for example:

In the hospitality industry unpredictability (of demand, of employees) is a major source of stress, but the high levels of responsibility that many managers bear can also be significant in stress causation, particularly as a sense of isolation may be experienced because of a unit's independence from other units and the larger organisation.[63]

Although a certain amount of stress may arguably be a good thing and helps to promote a high level of performance, it is also potentially very harmful. Stress is a source of tension, frustration and dissatisfaction. It can lead to difficulties in communication and interpersonal relationships. Research evidence points to the consequences of role conflict leading to lower job satisfaction, and an adverse effect on the level of individual performance.[64,65]

An example of role stress is Whyte's study of chefs and waiting staff discussed above. One reason was the constant conflict between the demands of the customers to be served quickly and pressure from the chefs who were unable to produce the food in time. The waiting staff were caught between two incompatible expectations and were pulled both ways. As a result, a number of waiting staff found the job very stressful and some of them often cried.

Reducing role stress

There is increasing evidence concerning stress-related illnesses and social problems, for example marriage breakdowns, which can have stress as a contributory factor. And decreasing efficiency resulting from work stress is extremely costly to organisations.[66] It is therefore important that managers make every effort to minimise the causes of stress. There are a number of ways in which management might attempt to avoid or reduce role conflict and the possibilities of role stress:

- increased clarity and specification of prescribed role expectations, for example through job descriptions;
- improved recruitment, selection and induction, the careful matching of abilities, motivations, personalities and interests to the demands of particular roles;
- a systematic approach to job training and retraining, staff development and career progression plans;
- review of organisation structure, for example the creation of new roles, assimilation of existing roles or reallocation of tasks and responsibilities;
- attention to group structures and group cohesiveness, and overcoming inter-group conflict, the possible use of autonomous working groups;
- changes in management systems and leadership style, for example the use of MBO, increased delegation, improved communications;
- advance notice and explanations of what is likely to happen, for example plans for a major refurbishment of the establishment, an unexpectedly large number of customers arriving together, preparations for a special banquet or conference;
- programme of medical examinations and health screening which may give early indications of potential stress-related problems.

Behaviour of individuals in groups

In order to understand and to influence the functioning and operation of groups, it is necessary to study patterns of interaction, and the parts played by individual members. For example, Green questions the characteristics that should be shown by the smooth-running team.

It should be obvious that it is unified, self-organised and self-supporting. Although team members should be recognised as individuals, each with a personality, likes and dislikes, and changing wants and needs, team members should feel a sense of belonging and should all pull in the same direction.[67] A method of analysing the behaviour of individuals in group situations is interaction process analysis.

Interaction analysis

Each member of a group may fulfil a distinctive role as part of the operations and processes of the group. The basic assumption behind interaction analysis is that behaviour in small groups may be analysed from the viewpoint of its function.[68] If the group is to be effective, then whatever its structure or the pattern of interrelationships among members, there are two main sets of processes or functions that must be undertaken – task functions and maintenance functions.

- Task functions are directed towards achieving the tasks and objectives of the group, and problem-solving activities. Most of the task-orientated behaviour will be concerned with 'production' activities, and the exchange and evaluation of information and ideas.

- Maintenance functions are directed towards maintaining the group as an effective working unit and the emotional life of the group. Most of the maintenance-orientated behaviour will be concerned with relationships among group members, giving encouragement and support, maintaining cohesiveness, and the resolution of conflict.

The appropriate combination and balance of task-orientated behaviour and maintenance-orientated behaviour is essential to the success and continuity of the group.

Classification of member roles

In addition to the fulfilment of task or maintenance functions, members of a group may say or do something to satisfy a personal need or goal. The display of behaviour in this way is termed self-orientated (or individual) behaviour. This gives three main types of functional behaviour which can be exhibited by members of a group: task-orientated, maintenance-orientated and self-orientated.

A popular system for the classification of member roles under these three broad headings is that devised originally by Benne and Sheats and summarised as follows.[69]

- *Group task roles* – these assume that the task of the group is to select, define and solve common problems. Any of the roles may be performed by the various members or the group leader. Examples include initiator, information seeker, opinion giver, coordinator, elaborator, evaluator–critic and recorder.

- *Group building and maintenance roles* – the analysis of member-functions is orientated towards activities which build group-centred attitudes or maintain group-centred behaviour. Contributions may involve a number of roles, and members or the leader may perform each of these roles. Examples include encourager, harmoniser, compromiser, gate-keeper, standard setter, observer and commentator.

- *Individual roles* – these are directed towards the satisfaction of personal needs. Their purpose is not related to either the group task or the group functioning. Examples include aggressor, blocker, recognition-seeker, play actor, dominator.

Analysis of behaviour

A number of different frameworks have been designed for observers to analyse patterns of behaviour of group members. Observers chart members' behaviour on specially designed forms. These forms may be used to focus on single individuals or to record the total small-group interactions. The interaction process can become complex, especially if non-verbal behaviour is included, and the headings of the observation sheet are not necessarily exclusive. It is important, therefore, to keep the framework simple, and easy to understand and to complete.[70] An example of the ten-point observation sheet used by the authors is given in Figure 8.10.

The system of categorisation may distinguish between different forms of behaviour in terms of the functions they serve. Completed observation forms can be used as a basis for discussing individual contributions or the group performance related to the strength/weaknesses of different functional behaviours. Different frameworks use varying categories for studying behaviour in groups. Observation sheets can be designed to suit the particular requirements of the group situation and the nature of the activity involved.

Skills of effective teamwork

ACAS suggests that teamwork can increase competitiveness by:

- improving productivity;
- improving quality and encouraging innovation;
- taking advantage of the opportunities provided by technological advances;
- improving employee motivation and commitment.[71]

According to Guirdham, the growth of teamwork has led to the increased interest in interface skills at work.

> More and more tasks of contemporary organisations, particularly those in service businesses, require teamwork. Taskforces, project teams and committees are key elements in the modern workplace. Teamwork depends not just on technical competence of the individuals composing the team, but on their ability to 'gel'. To work well together, the team members must have more than just team spirit. They also need collaborative skills – they must be able to support one another and to handle conflict in such a way that it becomes constructive rather than destructive.[72]

Stages of team development

Lashley cites Ellis and Dick's analysis of the phases and stages of team development (as opposed to Tuckman's stages of group development). Ellis and Dick point out that the experienced team leader aids the team through the various stages and recognises the danger of inaction and resentment that can occur if team members feel their efforts are not valued.[73]
Three stages are identified:

- *Searching stage* – when team members 'feel a thrill of enthusiasm' and show high commitment to the task. A feature of this stage is a reluctance to disagree with other group members. (Similar to the concept of 'Groupthink')
- *Exploring stage* – once objectives have been clarified, questions, suggestions and disagreement may follow. (Similar to Tuckman's 'Storming' phase)

Nature of group				
Nature of activity				
Date	Name of observer(s)			

Initial arrangement of group

```
                    C      D
              B                      E
A                                 F
```

Names of group members (or reference letters)

	A	B	C	D	E	F
Taking initiative – e.g. attempted leadership, seeking suggestions, offering directions						
Brainstorming – e.g. offering ideas or suggestions, however valid						
Offering positive ideas – e.g. making helpful suggestions, attempting to problem-solve						
Drawing in others – e.g. encouraging contributions, seeking ideas and opinions						
Being responsive to others – e.g. giving encouragement and support, building on ideas						
Harmonising – e.g. acting as peacemaker, calming things down, compromising						
Challenging – e.g. seeking justification, showing disagreement in *constructive way*						
Being obstructive – e.g. criticising, putting others down, blocking contributions						
Clarifying/summarising – e.g. linking ideas, checking progress, clarifying objectives/proposals						
Performing group roles – e.g. spokesperson, recorder, time keeper, humourist						
Other comments						

Source: Mullins, L. J., *Management and Organisational Behaviour*, 5th edn, Financial Times Pitman Publishing (1999) p. 498.

Figure 8.10 Observation sheet for behaviour in groups

● *Alliance stage* – at this stage the team share an understanding and a focus. Any disruption to team dynamics at this stage should be avoided. (Similar to Tuckman's 'Performing' phase)[74]

At each stage the team leader needs to adopt appropriate behaviour patterns, avoiding telling but asking in the earlier stage, allowing disagreement in the exploring stage, while helping and enabling the team to work towards the goal or objectives in the alliance stage. Clearly, to ensure that the team is as effective as possible the team leader needs to be aware of the stage that the team has reached and the potential dangers of each stage. This may require the team leader to balance the need to intervene, with the potential demotivation that this may lead to.

Critical review and reflection

'All this discussion about group membership and building successful teams is very interesting and sounds fine theoretically. However, it ignores the reality of the work environment in the hospitality industry, for example in managing groups of workers in a restaurant, kitchen or in a gay pub.'

What are your views?

Building successful teams

In addition to managing the situation during the various phases of team development, referred to above, the hospitality manager must be aware of, and pay attention to, a number of interrelated factors, including:

● clarification of objectives and available resources;

● organisational processes and the clarification of roles;

● empowerment, decision-making and channels of communication;

● patterns of interaction, and attention to both task and maintenance functions;

● social processes and the informal organisation;

● management systems and style of leadership;

● training and development.

The effectiveness of the team will also be influenced by the tasks to be undertaken, the nature of technology and the organisational environment. Ultimately, however, the performance of the team will be determined very largely by the characteristics of its members. The nature of group personality means that what works well for one team may not work well for an apparently similar team in the organisation.

We know everyone is different. When selecting people for your team, the most important thing to look for is ones who are decent, honest, bright and capable. You will find that good people will naturally work together as a team, will interrelate well and will want each other to succeed. And while I'm on the subject of teams, don't send people off on those terrible outward-bound weekends. Have a party instead.[75]

As Wilson points out, although teamworking, like most management ideas, is very simple, nevertheless this simplicity conceals a great challenge.

The principles of teamworking may be easily understood, but the task of installing it can be quite daunting. Introducing teamworking is not a straightforward grafting job, the simple matter of adding a new idea to those already in place. It is about making a fundamental change in the way people work. Every teamworking application is different. Each organisation, department and individual group is faced with unique problems and in some situations it is more about getting rid of old ways of doing things than injecting new ones.[76]

Exhibit 8.3 Tips for effective team-building

One way to build your business is by building the team. Developing your team should be an ongoing process, because with staff turnover at record highs, it's likely that your team will be constantly changing.

However, team leaders rarely take enough time to understand team members and find out the circumstances under which they perform best, so often teams will underachieve. When problems occur, many team leaders fail to put measures in place to make sure the same old issues don't return. These tips will help you create a successful team:

1 **Celebrate your differences** The strongest teams are made up of people who have complementary skills. Some members are ideas people, some are doers, some are thinkers and others are supporters. Make sure your team is made up of a variety of types. However, be aware that differences in personalities can cause conflict, so learn to understand your team and teach them to value their different skills.

2 **Support, not sabotage** Do you support team ideas and objectives or are you inclined to sabotage other people's plans because they aren't your own? Support is crucial to developing and maintaining group morale. If you don't agree, voice your objections, agree the way forward and then offer support.

3 **Meet regularly** Hold regular meetings to keep your team informed about what is going on in the company and what role each member plays. This will help motivate them and make them feel a valuable part of a team.

4 **Improve communication** One of the main reasons for despondency is lack of communication. You can use a variety of ways to communicate, such as newsletters, noticeboards, meetings and messages. Make communication a two-way process and keep it consistent and ongoing.

5 **Take initiative** Sometimes when a job has to be done, people think somebody else will do it, and as a result the job gets neglected. Make it a rule that if someone sees a job to do, they do it.

6 **Have fun** Try to inject fun into everything you do. Find out what makes your team feel positive. It may be a joke each day on the noticeboard, a share-a-smile scheme or just your infectious good humour. Whatever it takes, do something to make your team feel happy.

7 **Recognise the positives** People are often guilty of noticing the negatives and taking the positives for granted. As well as pointing out the negatives, praise the positives and make sure people feel they belong to the group.

8 **Believe in your team** Your expectations can affect your team's results. Do you expect failure or expect success? Make sure you have confidence in your team and give them a suitable period of time to get things in order.

9 **Delegate, train and develop** Your team will become more effective if you let them take on more responsibility. Delegate tasks and give them training.

10 **Have a focus** Work is easier if you have an aim. What are your business goals? Do your team know what they are? Share the company goals with your team and help them view the goals as their own. Then remember to share the results.

11 **Lead by example** Remember you are a leader and people will follow you. What frame of mind are you in when you come into work and when you walk around? Your people may notice if you are in a bad mood and it could affect their work.[77]

Skills for successful teamwork

The increasing need for collaboration and teamwork, together with recognition for the individual, has highlighted the need for attention to social skills and effective relationships (Figure 8.11). If people are not working together, they are essentially a collection of individuals. Douglas refers to the importance of helping people to master the so-called 'soft' skills:

> Organisations in most sectors – and especially in ones that are particularly demanding from a scientific or technical point of view – are operating in environments where collaboration, teamwork, and an awareness of the commercial consequences and implications of technical research are as important as scientific and technical skills themselves. Personnel with scientific and technical skills significantly disproportionate to their 'people' skills – by which I primarily mean people management capabilities and the knowledge of how to work with maximum effectiveness as part of a team – are increasingly unlikely to be as much of an asset to their organisation as they ought to be.[78]

However, Douglas points out that as we all interact with people to a greater or lesser extent in our everyday lives, there is a tendency to assume that people management skills are merely an extension of our natural abilities. In fact, people management skills are the more difficult and rare type of skill but to a large extent they can be learned.

Cloke and Goldsmith refer to the special skills required for successful teamwork and list ten skills team members can develop in order to build innovative self-managing teams. All of these skills are interrelated, mutually reinforcing and dependent upon each of the others.[79]

- **Skill of self-management** – overcoming obstacles together and in the process building a sense of ownership, responsibility, commitment and efficiency within each team member.
- **Skill of communication** – collaboratively developing their skills in becoming better listeners, commiserating with others, reframing communications so they can be heard, and communicating honestly about things that really matter.
- **Skill of leadership** – creating opportunities for each member to serve as leader. Employees need to be skilled in linking, organising, coordinating, collaborating, planning, facilitating, coaching and mentoring.
- **Skill of responsibility** – everyone is personally responsible not only for their own work but for the work of every other member of the team. Team members have to exercise responsibility in order to become self-managing.
- **Skill of supportive diversity** – collaborative experiences allow team members to overcome prejudices and biases and not create winners and losers, reject outsiders or mistrust people who are different.
- **Skills of feedback and evaluation** – essential to improving learning, team communication and the quality of products, processes and relationships. In a true team environment, self-critical perspectives are expected, welcomed, acknowledged and rewarded.
- **Skill of strategic planning** – to identify challenges and opportunities collaboratively and influence the environment in which problems emerge. Strategic planning encourages employees to think long-term, be proactive and preventative and focus on solutions rather than problems.
- **Skill of shaping successful meetings** – team meetings can be streamlined and made shorter, more satisfying and more productive, and result in expanded consensus.

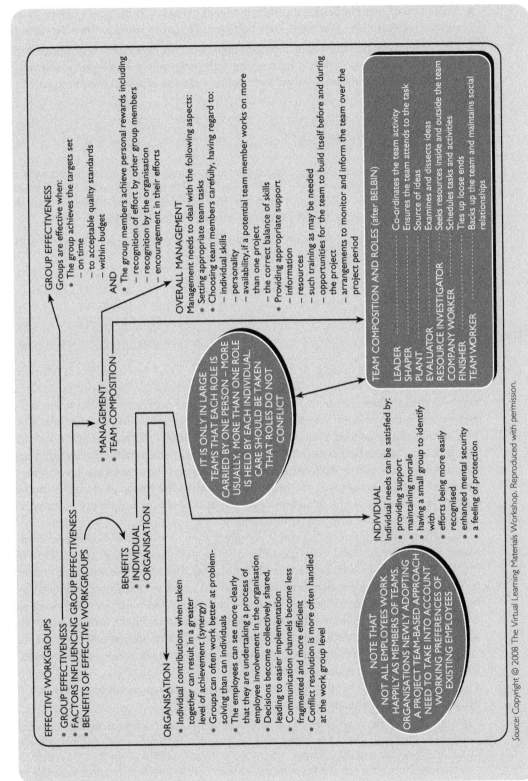

EFFECTIVE WORKGROUPS

- GROUP EFFECTIVENESS
- FACTORS INFLUENCING GROUP EFFECTIVENESS
- BENEFITS OF EFFECTIVE WORKGROUPS

BENEFITS
- INDIVIDUAL
- ORGANISATION

ORGANISATION

- Individual contributions when taken together can result in a greater level of achievement (synergy)
- Groups can often work better at problem-solving than can individuals
- The employees can see more clearly that they are undertaking a process of employee involvement in the organisation
- Decisions become collectively shared, leading to easier implementation
- Communication channels become less fragmented and more efficient
- Conflict resolution is more often handled at the work group level

NOTE THAT
NOT ALL EMPLOYEES WORK HAPPILY AS MEMBERS OF TEAMS. ORGANISATIONS NEWLY ADOPTING A PROJECT TEAM-BASED APPROACH NEED TO TAKE INTO ACCOUNT WORKING PREFERENCES OF EXISTING EMPLOYEES

GROUP EFFECTIVENESS

Groups are effective when:
- The group achieves the targets set
  - on time
  - to acceptable quality standards
  - within budget

AND
- The group members achieve personal rewards including
  - recognition of effort by other group members
  - recognition by the organisation
  - encouragement in their efforts

- MANAGEMENT
- TEAM COMPOSITION

OVERALL MANAGEMENT

Management needs to deal with the following aspects:
- Setting appropriate team tasks
- Choosing team members carefully, having regard to:
  - individual skills
  - personality
  - availability, if a potential team member works on more than one project
  - the correct balance of skills
- Providing appropriate support
  - information
  - resources
  - such training as may be needed
  - opportunities for the team to build itself before and during the project
  - arrangements to monitor and inform the team over the project period

IT IS ONLY IN LARGE TEAMS THAT EACH ROLE IS CARRIED BY ONE PERSON – MORE USUALLY, MORE THAN ONE ROLE IS HELD BY EACH INDIVIDUAL. CARE SHOULD BE TAKEN THAT ROLES DO NOT CONFLICT

TEAM COMPOSITION AND ROLES (after BELBIN)

LEADER .... Co-ordinates the team activity
SHAPER .... Ensures the team attends to the task
PLANT .... Source of ideas
EVALUATOR .... Examines and dissects ideas
RESOURCE INVESTIGATOR .... Seeks resources inside and outside the team
COMPANY WORKER .... Schedules tasks and activities
FINISHER .... Ties up loose ends
TEAM WORKER .... Backs up the team and maintains social relationships

INDIVIDUAL

Individual needs can be satisfied by:
- providing support
- maintaining morale
- having a small group to identify with
- efforts being more easily recognised
- enhanced mental security
- a feeling of protection

Source: Copyright © 2008 The Virtual Learning Materials Workshop. Reproduced with permission.

Figure 8.11 Concept map of effective work groups

- **Skill of resolving conflicts** – encouraging team members to improve skills in problem-solving, collaborative negotiation, responding to difficult behaviour and conflict resolution.
- **Skill of enjoyment** – most team members enjoy working together to accomplish difficult tasks. Their pleasure derives from meeting high performance challenges and producing results that benefit themselves and their teams, organisations and communities.

Critical review and reflection

'However, team leaders rarely take enough time to understand team members and find out the circumstances under which they perform best, so often teams will underachieve. When problems occur, many team leaders fail to put measures in place to make sure the same old issues don't return.' ('Tips for effective team building', *Caterer* (2003)).

To what extent do you agree with this statement? How can managers understand team members more effectively in the practical work environment?

Virtual teams

The combination of increasing globalisation and widespread developments in information and communications technology has given greater emphasis to the opportunities for, and need of, **virtual teams**. Instead of involving face-to-face proximity, virtual teams are collections of people who are geographically separated but still work together closely. The primary interaction among members is by some electronic information and communication process. This enables organisations to function away from traditional working hours, independent of the physical availability of staff. Computer-based information systems and increased wireless connectivity further the opportunities for virtual working. By their very nature, virtual teams are likely to be largely self-managed. The hospitality industry, in its broader definition, also involves virtual teams.

A study by Matlay and Westhead[80] considers the creation of entrepreneurial virtual teams across Europe developing specialist tourism packages, such as specialised family breaks, specific breaks such as 'vintage whisky and brandy clubs', bird watching or specialist fishing trips. They identify many advantages such as the availability of quality data and information, the pooling of human, financial and knowledge resources and sustainable customer bases across Europe. They also suggest there is a strong sense of 'virtual community' and high levels of 'virtual trust'. However, virtual teams are not without their disadvantages, which include the complexity of interacting across teams, lack of mechanisms to resolve conflict, and extended working hours.

According to Hall, the virtual team is a potential future compromise between fully fledged teams and well-managed groups.

I am watching the rise of this idea with interest but am sceptical that it will actually create a 'third way'. Real teams can only be forged in the crucible of personal interaction: videoconferences and net communications are still poor substitutes for this. Of course, once a team has formed it can use these media, as members will know each other well, but that's not the important bit. It's the forming, norming and storming that make a team.[81]

Management and communication skills

Parker highlights that remote working may also have an impact on the social aspects of organisational working with an increasing feeling of isolation.

> Remote teamworking is not simply a matter of ensuring staff have access to a laptop and telephone line, and assuming that they will be able to continue with their work. The management and communication skills that this new working culture requires are also key to success.[82]

A similar point is made by Norval who maintains that many remote workers can feel isolated and that the organisation is ignoring them, and this can affect their motivation. Without the visual sense and informal communications within the office, managers need to make a more conscious effort to build rapport and to rethink their management style.[83]

Symons considers that one advantage of virtual teamworking using asynchronous media is the clarity and richness of contributions when respondents are removed from the urgency of immediate interaction and that this can be particularly relevant in cross-cultural groups. However, as leaders cannot influence teams by their physical presence, and as hierarchies fade online, managing dispersed teams requires a range of subtly different leadership skills. It is important to develop mutual trust and a democratic approach of shared control and decision-making, and to adopt the role and style of a coach. 'The leader has to establish and maintain "credit" with the group, as "position power" has little or no currency in virtual working.'[84]

Garrett maintains that collaborating with other people in different cities or countries is not always a successful arrangement and lists the following suggestions for helping to organise the virtual team:

- **Say 'hello'** – the most successful teams spend time during their formation period face-to-face getting to know each other.
- **Build trust** – to hold the team together so that you can depend on other team members and feel comfortable opening up to them.
- **Recruit with care** – people who can communicate in the right way at the right time are more likely to be successful in virtual teams.
- **Don't rely on email** – the written word is easily misunderstood so supplement its use with other forms of communication.
- **Encourage dissent** – without face-to-face meetings people become reluctant to speak out but a healthy organisation needs people to speak out and challenge leaders and each other.
- **Use technology thoughtfully** – used badly, sophisticated tools can be a disaster, and people need to be trained to use the technology, not simply have it imposed on them.
- **Measure outcomes** – focus on the outcomes rather than time management, find a personal way to appraise performance, rather than email, and hold regular chats with members.
- **Do say** 'By proactively creating virtual teams we can go where talent is, extend our reach and work more efficiently.'
- **Don't say** 'We call them a virtual team because they're not quite the real thing.'[85]

One reason for the growth in virtual teams is because of increasing globalisation and team members working and living in different countries. This gives rise to potential difficulties of cultural diversity. As Francesco and Gold point out:

> The more culturally diverse the members, the more difficult it is to manage a virtual team. Cultural diversity, which will be increasingly common, adds to the complexity of managing virtual teams because different values, customs, and traditions require more leadership under conditions that reduce the ability to use direct leadership.[86]

Virtual working does not eradicate the sort of cultural misunderstandings that can arise in a face-to-face situation. 'Cultural or behavioural differences that can manifest themselves in face-to-face working situations can be exacerbated in virtual teamworking, particularly when the group has members from different backgrounds.'[87]

Critical review and reflection

'The nature of the hospitality industry is such that the development of virtual teams is unlikely to be of any relevance.'

To what extent do you believe this to be a valid point of view?

Cultural diversity in teams

The multicultural, diverse, nature of the hospitality industry means that work teams will often comprise individuals of different nationalities, backgrounds and cultures. Managing a team that contains so many differences clearly provides challenges to the leaders and managers of these teams. For example, cultural background and nationality can influence an individual's preferred role.

Inglehart's study of difference between European nationalities[88] suggests the French see their contribution as providing ideas, the Germans like to structure tasks, and finding the resources to perform a task is the preferred role of the Swedes.

Critical review and reflection

'The monocultural team is a thing of the past.' (Kwintessential translation and training)[89]

From your own experience in the hospitality industry, how far do you agree?

Hospitality teams and knowledge-sharing[90]

Hu, Horng and Sun consider the need for knowledge-sharing amongst work teams in the hospitality industry as customers are developing increasingly sophisticated demands.

To meet this new challenge there has recently been more emphasis on 'knowledge sharing' in the hospitality industry, and even on the notion of teamwork. Thus we are now seeing more and more 'organisational teams' within the industry.

They stress the importance of knowledge-sharing amongst teams considering that knowledge is a key factor in an organisation's success. Knowledge-sharing improves creativity in providing more creative products and services. The research streses the importance of a strong positive team culture and for the managers to 'focus more on individual team members in hospitality organisations, then all team members, that is, all employees will be encouraged to satisfy all the service needs of their organisation'.

Overall it was concluded that the relationships between and among a knowledge-sharing team culture and service innovation performance are significant and strong.

Synopsis

- Groups are a characteristic feature of all work organisations and social situations. They have a major influence on individual behaviour and performance. Work is a group-based activity especially in the hospitality industry. Harmonious working relationships and good team-work help make for a high level of staff morale and customer satisfaction.

- There are two major types of groups at work: formal, which are deliberately planned and created by management; and informal, which are based on personal relationships and serve to satisfy psychological and social needs. Individuals have varying expectations of the benefits from group membership relating to both work performance and social processes.

- Cooperation among members is likely to be greater in a strong, cohesive group. Many factors contribute to group cohesiveness and performance and can be summarised under the main headings of membership, work environment, organisational, and group development and maturity. There are, however, potential disadvantages from strong, cohesive groups.

- Group performance and the standard of decision-making can be influenced by the 'risky-shift' phenomenon and the concept of 'groupthink'. Consistently successful teams comprise a range of roles undertaken by various members. The concept of role is important to an understanding of group functioning. The manager should make every effort to minimise role conflict and role stress.

- The combination of increasing globalisation and widespread development in information communications and technology has given greater emphasis to the opportunities for, and need of, virtual teams. Even in the hospitality industry there are occasions when members are geographically separated but still need to work together closely.

- The effectiveness of the group/team will be influenced by the style of management, tasks to be undertaken, nature of technology and organisational environment. Ultimately, however, the characteristics and behaviour of the people involved, i.e. the manager, the team leader and the members of the group, will be the deciding factor in the success or otherwise of the group or team.

REVIEW AND DISCUSSION QUESTIONS

1 What is a group? Explain why it is important for a hospitality manager to understand the influence of group values and norms. Give practical examples from a hospitality organisation with which you are familiar.

2 How would you distinguish between a group and a team? To what extent do you believe the distinction has practical significance for managers?

3 Distinguish between formal and informal groups and provide your own supporting examples. What functions do informal groups serve in an organisation?

4 What actions would you, as a hospitality manager, take in order to create successful team-building? Explain the likely characteristics of an effective work team.

5 Discuss critically the advantages and disadvantages of a virtual team. To what extent are virtual teams a reality in the hospitality industry?

6 Identify the advantages and disadvantages of working with a multicultural team within the hospitality industry. Suggest a range of factors that should be considered when forming and developing a multi-ethnic, multicultural team.

7 Assess critically the likely standard of individual compared with group or team performance. Explain what is meant by (a) the risky-shift phenomenon, (b) groupthink, (c) brainstorming.

8 Explain fully the concept of role to an understanding of group processes and behaviour. Distinguish between role conflict and personality clash. As a manager, what actions would you take to reduce the problems of role stress?

ASSIGNMENT 1

The objective of the exercise is to apply the theoretical concepts of group and team development to a practical situation and to develop some innovative ideas in the development of team-building activities.

Scenario
You are the newly appointed restaurant manager of Stardos restaurant in a new marina development area. You have been allocated one day, two weeks before Christmas, to organise a team-building day to develop your team of restaurant staff. There are 10 staff; they include mixed ages, abilities and nationalities, full- and part-time.

Consider the examples in Appendix 1 'Smells Like Team Spirit' along with relevant theoretical approaches to team-building.

In small groups, plan an innovative team-building programme for the day, stating:

(a) The activities and the location selected.

(b) Your reasons for choice of activities. Include appropriate theory.

Present your ideas to the group.

ASSIGNMENT 2

Observe a small group at work.

1 Explain the extent to which the group progressed through the stages of: forming, storming, norming, performing and adjourning.

2 Provide examples of group values or norms which constituted 'proper' behaviour of group members.

3 Attempt to construct a simple diagram to display the structure of the group, and the frequency and duration of contacts among members.

4 Summarise the extent to which the behaviour of each individual member could be classified under:

- group task roles;
- group-building and maintenance roles; and
- individual roles.

5 Explain the conclusions you draw from your observation.

ASSIGNMENT 3

A self-perception inventory
This inventory was developed from a number of earlier versions which had been designed to give Henley members a simple means of assessing their best team roles.

Directions: For each section distribute a total of 10 points among the sentences which you think best describe your behaviour. These points may be distributed among several sentences: in extreme cases they might be spread among all the sentences or 10 points may be given to a single sentence. Enter the points in Table 8.1.

Table 8.1: Points table for self-perception inventory

I.	What I believe I can contribute to a team:	
	(a) I think I can quickly see and take advantage of new opportunities.	☐
	(b) I can work well with a very wide range of people.	☐
	(c) Producing ideas is one of my natural assets.	☐
	(d) My ability rests in being able to draw people out whenever I detect they have something of value to contribute to group objectives.	☐
	(e) My capacity to follow through has much to do with my personal effectiveness.	☐
	(f) I am ready to face temporary unpopularity if it leads to worthwhile results in the end.	☐
	(g) I can usually sense what is realistic and likely to work.	☐
	(h) I can offer a reasoned case for alternative courses of action without introducing bias or prejudice.	☐

II. **If I have a possible shortcoming in teamwork, it could be that:**

(a) I am not at ease unless meetings are well structured and controlled and generally well conducted. ☐

(b) I am inclined to be too generous towards others who have a valid viewpoint that has not been given a proper airing. ☐

(c) I have a tendency to talk too much once the group gets on to new ideas. ☐

(d) My objective outlook makes it difficult for me to join in readily and enthusiastically with colleagues.

(e) I am sometimes seen as forceful and authoritarian if there is a need to get something done. ☐

(f) I find it difficult to lead from the front, perhaps because I am over-responsive to group atmosphere. ☐

(g) I am apt to get too caught up in ideas that occur to me and so lose track of what is happening. ☐

(h) My colleagues tend to see me as worrying unnecessarily over detail and the possibility that things may go wrong. ☐

III. **When involved in a project with other people:**

(a) I have an aptitude for influencing people without pressurising them. ☐

(b) My general vigilance prevents careless mistakes and omissions being made. ☐

(c) I am ready to press for action to make sure that the meeting does not waste time or lose sight of the main objective. ☐

(d) I can be counted on to contribute something original. ☐

(e) I am always ready to back a good suggestion in the common interest. ☐

(f) I am keen to look for the latest in new ideas and developments. ☐

(g) I believe my capacity for judgement can help to bring about the right decisions. ☐

(h) I can be relied upon to see that all essential work is organised. ☐

IV. **My characteristic approach to group work is that:**

(a) I have a quiet interest in getting to know colleagues better. ☐

(b) I am not reluctant to challenge the views of others or to hold a minority view myself. ☐

(c) I can usually find a line of argument to refute unsound propositions. ☐

(d) I think I have a talent for making things work once a plan has to be put into operation. ☐

(e) I have a tendency to avoid the obvious and to come out with the unexpected. ☐

(f) I bring a touch of perfection to any job I undertake. ☐

(g) I am ready to make use of contacts outside the group itself. ☐

(h) While I am interested in all views I have no hesitation in making up my mind once a decision has to be made. ☐

V. **I gain satisfaction in a job because:**

(a) I enjoy analysing situations and weighing up all the possible choices. ☐

(b) I am interested in finding practical solutions to problems. ☐

(c) I like to feel I am fostering good working relationships. ☐

(d) I can have a strong influence on decisions. ☐

(e) I can meet people who may have something new to offer. ☐

(f) I can get people to agree on a necessary course of action. ☐

(g) I feel in my element where I can give a task my full attention. ☐

(h) I like to find a field that stretches my imagination. ☐

VI. **If I am suddenly given a difficult task with limited time and unfamiliar people:**

(a) I would feel like retiring to a corner to devise a way out of the impasse before developing a line. ☐

(b) I would be ready to work with the person who showed the most positive approach. ☐

(c) I would find some way of reducing the size of the task by establishing what different individuals might best contribute. ☐

(d) My natural sense of urgency would help to ensure that we did not fall behind schedule. ☐

(e) I believe I would keep cool and maintain my capacity to think straight. ☐

(f) I would retain a steadiness of purpose in spite of the pressures. ☐

(g) I would be prepared to take a positive lead if I felt the group was making no progress. ☐

(h) I would open up discussions with a view to stimulating new thoughts and getting something moving. ☐

VII. **With reference to the problems to which I am subject in working in groups:**

(a) I am apt to show my impatience with those who are obstructing progress. ☐

(b) Others may criticise me for being too analytical and insufficiently intuitive. ☐

(c) My desire to ensure that work is properly done can hold up proceedings. ☐

(d) I tend to get bored rather easily and rely on one or two stimulating members to spark me off. ☐

(e) I find it difficult to get started unless the goals are clear. ☐

(f) I am sometimes poor at explaining and clarifying complex points that occur to me. ☐

(g) I am conscious of demanding from others the things I cannot do myself. ☐

(h) I hesitate to get my points across when I run up against real opposition. ☐

To interpret the self-perception inventory you should look at the Analysis sheet at the end of the chapter.

Source: Reprinted with permission from Belbin R. M., *Management Teams: Why they succeed or fail*, Butterworth-Heinemann (1981), pp. 153–6.

CASE STUDY 8.1

The Eden Project

To turn one derelict, neglected corner of south-west England (the Gardens at Heligan) into a successful tourist business attracting millions of visitors is remarkable, to do it twice is astonishing. Yet this is what Tim Smit has done. The Eden Project is a top garden and eco-visitor attraction and an educational charity.

Case study 8.1 (*continued*)

Before Eden

Cornwall is one of several parts of the UK that has suffered economic decline during the latter part of the twentieth century. Its industrial heritage has all but disappeared in the wake of globalisation and the shifting nature of the industrial world landscape. Subsequently tourism has become one of the largest income-generating sectors in the area.

In 1990 Tim Smit, along with John Willis and John Nelson, began to restore the derelict gardens at Heligan, which is now a major tourist attraction in Cornwall. Smit is an archaeology and anthropology graduate who developed a love of gardens, so this Project enabled him to use many of his professional skills. While Heligan is horticultural archaeology, and the gardens today are, in essence, a living museum of nineteenth-century estate gardening, the Eden Project was a very different restoration Project that drew on Smit's skills as a rock music producer and showman. At Eden, Smit restored a large area of land, despoiled by the earlier excavation of china clay pits. The vision and purpose was looking to the future rather than the past.

Development of Eden

In the mid-1990s, the worked-out Bodelva china clay pit near St Austell looked like a derelict, polluted and worthless area with no fertile soil, essentially a 34-acre puddle. The project began in 1998. The first task was to shift 1.8 million tons of earth to reduce the pit side gradient and landscape the site. During this time a major problem was draining off the gallons of water that collected in the pit. This was used as an opportunity to apply the principles of sustainability, in using the water to service the site, for example watering the plants, running a waterfall and supplying the numerous toilets.

A central attraction at Eden are the two 'biomes' which are spectacular greenhouses that re-create different plant environments. The humid, tropical rainforest biome contains plants native to areas such as Malaysia and South America and the warm, temperate biome replicates a Mediterranean climate. The 'Core' is the education centre and more than half the area of the site is landscaped.

At the Eden Project, visitors can explore their relationship with nature, learn new things and be inspired. The website suggests what can be found there, including:

1 The world's largest enclosed rainforest, with steamy jungles and waterfalls

2 Cutting-edge architecture and buildings

3 Stunning garden displays all year round

4 World-class sculpture and art

5 Evening gigs, concerts and an ice rink in the winter

6 Educational centre and demonstrations to inspire all ages

7 Brilliant local, fairly-traded food in the restaurants and cafes

8 A new rainforest lookout that takes you above the treetops

9 A living example of regeneration and sustainable living

10 A free land train running on biofuel.

The purpose of Eden is essentially to educate people about the environment and the relationship of humanity with the plant world, but to do so in such a way as to set a conservation and sustainability example which is, above all things, spectacular fun.

Leadership

Smit generally dresses casually. He has the air of someone not used to spending his working day behind a desk. In a *Guardian* article, the interviewer noted some of Smit's key qualities:

'Smit's secret, if there is one, seems to be that he can bring people of very different disciplines and skills together, get them to brainstorm and collaborate, and come up with the extraordinary.' The Eden Project, he says, has attracted locals by the score, but also high-flying artists, businessmen, architects, scientists, engineers, educationalists, horticulturalists and ecologists from all over Britain. "It feels like a renaissance organisation" says one woman, who left a senior management job to work there as a director and has been amazed both at what gets done and the way it works. "It's attracted a critical mass of people, and there's a passionate belief, right through the project, that it belongs to everyone who works there, that it's a team thing. I guess it

Case study 8.1 (*continued*)

demonstrates that you can have an organisation that is highly effective, financially, environmentally and socially. It's a kind of experiment to show you can work in different ways." A local woman who has been with Eden since the start is more succinct. "It's the most equal place I've known' she says.

"This is a stage for change" says Smit, who admits that Eden can seem like a sect to outsiders. "Many people have made life choices to come here. Most could earn five times as much elsewhere. But I'm aware that if you want to effect real change, and we do, that you must not own it. You have got to make sure that it's owned by more than one person."

Although a key function of Eden is education, Smit is concerned that it is not stuffy or seen to be preaching, the educational process should be fun and exciting, and Eden should be a spectacle. This desire did at times bring him into conflict with the horticulturalists involved. Smit is also very "hands on", in that, although he may be integral to well-known events, he may also get involved in selling tickets or guiding visitors.

By 2008 the Project was employing 450 staff and 150 or more volunteers. The workforce is divided into a number of teams:

- The main team is the Destination Team that runs the front of house including organising the events, retail and catering operations. This team also includes the Green Team of horticulturalists, which is responsible for managing the planting and the biomes.

- The Foundation Team works with supporters of the project and develops educational and scientific projects.

- The Marketing Team and the Communications Team are responsible for in-house publishing and marketing communications such as the website.

- The Development Team is involved with major projects such as building and includes people

from external firms, such as architects and construction.

- The Finance Team manages the finances and stakeholder relationships.

- The Creative Team develops and produces the events.

- The Organisational Development Team looks after the staff, volunteers and the Eden culture.

- And finally the paying visitors are seen as their Visiting Team.

A blend of visionary and innovative leadership combined with a strong sense of the value of teamwork from Tim Smit has initiated a tremendously successful operation in both business and educational terms. The vision was realised in the physical development of the site, the benefits have been seen in the local economy, it has created over 400 jobs for local people and above all it has created memorable and exciting experiences for the millions of visitors.

Questions

1 To what extent do you think that the non-profit-making nature of this organisation enhances the sense of collaboration and teamwork between the various workforce teams?

2 Critically review the approach towards developing groups and teams. What are the strengths and risks about taking this view of people that work for you?

3 Analyse Tim Smit's leadership style using appropriate theory. Does it help or hinder his leadership that, as chief executive of a project about plants, he is not a horticulturalist?

4 How might Smit's approach to management be transferable to both profit-making and public-sector organisations whose stakeholder groups will be very different to those of Eden?

How to team-build: Smells like team spirit[91]

Last month we looked at the uplifting team-building events at the Bertinet Kitchen in Bath, where chefs were enthused by learning to make bread. In our second look at alternative training methods, we turn to the hotel sector, which has team-building activities of its own–some quite unusual. Emily Manson reports.

'With a cold steel rod pressed hard against the skin of my neck, I listen to the master begin his countdown. Five, four, three, two, one. Taking a deep breath, I lean in determinedly towards my 'buddy', who has the other end of the rod held firmly against her neck. Hey presto! We, two ordinary girls, bend a steel rod in half as easily as a hair pin, using only our necks and positive mental attitude. I still don't know how we did it.

Although it did build a team, not all team-building events need to be as potentially hair-raising as this, and several hotel operators have come up with some cracking ideas. At budget hotel chain Travelodge, they've adopted the format of hit TV show *The Apprentice* to bond regional managers and enthuse them about their areas.

The set-up

Hotel managers from a region are brought together and then split into two teams. Two of the delegates also fill the 'Nick' and 'Margaret' roles, monitoring the process and feeding back information to the 'Sir Alan' figure in the boardroom.

Tasks during the day-long event include visiting tourist attractions in the town, checking out the competition to note 'wow' factors and money-saving ideas, identifying areas of the town with the highest penetration of tourists, making contact with businesses in the area that don't currently use Travelodge, researching local history and discovering facts about regional architecture and landmarks.

Guy Parsons, managing director of Travelodge UK, says: 'As these managers are spread out across three counties in their own hotels, it is very revealing to see how they operate together as peers. It is an opportunity to identify the leaders in the group – who enjoys contributing, leading and who may lack confidence in a wider group. The events also help to foster a good team spirit across the group and breed confidence in the team as they get to know each other better.'

On top of these practical management skills, the set-up also encourages the managers to increase their local knowledge and reinvigorate their passion for tourism. Parsons adds: 'The managers get to know a key town in their area, they analyse tourism destinations, which areas of the town have the highest tourism penetration and even how the transport network aids the town.'

You're fired!

Of course, no replica of *The Apprentice* would be complete without the infamous boardroom scene where someone gets fired. Although Travelodge may be known for its cutthroat approach to prices, a more light-hearted attitude is taken towards this part of the day.

'We like to include an element of fun during the day, and the firing in the boardroom is very light and actually the most entertaining part of the process,' Parsons explains.

'Along the way there is often some friendly sabotage of the other team's performance or a touch of "creativity" – cheating – in delivering some of the results. It is often one of these culprits that gets fired and not, for example, a manager that is quiet or lacking confidence. The person that gets fired will be chosen to highlight a group trait or some Machiavellian behaviour rather than an individual's weaknesses and the penalty is generally to buy the first round of drinks in the evening.'

The results

Chris Wingrove, Travelodge district manager for Surrey, Sussex and Berkshire, who recently ran the day in Windsor, admits he was surprised by the levels of competitiveness that suddenly developed. 'Just putting the managers into two teams really sparked their enthusiasm and got the competitive juices flowing. They didn't want to lose,' he says.

But the process had other benefits, Wingrove adds: 'We have monthly meetings but they can be quite a sterile environment and this allowed less-experienced managers to come to the fore and even senior managers had to lead in a different way to normal. It was really good to mix everyone without the formality of work.' The day allowed one of the less-experienced managers of a small property, who normally has a low profile in the group, to shine unexpectedly. While he wasn't the team leader, explains Wingrove, by the end of day his methodical manner and leadership skills really made him stand out. He says: 'We've now capitalised on that and given him a special project that spans the district, enabling him to display his leadership qualities on a bigger stage, and this is rapidly developing him.'

The day is also a chance for the managers to have a day away from their hotel and use skills that they may not get to use in their daily work life. 'It drives enthusiasm for tourism and gives them time to get to know more about the area that they operate in,' Wingrove explains.

In true Travelodge style, the final plus is that the set-up is very cheap to implement. 'The prizes at the end of the day were some boxes of chocolates, but other than that it really didn't cost us anything,' Wingrove says.

Parsons adds: 'Travelodge is a fun place to work and likes to innovate with team-building. *The Apprentice* is probably one of the UK's best-watched programmes and is always a topic of conversation among managers and staff alike. 'This format was an opportunity to get groups of managers working together in a fun way that offers insights into how their peers [work], and the wider tourism market. It engendered a team spirit that wouldn't have been achieved by a round of golf or a drinks evening.'

Fencing: Kempinski Hotels

At Kempinski Hotels they favour a spot of fencing. Sebastian Herzog, director of sales and marketing at the Schloss Reinhartshausen Kempinski Eltville in Germany, holds the four-hour fencing session within the atmospheric wine cellars of the castle hotel and has engaged the help of a former Olympic fencing coach to run the courses.

Herzog explains the reasoning behind picking such a quirky activity as a team-building exercise: 'We wanted something special, and fencing is totally different. It's also something that hardly anyone has done before, so everyone starts from the same level. If you go golfing or climbing some people will already be more proficient than others, so it's nice for everyone to learn together. It's also good because it's not only fun but it also teaches you about watching your opponent. It's all about mirroring your sparring partner, and that translates well for how we communicate and work with each other.'

At around €140 per person, which includes all the equipment and trainers, Herzog admits the fact that it is good value for money is also a draw. 'In terms of training budgets, it's a fantastic investment,' he says. The scheme has proved so successful that Ursula von Platen, Kempinski's UK PR director, has taken up the sport with another colleague in her spare time, after attending the course when the company held an international workshop for Kempinski PRs. She says: 'You have to watch your opponent very carefully, read their body language and facial expressions, and then respond to those quickly. It's very interactive and it's not necessary to be strong. In fact, it's all about being flexible and quick-witted. It was very unusual and took everyone by surprise. Although initially we didn't know each other well, because we were in two teams, we ended up helping each other and everyone got really involved and enjoyed it immensely.'

Walks and tea parties: Red Carnation Hotels

Red Carnation Hotels has a range of team-building events. For the commis chefs there are educational visits every six months to widen their food knowledge.

Destinations include Billingsgate, Smithfields and New Covent Garden markets in London and an overnight visit to Mrs Tee's mushroom farm in the New Forest, where chefs get to pick their own mushrooms and then eat their haul in a specially created dinner.

Front-of-house staff from the London hotels are encouraged to conduct guided walks. The group's managing director, Jonathan Raggett, explains the rationale behind this: 'Not only does this provide them with a chance to get together outside the work environment, but it is also educational for staff, particularly for overseas team members. It enables them to talk with far greater confidence to guests about some of the less-familiar sightseeing activities.'

On top of these activities, each hotel has a monthly tea party hosted by the general manager and attended by as many employees as possible. Raggett explains that as well as being a good chance for staff from different departments to mix, ideas on improving service and environmental practices are also shared and awards are given out. 'But to lighten proceedings there's usually also a competition,' Raggett says. 'We have a version of *Who Wants to be a Millionaire?* which has proved particularly popular.'

All staff are also encouraged to take part in the company's Trading Places/In Your Shoes scheme, which involves spending one day working in another department. Participants so far have included a general manager changing into chef's whites for Shrove Tuesday to cook pancakes for staff and guests, a vice-president of marketing working as a concierge, a vice-president of sales trying his hand at being a doorman and Raggett himself spending a morning as a breakfast chef.

Travelodge's Apprentice-style team-building day ends with the traditional sacking . . . whoever gets fired has to buy the drinks.

Source: www.team-spirit.co.uk

Management teams: A self-perception inventory (Assignment 3)

Interpretation of total scores and further notes

The highest score on team role will indicate how best the respondent can make his or her mark in a management team. The next highest scores can denote back-up team roles towards which the individual should shift if for some reason there is less group need for a primary team role.

The two lowest scores on team role imply possible areas of weakness. But rather than attemting to reform in this area the manager may be better advised to seek a colleague with complementary strengths.

Self-perception inventory analysis sheet

Transpose the scores taken from Assignment 3, entering them section by section in Table 8.2 below. Then add up the points in each column to give a total team role distribution score.

Table 8.2: Self-perception inventory analysis sheet

Section		CW		CH		SH		PL		RI		ME		TW		CE
I	g		d		f		c		a		h		b		e	
II	a		b		e		g		c		d		f		h	
III	h		a		c		d		f		g		e		b	
IV	d		h		b		e		g		c		a		f	
V	b		f		d		h		e		a		c		g	
VI	f		c		g		a		h		e		b		d	
VII	e		g		a		f		d		b		h		c	
TOTAL																

Source: Belbin, R. M., *Management Teams: Why They Succeed or Fail*, Butterworth-Heinemann (1981), pp. 156–7.

Now refer to the details in Figure 8.12.

Type	Symbol	Typical features	Positive qualities	Allowable weaknesses
Company worker	CW	Conservative, dutiful, predictable.	Organising ability, practical common sense, hard-working, self-discipline.	Lack of flexibility, unresponsiveness to unproven ideas.
Chairman	CH	Calm, self-confident controlled.	A capacity for treating and welcoming all potential contributors on their merits and without prejudice. A strong sense of objectives.	No more than ordinary in terms of intellect or creative ability.
Shaper	SH	Highly strung, outgoing, dynamic.	Drive and a readiness to challenge inertia, ineffectiveness, complacency or self-deception.	Proneness to provocation, irritation and impatience.
Plant	PL	Individualistic, serious-minded, unorthodox.	Genius, imagination, intellect, knowledge.	Up in the clouds, inclined to disregard practical details or protocol.
Resource investigator	RI	Extroverted, enthusiastic, curious, communicative.	A capacity for contacting people and exploring anything new. An ability to respond to challenge.	Liable to lose interest once the initial fascination has passed.
Monitor – evaluator	ME	Sober, unemotional, prudent.	Judgement, discretion, hard-headedness.	Lacks inspiration or the ability to motivate others.
Team worker	TW	Socially orientated, rather mild, sensitive.	An ability to respond to people and to situations, and to promote team spirit.	Indecisiveness at moments of crisis.
Completer – finisher	CF	Painstaking, orderly, conscientious, anxious.	A capacity for follow-through.	A tendency to worry about small things. A reluctance to 'let go'.

Source: reprinted, with permission, from Belbin, R. M., *Management Teams: Why They Succeed or Fail*, Butterworth-Heinemann (1981), p. 78.

Figure 8.12 Useful people to have in a team

References

1 Berger, F. and Brownell, J., *Organizational Behaviour for the Hospitality Industry*, Pearson Prentice Hall (2009).

2 Adair, J., *Effective Teambuilding*, Gower (1986).

3 Schein, E. H., *Organizational Psychology*, 3rd edn, Prentice-Hall (1988), p. 145.

4 Crainer, S., *Key Management Ideas: Thinkers that Changed the Management World*, 3rd edn, Financial Times Prentice Hall (1998), p. 237.

5 ACAS, *Teamwork: Success Through People*, advisory booklet, ACAS (2007), p. 24.

6 Holpp, L., 'Teams: it's all in the planning', *Training & Development*, vol. 51, no. 4, April 1997, 44–7.

7 Vroom, V. H. and Deci, E. L., *Management and Motivation*, Penguin (1983).

8 Cane, S., *Kaizen Strategies for Winning Through People*, Pitman Publishing (1996), p. 116.

9 Belbin, R. M., *Beyond the Team*, Butterworth-Heinemann (2000).

10 Riches, A., 'Emotionally intelligent teams', *Organisational Change and Leadership Development*, www.anneriches.co.au, accessed 11 March 2003.

11 Mullins, L. J., 'Management and Managerial Behaviour', *International Journal of Hospitality Management*, vol. 4, no. 1, 1985, 39–41.

12 See, for example, Atkinson, P. E., 'Developing Cohesive Working Groups', *Hospitality*, no. 29, May 1983, 19–23.

13 Berger, F. and Vanger, R., 'Building Your Hospitality Team', *Cornell HRA Quarterly*, February 1986, 82–9.

14 Tuckman, B. W., 'Development Sequence in Small Groups', *Psychological Bulletin*, vol. 63, 1965, pp. 384–99 and Tuckman, B. W. and Jensen, M. C. 'Stages of small group development revised', *Group and Organisational Studies*, vol. 2, no. 3, 1977, 419– 27.

15 Bass, B. M. and Ryterband, E. C., *Organisational Psychology*, 2nd edn, Allyn & Bacon (1979).

16 Green, J., 'Are your teams and groups at work successful?', *Administrator*, December 1993, p. 12.

17 See also Jones, P. and Lockwood, A., *The Management of Hotel Operations*, Cassell (1989).

18 Rickards, T. and Moger, S., 'Creative leadership and team effectiveness: empirical evidence for a two barrier model of team development', working paper presented at the Advanced Seminar Series, University of Uppsala, Sweden, 3 March 2009. See also Rickards, T. and Moger, S., 'Creative leadership processes in project team development: an alternative to Tuckman's stage model?', *British Journal of Management*, Part 4, 2000, 273–83.

19 See, for example, Gullen, H. V. and Rhodes, G. E., *Management in the Hotel and Catering Industry*, Batsford (1983).

20 See, for example, Keiser, J. R., *Principles and Practices of Management in the Hospitality Industry*, 2nd edn, Van Nostrand Reinhold (1989).

21 Lysons, K., 'Organisational Analysis', *Supplement to The British Journal of Administrative Management*, no. 18, March/April 1997.

22 Law, S., 'Beyond the Water Cooler', *Professional Manager*, January 2005, 26–8.

23 See, for example, Venison, P., *Managing Hotels*, Heinemann (1983).

24 Simmons, P. and Teare, R., 'Evolving a total quality culture', *International Journal of Contemporary Hospitality Management*, vol. 5, no. 3, 1993, v–viii.

25 Jones, P. and Lockwood, A., *The Management of Hotel Operations*, Cassell (1989).

26 See, for example, Drummond, K. E., *Human Resource Management for the Hospitality Industry*, Van Nostrand Reinhold (1990).

27 Riley, M., *Human Resource Management in the Hospitality and Tourism Industry*, 2nd edn, Butterworth-Heinemann (1996), p. 60.

28 Berger, F. and Vanger, R., 'Building your hospitality team', *Cornell HRA Quarterly*, February 1986, 83–4.

29 Gardner, K. and Wood, R. C., 'Theatricality in food service work', *International Journal of Hospitality Management*, vol. 10, no. 3, 1991, 267–78.

30 Heller, R., *In Search of European Excellence*, HarperCollins Business (1997).

31 ACAS, *Teamwork: Success Through People*, advisory booklet, ACAS (2007), p. 6.

32 Lucas, E., 'And the winner is everyone', *Professional Manager*, January 2001, 10.

33 Adams, S., 'A-Class teams Achieve A-Class Results', *Manager, The British Journal of Administrative Management*, Autumn 2008, 21.

34 Cutler, A., 'Aspire to inspire', *Hospitality Leadership* (2010).

35 Tajfel, H. and Turner, J. C., 'The social identity theory of intergroup behavior', in Worchel, S. and Austin, L. W. (eds), *Psychology of Intergroup Relations*, Nelson-Hall (1986), pp. 7–24.

36 Guirdham, M., *Interactive Behaviour at Work*, 3rd edn, Financial Times Prentice Hall (2002), p. 118.

37 Haslam, S. A., *Psychology in Organizations: The Social Identity Approach*, 2nd edn, Sage Publications (2004), p. 17.

38 See, for example, Flynn, F. J., Chatman, J. A. and Spataro, S. E., 'Getting to know you: the influence of personality on impressions and performance of demographically different people in organizations', *Administrative Science Quarterly*, vol. 46, 2001, 414–42.

39 Hewstone, M., Ruibin, M. and Willis, H., 'Intergroup bias', *Annual Review of Psychology*, vol. 53, 2002, 575–604.

40 Seashore, S. E., *Group Cohesiveness in the Industrial Work Group*, Institute for Social Research, University of Michigan (1954).

41 Argyle, M., *The Social Psychology of Work*, 2nd edn, Penguin (1986).

42 See, for example, Allcorn, S., 'Understanding Groups at Work', *Personnel*, vol. 66, no. 8, August 1989, 28–36.

43 Bowey, A., *The Sociology of Organizations*, Hodder & Stoughton (1976).

44 Whyte, W. F., *Human Relations in the Restaurant Industry*, McGraw-Hill (1948).

45 Staw, B. M., 'Organisational psychology and the pursuit of the happy/productive worker', *California Management Review*, vol. 28, no. 4, Summer 1986, 40–53.

46 Schein, E. H., *Organizational Psychology*, 3rd edn, Prentice-Hall (1988).

47 Dann, D. and Hornsey, T., 'Towards a theory of interdepartmental conflict in hotels', *The International Journal of Hospitality Management*, vol. 5, no. 1, 1986, 23–8.

48 See, for example, Kogan, N. and Wallach, M. A., 'Risk-taking as a function of the situation, the person and the group', in Newcomb, T. M. (ed.), *New Directions in Psychology III*, Holt, Rinehart & Winston (1967).

49 Shaw, M. E., *Group Dynamics*, McGraw-Hill (1976).

50 Janis, J. L., *Groupthink*, 2nd edn, Houghton Mifflin (1982).

51 See, for example, Leane, C. R., 'A partial test of Janis' groupthink model', *Journal of Management*, vol. 11, no. 1, 1985, 5–17.

52 Osborn, A. F., *Applied Imagination*, rev. edn, Scribner (1957).

53 Bavelas, A., 'Communication patterns in task-oriented groups', in Lasswell, H. N. and Lerner, D. (eds), *The Policy Sciences*, Stanford University Press (1951).

54 Leavitt, H. J., *Managerial Psychology*, 4th edn, University of Chicago Press (1978).

55 Shaw, M. E., 'Communication Networks', in Berkowitz, L. (ed.), *Advances in Experimental Social Psychology*, vol. 1, Academic Press (1964).

56 Belbin, R. M., *Management Teams: Why They Succeed or Fail*, Heinemann (1981).

57 Belbin, R. M., *Team Roles at Work*, Butterworth-Heinemann (1993).

58 White, J., 'Teaming with Talent', *Management Today*, September 1999, 57–61.

59 For an example of a role-set for a unit manager, see Hales, C. and Nightingale, M., 'What are unit managers supposed to do?', *The International Journal of Hospitality Management*, vol. 5, no. 1, 1986, 3–11.

60 Jones, P. and Lockwood, A., *The Management of Hotel Operations*, Cassell (1989).

61 See, for example, Handy, C. B., *Understanding Organizations*, 4th edn, Penguin (1993).

62 Lockwood, A. and Jones, P., *People and the Hotel and Catering Industry*, Holt, Rinehart & Winston (1984).

63 Wood, R. C., *Organizational Behavior for Hospitality Management*, Butterworth-Heinemann (1994), p. 78.

64 Filley, A. C. and House, R. J., *Managerial Process and Organizational Behavior*, Scott Foresman (1969).

65 *Are Managers Under Stress? A Survey of Management Morale*, The Institute of Management, September 1996.

66 Hall, K. and Savery, L. K., 'Stress Management', *Management Decision*, vol. 25, no. 6, 1987, 29–35.

67 Green, J., 'Team Building in Practice', *Chartered Secretary*, November 1997, 34–7.

68 Bales, R. F., *Personality and Interpersonal Behavior*, Holt, Rinehart & Winston (1970).

69 Benne, K. D. and Sheats, P., 'Functional roles of group members', *Journal of Social Issues*, vol. 4, 1948, 41–9.

70 For a more detailed account of frameworks for behavioural analysis and their use, see Mullins, L. J., *Management and Organisational Behaviour*, 5th edn, Financial Times Pitman Publishing (1999).

71 See note 5.

72 Guirdham, M., *Interactive Behaviour at Work*, 3rd edn, Financial Times Prentice Hall (2002), p. 12.

73 Ellis, S. and Dick, P., *Introduction to Organisational Behaviour*, McGraw-Hill (2000).

74 Lashley, C. and Lee-Ross, D., *Organization Behaviour for Leisure Services*, Elsevier (2003).

75 Robinson, (Sir) G., *I'll Show Them Who's Boss*, BBC Books (2004), p. 183.

76 Wilson, J., 'Building teams – with attitude', *Professional Manager*, September 1998, 13.

77 Learn Purple, http://www.caterersearch.com/Articles/04/09/2003/50012/Tips-for-effective-team-building.html

78 Douglas, M., 'Why soft skills are an essential part of the hard world of business', *Manager, The British Journal of Administrative Management*, New Year 2003, 34–5.

79 Cloke, K. and Goldsmith, J., *The End of Management and the Rise of Organizational Democracy*, Jossey-Bass (2002).

80 Matlay, H. and Westhead, P., 'Virtual teams and the rise of e-entrepreneurship in Europe', *International Small Business Journal*, vol. 23, 2005, 279, Sage.

81 Hall, P., 'Team solutions need not be the organisational norm', *Professional Manager*, July 2001, 45.

82 Parker, C., 'Remote Control – a Case Study', *Manager, The British Journal of Administrative Management*, March/April 2002, 30.

83 Norval, D., in conversation with Law, S., 'Beyond the Water Cooler', *Professional Manager*, January 2005, 26–8.

84 Symons, J., 'Taking Virtual Team Control', *Professional Manager*, vol. 12, no. 2, March 2003, 37.

85 Garrett, A., 'Crash Course in Managing a Virtual Team', *Management Today*, September 2007, 20.

86 Francesco, A. M. and Gold, B. A., *International Organizational Behavior*, 2nd edn, Pearson Prentice Hall (2005), p. 118.

87 Murray, S., 'Virtual teams: global harmony is their dream', *Financial Times*, 11 May 2005.

88 Inglehart, R (1997) www.worldvaluessurvey.org/wvs/articles/folder_published/article_base_54, accessed 1.3.12

89 http://www.kwintessential.co.uk/cross-cultural/team-building.html

90 Hu, M., Horng, J. and Sun, Y., 'Hospitality teams: Knowledge sharing and service innovation performance, *Tourism Management*, vol. 30, issue 1, Feb. 2009, 41–50.

91 Manson, E., 'Smells like team spirit', May 2009, www.caterersearch.com, accessed 15.5.12.

Chapter 9

Managing challenging situations

Learning outcomes

After completing this chapter you should be able to:

- explain the nature and main sources of conflict within hospitality organisations;
- assess causes and influence of stress within the work environment;
- detail challenging situations facing the hospitality managers;
- explore the management of bullying and harassment in the workplace;
- examine the need for, and effect of, management control;
- review concepts and practice behind managing and resolving conflict.

Introduction

Earlier chapters emphasise current beliefs that staff should be trusted rather than controlled and that empowerment may lead to a stronger workforce and better provision of service; it must be recognised, however, that there are times when empowerment does not bring the expected results.

Managers in the hospitality industry encounter more challenges in the management of people than in many other work environments. The nature of the workforce and the nature of the work environment can present managers with particular industry-related problems. Managing any workforce will involve the resolution of conflict. This chapter will focus on the challenges to be found in the hospitality industry.

Critical review and reflection

On return from industry placement, a student reported to the placement tutor that the hotel staff were 'a load of fruit loops'.

From your own experience, would you agree that hospitality organisations employ staff with more than the average number of social and personal problems?

Organisational conflict

Conflict is an inevitable feature of organisational life, and a reality of management and the behaviour of people at work. Within the hospitality industry conflict situations are a common occurrence and manifested largely at the individual, group or unit level rather than on a collective bargaining basis. Organisational conflict is a common theme in discussions on the general nature of working in the industry such as interdepartmental competition,[1] or organisation structure and operation of rules,[2] or related to specific features, for example high staff turnover.[3]

Common definitions of conflict are usually associated with negative features and situations which give rise to inefficiency. Conflict is the harmful side of differences within organisations.[4] The traditional view of conflict is that it is potentially dysfunctional and represents forms of deviant organisational behaviour which should be controlled and changed.

However, it is also arguable that, properly managed, conflict can, at least to a point, have potentially positive outcomes.[5] It can have an energising and vitalising effect within an organisation. Conflict can be seen as a 'constructive force' and in certain circumstances it may be welcomed or even encouraged.

Clearly, conflict situations can give rise to emotional and physical stress and in extreme cases can have very upsetting consequences for some people. Conflict can also have adverse effects on organisational performance and effectiveness. It is important therefore that management makes every reasonable effort to avoid the harmful consequences of conflict. An important, and central, feature of attempts at the resolution of conflict include management strategies related to establishing and maintaining effective employee relations.[6] Improved training and development for empowerment and employee participation may be applied as a change strategy to help employees in the hospitality industry to deal effectively with conflict management and resolution.[7]

Contrasting perspectives of work organisations

An appreciation of the nature of conflict can help an understanding of social and organisational behaviour, the nature of employee relations and applications of human resource management. Differing views on the explanation and outcomes of conflict can be related to contrasting unitary or pluralistic perspectives of work organisations.

For example, it might be expected that a healthy climate would be reflected by complete harmony in working relationships, and loyalty and common commitment to the goals and objectives of the organisation. This view of work organisations as 'happy families' is a worthwhile and creditable ideal, and as such is implied by many leading management writers.[8] Such a view suggests a unitary perspective of the organisation.

The unitary perspective

With the unitary perspective, the organisation is viewed as a team with a common source of loyalty, one focus of effort and one common leader. There is an image of the organisation as being an integrated whole, with supportive and cooperative structures. Management and workers are viewed as sharing a common interest, namely the success of the organisation. Trade unions are seen by the organisation as an unnecessary evil, and restrictive practices outmoded or caused by troublemakers.

The unitary perspective views authority as vested in management. Where conflict exists it represents a malfunction within the organisation and is attributed to poor communications, personality clashes or the work of agitators. Human resources policies and managerial development can be seen as reflecting a unitary ideology. Developments in human resource management can also arguably be seen as imposing new forms of control and a managerial approach to facilitating organisational goals and the involvement of employees which furthers a unitarist perspective.[9] This is an approach often embodied by owner managers in small hospitality organisations.

The pluralistic perspective

The pluralistic perspective presents an alternative view in which the organisation is viewed in terms of competing sub-groups with their own legitimate loyalties, goals and leaders.[10] These competing sub-groups are almost certain to come into conflict. From the pluralistic perspective, conflict is seen as an inherent and accepted feature of work organisations and induced in part by the very structure of the organisation. Conflict can be an agent for evolution, and internal and external change.

Restrictive practices may be seen as a rational response from a group which regards itself as being threatened. Conflict is generated through individuals and groups pursuing their own diverse goals.

> Managers and owners on one hand and employees on the other have quite different sets of needs from the organisation. The link between pay, costs and profits, and terms and conditions of employment are just two examples of issues where employers and the employed have different and thereby potentially conflicting needs.[11]

It is the job of the manager to manage and accommodate the competing interests of different parties. Belief in the principles of a pluralistic perspective can therefore restrict the implementation of a unitary approach to employee relations.

The radical perspective

The radical approach, which is associated with the ideas of writers such as Karl Marx and the structuralist approach to organisations and management, challenges the traditional view of conflict. The radical approach views organisations in terms of the disparity in social power and control. This disparity mirrors the inequalities in society as a whole. Thus, organisational conflict is a feature of the unequal nature of organisational life and is a means of bringing about change.[12] This perspective does not value collective bargaining as particularly helpful, in a system stacked against the workers. Organisational conflict is a natural part of the class struggle between owners and controllers of economic resources and the means of production, and the workers and wage earners.

According to the radical approach, the design of organisation structure, management systems and the choice and use of technology all form part of the struggle for power and control within the work organisation. Greater attention should be given to relationships between the formal and informal aspects of the organisation and the study of conflict between the needs of the individual and those of the organisation, and between workers and management.

Broader interpretation of conflict

A more recent view of conflict is the **interactionist perspective**, which believes that conflict is a positive force and necessary for effective performance. This approach encourages a minimum level of conflict within the group in order to encourage self-criticism, change and innovation, and to help prevent apathy or too great a tolerance for harmony and the status quo.[13]

Conflict *per se* is not necessarily good or bad but an inevitable feature of organisational life and should be judged in terms of its effects on performance. Even if organisations have taken great care to try to avoid conflict, it will still occur. Conflict will continue to emerge despite management attempts to suppress it.

The current view appears to recognise that conflict can be interpreted more broadly than in the traditional view, even as a sign of a healthy organisation.

Positive and negative outcomes

Conflict is not necessarily a bad thing. It can be seen as a 'constructive' force and in certain circumstances it can be welcomed or even encouraged. For example, it can be seen as an aid to incremental improvement in organisation design and functioning, and to the decision-making process. Conflict can be an agent for evolution, and for internal and external change. Properly identified and handled, it can help to minimise the destructive influences of the win–lose situation.

From a survey of practising managers, who reported that they spend approximately 20 per cent of their time dealing with conflict situations, Schmidt records a number of both positive and negative outcomes of conflict.[14] Positive outcomes include:

- better ideas produced;
- people forced to search for new approaches;
- long-standing problems brought to the surface and resolved;
- clarification of individual views;
- stimulation of interest and creativity;
- a chance for people to test their capacities.

Negative outcomes include:

- some people feeling defeated and demeaned;
- an increase in the distance between people;
- development of a climate of mistrust and suspicion;
- individuals and groups concentrating on their own narrow interests;
- development of resistance rather than teamwork;
- an increase in employee turnover.

Critical review and reflection

'Conflict should be accepted as a reality of management and organisational behaviour, and properly managed it can be an energising and vitalising force within groups and the organisation. Managers should therefore be encouraged to invoke constructive conflict.'

What is your opinion of the above statement in the context of managing people in the hospitality industry?

Conflict and 'difficult people'

The idea of conflict as inevitable is discussed by Irvine, who suggests that if you ask a group of managers about the nature and level of conflict they experience, the majority will tell you honestly that apart from the odd minor tiff, there is not much conflict about. There are, however, 'difficult people'.

> Perhaps our reluctance to identify, and then directly address, conflict within organisations is based upon the widely held belief that conflict is inevitable, negative and unmanageable. There is a tendency to see conflict as a result of one person's personality. Conflict may be inevitable, but how dramatically situations could be changed if we could also view it as positive and manageable! What if we think of these situations as raising **questions of difference**? What if we were to make a shift away from blaming individuals and their personalities, recognising instead that it is through normal human interaction that outward expressions of difference are produced?[15]

According to Mannering, conflicts, misunderstandings and personality clashes are usually at the root of the problem when employees become unhappy at work. There is an erosion of our social framework, and the work environment has become more competitive with pressure to have the best jobs and gadgets. People are placed into teams with people they would possibly never choose to associate with. Mannering suggests that people can be 'difficult' for a number of reasons but it is important not to concentrate on the negative points. Negativity is the most difficult behaviour to overcome or change as it constantly undermines what the team is trying to achieve. In order to help defuse conflict, it is important to draw a fine line between firm management and aggressive behaviour. Humour may help defuse a situation but it is more important to stay calm and professional. Improved communications and relationships may help but if someone is determined not to cooperate, then there will be conflict. Mannering makes the point that although you cannot please everyone all the time, avoidance is not an option for dealing with difficult people. Managers must develop solid coping mechanisms and do their best in the particular situation.[16]

Berger and Brownell categorise some of the more common 'types' of difficult people and suggest that managers may need to adopt different strategies in managing each of these 'types'.

For example, they suggest there are those with *'overbearing behaviour'* who need to be encouraged to earn people's respect rather than bullying them; *'shrinking violets'* who need to gain self-confidence through being guided and encouraged; *'nonconformists'* who need to have the difference between their way of doing things, and the required way, explained to them ; *'cynics'* who may have developed negative attitudes over time and need to have the effects of their negativity pointed out to them; and those with *'passive-aggressive'* behaviour, who express their negative reaction to authority by creating obstacles to good performance for themselves and others.

Before managers can adopt appropriate approaches to dealing with each type, it is necessary to identify these different behavioural patterns.[17]

CASE STUDY 9.1

Managing difficult people

The trouble with Wayne

Wayne was employed as a general assistant in a contract catering environment. The catering complex provided meals, snacks, and beverages for a number of diverse organisations in an industrial park in the south of England. The catering facility was open from 7.00 am to 5.00 pm, Monday to Friday. Peak times, including lunch time, needed to be covered adequately, so staff needed to work flexibly, which included early and late starts, allocated on a rota basis.

Wayne's duties were to serve meals and coffees, clean, arrange displays – typical work for a catering assistant. He came from a troubled background, and had few educational qualifications. Having never previously secured full-time employment, he was delighted to be offered a job at the age of 18 as part of a job creation scheme. The scheme offered the opportunity to take NVQ training qualifications if he performed well.

He did work very well. He was enthusiastic, appeared highly motivated and showed much initiative. He was considerably better than many of the other staff and was a valued team member. The catering manager described him as 'superb'.

Unfortunately, Wayne was an extremely poor timekeeper. He was regularly late to work, and also took days off sick. When interviewed he always appeared to have valid personal reasons for his lateness and sick days. After a while, in an attempt to change his behaviour, he received a series of four formal warnings, which, initially, had the desired effect. However, after about six months, he reverted to his previous behaviour of being late and taking unauthorised absences.

He again went through the formal warning process and reached the point where the disciplinary procedure indicated that he should be dismissed.

The catering manager was faced with a dilemma. On one hand, she was reluctant to dismiss him, having sympathy for his problems and knowing it was difficult to recruit good staff. He would be difficult to replace. Yet, on the other hand there was the need to consider the effect on other staff, who were unhappy at having to cover for Wayne's lateness and his many absences, as well as at the catering manager's perceived favouritism towards Wayne.

Questions

1 Identify the management issues involved in this case.

2 How would you deal with the situation if you were the catering manager?

3 Justify your actions.

The sources of conflict

Much has been written about the implications of conflict as a social process. Whilst recognising the importance of this debate, it is not the intention here to enter into a detailed discussion of the ideologies of conflict. The important point is not so much the extent to which it is possible to create a totally harmonious working environment, or whether competing sub-groups and conflict are seen as inevitable consequences of organisation structure, but how conflict when found to exist is handled and managed.

There are many potential sources of organisational conflict. The main ones can be summarised as follows:

- **Differences in perception.** We all see things in different ways and have our own set of values, beliefs and opinions. We all have our own, unique picture or image of how we see the 'real' world. Differences in perception result in different people attaching different meanings to the same stimuli. The underlying issue may have nothing specifically to do with work but since perceptions become a person's reality, value judgements can be a potential major source of conflict.

- **Limited resources.** Most organisational resources are limited and individuals and groups have to fight for their share, for example at the time of the allocation of the next year's budget or when cutbacks have to be made. The greater the limitation of resources, then, usually, the greater the potential for conflict. In an organisation with reducing profits or revenues, the potential for conflict is likely to be intensified. This is of particular relevance in the hospitality industry, where profit margins may be small.

- **Departmentalisation and specialisation.** Most work organisations are divided into departments with specialised functions. Because of familiarity with the manner in which they undertake their activities, managers tend to turn inwards and to concentrate on the achievement of their own particular goals. When departments need to cooperate, this is a frequent source of conflict. Differing goals and internal environments of departments are also a potential source of conflict.

- **The nature of work activities.** Where the task of one person is dependent upon the work of others there is potential for conflict. An example, frequently cited in the hospitality industry, is restaurant staff being reliant on the food being produced by the kitchen and the kitchen delaying production. Alternatively, the kitchen may produce dishes and there is a delay in serving so that, when received by the customers, the food is not at its best.

- **Role conflict.** A role is the expected pattern of behaviours associated with members occupying a particular position within the structure of the organisation. In practice, the manner in which people actually behave may not be consistent with their expected pattern of behaviour. Problems of role incompatibility and role ambiguity arise from inadequate, or inappropriate, role definition and can be a significant source of conflict.

- **Inequitable treatment.** A person's perception of unjust treatment, for example in the operation of human resource policies and practices or in reward and punishment systems, can lead to tension and conflict. For example, according to the equity theory of motivation the perception of inequity will motivate a person to take action to restore equity, including changes to inputs or outputs, or through acting on others. The issue of tipping and fairness of their allocation can frequently lead to tension within the working environment.

- **Violation of territory.** People tend to become attached to, and jealous of, their own 'territory' within work organisations: for example, to their own area of work, or to their own room, chair or parking space or 'their own' customers. They may also be jealous of what other people may have, such as access to information, or possibly group membership.[18] Ownership of territory may be **conferred formally**, for example by organisation charts, job descriptions or management decisions; it may be **established through procedures**, for example circulation lists or membership of committees; or it may **arise informally**, for example through group norms, tradition or perceived status symbols. The place where people choose to meet can have a significant symbolic value. For example, if a subordinate is summoned to a meeting in a manager's office this might be taken to mean that the manager is signalling higher status. If the manager chooses to meet at the subordinate's place of work, or on neutral territory, this may be a signal that the manager wishes to meet the subordinate as an equal. If a person's territory is violated this can lead to the possibility of retaliation and conflict.

- **Environmental change.** Changes in an organisation's external environment, such as shifts in demand, increased competition, government intervention, new technology or changing social values, can cause major areas of conflict.

Other potential sources of organisational conflict include:

- **individual** – such as attitudes, personality characteristics or particular personal needs, illness or stress;

- **group** – such as group skills, the informal organisation and group norms;

- **organisation** – such as communications, authority structure, leadership style, managerial behaviour;

- **the age gap** – as in relationships between older employees and younger managers, where experience is on one side and power on the other. Hart discusses how this can lead to conflict:

> The problem for the inexperienced manager in conflict with an older employee is that it is all too easy to label someone 'difficult' rather than intelligently trying to explore the reasons behind their behaviour. If steps are not taken to improve the relationship both manager and employee can end up feeling threatened and undermined.[19]

Strategies for managing conflict

Although a certain amount of organisational conflict may be seen as inevitable, there are a number of ways in which management can attempt to avoid the harmful effects of conflict. The strategies adopted will vary according to the nature and sources of conflict outlined above. Managing conflict takes time and effort, but attempting to establish a climate of mutual trust, consideration and respect is worthwhile.

- **Clarification of goals and objectives.** The clarification and continual refinement of goals and objectives, role definitions and performance standards will help to avoid misunderstandings and conflict. Focusing attention on superordinate goals that are shared by the parties in conflict may help to defuse hostility and lead to more cooperative behaviour.

- **Resource distribution.** Although it may not always be possible for managers to increase their allocated share of resources, they may be able to use imagination and initiative to help overcome conflict situations – for example, making a special case to higher management; being flexible in transferring funds between budget headings; delaying staff appointments in one area to provide more money for another area.

- **Human resource management policies and procedures.** Careful and detailed attention to just and equitable HRM policies and procedures may help to reduce areas of conflict (see the section on the equity theory of motivation in Chapter 7). Examples are job analysis; systems of reward and punishment; appeals, grievance and disciplinary procedures; training managers in coaching and negotiation skills.

- **Non-monetary rewards.** Where financial resources are limited, it may be possible to pay greater attention to non-monetary rewards. Examples are job design; more interesting, challenging or responsible work; increased delegation or empowerment; improved equipment; flexible working hours; attendance at courses or conferences; unofficial perks; or more relaxed working conditions.

- **Development of interpersonal/group process skills.** This may help engender a better understanding of one's own behaviour, the other person's point of view, communication processes and problem-solving. It may also assist people to work through conflict situations in a constructive manner. Where possible one should encourage addressing disputes early on a one-to-one basis.

- **Group activities.** Attention to the composition of groups and to factors that affect group cohesiveness may reduce dysfunctional conflict. Overlapping group membership, so that each group will have one member who is also a member of another group, and the careful selection of project teams or task forces for dealing with problems that affect more than one group, may also be beneficial. This ensures that each group has a wider view, and understanding, of how their work links with that of other groups.

- **Leadership and management.** A more participative and supportive style of leadership and managerial behaviour is likely to assist in conflict management – for example, showing an attitude of respect and trust; encouraging personal self-development; creating a work environment in which staff can work cooperatively. An open-door policy and early identification of potential causes of disputes may help avoid conflict.

- **Organisational processes.** Conflict situations may be reduced by attention to such features as the nature of the authority structure; work organisation; patterns of communication and sharing of information; democratic functioning of the organisation; avoidance of unnecessary adherence to bureaucratic procedures and official rules and regulations.

- **Socio-technical approach.** Viewing the organisation as a socio-technical system, in which psychological and social factors are developed, in keeping with structural and technical requirements, will help in reducing dysfunctional conflict.

Organisational stress

In addition to organisational conflict, a major and related influence on the working environment is the extent to which employees suffer from organisational stress. **Stress** is a complex and dynamic concept. It is a possible source of tension and frustration, and can arise through a number of interrelated influences on behaviour, including the individual, the group, and organisational and environmental factors. The nature of the hospitality industry makes it particularly prone to stress because employees are frequently required to work long, unsocial, hours in pressurised environments, coping with unforeseeable peaks and troughs of demand, and subsequent workload.

The Health and Safety Executive (HSE) defines stress as: 'The adverse reaction people have to excess pressure or other types of demands placed on them. There is clear distinction between pressure which can create a "buzz" and be a motivating factor and stress, which can occur when this pressure becomes excessive.'[20]

However, York contends that despite all the business-speak, people get seriously vague when it comes to definitions. He raises the question: **what is stress?** Is it a new name for an old-fashioned condition such as unhappiness or overwork, or is it peculiar to our uniquely pressured times? York suggests there is something in the idea that stress isn't just about hard work or unhappiness, but about conflict, confusion and frustration. It's about the anxiety generated by multi-tasking and balancing priorities; meeting contradictory demands; about knowing where to start; and papering over the cracks when you want to do too much.[21]

The effects of stress

An increasing number of surveys report perceived or actual increases in levels of stress and contend that stress at work is one of the biggest problems in European companies and one of the major adverse influences on the quality of working life and work performance. There have also been a number of highly publicised reports of successful legal claims based on the effects of stress.

Research by organisations such as the Health and Safety Executive have identified stress, anxiety and depression as among the most commonly reported illnesses, and wider research has also indicated that stress, brought about through work intensification and conflicts between home and work, is related to the risks of disease and ill-health.[22]

> The results of unrelieved stress on the individual and on business are worrying. The result may be higher accident rates, sickness absence, inefficiency, damaged relationships with clients and colleagues, high staff turnover, early retirement on medical grounds, and even premature death ... The cost of stress is huge. It is devastating to the individual and damaging to the business at a time when the need to control business costs and ensure an effective and healthy workforce is greater than ever. It is in everyone's interest to tackle the taboo on talking about emotional problems because it is this which inhibits individuals from seeking help.
>
> (Simon Armson, Chief Executive, The Samaritans)[23]

Is stress necessarily to be avoided?

The Yerkes – Dodson law, illustrated overleaf, shows their contention that a certain amount of stress is necessary to achieve optimal performance, but that once this point has been reached, increasing stress further causes a decrease in performance.

Berger and Brownell[24] cite Forbes' model which identifies that both low stress (underload) and high stress (overload) are non-productive, optimal performance being obtained at the point where the individual is moderately stressed. They suggest that an effective manager watches for signs that employees are operating under an acceptable level of stress.

The problem for the manager is identifying this acceptable level since it differs from person to person, and indeed, it differs for an individual from time to time and circumstance

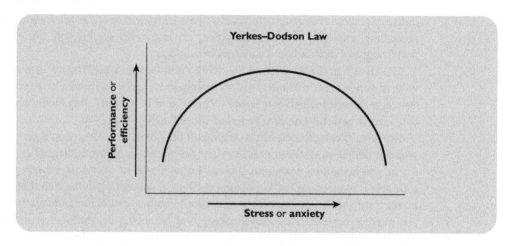

to circumstance. This means that what may be acceptable today may well be unacceptable, say, one month later. We could refer to this as 'felt stress' to indicate this variability in the effects.

Thus a certain amount of stress is not necessarily a bad thing; it may, arguably, even help promote a higher level of intensity and motivation to get work done. It is important to bear in mind, however, that stress is potentially very harmful, not only because it can be counterproductive to good performance, but, more importantly, because it can be physically and psychologically harmful to the individual (the earlier quote from The Samaritans' Chief Executive underlines this point). It must be borne in mind that employers do have a duty of care to their employees.

Table 9.1 details some of the different physical and psychological states and behaviours associated with the different levels of felt stress.

Whilst the above model talks of levels of stress, many would refer to **pressure** as a positive factor in achieving performance, only becoming **stress** at the overload phase. Thus, 'pressure' can be seen as a positive factor that may be harnessed to help people respond to a challenge and function more effectively. 'Stress' may be regarded as a continuous negative response arising from extreme pressure or other demands, and the individual's inability to cope.

Orpen also suggests that stress at work can be a positive thing. Just as there are circumstances when individuals may have too much stress, there are also circumstances when individuals may have too little stress for effective performance.[25] This view also appears

Table 9.1 Levels of felt stress

Underload	Optimal performance	Overload
Boredom	Exhilaration	Irritability
Accidents	Mental alertness	Accidents
Lethargy	High energy	Poor judgement
Alcoholism	Improved memory and recall	Diminished memory and recall
Absenteeism	Sharp perception	Absenteeism
Negativity	Calmness under pressure	Strained relationships
Erratic behaviour	Realistic analysis of problems	Increased errors

to be supported by Gwyther, who points out that although stress appears to have become public health enemy number one and is viewed as the culprit of myriad complaints, the term is bandied about far too readily and there is a need to stand back and attempt to get things into some sort of perspective. A measure of stress is natural. A degree of stress at work is no unhealthy thing and without it nothing would ever get done.[26]

However, it is important to bear in mind that although management may believe that a moderate level of stress can be a spur to increased work performance, employees are unlikely to perceive this in the same way and may dispute what is regarded as an acceptable level of stress or excessive pressure. As ACAS point out, whilst some amount of stress can be useful as a spur to motivation the key phrase in the HSE definition is 'adverse reaction'. This can include physical symptoms such as headaches, stomach problems and muscle tension, and mental symptoms such as anxiety and depression. These reactions can be extremely debilitating and result in reduced productivity, absenteeism and poor morale in the workplace.[27] As we have suggested above, the manager needs to be sensitive to the point where, for an individual, the healthy pressure turns into unhealthy stress.

Causes of stress

Whatever the effects, it is generally acknowledged that stress is potentially part of everyday working life. It occurs for a variety of reasons, including individual differences and types of personality; occupation and actual nature of the job, whether working in the private or public sector; and organisational conflict (discussed earlier in this chapter).

Other sources of stress at work include the following:

- Restructuring of organisations and reductions in staffing levels resulting from demands for improved business competitiveness and lower operating costs. This has placed greater pressures on remaining staff and resulted in a growing number of work-related health problems, work stress and a less efficient workforce.

- The long-hours culture, increased workloads and work intensification, together with unreasonable deadlines.

- Excessive rules and regulations, and greater bureaucratic burdens.

- Developments in information and communications technology (ICT) that mean staff are far more constantly and easily contactable and expected to deliver everything faster. This can lead to greater pressure on individuals, a reluctance to switch off and a blurring between work and home life.

- Organisational changes such as redundancies and the loss of key members of staff that place extra demands on staff.

- Interpersonal relationships at work, especially with immediate superiors; poor communications.

- Lack of delegation and autonomy over control of work.

- Organisation structure and role relationships. Lack of clarity about expected patterns of behaviour, or role conflict, is a potential source of stress. In the case of customer service, Jamison suggests that if there is a conflict between the requirements of a customer and the requirements of the organisation, this will induce unhelpful behaviour as a result of stress.[28]

Berger and Brownell suggest the growing incidence of stress in the hospitality industry is mainly caused by 'increasing competiveness in business and inability of most managers to manage stress in their workplaces'.[29]

Increasing competitiveness is a feature of modern life and the modern working environment. Managers need to attempt to control stress in their working lives and, through awareness of the nature of stress and its consequences, attempt to control the causes of stress in the working lives of their staff.

Cultural differences

To what extent do causes of stress vary according to different cultures? There is some evidence to suggest that the incidence of stress does not vary noticeably among different cultures. For example, Type A personalities (discussed in Chapter 2) exhibit similar levels of stress across the United Kingdom, Hungary, Italy, Israel and the United States.[30] Another study of a diverse set of countries across the Anglo world, China and Latin America suggests that stress caused by long work hours can be mitigated by a strong social support network such as families or friends.[31]

Exhibit 9.1 Stress in the fast food sector in Malaysia

In the following study of the fast food industry in Malaysia, Ryan et al.[32] discuss the link with stress and staff turnover. He suggests the intention to leave is influenced by friends, and is also influenced by the Malaysian Islamic culture. He identifies that friendship ties and being part of a team often encouraged individuals to stay with an organisation. On the other hand, job stress and 'burnout' were frequently important factors in the decision to leave.

Firth et al.[33] suggest that job stress is strongly related to role ambiguity, role conflict, work overload and work – life balance.

From this brief summary it is suggested that an intention to leave is related to job stress. Factors that militate against stress include peer support systems, levels of commitment, both situational and continuing, and feelings of being positively recognised for contributions made. Items that may create stress relate to poor management, for example a lack of clear instructions, a location not found to be satisfactory and, in Malaysia, an insensitivity towards the religious needs of those of the Islamic faith.

Consequently the literature review raised a series of propositions that informed the research, and these included:

- A positive relationship exists between feelings of being stressed and intention to leave a job.[34]

- A negative relationship exists between feelings of work group support on the one hand and feeling stressed on the other, that is, if a respondent feels that they are working within a supportive social setting this reduces the intention to leave a job.[35,36]

- Those with least experience and younger years may be more likely to show uncertainty as to job commitment than those with more experience.[37,38]

- Perceived differences between the roles of being an employee and family-related responsibilities may lead to higher intentions to leave because of the nature of shift work in the industry.[39]

- Role ambiguity may be a source of stress and thereby contribute to a wish to leave a job (e.g. Firth et al. used role ambiguity as a measure of job stress, as do Derry and Shaw).[40]

- The higher the level of positive managerial recognition of employee contribution, the higher

---

the self-esteem, and thus the lower the intention to leave (Leidner, 1993;[41] Silva, 2006[42]).

Within the Malaysian fast food industry it is suggested that, as it is 20 per cent of staff approximately who may be susceptible to higher intentions to leave, to simply work on such human resource characteristics without reference to a more careful cost analysis of the implications of the alternative modes of recruitment and selection intention would be inadequate. In countries such as the US the fast food industry has come to play a role where, for many young Americans, it is their first experience of structured employment, and while not subsequently seeking a career in the industry, and only having fulfilled a temporary role within a given workplace, it might be argued that the majority have met the franchisee's expectations and gained disciplines that subsequently stand the employee in good stead in future work. While it is conventional to argue that high labour turnover is something to be avoided and to be addressed through staff empowerment schemes and knowledge systems that disseminate understandings from and to all staff levels, it is important to understand the routinised nature of the fast food industry and the brutal fact that not all posts possess intrinsically high levels of satisfaction for many workers. Hence, to conclude, future studies may have to consider wider social frameworks when interviewing past workers in the fast food industry, and an assessment of how work discipline skills are translated into other arenas if a better understanding of labour turnover is to emerge.

Critical review and reflection

To what extent do you feel that the above Malaysian example is applicable to the fast food outlets in the UK?

Is job stress, as a factor causing individuals to leave fast food organisations in the UK, more or less important than the researchers suggest?

Should fast food organisations in the UK be concerned about high labour turnover or accept it as a characteristic of the job?

Coping with stress

There are a number of measures by which individuals and organisations can attempt to reduce the causes and harmful effects of stress. There are also many suggested techniques to help individuals bring stress under control – for example, changing one's viewpoint, identifying causes of distress, effective time management, expanding one's social network, laughing and telling jokes, relaxation training, working on stress reduction and appreciating that some stress can be useful. However, there are not always easy remedies for stress and much depends upon the personality of the individual. Techniques such as relaxation therapy may help some people, although not others, but still tend to address the symptoms rather than the cause. It could be argued that this is unsurprising.

Since there is such variation in the effects of pressure and stress on individuals, it is easy to see that dealing with stress is an issue for the affected individuals themselves. However, as we have seen, it is the individual's reaction to the work situation and the actions, policies and procedures of organisations and their managers which causes unacceptable and unhealthy levels of stress. Therefore it is necessary for organisations to consider the nature and extent of stress-inducing hazards.

As Vine and Williamson point out, stress-inducing hazards are hard to pin down, much less eliminate. It is important to know how people feel about the things that cause them stress as well as which 'stressors' are most common in a particular industry and occupation. Human resource policy should include several stress management building blocks within the organisation structure, including management education, employee education, counselling and support, critical incident briefing, and good sound management.[43] The CIPD identify that organisations also need to give greater attention to training, support and counselling and to the work organisation and job design.[44]

Effective communications and conversation

Effective two-way communications at all levels of the organisation are clearly important in helping to reduce or overcome the level of stress. Staff should feel able to express their true feelings openly and know they will be listened to. However, in addition to good communications, Reeves refers to the importance of conversation for maintaining relationships and suggests a case for a conversation culture. The ability to hold good-quality conversations is becoming a core organisational and individual skill. Unlike communication, conversations are intrinsically creative and roam freely across personal issues, corporate gossip and work projects. 'Conversations are a defence against stress and other mental health problems. People with good social relationships at work are much less likely to be stressed or anxious.'[45]

Reducing uncertainty

Informing members of staff in the first place about what is happening, especially at times of major change, involving them proactively in the change process, and allowing people to feel in control and exercise their own discretion reduces uncertainty and can help minimise the potential for stress.

Supportive work environment

Managers can do much to create a psychologically supportive and healthy work environment. Treating people with consideration, respect and trust, giving full recognition and credit, getting to know members of staff as individuals and placing emphasis on end results can all help to reduce stress. Managers should attempt to be role models and through their language and body language indicate to others that they are dealing effectively with their own work pressures.

HSE's stress management standards

As part of its 'Fit for Work, Fit for Life, Fit for Tomorrow' strategic programme, the HSE is working with businesses on health issues, including work-related stress, to enable them to be managed more effectively in the workplace. With input from a range of businesses, professional bodies and trade unions, the HSE has developed a new approach to tackle this problem. The Management Standards for Work-related Stress encourage employers and employees to work in partnership to adopt agreed standards of good management practice to prevent stress at an organisational level.

The adoption of the Management Standards is a key element in bringing about reductions in worker ill-health absence. The Standards provide a framework that allows an assessment to be made about the degree of exposure to six key areas of work design – demands, control, support, relationships, role and change – which, if not properly managed, are associated with poor health and well-being, lower productivity and increased sickness absence.

European Union agreement on stress

The European Commission magazine reports that within the EU, work-related stress can be approached on different levels – individual worker, work organisation, national and EU level. Aside from the legal obligations, stress is a problem for the individual, their work organisation and society, and work-related stress problems are increasing. The European social partners have negotiated a framework agreement to identify and manage problems related to work stress. The agreement identifies anti-stress measures dealing primarily with management and communications; ensuring adequate management support for individuals and teams; matching responsibility and control over work; improving work organisation and processes, working conditions and environment.

Critical review and reflection

'Organisations need to pay more attention to work factors, such as job design, and work intensification rather than attempting to change individual employees' psychologies, so that they can cope with what the organisation sees as legitimate pressure.'

What are your views? Do people really feel stressed at work? Is it their responsibility or due to the way that their organisations manage the work?

Managing challenging situations in the hospitality industry

Management of people in any environment will bring challenges. The hospitality industry possibly has more problems than many others. These problems arise because of a number of factors. These include long hours, often in excess of 65 hours per week,[46] alongside relatively low pay which is partly due to the fact that many in the industry are part-time and work few hours; low rates of pay, frequently the legal minimum; a pressurised working environment; along with a highly transient workforce, often with particular social issues. These and other problems provide hospitality managers with serious challenges.

Management's key responsibility in any organisation is to ensure that the organisational objectives are achieved. At the same time, management has a duty of care to all of its employees. These two key responsibilities can be difficult to reconcile, particularly when dealing with vulnerable people.

Challenging issues

The essential nature of the hospitality industry is that it is people-intensive, and customers require the people providing service, for which they are paying, to be available when required. It is also very competitive and price-sensitive, which means that organisations must keep firm control of wage costs if they are to survive. Taken together, this forces managements to use all of their resources, but particularly their human resources, efficiently. In this sense 'efficiently' means maximising output, including quality as well as quantity, whilst minimising cost.

Managements' attempts to be efficient in their use of labour clearly require work intensification, if they are to achieve their targets and organisational objectives, which can militate against the second key responsibility – the duty of care for their employees.

For managers to achieve their targets, they need to attempt to ensure that everyone is under sufficient pressure to maintain optimal output, whilst being aware that too much pressure can lead to overload. As has been noted earlier, judging when pressure becomes unwelcome stress is extremely difficult and there will be times when, under extreme pressure themselves, managers will demand too much and cause consequent health and performance problems for the people they manage.

Staff working under these conditions may feel that the situation is too demanding and seek alternative employment. But where better alternatives are unavailable, if they are to deal with the unwelcome situation, they may develop their own coping mechanisms.

Murray-Gibbons and Gibbons'[47] research indicates that chefs' five major coping responses for dealing with occupational stress are under/overeating; not exercising; drinking; ignoring stress; and smoking. Berger and Brownell[48] identify the major behavioural consequences of organisational stress in the hospitality industry as being eating disorders, increased smoking, alcohol and drug abuse, violent tendencies and accident proneness.

Alcohol abuse

As indicated above, alcohol abuse is a problem in the hospitality industry. In certain jobs, individuals may be working long hours, unsupervised, and can suffer from overload at some times and underload at others. In the latter situation, and where alcohol is being served, there is both reason for the behaviour (the individual may be bored or stressed) and opportunity (alcohol is readily available).

The consumption of alcoholic beverages is an integral part of many sectors of the hospitality industry.[49] Staff frequently turn to alcohol in response to the long hours encouraging a source of quick relaxation after work, and in response to the pressurised work environment encountered in the industry. The culture amongst kitchen staff, for example, almost encourages the consumption of alcohol. It is readily available for use in cooking. It is often seen as 'normal' to drink during work hours: '. . . *booze worked best of all because it was part of the industry. Chefs drank and when I drank I felt as good as anyone else*'.[50,51]

Not only is the consumption of alcohol a potential health risk, it can lead to accidents and other behavioural consequences. In some cases these consequences can be extremely damaging to the individual, to others, and to the organisation. In particular, alcohol addiction can completely ruin people's lives. *'Catering is like any other industry – you will encounter those with addiction issues, but statistically, like professional athletes, people in the catering industry show a higher propensity to the disease.'*[52]

Critical review and reflection

Peter Kay of the Ark Foundation[53] regularly speaks to students regarding dealing with alcohol and drug abuse in the industry. He often poses the question: 'If you had an excellent chef who produced excellent product at the correct gross profit, always turns up to work, always delivers a good product, but you are aware he takes illegal drugs, how would you manage the situation?'

Consider this scenario – how would you respond? Would your response differ if this chef was continually drinking heavily?

Clearly each individual must take responsibility for any abuse of alcohol, but at the same time the organisation cannot entirely escape responsibility for the pressure that contributes to the behaviour, the culture in which such behaviour is condoned, any lack of controls on alcohol availability, and failure to clearly specify and uphold appropriate policies and procedures. Strategies need to be developed, by human resource departments and/or senior management, and put into place. It is the responsibility of line managers to ensure that these policies are enforced. Enlightened managers need to address these issues through the use of policies including a clear disciplinary procedure.[54]

As the people who work with the staff on a daily basis, it will be primarily the line managers' responsibility to ensure that the problems are faced and dealt with properly. CIPD's suggestions for organisations and managers include:

- providing clear rules on the use of alcohol
- providing awareness training
- treating an individual's problem with alcohol as an illness requiring support
- ultimately utilising the disciplinary procedure.

Critical review and reflection

'It's all very well for the employer to try to help the alcoholic, or near alcoholic, but surely if people want to smoke or overeat, that is up to them?'

Do you agree? To what extent do you think that the problems are contributed to by the employer and what might an employer do to protect the health of its employees in these areas?

An organisation may find that a new employee has a drug or alcohol problem. Perhaps the person is attracted to the job because of the relative ease of access to drugs and/or alcohol that the working environment provides. An employee may develop problems, partly due to the stress of the job and the opportunities for abuse that working in the hospitality industry offers. In any event, the manager needs to be aware of the problem and deal with it promptly, for the good of the organisation, the individual and other staff and guests.

Peter Kay suggests that managers need to be aware of the following signs that may indicate there is a problem:

- unexplained mood swings
- paranoia – some users feel that they're being persecuted or that people are out to get them
- anxious to leave work (before the bars shut)
- unexplained theft, such as stock loss from the bar
- unusual amount of alcohol ordered for cooking
- close relationships between bar staff and chefs
- severe upward improvement in mood if returning to work after a break or split shift
- phoning in sick on a regular basis, more often than not on Mondays
- blaming others for mistakes.[55]

Bullying

Bullying can occur in any context in which human beings interact with each other; it is the continuous harassment of another individual and can take the form of verbal, emotional or physical abuse. In general terms, the bully is in a position of perceived strength, or is more powerful than the victim. This power imbalance may be caused by many factors but in the case of bullying at work, it often takes the form of hierarchical power.

In recent years the subject of bullying in the workplace has become an important focus of attention. Bullying in the hospitality industry, notably in the kitchens of prestigious establishments, has become a particular cause for comment and concern. The somewhat macho culture, publicised and to an extent glamourised by high-profile 'television chefs', has come in for particular criticism. 'Several chefs have also claimed that giving and receiving abuse is part of the socialisation process that creates the "hardiness" needed to function in a commercial kitchen or restaurant.'[56]

This culture, far from receiving justifiable admiration, is surely misplaced. 'Bullying is not just an employee health issue: it is a business issue, as it leads to poor morale and under performance' (Cooper[57]).

While it is the chefs who tend to be accused of bullying, for anyone to engage in institutional bullying it requires the support and, at least tacit, approval of managers. This is therefore a managerial issue of concern. A survey reported in *Personnel Today* suggested that over a third (35 per cent) of hospitality workers believe their bosses actively condone bullying and harassment.[58]

What is workplace bullying?

It may be offensive, intimidatory, insulting or malicious behaviour and can involve workplace colleagues who, for some, or no, reason 'pick on' one of their fellow workers. In this case it is the power of the group that is abused. But it may also be a managerial abuse of power, where a manager, or other person in a position of authority, misuses that power through one of the behaviours referred to above, in order to achieve legitimate or illegitimate goals.

Bloisi and Hoel,[59] talking of workplace bullying, quote Einarsen *et al.*

> Bullying at work means harassing, offending, socially excluding someone or negatively affecting someone's work tasks. . . . A conflict cannot be called bullying if the incident is an isolated event or if two parties of approximately equal 'strength' are in conflict.[60]

However, this seems problematic, depending upon the severity of the incident and whether there is an implied threat of a further attack at some time in the future.

The effects of bullying are well known; they include poor morale, lower performance, stress, increased staff turnover.

Bullying in commercial kitchens

There is debate regarding the scope of bullying in kitchens.

The 'macho' kitchen culture has been in place for many years. Auguste Escoffier, the famous early twentieth century chef, is said to have stated that commitment is vital and that working long hours can demonstrate this commitment. It is not unusual for chefs to work 80 hours per week and, somehow, this has become an accepted norm. Working shorter hours is seen by some as a sign of weakness.

Bloisi and Hoel[61] point out that the pressure of work in hot crowded kitchens, the lack of managerial and supervisory training for chefs, the organisational setting of a commercial kitchen and the fragmentation of the industry with high labour turnover all encourage a culture that fosters 'bullying'-type behaviour. To this one could add managerial acceptance of the legitimacy of this behaviour as another factor.

Furthermore there is the factor of imbalance of power. The nature of the staff employed in kitchens is such that they may feel vulnerable and lack confidence. In times of recession fear of job loss prevents staff from complaining. They may even be illegally employed and fear deportation.

Research has shown that part of the socialisation of chefs starts in colleges, instilling a culture of condoning, even encouraging, bullying. Chef lecturers instil the culture of the macho environment through what could, by some, be considered abuse.[62]

The effects of bullying in the catering industry

Bullying is generally unacceptable on moral grounds as well as being bad for business. Johns and Menzel,[63] in their article on kitchen violence, point out that workplace bullying can lead to adverse physical and psychological effects, difficult relationships, alcoholism and heavy smoking, all of which combine to produce stress and reduce job satisfaction. In turn, increasing staff turnover and absenteeism reduce productivity through low morale.

Suggestions for combating these problems include:

- providing clear anti-bullying policies that make it clear to staff that they should feel able to report the occurrence of bullying without fear of reprisals;[64]
- tackling the issue on a national scale, involving all stakeholders in the industry;
- publicising and raising awareness of the issue and its social consequences;
- improving working conditions, to reduce physical stress;
- reducing overall hours, with fewer split shifts.[65]

Control

In earlier discussion of the role of the manager, attention was drawn to the motivation of staff, along with the benefits of trust and empowerment. However, managers cannot rely upon their staff to always do the right thing, no matter how well motivated they may be. There needs to be a measure of control to ensure that all staff perform as required, and that each person's efforts are compatible with each other and the requirements of the organisation. Thus, control systems for the regulation of behaviour are seen as a necessity in most work environments, despite control often having an emotive connotation and being interpreted in a negative manner to suggest direction or command by the giving of orders. Baum [66] draws attention to the conflict between empowering staff to provide the increasingly individualised service required by guests, which is best provided by an empowered and motivated staff, and the increased standardisation needed today to control costs in the industry.

No matter how far an organisation goes in empowering staff, and no matter how effectively managers delegate to their subordinates, managers remain accountable to their superiors for the conduct of activities in their areas. For this reason, managers must exercise control over the actions and decisions of subordinates and this requires that they monitor the behaviour and actions of staff in order to ensure they maintain the required level of performance.

> The essence of the delegation problem lies in the trust – control dilemma. The dilemma is that in any one managerial situation, the sum of trust–control is always constant. The trust is the trust that the subordinate feels that the manager has in him. The control is the control that the manager has over the work of the subordinate. [67]

Control is therefore an integral part of a system of delegation. It is necessary to ensure the effective coordination of activities and to maintain the chain of command. (Figure 9.1) There is a risk, when setting up control mechanisms within an organisation, that by so doing the organisation will stifle enthusiasm and innovation – the very things that make the difference, particularly in a service-based organisation. For example, the waiter serving

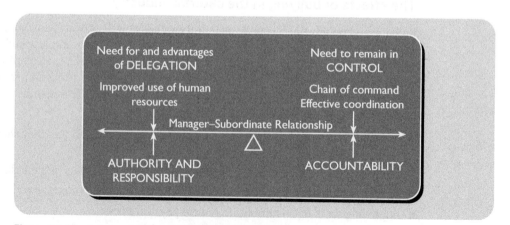

Figure 9.1 The balance between delegation and control

a customer needs to empathise with that person, unlike a person working in manufacturing who needs to ensure that the product being made is of uniform shape, size and quality. The difficulty for hospitality managers is, through appropriate control, to ensure that work is carried out in the proper manner, rules are followed and standards maintained, while allowing as much autonomy as possible to the staff to do the job in their own way. Simply put, one could say that staff need to be **told what** needs to be done and, as far as possible, staff should **decide how** to do it.

There are a number of areas where it is necessary for the organisation to establish rules and ensure that they are followed absolutely. Examples of these would include matters of health and safety, law, and security. In addition to these areas, the hospitality organisation will need to establish further rules, to ensure that staff maintain the organisation's standards of conduct and behaviour.

According to McKenna, codes of conduct can constitute a form of control:

> Developing and distributing a code of conduct is a form of control that sets out the rules of behaviour and values with which an organisation's senior managers expect their subordinates will conform. Such a code will only be accepted if subordinates observe that managers at all levels live this code in their actions, beliefs and involvement in collective learning.[68]

Pilferage and theft

Critical review and reflection

'The pay and conditions in the hospitality industry are so poor that staff are bound to steal from their employer. Taking food, towels, glasses, bottles of wine is all part of normal practice. It is no worse than office staff using company stationery or making phone calls on company phones and is minor compared with excesses in other sectors.'

To what extent do you agree with this statement?

In Chapter 2 we looked at employees and the psychological contract. Briefly, this is an extension of the normal wages for work, whereby the employee gives up time and supplies effort in exchange for financial reward. The psychological contract involves the employee committing to the organisation, making additional effort, showing flexibility and so on, beyond what that employee is paid for and, in exchange, the person expects a degree of consideration and respect, maybe trust, maybe flexibility on the part of the organisation. Each individual will have their own version of the psychological contract based on an unspoken calculus of what seems fair to them.

This works well, as it covers those little, unexpected situations and often reinforces the social bonds between employee and manager. Problems arise when, for some reason, the employee feels that the psychological contract is unfair, or has been broken by the employer in some way. The employee might then take some compensatory action.

There could be problems with the wage–work bargain, also. If the employee feels that this is unfair then, as previously discussed in the section on equity theory in Chapter 7, again that person might well take some action to either reduce effort or increase the reward received. Mars and Mitchell suggest that where employees feel under-rewarded, significant pilfering can take place.[69]

Another factor that can lead to small-scale, and sometimes large-scale, pilfering is that 'everybody is doing it'. Group pressures can legitimise theft, and sometimes put pressure on individuals to commit it. (See Chapter 8 on group norms.)

The situation throughout the hospitality industry, of long hours, low pay for many, and a lack of continuous supervision, almost encourages such practices by giving reasons and opportunities for them. Baum indicates that these practices are endemic, suggesting that far from taking minor theft seriously, management's attitude is as follows: 'fiddles, pilferage can be seen to be tacitly accepted within tourism hospitality and leisure as part of the overall package and arguably a justification for suppressing formal and taxable pay'.[70]

Mars and Mitchell[71] suggest that this attitude increases management's power by laying down parameters within which fiddles are acceptable, using them to redress the balance in the wage – work bargain whilst, at the same time, providing them with a ready-made reason for dismissal should a 'fiddling' employee displease them.

However, Boella and Goss-Turner question the importance of the issue: 'such practices must be seen in proper perspective, bearing in mind that some other trades and professions provide vastly more lucrative opportunities than those provided in the hospitality industry'.[72]

Whatever the situation, it is an issue for management to manage.

CASE STUDY 9.2

'Just a pack of butter'

Lily had worked in the still-room of a large city-centre 4-star hotel for 16 years. Her job involved preparing teas, coffee, toast, butter – the usual range of still-room items. The work was boring and monotonous but she turned up regularly at 6.00 am every morning to ensure coffee and tea were made and that everything was ready for the busy breakfast service.

She was a reliable and conscientious worker, and over the 16 years had taken very little time off sick. She was paid the minimum legal hourly rate. (She lived in a small council house with her family.)

It was not unusual for staff to help themselves from the kitchen; after all, much food was wasted, with toast and butter thrown away. Lily was often asked to send tea, coffee and bread up to the hotel manager in the flat where he lived with his family. It was clearly acceptable for people to take hotel food while at work, so like everyone else, Lily helped herself to tea, coffee, bread and butter while at work. On most days she also took a little bread and butter and tea bags home for her family.

This 'perk' continued until a new manager joined the hotel. Managers tended to change every three or four years so Lily had worked for several different managers, without any serious changes to terms and conditions, or ways of working. The manager had been given instructions to address the issue of a low gross profit on food. He knew he needed to take strict action to avoid food pilferage and shortly after on his arrival he instigated bag checks as staff left the kitchen.

One day Lily's bag was checked and a loaf of bread, butter and teabags were found in her bag. Lily could not deny she was taking the food home. She was dismissed.

Case study 9.2 *(continued)*

Questions

1 What issues are raised with this case?

2 How fair was the dismissal?

3 If there had been a recognised trade union, would the outcome have been different?

4 What are the ethical issues raised in this case?

5 More generally, how can pilferage within hotels be more closely controlled?

In the summer of 2010, a number of major hospitality organisations, including Starbucks, Costa Coffee, EAT, Compass Group, Greggs and Harrods, set up The Cafe, Dining and Hospitality Loss Prevention Forum. The aim was to share best practice, in a bid to tackle crime and the losses felt by restaurants, cafes and hospitality venues. A year later, the Institute of Hospitality reported on the Forum's attempts to deal with theft by employees.

Exhibit 9.2 Employee theft

Summary of Findings and Suggestions of the Cafe, Dining and Hospitality Loss Prevention Forum, Summer 2011[64]

- 10 per cent of employees will find ways to steal. 10 per cent will never steal and the remaining 80 per cent may, if given the opportunity.
- Theft is usually an emotional act that involves self-justification and can occur at any level in a business.
- Employee theft is a concern that needs to be managed on a daily basis.
- it is not necessarily the lower paid staff who are the main cause of concern (for one company the majority of employees who stole (80 per cent) were supervisors).
- It is acknowledged, however, that lower levels of pay could result in a highly transient workforce whereby employees felt it was both easy to join and easy to leave.
- It is believed that increasing basic wages would not reduce employee theft.
- Creating a positive culture of belonging is more important in mitigating employee theft than the level of pay.
- However it is noted that the business with both the best family-style culture and the best levels of pay had the lowest levels of employee theft.[73]

Critical review and reflection

What might be the benefits of installing electronic surveillance systems in key areas of a hotel/other hospitality outlet?

What implications might this have for the balance between trust and control, and how might that affect the relationships between managers and staff?

Different approaches to management control

Different approaches to organisation and management illustrate contrasting approaches to the nature of management control. The **classical approach** places emphasis on the technical requirements of the organisation and tends to support a high level of control as necessary for efficiency. It may be recalled, for example, that a criticism of scientific management is the high level of management control over workers and the actual process of work.

Those writers who place emphasis on a **human relations approach** and the social needs of individuals see a high level of control as self-defeating. It produces a negative response, increases internal conflict and results only in short-term improvement in performance.[74] Control should not be seen therefore only in the sense that it suggests close and constant supervision or as a constraint on freedom of action by the individual. In terms of the **systems approach**, control relates both to the measurement of organisational effectiveness, and to the inputs and series of activities by which inputs are transformed into outputs. Control emphasises the interrelationships among the different sub-systems of the establishment.

The **contingency approach** views management control as an organisational variable. The most appropriate methods of control will depend upon the contingencies of particular situations.

Improvement in performance

Control can be interpreted in different ways. It is far-reaching and can be manifested in a number of different forms. Control systems can be concerned with general results, specific actions or day-to-day operational activities, with an evaluation of overall performance of the establishment as a whole or with particular parts of it.

Whatever the different forms of management control, the underlying feature is checking and reviewing progress towards the attainment of stated objectives. The whole purpose of management control is the improvement in performance. Lord Forte, for example, made the following point: 'we have an intensive system of controls. The word is often misinterpreted. I do not mean controls in the sense of cutting down on quality, but of setting standards and seeing that the operation conforms'.[75]

Control can be seen to operate at both the individual and the organisational level (Figure 9.2).

The individual level

At the individual level members of staff want to know what is expected of them, and if they are performing well and in the right areas. Control is a basis for training needs, the motivation to achieve standards and for the development of individuals. Whenever a person inquires 'I would like to know how well I am doing', this can be seen in effect as asking for control. An effective control system places emphasis on the exchange of information, and feedback on actual results against planned targets.[76]

The concept of ultimate responsibility gives rise to the need for effective management control. Managers must exercise control over the actions and decisions of subordinates and be kept informed of the relevance and quality of their work. Managers need to monitor the behaviour and actions of staff in order to ensure they maintain a satisfactory standard of performance.

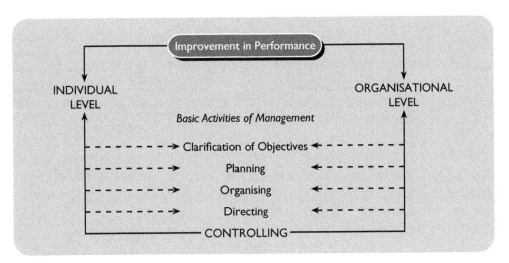

Figure 9.2 The operation of management control

The organisational level

At the organisational level control completes the cycle of managerial activities. It involves reviewing the planning and organisation of the work of the establishment, and guiding and regulating the activities of staff. Management control is concerned with organisational effectiveness and determining whether the objectives of the establishment are being achieved.

The purpose of organisational control is to prevent impropriety, to monitor the use of resources, to check up on the progress of work and provide feedback on the success or failure of operations. Control is an inherent characteristic of the work situation and an important feature of the people–organisation relationship.

Within a service industry such as hospitality the demand for quality assurance places particular emphasis on the importance of effective control procedures. (This is considered in more detail in Chapter 10.)

> Control is also an important management function, no less important in the delivery of quality than in other aspects of management activity. Indeed, to the extent that the essence of quality is consistency, most of the delivery of quality is a matter of good control.[77]

Main stages in control systems

Whatever the nature of control in any specific organisation, and whatever form it takes, there are five essential elements in an organisational control system (see Figure 9.3). They are:

- planning what is desired to be achieved;
- establishing standards of performance;
- monitoring actual achievement;
- comparing the actual achievement to the planned achievement;
- rectifying any deviation and taking corrective action.

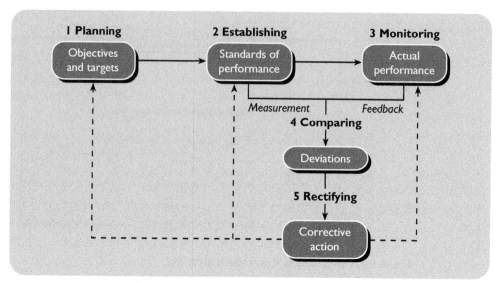

Figure 9.3 The five essential stages of organisational control

Clear objectives and targets

Planning provides the framework against which the process of control takes place. It is important that staff understand their duties and responsibilities, and know exactly what is required of them. Objectives and targets should be stated clearly in order to establish defined standards of performance against which the level of achievement can be determined. This requires realistic means of measurement, which wherever possible should be stated in quantitative terms.

The importance of feedback

There must be some system of feedback and reporting of information in order to monitor progress and review results. The information should be accurate, relevant, timely and easily understood by all concerned. It should be in a form which enables management to compare actual performance against planned targets, and which highlights any deviations. This information should be fed back to the staff concerned to let them know how well they are doing.

   If it is to be effective, feedback should identify probable causes of any deviations and provide the basis for decisions on taking any corrective action. This might involve consideration of what can or should be done to improve the level of actual performance, revisions to the original objectives and targets, or adjustments to the standards of performance or the operation of the control system itself. Feedback and review should be a continual part of a management control system.

Financial and accounting controls

Arguably the most important part of any management control system, financial and accounting systems are especially important in the hospitality industry.[78] The reasons for this are easy to understand.

- The stewardship of financial resources and the need to demonstrate value for money is of vital concern to the organisation. Control systems are often geared to highlighting the easily identifiable performance of sales, costs and profits.

- Organisational aims, objectives and targets are often expressed in financial terms and measured in terms of profitability. Results are measured and reported in financial terms.

- Money is quantifiable and a precise unit of measurement. It is easily understood, and is often used as a common denominator and as a basis for comparison.

- Financial limits are easy to apply as a measure of control or limit to authority, and are easy to relate to. We have seen, for example, that control is a necessary part of delegation. A manager might delegate to a subordinate the authority to incur expenditure on certain items up to a given financial limit.

Managers rely on an accurate information system as a basis for control and this information is often expressed in financial terms. Management accounting tools such as budgets, ratio analysis and standard costing provide helpful information for control of the operations of the various departments and activities of the hotel. As Venison, for example, emphasises: 'the production of correct and up-to-date accounts is absolutely vital to the success of any hotel venture ... As an hotel manager ... you have a primary duty to ensure that somebody is effectively handling the accounts function'.[79]

Attention to behavioural factors

There is of course nothing wrong with the use of financial or accounting systems of control. The important point is the manner in which such controls are applied and their effects on the behaviour of staff. Consideration must be given to the behavioural factors and the motivation for staff to improve their performance.[80]

Accounting control systems such as internal audit, management by exception and budgetary control tend to operate in a negative way and to report only on unfavourable performance, or on variances which may have adverse consequences. As a result there is no specific recognition from management and only a limited sense of achievement for favourable performance. There is little, if any, positive motivation. Budgetary control may be perceived as a means of exerting pressure on staff and can also be seen as imposing restriction on individual freedom of action.[81]

As with other forms of control, financial and accounting systems have positive as well as negative effects. If control systems are to be successful in leading to improved performance, they should be designed and implemented in a constructive and rewarding way. To do this, they must take account of the individual, social and organisational factors which determine people's patterns of behaviour.

Critical review and reflection

Why are financial and accounting systems of control so important to a hospitality organisation?

To what extent and in what ways can a concentration on financial information and targets cause problems for a hospitality organisation?

◼ Concern for the whole process of management

Whilst it is essential for hospitality organisations to focus on profitability, in the past there has tended to be a concentration on short-term cost-consciousness. However, management control embraces far more than just financial or accounting considerations. It should be concerned with the whole process of management: with the extent to which the aims and objectives of the hospitality organisation are being achieved and with improvement in performance.

Control includes consideration of such factors as quality, judgement, customer satisfaction, social responsibilities, and the human factor and the effective management of people. Regrettably, however, it appears that the industry has given little attention to evaluating the contribution and worth of its human resources or to accounting for the value of its employees.[82]

Synopsis

- Conflict at work is a reality. It is commonplace within the hospitality industry, at individual, group and unit level. An explanation of the nature and outcome of conflict can be related to contrasting perspectives of work organisations. It is important that the manager is aware of and can understand the reasons for, and implications of, conflict.

- One outcome of conflict can be the manifestation of stress in the working environment. The hospitality industry working environment is particularly prone to inducing stress in the workforce and management, due to the pressure placed on people by the particular requirements of the work. It is important that the manager appreciates the sources of stress, and is conscious of the relationship between stress and performance. The manager also needs to be aware of how individuals react differently to stress and adjust the management style according to the needs of individual members of staff.

- The stresses of working in the hospitality industry, and the working environment, tend to make individuals vulnerable to a number of unhealthy and/or dangerous coping strategies, such as over/undereating, smoking and drinking. A subject of particular concern in the hospitality industry is that of alcohol and drug abuse; this is not only counterproductive to the organisational objectives, but also causes short-term and long-term damage to people's health. The hospitality manager needs to be aware of the duty of care that organisations have towards their employees and take that into account in the management of the employees.

- Bullying is seen to be an issue of particular concern in the hospitality industry. The nature of the industry means that there is considerable pressure on managers and staff to work long hours, and to deliver a quality service on demand. There has been a 'macho' culture in some kitchens and an acceptance of, and, some would say, a requirement for, bullying. Whilst the conditions in some kitchens are indisputably difficult and may lead to stress and short tempers, bullying has to be seen as counterproductive to achieving the organisational objectives. Managers need to be aware of the costs to the organisation of condoning a bullying culture, and the costs to the individuals involved. They need to be conscious of the duty of care to employees and address the culture and incidents of bullying and take appropriate action.

- Pilferage and theft is a serious problem in the hospitality industry as a whole. It occurs at all levels of organisations. It may, however, be seen as an explicable reaction to low pay, and poor terms and conditions of service. Management may informally set limits on what are the acceptable limits of pilferage. Management may also condone the behaviour as compensation for poor wages, reserving the right to dismiss employees whom they may wish to lose for other reasons.

- Individuals produce the performance that enables an organisation to attain the organisational objectives. Current thinking is that to enable individuals to produce their best performance they need to be empowered. On the other hand, it is necessary for managers to control the employees, so that the workforce, as a whole, attains the organisational objectives. Managers need to find the right balance between trusting subordinates and controlling them.

- Financial and accounting control systems are key to an organisation, none more so than a hospitality organisation. Measuring financial performance makes evaluation of performance and trends relatively straightforward. However, over-concentration on financial matters can result in a failure to perceive other factors that may have significant effects on both the short-term and long-term performance of the organisation.

REVIEW AND DISCUSSION QUESTIONS

1 Discuss the extent to which you consider that staff within the hospitality industry are prone to greater problems than staff within other industries.

2 As an enlightened manager, how would you deal with a member of staff who you knew was taking illegal drugs? Discuss the approaches that should be taken in cases of alcohol or drug abuse.

3 Define the term 'bullying'. How does this differ from harassment? How could problems related to these issues be reduced within an organisation?

4 What do you understand by the terms unitary and pluralist perspective? Why do you consider these different perspectives occur in the hospitality industry?

5 Discuss the extent to which you believe conflict is an inherent feature of work organisations. Explain your understanding of the radical approach to organisation conflict.

6 It is often claimed that pilferage is bound to occur in the hospitality industry. Discuss the extent to which this may be the case, and what actions should be taken by management to reduce its occurrence.

7 Give your own views on the controversial nature of management control. What do you see as the purposes of management control in hospitality work situations?

8 Identify the main causes of stress within the hospitality working environment. What actions can be taken by management and by the individual to reduce the levels of stress encountered in the working environment?

CASE STUDY 9.3

The successful executive

This is the story of Annette Thomas, who is a very successful training consultant in the hospitality industry. She started out as a human resources manager/duty manager in a large hotel company but then decided to specialise in training consultancy. Her employers set her the objective of growing this aspect of the business, and agreed to pay her a percentage of the profit that her efforts generated for them. For the first three years, Annette balanced the task of designing and also running training programmes for her employer and a select group of clients.

As time progressed, Annette's workload became increasingly difficult to cope with. She travelled extensively in the UK providing programmes for her clients. At the same time, she looked after her own financial control, administration and research and continued to market her consultancy, which often involved attending evening functions of local professional organisations.

Gradually Annette's workload increased to such an extent that she found herself working seven days a week. She felt she could cope as her office was at home. However, Annette's constant fear was that she would become ill and would not be able to work. She also had a home, a husband, a child, and a dog to think about and make time for.

Annette did not feel her earnings justified the hire of a secretarial assistant or researcher so she continued to work increasing hours. She felt compelled to take on more work and increased her travel, so as to make a name for herself and to grow and develop professionally.

Annette believed in networking as a way to increase business. She joined two committees to assist this. Soon she found herself on a subcommittee with more responsibilities. She agreed to run a monthly programme, without a fee, for the local unemployed. This was a good networking strategy and she felt she was helping the community.

Adding further pressure, in the third year of running her own business, Annette began to produce a web page for her clients. This provided her with additional contacts to develop the business within the hospitality industry.

In year four, Annette began to feel the physical repercussions of her activities. More tired than usual, one day she found herself almost unable to get out of bed. This frightened her as she prided herself on eating well and staying healthy, although she had given up going to the gym on a regular basis due to lack of time.

She tried to adhere to a routine of fitness. Even so, she often had to rise at 5.00 am to reach her destination and worked with her clients until late into the evening. When running training courses for hotels, this was generally expected. It was also expected that she would socialise with the delegates in the bar in the evening.

What had gone wrong? Annette began a round of visits to her doctor and the hospital for tests. The tests showed she was very fit. No blood pressure problems and so forth. Yet she was beginning to feel more and more ill. She began to have regular headaches, lose her natural clear complexion, suffer weight gain and find her energy level severely depleted. She also found herself bursting into tears at inappropriate times and for no real reason.

Despite the signals Annette felt she had no choice but to persevere with her strenuous programme. She had spent several years building up the business and did not want to let her clients down. One day she found she could not go on. Her system collapsed.

Out of sheer desperation, Annette went to an acupuncturist and naturopathic doctor. This doctor discovered the problem. He diagnosed an infection of the liver and the malfunction of her adrenal glands – the accelerator pedal of the body. This came as great shock to Annette, who could not understand how this had happened to her. She had no choice but to cancel most of her engagements for the next two-month period and began a strict dietary regime, taking recommended minerals, vitamins and medicines to eliminate the liver and adrenal problems. Gradually over a period of six months Annette began to recover her mental and

Case study 9.3 (*continued*)

physical well-being. However, her illness caused her to look seriously at her working life. She realised that some radical changes were necessary. But where to begin?

Questions

1 What could Annette have done differently to deal with the pressures and cope with the immense stress she was under?

2 What would you recommend she do, once she reached the point of having to submit to her illness and cancel some of her work?

3 What can you do, as an individual, to plan a strategy for managing stress in order to avoid a situation similar to that of Annette?

4 What needs to be done at organisational level by management to help all of its employees recognise the symptoms and causes of stress and ultimately cope?

CASE STUDY 9.4

The Clink Restaurant, HMP High Down[83]

It might be any training restaurant, smart, modern with a four-course menu. The meals are well cooked and well served, typical of any College or University training restaurant. However, the security search, entry through locked gates, barbed wire and high walls suggest something different about this training restaurant. Guests are not permitted to enter with any sharp items, mobile phones, lipstick or cameras. They are security checked in advance when making reservations and must produce photo ID before they enter.

The Clink is a 92-seater training restaurant situated within High Down Prison near Sutton, which takes Category B[84] prisoners, many of whom have been imprisoned for drug offences. The trainees in both the restaurant and kitchen are all inmates being trained ready for employ-

Case study 9.4 (*continued*)

ment in the hospitality industry. Those who join the courses are due for release in the next few months.

The aim of the Clink is to prepare prisoners for life outside and to reduce reoffending. Some of those trained as trainers are also prisoners. The students are preparing for NVQ 1, 2 and 3 in Food Production and NVQ 1 and 2 Food Service. However, they cannot take qualifications that require working with alcohol. Most have never worked in a kitchen or even in catering before, and some have never worked.

The trainees work from 6.00 am–4.00 pm. It is a popular training programme and is the highest-paid 'job' in the prison. They start in the restaurant, learning food service, then progress to the kitchen.

Approximately 24 trainees work in the kitchen and restaurant areas at any one time under the supervision of trainers, the restaurant manager, a former prisoner himself, and the head chef. Particular care has to be taken over security. There is careful control over the issue of knives in the kitchen and a shadow box is used to check that all equipment is replaced at the end of the shift. Only plastic cutlery is used in the restaurant and no alcohol is served. In all other aspects the restaurant has the appearance of any good restaurant. Interestingly, the hand-crafted chairs and tables were all designed and constructed by the prisoners in workshops. Managing these trainees brings its own special issues. According

to the restaurant manager the trainees are highly motivated.

Once released, prisoners are placed into the ex-offender career mentoring scheme supported and run with the help of hospitality education charity Springboard.[85] After release they receive support from a mentor to seek full-time employment and to find accommodation, open bank accounts and other tasks involved in settling into the world of work.

In 2011, 85 prisoners had been, or were currently being, trained in The Clink Restaurant; 25 have successfully been released into full-time employment.

Following the success of the Clink, a similar programme is due to open in three other UK prisons in 2012–13.

Questions for discussion

1 What do you consider may be some of the issues in managing these trainees at work within the Clink, in terms of motivation and practical security aspects?

2 The aim of the programme is that on release these 'graduates' will be employed within the hospitality industry. As a manager within the hospitality industry, consider the issues that would need to be addressed when employing these staff within hotels or commercial catering establishments.

3 Identify and consider the benefits of employing these potential staff to the individuals, the hospitality organisation and to society generally.

References

1 Wood, R. C., *Working in Hotels and Catering*, 2nd edn, International Thomson Business Press (1997).

2 Carmouche, R. and Kelly, N., *Behavioural Studies in Hospitality Management*, Chapman & Hall (1995).

3 Riley, M., *Human Resource Management in the Hospitality and Tourism Industry*, 2nd edn, Butterworth-Heinemann (1996).

4 Handy, C. B., *Understanding Organizations*, 4th edn, Penguin (1993).

5 See, for example, Townsend, R., *Further Up the Organisation*, Coronet Books (1985).

6 See, for example, Lucas, R. E., *Managing Employee Relations in the Hotel and Catering Industry*, Cassell (1995).

7 Erstad, M., 'Empowerment and organizational change', *International Journal of Contemporary Hospitality Management*, vol. 9, no. 7, 1997, 325–33.

8 For example, see Drucker, P. F., *The Practice of Management*, Pan Books (1968).

9 See, for example, Horwitz, F. M., 'HRM: an ideological perspective', *International Journal of Manpower*, vol. 12, no. 6, 1991, 4–9.

10 Fox, A., *Industrial Society and Industrial Relations*, HMSO (1966).

11 Lashley, C., 'Discovering hospitality: observations from recent research', *International Journal of Culture, Tourism and Hospitality Research*, vol. 1, no. 3, 2007, 214–26.

12 Salaman, G., *Class and Corporation*, Fontana (1981).

13 See, for example, Robbins, S. P., *Organizational Behavior: Concepts, Controversies, Applications*, 8th edn, Prentice Hall (1998).

14 Schmidt, W. H., 'Conflict: a powerful process for (good or bad) change', *Management Review*, issue 63, December 1974, 4–10.

15 Irvine, L., 'Conflicts of Interest', *The British Journal of Administrative Management*, March/April 1998, 8–10.

16 Mannering, K., 'Working with "prickly" people', *Professional Manager*, vol. 19, no. 1, January 2009, 32–4.

17 Berger, F. and Brownell, J., *Organizational Behavior for the Hospitality Industry*, Pearson Prentice Hall (2009).

18 See, for example, James, J., *Body Talk at Work*, Judy Piatkus Limited (2001).

19 Hart, J., 'Mind the gap', *Professional Manager*, November 2002, 22–3.

20 Health and Safety Executive, 'Tackling stress: the management standards approach', July 2005.

21 York, P., 'Getting a grip on stress', *Management Today*, October 2001, 105.

22 'Work–life balance: evidence from across the UK', *European Industrial Relations Review*, issue 380, September 2005.

23 Armson, S., 'Putting stress on the bottom line', *Management Today*, September 1997, 5.

24 Forbes, cited in Berger, F. and Brownell, J., *Organizational Behavior for the Hospitality Industry*, Pearson Prentice Hall (2009), pp. 180–181.

25 Orpen, C., 'Want the best? Get stressed!' *Chartered Secretary*, August 1996, 18–20.

26 Gwyther, M., 'Stressed for success', *Management Today*, January 1999, 22–6.

27 *ACAS News*, issue 11, Spring 2008.

28 Jamison, C., 'Top 10 Myths of Customer Service', *The British Journal of Administrative Management*, July/August 1999, 19–21.

29 Berger, F. and Brownell, J., *Organizational Behavior for the Hospitality Industry*, Pearson Prentice Hall (2009).

30 Liu, C., Spector, P. E. and Shi, L., 'Cross-national job stress: a quantitative and qualitative study', *Journal of Organisational Behavior*, February 2007, 209–39.

31 Spector, P. E., 'A cross-national comparative study of work-family stressors, working hours and well-being: China and Latin America versus the Anglo World', *Personnel Psychology*, Spring 2004, 119–42.

32 Ryan, C., Ghazali, H. and Mohsin, A., 'Determinants of intention to leave a non-managerial job in the fast-food industry in West Malaysia', *International Journal of Contemporary Hospitality Management*, vol. 23, no. 3, 2011, 344–60.

33 Firth, L., Mellor, D. J., Moore, K. A. and Loquet, C., 'How can managers reduce employee intention to quit?', *Journal of Managerial Psychology*, vol. 19, no. 2, 2004, 170–87.

34 Moore, K. A., 'Hospital restructuring: impact on nurses mediated by social support and a perception of challenge', *Journal of Health and Human Services Administration*, vol. 23, no. 4, 2002, 490–517. See also Firth *et al.*, note 33.

35 Kalliath, T. J. and Beck, A., 'Is the path to burnout and turnover paved by a lack of supervisory support? A structural equations test', *New Zealand Journal of Psychology*, vol. 30, 2001, 72–8.

36 Lichtenstein, R., Alexander, J. A., McCarthy, J. F. and Wells, R., 'Status differences in cross-functional teams: effects on individual member participation, job satisfaction, and intent to quit', *Journal of Health and Social Behavior*, vol. 45, no. 3, 2004, 322–35.

37 Krackhardt, D. and Porter, L. W., 'Turnover embedded in communication network', *Journal of Applied Psychology*, vol. 71, no. 1, February 1986.

38 Munasinghe, L. and Sigman, K., 'A hobo syndrome? Mobility, wages and job turnover', *Labour Economics*, vol. 11, 2004, 191–218.

39 Ghiselli, R. F., La Lopa, J. M. and Bai, B., 'Job satisfaction, life satisfaction and turnover intent', *Cornell Hotel and Restaurant Administration Quarterly*, vol. 42, no. 2, 2001, 28–37.

40 For Firth *et al.* (2004), see note 33. Derry, M. and Shaw, R.N., 'An exploratory analysis of turnover culture in the hotel industry in Australia', *International Journal of Hospitality Management*, vol. 16, no. 4, 1997, 375–92.

41 Leidner, R., *Fast Food: Fast Talk: Service Work and Routinization of Everyday Life*, University of California Press (1993).

42 Silva, P., 'Effects of disposition on hospitality employee job satisfaction and commitment', *International Journal of Contemporary Hospitality Management*, vol. 18, no. 4, 2006, 317–28.

43 Vine, P. and Williamson, J., 'Run down, stressed out', *The British Journal of Administrative Management*, January/February 1998, 14–17.

44 For further guidance see *Stress and mental health at work,* www.cipd.co.uk, September 2010.

45 Reeves, R., 'Reality bites', *Management Today*, March 2003, p. 35.

46 Murray-Gibbons, R. and Gibbons, C., 'Occupational stress in the chef profession', *International Journal of Contemporary Hospitality Management',* vol. 19, no. 1, 2007, 32–42.

47 See note 46.

48 See note 29.

49 Goss-Turner, S., *Managing People in the Hospitality Industry*, Croners (1992).

50 Kay, P., 'Back from the Brink', *Caterer and Hotelkeeper*, 25 November 2004.

51 http://www.caterersearch.com/Articles/13/01/2010/331742/peter-kay-back-from-the-brink.htm

52 'Phil Howard: Drugs don't work', *Caterer and Hotelkeeper*, 4 September 2009.

53 Ark Foundation, http://www.hospitalityaction.org.uk/, accessed 6.3.12

54 CIPD Alcohol and Drug Abuse policies, www.cipd.co.uk/hr-topics/alcohol-drug-abuse.aspx, accessed 25.10.12

55 See note 51.

56 Bloisi, W. and, Hoel, H., 'Abusive work practise and bullying among chefs. A review of the literature', *International Journal of Hospitality Management*, 27, 2008, 649–56.

57 Cooper, C., *Beating the Bullies,* www.charteredsecretary.net, March (2010).

58 *Personnel Today*, 24 January 2008.

59 See note 56.

60 Einarsen, S., Hoel, H., Zapf, D. and Cooper, C., 'The concept of bullying at work: the European tradition', in Einarsen, S., Hoel, H., Zapf, D. and Cooper, C., *Bullying and Emotional Abuse in the Workplace: International perspectives in research and practice*, Taylor and Francis (2003), pp. 3–30.

61 See note 56.

62 See note 56.

63 Johns, J. and Menzel, P., 'If you can't stand the heat!'. . . kitchen violence and culinary art, *Hospitality Management,* vol. 18, 1999, 99–109.

64 Paz, M., 'Dealing with bullying at work', *Caterer and Hotelkeeper*, 26 March 2010, accessed 6.4.12 from www.caterersearch.com

65 See note 63.

66 Baum ,T., *Human Resource Management for Tourism, Hospitality and Leisure*, Thompson (2006).

67 Handy, C. B., *Understanding Organizations*, 4th edn, Penguin (1993), p. 283.

68 McKenna, R., *New Management*, Irwin/McGraw-Hill (1999), pp. 430–1.

69 Mars, G. and Mitchell, P., *Manpower Problems in the Hotel and Catering Industry*, Heinemann (1979).

70 See note 66.

71 Mars, G. and Mitchell, P., *Manpower Problems in the Hotel and Catering Industry*, Heinemann (1979).

72 See Boella, M. J. and Goss-Turner, S., *Human Resource Management in the Hospitality Industry*, Elsevier (2005).

73 Institute of Hospitality, 'Dealing with theft by employees', *Hospitality*, Issue 22, Summer 2011.

74 See, for example, Blake, R. R. and Mouton, J. S., *The Managerial Grid III*, Gulf Publishing Company (1985).

75 Forte, Charles (Lord), *Forte: The Autobiography of Charles Forte*, Sidgwick & Jackson (1986), p. 190.

76 Mullins, L. and Banks, G., 'How well am I doing?', *Euhofa Journal*, International Association of Directors of Hotel Schools, Switzerland, no. 18, June 1986.

77 Lockwood, A., Baker, M. and Ghillyer, A. (eds), *Quality Management in Hospitality*, Cassell (1996), p. 158.

78 See, for example, Medlik, S., *The Business of Hotels*, 3rd edn, Butterworth-Heinemann (1994).

79 Venison, P., *Managing Hotels*, Heinemann (1983), p. 107.

80 Mullins, L. J., 'Behavioural Implications of Management Accounting', *Management Accounting*, vol. 59, no. 1, January 1981, pp. 36–9.

81 See, for example, Prior, P., 'Communicating: an enthusiast's view', *Accountancy*, vol. 95, no. 1089, May 1984, 69.

82 Maher, A., 'Accounting for human resources in UK hotels', *Proceedings of CHME Research Conference*, Manchester Metropolitan University, April 1993.

83 www.theelinkcharity.com

84 Catagory B prisoners are those who do not require maximum security, but for whom escape needs to be made very difficult.

85 Springboard, http://springboarduk.net/

Chapter 10

Managing the changing environment

Learning outcomes

After completing this chapter you should be able to:

- outline the meaning and nature of organisation development;
- examine the nature and main features of organisational culture;
- detail characteristics of organisational climate;
- explain approaches to improving organisational performance and effectiveness;
- examine the nature of management change and reasons for resistance to change;
- explore the successful implementation of change.

Introduction

A central feature of the successful hospitality organisation is the diagnosis of its culture, health and performance along with the ability of the organisation to adapt rapidly to change. The hospitality industry is particularly influenced by the changing environment and must respond, not only to succeed, but to survive in a highly competitive market. Adapting to change involves applications of organisational behaviour and recognition of the social processes of the organisation. The manager needs to understand the nature and importance of organisational culture and climate, organisational development, employee commitment, and the successful implementation and management of change.

Critical review and reflection

'It is generally accepted that the hospitality industry must respond rapidly to change but there is a hesitancy, in many sectors of the industry, to move forward.'

What is your view?

Organisational effectiveness

This book has been concerned with interactions among the structure and operation of hospitality organisations, the role of management and the behaviour of people at work. The central theme has been improved organisational performance through the effective management of people. Organisations need to be **efficient** in doing the right things with the optimum ratio of outputs to inputs, and in the use of their resources. But they also need to be **effective** in doing the right things, and their outputs need to be related to a specific purpose, objective or task. **Performance** should be related to such factors as increasing profitability, improved service delivery, or obtaining the best results in important areas of organisational activities. Organisations must also ensure that they meet satisfactorily, or exceed, the demands and requirements of customers, and that they are **adaptable** to specific requirements, changes in the external environment and demands of the situation.[1] Organisational performance is affected, then, by a multiplicity of individual, group, task, technological, structural, managerial and environmental variables.

Attributes for successful performance

In their study of 62 American companies (including service companies) with outstandingly successful performance, Peters and Waterman identify eight basic attributes of excellence which appear to account for success.[2]

- *A bias for action* – action-orientated and a bias for getting things done.
- *Close to the customer* – listening and learning from the people they serve, and providing quality, service and reliability.
- *Autonomy and entrepreneurship* – innovation and risk-taking as an expected way of doing things.
- *Productivity through people* – treating members of staff as the source of quality and productivity.
- *Hands-on, value-driven* – having well-defined, basic philosophies and top management keeping in touch with the 'front lines'.
- *Stick to the knitting* – in most cases, staying close to what you know and can do well.
- *Simple form, lean staff* – simple structural forms and systems, and few top-level staff.
- *Simultaneous loose–tight properties* – operational decentralisation but strong centralised control over the few, important core values.

The 7-S framework

From their research, Peters and Waterman suggest that any intelligent approach to organising needs to encompass at least seven, interdependent variables (the McKinsey 7-S Framework):

- strategy;
- structure;
- staff;

- (management) style;
- systems (and procedures);
- (corporate) strengths or skills;
- shared values (i.e. culture).

Although many of the original 'excellent' organisations have since fallen from grace, it should be remembered that the formulas for their success did appear appropriate in the 1980s and the study highlighted the importance of culture and organisational renewal. Important lessons can always be learned and the 7-S model continues to provide a helpful framework as a basis for organisational analysis.

Heller's study of European excellence

In his study of European companies and managers, seeking excellence for those companies, Heller identifies ten key strategies:

1 Developing leadership – without losing control or direction.
2 Driving radical change – in the entire corporate system, not just in its parts.
3 Reshaping culture – to achieve long-term success.
4 Dividing to rule – winning the rewards of smallness while staying or growing large.
5 Exploiting the 'organisation' – by new approaches to central direction.
6 Keeping the competitive edge – in a world where the old ways of winning no longer work.
7 Achieving constant renewal – stopping success from sowing the seeds of decay.
8 Managing the motivators – so that people can motivate themselves.
9 Making teamworking work – the new, indispensable skill.
10 Achieving total management quality – by managing everything much better.[3]

Heller suggests that there are many examples of progressive, and successful, companies employing each of the above strategies in their attempts to become, and continue to be, effective.

Organisational development

Organisational development (OD) is a generic term embracing a wide range of loosely defined intervention strategies into the social processes of an organisation. These intervention strategies are aimed at the development of individuals, groups, and the organisation as a total system. It is concerned with the diagnosis of organisational health and performance, and the ability of the organisation to adapt to change. In a very general sense OD is concerned with attempts to improve the overall performance and effectiveness of an organisation.

Given the importance of people to effective organisational performance, particularly in the hospitality industry, topics normally included under the heading of organisational behaviour can be seen as particularly relevant to the study of OD. This would include many of the topics identified earlier in the book as being of particular importance to the hospitality industry, such as team-building and empowerment. Other areas of relevance such as culture, organisation change and quality assurance will be discussed later.

Since the hospitality industry is highly competitive, the dimensions of OD, which include the role of top management, organisational culture, organisational climate and the management of change, are important considerations. However, it should be noted that the emphasis of OD is more on the development of the organisation than the actual processes of organisation and management.

The role of top management in organisational development

Effective management is at the heart of organisational development and improved performance. This applies as much to service organisations and the hospitality industry as to any other industry. The role of management is one of the most important factors in the success of any hospitality organisation. At the corporate level, top management have a responsibility for determining the direction of the organisation as a whole and for its survival, development and profitability. For example, in the words of Kanter: 'Managing means managing an entire context. If you strip out one element and apply one methodology, it won't work.'[4]

In Chapter 5 we discussed the nature of managerial work, and the importance of the role of management as an integrating activity and the cornerstone of organisational effectiveness. Top management have a particular responsibility for determining the objectives and formulation of policy for hospitality operations as a whole. For example, top management play a crucial role in formulating human resource management policies, establishing underlying philosophy and attitudes, and attempting to maintain a level of morale and commitment of all members of staff in order to secure optimum operational performance.

Attention to key features

Top management clearly have an essential part to play in improving organisational performance and the effective management of human resources. They need to give attention to such features as the following:

- Clarification and communication of corporate aims and objectives. The identification of key areas of performance and results, including social responsibilities.
- Interactions with and responsiveness to external environmental influences, and the effective management of change.
- Pursuing corporate goals in accordance with an ethical and operational foundation, and recognition of the psychological contract.
- Design of an organisation structure which takes account of the socio-technical system and is most suited to organisational processes and the execution of work.
- Organisational strategies and practices, for example relating to human resource planning and the management of staff turnover.
- Welding a coherent and coordinated pattern of work activities, and harnessing the efforts of staff.
- Clear, consistent and equitable policies and procedures, for example relating to the personnel function, including training and development.
- A style of managerial behaviour which adopts a positive policy of investment in people.

- Recognition of the needs and expectations of people at work and systems of motivation, job satisfaction and rewards.

- Effective control of those critical activities important to the overall success of the organisation.

- Creating an organisational climate which encourages members of staff to work willingly and effectively.

The process of management

Top management have a particular concern for the community or institutional level and for the work of the organisation as a whole. But it is the role of management *throughout all levels of the organisation* to act as an integrating activity and to coordinate, direct and guide the efforts of members towards the achievement of goals and objectives. The process of management, however, takes place not in a vacuum but within the context of the organisational setting. Applications of organisational behaviour and the effective management of human resources are dependent, therefore, not only upon the nature of the hospitality industry, but also upon the characteristic features of the individual organisation – and its organisational culture and climate.

Organisational culture

Although most of us will understand in our own minds what is meant by organisational culture, it is a general concept which is difficult to define or explain precisely. The concept of culture has developed from anthropology. There is no consensus on its meaning or its applications to the analysis of work organisations.[5]

However, it involves an appreciation of the assumptions people share about an organisation's values, beliefs, norms, symbols, language and rituals.[6] A popular and simple way of defining culture is: 'how things are done around here'. Or as Atkinson explains:[7] 'what is acceptable and not acceptable'. A more detailed definition is 'the collection of traditions, values, policies, beliefs, and attitudes that constitute a pervasive context for everything we do and think in an organisation'.[8]

Culture is reinforced through the system of rites and rituals, patterns of communication, the informal organisation, expected patterns of behaviour and perceptions of the psychological contract.

Schein suggests a view of organisational culture based on distinguishing three levels of culture: artefacts and creations; values; and basic underlying assumptions.[9] From a study of five US restaurant companies, Woods sees much of culture as invisible, or at least unspoken, and identifies at least three main levels:

- *the visible or manifest level* – such as slogans, ceremonies, myths, sagas and legends, uniforms, building design;

- a second level not immediately visible to customers is *the strategic level*, such as beliefs about strategic vision, capital market, product market expectations, and internal approaches to management;

- the third level is most deeply submerged and is *the level of deep meaning*, which embraces the values and assumptions with which the organisation operates. Ideally, the values and assumptions espoused by top management will be the same as those held by hourly workers.[10]

Main types of organisation culture

Developing the ideas of Harrison,[11] Handy describes four main types of organisation culture: power culture; role culture; task culture; and person culture.[12]

- *Power culture* depends on a central power source with influence disseminating from the central figure throughout the organisation. A power culture is frequently found in small entrepreneurial organisations. It is based on trust and personal communication with little bureaucracy and few rules or regulations.

- *Role culture* is often stereotyped as bureaucracy and based on logic and rationality. Role culture rests on the strength of strong organisational 'pillars' and the functions of specialists in, for example, purchasing, production and finance. Work is controlled by procedures and rules and coordinated by a small band of senior managers.

- *Task culture* is job-orientated or project-orientated. It is represented by a net. People generally work in teams and task culture seeks to utilise the unifying power of the group. There are few levels of authority, and influence is widely spread and based more on expert power than positional or personal power.

- *Person culture*, where the individual is the central focus and any structure exists to serve the individuals within it. Individuals generally work alone, or several may decide it is in their own interests to band together. Management hierarchies and control mechanisms are possible only by mutual consent. This culture is common with professionals.

Every organisation will have its own unique culture and most large businesses are likely to be something of a mix of cultures with examples for each of the four types in varying areas of the organisation. Different people enjoy working in different types of organisation culture and they are more likely to be happy and satisfied at work if their attributes and personalities are consistent with the culture of that part of the organisation in which they are employed.

Four generic types of culture

From an examination of hundreds of business organisations and their environments, Deal and Kennedy categorised corporate cultures according to two determining factors in the marketplace:

- the degree of risk associated with the organisation's activities; and
- the speed at which organisations and their employees receive feedback on the success of decisions or strategies.

These factors give rise to four generic types of culture: the tough-guy, macho culture; the work-hard/play-hard culture; the bet-your-company culture; and the process culture.[13]

- **Tough-guy, macho culture** – an organisation of individualists who frequently take high risks and receive quick feedback on the right or wrong of their actions. Examples cited include police departments, surgeons, construction, cosmetics, management consulting and the entertainment industry. Financial stakes are high and there is a focus on speed. The intense pressure and frenetic pace often result in early 'burn-out'. Internal competition and conflict are normal, stars are temperamental but tolerated. A high staff turnover can create difficulties in building a strong cohesive culture.

- **Work-hard/play-hard culture** – characterised by fun and action where employees take few risks, all with quick feedback. There is a high level of relatively low-risk activity. Examples include sales organisations such as estate agents and computer companies, mass consumer companies such as McDonald's, office equipment manufacturers and retail stores. Organisations tend to be highly dynamic and the primary value centres on customers and their needs. It is the team who produce the volume, and the culture encourages games, meetings, promotions and conventions to help maintain motivation. However, although a lot gets done, volume can be at the expense of quality.

- **Bet-your-company culture** – where there are large-stake decisions with a high risk but slow feedback so that it may be years before employees know if decisions are successful. Examples include oil companies, investment banks, architectural firms and the military. The focus is on the future and the importance of investing in it. There is a sense of deliberateness throughout the organisation typified by the ritual of the business meeting. There is a hierarchical system of authority with decision-making from the top down. The culture leads to high-quality inventions and scientific breakthroughs, but moves only very slowly and is vulnerable to short-term fluctuations.

- **Process culture** – a low-risk, slow-feedback culture where employees find difficulty in measuring what they do. Typical examples include banks, insurance companies, financial services and the civil service. The individual financial stakes are low and employees get very little feedback on their effectiveness. Their memos and reports seem to disappear into a void. Lack of feedback forces employees to focus on how they do something, not what they do. People tend to develop a 'cover your back' mentality. Bureaucracy results, with attention to trivial events, minor detail, formality and technical perfection. Process cultures can be effective when there is a need for order and predictability.

Influences on the development of culture

The culture and structure of an organisation develop over time and in response to a complex set of factors. We can, however, identify a number of key influences that are likely to play an important role in the development of any corporate culture. These include: history, primary function and technology, goals and objectives (strategy), size, location, management and staffing, and the environment.[14]

History

The reason, and manner in which, the organisation was originally formed, its age, and the philosophy and values of its owners and first senior managers will affect culture. A key event in the organisation's history such as a merger or major reorganisation, or a new generation of top management, may bring about a change in culture. Failure in mergers and acquisitions can arise from cultural clashes and failure to integrate different cultures.[15]

Primary function and technology

The nature of the organisation's 'business' and its primary function have an important influence on its culture, for example the range and quality of products and services provided, the importance of reputation and the type of customers. The primary function of the organisation will determine the nature of the technological processes and methods of undertaking work, which in turn also affect structure and culture. Compare, for example, a traditional, high-class hotel, particularly noted for its cuisine, with a popular mass-production fast food chain.

Goals and objectives (strategy)

Although a business organisation may pursue profitability, this is not by itself a very clear or sufficient criterion for its effective management. For example, to what extent is emphasis placed on long-term survival or growth and development? How much attention is given to avoiding risk and uncertainties? How much concern is shown for broader social responsibilities? The organisation must give attention to objectives in all key areas of its operations. The combination of objectives and resultant strategies will influence culture, and may themselves be influenced by changes in culture.

Size

Usually, larger organisations have more formalised structures and cultures. Increased size is likely to result in separate departments and possibly split-site operations. This may cause difficulties in communication and interdepartmental rivalries with the need for effective coordination. A rapid expansion, or decline, in size and rate of growth, and resultant changes in staffing, will influence structure and culture.

Location

Geographical location and the physical characteristics will have a major influence on culture, for example whether the organisation is located in a quiet rural location or a busy city centre. This will influence the types of customers and the staff employed. It can also affect the nature of services provided, the sense of 'boundary' and distinctive identity, and opportunities for development.

Management and staffing

Top executives can have considerable influence on the nature of culture but all members of staff help to shape the dominant culture of an organisation, irrespective of what senior management feel it should be.

Culture is also determined by the nature of staff employed and the extent to which they accept management philosophy and policies or only pay 'lip service'. Another important influence is the match between corporate culture and employees' perception of the psychological contract.

The environment

In order to be effective, the organisation must be responsive to external environmental influences. For example, if it operates within a dynamic environment, it requires a structure and culture that are sensitive and readily adaptable to change. An organic structure is more likely to respond effectively to new opportunities and challenges, and risks and limitations, presented by the external environment.

Exhibit 10.1 Management and organisation culture

Management responsibility for the culture and values of an organisation

All organisations display attributes that relate to their culture and values. This is particularly important in the hospitality industry where the 'environment' is the background against which the product is judged. Although the facilities and physical setting are important components of the environment, no amount of investment in these can make up for a shortfall in ambience or 'feel'. To make matters more difficult for those of us who aspire to excellence in hospitality, these attributes are highly subjective and notoriously difficult to influence and control. However, because the feel of an environment is the result of the interaction of people, it is the responsibility of the management. Successful organisations match the skills, attitudes and behaviours of the staff with the needs and expectations of the customers.

Very often a strong culture grows within a company reflecting the attitudes and behaviours of the most senior people. The company culture does not have to be defined in order for its people to 'know it'. New staff either adapt to, and become part of, the culture, or do not fit and usually do not stay. This is particularly true of owner-managed hospitality businesses and was certainly the case at Highgate House Conference Centre. Highgate House had developed over 25 years under the guidance of an exceptionally energetic and talented mother-of-nine who was determined that behaviour standards and individual well-being were paramount. The culture ran right through the business, which established a superb reputation as a high-quality 95-bed residential conference centre.

When the management of the business passed to the next generation there was a very real danger that attitudes could change. This risk was increased when the decision was taken to grow the business to more than one centre with the launch in 1998 of The Sundial Group. Because the feel of Highgate House was identified by the customers as a key reason for their repeat business, the senior management decided that it was important to try to pin down the culture and find ways to describe it. They wanted to ensure that the culture continued as far as possible as the company grew. They identified and published four core values, making them part of the marketing image for customers and the behaviour standards for staff. By being open about what behaviours are expected it became very much easier for the management to safeguard them.

The following is an extract from the document that was circulated to customers and staff at the launch of The Sundial Group and forms part of the induction of all staff, also appearing in the employee handbook.

- We are committed to creating an environment that genuinely encourages learning and creative thinking, for our clients and for our staff.

- We believe that our people make us the best conference and training services group in the country. Our values are embodied every day in their professionalism, experience, quality and respect for our guests and each other.

- *Professionalism*. The discreet, seamless hospitality that is Sundial's hallmark is ideally suited to our customers' very specialised needs. Successful business meetings, training courses, and smaller conferences benefit greatly from our attention to detail, secure privacy and focus.

- *Experience*. Understanding customers' needs and providing responsive service are the important long-term benefits Sundial gains from attracting and keeping staff with the right skills and positive attitudes. This continuity enables us to draw on a wealth of experience and helps us to earn the confidence of the organisations we work with.

- *Quality*. Our standards are uncompromising with a relentless drive for value for money and continuous improvement appropriate to needs. Our policies are designed to help our staff learn and develop, encouraging them to use their initiative and provide what's needed, when it's needed. We thrive on feedback and innovation.

- *Respect*. Sundial is a family business. We started the first independent conference centre over 35 years ago. A lot has changed since then, but not our core belief in respect for those around us. 'Treat people as you would like to be treated' is a golden rule everyone can understand and appreciate, and one which we use to put our services and hospitality into context.

These statements form a manifesto and contain commitments that help set the expectations of customers and staff. Equally they give a clear message to staff and especially to managers about how to behave. However, to translate into organisational culture, it is critical that every level of leadership in the business subscribes to and demonstrates these values consistently.

Expanding from a close-knit business, where the entrepreneurial owner knew everything that went on and made pretty much every significant decision, to a multi-site group, required far-reaching changes in management and responsibility. Committing to values that can be easily described and understood provides a framework against which decisions can be taken. The right answer is always the one which best fits these values.

In order for Sundial Group to live up to this manifesto it became clear that policies and strategies needed to be developed. Our commitment to Professionalism led us to accreditation under Investors in People, ensuring that we link training and development to business objectives. Experience can only be achieved through a positive approach to controlling staff turnover. Quality must be appropriate to need; we are now much more aware of our customers' expectations and competitors' performance. Respect depends on empathy; we have a much better understanding of the attitudes that need to be demonstrated by prospective staff in order for them to succeed with us.

Although it is still early days in the development of The Sundial Group, we can begin to see the effectiveness of our commitments. Our staff turnover levels have remained well below the industry standard, repeat business levels are also remaining very good and profitability shows a marked improvement. UK conference buyers recently voted Highgate House venue of the year and together the three Sundial venues polled in excess of 50 per cent of the vote in a field of 30 nominated top venues.

The achievement of Investors in People provided a valuable external benchmark and our work with The European Quality Model self-assessment process is providing further valuable feedback.

Improved availability of feedback data such as Trip Advisor also ensures the company remains close to its customers, while participating in industry benchmarking, provided by BRC Continental via their feedback web portals, also provides enhanced opportunity for customer feedback.

However, we operate in a highly competitive marketplace and are not prepared to rest on our laurels; healthy paranoia is a useful driver for continuous improvement!

(The Sundial group currently consists of Highgate House in Northamptonshire, Barnett Hill in Surrey, Woodside in Warwickshire and Sundial Options and Solutions, our venue finding service. www.sundialgroup.com)

Source: The authors are grateful to Tim Chudley, Managing Director of The Sundial Group, for providing this information.

Critical review and reflection

The Sundial Group recognises that the importance of feedback from customers through Trip Advisor is essential.

To what extent do you consider media, such as Trip Advisor *or* Twitter, *are vital sources of information for the improvement of standards in the hospitality industry and how may they influence the culture of an organisation?*

The cultural web

In order to help describe and understand the culture of an organisation, Johnson, Scholes and Whittington present a cultural web, which brings together different aspects for the analysis of organisational culture (see Figure 10.1).

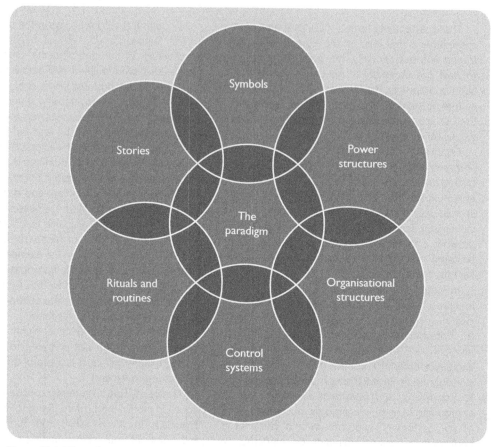

Figure 10.1 The cultural web of an organisation

- **Rituals and routines** – rituals are the particular activities or special events through which the organisation emphasises what is particularly important; and can include formal organisational processes and informal processes. Routine behaviours are the ways in which members of the organisation behave towards each other and towards those outside the organisation: they make up how things are done, or how things should happen.

- **Stories** told by members of the organisation that embed the present and flag up important events and personalities, and typically have to do with successes, failures, heroes, villains and mavericks.

- **Symbols** – such as logos, uniforms, titles, type of language or terminology commonly used – which become a shorthand representation of the nature of the organisation. For example the use of the term 'K.P.' for kitchen porter, or always responding to the chef in the kitchen with the acknowledgement, 'yes, Chef'.

- **Power structures** – the power of the most powerful individuals or groups in the organisation may be based on management position and seniority, but in some organisations power can be lodged with other levels or functions.

- **Organisational structures** – which reflect power structures and delineate important relationships and activities within the organisation, and involve both formal structure and control and less formal systems.
- **Control systems** – the measurement and reward systems that emphasise what it is important to monitor, and to focus attention and activity upon – for example, stewardship of funds or quality of service.
- **The paradigm** of the organisation, which encapsulates and reinforces the behaviours observed in other elements of the cultural web.[16]

Other interpretations of culture

There are, however, many other ways in which people attempt to describe and understand what constitutes organisational culture, and different areas of attention for analysing the elements of culture. Wilson suggests that culture is a characteristic of the organisation, not of individuals.

> One way of examining the culture of an organisation is to look at its corporate image to see what and who is valued in the organisation. A corporate image is the mental picture the clients, customers, employees, and others have of an organisation. The impression is the combination of unconscious, unintended, conscious, and intended factors that arise.[17]

ACAS distinguishes two different organisation cultures and different ways of doing things:

- **control culture** with the emphasis on rules and procedures, control and compliance with precedent providing guidelines; and
- **quality of working life culture** with the emphasis on core values, with mission statements providing guidance and commitment via shared goals, values and traditions.[18]

The importance of culture

Culture can help reduce complexity and uncertainty. It provides a consistency in outlook and values, and makes possible the processes of decision-making, coordination and control.[19]

Culture is clearly an important ingredient of effective organisational performance. Organisation culture will influence the pride that people have in their jobs and the appropriateness of the manager's methods of motivation. Culture is also a major determinant of organisational performance and effectiveness. In the hospitality industry culture is a vital component in the standards of delivery of service to the customer. It is important therefore to recognise the essential characteristics of service organisations and to develop a culture which encourages group motivation, harmonious working relationships and good teamwork.

Culture and ineffectiveness

According to Glover, a properly developed corporate culture can be a management tool for building product quality and staff productivity. However, if management misunderstands the effects of corporate culture, the quality of products and services in hospitality operations may suffer through a 'cult of ineffectiveness'.[20]

Glover identifies a number of organisational characteristics that commonly give rise to a cult of ineffectiveness.

- *Missing standards* – through lack of agreement on expectations, inconsistent delivery of products and services, lack of measuring and managing quality, and evaluation based on activity not results.

- *Unbalanced accountability* – although financial accounting is highly developed, effective controls over the people area, and accounting procedures for measuring the effectiveness of managers and supervisors, are less precise.

- *Ineffective communications* – ideas and responses from employees are seldom sought, and comments from guests not appreciated. Neither group is considered in management decision-making. Top-down communication, as well as broken or misunderstood communication, engenders a cult of ineffectiveness.

- *Symptoms, not causes* – emphasis is placed on remedies for symptoms, rather than delving for the underlying cause of problems. For example, the rudeness of a waiter may have less to do with the waiter and more to do with inappropriate selection and training or poor management practices.

- *Lack of recognition* – most managers admit that they rarely let employees know when a job has been done well. Many employees only hear from their manager when there is a problem.

- *Absence of teamwork* – many corporate cultures reward competition among employees and may encourage conflict. If employees are rewarded on the basis of individual action, this can thwart the development of teams. Yet the nature of hospitality operations demands effective teamwork.

- *Inadequate training* – a common means of training new members of staff is by 'trailing' an experienced employee. This transfers the most important managerial responsibility to a line employee who may not have a clear view of the company's objectives. Also, managers and supervisors are often expected to sink or swim as they are introduced to new responsibilities.

- *Recriminations* – complaints or other problems are often an occasion for blame, finger-pointing and defensiveness rather than being taken as an opportunity to improve operations. Management has a responsibility to limit problems in the first place.

- *The need for effectiveness* – many hospitality managers fail to recognise the difference between effectiveness and efficiency. 'Getting the job done' should include effective delivery of the product or service and result in achieving established standards.

- *Actions of top management* – an organisation is more than the sum of all its operations and departments. It also includes a culture that is shaped by the actions of top management. The informal social organisation affects all levels of the company, and influences its ability to deliver products and services to the customer.

Culture in short-life organisations

The importance of culture raises interesting questions relating to its nature and influence in 'short-life' organisations – that is, organisations created to run for only a short period of time such as arts festivals, national garden festivals or event catering. For example, how does culture develop when the organisation has little or no prior history, has short-term goals and objectives and has only limited time for top management to exercise influence? How do managers in such organisations attempt to inculcate culture? From a study of Garden Festival Wales, Meudell and Gadd found that success in creating a culture occurred as a direct result of their recruitment and training initiatives. However, it is not only culture but climate that is important for organisational effectiveness. 'Rigorous training in customer care/corporate culture might produce an automatic "Have a nice day" but only the engendering of a suitable climate will encourage people to say it and mean it.'[21]

Critical review and reflection

'The socialisation of new members into an organisation's culture and climate is no more than a management control system based upon the manipulation of an individual. It is therefore unethical and should be condemned.'

How would you challenge the validity of this statement? What has been your personal experience in the hospitality industry?

Organisational climate

In addition to arrangements for carrying out organisational processes, management has a responsibility for creating a climate in which people are motivated to work willingly and effectively. Organisational climate can be said to relate to the prevailing atmosphere surrounding the hospitality organisation, to the level of morale and to the strength of feelings of belonging, care and goodwill among members.

The perception of employees

Whereas organisational culture describes what the organisation is about, organisational climate is an indication of the employees' feelings and beliefs of what the organisation is about. Climate is based on the **perceptions** of employees towards the quality of the internal working environment.[22] The extent to which employees accept the culture of the organisation will have a significant effect on climate.

Climate also relates to the recognition of the organisation as a social system and the extent to which membership is perceived as a psychologically rewarding experience. It can be seen as the state of mutual trust and understanding among members of the organisation.

Meudell and Gadd contend that the distinction between organisational culture and climate is of particular importance in service industries, not only from the point of view of guest perception of staff but also from the point of view of teamworking:

> The culture may, for example, encourage a hotel-wide quality circle but it is only a suitable climate which will prevent verbal and, possibly, physical violence when a laundry worker suggests changes in procedures for issuing kitchen whites which could improve efficiency![23]

Characteristics of a healthy organisational climate

Organisational climate is characterised, therefore, by the nature of the people–organisation relationship and the superior–subordinate relationship. These relationships are determined by interactions among goals and objectives, formal structure, the process of management, styles of leadership and the behaviour of people. A healthy organisational climate might therefore be expected to exhibit such characteristic features as:

● the integration of organisational goals and personal goals;
● the most appropriate organisation structure based on the demands of the socio-technical system;
● democratic functioning of the organisation with full opportunities for participation;
● justice in treatment with equitable personnel and employee relations policies and practices;
● mutual trust, consideration and support among different levels of the organisation;
● the open discussion of conflict with an attempt to avoid confrontation;
● managerial behaviour and styles of leadership appropriate to the particular work situations;
● acceptance of the psychological contract between the individual and the organisation;
● recognition of people's needs and expectations at work, and individual differences and attributes;
● equitable systems of rewards based on positive recognition;
● concern for the quality of working life and job design;
● opportunities for personal development and career progression;
● a sense of identity with, and loyalty to, the organisation and a feeling of being a valued and important member.

The management of organisational climate

If organisational climate is to be improved, then attention should be given to the above features. The climate created by managers will have a significant influence on the motivation and behaviour of employees, and is, therefore, an important means of improving productivity and standards of work performance.

In hospitality operations, customer satisfaction relies heavily on group-based activities and the need for different departments to work closely together. It is particularly important, therefore, to develop an organisational climate which encourages good teamwork. However, although similar types of organisations may share certain common features, each will have its own distinctive characteristics. Every organisation has its own climate, or internal environment, or 'personality'.

Main dimensions of climate

Climate will influence the level of morale and attitudes which members of the organisation bring to bear on their work performance and personal relationships. Although morale is difficult to measure objectively, a carefully designed and conducted description questionnaire (or attitude survey) will help to establish the true feelings of members on factors contributing to organisational climate.

There are many possible survey instruments with which to gauge climate. Different questionnaires vary greatly in the number of items and in the number of categories. Mill, for example, suggests that climate can be described in terms of six main dimensions: clarity, commitment, standards, responsibility, recognition and teamwork (Figure 10.2).[24]

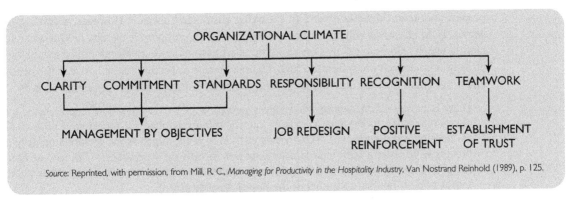

Source: Reprinted, with permission, from Mill, R. C., *Managing for Productivity in the Hospitality Industry*, Van Nostrand Reinhold (1989), p. 125.

Figure 10.2 Organisational climate and management action

If clarity, commitment or standards are low, this suggests the need for a system of management by objectives. This involves the setting of clearly stated objectives and targets, and developing commitment among employees through involving them in agreeing standards of performance.

Where responsibility is low, this suggests the need for attention to job redesign and passing on to employees increased autonomy for the planning, organising and control of their jobs.

When recognition is lacking, management should provide positive reinforcement by giving employees rewards and encouragement when they do something right.

If teamwork is lacking, then management should attempt to develop a feeling of trust and supportive relationships with employees and among groups of employees.

Gray claims, from his research, to have found a clear correlation between successful workplace outcomes and a range of climate characteristics. He maintains that a climate conducive to successful outcomes also tends to be conducive to individual happiness. The climate of an organisation has a significant impact on the quality and quantity of work that gets done and on the well-being of employees.[25]

Organisational performance

Quality

One particular feature of organisational performance and effectiveness is attention to quality, and this is especially important in service industries, including hospitality organisations. The successful hospitality organisation should as a matter of policy be constantly seeking opportunities to improve the quality of its products, services and processes. The organisation must also couple quality with a required level of productivity. Such a philosophy is increasingly encompassed as part of a total quality management (TQM) culture. Alongside this approach to achieving quality is the continuing and essential requirement for quality assurance (QA).

Total Quality Management

The key elements of TQM include *a total process* involving all operations and management units in the organisation and led from the top and *the customer as king* with every strategy, process and action directly related to satisfying customers' needs.[26] However, according to James, TQM initiatives will not succeed unless rooted in a supportive Quality of Working Life culture which creates a fear-free organisation in which employee involvement is pursued vigorously. It is necessary to generate a high degree of reciprocal commitment between the needs and developments of the individual, and the goals and development of the organisation.[27]

> TQM is a way of managing which gives everyone in the organisation responsibility for delivering quality to the final customer; quality being described as 'fitness for purpose' or as 'delighting the customer'. TQM views each task in the organisation as fundamentally a process which is in a customer/supplier relationship with the next process. The aim at each stage is to define and meet the customer's requirements with the aim of maximising the satisfaction of the final consumer at the lowest possible cost.[28]

Quality assurance

A significant aspect of moving a hospitality organisation forward, and responding to change, is the achievement of standards. These are constantly being tested in this increasingly competitive sector.

Earlier it was seen that profit can be an incentive for the organisation to carry out its activities effectively. In order to survive, the organisation needs to grow and develop with most sections achieving a steady, continuous, level of profitability. The successful hospitality organisation should, therefore, be constantly seeking opportunities to improve the quality of its products, services and processes.

The need for quality assurance comes from a combination of the following:

- the natural outcome of good business and the need to provide high quality goods and services in order to ensure survival , competitiveness and economic success;
- the labour-intensive nature, and staffing characteristics, of the industry;
- the desire to achieve and display some 'tangible' measure of quality through certification;
- the need to satisfy an absolute requirement, for example a legal liability such as that established by the Food Safety Act 1990;
- part of the exercise of the broader social responsibilities of management;
- increasing customer expectations.

It has been seen that organisational effectiveness will be influenced by many interrelated factors such as climate, top management, appropriate OD involving all the variables discussed earlier.

Measures of performance and control are necessary to measure the success of the organisation's operational standards and quality control.

Critical review and reflection

Hospitality organisations clearly need to achieve 'quality'.

To what extent do you feel that the TQM approach is likely to achieve that requirement and to what extent should hospitality managers adopt QA techniques to ensure that the required quality standards are achieved?

TQM and human resource management

There are numerous definitions of TQM which are generally expressed in terms of a way of life for an organisation as a whole, commitment to total customer satisfaction through a continuous process of improvement, and the contribution and involvement of people. TQM emphasises the importance of people as the key to quality and the satisfaction of customers' needs.[29] Staff should be properly trained and in a position to take action about quality defects as they notice them. This involves the convergence of quality assurance and human resource management.

TQM therefore requires the creation of a corporate identity, a total organisational approach, and the participation and commitment of staff at all levels, starting with the active support and involvement of top management. It also involves a strategic focus on training for total quality. As an example, Scott's Hotels training programme for quality was based on the managing director's conceptual model of TQM[30] (see Figure 10.3).

TQM involves an increased level of empowerment and providing staff with greater authority and responsibility for self-checking, decision-making and problem-solving. The introduction of TQM can therefore add to the pressures for a restructuring of the organisation and the move towards flatter hierarchies with the removal of a layer of managers/supervisors.

Benchmarking

As part of TQM standards, a process of benchmarking may be adopted. This is intended to measure an organisation's effectiveness compared to similar enterprises, and to provide a basis against which service and performance can be evaluated. Benchmarking may be both 'competitive', involving a comparison of products, service provision and delivery against competitors, and 'internal', involving an audit of activities and service within the group/organisation and a review of whether these could be performed more efficiently or effectively.

Kaizen

An integral part of a total quality approach is the Japanese concept of **Kaizen**, which literally means 'improvement' and is often interpreted as gradual progress or incremental change. Kaizen was introduced in several Japanese organisations after the Second World War and is particularly associated with Toyota. This focuses on the people aspect of improvement and the acceptance of change. The concept is based on a daily activity of continual evolutionary change and on the belief that the individual workers know more about their own jobs than anyone else. Cane suggests that the traditional Kaizen approach embeds it in a hierarchical structure, although it gives considerable responsibility to employees within certain fixed boundaries. The approach:

- analyses every part of a process down to the smallest detail;
- sees how every part of the process can be improved;
- looks at how employees' actions, equipment and materials can be improved; and
- looks at ways of saving time and reducing waste.[31]

According to the Kaizen Institute, Kaizen is a Japanese term meaning 'change for the better'. Applied to business organisations, it implies continuing improvement, involving everyone, that does not cost much. Kaizen organisation culture is based on three superordinate principles:

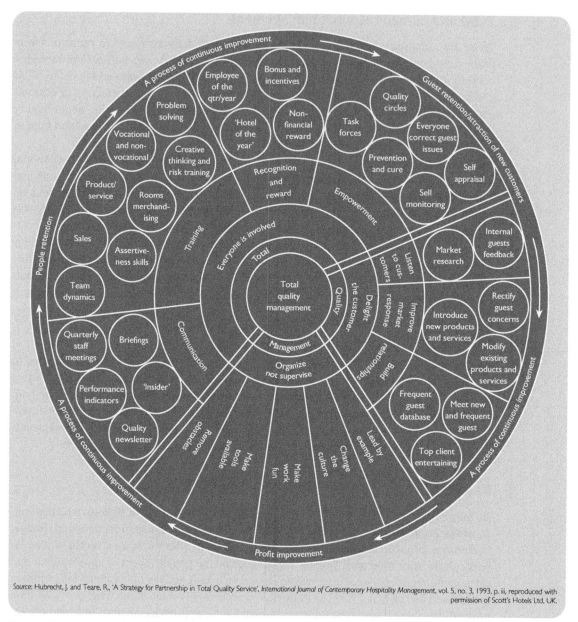

Source: Hubrecht, J. and Teare, R., 'A Strategy for Partnership in Total Quality Service', *International Journal of Contemporary Hospitality Management*, vol. 5, no. 3, 1993, p. iii, reproduced with permission of Scott's Hotels Ltd, UK.

Figure 10.3 Conceptual model of TQM

process and results; systematic thinking; and a non-judgemental, non-blaming approach. Kaizen strategy begins with customers' needs concerning quality, cost and delivery and is founded on a people-orientated culture.[32]

The EFQM Excellence Model[33]

Total quality is the goal for many organisations, but it has been difficult until relatively recently to find a universally acceptable definition of what this actually means. The

European Foundation for Quality Management (EFQM) Excellence Model[34] builds on the experience of previous models and was adopted by the British Quality Foundation in 1992 as the basis for both self-assessment and the UK Quality Award for Business Excellence, launched in 1994. Oakland provides the following description:

> The EFQM Excellence Model recognises that processes are the means by which a company or organisation harnesses and releases the talents of its people to produce results performance. Moreover, improvement in the performance can only be achieved by improving the processes by involving the people.[35]

The 'Model' is based on the concept that an organisation will achieve better results by involving all the people in the organisation in the continuous improvement of their processes; it provides a focus for integrating all contributors to the organisation's performance. It is a practical tool that facilitates measurement of where an organisation is on the path to excellence, helping them to understand where there are gaps and stimulating solutions. The 'Model' is designed to be non-prescriptive but is there to provide guidelines. Organisations are able to benchmark themselves against others both within and outside their sectors. (See figure below.) [36]

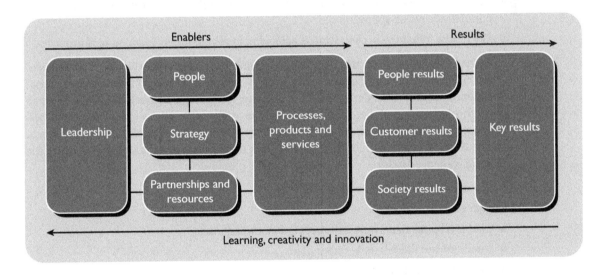

The basic assumption of the 'Model' is that excellent results to Performance, Customers, People and Society (the Results) are achieved through Leadership driving Policy and Strategy, People, Partnership and Resources, and Processes (The Enablers). Learning, Creativity and Innovation are key to improving enablers that, in turn, improve results.

Nine criteria of the Model

Each of the nine criteria featured in the 'Model' are described by the British Quality Foundation as follows:

1 *Leadership.* How leaders develop and facilitate the achievement of the mission and vision, develop values and ethics for long-term success and implement these via appropriate actions and behaviours, and are personally involved in ensuring that the organisation's management system is developed and implemented.

2 *Strategy.* How the organisation implements its mission and vision via a clear stakeholder-focused strategy, supported by relevant policies, plans, objectives, targets and processes, ensuring economic, societal and ecological sustainability.

3 *People.* How the organisation manages, develops and releases the knowledge and full potential of its people at an individual, team-based and organisation-wide level, and plans these activities in order to support its policy and strategy and the effective operation of its processes, allowing mutually beneficial achievement.

4 *Partnerships and resources.* How the organisation plans and manages its external partnerships and internal resources in order to support its policy and strategy and the effective operation of its processes.

5 *Processes, products and services.* How the organisation designs, manages and improves its processes, products and services in order to support its policy and strategy and fully satisfy, and generate increasing value for, its customers and other stakeholders.

6 *Customer results.* What the organisation is achieving in relation to its external customers.

7 *People results.* What the organisation is achieving in relation to its people.

8 *Society results.* What the organisation is achieving in relation to local, national and international society as appropriate.

9 *Key results.* What the organisation is achieving in relation to its planned performance.

Each of the above criteria are supported by a number of sub-criteria which pose a number of questions that should be considered in the course of self-assessment during which an organisation is encouraged to consider the results it is aiming for, the approaches that have been put in place, the deployment of these approaches and the assessment and review of the approaches. This system, which is at the heart of the Excellence Model, is known as the RADAR approach.

The British Quality Foundation recommends the following methodology for using the EFQM Excellence Model:

- develop commitment to self-assessment;
- plan self-assessment;
- establish teams to perform self-assessment and educate;
- communicate the self-assessment plans;
- conduct self-assessment;
- establish an action plan and;
- implement the action plan.[37]

Contemporary hospitality models

Excellence through people[38] is a scheme to help both small and large organisations in the hospitality, leisure, travel and tourism industry attract quality people into quality jobs to deliver quality service.[39]

Best Practice Forum is encouraging businesses in the hospitality, leisure, travel and tourism industry to introduce new ideas and innovation by adopting or adapting best practice – so raising their efficiency, productivity and competitiveness to world-class levels.

Hospitality Assured is based on international best practice; this standard has been created by the Institute of Hospitality in response to government and industry concerns about low standards of performance in many hospitality operations. Hospitality Assured provides a definitive standard for service excellence and identifies nine steps (see figure below) that any size or type of hospitality business has to address in running its operation effectively if consistent quality of service to meet customers' needs is to be maintained.

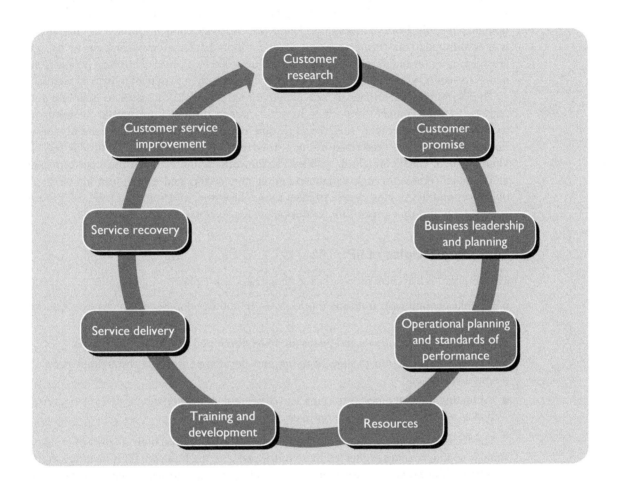

The Hospitality Assured framework is recognised by the British Quality Foundation and Quality Scotland as meeting the criteria of the EFQM Excellence Model (see above), which can be applied to any service business and offers the following advantages to a business:

- an opportunity to demonstrate to the customer its commitment to service excellence;
- a template for business improvement based on best practice;
- an industry-specific self-assessment diagnostic tool to identify and prioritise action;
- the opportunity for accreditation and national recognition; and
- the opportunity to benchmark and work together with like-minded businesses.

(The authors are grateful to Martin Brunner for providing the above information on the EFQM Excellence Model.)

Investors in People (IiP)

Investors in People is a standard for the training and development of people within an organisation. The standard was seen as coming originally from business as there was a need to recognise the importance of people as a strategic resource. In response, the IiP Standard was launched in 1991 as the national standard of good practice for the training and development of people. In 1993 Investors in People UK (a private company limited by guarantee) was established to take ownership of the Standard, protect its integrity, and ensure its successful promotion and development. The company is led by a board of business people from across the country, representing large and small firms from a variety of industrial sectors.

The IiP initiative continues to 'provide a national framework in order to maintain and increase the UK's competitive position in world markets through its increased commitment to developing a more highly skilled and flexible workforce'.[40] It seeks to reward organisations that achieve the prescribed training standards which allows them to display the IiP kitemark logo. The IiP Standard provides a framework for improving business performance and competitiveness through a planned approach to setting and communicating business objectives and developing people to meet these objectives. The Standard is held for three years after which time organisations must apply for reassessment to retain it.

Four key principles of IiP

The Standard is a cyclical process based on four key principles:

- a public commitment from the top to invest in and develop people in order to achieve business goals;
- planning how individuals and teams are to be developed to achieve these goals;
- taking relevant action to meet training and development needs throughout people's employment; and
- evaluating the outcomes of training and development for individuals and the organisation as a basis for continuous improvement.

The focus is not on training and development *per se*, but is purposely aligned to business strategy so that training is directed more to the needs of the business. IiP is investing in the members of the workforce, developing them and helping them to achieve not only their own personal goals but the goals and objectives of the organisation. Investors in People is recognised as one of the most successful quality awards ever introduced. It can be viewed as part of a wider quality management process with natural progression to total quality management (TQM).

IiP and service quality

From a study of case histories of hospitality organisations, Lockwood *et al.* comment that every one of the case studies demonstrates the importance placed on training by organisations committed to service quality.

> Most of the case study companies have found that IiP complements their strategies. This is not surprising. IiP sets out to develop, in the firm's employees, the abilities they need to achieve the company's business goals. In service industries, particularly, the employees' performance can make a critical contribution to the customers' expectations of the product. Consequently, training can change significantly the customers' perception of value for money.[41]

The Headland Hotel case study illustrates a success in IiP.

CASE STUDY 10.1

The Headland Hotel

Profile

Size: 101–250
Sector: Hotels and Leisure
Location: South West
Theme: Leadership and management
           Increased productivity

The organisation

The Headland Hotel is a luxury hotel in Newquay, and is a blend of Victorian grandeur and casual luxury. A classic icon of the stunning coastline on which it stands, this four-star hotel is a family-run establishment with charming staff whose aim is to engage with guests and make them feel welcome.

The Headland Hotel has been recognised regionally and nationally, winning many awards, both for its high-quality accommodation and food, and also for its approach to employing and developing staff. The Headland was the first company in Cornwall to gain Investor in People status in January 1993 and has recently taken part in the pilot of the new approach from Investors in People as they take training and development of their team very seriously.

The challenge

Whilst the management team were keen on having good practice recognised, they also wanted to focus on improving their performance. The new approach provided a cost-effective means of identifying current strengths that would support the effective management of change, but would also highlight areas that might be improved. The main body of the report centred on good practices within the hotel which supported effective change management and potential for improvement.

The Standard identified both good practice achieved and where and how it was established. This evidence put them in a great place to gain the most from the standard and demonstrated how the process was not a 'one-off' but could develop with them and continue to provide company growth.

Focus was on the planning of key issues to take forward and facilitate the practical delivery of improvements to support change management.

The action plan considered four themes for further improvement:

- Vision and strategies for change
- Communication
- Performance indicators
- Developing management capacity.

Additional 'paper' evidence was accumulated as the review progressed, at the suggestion of interviewees, offering a document as a good example to illustrate a particular practice.

The strategy

They compiled a review plan tailored to reflect the information relevant to the new approach from the Investors in People planning process following discussions with their assessor. The appropriate evidence requirements across the framework were identified, again drawing from (but not duplicating) the mapping example, and a matrix was incorporated within the review plan.

The results

The new approach from Investors in People enabled The Headland Hotel to explore some of the factors that they felt needed to move forward in order to implement change successfully, for example: communicating with and engaging staff more fully in change; empowering staff to implement new ways of working; line managers being more proactive in delegating to team members, etc. Top management have a very proactive approach in involving staff in plans for improving the Hotel and its performance. But it was felt that this could be taken further, and cascaded more effectively within individual departments. However, communication was identified as exceptionally strong across the business which is

➡

something they hold as a high priority especially within their sector.

Staff retention has undoubtedly improved year on year since participating in Investors in People and new staff often approach them because of the Standard. As a company they are exceptionally people-driven which puts them at the heart of the business. They therefore offer exceptional staff benefits and career progression which is seen as a paramount part of their employment. Even though progression with Investors in People has meant they expect more from their people, this is reflected in what they get back, demonstrated by the fact they have achieved a high consistency with their current management team. People want to work at the hotel and they attract the right staff because of the clear path The Standard demonstrates, encouraging applications even when no jobs are advertised!

The framework of the new approach from Investors in People was seen as very straightforward and was easily tailored to support their changes and particularly to help the management team to engage staff. Staff were aware of the way Investors in People has helped the hotel to manage their business issues effectively. They now feel more able to raise issues but also come up with solutions because they are passionate about what they do and want themselves and the business to thrive. It helped them to see the value in their participation, thus ensuring that their contribution was very constructive. It also helped employees focus on what they required from the restaurants to make them work seamlessly following all the changes.

Working with The Standard, the Hotel Directors and HR Manager's objective was to confirm understanding of the feedback contained within the report. This gave transparency to what they hoped to achieve which in turn helped to drive staff through the changes that were imminently going to happen. Investors in People principles now sit alongside their action plan making sure that as a collective they all understand the key objectives.

Key points from the feedback were:

- The report format was thorough, understandable and 'made sense'.
- It 'firmed up' areas that need improving and will help to engage staff in moving the hotel forward.
- It gave a thorough understanding of the breadth of good practices in place.
- The draft action plan was very useful in summarising improvement areas and to assist with practical action planning.
- Overall an effective approach for a review and delivered good value for money.

Investors in People assessor comments

Clive Tabiner, Investors in People assessor, comments: 'This review demonstrates that the new approach from Investors in People can be fairly short – in this case seven weeks – but have a deep impact. We reaffirmed their action plan and the senior managers involved consulted widely with their departmental managers, to ensure that there was good "buy in" throughout the hotel.'

Human Resources manager comments

Michelle Brown, Human Resources manager, comments: 'This new approach helped us maximise skills and capabilities linked to employee benefits, and the organisational strategy, to effectively bring into line people and objectives for the business. By managing change effectively we feel we have ensured that we continue to exceed customer expectations and for such a simple process what we gained was beyond our expectations and our people's.'[42]

Service quality and business performance

Harrington and Akehurst suggest that empirical studies have, in the main, not included analyses of service quality in the hotel industry and relatively few researchers have addressed the proposition that service quality leads to improved performance and competitiveness. From an exploratory study of 250 UK hotel units with a size of over 100 beds, Harrington and Akehurst suggest four implications for management: (1) the results emphasise the need for hotels to develop more effective internal communications relating to quality service for the customer; (2) the requirement for managers to adopt more representative procedures for evaluating service quality at the unit level; (3) the significance for managers of developing and operationalising service strategies at business and unit level; and (4) concern about the low ranking for image in quality terms.

In conclusion, Harrington and Akehurst observe that:

> whilst a large proportion of respondents acknowledge the importance of developing, promoting and measuring service quality, it would appear that few managers, at the hotel unit level, have systems in place to effect implementation. Indeed, responsibility for implementing service quality initiatives remains for the most part with senior management.[43]

Managerial perceptions and attitudes

Harrington and Akehurst also draw attention to the need for further research to be carried out to investigate the nature of service quality implementation in UK hotels. The quality concept has attracted increasing interest in the service sector and there is a growing body of literature on the subject. Results from the study suggest a growing awareness, within hotels, of the need to manage quality in a complex and competitive marketplace. However, the findings also emphasise the importance of distinguishing *awareness* from *actionable policy* and suggest cause for concern in the attitudes shown by middle managers towards their hotels' quality efforts. There is a need to direct attention towards a critical examination of the effectiveness of implemented quality initiatives.[44]

In order to measure service quality implementation practices, Harrington and Akehurst undertook a further survey of 133 general managers in three-star UK hotel organisations. The reported results add emphasis to the need to closely align human resource considerations with overall strategic concerns in the achievement of quality objectives, and the consideration of people management issues in quality implementation. Although managers may subscribe to the notion of human relations dimensions underpinning the quality implementation process, this is not necessarily practised in the organisations surveyed. Further research is needed to examine managerial attitudes to, and opinions of, the *actual* practice of quality management in hotel organisations.[45]

Myths of customer service

In an interesting and thought-provoking account on the provision of customer service, Jamison argues the need to maintain a balance in the belief that 'the customer is always right' and suggest ten myths of customer service.[46]

- *Myth 1: 'Give the customers what they want'* – customers are not able to imagine creative solutions to what they want. Profit-making creative solutions must be designed internally and presented properly to customers in order to stimulate a response.
- *Myth 2: 'The customer is always right'* – this is clearly not evident as there are customers who steal or seek to defraud, and people who try to profit from the high-profile image of a particular company.
- *Myths 3 and 4: 'Always delight your customers and exceed their expectations'. 'Always provide the best quality service'* – not every company should seek to provide the best quality

457

service unless it wishes to go out of business. What is appropriate for the prestigious Ritz-Carlton Hotel chain would clearly be inappropriate for a mass caterer such as McDonald's.

● *Myth 5: 'Empower all your staff'* – causes of poor quality are not always lack of awareness or the wrong attitude among staff but more often the definition of the role they are asked to perform, or the procedures they are expected to follow.

● *Myth 6: 'Reduce the number of complaints'* – it is better to regard complainers not in a negative vein but as customers trying to help the company perform better. Encouraging customers to complain direct to the company provides the opportunity to turn them into advocates.

● *Myth 7: 'You must introduce a loyalty card'* – loyalty consists of far more than a loyalty card. Managers need to design a customer care programme that is relevant and specific to their company.

● *Myth 8: 'Good customer service is just smiling at customers and wishing them a nice day'* – customer service differs from culture to culture. What may work in the United States does not always work here. McDonald's had to apologise because it infuriated the British public by training its staff to wish everyone to 'have a nice day'.

● *Myth 9: 'You must try to please all the people all the time'* – customers have different service requirements, and it's not possible to provide one bland service offer to them all.

● *Myth 10: 'Much service improvement is operational and tactical'* – there is a strategic dimension to customer care and service should be as different as their products. It is senseless for a 'least cost' supplier (like Travelodge) to try to offer the best service in the industry (like Ritz-Carlton).

Critical review and reflection

'If an individual or group is set a target, they will meet it, even if this results in failing to achieve the organisation's real objectives.'

To what extent do you agree with this statement? Give examples of situations where targets have been met without regard to quality standards or ethical considerations. As an example, what might a chef do to ensure that a target of a certain gross profit on food is achieved?

The management of change

Critical review and reflection

'You think you understand the situation. What you don't understand is the situation just changed.'[47]

What might be the implications of the above statement? Give examples.

Change is an inevitable and constant feature of life. It is an inescapable part of individual, social and organisational life. At the individual level there could for example be a **personal transformational change** where circumstances have not changed but, because of some emotional or experiential happening, the individual was transformed or changed. This could have an effect on the individual's behaviour or attitudes at, or to, work.

Looking specifically at organisations, organisational change can be initiated deliberately by the manager; it can evolve slowly within a department. It can be imposed by specific changes in policy or procedures or it can arise from external pressures. Change can affect all aspects of the operation and functioning of the organisation.[48]

The hospitality industry is concerned with both production and service, and is particularly susceptible to environmental influences. In order to ensure its survival and future success, the hospitality organisation must be able to adapt readily to the changes affecting it. The ability to deal with change is a key attribute of a successful hospitality organisation.

Forces of change

A hospitality organisation can only perform effectively through interactions with the broader external environment of which it is part. The structure and functioning of the organisation must reflect, therefore, the nature of the environment in which it is operating. There are factors which create an increasingly volatile environment, such as:

- uncertain economic conditions;
- globalisation and fierce world competition;
- government intervention;
- European Union social legislation.

Other major forces of change might be seen to include:

- *Knowledge explosion* – for example the number of people in some form of education, new ideas and methods of working, the increasing number of hospitality management students, the speed and availability of information via the internet.
- *Rapid product obsolescence* – changes in consumer preference, together with changing technology such as increased demand for different and unusual foods.
- *Scarcity of natural resources* and strengthening of green issues.
- *Changing nature of the workforce* – for example the flow of possible staff from parts of Europe or the rest of the world, such as a substantial increase in the number of Polish staff available, followed by their return to Poland as economic conditions changed.
- *Quality of working life* – for example the increased attention to the satisfaction of people's needs and expectations at work, the expectations of flexible working, and increased maternity and paternity leave allowances.
- *Rapid developments in new technologies and the information age* – for example advances in computing and control systems or changes in food production systems. These changes can result in de-skilling in some areas such as kitchens and the increasing need for IT skills in others such as for those working in reception.

Technology and change

The rapid development, and increasing use, of technology is undoubtedly one of the most significant drivers of changes in work and working practices in the hospitality industry.

Ip, Leung and Law discuss the need to enhance operational efficiency, improve service quality and reduce costs. They indicate that practitioners in the hospitality industry have widely adopted and implemented information and communication technologies in their businesses, whilst maintaining that much more should be done in this area.[49]

They identify seven areas where organisations should use appropriate technology to increase operational efficiency:

1 *Human resources and web-based training.* Although hospitality organisations are using web-based training for their staff, there is potential for wider use of this resource.

2 *Security*

3 *Computerised reservation systems*

4 *Revenue management*

5 *Marketing.* The development of e-marketing strategies is crucial to success. Increasingly hospitality practitioners are collecting detailed information about their customers which enables the offer of personalised services to specific customers. This information also allows for targeted marketing.

6 *Guest services/guest satisfaction surveys.* The study concluded that the effective use of ICTs not only improves service quality but also maximises guest satisfaction, thereby increasing profitability.

7 Strategic and operational management.

Ip, *et al.* also point out some of the negative implications of the increase in the use of ICTs. This includes so-called 'cyberslacking', meaning that some staff are guilty of time-wasting on the internet. Another major issue is that of potential infringement of customers' personal privacy.

> The tendency of potential customers to use the internet, including comparison sites, to obtain good deals has obvious implications for organisations' profitability and the inability or unwillingness of small organisations to produce attractive, and informative websites, clearly affects their ability to compete. Lack of knowledge of potential ICT applications also has a detrimental effect on some organisations' business.

Connolly and Olsen[50] similarly identify that ICTs are the largest forces that affect the changes in hospitality and tourism.

According to a survey from the Management Consultancies Association, four interrelated forces are driving change, each of which brings organisations and individuals into conflict:

1 outsourcing and the continual redefinition of what constitutes an organisation's core business;

2 the distribution of work across different people, organisations and locations, and the extent to which this makes work fragmented;

3 changing demographics and expectations that create an employees', rather than employers', market;

4 the double-edged sword of technology, which enables people to do more but tempts organisations to do too much.[51]

Critical review and reflection

'Change is nothing new and a simple fact of life. Some people actively thrive on new challenges and constant change, while others prefer the comfort of the status quo and strongly resist any change. It is all down to the personality of the individual and there is little management can do about resistance to change.'

To what extent do you accept this contention? What is your attitude to change?

Planned organisational change

Most organisational change is triggered by the need to respond to or anticipate the factors referred to above. Planned change represents an intentional attempt to improve, in some important way, the operational effectiveness of the organisation.

The basic underlying objectives can be seen in general terms as:

● modifying the behavioural patterns of members of the organisation; and

● improving the ability of the organisation to cope with changes in its environment.

ACAS refers to initiating and maintaining a Quality of Working Life (QWL) change programme. Such initiatives could stem from a variety of issues that might provide 'a window for change' to management and/or worker representatives. Examples include:

● a general sense that the organisation could perform better;

● the need to improve organisation flexibility, quality or to develop new customer concern;

● a sense that skills and abilities of people are under-utilised or concerns about a lack of commitment from employees;

● the need to introduce changes in technology or working practices;

● workers feeling over-controlled by supervision or by the process or jobs seen as being boring;

● concerns about ineffective communications or poor performance indicators;

● fractious relationships between managers and the managed.[52]

Resistance to change

Managerial resistance to change

Although the organisation has to adapt to its environment, there is often resistance at the managerial level against change.

● Major change often requires large resources which may already be committed to investments in other areas or strategies. Assets such as buildings and furnishings, technology, equipment and people cannot be altered easily.

● Attention is often focused on maintaining stability and predictability, especially in large-scale organisations. The need for formal structures, the division of work and established rules, procedures and methods of work can result in resistance to change.

● Management may feel comfortable operating within the structure, policies and procedures which have been formulated to deal with a range of past or present situations. Managers may set up defences against change and prefer to concentrate on the routine things they perform well.

● Change may also be seen as a threat to the power or influence of management, such as their control over decisions, resources or information. As an example, middle management may be resistant to the introduction of quality circles because the increased empowerment of members is seen as an encroachment on their traditional areas of authority and responsibility.[53]

Individual resistance to change

People are naturally wary of change and, although there may be potential positive outcomes, resistance to change – or the thought of the implications of change – appears to be a common phenomenon. Resistance to change can take many forms and may arise from a combination of factors. It is therefore often difficult to pinpoint the exact cause but some common reasons for individual resistance to change include the following.

Fear of the unknown

Many major changes present a degree of uncertainty, for example the possible effects of new technology or methods of working. A person may resist promotion because of uncertainty over changes in responsibilities or the increased social demands of the higher position. Changes which confront people with the unknown tend to cause anxiety or fear. A proposed change which is likely to break up a cohesive working group or to move an individual to a new work group may be resisted.

Habit

People tend to respond to situations in an established and accustomed manner. Habit may serve as a means of comfort and security, and as a guide for decision-making. Proposed changes to habits, especially if well established and requiring little effort, may well be resisted. If there is a clearly perceived advantage, for example a reduction in working hours without loss of pay, there is likely to be less resistance to the change. However, because of habit, some people may still find it difficult to adjust to the reduced hours of work.

Inconvenience or loss of freedom

If the change is seen as likely to prove inconvenient, make life more difficult, reduce freedom of action or result in increased control, there is likely to be resistance. For example, a manager may resist being moved to another establishment or location, especially if this involves greater travelling or moving house. Staff are likely to resist new working practices which require learning new skills or result in closer management control.

Economic implications

People are likely to resist change which is perceived as reducing either directly or indirectly their pay or other rewards, or requiring an increase in work for the same level of pay. Staff may resist a move to another job, even at the same level of basic pay, if they fear they may receive less in overtime payments, gratuities or other perks.

Security in the past

Some people tend to find a sense of security in the past. In times of frustration or difficulty, or when faced with new or unfamiliar ideas or methods, people may reflect on the past and wish to retain old and comfortable ways. There may be a tendency to cling to well-established and well-known procedures as giving a feeling of security.

Threat to status or symbols

Any perceived threat to the status or symbol attached to a job or position is likely to be resisted, for example proposals to remove a private office, reserved car parking space, special uniforms or a private locker.

Selective perception

People tend to have their own, biased view of a particular situation, which fits most comfortably their own perception of reality. This can cause almost a 'built-in' resistance to change. For example, strong trade unionists may have a stereotyped view of management as untrustworthy and therefore oppose any management change, however well-founded might be the intention. Managers may have a particular bias towards a particular theory or practice of organisational behaviour and discard new ideas which they feel to be of no concern or value to them.

Resistance to change in hospitality organisations

From an in-depth investigation of nine hotels in the UK, Okumus and Hemmington conclude that there are important similarities between hotel firms and manufacturing firms in terms of facing and overcoming barriers and potential resistance to change. They identified main barriers and resistance to change in hotel firms as: financial difficulties; cost of the change; lack of resources; fear of losing the existing customer; time limitation; priority of other businesses; lack of cooperation and skills; fear of insecurity; losing something valuable; and internal politics.

Okumus and Hemmington point out that managers require to understand the nature and forces of change, reasons for resistance and the effective implementation of change. Hotel managers need to adopt multiple strategies to help to overcome potential barriers to change and hotel firms should provide managerial staff with development to help them to cope with complex change situations.[54] However, as Cunningham points out, it is not impossible to get individuals to accept change:

> What seems to get in the way is the continual chanting of the untrue generalisation that 'people resist change'. People resist some change – if they perceive that they are going to lose out. People welcome change that makes things better.[55]

Successful implementation of change

Continual change is inevitable and the effective implementation of change is an increasingly important managerial responsibility. New ideas and innovations should not be perceived as threats by members of staff. But there is often resistance to change from people at all levels of an organisation. Overcoming this resistance can be difficult if their perception is that the change will be adverse to them. For the change to be introduced successfully, changes of both attitudes and behaviour will be necessary.

Behaviour modification

It may be useful to consider the work on behaviour modification carried out by Lewin who developed a programme of planned change and improved performance. This involves the management of a three-phase process:

- **unfreezing** – reducing those forces which maintain behaviour in its present form, recognition of the need for change and improvement to occur;
- **movement** – development of new attitudes or behaviour and the implementation of the change;
- **refreezing** – stabilising change at the new level and reinforcement through supporting mechanisms, for example policies, structure or norms.[56]

French, Kast and Rosenzweig list eight specific components of a planned-change effort related to the above process (see Figure 10.4).[57]

One of the most important factors in the successful management of change is the style of managerial behaviour adopted.

Never is leadership more sought after than in times of change and uncertainty. Effective change leadership is the key to shifting people's perceptions from seeing change as a threat to seeing it as an exciting challenge.[58]

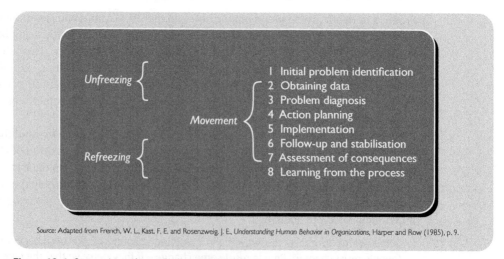

Source: Adapted from French, W. L., Kast, F. E. and Rosenzweig. J. E., *Understanding Human Behavior in Organizations*, Harper and Row (1985), p. 9.

Figure 10.4 Stages in a planned-change effort

In certain situations it may be necessary for management to use compulsion and the hierarchical authority to impose change. This *may* be appropriate, for example, if change is clearly going to be detrimental to staff and they are unlikely to be persuaded that it will not be detrimental. It should also be recognised that some people may prefer, and respond better to, an autocratic, directed and controlled style of management.

In most cases, however, the introduction of change is more likely to be effective with a participative style of management. If staff are kept fully informed of proposals, are encouraged to adopt a positive attitude and have personal involvement in the implementation of the change, there is a greater likelihood of their acceptance of the change. Use of the Lewin model, above, may be particularly useful.

Human and social factors of change

Managers must be responsive to change. However, activities managed on the basis of technical or economic efficiency alone are unlikely to lead to optimum improvement in performance. The efforts made by management to maintain the balance of the socio-technical system will influence people's attitudes, the behaviour of individuals and groups, and thereby organisational performance and effectiveness. Management must therefore take proper account of the importance of human and social factors of change. This demands that management:

- create an environment of trust and shared commitment, and involve staff fully in decisions and actions which affect them;
- maintain full and open communications, and the genuine participation of all staff concerned, preferably well before the actual introduction of the change;
- emphasise benefits of, and potential opportunities presented by, the change;
- encourage team management and a cooperative spirit among staff;
- give attention to job design, methods of work organisation and the development of cohesive groups;
- provide suitable economic incentive schemes to safeguard potential loss of earnings or job security, and ensure an equitable allocation of any financial savings resulting from the change;
- design a human resource management action programme directed to a review of recruitment and selection, natural wastage of staff, training and re-training, provisions for early retirements, and other strategies to reduce the possible level of redundancies or other harmful effects on staff.[59]

In certain situations it may be necessary for management to use compulsion and the hierarchical authority to impose change. This *may* be appropriate, for example, if change is clearly going to be detrimental to staff. It should also be recognised that some people may prefer, and respond better to, an autocratic, directed and controlled style of management. In most cases, however, the introduction of change is more likely to be effective with a participative style of management. If staff are kept fully informed of proposals, are encouraged to adopt a positive attitude and have personal involvement in the implementation of the change, there is a greater likelihood of their acceptance of the change.

Exhibit 10.2 Managing change at Novotel

Calori, Baden-Fuller and Hunt conducted a study of the change process at Novotel in the 1990s, which remains relevant at the time of writing. Their change programme provides an example of stages that may be followed in a situation of major change in a hospitality organisation.

Novotel perceived that there was a problem of falling occupancy and consequent profitability. Contraction to reduce costs and/or increasing prices to maintain profits were not seen as viable options. As a result of this initial analysis the organisation developed the following strategy:

- **Recognise customer needs** – recognition that falling occupancy was more important than rising profits, and to achieve this first-hand customer data was important.
- **Form and motivate new top team** – appoint two co-presidents with different skills and styles and form a team strongly committed to change.
- **Change as a project** – lead and coordinate organisational change, as a project.
- **Develop new competencies and capabilities** – develop new competencies in staff, for example having multi-skilled and flexible front-line workers; gear incentives to competence building; bringing in new routines for tasks such as room-cleaning.
- **Obtain external stakeholder support** – obtaining support from the main board to large-scale change and the consequent costs.
- **Redistribute power and change the structures** – increase the span of control and remove layers of management to give more power to front-line workers.
- **Design the communication strategy** – remove layers of hierarchy and organise regular meetings and progress groups.
- **Shape new behaviours** – recruit new people and eliminate top managers not committed to the change; fully involve middle managers; publicise key individual actions at local level; and hold local activities in hotels to reinforce the balance between standardisation and individuality. [60]

Exhibit 10.3 Managing change at the Swan and Dolphin Hotels, Walt Disney World Florida

Ford, Heisler and McCreary[61] provide a practical example of the management of change at the Swan and Dolphin Hotels in Walt Disney World, Orlando, Florida. In 1998 the Starwood Corporation bought the Swan Hotel from Westin Hotels and, shortly afterwards, the Dolphin Hotel from the Sheraton Hotel Corporation.

These two hotels were more or less adjacent, which seemed to offer an opportunity to merge a lot of their management and operations, thereby creating one, bigger and more efficient, operation. In a sense, the merging of systems was the easy part; what was more difficult was dealing with the staff, who were used to the different cultures of the 'old' hotels and were not happy about things changing.

The smaller Swan hotel, under Westin ownership, had deemed itself superior to the Dolphin when owned by Sheraton, and this led to considerable tension between the staffs, after the merger. The new owners, Starwood, needed to find a way of overcoming these tensions, getting all staff to accept that they were now part of the same organisation. It was extremely important that attitudes and behaviours changed to the point that everyone worked well and happily together. An effective change process was needed.

The consultants recommended using a 5-P model of change (which built upon the previous McKinsey 7-S model), comprising the following stages:

> **purpose**; specific targets of change should be identified and **prioritized**; **people** potentially affected by the change should be identified and brought into the change process; the **process** should use appropriate levels of direction, participation, and consultation; and the **proof** should demonstrate visibly and believably what the change accomplished.

While the Swan–Dolphin merger was not without its problems, the approach resulted in a successful change implementation that saved $4 million in annual expenses.

The stages of the merger process can be summarised as follows:

Purpose – The specific targets of change, referred to above, were seen to be the three stakeholder groups: the managers, the employees and the customers. In defining the purpose it was appreciated that effective change management must have a clear purpose, a goal or vision or a compelling problem. The major problem here was that, for the employees, and to some extent the managers, making a lot of money for the Starwood corporation was not a compelling argument for change. However, being part of a prestigious and successful hotel organisation was more acceptable and if all the unsettling changes were to lead to that, then employees might be expected to embrace them.

Staff were not informed of all targets at the outset of the change process but given them in manageable stages. The progress towards the unified organisation was marked by identifying and celebrating 'small victories' as the new organisation moved forward.

Priorities – The required changes were prioritised following analysis using the McKinsey 7-S model, i.e. looking at **S**trategy, **S**tructure, **S**ystems, **S**taff, **S**tyle, **S**kills and **S**hared Values.

People – clearly, some were in favour of the changes, but some resisted change when they felt their jobs were threatened. *One example of resistance to change was when the 'Swan' chefs produced a carving of a dolphin eating a swan.*

The attitudinal change needed was achieved by giving the staff an overabundance of information, treating them with respect and dignity and employing a team to identify problem areas and resistance.

Process – throughout the change process, great care was taken to encourage participation and consultation, and appropriate management styles were adopted at all levels.

Proof – the result of the change programme was that the new merged hotels achieved $4 million savings and the Swan and Dolphin won an award as 'One of the best places to work – 2010'.

One of the best places to work[62]

'The Walt Disney World Swan and Dolphin was recognized by *Orlando Business Journal* as one of the "Best Places to Work 2010" and was also honored as the top placing company for our size (1,000+ employees).

'In addition, we were recognized by the Orlando Sentinel's Top 100 for Working Families, where once again we placed in the Top 25! This award honors those companies who make family a priority and offer benefits both traditional (medical, dental, 401k etc) and unique (anniversary recognition, holiday parties etc). This year the Orlando Sentinel also recognized our very own Adriana Zamot as the winner of the "Family Champion" award. The Family Champion award is given to an individual who strives to help make their company an environment where family-friendly is encouraged.'

http://www.swandolphin.com/63

The future

Director of Human Resources of Compass Catering, Vicky Williams, interviewed in August 2011, suggested that the key changes affecting the hospitality industry today, and likely to occur in the foreseeable future are as follows:

- An increasingly multi-ethnic workforce. This suggests a workforce comprising people with a variety of cultures, some of whom might not have English as their first language.

- Managing a highly qualified workforce, often with degrees and postgraduate qualifications, working for the minimum wage. The challenge is addressing their discontent in being employed in non-graduate roles with low rates of pay and keeping them motivated.

- Managing the older workforce, as more people with inadequate pensions are required to continue working for financial reasons.

- The changing social expectations and attitudes of the workforce towards issues such as corporate social responsibility and the wider environment.

- Motivating staff using means other than financial rewards in a tight economic climate.

Critical review and reflection

To what extent do you agree with Vicky Williams' analysis above?

What major changes do you anticipate within the hospitality industry within the next five years?

Synopsis

- Organisational development is a generic term embracing a wide range of intervention strategies into the social processes of organisations. It is concerned with attempts to improve overall performance and effectiveness. Two central and critical features of OD are organisational culture and organisational change.

- Applications of the effective management of people are dependent upon the characteristic features of the individual organisation and its culture. Culture is difficult to explain precisely. It helps to explain what the organisation is all about and how things are performed in different organisations. There are a number of different ways in which to understand what constitutes organisational culture. It develops over time and in response to a complex set of factors.

- Organisational effectiveness is influenced by a multiplicity of variables. One particular feature of successful performance in the hospitality industry is concern for quality and standards. This must be coupled with a required level of productivity. The adoption of a total quality management culture involves the convergence of quality assurance and human resource management. As part of a TQM approach a process of benchmarking may be adopted.

- The EFQM Excellence Model recognises that processes are the means by which a company or organisation harnesses and releases the talents of its people to produce results. Other major contemporary hospitality models include Excellence through People and Hospitality Assured. It is important for the hospitality industry to give attention to the measurement of productivity, and to quality standards and business performance.

- Hospitality organisations operate within an increasingly volatile environment and are in a state of constant change. There is a wide range of forces acting upon organisations which make the need for change inevitable.

- Resistance to change can take many forms. A key feature in organisational behaviour is the successful management of change and interactions with the external environment. Managers need to give attention to the effective implementation of change, including due emphasis on human and social factors, and to overcoming the barriers and resistance to change and to encouraging the positive embracing of new ideas and developments.

REVIEW AND DISCUSSION QUESTIONS

1 Explain what is meant by organisational culture. How might corporate culture influence the effectiveness of hospitality operations?

2 What do you understand by organisational climate? Discuss with practical examples the main areas in which action could be taken to help improve organisational climate in the hospitality industry.

3 Explain the key elements of Total Quality Management (TQM) and how this differs from Quality Assurance (QA).

4 With examples, discuss how the use of technology is affecting the management of people in the hospitality industry.

5 Why do individuals and organisations tend to resist change? To what extent do you believe such resistance can be effectively overcome?

6 Explain fully the most important features of two of the models for the successful implementation of organisational change.

7 How are changes in the working environment likely to impact on managing the workforce in the hospitality industry in the future?

ASSIGNMENT 1

In June 2006 an article in the *Caterer and Hotelkeeper* identified '12 things that changed hotels'.[64]

They were:

- the internet
- the celebrity chef
- better hotel restaurants
- the boutique hotel
- the budget hotel
- easy air travel
- the spa
- Eastern European labour
- the death of stiff service
- the high-fashion hotel bar
- the vacuum wine saver
- no more single beds.

1 To what extent do you feel that the above list is appropriate today?

2 What other factors do you think are changing the hospitality industry today?

3 Give reasons for your choices.

4 How, and why, does your list vary from the list above?

ASSIGNMENT 2

Identify uses of technology within an establishment with which you are familiar. Evaluate the extent to which they enhance

    (a) productivity;

    (b) the working environment and job design of staff.

CASE STUDY 10.2

Driving change and managing tradition

EP (EP Business in Hospitality Magazine) went behind the scenes at Buckingham Palace to talk to the Deputy Master of the Household, Edward Griffiths. We asked him and many of his team about what it is actually like to work in the Royal Palace and about the challenges and successes of driving modernisation and change while ensuring traditions are maintained.

It is iconic; the Palace draws millions of tourists a year, as does its famous inhabitant, the Queen. However, despite passing this place frequently, and hearing or reading about the monarchy on an almost daily basis, I had never given much thought to what went on behind the scenes. So it was with a sense of excitement, yet also trepidation, that I went to meet with Edward Griffiths and his team to learn more and see a little of 'a day in the life of...'

Edward joined the Royal Household as Deputy Master nine years ago, coming from a career in hotels, restaurants and contract catering. He was previously managing director of Roux Restaurants and Roux Fine Dining. Was the Palace a shock to the system?

'I was brought into this newly created role as one of two Deputy Masters of the Household in order to bring together the three previously independent departments of Food, Service and Housekeeping, which had all previously reported as separate departments', explains Edward. 'The brief was to bring cohesion to the departments and to drive an evolution of change drawing on my previous experience in business. It is a common misconception that the Palace is old-fashioned, and yet when I came on board I was pleasantly surprised by the professional, forward-thinking organisation that I had joined. However, we needed to introduce further change and evolve continuously; this is not about changing five things then the job is done.

'We started by bringing the departments together and focusing on cross-training and improving the skills of the team across all aspects of our work. I can most liken my position to that of a hotel managing director; we have most of the same departments across hospitality and domestic services but with a few key differences. Firstly, we have to be portable

as we are predominantly based at Buckingham Palace but must move with the Queen to the other royal residences as required. This is both interesting and exciting for the team, but it also presents certain challenges.

'Secondly, we are guardians of heritage buildings, traditions and priceless items. Our teams require certain skills and training that would never be necessary in a hotel environment. Our housekeeping staff and Palace attendants are responsible for the cleaning, upkeep and movement of antique furniture and incredibly delicate objects and must be specially trained in the treatment and conservation of these items. In a way this aspect is more like running a museum or art gallery than a hotel. Our footmen are handling china, glass, silver and gilt that are both very valuable and often old and delicate. We have no budget line in our P&L for breakage, it simply cannot happen! Can you imagine that in a hotel?

'And finally, we do not work in a hotel or a business, but in a private home, albeit one with both public and private spaces. This is where the Queen lives and our teams from the chefs to the housekeeping staff cater for everything in the Palace, from private "family" dinners to state dinners and garden parties, always with a respect for the fact that this is the Queen's home.'

So what has changed in the nine years since Edward took the helm? 'One of the main areas for change has been the cross-training of our workforce. Previously there was a lot more hierarchy in the departments, for example there were footmen who would serve at dinners and receptions and under butlers who set up, laying tables and preparing the event.

'We have altered this; all footmen work across an event from beginning to end. We have also ensured that our footmen and our housekeeping staff are cross-trained. We used to rely a lot on a casual labour pool for larger events but this can be problematic both from a financial perspective and also from a security point of view. Our housekeeping team are now all trained in the food and beverage side of our work and will serve and be

Case study 10.2 (continued)

involved in larger front-of-house events; similarly, all footmen train in housekeeping.

'This has all been supported by the development of the new Butler's Diploma written by Nigel McEvoy, the Palace Steward, in conjunction with the Savoy Educational Trust, City and Guilds and Thames Valley University.

'Just like any organisation, we have had to adapt, modernise and become more efficient. Since the civil list funding was fixed ten years ago and the Queen's programme has become busier and busier we are effectively doing three times more "business" than we were ten years ago on a decreasing budget. It is vital to drive efficiencies so that we can maintain and improve the standard and quality of the environment and service.

'Some of this efficiency is through the cross-skilling initiatives led by Stephen Gourmand, the Assistant Master responsible for service and housekeeping. However, we also make use of an in-house craft team based in Windsor to enable us to maintain and improve the fabric of the Palaces without incurring the costs associated with outsourcing. We have to prioritise and continue to work on the most important areas – it has been said that you never finish painting the Forth Bridge, as once you get to one end you start again from the other. It can feel a little like that!'

Nine years on, how does Edward feel about the future?

'Motivation is high. We have a continued challenge ahead, and a lot to do. However, it is rewarding and we have an incredibly enthusiastic team with the same values. What is even more inspiring is that the team are actively contributing to the development of our collective values; we are living proof that good ideas feed in from all areas.'[65]

Questions

1 Identify the similarities and differences involved in managing at Buckingham Palace and managing in other hospitality settings.

2 Examine the factors that required a change within the organisation. Identify the possible resistance to change and suggest how it was overcome.

3 Looking at a hospitality organisation of your choice, suggest how the difference between that organisational culture and the organisational culture in the Palace affects the way that major change is addressed.

CASE STUDY 10.3

The Walt Disney Company

Disney begins tugging on the heartstrings of employees even before they are hired. Think about the typical recruiting office in the hospitality industry – a windowless cubbyhole in the sub-basement between the laundry and the boiler room. Then walk into Disney World's capacious 'casting center,' and you're in Wonderland. Well, not exactly, but the doorknobs on the entrance do replicate the ones Alice yanked during her adventures. Just inside the portals, perched on high pedestals, are statues of 15 mock-gilded Disney characters, including, of course, the world's most famous rodent. Ascend a gently sloping hallway, whose walls are decorated with whimsical murals, and you're in a vast anteroom where the centerpiece is the original model of Snow White's castle. Some 50,000 aspiring employees funnel through the Lake Buena Vista casting center every year, seeking jobs that start with pay as low as $5.95 per hour. (Disney's other theme parks, in California, Japan, and France, do their own hiring.) Eight thousand emerge as freshly minted food servers, parade marchers, souvenir sellers, bus drivers, room cleaners, and other assorted 'cast members'. What are Disney World's 40 interviewers – all of whom started as front-line workers – most interested in? Not cognitive ability. Only applicants seeking a job that involves handling cash take a simple math test. Says Duncan Dickson, director of casting: 'We're looking for personality. We can train for skills. We want people who are enthusiastic, who have pride in their work, who can take charge of a situation without supervision.' Like Marriott, Disney has overhauled its approach to orientation, putting less emphasis on policies and procedures and more on emotion. Traditions, the two-day initial training session attended by all new cast members, is part inculcation, part encounter group. Guided by two unfailingly upbeat cast members, neatly dressed neophytes seated at round tables in a small classroom discuss their earliest memories of Disney, their visions of great service, their understanding of teamwork. Next comes the movie, a panegyric to Walt Disney himself. The film depicts the founder as a creative risk taker who overcame setbacks (his first character, destined for obscurity, was named Oswald the Lucky Rabbit), believed in teamwork (he and brother Roy were partners), and preached the importance of exceeding the expectations of his guests. Yes, Walt actually embraced that concept, now being peddled as a new management mantra, way back in 1955. Trainer Robert Sias reminds the class that the entire Disney empire began with a mere mouse. He adds, 'you never know when something seemingly insignificant out in the workplace is going to have an enormous impact on a guest'. Sias recounts how he witnessed one of these 'magic moments' unfold on the grounds of the Disney-MGM Studios theme park. Emerging from the Chinese Theatre, a mother buys her young son a box of popcorn from an open-air stand. Seconds later, the lad, who looks to be about four, trips and falls. The popcorn spills, the boy bawls, the mother screams. A costumed cast member on his way to another attraction happens by. Barely breaking stride, he scoops up the empty cardboard box, takes it to the popcorn stand for a refill, presents it to the shattered child, and continues on his way. By encouraging such spurts of spontaneity like this impromptu *pas de deux* involving the costumed character and the popcorn seller, Disney World tries to instill verve in jobs that are otherwise tightly regimented. The 36-page cast members' appear-

ance guide, for example, includes excruciatingly detailed ukases on length and style of hair, color and quantity of cosmetics, and hues and textures of hosiery. This combination of precision and pixie dust produces results. Although revenue growth at all Disney resorts has slowed in recent years, 1993 receipts still reached $3.4 billion, more than treble their level a decade ago. Even the troubled Euro Disney, outside Paris, is inching toward recovery. Disney World, where the average age of cast members is 37, loses only about 15 per cent of its front-line employees to attrition each year, compared with a rate of 60 per cent for the hospitality industry as a whole. Why do so many cast members stay on? Wages are competitive, benefits are good, and opportunities for advancement abound. Disney acquires two-thirds of all salaried employees – such as managers, designers, and marketers – from within the company. But don't underestimate the power of sentiment. Listen to Ricky Anderson, 20, a host in Tomorrowland: 'Sometimes, you get hot in your costume, you get fed up dealing with angry guests who are tired of waiting in line. But then a kid asks you a question, you answer it, and she breaks into a smile. You can make someone happy.' Anderson, an intense, part-time college student who hopes to become an electrical engineer in Disney's 'imagineering' subsidiary, also treasures the times when the theme park hosts terminally ill children. Says he: 'I realize that what I'm doing is actually important and not to be taken for granted.' [66]

Culture at Disney[67]

'Each of our companies has a unique ability to harness the imagination in a way that inspires others, improves lives across the world and brings hope, laughter and smiles to those who need it most. Together as one team, we embrace the values that make The Walt Disney Company an extraordinary place to work:

- **Innovation**
  - We are committed to a tradition of innovation and technology.

- **Quality**

Case study 10.3 (continued)

- We strive to set a high standard of excellence.
- We maintain high-quality standards across all product categories.
- **Community**
  - We create positive and inclusive ideas about families.
  - We provide entertainment experiences for all generations to share.
- **Storytelling**
  - Timeless and engaging stories delight and inspire.
- **Optimism**
  - At The Walt Disney Company, entertainment is about hope, aspiration and positive outcomes.
- **Decency**
  - We honor and respect the trust people place in us.
  - Our fun is about laughing at our experiences and ourselves.

These values live in everything we do. They create a unified mission that all our people believe in and work toward. And to recognize individual efforts, we have a variety of reward programs, including:

- Quality of Work
- Length of Service
- Community Volunteerism
- Employee of the Month Recognition

These are just some of the ways The Walt Disney Company commits to providing a rewarding, inclusive and supportive work environment.'

Questions

1 How would you characterise the culture of Disney?

2 How did the company encourage recruits to fit in with this culture?

3 How did some employees resist company norms and were they justified in so doing?

4 To what extent do you consider the culture in Disney today may be the same as in 1994?

References

1 For a fuller discussion see, for example, Baguley, P., *Improving Organizational Performance: A Handbook for Managers*, McGraw-Hill (1994).

2 Peters, T. J. and Waterman, R. H., *In Search of Excellence*, Harper & Row (1982).

3 Heller, R., *In Search of European Excellence*, HarperCollins Business (1997), p. xiv.

4 Merriden, T., 'The Gurus: Rosabeth Moss Kanter', *Management Today*, February 1997, 56.

5 See, for example, Smircich, L., 'Concepts of culture and organisational analysis', *Administrative Science Quarterly*, vol. 28, 1963, 339–58.

6 Bloisi, W., *Management and Organisational Behaviour*, McGraw-Hill (2003).

7 Atkinson, P. E., 'Creating cultural change', *Management*, vol. 24, no. 7, 1990, 6–10.

8 McLean, A. and Marshall, J., *Intervening in Cultures*, Working Paper, University of Bath (1983).

9 Schein, E. H., *Organizational Culture and Leadership: A Dynamic View*, Jossey-Bass (1985).

10 Woods, R. H., 'More alike than different: the culture of the restaurant industry', *Cornell HRA Quarterly*, vol. 30, no. 2, August 1989, 82–97.

11 Harrison, R., 'Understanding your organization's culture', *Harvard Business Review*, vol. 50, May/June 1972, 119–28.

12 Handy, C. B., *Understanding Organizations*, 4th edn, Penguin (1993).

13 Deal, T. E. and Kennedy, A. A., *Corporate Cultures: The Rites and Rituals of Corporate Life*, Penguin (1982).

14 See, for example, Handy, C. B., *Understanding Organizations*, 4th edn, Penguin (1993); and McLean, A. and Marshall, J., *Cultures at Work*, Local Government Training Board (October 1988).

15 See, for example, Beckett-Hughes, M., 'How to integrate two cultures', *People Management*, vol. 11, no. 5, 10 March 2005, 50–1.

16 Johnson, G., Scholes, K. and Whittington, R., *Exploring Corporate Strategy*, 7th edn, Financial Times Prentice Hall (2005).

17 Wilson, F., *Organizational Behaviour and Work: A Critical Introduction*, 2nd edn, Oxford University Press (2004), p. 185.

18 'Effective Organisations: The People Factor', Advisory Booklet, ACAS, November 2001.

19 Gorman, L., 'Corporate culture – why managers should be interested', *Leadership and Organization Development Journal*, vol. 8, no. 5, 1987, 3–9.

20 Glover, W. G., 'The Cult of Ineffectiveness', *Cornell HRA Quarterly*, February 1987, reprinted in Rutherford, D. G. (ed.), *Hotel Management and Operations*, Van Nostrand Reinhold (1990), pp. 29–33.

21 Meudell, K. and Gadd, K., 'Culture and climate in short-life organizations: sunny spells or thunderstorms?', *International Journal of Contemporary Hospitality Management*, vol. 6, no. 5, 1994, 27–32.

22 Tagiuri, R. and Litwin, G. H. (eds), *Organizational Climate*, Graduate School of Business Administration, Harvard University (1968).

23 Meudell, K. and Gadd, K., 'Culture and climate in short life organizations: sunny spells or thunderstorms?' *International Journal of Contemporary Hospitality Management*, vol. 6, no. 5, 1994, 28.

24 Mill, R. C., *Managing for Productivity in the Hospitality Industry*, Van Nostrand Reinhold (1989).

25 Gray, R., *A Climate of Success*, Butterworth Heinemann (2007).

26 Pentecost, D, 'Quality management: the human factor', *European Participation Monitor*, no. 2, 1991, 8–10.

27 James, G., 'Quality of Working Life and Total Quality Management', ACAS, Occasional Paper, no. 50, November 1991.

28 'Total quality: getting TQM to work', Checklist 030, Chartered Management Institute, June 2005.

29 See, for example, Lammermeyr, H. U., 'Human Relationships – The Key to Total Quality Management', *Total Quality Management*, vol. 12, no. 2, 1991, 175–180.

30 For an account of the application of total quality management in Scott's Hotels Ltd, see Hubrecht, J. and Teare, R., 'A strategy for partnership in total quality service', *International Journal of Contemporary Hospitality Management*, vol. 5, no. 3, 1993, i–v.

31 Cane, S., *Kaizen Strategies for Winning Through People*, Pitman Publishing (1996), p. 8.

32 www.kaizen-institute.com, accessed 4 June 2009.

33 http://www.efqm.org/en/, accessed 22.3.12.

34 I am grateful to Martin Brunner, for his contribution of The Excellence Model.

35 Oakland, J. S., *Total Organizational Excellence: Achieving World Class Performance*, Butterworth-Heinemann (1999), p. 99.

36 http://www.efqm.org/en/tabid/132/Default.aspx, accessed 17.2.12

37 http://www.efqm.org/en/Home/TheEFQMExcellenceModel/TheCriteria/tabid/392/Default.aspx

38 http://bestpracticeforum.org/excellence-through-people.aspx

39 http://bestpracticeforum.org/excellence-through-people.aspx, accessed 17.2.12

40 *The Investors in People Standard*, Investors in People UK (1995).

41 Lockwood, A., Baker, M. and Ghillyer, A. (eds), *Quality Management in Hospitality*, Cassell (1996), pp. 160–61.

42 From Investors in People website, accessed 17.2.12.

43 Harrington, D. and Akehurst, G., 'Service Quality and Business Performance in the UK Hotel Industry', *International Journal of Hospitality Management*, vol. 15, no. 3, 1996, 283–98.

44 Harrington, D. and Akehurst, G., 'An exploratory investigation into managerial perceptions of service quality in UK hotels', *Progress in Tourism and Hospitality Research*, vol. 2, John Wiley & Sons (1996), pp. 135–50.

45 Harrington, D. and Akehurst, G., 'An Empirical Study of Service Quality Implementation', *The Services Industries Journal*, vol. 20, no. 2, 2000.

46 Jamison, C., 'Top 10 Myths of Customer Service', *Manager: The British Journal of Administrative Management*, July/August 1999, 19–21.

47 Michael Nowliss, London Business School, quoted in EP Condense 28.6.11

48 For a discussion of change in relation to the complexities of organisational life see Senior, B. and Fleming, J., *Organisational Change*, 3rd edn, Financial Times Prentice Hall (2006).

49 Ip, C., Leung, R. and Law, R., 'Progress and development of information and communication technologies in hospitality', *International Journal of Contemporary Hospitality Management*, vol. 23, no. 4, 2011, 533–51.

50 Connolly, D. J., and Olsen, M. D., *An environmental assessment of how technology is reshaping the hospitality industry*, Tourism and Hospitality Research, vol. 3, no. 1, Ebsco Publishing (2002).

51 Czerniawska, F., *From Bottlenecks to BlackBerries: How the Relationship between Organisations and Individuals Is Changing*, Management Consultancies Association (September 2005).

52 'Effective organisations: the people factor', Advisory Booklet, ACAS, November 2001.

53 See for example: Dale, B. and Barlow, E., 'Quality Circles: The View From Within', *Management Decision*, vol. 25, no. 4, 1987, 5–9.

54 Okumus, F. and Hemmington, N., 'Barriers and resistance to change in hotel firms: an investigation at unit level', *International Journal of Contemporary Hospitality Management*, vol. 10, no. 7, 1998, 283–88.

55 Cunningham, I., 'Influencing people's attitudes to change', *Professional Manager*, vol. 14, no. 3, May 2005, 37.

56 Lewin, K., *Field Theory in Social Science*, Harper and Row (1951).

57 French, W. L., Kast, F. E. and Rosenzweig, J. E., *Understanding Human Behavior in Organizations*, Harper and Row (1985).

58 Hooper, A. and Potter, J., 'Take it from the top', *People Management*, 19 August 1999, p. 46.

59 For a more detailed account, see Mullins, L. J., 'Information technology – the human factor', *Administrator*, vol. 5, no. 8, September 1985, 6–9.

60 Calori, R., Baden-Fuler, C., and Hunt, B., 'Managing Change at Novotel: Back to the Future', *Long Range Planning*, vol. 33, no. 6, 2000, 779–804.

61 Ford, R., Heisler, W. and McGeary, W., 'Leading change with the 5P model: complexing the Swan and Dolphin Hotels at Walt Disney World', *Cornell University*, vol. 29, issue 2, 2008, 191–203.

62 http://www.swandolphin.com/aboutus/staff.html, accessed 11.3.12

63 http://www.swandolphin.com/, accessed 11.3.12

64 Harris, D., '12 things that changed hotels', *Caterer and Hotelkeeper*, 15 June 2006.

65 'Driving change and managing tradition', *EP Business In Hospitality*, issue 35, September 2010, 26–9. http://www.epmagazine.co.uk/driving-change-and-managing-tradition/

66 Abridged from Henkoff (1994) 'Finding and keeping the best service workers', http://corporate.disney.go.com/corporate/conduct_standards.html

67 http://disneycareers.com/en/working-here/culture-diversity/, accessed 1.4.12

Index

Index

Index